ESSAY ESSENTIALS
WITH READINGS

FIFTH EDITION

ESSAY ESSENTIALS
WITH READINGS

SARAH NORTON

BRIAN GREEN

NELSON EDUCATION

NELSON / E D U C A T I O N

Essay Essentials with Readings,
Fifth Edition

Sarah Norton and
Brian Green

**Vice President and
Editorial Director:**
Evelyn Veitch

Editor-in-Chief:
Anne Williams

Executive Editor:
Laura Macleod

Marketing Manager:
Amanda Henry

Developmental Editor:
Theresa Fitzgerald

Permissions Coordinator:
Joanne Tang

**Senior Content Production
Manager:**
Natalia Denesiuk Harris

Copy Editor:
June Trusty

Proofreader:
Kate Revington

Indexer:
Edwin Durbin

Production Coordinator:
Ferial Suleman

Design Director:
Ken Phipps

Managing Designer:
Franca Amore

Interior Design:
Sonya V. Thursby, Opus House
Incorporated

Cover Design:
Dianna Little

Cover Image:
Photographic Ephemera by Gracie

Compositor:
Carol Magee

Printer:
Edwards Brothers

**Library and Archives Canada
Cataloguing in Publication**

Norton, Sarah, date
    Essay essentials with readings /
Sarah Norton, Brian Green. — 5th
ed.

Includes index.
ISBN 978-0-17-650187-7

    1. Essay—Authorship-
Textbooks. 2. Report writing—
Textbooks. 3. English language—
Rhetoric—Textbooks. 4. College
readers.
I. Green, Brian II. Title.

PE1471.N69 2010   808'.042
C2009-907335-8

ISBN-13: 978-0-17-650187-7
ISBN-10: 0-17-650187-8

Contents

PART 7: Workbook

Readings: Contents by Subject

Communication and Writing

The Contemporary Scene

Media and the Arts

Science, Technology, and the Environment

Ethics and Morality

Preface: To the Instructor

Essay Essentials with Readings, Fifth Edition, is designed for Canadian post-secondary students who are learning to write academic and professional prose. The book has been substantially revised.

A major change is the introduction of a new section (Part 6) that contains 23 contemporary readings, 17 of which are new to the book. Two new essays by student writers illustrate the MLA and APA formatting and documentation styles. We have added a table of contents by subject for teachers who prefer to organize their courses around themes rather than organizational structures. Chosen for their value as prose models as well as their appeal to a broad range of interests, the readings represent the middle range of the language register. We have avoided both stiffly formal and slangy popular pieces; the reading selections are written in levels of diction appropriate to academic, technical, business, and public writing. And in an effort to appeal to both students and teachers, we have included a number of humorous pieces.

Part 4, The Research Paper, constitutes another major change. We have brought the section on APA style forward from an appendix to the body of the book, and we have included many more examples of electronic and other nonprint sources. Source citations are based on the most recent versions of APA and MLA styles. Students who need to write research papers for humanities courses and social sciences courses should find this section of the text both helpful and convenient.

Essay Essentials with Readings is divided into seven parts. Parts 1 through 4 explain, exemplify, and provide practice in planning, drafting, and revising transactional prose, as well as in researching and writing properly formatted and documented essays. Because most adults learn better and with more satisfaction when they work with other learners, many of the exercises are interactive.[1] Some involve the whole class, but most are designed to be done in pairs or groups, either in class or online.[2]

---

[1] Answers to exercises marked with an asterisk are provided in Appendix B.

[2] These group exercises can be adapted to individual assignments if the instructor prefers or the course requires.

A principal goal of this book is to convince students that good writing necessarily involves rewriting and editing. Part 3, Revising, has been revised to clarify the distinct but overlapping tasks of rewriting, editing, and proofreading, and we have developed new exercises to help students identify and execute these tasks. To reinforce our goal, we have incorporated rewriting and editing in exercises throughout the text.

Part 5, Patterns of Development, begins with a new chapter defining and illustrating description, narration, and example: three developmental strategies that can be useful in all forms of nonfiction prose. Chapters 16 through 19 provide instruction and examples of the traditional patterns of exposition. Chapter 20 focuses on argumentation, the most challenging kind of writing that students will encounter in school and in the workplace. Each chapter in this unit concludes with two short essays, one of which is annotated to illustrate the construction of the essay and the development of its paragraphs. Students are asked to annotate the second essay in a similar fashion. These exercises, together with numerous others in the book, show students how nonfiction prose is put together. We believe that without a clear understanding of how paragraphs are built and how they can be organized to create an extended document, students will not be able to produce clear, well-organized, adequately developed essays, reports, proposals, or memoranda.

The questions following the essays in Parts 5 and 6 are designed to provoke thinking and discussion as well as to promote students' understanding of structure and development. Teachers will find suggested answers to these questions in the *Instructor's Manual* and on the *Essay Essentials* website at http://www.essayessentials5e.nelson.com.

Part 7, the Workbook, reviews the basics of syntax, grammar, punctuation, and spelling. Many students will be required to work through this workbook on their own; answers to the asterisked exercises are provided in Appendix B. Answers to the Mastery Tests are provided in the *Instructor's Manual* and on the Instructor's Page of the website. The four units of the workbook can be covered in any order, but the sections within each unit are interdependent and should be studied sequentially; competency in later chapters often depends on mastery of previous ones.

Inside the front cover is a Quick Revision Guide. We encourage students to use it as a checklist to consult as they revise and edit their work. Instructors can duplicate the guide, attach a copy to each student's paper, and mark ✔ or ✗ beside each item in the guide to identify the paper's strengths and weaknesses. This strategy provides students with specific feedback in a consistent format. It also saves hours of marking time.

Essay Essentials is accompanied by a comprehensive website that supports both students and teachers (http://www.essayessentials5e.nelson.com).

Learners who need more practice than the text provides will find additional exercises and practice tests on the website. These exercises and tests are electronically scored, so students receive instant feedback.

The website also provides information that could not conveniently be included in the text itself. For example, to augment the brief introduction to argumentation in Chapter 20, the website offers an introduction to logical reasoning (inductive and deductive), together with definitions and examples of common logical fallacies. In addition, the website provides students with definitions and examples of the parts of speech, sentence patterns, ESL tips, links to reference sites, a write-in "Ask the Authors" feature, and much more.

The Instructor's Page includes a teaching manual, suggested answers for most of the questions in Parts 1 through 6, answers to the chapter Mastery Tests in Part 7, PowerPoint slides and transparency masters, *The Essentials iTest* (a comprehensive bank of multiple-choice diagnostic and pre- and post-tests), and a writers' forum—a direct link to the authors. We are eager to hear your comments, criticisms, and questions about the text, about your experience with *Essay Essentials with Readings* in the classroom, and about any related matter you'd like to discuss with us.

Acknowledgments

Much of the new material in this edition is attributable to the support of colleagues and friends across Canada. We wish to record our special thanks to Deborah Bowen and John C. Van Rys (Redeemer University College), Michael O'Hea (Grant MacEwan University), Holly Nelson (Trinity Western University), and Maureen Niwa-Heinen (Camosun College), who provided us with excellent examples of student writing. We welcome our new student contributors: Rubi Garyfalakis and Amanda van der Heiden, two fine writers whose work we are proud to introduce.

Our reviewers offered helpful comments and suggestions: Janet Bowes (Mount Royal University), Paul Hutchinson (Niagara College), Annette Isber (Niagara College), Jodi Lundgren (Camosun College), Roneen Marcoux (University College of the Fraser Valley), and Dennis Vanderspek (Fleming College). Eva Tihanyi, a long-time contributor to the book, earned our gratitude by surveying her department and summarizing for us their comments on the fourth edition. In an effort to answer the question "What engages today's students?" a number of instructors gave generously of their time and expertise to a series of discussions we called "The *Essay Essentials* Book Club." We thank the instructors from Fleming College, Kwantlen Polytechnic University, Camosun College, and Vancouver Island

University for the detailed and helpful feedback they provided on what works in their classrooms.

We are especially indebted to Patricia Labonte, former director of Teaching and Learning Resources at Niagara College, for her comprehensive revision of the chapters on research and documentation. We thank Centennial College for permission to reproduce portions of *The Revised Style Sheet* in Part 4 of the book and *Preventing Plagiarism: Why? What? How?* on the website.

We are most grateful to our publishing team at Nelson Education Ltd. Without the encouragement of Laura Macleod and the support of Theresa Fitzgerald, Natalia Denesiuk Harris, and Amanda Henry and her sales force (Dustin Tysick deserves mention here), there would have been no fifth edition. And finally, a special "Thank you" goes to our copy editor, June Trusty, who almost invariably catches us when we slip.

Sarah Norton
Brian Green

Introduction: Why, What, and How to Learn to Write

Few people enjoy writing; it's hard work. Writing is a complex process, a learned skill that requires patience, concentration, and persistence. Unlike most of the skills you acquire in a career program, however, writing is not job-specific. **The skills you learn from this book will be useful to you in all your college or university courses** and **in every job you hold throughout your working life.** If you have graduated from college or university, your prospective employer will assume that you are able to write quickly and skilfully. The higher you climb on the organizational ladder, the more you will write and the more complex your writing tasks will become. And evaluations of your performance in any job will be based in part on your communication skills.

Essay Essentials with Readings will teach you to write standard English prose, the kind you can apply to any writing task. The word "essay" comes from the French *essayer*, to try or attempt. Broadly speaking, an essay is an attempt to communicate information, opinion, or emotion. In college or university, an essay is an exercise that requires students to explore and explain their own and others' thoughts about a subject. In the larger world, essays appear in print and online newspapers and magazines as editorials, reviews, opinion pieces, and commentaries on news and public affairs.

Thinking, organizing, and researching are basic to all practical writing tasks. **In this book, you will learn how to find and organize thoughts, to develop ideas in coherent paragraphs, and to express yourself clearly, correctly, and concisely.** Once you've mastered these basics, you can develop any job-specific writing styles that may be required of you. If you can write well-organized, convincing, and error-free essays, you will have no difficulty adapting your skills to business or technical reports, instructions, proposals, memoranda, sales presentations, commercial scripts, legal briefs, or websites.

The fact that literacy is in decline does not make the ability to write less important; rather, it means that those who can write competently are in high demand. **You can learn to write well if you are willing to work at it.** We have designed this text to enable you to master the theory of good writing and to practise it successfully. Because it is more fun and more efficient to learn with others than it is to struggle alone, we have included many group-based exercises. To make the process less onerous, we have also introduced a few humorous essays, and, in Part 7, as many entertaining exercises as we could think of. If you follow the guidelines in this book, you will produce effective essays in school and creditable communications in your career.

THE WEBSITE

In addition to the material in this book, you will find useful information and helpful exercises on our website. Go to http://www.essayessentials5e.nelson.com and click on "Student Resources" to find the menu of options available to you. Under "More Information" you will find helpful supplements to the book, and under "More Practice" you will find additional exercises for the sections in Part 7. The answers to these exercises are marked automatically, so you will know instantly whether you have understood the material.

Also on the website are practice tests, reference links, and an "Ask the Authors" button that enables you to send us any questions you have about *Essay Essentials* or about your writing. We take your questions seriously and will answer as soon as we get your message. Purchase of this book also entitles you to free access to InfoTrac®, an easy-to-use online library of source materials you can use for your research in this and other courses. You will learn more about InfoTrac® and other databases in Chapter 11.

WHAT THE SYMBOLS MEAN

This symbol in the margin beside an exercise means the exercise is designed to be done by two or more students working together. Carefully read the directions that introduce the exercise to find out how many students should participate and what task is to be performed. Often you are instructed to begin work in a pair or group, then to work individually on a writing task, and finally to regroup and review your writing with your partner(s).

This symbol means "note this." We've used it to highlight writing tips, helpful hints, hard-to-remember points, and information that you should apply whenever you write, not just when you are dealing with the specific principle covered in the paragraph marked by the icon.

This icon attached to an exercise means that the exercise is a mastery test designed to check your understanding of the chapter you have just completed. The answers to these exercises are not in the back of the book; your instructor will provide them.

GO TO WEB

EXERCISE

This symbol means that the *Essay Essentials* website has exercises to supplement the chapter you are working on. Log on to the website and then click on "Web Exercises." The exercises are arranged by chapter or workbook section, so to get to the exercises for the apostrophe, for example, click on "Workbook Section" 7.17, and do the numbered exercises listed below the icon.

THE PROCESS OF WRITING

Writing is a three-step process consisting of
1. planning or prewriting
2. drafting
3. revising

This book explains and illustrates two approaches to the process of writing: conceptual and experimental. The **conceptual** (or top-down) approach is the one you choose when you know what you want to say before you begin to write. You identify your subject and main points, and draft a thesis statement (a statement that previews the content of your paper for your readers). Research papers, business reports, and essay questions on exams are examples of writing that require a conceptual approach.

The **experimental** (bottom-up) approach is useful when you do not know ahead of time what you want to say. You discover your thesis gradually, incrementally, through trial and error, and through several drafts. Experimental writers often rely on prewriting strategies such as brainstorming and freewriting to kick-start the process.

You should learn to use both approaches. Sometimes you will discover your subject through writing; at other times, using "top-down" strategies will help you to express clearly what you already know. If you are familiar with both approaches, you can comfortably choose whichever is more appropriate for a particular writing task.

WHAT YOUR READERS EXPECT

Whichever approach you use, your goal is to make your finished essay easy for your readers to read and understand. To achieve that goal, you must meet your readers' expectations.

Readers have five unconscious expectations when they begin to read a piece of extended prose. They expect to find

- a preview (in the introduction) of the content and organization of the paper
- paragraphs
- a sentence (usually the first) in each paragraph that identifies its topic
- unified paragraphs, each of which explores a single topic
- connections (transitions) within and between paragraphs

Keep in mind that readers want to obtain information quickly and easily, without backtracking. They rely on the writer—you—to make efficient reading possible.

Your readers will read more easily and remember more of what they have read if you include a thesis statement to introduce them to the content and organization of the paper, and if you begin each paragraph with a topic sentence. If you do not organize and develop your paper and its paragraphs in a clearly identifiable way, readers will impose their own organization on it. The result will be longer reading time, difficulty in understanding and remembering the content, or, worse, the assumption that a paragraph or even the whole paper has a meaning other than the one you intended. You can help your readers to read efficiently if you follow the old adage: "Tell them what you're going to tell them; tell them; then tell them what you've told them."

HOW TO BEGIN

Having a conversation with someone who never seems to get to the point is a tiresome and frustrating experience. Similarly, an essay—or any other form of written communication—that has no point and that rambles on will turn readers off.

How can you avoid boring, confusing, or annoying your readers? To begin with, you need to have something to say and a reason for saying it. Very few people can write anything longer than a few sentences from start to finish without taking time to think about and plan what they'll say. Prewriting will help you to plan and develop your writing projects more efficiently. We will explore some prewriting strategies in Chapter 2.

Once you've determined what you want to say, the next step is to arrange your main points in the most effective order possible. If you organize your ideas carefully, you won't ramble. Writing an essay is like building a house: If you have a clear plan or blueprint, you can construct the house without the frustration of having to double back or even start all over again. A good plan saves time.

As a general rule, the more time you spend on prewriting and planning, the less time you'll need to spend on drafting and revising. Careful planning will enable you to produce papers that your readers will find clear and understandable.

THE PARTS OF AN ESSAY

An essay, like any document, has a beginning, a middle, and an end. Most students come to college or university with some familiarity with the five-paragraph theme, the most basic form of essay composition, so we will start with it and then move on to adaptations and variations of this basic format. Think of this tightly structured form of prose not as a straitjacket that stifles your creativity, but rather as a pattern to follow while you develop the skills and abilities you need to build other, more complex prose structures.

The beginning, or **introduction**, tells your reader the thesis (i.e., the single main idea you will explain or prove) and the scope of your essay. If your introduction is well crafted, its **thesis statement** will identify the points you will discuss in the paragraphs that follow.

The middle, or **body**, consists of paragraphs that discuss in detail the points that have been identified in the introduction. In a short essay, each paragraph develops a separate main point. Each paragraph should contain three essential components:

1. a **topic sentence**, which identifies the point of the paragraph
2. development, or **support**, of the topic sentence; supporting sentences provide the detailed information the reader needs in order to understand the point
3. a **concluding sentence** that either brings the discussion of the topic to a close or provides a transition to the next paragraph

The end, or **conclusion**, is a brief final paragraph. Unless your essay is very short, you summarize the main points to reinforce them for the readers, and then end with a statement that will give your readers something to think about after they have finished reading your essay.

Bertrand Russell's "What I Have Lived For" is a classic example of a well-structured essay. The introduction contains a clear thesis statement. Each paragraph of the body consists of a clearly identifiable topic sentence, development sufficient to explain it, and a concluding sentence. The conclusion is brief, pointed, and memorable. Study it carefully, for this is the kind of short essay that you need to be able to write before you attempt more complex prose assignments.

WHAT I HAVE LIVED FOR
Bertrand Russell

INTRODUCTION
Thesis statement

Three passions, simple but overwhelmingly strong, have governed my life: the longing for love, the search for knowledge, and unbearable pity for the suffering of mankind. These passions, like great winds, have blown me hither and thither, in a wayward course, over a deep ocean of anguish, reaching to the very verge of despair.

BODY
Topic sentence

Support

Concluding sentence

I have sought love, first, because it brings ecstasy—ecstasy so great that I would often have sacrificed all the rest of life for a few hours of this joy. I have sought it, next, because it relieves loneliness—that terrible loneliness in which one shivering consciousness looks over the rim of the world into the cold unfathomable lifeless abyss. I have sought it, finally, because in the union of love I have seen, in a mystic miniature, the prefiguring vision of the heaven that saints and poets have imagined. This is what I sought, and though it might seem too good for human life, this is what—at last—I have found.

Topic sentence

Support

Concluding sentence

With equal passion I have sought knowledge. I have wished to understand the hearts of men. I have wished to know why the stars shine. And I have tried to apprehend the Pythagorean power by which number holds sway above the flux. A little of this, but not much, I have achieved.

Topic sentence

Support

Concluding sentence

Love and knowledge, so far as they were possible, led upward toward the heavens. But always pity brought me back to earth. Echoes of cries of pain reverberate in my heart. Children in famine, victims tortured by oppressors, helpless old people a hated burden to their sons, and the whole world of loneliness, poverty, and pain make a mockery of what human life should be. I long to alleviate the evil, but I cannot, and I too suffer.

CONCLUSION

This has been my life. I have found it worth living, and would gladly live it again if the chance were offered me.

PART 1

Planning

Grasp the subject. The words will follow.
Cato the Elder, 234–149 BCE

What is written without effort is . . . read without pleasure.
Samuel Johnson, 1709–1784

A great many people think they are thinking
when they are merely rearranging their prejudices.
William James, 1842–1910

If you don't have time to do it right,
you'd better have time to do it over.
Anonymous

Lack of planning on your part does not constitute
an emergency on my part.
Anonymous

1

Your Audience and You

Before you begin to write anything—an essay, a report, an e-mail message, or a set of instructions—you must have something to write about (your subject) and someone to write for (your audience). Writing is communication, and for communication to take place, you (the writer) must be able to make your ideas or message clear to your readers.

Addressing Your Readers

As you plan, draft, and revise your paper, ask yourself the following questions:

- How old are your readers?
- What is their level of education?
- What do they do for a living?
- What is their income?
- What is their cultural background?
- Are they male or female?

While you must be careful to avoid generalizing or stereotyping, the answers to these questions do influence most people's views, and you would be wise to consider them before you begin to write. For most college and university assignments, you should assume that your instructor and your classmates are your audience. Some teachers will specify external audiences for short papers. The purpose of such exercises is to warm up your writing muscles.

Naturally, your instructor will be reading your early (and your late) assignments, but, if you are given the opportunity, experiment with writing for other readers: your high-school principal, for example, or a recent immigrant, a union official, a member of the Liberal Party, a religious leader, the CEO of a polluting company, or the manager of your school cafeteria.

Keeping your reader in mind will help you to plan, develop, and revise your assignment in a tone and style appropriate to your message.

Spend some time thinking about your subject in relation to your audience. Consider the following three questions when you are deciding what information your essay should include.

1. What does my reader know about my subject?
2. What is my reader's attitude toward my subject?
3. What are my reader's needs in regard to my subject?

READERS' KNOWLEDGE

The first question will help you choose the kind and amount of information that should be included. Are you writing for someone who knows little about your subject, or for someone with fairly detailed knowledge? Do you have to cover all the basics, or can you take it for granted your audience is familiar with them? You don't want to bore your readers by telling them things they already know. On the other hand, if you fail to provide information they need in order to understand your message, you'll turn them off or lose them entirely.

READERS' ATTITUDES

The second question helps you decide how to approach your subject. Will your readers be sympathetic to what you have to say? If so, you will aim to reinforce their agreement. You will probably state your opinion up front, to show you're on their side. If, however, you think they may be hostile to what you have to say, you might lessen their resistance by providing reasons and support for your ideas before revealing your point of view. Gentle persuasion is usually more effective than confrontation in writing, as it is in life.

READERS' NEEDS

The third question helps you to decide whether to persuade or inform, to compare or classify, to describe or analyze. Which approach will give your readers the information they need to know about your subject? The answers to this question will determine whether your remarks should be fairly general or quite specific. Do you intend to add to or reinforce your audience's general knowledge, or do you want your readers to apply your information only in specific situations?

Reflecting Yourself

Once you are clear about who your readers are, what they know, and what they need to know, you should think about your role in the communication process. Any time you speak or write, you present yourself in a particular way to your audience. We all play a variety of roles. We choose a role, often unconsciously, that we hope will suit the expectations of the people we are communicating with. These roles are not false or hypocritical; they are simply facets of our personality that we try to match to the needs of each situation. Choosing and maintaining an appropriate role is essential in successful communication.

Each day, for example, you meet a variety of people. Some of them you know well—parents, siblings, friends, classmates, instructors, co-workers, and supervisors. Others you know only casually—the cashier in the restaurant, the police officer at the radar trap, the enumerator for the upcoming election, the checkout person in the grocery store. With each of these people, whether the contact is casual or intense, you consciously or unconsciously adjust your language in order to communicate. If you speak to your spouse as you might to your dog, you'll be sleeping on the couch. If you speak to a salesperson as you would to a love interest, you'll be arrested.

Consider the following three questions when you are deciding what role would be most appropriate in a particular communication situation.

1. What is my purpose in writing?
2. What is my attitude toward my subject?
3. What are my readers' expectations of me in this communication?

YOUR PURPOSE

The most common purposes of writing are to inform, to persuade, and to entertain. All essays are to some degree persuasive, in that they attempt to convince the reader that the writer has accurately depicted the event, object, or idea that is the topic of the paper. Most college and university writing assignments fall into one of the first two categories. Unless you are in a creative writing course, you probably will not be assigned to write a paper that is intended to entertain the reader. Your purpose will depend largely on the needs and expectations of your readers. It will influence your choice of supporting details to develop your points and will affect your tone. *How* you say something often has more impact on your audience than *what* you say.

YOUR ATTITUDE

The second question requires you to clarify your attitude toward your chosen subject. This involves more than simply asking, "Am I for or against it?" You should consider how strongly you feel about the subject because your attitude will influence your tone as well as the kinds of evidence you present. You should also think about how personal you want to be in presenting your ideas, or how balanced and objective you wish (or are able) to be. Consider how closely your attitude toward the subject aligns with your audience's attitude. If your views coincide, then a fairly informal approach may be appropriate; if they differ, then an impersonal, objective approach is preferable.

YOUR ROLE

The third question requires you to think about what role your audience is likely to expect of you. If you write as an authority, will you be credible? If you write as a peer or colleague, will you be effective? What are your readers likely to expect from someone in your position writing to them on this subject? Taking the time to think about your readers' expectations will help you to make appropriate choices with respect to the point of view you take, the examples and support you provide for your ideas, and the level of language you use.

Levels of Standard English Writing

Good writing involves more than the meaning of words and sentences. It also requires the choice of appropriate language. No one would submit a book review that began, "This is an awesome book with, like, ideas that sort of make you think, you know?" You know instantly that the language is inappropriate. Similarly, if you were discussing the book with friends over coffee and announced, "This book contains provocative and stimulating ideas that engage and challenge the reader," your language would be equally inappropriate.

Written English (except for instant messaging) is usually more formal than spoken English. Because writers have time to consider what they want to say and how best to say it, they can choose their words carefully, arrange them in meaningful sentences, and organize ideas into logical paragraphs. An appropriate level of language is an essential part of effective writing.

Choose a level that suits both your topic and your reader. There will be times when you need to compromise; for example, when you send one message to several people. In such cases, the safe bet is to aim at the highest level of receiver and trust that the others will understand.

Sometimes it isn't clear what level you should be using. At such times, your reader's preference should determine your choice. Many colleges and universities expect students to write academic papers in formal English, which requires, among other things, third-person pronouns (*he, she, one, they*). Informal writing, with its first- and second-person pronouns (*I, me, you*), may not be acceptable. (See pages 446–48 for an explanation of "person.") Ask your instructor about his or her policy and follow it. (*Note:* Not all instructors require the same level of language. Some are sticklers for formality; others are more relaxed. Don't waste time arguing; tailor each assignment to your instructor's requirements.)

Similarly, because most employers tend to favour formal letters of application over casual ones, if you want to get the job, you will write a formal letter. For a talk you give to your class, an informal, conversational style may be appropriate. Most of what you read and write falls somewhere in the middle. Business documents, for example, are usually written in general-level Standard English.

There are no fixed divisions of language use: the three levels we've identified often overlap. To help you choose the most appropriate level for your message and audience, the table below outlines the basic features of informal, general, and formal written English.

	Informal	General	Formal
Vocabulary and Style	Casual, everyday; usually concrete; some slang, colloquial expressions, contractions. Usually written in 1st or 2nd person.	The language of educated persons; nonspecialized; balance of abstract and concrete; readily understood. Can use 1st, 2nd, or 3rd person.	Often abstract, technical, or specialized; no contractions or colloquialisms. Written in 3rd person.
Sentence and Paragraph Structure	Sentences short, simple; some sentence fragments; paragraphs short.	Complete sentences of varying length; paragraphs vary, but are often fairly short.	Complete sentences, often long, complex; paragraphs fully developed, often at length.
Tone	Conversational, casual; sounds like ordinary speech.	Varies to suit writer's message and purpose.	Impersonal, serious, often instructional.
Typical Uses	Personal notes, some fiction, some newspapers, much advertising.	Most of what we read: websites, newspapers, magazines, novels, business correspondence.	Academic writing, some textbooks, scientific reports, journal articles, legal documents.

No one level is "better" than another. Each has its place and function. Your message, your audience, and your purpose in writing are what should determine the level you choose.

Read the following selections and consider each writer's purpose, the audience for whom the message is intended, and why the writer's level of language is appropriate to the readers, the subject, and the purpose.

INFORMAL

Love him or hate him, Michael Moore has turned the world of documentary film on its ear. Documentaries are stuffy and boring, aren't they? They certainly aren't supposed to be wildly popular or turn their directors into media stars. But starting with *Roger and Me* back in 1989, Moore has almost single-handedly made the documentary fun, personal, and popular. Like most film students, I began thinking I wanted someday to make blockbuster Hollywood hits like the movies Canadians Norman Jewison and James Cameron are famous for, but now I'm a convert to documentaries and that other Canadian production star: the National Film Board of Canada.

Who is the intended audience? This paragraph is intended for general readers, not people who are looking for a scholarly discussion of film. The writer assumes some interest in and knowledge of Michael Moore and his films.

What is the writer's role? The writer wants to inform readers in a personal way about her point of view. She plays the role not of expert or teacher, but rather of a friend or acquaintance supplying the information for discussion in a casual way.

Why is the level of language appropriate? The use of contractions and colloquialisms ("the world . . . on its ear," "stuffy and boring") and especially the use of first and second persons in direct address clearly mark this as an informal and friendly communication. Short sentences and a conversational style add to the informal tone.

GENERAL

What is a documentary film? The so-called father of documentary film, the late John Grierson, called it "the creative treatment of reality," but that definition is uncomfortably broad. For example, is *Valkyrie* a documentary? What about *Defiance* or *Amadeus* or *Milk* or *Lawrence of Arabia*? All are about real people and contain a version of historical events, but few would classify them as documentaries. The purpose of these films is to entertain (if you discount their real purpose: to make money), and perhaps purpose lies at the heart of the definition. The primary purpose of a documentary film is to inform.

Who is the intended audience? Readers of this paragraph will be knowledgeable enough about films to have seen at least one of the five major releases mentioned, and interested enough in film to want to know more about the documentary genre.

What is the writer's role? The writer is providing information from an expert point of view, but in a friendly way rather than as a lecture or formal instruction. The use of humour and casual language makes the information easy to absorb, and the direct address and use of questions add a friendly tone to the paragraph.

Why is the level of language appropriate? The vocabulary and writing style are easily understood by general readers. The use of second person ("if you discount their real purpose") adds to the personal nature of the language, as do the questions directed to the reader. This message is designed to appeal to the widest audience possible.

FORMAL

The late John Grierson, best known as "the father of documentary film" and the founder of the National Film Board of Canada, called documentary "the creative treatment of reality." Since its inception in 1939, the NFB has been presenting reality to Canadians and the rest of the world in creative ways. While it has earned recognition in other cinematic fields (notably animation), the NFB has achieved most of its international acclaim from more than 70 years of producing first-class documentary films, many of them Academy Award winners.

Who is the intended audience? The readers of this passage are literate and well read. They are people whose education and experience have enabled them to appreciate that good films can be informative as well as entertaining.

What is the writer's role? The writer's purpose is to highlight the achievements of the NFB to an audience of educated peers who share his aesthetic interests. The writer presents himself not as an expert addressing non-experts, but rather as an enthusiast who wants to share knowledge with a receptive audience.

Why is the level of language appropriate? The vocabulary is fairly sophisticated, and the sentences are relatively long and complex. There are no contractions or colloquialisms, no first- or second-person pronouns. The writer addresses his audience as peers—other film enthusiasts—but not as close friends. The objective tone would be suitable for an article in a professional magazine.

Exercise 1.1*

Read the excerpts below and discuss the intended audience, the author's role, and the appropriateness of the language. Answers for this chapter begin on page 534.

1.   One of the most frequent complaints about Walmart, which employs 1.4 million people worldwide, is its failure to pay workers a living wage. Store employees are paid 20–30 percent less than the industry average, making many of them eligible for social assistance. It is estimated that American taxpayers fork out $2.5 billion a year in welfare payments to Walmart employees (Head, 2004). Because the retailer hires hard-to-place workers, like recent immigrants, seniors, and single mothers, its employees are often afraid they will not find work elsewhere. The kind of work Walmart does offer is gruelling: stores are intentionally understaffed—the strategy behind the company's legendary productivity gains—so that existing employees will work harder (Head, 2004). It is alleged that systemic discrimination against women within the corporation has denied the majority of Walmart workers the chance at promotion, a charge that is now the subject of the largest civil-rights suit in U.S. history.

Parmar, Deenu. "Labouring the Walmart Way." *Essay Essentials with Readings*. 5th ed. Toronto: Nelson Education Ltd., 2010. 317–19. Print.

Who is the intended audience? _____

_____

_____

_____

_____

What is the writer's role? _____

_____

_____

_____

_____

Why is the level of language appropriate? _____

_____

_____

_____

_____

2.   The "inletting" or "butt mortise" plane is designed to cut precise mortises for butt hinges, lock fronts, and strike plates, or to repair jambs, doors, furniture, and millwork, wherever the ability to do inletting is important. The plane has a completely open throat so that you can watch what you are doing. The 3/4" wide cutter is set at a 40 degree pitch for general work. This can be increased to 70 degrees (plus or minus) for difficult grain simply by inserting the blade bevel-up. For inletting, such as hinges, you set the blade extension at the hinge leaf thickness, score the outline and plane to depth, using overlapping strokes for a smooth bottom. The same technique would be used for a veneer repair on solid wood.

_____

Lee Valley Catalogue. Tenth Anniversary Issue, 1987–88: 23. Print.

Who is the intended audience? _____

_____

_____

_____

_____

What is the writer's role? _____

_____

_____

_____

_____

Why is the level of language appropriate? _____

_____

_____

_____

_____

3.   Doing business with the Chinese is an enterprise fraught with peril for the unwary Western business person. While in the West most business is ultimately conducted face to face between the principals, negotiations seldom if ever achieve this intimacy in the Orient. It is common for gatherings of ten or more to take part in the early stages of agenda-setting and prioritizing, and the hapless Westerner who has not engaged the services of a Chinese guide will have to sort out the Party overseers from the ineffectual hangers-on and try to hone in on the power brokers who often remain in the background to assess and evaluate before making themselves known. Often the early stages of business relationships are conducted in the very formal atmosphere of banquets, with hierarchical seating arrangements and ritual toasts. Coping with the exotic atmosphere, the oblique method of negotiation, the recondite formality, and the unidentifiable food is a formidable challenge: one that should be undertaken without assistance by only the most intrepid and experienced of Western entrepreneurs.

_____

Czereczovich, Katlin. "Business Abroad." *Canadian Women Entrepreneurs* Spring 2002: 91. Print.

Who is the intended audience?   _____

_____

_____

_____

_____

What is the writer's role?   _____

_____

_____

_____

_____

Why is the level of language appropriate?   _____

_____

_____

_____

_____

4.   In Paris there is open season on pedestrians all year round. Find an elderly Parisian pedestrian and you'll have the ultimate in cunning and agility. Watch him cross the street, inciting a bus to charge, then nipping

nimbly behind a stalled taxi that has flooded its carburetor in the excitement of trying to nail him. Beautiful footwork. The Paris traffic policeman puts a nice rhythm into the chaos by standing in a concrete pillbox and waving cars in all directions. He is especially useful in the large, busy squares. These squares, which are round, give the motorist a chance to circle and take another crack at a pedestrian. The pedestrian's only defence here is to run with other pedestrians in a pack. Most European cars, being small and light, will not take on more than five people, or two bicycles, at once. The Paris taxi will take on anything except passengers.

Nicol, Eric. *Still a Nicol: The Best of Eric Nicol.* Whitby: McGraw-Hill, 1972. Print.

Who is the intended audience? _____

_____

_____

_____

_____

What is the writer's role? _____

_____

_____

_____

_____

Why is the level of language appropriate? _____

_____

_____

_____

_____

5.   If only the problem were that simple. For those who like tidy problems with clear solutions, it is disturbing to find that there is another side to the sweatshop debate. To begin with, sweatshops are "the first rung on the ladder out of extreme poverty" (Sachs 11). They allow developing countries to expand their exports and consequently to improve their economies (Arnold and Hartman 2.) Workers (usually women) choose to work in sweatshops because they are often the only means by which women can further their own ends. By working in a sweatshop, women make a small income, learn about business practices, and benefit from the improved

social and economic conditions that come with economic growth. Arnold and Hartman explain that as the economy grows, more jobs are created; the labour market tightens, and companies are forced to improve their working conditions in order to attract employees (2–3). Theoretically, this analysis makes sense, but does it apply in practice? Do employees really benefit from working in sweatshops?

Garyfalakis, Rubi. "No Sweat?" *Essay Essentials with Readings.* 5th ed. Toronto: Nelson Education Ltd., 2010. 336–41. Print.

Who is the intended audience? _____

_____

_____

_____

_____

What is the writer's role? _____

_____

_____

_____

Why is the level of language appropriate? _____

_____

_____

_____

_____

Exercise 1.2

As a class, select one of the five paragraphs found on pages 16–20. First, be sure you all agree on the intended audience and purpose of the paragraph. Your objective is to "translate" the paragraph for a different audience. The purpose of your revision will be the same as that of the original, but the language and tone will be adapted to suit the new audience for whom the message is intended.

Next, in groups of three, choose an audience for your revision from the following list. (Each group must select a different audience.)

- your supervisor at your part-time job
- your *Facebook* friends
- a parent
- a high-school drop-out
- your academic advisor
- a blind date

Once all groups have completed their "translations," compare the results by reading the revised paragraphs aloud. Try to guess who each group's intended audience is. How do you know? How does the language work to meet the needs of the new audience?

The following exercise will give you practice in communicating effectively by adjusting your level of language to suit your purpose, your message, and your audience.

Exercise 1.3

Imagine, in each of the following situations, that you must deal with three different audiences face to face. Before you begin, analyze each audience in terms of knowledge, attitudes, and needs; then clarify the purpose of your message, your attitude toward your subject, and your audience's expectations of you.

1. You prepared your company's sales presentation in PowerPoint and stored it on the hard drive of your notebook computer. On your way to a meeting with clients in Detroit, your notebook was handled roughly by Customs inspectors at the airport. When you got to the sales meeting, your computer would not open in PowerPoint.

   You made the sales presentation as well as you could, but the clients were not impressed, and your company did not get the contract. Explain these circumstances to

   - your supervisor in the sales department
   - the U.S. Customs complaint bureau
   - a representative of the computer company, which claims its notebook computers are practically indestructible

2. You applied for a bursary that would allow you to continue your studies abroad and give you enormously valuable experience before you graduate. You receive a letter of congratulations and a large cheque, but, while the cheque is made out to you, the letter is clearly referring to someone else—a mix-up has occurred. Are you the recipient of the bursary, or should the money have gone to the person

named in the letter? What letter did that person receive? These are some of the questions that occur to you. Describe your dilemma and your course of action to

- a professor whom you like and whose opinion you respect
- the person who sponsored your application
- the organization granting the bursary

3. To celebrate the Grey Cup, you invited 15 close friends over to watch the game on your landlord's 54-inch plasma TV. After promising to provide food, you became nervous about your cooking abilities and asked a friend who works as an apprentice chef to provide a huge vat of chili. She made the chili, along with mounds of garlic bread and homemade nachos. Your friends were so impressed that you couldn't resist taking credit for the food, claiming you had used an old family recipe. Unfortunately, everyone got food poisoning and was sick for three days. How would you explain the situation to

- your very sick friends?
- the friend who cooked the food?
- your landlord, who had to clean up his recreation room after some people had been sick there?

4. Following a round of layoffs and pay cuts, your employer is making an effort to improve flagging morale. She announces that the person who submits the best idea for improving morale will get an extra week of paid vacation. Your idea is to provide 10-minute breaks twice a day, during which lively music will be played in the office and workers will be encouraged to "kick back and chill out." Sell your idea to

- your employer
- a co-worker who is a classical music fan
- the man who works at the desk next to you; he is a workaholic who never takes a break, not even for lunch

5. You are short of money—so short you can't even buy gas for your car. If you can't get gas money, you will be late for work, and your boss is annoyed because you've been late twice this week already. Ask for money from

- your parents
- a friend
- someone who owes you money

6. Turn one of the 15 role-playing situations above into a written assignment.

Exercise 1.4

This exercise is designed to reinforce your understanding of the importance of knowing your reader. An effective communicator figures out ahead of time not only what his or her readers need to know, but also what they do not need to know. Some information is necessary and some is superfluous, with the mix varying widely from audience to audience. With this in mind, describe one of the following topics to three different audiences: Choose one from each of the three groups listed below.

> Topics: A favourite musician or group, a favourite stand-up comic or other performer
>
> Group A: A grandparent, a teacher, an employer
>
> Group B: A co-worker, a classmate, an old friend you haven't seen in years
>
> Group C: The president of your college or university or the Student Council Social Committee, whom you are trying to persuade to support a fundraising event featuring your topic

Exercise 1.5

1. The short article below was written to appeal to music enthusiasts. The level of language is informal, full of colloquialisms and slang expressions, some of which are outdated. Read it through, highlighting any terms or phrases that might confuse your parents (or that confuse you). In small groups, clarify the meaning of these terms.

2. Rewrite this article in general-level language so that it makes sense to a wider audience.

3. Exchange revisions with a partner. Identify and discuss any phrases you still don't fully understand.

THE NEEDLE AND THE DAMAGE DONE

Matthew McKinnon

Has there ever been a perfect medium for music? Listening to a CD is like watching Deep Blue play chess—technically flawless, but there's no ghost inside the shell. Compression formats like MP3 and AAC typically make music sound even worse. At their atomic level, iPod libraries comprise marathon strings of binary code: 1 or 0, true or false, black or white. Digital music knows no other colours.

And the alternatives? In the 1970s, audiocassettes helped music become portable and personal, but they hissed, crackled, and popped on playback. The 8-track era never happened, no matter what *Wikipedia* says. That leaves vinyl—too big to carry, so easily scratched. And yet. . . .

Music on wax remains an audio junkie's dearest love. The LP's analog sound is warm, a special vibration that is as tonally rich as it is deep. Listening to vinyl, as described by rock super-producer Butch Vig (Nirvana, Sonic Youth, Garbage), means you get to hear music's "3-D characteristics: the reverb, the little tails of echoes, the stereo left–right feel."

Vinyl is hanging tough as the traditional music industry crumbles around it. Compact discs look like the dodo bird of the decade to come: Since 2000, CD sales have declined more than 36 percent. Apple's iTunes Store, with more than 5 billion songs sold during its first five years of operation, recently passed Walmart to become America's top music retailer. Meanwhile, vinyl record sales rose by 36 percent last year, and turntables spiked 80 percent—a remarkable feat in the age of downloading.

Mid-level stalwarts are leading vinyl's charge. Matador, New York's steadiest supplier of indie rock, offers LP versions of more than 50 current and classic releases. Stones Throw, the middleweight champ of urban music (home to Madlib, James Pants, and Koushiki), presses more vinyl than your average flooring installer. Even major labels seem excited about LPs. Many of this year's biggest releases are available at Amazon.com's vinyl boutique ("the spiritual home of audio purists and DJs").

And who said vinyl isn't portable? Touring bands like Chicago's Yakuza are surviving on the road by selling records at their live shows. "Lovely, gorgeous, double gatefold, colour, limited-edition vinyl—$25 a pop. If we have a bad show and sell three, that's $75 we weren't planning on," Yakuza's Bruce Lamont said earlier this summer. "We're all audiophile nerds, so we're way into the whole vinyl thing. We're really proud to have our own music on that medium."

2

Selecting a Subject

Approximately one-third of the time you devote to an essay should be spent on the planning stage. (The remainder is devoted to drafting and revising.) If you take the time to analyze your audience, find a good subject, and identify interesting main points to make about that subject, you will find that the mechanics of writing fall into place much more easily than if you try to sweat your way through the paper the night before it's due. After you have considered your readers' background, needs, and expectations, the next step is to choose a satisfactory subject to write about.

Even when you are assigned a topic for an essay, you need to examine it, focus it, and consider different ways of approaching it. Depending on your knowledge of the topic and the readers you are writing for, the range of specific subjects for any broad topic is almost endless. For example, given the broad topic "research sources," here are some of the approaches from which you might choose.

- Can you trust Internet sources?
- Interviewing to develop original source material
- Books: Still the best "random access device"
- Journal indexes: An underused source of mountains of material
- How to do an effective Internet search

Your first task, then, is to choose a satisfactory subject, one that satisfies the basic principles of the **4-S test:**

A satisfactory subject is significant, single, specific, and supportable.

If it passes the 4-S test, your subject is the basis of a good essay.

MAKE YOUR SUBJECT SIGNIFICANT

Your subject must be worthy of the time and attention you expect your readers to give to your paper. Can you imagine an essay on "How to buy movie tickets" or "Why I hate pants without pockets," for example, as being meaningful to your readers?

Exercise 2.1*

From the list below, choose those subjects that would be significant to a typical reader. Revise the others to make them significant, if possible. If not, suggest another, related subject that is significant. When you have finished this exercise, compare your answers with those provided on page 535.

1. Tips for using *Facebook* and/or *MySpace* wisely
2. How to identify good online sources
3. How to take notes from a textbook
4. The perfect vacation destination
5. How to use a cellphone
6. Television—a threat to Canadian independence
7. Winter weather

MAKE YOUR SUBJECT SINGLE

Don't try to crowd too much into one paper. Be careful that your subject is not actually two or three related subjects masquerading as one. If you attempt to write about a multiple subject, your readers will get a superficial and possibly confusing overview instead of the interesting and satisfying detail they expect to find in a well-planned paper. A subject such as "The problem of league expansion in hockey and other sports" is too broad to be dealt with satisfactorily in one essay. More manageable alternatives are "The problems of league expansion in the NHL" or "Why Hamilton can't get an NHL franchise."

Exercise 2.2*

From the following list, choose the subjects that are single and could be satisfactorily explored in a short essay. Revise the others to make them single.

1. Causes of unemployment among college and university students and new graduates
2. Pub night at different campuses
3. Why *Twitter* and *Facebook* are so popular
4. The importance of accuracy in blogs and news sites

5. Methods of preventing the spread of STDs
6. Causes of injury in industry and pro sports
7. Wildlife management and gerontology: rewarding careers

MAKE YOUR SUBJECT SPECIFIC

Given a choice between a broad, general topic and a narrow, specific one, always choose the specific one. Most readers find concrete, specific details more interesting than broad generalizations. It would be difficult to say anything very detailed about a huge subject such as "the roles of women in history," for example. But with some research, you could write an interesting paper on "the roles of 19th-century prairie women" or "famous female pilots."

You can narrow a broad subject and make it more specific by applying one or more *limiting factors* to it. Try thinking of your subject in terms of a specific *kind, time, place, number,* or *person* associated with it. By applying this technique to the last potential subject above, you might come up with "Amelia Earhart's last flight."

Exercise 2.3*

In the list below, identify the subjects that are specific and could be explained satisfactorily in a short essay. Revise the others to make them specific by applying one or more of the limiting factors to each one.

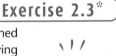

1. Summer employment opportunities in my career field
2. Canada's military heroes
3. How to enjoy winter weather
4. The effects of government bailouts of failing industries
5. The problems of urban living
6. How to repair home appliances
7. Adolescents' addiction to instant messaging

MAKE YOUR SUBJECT SUPPORTABLE

You must know something about your subject (preferably more than your readers know), or you must be able to find out about it. Remember, your readers want information that is new, interesting, and thought-provoking—not obvious observations familiar to everyone. You must be able to include *specific examples, facts, figures, quotations, anecdotes,* or other *supporting details.* Supporting information can be gathered from your own experience, from the experience of other people, or from both. If you don't know enough about your topic to write anything but the obvious, be prepared to do some research.

Exercise 2.4*

From the subjects given below, choose those that are clearly supportable in a short essay. Revise the others to make them supportable.

1. Journalism as a career
2. Movie review: *Avatar*
3. Crisis in the Canadian automotive industry
4. The North Korean secret service
5. Time travel
6. Art through the ages
7. The hazards of working in a fast-food outlet

Exercise 2.5*

Together with a partner, discuss the acceptability of the potential subjects listed below. Indicate with check marks (✔) whether each subject passes the 4-S test by being significant, single, specific, and supportable. Revise each unsatisfactory subject (fewer than four check marks) to make it a satisfactory subject for a short essay.

Subject	The 4-S Test				
	significant	*single*	*specific*	*supportable*	Revision
1. Portable computers	☐	☐	☐	☐	_____
2. Insomnia, hypertension, and other stress-related disorders	☐	☐	☐	☐	_____
3. The Arctic 200 years from now	☐	☐	☐	☐	_____

Subject	*significant*	*single*	*specific*	*supportable*	Revision
4. Healthy lunches for busy people	☐	☐	☐	☐	_____
5. Architectural trends	☐	☐	☐	☐	_____

Exercise 2.6

Write down three subjects that you think pass the 4-S test. When you've finished, exchange papers with another student and carefully check each other's work.

Once you have selected an appropriate subject, it's time to move on to the next stage: identifying solid main points to support that subject.

3

Managing the Main Points

While you were selecting subjects and testing them against the four principles presented in Chapter 2, you were thinking, consciously or unconsciously, about what you could say about them. **Main points** are the two or three or four most important things you have to say about your subject. Selecting them carefully is a vitally important part of the writing process.

Generating Main Points: The Bottom-Up Approach

If you are feeling intimidated by your task and unsure about how to present your subject, some prewriting activities can be helpful. The goal of any prewriting activity is to help you find out what you know about your subject and to prepare you for the drafting process. Before we look at some potentially helpful prewriting strategies, we would like you to consider the old truism "The more you read, the better you write." Reading is not just essential to learning about subject matter; it also influences the quality of your writing. Reading broadly will expose you to a wide variety of styles as well as points of view, and as you work consciously at mastering the content of what you read, your brain is working unconsciously to absorb the qualities of different kinds of writing.

Writers use several methods to stimulate thinking. Three are especially effective: talking, freewriting, and brainstorming. All will make your creative juices flow. We recommend that you try all three to see which works best for you in a particular writing situation. Understand that these techniques work only when you already have some ideas in your head. Either you will be writing from personal experience or you've done some research. (You'll learn about research in Part 4.)

TALKING

Students love to talk and often experience frustration in classes because there is no time to "just talk" about what they're learning. But note that this prewriting strategy works only if the students participating in the exercise are clearly and tightly focused on a specific subject. **Focused dialogue** works best in groups of three or four students, all of whom are interested in the subject. As long as they don't wander off-topic, many students find small-group discussion a nonthreatening way of clarifying what they know and don't know about a topic. If your group is disciplined enough to stay focused, you can learn a lot by hearing what your peers think. You can build on the ideas of others, discover what you yourself think, and evaluate the clarity of your reasoning.

Like any other skill, keeping on topic during a focused dialogue becomes easier with practice. If you haven't tried this prewriting strategy before, you may want to use the questions on page 37 as a guide to help you stay on-topic or to bring you back if you find yourselves straying. And, like any other skill, it's a good idea to start small and work up. At first, 10 minutes may exhaust your group's thoughts. With practice, 15 to 20 minutes may be necessary to allow everyone a chance to voice an opinion and for the group to discuss, modify, and build on each person's contribution.

In a focused dialogue, we suggest that every participant take notes. What seems significant to one student may not seem so to another, and since the point of the exercise is to discover ideas in preparation for the paper you will write on your own, only you know what you may need as a written record of the discussion.

FREEWRITING

Freewriting is talking written down. It does what its name implies—it sets you free to write without worrying about any of the errors you may make that block the flow of your ideas. Forget about grammar, spelling, word choice, and so on, until you get some ideas down on the page. Here's how to go about freewriting:

1. Put your watch and a pad of paper on your desk. If you can type faster than you can write, open a new document on your computer. (Some writers find it helpful to turn off the monitor.) Write your subject at the top of the page or tape it to the top of your computer monitor. Ideally, your subject will have passed the 4-S test, but if you're really stuck, you can begin with just a word or a phrase.

2. Make a note of the time and start writing. Don't stop until you have written for three, five, or even ten minutes straight. Write anything that comes to mind, even if it seems boring or silly. If you get stuck for words, write your subject or even the last phrase you've written over and over until something new comes to mind. (Don't worry, it will!)

3. Write as quickly as you can. Don't pause to analyze or evaluate your ideas, and don't scratch out or delete anything. This technique is designed to get thoughts into words as quickly as possible without self-consciousness.

4. When the time is up, stop and stretch. Then read over what you've written. Highlight anything that is related to your subject. Much of your freewriting will be irrelevant nonsense that you can delete. But what you have highlighted will be useful in the next step: identifying the main points you will use to explain your subject.

5. Turn the highlighted phrases, fragments, and sentences into clear, understandable points. If you don't end up with at least 10 points, continue freewriting for another few minutes and see what new ideas you can discover.

6. On a separate piece of paper, list the points you have identified. Study the possible relationships among these points and cluster them under two or three headings. These are your main points. Now you can move on to the next step: testing each main point to be sure it is satisfactory for your essay.

Here is an example of the freewriting technique. The assigned topic, for a course in law enforcement fundamentals, was "crime and punishment." Victor Chen, one of the writers featured in the readings in Part 6, was interested in the difference between crime as it is portrayed in the media and the reality of Canada's justice system. After doing some research and finding statistics that he thought might be useful, he drafted the following on his computer in 15 minutes.

What's really happening in our system in terms of crime and punishment is really different from what we see in the media. Look at TV crime shows, it used to be that all the courtroom shows were about defence lawyers trying to prove their clients' innocence. The prosecutors were the bad guys doing everything they could to put the defence attorney's client in jail or worse. There has been a big shift in the last five years or so and now we seem to have developed a taste for law and order. Now it's the prosecutors who are the good guys and the defence attorneys are trying to prevent their sleazy clients from escaping justice. The sad thing is that we form opinions about what goes on in real courtrooms based on stories like these. Almost all of the courtroom dramas on TV are American and what goes on in American courtrooms is different in

Canada, so we are definitely not very aware of how our justice system really works.

To prove this, look at the study that was done by Roberts and Doob. They took a group of people and gave them newspaper articles about a trial. When they had read the stories, they were asked about the trial. Most of them thought the criminal had gotten a sentence that was too light and only 15 percent thought the sentence was too tough. Then they took another group and gave them the court documents and transcripts of what actually went on in the trial. This group was reversed, more than half of them thought the sentence was too tough. Less than 20 percent agreed with the majority in the other group that the criminal should have got a longer sentence. This shows that we are getting a distorted impression of reality when we read about violent crime in the papers or on TV. It's like we're living in two worlds, the imaginary media one and the real one we don't know about. Also the news distorts violence. Reading the papers or watching TV, you'd think there was an epidemic of crime and that our streets are unsafe and murder was a common occurrence. This is so they can sell more papers and attract more viewers. In fact crime rates are falling. About half the crime reported in the news is violent while violent crime is actually less than 12 percent of cases that are reported. Murders are less than 1 percent of violent crimes but they are 25 percent of crime stories. If all you did was read the papers and watch TV you'd think that murders were very common but actually they are quite rare. It's easy to see how we get the idea that violence in our society is a real problem. So it's really important that the people who make the laws don't rely on the media, because it is very distorted information.

After completing this freewriting exercise, Victor highlighted all the points that he considered significant, supportable, and related to the subject. He quickly realized that the paper would be too long, and that one of his points was based on personal observation rather than provable facts. He crossed out everything related to television shows and then rearranged the other information into a rough outline of an essay with two main points.

Intro: The reality of the justice system and the media accounts of it are two different things. Take two examples: violence and court proceedings.

1. Crime
   - murders in reality vs. murders in the media
   - violent crime in reality vs. violent crime in the media
2. Courts—the Roberts and Doob study
   - opinions of group that read newspaper accounts of a trial
   - opinions of group that read court documents of a trial

Conclusion: Lawmakers need to base decisions on reality and not on the media or public opinion.

Working from this rough outline, Victor developed a first draft. In reading it over, he noted where he needed to add more support to make the contrast clearer and more emphatic. After two more revisions and a careful edit, he submitted "Justice and Journalism," which you will find on pages 312–14.

Exercise 3.1

Choose a subject, or work with an assigned subject. Follow the six steps outlined on pages 31–32 to see what main points you can come up with. Don't worry if your work is messy. Freewriting is a record of your thoughts, and thinking is messy.

BRAINSTORMING

In **brainstorming**, you write down a list of every idea you can think of about a specific subject. You can brainstorm alone, with a partner, or—best of all—in a group. If you run out of ideas too quickly, then try the age-old journalist's technique: ask the questions *who, what, why, when, where,* and *how* about your subject. Here's how to proceed. (The first three steps below assume you are working with a partner or in a small group. You can also do them by yourself, but you'll have less fun.)

1. Write your topic at the top of the page. Again, you will save time if you've checked your subject against the 4-S test. Decide how much time you will spend on this exercise: three, five, or more minutes. As in freewriting, working against the clock can bring surprising results.
2. Write down in short form—words or phrases—every idea you can think of that is even vaguely related to your subject. Choose the fastest writer in your group to be the recorder. Work quickly. Don't slow yourselves down by worrying about grammar or repetition.
3. When the time is up, relax for a minute, then go over the list carefully. Highlight the points that seem most clearly related to your subject and cross out any duplicates or any ideas that are vague, trivial, or irrelevant. If you don't end up with at least three or four points that are meaningful to you, brainstorm again for a few minutes, using the six journalist's questions to generate more ideas.
4. Working alone now, take your three or four most significant points and rephrase them in clear sentences on a new sheet of paper. Now you're ready to move on to the next step: testing your main points to ensure that they are suitable for use in your essay.

The following example demonstrates how brainstorming can be used to overcome the most frustrating inertia. The subject is "your college English course." As you might expect, the class groaned when the subject was assigned, but one group's quick brainstorming produced some interesting approaches to the topic. The time limit given for this exercise was four minutes. After brainstorming, at least one student was convinced that her career opportunities would improve if she learned how to communicate better.

Your College English Course

- have to take it
- should like it but I don't
- writing is important
- speaking's easier than writing
- bosses will hire you if you can write
- you can get a job
- letter of application
- have to write on the job
- have to write to the boss, other departments
- have to write to customers
- embarrassed about my writing
- people don't respect a poor writer
- writing helps you think
- writing helps you read better
- have to write reports
- need to know how to write a good report
- have to prepare slides for presentations
- need to write to get promoted

This list contains several significant points along with some irrelevant and trivial ones, which the group deleted. Then they talked about possible relationships among the remaining items on the list.

At this point, each student began working alone. After one student had highlighted the points she felt were most important, she noticed that these points could be divided into two related ideas: what college English teaches and why it is useful. She then combined these ideas into a thesis (a point of view about a subject). Here is her list of revised points.

College English is useful because
- it improves writing and thinking skills
- you will communicate better on the job
- job promotion requires good communication skills

Exercise 3.2

In groups of four or five, brainstorm to identify as many topics as you can in five minutes. Do not censor or cut any ideas. You should end up with at least 20 topics. Then exchange papers with another group and edit that group's topics, crossing out any that are too broad or too narrow. Switch papers again, but with a different group, and choose four topics that pass the 4-S test. Finally, select the best of the four topics and present it to the rest of the class, explaining why it's a good choice for an essay.

Exercise 3.3

Choose one of the three prewriting techniques presented in this chapter: talking, freewriting, or brainstorming. Generate as much information as you can in five minutes about one of the topics presented to the class in Exercise 3.2. Then narrow your information down to an opinion supported by two or three main points. Finally, write a brief outline (about as long as the example given at the bottom of page 35) for a short essay.

Generating Main Points: The Top-Down Approach

Another way to find out what you have to say about a subject is to ask specific questions about it. Questioning lets you "walk around" your subject, looking at it from different angles, taking it apart and putting it back together again. Each question is a probe that enables you to dig below the surface and find out what you know. The top-down approach is more structured than the strategies we have discussed so far, but it has the advantage of producing clear main points with few or no off-topic responses. It also identifies for you the kinds of development you can use in your essay.

Questioning your subject works best if you know it well or have done some research but are not sure how to approach it. Any subject can be approached in a number of ways. Your purpose in writing should determine the approach you choose.

Here's how to use the questioning technique to generate ideas:

1. Begin by writing your proposed subject at the top of the page, or tape it to your monitor.

2. Now apply the 12 questions listed below, one at a time, to your subject to see which ones "fit" best. That is, find the questions that call up in your mind answers that could be used as points to develop your subject. As you go down the list, you will probably find more than one question for which you can think up answers. Do not stop with the first question that produces answers. The purpose of this idea-generating technique is to discover the *best* approach for your target audience and writing purpose.

3. Go through the entire list and record your answers to any questions that apply to your subject. Ignore the questions that make no sense in relation to the subject.

4. Finally, study the questions that produced answers and choose the one that generated the ideas that are closest to what your reader needs to know and what you want to say.

The questions listed in the left-hand column lead to the kinds of essay development listed in the column on the right. Don't worry about these now. We'll discuss them in detail in Part 5.

The Answers to This Question	Produce This Kind of Paper
1. How is your subject *made* or *done*? 2. How does your subject work?	*Process*
3. What are the main *kinds* of your subject? 4. What are the component *parts* of your subject? 5. What are the significant *features*, *characteristics*, or *functions* of your subject?	*Classification/ Division*
6. What are the *causes* of your subject? 7. What are the *effects* or *consequences* of your subject?	*Cause/Effect*
8. What are the *similarities* and/or *differences* between your subject and *X*?	*Comparison/ Contrast*
9. What are the main *advantages/disadvantages* of your subject? 10. What are the reasons *in favour of/against* your subject?	*Argument/ Persuasion*
11. What does your subject *look, feel, sound, smell*, and/or *taste* like?	*Description*
12. How did your subject *happen*?	*Narration*

Here is an example of how the process works. Alice Tam, a recent college graduate, has decided to write about her first job as a management trainee. Her target audience is general readers, not experts in her field. The subject passes the 4-S test: it is significant, single, specific, and supportable.

1. How is my job done?
   The answer to this question is basically a job description, which would be of little interest to anyone other than Alice's close friends, her supervisor, or the person hired to replace her. Let's move on.

2. How does my first job work?
   All jobs are different; this question doesn't take us anywhere.

3. What are the main kinds of first jobs?
   This question might lead to an acceptable topic for a research paper on the kinds of entry-level jobs that graduates from specific programs can expect to get, but the answers won't produce the sort of personal experience essay Alice wants to write.

4. What are the component parts (i.e., main requirements) of my job?
   Our writer might use this question as a starting point for a discussion of her main job functions, but this information would be of interest only to those in her career field, not to a broad, general audience.

5. What are the significant features of my job?
   This question has possibilities. Alice could tell her readers about those aspects of her job that apply to all first-time employees, perhaps limiting her focus to the aspects of the working world that she hadn't expected—that, in fact, surprised her.

6. What were the causes of my first job?
   Broadly interpreted to mean "Why did I want my first job," this question probably wouldn't produce useful answers. Most people work because they have to support themselves.

7. What are the effects of my first job?
   This question raises some interesting answers. What effect has full-time employment had on Alice's life? She might discuss the self-esteem that replaced her earlier insecurity and fear of the job search; she might discuss her new independence, both financial and social.

8. What are the similarities (or differences) between my first job and . . . what? A second or third job?
   Our writer is still in her first job and so can't answer this question.

9. What are the main advantages (or disadvantages) of my first job?
   This question produces answers that are easy to explain—and that's the problem with it. Unless Alice has a very unusual first job, the answers

to this question are predictable and therefore unlikely to be of interest to a broad audience.

10. What are the reasons in favour of (or against) my first job?

    This question leads to answers that overlap with those produced by question 9. It would lead to an average essay, but not to anything outstanding or memorable.

11. What does my job feel like?

    At first glance, this question doesn't make much sense. A *job* can't feel; the *employee* does. However, by interpreting the question loosely, Alice could describe her nervousness, her desire to do well, the pressures she felt, and the rewards of the job.

12. How did my job happen?

    This question doesn't sound promising. How Alice landed her job would be of interest to her family and friends, but probably would not appeal to a broader audience unless her experience was highly unusual or could be instructive to others.

After patiently going through the list, our writer found two questions, 5 and 7, that produced answers she felt she could work with. She especially liked the possibilities suggested by question 5. As Alice focused her thoughts, she realized that what she wanted to write about was the unexpected challenges she confronted when she joined the world of work. So she refined the question to capture what she wanted to write about ("What are the most significant challenges I faced in my first job?") and came up with three solid answers: the expectations of her boss, her co-workers, and herself. The essay that resulted from this process, "On-the-Job Training," appears on pages 243–44.

Generating main points is a time-consuming but worthwhile process. The more time you spend at this stage, the less time it will take you to draft your essay. To sharpen your skills, study the examples given below. Each consists of a 4-S test-approved subject, a question about that subject, and some answers the question produces that would form solid main points to support, explain, or prove the subject of the essay.

Subject	Selected Question	Main Points
Hockey violence	What are the reasons in favour of violence in hockey?	• releases aggression • keeps players alert • attracts fans
Law enforcement officers	What are the main functions of law enforcement officers?	• preventing crime • apprehending criminals • enforcing the law • acting as role models

Subject	Selected Question	Main Points
Job interviews	How do you make a negative impression in a job interview?	• be late • be inappropriately dressed • be ignorant about the company • complain about former employers
Essay topics	What are the characteristics of a satisfactory essay topic?	• single • significant • specific • supportable

Exercise 3.4

Working in pairs, apply the questions on page 37 to each of the subjects listed below. Select the question that produces the answers you both like best, and list three or four of these answers as main points.

Subject	Selected Question	Main Points
1. Procrastination		• • • •
2. Instant messaging		• • • •
3. EVs (electronic vehicles)		• • • •

4. Business dress
   codes

    •

    •

    •

    •

5. Your favourite meal

    •

    •

    •

    •

Exercise 3.5

In pairs, choose two subjects that you think would be suitable for short essays. Be sure both are significant, single, specific, and supportable. For each subject, list at least three strong main points. Use the questions on page 37 to help you identify main points. When you've finished, exchange your ideas with another team, critique each other's main points, and make suggestions.

Subject   _____

Selected Question   _____

Main Points   •

    •

    •

Subject   _____

Selected Question   _____

Main Points   •

    •

    •

Testing Your Main Points

Now that you've practised identifying main points using talking, freewriting, brainstorming, and the questioning approach, the next step is to examine the points you've come up with to make sure each is going to work as a major component in your essay. Some may be too minor to bother with; some may overlap in meaning; some may even be unrelated to your subject. Here's how to test your main points to be sure they are satisfactory. Whether you've arrived at your main points through talking, freewriting, brainstorming, or questioning, the test is the same.

> Main points must be significant, distinct, and relevant.

ARE YOUR MAIN POINTS SIGNIFICANT?

Each main point should be worth writing and reading about. If you can't write at least one interesting and informative paragraph about a point, it is probably not significant enough to bother with. Don't waste your readers' time with trivial matters. In the following example, one of the main points does not have the same importance as the others; it should be eliminated or replaced. Which one would you discard?

Reasons for attending college
- to learn career skills
- to improve one's general knowledge of the world
- to enjoy the social life
- to participate in student government

ARE YOUR MAIN POINTS DISTINCT?

Each of the main points you choose must be different from all the others; there must be no overlap in meaning. Check to be sure you haven't given two different labels to what is really only one aspect of your subject. Eliminate or replace any main points that duplicate other points or that can easily be covered under another point. Here's an example of a list that contains a redundant main point. Which point would you eliminate?

Advantages of cycling	• improves fitness
	• stimulates enjoyment of surroundings
	• keeps one in shape
	• doesn't damage the environment

ARE YOUR MAIN POINTS RELEVANT?

The main points you choose must be clearly and directly related to your subject. They all must be aspects of that subject and must add to the development of your readers' information on the subject. In this example, the third main point listed should be eliminated because it does not relate to the stated topic.

Why buy all-season tires?	• better control on turns
	• increased traction in loose snow
	• added expense
	• decreased stopping distance

Exercise 3.6*

At least one main point in each item below is unsatisfactory. Identify each faulty point and explain why it should be deleted. When you have finished, compare your answers with those on page 536.

1. Business communication devices
   • telephone
   • e-mail
   • fax
   • mail
   • cellphone

2. Advantages of locating a business outside the city
   • cheaper cost of living
   • calmer pace
   • distance from suppliers and markets
   • government subsidies and tax benefits

3. Kinds of television commercials
   • boring
   • clever
   • misleading
   • puzzling
   • repetitive

4. Causes of college
   and university failure
   - lack of preparation in high school
   - procrastination
   - poor study habits
   - irregular attendance

5. How to choose a place to
   live
   - determine your needs
   - determine your budget
   - find a reliable real estate agent
   - seek expert advice

6. Reasons for high
   staff turnover
   - salary lower than industry standard
   - no chance for advancement
   - uncomfortable work environment
   - competitors offer better pay

Organizing Your Main Points

After you've identified the main points for your essay and checked to make sure they are satisfactory, your final task in the planning process is to list them in the order in which you will present them. (This list of points is sometimes called a *plan of development* or a *path statement*.) Main points are like menu items on a website: the more logically they are arranged, the easier it is to navigate your way through them.

There are four ways to order your main points:
chronological, climactic, logical, and random.

CHRONOLOGICAL ORDER

When you present your points in order of time from first to last, you are using **chronological order**. You will find it most appropriate in process essays, but it can be used in other types of essays as well. Here are two examples.

Subject	Main Points
The process of writing a paper	• select an appropriate subject • list and edit the main points • write a thesis statement • write an outline for the paper • write a first draft • revise, edit, and proofread
The evolution of a relationship	• meeting • attraction • discovery • intimacy • disillusionment

CLIMACTIC ORDER

Persuasion most often uses a climactic arrangement, but climactic order is also common in papers based on examples, comparison or contrast, and classification or division. In **climactic order**, you save your strongest or most convincing point for last (the climax of your argument). You lead off your essay with your second-strongest point, and arrange your other points in between, as in this example.

Subject	Main Points
Advantages of a postsecondary education	• development of skills and knowledge • friendships and contacts with compatible people • potential for higher income • discovery of one's own potential

LOGICAL ORDER

Cause-and-effect essays, or any writing in which one point must be explained before the next point can be understood, are based on **logical order**. Your main points have a logical relationship, and you cannot discuss them out of order without confusing your readers. Consider the following sequence.

Subject	Main Points
Main causes of youth crime	• lack of opportunity for work • lack of recreational facilities • boredom • craving for excitement

The logical links here are clear: because of unemployment, recreational facilities are needed. Because of both unemployment and inadequate recreational facilities, boredom and the craving for excitement become problems. Readers must grasp each point before the next can be explained and understood.

RANDOM ORDER

On the rare occasions when your points can be explained in any order without affecting your readers' understanding, you can use **random order**. A random arrangement is possible only if all your main points are of equal significance and if they are not linked together logically or chronologically. In this example, all three points have equal weight.

Subject	Main Points
The garbage disposal crisis	• disposal sites are hard to find • cartage costs are high • new technologies are not yet fully developed

Exercise 3.7*

Choose the type of order—chronological, climactic, logical, or random—you think is most appropriate for each of the following subjects. Arrange the main points in that order by numbering them in the spaces provided.

Subject	Order	Main Points
1. How to impress a client	_____	____ firm handshake ____ friendly closing ____ well-prepared sales presentation ____ knowledge of client's needs ____ appropriate business attire
2. How to handle tax preparation	_____	____ do your own ____ don't bother to file a return ____ go to a franchise tax-preparation company ____ hire an accountant

3. Reasons for
   listening to
   CBC Radio _____

____ It offers informative
   programs.
____ Your taxes are paying for it.
____ It encourages a sense of
   Canadian unity.

4. Methods of
   quitting smoking _____

____ nicotine patch
____ cold turkey
____ gradual withdrawal

5. Causes of
   dissatisfaction
   with employment _____

____ incompetent or unfriendly
   supervisor
____ incompatible co-workers
____ inappropriate pay for skills
   and effort
____ unfulfilling work
   assignments

GO TO WEB

EXERCISE 3.1

Exercise 3.8

Now go back to the subjects and main points that you developed in Exercise 3.5. First, reconsider your main points: Are they all significant, distinct, and related to the subject? Next, put the main points in the order that is most appropriate for the subject to which they belong.

When you've finished this task, exchange papers with another student and check each other's work. Can your partner identify the order of points you have chosen? Does he or she agree with your choice?

In this chapter, you've learned how to identify main points, how to test them for suitability, and how to arrange them in the most appropriate order. You're ready now to go on to the next step: writing the thesis statement—probably the most important sentence in your paper.

4

Writing the Thesis Statement

The key to clear organization in any paper is a thesis statement near the beginning that announces the paper's subject and scope. The thesis statement not only helps a reader to see how you are going to approach the subject, but also serves to keep you, the writer, on track.

A **thesis statement** is one or more sentences that clearly and concisely indicate the subject of your paper, the main points you will discuss, and the order in which you will discuss them.

In business communication, technical writing, and some academic writing (e.g., research papers and dissertations) it is important to indicate the subject and scope of your paper at the outset. Readers expect this sort of preview.[1]

The number of sentences in a thesis statement depends on what the subject is, how best to phrase it, how many points there are, and how complex they are. A thesis statement in a short paper is usually a single sentence at the end of the first paragraph, but in a lengthy paper on complicated issues, it might be several sentences or even a paragraph long. Occasionally (in a technical description, for example), a writer will choose a short thesis and omit the main points from the thesis statement.

To write a thesis statement, you combine your subject and your main points. A simple formula for constructing a thesis statement appears at the top of the next page.

---

[1] In less formal writing, such as newspaper or magazine articles and informal essays—including some of the essays in this book—a thesis statement is not necessarily required.

subject	link	main points
S	consists of	1, 2, 3 . . . etc.

These three elements can be combined in various ways. For example:

The most prolific producers of unnecessary jargon are politicians, sports-writers, advertising copywriters, and educators. (Subject and main points are linked by *are*.)

Three powerful factors are responsible for the development of anorexia nervosa in young women: the pressures of adolescence, the expectations of family and peers, and the potent influence of mass media. (Subject and main points are linked by a colon.)

Because the United States influences Canada's foreign policy, dominates its culture, and controls its economy, Canada is little more than an American satellite. (Main points precede subject and are linked to the subject by *Because*.)

Fad diets are not the quick fix to weight problems that they may appear to be. On the contrary, they are often costly, ineffective, and even dangerous. (Subject is one sentence. Main points are in second sentence, linked to the first by *On the contrary*.)

Once you have mastered the basic formula, you can experiment with creative ways of expressing a thesis statement. Just be sure that it is appropriate in form, language, and tone to the kind of paper you are writing. The thesis statements in the exercise below range from short to long, formal to informal, and serious to flippant. The first four items are straightforward; you should have no trouble analyzing them. The last three are increasingly complex and challenging. Work with a partner to identify their elements.

Exercise 4.1*

In each of the following thesis statements, underline the subject with a double line and the main points with a single line. When you have finished all seven, compare your answers with those on pages 536–37.

1. Students who try to combine a full-time job with a full-time program

   face problems at school, at work, and at home.

2. To be successful in a broadcasting career, you must be talented, motivated, and hard-working.

3. Establishing a local area network would promote teamwork and increase efficiency in the office.

4. The business traveller can learn much from the turtle. Carry everything you need with you. Move slowly but with purpose and consistency. Keep your head down until you are sure you know what's going on.

5. Cellphones must be turned off during class because they disrupt everyone's concentration, they prevent the user from learning, and they distract and annoy the teacher, to the detriment of all.

6. Although easily dismissed as merely animated entertainment, *The Simpsons* is effective social commentary, tackling with humour and gusto such issues as the environment, social justice, and race relations.

7. Large energy producers and some provincial governments say we cannot afford to live up to the terms of the Kyoto and Copenhagen agreements, which seek to reduce the production of greenhouse gases. But can we afford not to comply? Can we afford to compromise the health of Canadians by continuing to pollute? Can we afford to risk the effects of climate change on our environment? Can we afford to fall behind the rest of the world in research and development leading to a solution to the problem of greenhouse gases?

Exercise 4.2

Each of the five introductions below contains a thesis statement. Working with a partner or in groups of three or four, identify the thesis statement in each paragraph.

1. What does an interviewer look for in a job applicant? Good credentials, good preparation, good grooming, and good communication skills are essential features for anyone who wants a job. No interviewer would seriously consider an applicant who comes to an interview without the

required educational background and work experience, without information about the job and the company, without appropriate clothing, and without the ability to present ideas clearly in the interview.

2. The numbers from Statistics Canada tell the story: a record one in seven of us is 65 or older; the median age is up; the average age of seniors is up; the number of centenarians is up; and the Baby Boomers constitute the largest generation in our population. This situation presents us with many difficult challenges in the years to come, but it also provides significant opportunities for those able and willing to take advantage of the trend. Postsecondary-aged Canadians who want secure and useful employment should be looking to gerontology, medicine, and recreation for their career prospects and their investment opportunities.

3. Suddenly a man steps into the road in front of me. He's wearing a uniform and he's waving his hand for me to pull over to the side. My heart pounds and my skin prickles with anxiety. I feel guilty, but I don't know what I've done wrong—maybe speeding 10 kilometres over the limit, but no more. Anyone who has been caught in a radar trap knows these momentary feelings of panic, guilt, and resentment. We fear that the police officer will be brusque and accusing, but we are often surprised. There are as many kinds of police officers as there are people. Four kinds, however, dominate the profession: the confident veteran, the arrogant authoritarian, the cocky novice, and the friendly professional. As I roll down my window, I wonder which kind of police officer has stopped me.

4. After a hard day's work, do you relax with two or three stiff drinks? Do you enjoy a few beers while watching a game on TV? Do you believe alcoholic drinks make a party more fun? Do you cool off with gin fizzes on a hot afternoon? If you answered "yes" to most of these questions, you are probably abusing alcohol. The line between excessive social drinking and a serious addictive habit is a blurry one. Most alcoholics don't know they are hooked until they try to stop drinking. What are the signs that a drinker is no longer drinking for pleasure only? If a person "needs" a drink, or drinks alone, or can fall asleep only after a few drinks, or can find enjoyment only when drinking, that person is probably in trouble.

5. Ours is a transient society. Most of us travel more kilometres in a year than our grandparents travelled in a lifetime. We move from one city to another, one province or territory to another, and one country to another. In the course of moving, we inhabit many homes. The family home of the past may have been inhabited by several generations, consecutively or concurrently. Today's average Canadians will probably have 10 or more addresses during their adult lives. Our restlessness is particularly hard on the children in our migrating families: they have to leave familiar surroundings and friends, and they must adjust to a new environment, new habits, and sometimes a new language. These children pay a heavy price for the mobility of modern impermanence.

Phrasing Your Statement of Subject

The first part of a thesis statement is the statement of subject. It identifies *your idea about* or *your approach to* your subject and states a viewpoint that must be explained or proved. (The main points provide the explanation or proof.) Your statement of subject should be as clear and concise as you can make it. It must NOT be boring.

Beginning writers often fall into the trap of stating the obvious: "In this paper, I am going to discuss . . ." or "The subject of this report is. . . ." Your readers *know* it's your paper; you needn't hit them over the head by telling them so. Here are three examples of faulty subject statements and our suggested revisions.

Poor	Better
In this essay, I am going to discuss violence in hockey. (What about it?)	Violence in hockey is misunderstood by the nonplaying public.
This paper is about Canada's multiculturalism policy. (What about it?)	Canada's multiculturalism policy is neither practical nor desirable.
I am going to examine the influence of Walmart in Canada. (What about it?)	With over 200 stores in Canada and plans for expansion, Walmart's effects on labour are worth considering.

As soon as you write, "In this essay . . ." or "I am going to discuss (write about, explore) . . . ," you trap yourself into simply announcing your subject, not stating your idea or opinion about it. Avoid these traps. Always let your reader know *what it is about your subject* that your paper will explain or prove. In Part 4, we will look at the different ways you can tackle your subject.

Phrasing the Main Points

When you combine your statement of subject with your main points to form a thesis statement, be sure that all your main points are phrased the same way: in grammatically parallel form. If point 1 is a single word, then points 2, 3, and so on must also be single words. If point 1 is a phrase, then all the points following it must be phrases. If point 1 is a clause or a sentence, then the succeeding points must also be clauses or sentences. Only the most experienced writers can produce a perfect thesis statement in one try. The rest of us need to draft, revise, reconsider, revise again—and probably do it all yet again—to produce a grammatically parallel thesis statement.

The following sentence is not grammatically parallel:

Of the many qualities that combine to make a good nurse, the three most important are strength, intelligence, and she must be compassionate.

Revised to be grammatically parallel, the sentence might read like this:

Of the many qualities that combine to make a good nurse, the three most important are strength, intelligence, and compassion.

Or like this:

Of the many qualities that combine to make a good nurse, the three most important are that he or she be strong, intelligent, and compassionate.

If you have trouble with grammatical parallelism, turn to Part 7, Section 7.5, before you try the exercise below.

Exercise 4.3

In each of the following lists, one point is not parallel with the others. Rephrase the incorrect item so that all are in grammatically parallel form.

1. Our employees are
   a. motivated
   b. good training
   c. knowledgeable
2. Our doctor is
   a. full of compassion
   b. competent
   c. hard-working
3. I've noticed that my friends are increasingly
   a. concerned about their diets
   b. interested in fitness
   c. environmental awareness
4. To upgrade our educational system, we need
   a. more effective teacher training
   b. better liaison between levels of education
   c. students must be motivated to learn
5. An investment strategy must be
   a. based on current information
   b. appropriately diversified
   c. the client has to be tolerant of the degree of risk

Exercise 4.4

Work in pairs to develop two thesis statements for potential essays. Phrase the two thesis statements so that one has a poor statement of subject and the other lacks parallelism. Exchange your creations with another team and identify each other's problems. Then correct the sentences. Exchange papers again. Did the other team identify and correct the problems you thought you'd created? If not, revise your own team's faulty sentences.

Exercise 4.5

Working with a partner, combine each of the following subjects with its main points to form a clear thesis statement that is expressed in grammatically parallel form.

1. Causes of stress
   - being laid off
   - financial problems
   - the loss of a family member

Thesis statement: _____

_____

_____

_____

_____

2. Steps in finding a job
   - conduct an Internet job search
   - prepare a letter of application
   - perform well in the interview

Thesis statement: _____

_____

_____

_____

_____

3. How to save money
   - automatic payroll deductions
   - keep a record of expenditures
   - reduce impulse buying
   - establish and maintain a budget

Thesis statement: _____

_____

_____

_____

4. Evolution of a recession
- Unemployment causes general economic slowdown
- Consumer buying decreases, resulting in inflation
- Inflation causes fear and a further decrease in consumer demand

Thesis statement: _____

_____

_____

_____

5. Evolution of a revolution
- Those in power oppress those they rule
- Oppression leads to revolution
- Revolutionaries take power
- Those in power oppress those they rule

Thesis statement: _____

_____

_____

_____

_____

Exercise 4.6

Working independently, combine each of the following subjects with its main points to form a grammatically parallel thesis statement.

1. Comparison between McDonald's and Wendy's (or any other two fast-food restaurants)
- food
- atmosphere
- service
- price

Thesis statement: _____

_____

_____

_____

_____

2. Effects of urban
   overcrowding
   - traffic jams
   - air pollution
   - high rate of homelessness
   - violence on the streets
   - domestic violence

Thesis statement: _____

_____

_____

_____

3. Characteristics of a
   successful small business
   - adequate capital
   - marketable product
   - personnel that are dedicated
   - workable business plan

Thesis statement: _____

_____

_____

_____

_____

Exercise 4.7*

In groups of three or four, share the thesis statements you developed for Exercise 4.6 and discuss your decisions. As a group, revise each statement until you are all satisfied they meet the criteria for satisfactory thesis statements. Then compare your results with our suggestions on page 537.

You have now covered all the steps leading to the construction of a good thesis statement. The exercises above have given you practice in the skills you need to phrase subjects and main points correctly and effectively.

Exercise 4.8 will walk you through the process of developing a thesis statement for a subject of your own choice. As you fill in the blanks in this exercise, you will be reviewing the first four chapters of this book and also testing your mastery of the writing skills they presented.

Exercise 4.8

1. Select a subject.

   _____

   _____

2. Test whether your subject is significant, single, specific, and support-able.

3. Using either a bottom-up or a top-down approach to generate ideas, identify three to five main points in support of your subject.

   _____

   _____

   _____

   _____

   _____

4. Test whether your main points are all significant, distinct, and clearly related to your subject.

5. Arrange your main points in the order that is most likely to guarantee your readers' understanding of your subject: chronological, climactic, logical, or random.

   _____

   _____

   _____

   _____

   _____

6. Rewrite your main points so that they are grammatically parallel: all single words, all phrases, or all clauses.

_____

_____

_____

_____

_____

7. Combine your statement of subject with your main points to produce a thesis statement.

_____

_____

_____

_____

_____

The seven points listed in Exercise 4.8 summarize the steps to follow in planning an essay. Keep this outline handy and refer to it when you start your next paper or research report.

5

Preparing an Outline

Writing a paper is like building a house: you save much time and frustration if you start with a plan. For anything longer than about 400 words, writers need a plan or outline to guide them as they begin to build words into sentences, sentences into paragraphs, and paragraphs into the final product, whether it's a term paper, a research report, a business plan, or a market analysis.

Wise writers treat an outline as tentative, not something chiselled in stone. As you draft your paper, you may discover new ideas or a new structure that better suits your purpose. If so, change your thesis statement and outline to accommodate it. (It's a good idea to make these changes in pencil or as a new file because you may decide at the end of the draft that these new ideas weren't so great after all.)

If you have access to a word-processing program with an outline feature, try it out. These programs can be a great help to an inexperienced writer with little knowledge of how to plan a writing assignment.

As we have seen, all written messages consist of an introduction, a body, and a conclusion, but each of these may vary from one to several paragraphs in length, and from simple to sophisticated in style. The model format on the next page is an outline for a simple five-paragraph essay. Once you've mastered this basic structure, you can modify, expand, and develop it to suit any of the kinds of writing you'll be called upon to do.

Outline Format

Title	_____

INTRODUCTION   _____

Attention-getter*   _____
_____
_____
_____

Thesis statement   <u>Subject consists of 1, 2, and 3.</u>

BODY   <u>Topic sentence introducing main point 1 goes here.</u>

Support for first main point
_____
_____
_____
_____
_____

<u>Concluding sentence goes here.</u>

<u>Topic sentence introducing main point 2 goes here.</u>

Support for second main point
_____
_____
_____
_____
_____

<u>Concluding sentence goes here.</u>

<u>Topic sentence introducing main point 3 goes here.</u>

Support for third main point
_____
_____
_____
_____
_____

<u>Concluding sentence goes here.</u>

CONCLUSION   _____

Summary   _____
_____

Memorable statement*   _____
_____ .

---

*Terms marked with an asterisk are explained and illustrated in Chapter 7.

The outline below follows the format on page 60. The final version of "Ready, Willing . . . and Employable" appears after the outline.

Ready, Willing . . . and Employable	*Essay title*
What are employers looking for today?	*Attention-getter*
Employers are looking for a new breed of employee: one who has knowledge, flexibility, and the right attitude.	*Thesis statement*
Knowledge is still first on the list.	*1. Topic sentence*
• colleges offer a broad range of programs to meet employers' needs • graduates must know current trends as well as theory • some employers test for knowledge • some rely on school's reputation plus recommendations of professors and recruiters	*Support for first main point*
Adaptability is essential for a prospective employee.	*2. Topic sentence*
• today's jobs require multitasking • flexible workers are more cost-effective and better problem solvers • flexible workers can adapt to change • students need to broaden their education and learn a variety of skills	*Support for second main point*
Employers complain about graduates' poor attitude.	*3. Topic sentence*

• graduates lack the ability to take direction, use team skills, communicate well, and motivate themselves
• similar problems show up in class
  —chronic lateness
  —lack of cooperation
  —laziness
• students need to correct these attitude problems on their own
	Support for third main point

Students must be ready, able, and willing to work.	*Summary of main points*
With these skills, a good résumé, and professional contacts, graduates can enter the workforce with confidence.	*Memorable statement*

READY, WILLING . . . AND EMPLOYABLE

Attention-getter

Thesis statement

What are employers looking for in today's job market? Several recent surveys point to a subtle shift in the requirements of businesses looking to hire college and university graduates. Only a few years ago, knowledge was the prerequisite to employment in most industries. Employers needed workers with the highly specialized skills of an emerging high-tech workplace. Now many of those skills are taken for granted, and other characteristics have become increasingly important. Employers are seeking a new breed of employee: one who has the knowledge required to do the job, the flexibility to adapt, and—most important—the attitude to succeed.

Topic sentence

Support for first main point

Knowledge of how to do the job is, understandably, still first on the shopping list that employers bring to job fairs. Colleges and universities across the country have responded to marketplace requirements with an array of programs designed to prepare students to meet the needs of industries from broadcasting to photonics, from microelectronics to winemaking. Graduates are expected to have up-to-the-minute information on current trends in their fields, as well as solid grounding in the theory and practice of their specialty. Some employers test applicants for this knowledge; others rely on the reputation of the institution, the recommendation of professors with whom they have professional connections, and the insights of recruiters. As valuable as knowledge is to the employer, however, an employee's flexibility is quickly becoming just as important.

Concluding statement and transition

Topic sentence

Support for second main point

"Multitasking" is a buzz word often used to describe the ability to move quickly and easily between projects and work environments, bringing a wide range of skills to bear on a variety of situations. Adaptability is an essential characteristic of any prospective employee. Workers who can use their expertise simultaneously on several different tasks within a project are valuable not only because they are more cost-effective than several single-task specialists, but also because they tend to see projects holistically and are better problem solvers as a result. In addition, flexible workers are those who most quickly and easily adapt to changes in technology or work practice, and such changes are a way of life in today's work environment. Students must prepare themselves to be flexible workers by broadening their education and by learning as many skills as possible. Unlike their parents, workers in the current generation have little hope of finding a job that will require only one skill set over the course of a career. Adaptability is a critical skill, but even when combined with knowledge, it is not enough to ensure employability. Increasingly, attitude is the determining factor in who gets hired—and promoted!

Concluding sentence

Transition to next paragraph

Employers continually complain to colleges and universities that students *Topic*
on placement and graduates in their first position fail to impress, not from lack *sentence*
of knowledge, skill, or preparation, but from a broad range of inadequacies best
summed up as "poor attitude." Among the faults cited under this broad
heading are inability to take direction, failure to work well with colleagues,
inability to communicate effectively, and lack of enthusiasm and initiative. How
can such problems be corrected before graduates reach the workplace? Schools
do not offer courses in attitude adjustment, but perhaps they should. Most of
these problems have surfaced in classes long before graduation. Students who *Support for*
are chronically late, frequently uncooperative, constantly complaining, or vis- *third main*
ibly lazy are those who, with all the skills and ability in the world, will not suc- *point*
ceed in any job worth having. Even highly motivated and ambitious graduates
have sometimes had difficulty adjusting to entry-level positions when they find
themselves working under the supervision of people they consider to be less talented or skilled. It is up to students themselves to correct their attitudinal defi-
ciencies. They need to pay attention to the criticisms of teachers, classmates,
even family members, and make an honest evaluation of consistently noticed
faults. Only when such attitude faults have been identified and acknowledged *Concluding*
can they be corrected, and only when they have been corrected will the stu- *sentence*
dent be an asset to an employer.

As graduation draws near, most students view their coming transformation *Summary*
into workers with eagerness liberally mixed with anxiety. Statistics tell us that *and*
most college and university graduates find employment in their fields within a *memorable*
year of graduation. Armed with this encouraging information, together with a *statement*
good résumé, professional contacts, and the knowledge, flexibility, and attitude
to succeed, graduates can face employers and the workplace with confidence.

Exercise 5.1

Read "Getting Pancake Sauce from Trees" (pages 293–95). Identify the sen-
tences that correspond to the major structural items in the outline format that
follows. If you're working through this textbook in order, you may not have
studied some of the terms mentioned, but you should be able to make a good
guess at identifying the attention-getter and the memorable statement. To
make your task easier, the sentences in the essay have been numbered.

After you have completed the task, compare your results with those of a
classmate. Discuss any differences you discover and try to resolve them.
"Getting Pancake Sauce from Trees" is a slight variation on the basic pattern,
so analyze each paragraph carefully. Let meaning be your guide.

Getting Pancake Sauce from Trees

INTRODUCTION

Attention-getter   Sentence(s)   _____

Thesis statement   Sentence(s)   _____

BODY PARAGRAPH #1

Topic sentence   Sentence(s)   _____

Support for first main point   Sentence(s)   _____

Conclusion   Sentence(s)   _____

BODY PARAGRAPH #2

Topic sentence   Sentence(s)   _____

Support for second main point Sentence(s)   _____

Conclusion   Sentence(s)   _____

BODY PARAGRAPH #3

Topic sentence   Sentence(s)   _____

Support for third main point   Sentence(s)   _____

Conclusion   Sentence(s)   _____

CONCLUSION

Summary/Reinforcement   Sentence(s)   _____

Memorable statement   Sentence(s)   _____

PART 2

Drafting

A journey of a thousand miles must begin with a single step.
Lao Tzu, circa 6th century BCE

He who has made a beginning has half the deed done.
Horace, 65–8 BCE

Failure to prepare is preparing to fail.
Benjamin Franklin, 1706–1790

Almost all good writing begins with terrible first efforts. You need to start somewhere. Start by getting something—anything—down on paper. . . . [T]he first draft is the down draft—you just get it down.
Anne Lamott, 1954–

6

Understanding Paragraph Form and Function

What Does a Paragraph Look Like?

Essays are divided into paragraphs. **Paragraphs** are sentence groups that are separated from each other in their physical presentation and in their content. They usually have an indentation at the beginning (on a typed page, the first word begins five spaces in from the left margin) and some white space at the end (the paragraph's last word is followed by a hard return). Between the indentation and the final period comes the paragraph— a group of sentences that explains a single idea or topic.

If you were to draw a blueprint for a single paragraph, it would look like this:

A sentence that introduces the **topic** (or main idea) of the paragraph goes here.

Three or more sentences that specifically support or explain the topic go in here.

A sentence that concludes your explanation of the topic (and may provide a transition to the next paragraph) goes here.

Consider the following paragraph. Is it an acceptable paragraph?

[1]Scientists have discovered that eating blueberries and having friends are good for the memory and that pregnancy and smoking are bad for it. [2]Nautiluses can remember useful things, but only for a day, whereas cuttlefish,

which are much more sophisticated [organisms] observe and form preferences for their future prey when they are still embryos. [3]Swiss biologists determined that stupid flies live longer than smart flies because intelligence wears out flies' brains, and Canadian researchers said that straining to recall information on the tip of the tongue makes us learn our mistaken guesses rather than the correct answers we eventually remember. [4]Strokes were found to generate depolarization waves that spread outward from the affected area and damage other parts of the brain. . . . [5]Neuroscientists found that sloths sleep around nine and a half hours a day. [6]Previous research had studied only captive sloths, which sleep on average sixteen hours a day, possibly because they are bored and depressed.

Plant, Robert. "Memory Song." *Harper's Magazine* 6 Aug. 2008: 84. Print.

The above passage looks like a paragraph: it is indented, contains six sentences, and leaves blank the space between the last word and the margin. But it is not a paragraph. It does not develop a single idea. There is no topic. True, all of the sentences in this passage have something to do with the brain: memory, intelligence, and malfunction, but the sentences don't support any one idea. They are not linked together in any logical way. In fact, you could rewrite this passage beginning with the last two sentences and working back to the first. It would make just as much (non)sense. Try it!

How Does a Paragraph Function?

Readers expect a paragraph to present a unit of thought or a single, developed idea. The white space at the beginning and end of each paragraph defines your thought units and also serves two other functions.

1. Paragraphs provide visual cues that make your writing "reader-friendly." Imagine how intimidating the page you are now reading would be if it were one continuous block of print: no headings, no indentations, no paragraphs.
2. Paragraphs divide your writing into linked but separate sections. Without paragraphs, ideas would blur and blend into each other. Readers would find it difficult to identify them, let alone follow the development of the writer's thinking.

In a typical essay, an introductory paragraph is followed by paragraphs that add details and depth to the ideas set out in the introduction. A concluding paragraph brings all the ideas together again and leaves the reader with a complete understanding of the writer's thoughts about the topic.

Readers can tell a great deal about your thinking just by glancing at a page of your paper. A number of short paragraphs indicates a series of ideas, briefly (and perhaps superficially) explained. Long paragraphs—half a page or longer—suggest complex ideas that require explanation and details. They signal serious thought but are more difficult to read because they require close attention.

As a general rule, you explore one major idea or main point in each paragraph. When you have finished exploring one topic and wish to move on to another, you signal this shift to your readers by beginning a new paragraph.

How Long Should a Paragraph Be?

The answer to this question depends on the topic, your readers' familiarity with it, and your purpose in writing. If your topic is complex, your readers' knowledge is limited, and your purpose is to persuade readers who do not share your point of view, then you'll probably need a fairly long paragraph to accomplish your goal. On the other hand, if you're writing about a topic your readers are familiar with, and your purpose is simply to share with them your understanding of that topic, you may be able to accomplish your task in a few sentences.

Exercise 6.1

Divide the class into five groups. Each group will take one of the paragraphs below to read and analyze by answering the following questions. Share your analysis with the class.

- What is the topic of the paragraph, stated in a few words?
- How much knowledge of the topic does the writer assume the readers have?
- What is the writer's purpose in this paragraph?

1. Violence as a way of achieving racial justice is both impractical and immoral. It is impractical because it is a descending spiral ending in destruction for all. The old law of an eye for an eye leaves everybody blind. It is immoral because it seeks to humiliate the opponent rather than win his understanding; it seeks to annihilate rather than to convert. Violence is immoral because it thrives on hatred rather than love. It destroys community and makes brotherhood impossible. It leaves society in monologue rather than dialogue. Violence ends by defeating itself. It creates bitterness in the survivors and brutality in the destroyers. A voice echoes through

time saying to every potential Peter, "Put up your sword." History is cluttered with the wreckage of nations that failed to follow this command.

King, Martin Luther, Jr. "Three Types of Resistance to Oppression." *Stride toward Freedom*. New York: Harper & Row, 1958. 215. Print.

2.   Take William Lyon Mackenzie King, our prime minister through the war and, so it seemed, for all time until Pierre Trudeau came along and seemed to be prime minister for all time. King held power longer than any other Western politician in this century. How did such a pudgy, mundane little man do it? The truth is, he did it deliberately. He was shrewd and self-effacing, and he told his friends that he made every speech as boring as possible because then no one would ever remember what he said and hold it against him. Twenty-two years in power, droning on and on over the airwaves, and meanwhile, he was as crazy as a loon.

Callaghan, Barry. "Canadian Wry." *Canadian Content*. Ed. Sarah Norton and Nell Waldman. 2nd ed. Toronto: Harcourt, 1992. 92. Print.

3.   *Vinaya* means humility; it is the complete surrendering of the self on the part of the *shishya* [the disciple] to the *guru*. The ideal disciple feels love, adoration, reverence, and even fear toward his *guru*, and he accepts equally praise or scoldings. Talent, sincerity, and the willingness to practise faithfully are essential qualities of the serious student. The *guru*, as the giver in this relationship, seems to be all-powerful. Often, he may be unreasonable, harsh, or haughty, though the ideal *guru* is none of these. Ideally, he should respond to the efforts of the disciple and love him almost as his own child. In India, a Hindu child, from his earliest years, is taught to feel humble toward anyone older than he or superior in any way. From the simplest gesture of the *namaskar*, or greeting (putting the hands palm to palm in front of the forehead and bowing), or the *pranam* (a respectful greeting consisting of touching the greeted person's feet, then one's own eyes and forehead with the hands held palm to palm) to the practice of *vinaya* or humility tempered with a feeling of love and worship, the Hindu devotee's vanity and pretension are worn away.

Shankar, Ravi. "Studying Music in India." *My Music, My Life*. Delhi: Vikas Publications, 1968. 11-12. Print.

4.   When I found [the snakeskin], it was whole and tied in a knot. Now there have been stories told, even by reputable scientists, of snakes that have deliberately tied themselves in a knot to prevent larger snakes from trying to swallow them—but I couldn't imagine any way that throwing itself into a half hitch would help a snake trying to escape its skin. Still, ever cautious, I figured that one of the neighborhood boys could possibly have tied it in a knot in the fall, for some whimsical boyish reason, and left it there, where it dried and gathered dust. So I carried the skin along thoughtlessly as I walked, snagging it sure enough on a low branch and rip-

ping it in two. . . . I saw that thick ice still lay on the quarry pond and that the skunk cabbage was already out in the clearings, and then I came home and looked at the skin and its knot.

Dillard, Annie. *Pilgrim at Tinker Creek*. New York: Harper's Magazine Press, 1974. 73. Print.

5.   [T]here needs to be a thorough revision of the maximum-penalty structure to remove the incongruities that riddle the current Criminal Code. Should forgery or certain kinds of fraud really have the same maximum penalty as sexual assault with a weapon? The maximum penalties are also much too high; most were created many decades ago, when our perceptions of the seriousness of various crimes differed from those today. The maximum penalty for breaking and entering is life imprisonment, for example, but in practice the average sentence is well under one year. This is called "bite and bark" sentencing; the system barks more loudly than it bites, and creates false expectations among the public.

Roberts, Julian V. "Three Steps to Make the Punishment Fit the Crime." *Globe and Mail* 7 Dec. 1993: A25. Print.

Exercise 6.2

Write a short paragraph (five to seven sentences) that demonstrates your understanding of paragraph form and function. Choose any topic you like. When you have finished, exchange papers with another student and check each other's paragraph for

- Form: Is there a clear introduction to and conclusion of the topic?
- Function: Does the paragraph develop one main idea or topic? Are all sentences clearly related to the topic? Is the topic explained in enough detail to satisfy the reader's understanding?

Crafting the Topic Sentence

The **topic sentence** in each paragraph is the sentence that clearly identifies what the paragraph is about—its main idea. The topic sentence focuses the paragraph, helps to unify it, and keeps you and your readers on track. In professional writing, the topic sentence is not always the first sentence of the paragraph. Sometimes it is more effective to announce the topic in the second, third, or even the last sentence. But professional writers, through years of practice, have earned the right to break the rules. Beginning writers should remember this: *most readers assume that the first sentence of a paragraph identifies the topic of that paragraph.* If your first sentence doesn't do this, then your readers may go through your paragraph assuming the topic is something other than what you intended. Miscommunication frustrates readers and wastes their time. To be absolutely clear, identify your topic up front.

A good topic sentence does three things:

1. It introduces the topic of the paragraph.
2. It makes a point about the topic.
3. It makes a statement that is neither too broad nor too narrow.

Readers appreciate writers who get to the point quickly, make the point clearly, and support or explain it adequately. They also appreciate writers who can make their points in an interesting way. Take the time to write topic sentences that are something more than straightforward, flat announcements of your main idea. Compare the following pairs of topic sentences.

Weak	Strong
I am going to explain why I love blogs.	The beauty of blogs is that they promote genuine democracy.
This paragraph is about violence.	Violence as a way of achieving racial justice is both impractical and immoral. (Martin Luther King, Jr.)

A good way to introduce the topic so that it is both interesting and effective is to make a point about it. You save your readers' time and eliminate the risk of confusion if you make clear at the outset your idea about or your attitude toward your topic. Consider these examples:

Weak	Strong
Many people around the world enjoy music.	Nothing bridges gaps between cultures like music.
Canadians are different from Americans.	Canadians should be thankful for their differences from Americans.

Finally, the topic you choose must be the "right size"—neither so broad that you cannot support it adequately in a single paragraph, nor so narrow that it doesn't require support. The 4-S test that you used to determine whether a subject was suitable for a paper can also be applied to potential paragraph topics. If your topic is single, significant, specific, and supportable, it should also be the basis for a solid paragraph. Take a look at these topic sentences.

Weak	Strong
The legal system in Canada discriminates against men. (too broad)	Single fathers who seek custody of their children are often treated unfairly in family court.
My children won't eat peas, broccoli, or spinach. (too narrow)	Getting young children to eat a balanced diet is not an easy task.
Cars should be banned from city streets. (too broad)	Cars should be banned from the downtown core from 7:00 a.m. to 7:00 p.m.

Exercise 6.3*

Read through each of the following paragraphs, then underline the topic sentence.

1. The third consideration is perhaps the most important. Canada makes no economic sense. There may be excellent reasons for Canada's existence historically, socially, culturally, and even geographically, but the lines of trade and commerce flow north–south. If a government's chief concern is the economy, that government will naturally draw the country closer and closer to the United States, cinching in those belts of commerce that bind Canada to her southern partner. Only governments whose major goals are cultural or social will loosen the longitudinal ties and seek east–west bonds.

2. Winston Churchill said, "Golf is a game whose aim it is to hit a very small ball into an even smaller hole with weapons singularly ill-designed for the purpose." It has been said that baseball is an activity where fourteen men stand idly by while two play catch. In fact, all sports can be made ridiculous because the essence of sport is rules. If you really want to put a ball into a hole in the ground, it's very easy to do: pick it up, carry it to the hole, and drop it in. The fun in golf, as in all sports, is that the task is made challenging by rigid and complex regulations. Reduced to its essential, sport is the attempt by one person or group to win dominance over another while encumbered by complicated rules. The rules in a game like hockey or baseball are enormously complex, while those in soccer and bowling are less so; however, the objective of all games is the same as the objective of war. Luckily, civilized humans have a love of rules and laws, and can take out their aggressions within the strict confines of the rule book.

3. Seen by scanning electron microscope, our taste buds look as huge as volcanoes on Mars, while those of a shark are beautiful mounds of pastel-colored tissue paper—until we remember what they're used for. In reality, taste buds are exceedingly small. Adults have about 10,000, grouped by theme (salt, sour, sweet, bitter), at various sites in the mouth. Inside each one, about fifty taste cells busily relay information to a neuron, which will

alert the brain. Not much tasting happens in the center of the tongue, but there are also incidental taste buds on the palate, pharynx, and tonsils, which cling like bats to the damp, slimy walls of a cave. Rabbits have 17,000 taste buds, parrots only about 400, and cows 25,000. What are they tasting? Maybe a cow needs that many to enjoy a relentless diet of grass.

Ackerman, Diane. *A Natural History of the Senses.* New York: Vintage-Random House, 1991. 138. Print.

4.   Scholarly explanations of humor fall into three major categories. According to superiority theories, we laugh at the henpecked husband and the woman hit with a banana cream pie because the misfortunes of others make us feel better about our own lot. The 17th century philosopher Thomas Hobbes, for example, described laughter as a result of the "sudden glory" of increased self-esteem at the expense of others. Incongruity theories . . . stress the cognitive jolt of bringing together unrelated ideas. Thus the infant who chuckles when Mommy eats the baby food is savoring the incongruity of a grown woman making a fool of herself. Finally, tension-relief theories attribute our laughter to a sudden release from strain. Freud argued that our jokes, like our dreams, allow pent-up sexual and aggressive images to suddenly leap into consciousness, albeit in a disguised form.

"What's So Funny?" *Psychology Today* June 1978: 101. Print.

5.   "Why do you want it?" This should be the first question a good computer salesperson asks a prospective customer. With the huge variety of computers now on the market, the determining factor in a purchase should be the job the machine will be expected to do. While an HDTV card, a premium audio system, and a 30-inch LCD are great for watching movies, a user who wants a basic word processor would be throwing away money to buy them. Home users and small businesses often get carried away with the desire for gigantic memory capacity, lightning speed, and high-resolution capability, but these are advertising gimmicks rather than useful purchases for most small users. On the other hand, it can be a costly error for a buyer to underestimate long-term computer needs and buy a machine that must be upgraded or replaced in a year.

Now compare your answers with ours on page 537.

Exercise 6.4

Each of the following thesis statements contains a subject and main points. Working with a partner or in a small group, develop the main points of each thesis statement into effective topic sentences.

1. Volunteering is a valuable addition to a college or university education because it provides work experience, develops professional contacts, and enhances self-esteem.
2. Unemployment, poverty, and loneliness are factors that may lead to depression.
3. Canadians immigrate to other countries for three main reasons: a warmer climate, better job opportunities, and new cultural experiences.

Exercise 6.5

For each of the thesis statements below, develop the main points into effective topic sentences. Make sure each topic sentence you write introduces the topic clearly, makes a point about the topic, and is neither too broad nor too narrow.

1. The driver who caused your accident last weekend was probably one of four types: a road hog, a tailgater, a speed demon, or a Sunday driver.
2. There are three types of supervisor in this world: the good, the bad, and mine.
3. The thought of moving to the country is attractive to many city dwellers because of the slower pace, the healthier environment, and the closer-knit communities.

Developing the Topic

Once you've written your topic sentence, the next step is to develop it. An adequately developed paragraph gives enough supporting information to make the topic completely clear to the readers. Unless you are writing from a detailed outline listing all the supporting material you need, it's time to focus once again on your intended audience. Put yourself in your readers' place.

- How much information do your readers already have about your topic?
- Are they inclined to agree or disagree with you?
- What do your readers need to know to understand your point clearly?

There are seven ways to develop a topic. Not all will be appropriate in every case, and some will be more effective than others. Let your topic, your writing purpose, and your audience guide you in choosing the most appropriate kind(s) of development.

1. **Tell a story.** Everyone loves to read a story—if it's relevant and well told. An anecdote can be an effective way to help your readers not only

understand your idea but also remember it. Below are two examples that illustrate the use of narration to develop a topic.

> I first experienced culture shock when I travelled to Egypt. I was walking down the main street on the day of my arrival when it suddenly struck me that the crowds on the street were stepping aside to make way for me. It was 1990, and my height, blond hair, and blue eyes were so unusual to the Egyptians that I was an object of intense curiosity. The staring and pointing followed me everywhere. Finally, unable to cope any longer with being constantly on display, I took refuge in the Canadian Embassy and spent a couple of hours quietly leafing through back issues of *Maclean's* magazine.

> Imagine that two accountants do similar jobs for similar companies. One day they make the same discovery: with almost no chance of getting caught, they can embezzle a large sum from their employers. They can both use the money to pay off debts or buy a new car. The first accountant right away says to himself, "It's wrong to steal," and never considers the matter again. But the second accountant is torn. She, too, knows that stealing is wrong, but she's tempted and at first decides to go ahead. Then she decides she won't, and then that she will. Finally, after weeks of agonizing, she decides not to embezzle. Who is the morally better person?

Hurka, Thomas. "Should Morality Be a Struggle? Ancient vs. Modern Ideas about Ethics." *Principles: Short Essays about Ethics.* Toronto: Harcourt Brace, 1994. 83. Print.

Exercise 6.6

Using a story to develop your topic, write a paragraph on one of the following, or choose a topic of your own.

1. A road-rage experience
2. The day I became an adult
3. The customer is not always right
4. How not to treat employees
5. Defusing a tense situation

2. Define your topic. The definition paragraph explains and clarifies the meaning of a word or idea. Use a definition paragraph to explain a term that may be unfamiliar to your readers. (Write your own definition, please. Quoting from a dictionary is an overused and boring way to start a paragraph.) Below are definitions of two terms that the authors wanted to be sure their readers would understand from the *writers'* point of view.

Culture shock is the inability to understand or cope with experiences one has never encountered before. It commonly affects travellers who journey to lands whose climate, food, language, and customs are alien to the traveller. In addition to confusion and anxiety, culture shock may produce physical symptoms such as chills, fever, trembling, and faintness.

A hybrid is a cross between two established varieties of plant, animal, . . . or technology. The hybrid bicycle, for example, combines the features of a road bike with those of an off-road bike to produce a comfortable and efficient bicycle for short-distance cycling. For most people, however, the word "hybrid" signifies a fuel-efficient, low-emission automobile. Hybrid car technology combines a gasoline or diesel internal combustion engine with a battery-powered electric motor. Its objective is to maximize the best properties of both the gas engine and the electric motor.

Howerth, Sara R. "The Gas–Electric Hybrid Demystified." *Essay Essentials with Readings.* 5th ed. Toronto: Nelson Education, 2010. 310-12. Print.

You should include a definition, too, if you're using a familiar term in an unusual way. Here Martin Luther King defines what he means by "the length of life":

Now let us notice first the length of life. . . . [T]his is the dimension of life in which the individual is concerned with developing his inner powers. It is that dimension of life in which the individual pursues personal ends and ambitions. This is perhaps the selfish dimension of life, and there is such a thing as moral and rational self-interest. If one is not concerned about himself he cannot be totally concerned about other selves.

King, Martin Luther, Jr. "The Dimensions of a Complete Life." *The Measure of a Man.* 1959. Philadelphia: Pilgrim Press, 1969. Print.

Exercise 6.7

Choose one of the following topics (or select one of your own) and write a paragraph in which you develop the topic by defining it.

1. Burnout
2. A good boss (employee, customer, colleague)
3. An extrovert (introvert)
4. A great artist (musician, actor, writer, etc.)
5. A bad habit

3. Use examples. Giving examples is probably the most common method of developing an idea and supporting a statement. Readers can become confused or suspicious when they read unsupported statements of "fact," opinion, or ideas. One of the best ways to support your topic is by providing clear, relevant examples.

Sometimes, as in the paragraph below, one extended example is enough to allow your readers to see clearly what you mean.

Culture shock can affect anyone, even a person who never leaves home. My grandfather was perfectly content to be an accountant until he retired, and was confident that his company would need his services for the foreseeable future. Computers were "silly toys" and modern business practices just "jargon" and "a new fad." When he was laid off four years before his scheduled retirement, he went into shock. It wasn't just the layoff; it was the speed of change—the idea that he was stranded in a new and unfamiliar culture for which he was unprepared, and in which he had no useful role.

Sometimes a number of examples may be necessary to develop a point, as in this paragraph.

Even in the Middle Ages, before electricity, there were many things you could do to torment a person. You could tie him up in an iron belt that held the arms and legs up to the chest and left no point of rest, so that all his muscles went into spasm within minutes and he was driven mad within hours. This was the twisting stork, a benign-looking object. You could stretch him out backward over a thin piece of wood so that his whole body weight rested on his spine, which pressed against the sharp wood. Then you could stop up his nostrils and force water into his stomach through his mouth. Then, if you wanted to finish him off, you and your helper could jump on his stomach, causing internal hemorrhage. This torture was called the rack. If you wanted to burn someone to death without hearing him scream, you could use a tongue lock, a metal rod between the jaw and collarbone that prevented him from opening his mouth. You could put a person in a chair with spikes on the seat and arms, tie him down against the spikes, and beat him, so that every time he flinched from the beating he drove his own flesh deeper onto the spikes. This was the Inquisitor's chair. If you wanted to make it worse, you could heat the spikes. You could suspend a person over a pointed wooden pyramid and whenever he started to fall asleep, you could drop him onto the point. If you were Ippolito Marsili, the inventor of this torture, known as the Judas cradle, you could tell yourself you had invented something humane, a torture that worked without burning flesh or breaking bones. For the torture here [was sup]posed to be sleep deprivation.

Rose, Phyllis. "Tools of Torture: An Essay on Beauty and Pain." *Never Say Goodbye*. 1990. Reprinted in *Paragraph Essentials* (p. 132) by permission of Georges Borchardt, Inc., for the author. Print.

Exercise 6.8

Using examples to develop your topic, write a paragraph on one of following, or choose a topic of your own.

1. Addiction to *Facebook* (*MySpace*, Smartphones, *Twitter*)
2. Parents and privacy
3. Television: Life's biggest time-waster
4. Childless by choice
5. The incompetence (incomprehensibility) of men (women)

---

4. Use a quotation or paraphrase. Occasionally you will find that someone else—an expert in a particular field, a well-known author, or a respected public figure—has said what you want to say better than you could ever hope to say it. Relevant and authoritative quotations, as long as they are kept short and are not used too frequently, are useful in developing your topic. Two sources of quotations on practically any subject are *John Robert Colombo's Famous Lasting Words: Great Canadian Quotations* (Vancouver: Douglas & McIntyre, 2000) and *Bartlett's Familiar Quotations* (New York: Bartleby.com, 2000). **Never forget to acknowledge the source of your quotation.** In the paragraph below, the writer introduces his topic with a thought-provoking quotation.

"Although one can experience real pain from culture shock, it is also an opportunity for redefining one's life objectives. Culture shock can make one develop a better understanding of oneself and stimulate personal creativity." As with any experience that forces us out of our comfort zone and shatters our complacency, culture shock can be an opportunity for growth and development, as this quotation from Dr. V. Patel, dean of the faculty of education at San Diego State University makes clear. The trick is to recognize this unpleasant experience as a starting point for personal change. Here's an opportunity to re-examine our preconceptions about our place in society, about our interactions with others, even about the path we have chosen to take in life: has it become a rut?

A **paraphrase** is a summary in your own words of someone else's idea. Remember to indicate whose idea you are paraphrasing, the way the author of "The Myth of Canadian Diversity" does in the following paragraph.

> . . . [O]ur much-discussed ethnic differences are overstated. Although Canada is an immigrant nation and Canadians spring from a variety of backgrounds, a recent study by the C. D. Howe Institute reports that the idea of a "Canadian mosaic"—as distinct from the American "melting pot"—is a fallacy. In *The Illusion of Difference*, University of Toronto sociologists Jeffrey Reitz and Raymond Breton show that immigrants to Canada assimilate as quickly into mainstream society as immigrants to the United States do. In fact, Canadians are less likely than Americans to favour holding on to cultural differences based on ethnic background. If you don't believe Mr. Reitz and Mr. Breton, visit any big-city high school, where the speech and behaviour of immigrant students just a few years in Canada is indistinguishable from that of any fifth-generation classmate.

Published in the *Globe and Mail*, June 13, 1994, A12. Reprinted with permission of the *Globe and Mail*.

Exercise 6.9

Choose one of the following topics (or select one of your own) and write a paragraph in which you develop the topic by using quotations and/or paraphrase.

1. Canada's best blogger
2. My favourite stand-up comic
3. The best movie of the year
4. The wisdom of children
5. A songwriter whose lyrics move me

5. Use a comparison. A comparison shows similarities between things; it shows how two different things are alike in a particular way or ways. If you have a difficult or abstract topic to explain, try comparing it to something that is familiar to your readers, as this writer does.

> Being left on your own in a foreign land is a bit like being forced to play a card game when you're the only one who doesn't know the rules. As the stakes get higher and the other players' excitement and enjoyment increase, you get correspondingly more frustrated and miserable. Finally, in desperation, you want to throw your cards on the table, absorb your losses, and go home.

In this next paragraph, the writer uses an **analogy**—an extended comparison—between a date and a car to make her point both clear and interesting.

The economy-model date features cramped conditions and a lack of power. The econo-date thinks that his personality can make up for the fact that you never go anywhere except for walks and never do anything that costs money. He tends to be shy, quiet, and about as much fun as an oil leak. It's not that he doesn't have money to spend; it's that he doesn't use any imagination or creativity to compensate for his lack of cash.

Exercise 6.10

Choose one of the following topics (or select one of your own) and write a paragraph in which you develop the topic by using comparison.

1. Being self-employed
2. A horrible class
3. Two consumer products
4. Canadians
5. Engineering (or computer science, arts, or nursing) students

6. Explain steps or stages in a process. Sometimes the most effective way to develop the main idea of your paragraph is by explaining how something occurs or is done—that is, by relating the series of steps involved. Make sure you break down the process into its component parts and detail the steps logically and precisely.

The first sign of culture shock is usually anxiety. The traveller feels uncomfortable and ill at ease; nothing looks, smells, sounds, or tastes familiar. Next, he may become resentful, even angry, and withdraw from his new surroundings, seeking isolation in safe, familiar territory—his room. Unfortunately, solitude reinforces anxiety and makes the situation worse. Over time, the victim of culture shock may begin to perceive the environment not as strange but neutral, but as strange and hostile. Friendly interaction with others and positive experiences in the new culture are the cure, but one is not likely to encounter either while cocooned in a small boarding house or hotel room. Fortunately, most travellers find that culture shock diminishes with rest. As anxiety lessens, curiosity grows, and they begin to venture out to participate in the life of the new country. In extreme cases, however, travellers suffering from culture shock can develop flu-like symptoms: fever, chills, sleeplessness, and a debilitating loss of energy. When these symptoms strike, it's time to call home for moral support and encouragement to get out and enjoy the sights and scenes one has travelled so far to experience.

In writing a process paragraph, you need to pay particular attention to transitions, which are discussed in the next chapter. If you don't, you'll leave your readers gasping in the dust as you gallop through your explanation. The paragraph below illustrates a simple yet effective use of transitions.

In 1983, a Harvard Medical School team led by Dr. Howard Green found a revolutionary way to repair burned skin. Here is how it is done. Doctors cut up a small patch of skin donated by a patient, treat it with enzymes, then spread it thinly onto a culture medium. After only ten days, colonies of skin cells begin linking up into sheets, which can then be chopped up and used to make further sheets. In twenty-four days, enough skin will be produced to cover an entire human body. About ten days later, the gauze is removed, and the skin soon grows into a surface much smoother and more natural-looking than the rough one a normal skin-graft usually leaves.

Ackerman, Diane. *A Natural History of the Senses.* New York: Vintage-Random House, 1990. 69-70. Print.

Exercise 6.11

Choose one of the following topics (or select one of your own) and write a paragraph in which you develop the topic by describing the series of steps or stages involved in the process.

1. Buying a used car
2. Teaching a 16-year-old to drive
3. Learning to live with a roommate
4. Persuading parents to send more money
5. Getting out of debt

7. **Provide specific details.** Concrete, specific, descriptive details can be an effective way to develop your main idea. In the following paragraph, the writer uses specific detail to describe treatment for culture shock.

Culture shock can be alleviated by taking action to reduce the impact of the cause, and then treating each of the symptoms separately. Prevention is the best cure: introduce yourself gradually to a new environment. Explore in small stages, while keeping contact with safe and familiar surroundings. Don't plunge into the bazaar within an hour of your arrival in Marrakesh, but begin your exploration in the Western quarter and gradually expose yourself to the sights, sounds, and smells of areas that seem threateningly foreign. If you should come down with symptoms of shock, go to bed, stay warm, drink lots of bottled water, and sleep as much as you can. When you begin to feel better, take things slowly and avoid stressful situations where you have to make decisions or confront the unexpected. A guided bus tour of the city is a good way to begin familiarizing yourself with a new physical and cultural environment, and to discover what's available that you want to explore.

In some paragraphs, numerical facts or statistics can be used to support your point effectively. However, in keeping with Benjamin Disraeli's immortal comment ("There are three kinds of lies: lies, damned lies, and statistics"), critical readers tend to be suspicious of statistics. Be very sure that your facts are correct and that your statistics are current.

Canadians are great travellers. We not only travel around our own country, exploring every nook and cranny from Beaver Creek in the Yukon Territory to Bay Bulls in Newfoundland, but we also can be found touring around every other country on Earth. Statistics Canada (2008) reports that we take more than 175 million overnight trips a year within our own borders. Abroad, we favour our next-door neighbour by a wide margin above other destinations, averaging around 16 million overnight trips a year to the United States. Mexico is our second-favorite destination, with over 841 000 visits, followed by the United Kingdom (778 000) and France (645 000). Of the Caribbean Islands, Cuba is our favourite winter escape, ranking fifth overall, with about 350 000 visits a year by Canadians. China (including Hong Kong) ranks ninth in popularity with 400 000 visits by Canadians, just behind the Dominican Republic and ahead of Germany and Italy. Canadians' top 15 travel destinations are rounded out by more European nations: the Netherlands, Spain, Switzerland, Ireland, and Austria. We can make a rough estimate from these figures that, on average, Canadians travel five times a year within Canada, and outside of Canada twice in three years.

Exercise 6.12

Using specific details to develop your topic, write a paragraph on one of following, or choose a topic of your own.

1. A Web page
2. A migraine headache
3. The myth of the shorter workweek
4. The best team in basketball (baseball, football, soccer, lacrosse)
5. Money can't buy happiness.

When writing your own paragraphs, you will often need to use more than one method of development to explain your point. The seven methods described in this chapter can be used in any combination you choose. You will choose the most effective combination by keeping in mind the main purpose of your essay (to inform, convince, or entertain), your thesis, and your reader.

How Do You End a Paragraph?

A good paragraph doesn't just end; like a door, it should close firmly, with a "click." Finish your paragraph with a statement that serves either as a **clincher**—an unmistakable and appropriate conclusion—or a **transition** to the new idea that will be developed in the next paragraph.

Exercise 6.13

Turn back to the paragraphs in Exercise 6.1 (pages 69–71). Reread each one and decide whether it ends with a clincher or a transition sentence.

Exercise 6.14

To stretch your imagination and improve your mastery of the kinds of support you can choose from to develop a topic, write a paragraph on one of the following topics, using two or more methods of development. Your target audience is your instructor and your classmates.

1. Getting along with co-workers
2. Performance appraisal
3. Training a new boss
4. Life is like a game of _____
5. Canadians don't appreciate how lucky they are.

7

Writing Introductions and Conclusions

Two paragraphs of your paper—the first and the last—serve special functions and deserve special care. Many writers wait until after they have worked through a draft or two of the body of an essay before tackling these two critical paragraphs. To introduce and conclude your subject effectively, you need to know what main ideas your paper explores and how these ideas are arranged and developed. Only then can you integrate the beginning and the ending of your essay into the whole.

All too often, the introduction and the conclusion of a paper are dull or clumsy and detract from its effectiveness. Here's how to avoid dull and clumsy and write good ones.

The Introductory Paragraph

The introduction is worth special attention because that's where your readers either sit up and take notice of your paper or sigh and pitch it into the wastebasket.

There are two parts to an introductory paragraph:
1. an attention-getter
2. a thesis statement

Getting and Holding
Your Readers' Attention

Your readers must be attracted to your thesis or there's no point in putting pen to paper or fingers to keyboard. The attention-getter must be appropriate to the content of your essay and to your intended readers. If your audience is known for a solemn approach to life and your topic is serious (environmental ethics, for instance, or equal opportunity policies in the workplace), there is no point in leading off with a pun or joke, no matter how witty. Such an opening would be inappropriate and probably offensive to your readers.

Your attention-getter does not have to be a single sentence; in fact, good ones are often several sentences long. Your readers will be committing varying amounts of personal time to reading your writing. You owe it to them to make your opening sentences clear, interesting, and creative.

An effective attention-getter should be followed by an equally effective thesis statement, one that slides smoothly and easily into place. Your readers should be aware only of a unified paragraph, not of two separate parts in your introduction.

Below are eight different kinds of openings you can choose from to get your readers' attention and lead up to your thesis statement. In each of the example paragraphs, note how the attention-getter and the thesis statement are solidly linked to form a unified whole. To demonstrate that you can take many different approaches to a subject, depending on your purpose and your audience, we have used the same subject—physical fitness—in all of the introductions.

1. Spell out the significance of your subject. If your subject's significance can catch your readers' interest, they will want to know more about it, especially if it is a subject that affects them directly.

More and more young people are dying of heart disease. Despite the statistics that say most people in our society are living longer thanks to advances in medicine and surgery, the figures can be misleading. It is a fact that people in their thirties and forties are dying from coronary problems that once threatened people in their fifties and sixties. What has caused this change? Certainly, the increase in stress, the fatigue of overwork, the rise in obesity, and the decline in physical activity are all contributing factors. To combat the risk of cardiovascular disease, we need physical activity. Regular exercise can forestall the ravages of heart disease and promote longevity.

2. Begin with a well-phrased quotation. You might choose a famous statement, a popular slogan, or a common saying. Use a quotation when it sums up your point of view more succinctly and effectively than your own words could. As a rule, you should identify the source of the quotation.

"Who can be bothered?" "I'm much too busy." "I get all the exercise I need at the office." We've all heard excuses like these, excuses for avoiding regular exercise. Modern life, with its distractions and conveniences, tends to make people sedentary and lazy, but the human organism cannot tolerate inactivity and stress indefinitely. Eventually, it begins to break down. Those who want to keep in shape for the challenges of modern life should consider the benefits of working out a few times a week. Regular exercise can rejuvenate the body, refresh the mind, and improve self-confidence.

3. Use a startling statement. Sometimes a surprising remark (NOT an insult or a false exaggeration) is effective in getting readers' attention. A little-known or striking fact will have the same effect.

After the age of 30, the average North American puts on 10 to 20 kilograms of fat. Presumably, the cause for this startling increase in avoirdupois is a combination of metabolic changes, decreased physical activity, and hundreds of kilos of junk food ingested since childhood. It's difficult to stop the spread of middle-aged corpulence, but experts tell us we *can* resist the rise in flab by reducing our caloric intake and increasing our physical activity. Regular exercise can rejuvenate the body, refresh the mind, and improve self-confidence.

4. Ask a question or two. Questions are often an effective way to encourage interest because your readers will find themselves thinking of answers. Some questions are rhetorical; that is, they will not have specific answers. Others might be answered in your essay.

Have you been feeling sluggish and exhausted lately? Has your blood pressure increased along with your waistline in the past few years? Are you stalled in front of the television set every night with potato chips and a beer? If so, you are probably suffering from a common middle-aged ailment called *flabitis*. This malady strikes most people over 30: they put on weight, have trouble concentrating, tire easily, and prefer watching sports to participating in them. Fortunately, there is a cure for flabitis: a three-times-weekly dose of exercise. With regular exercise, you can rejuvenate your body, refresh your mind, and improve your self-confidence.

5. Begin with a generalization related to your subject. Generalizations can be useful for suggesting the context and scope of your subject. They must, however, be narrowed down carefully to a focused thesis statement.

Until the 20th century, physical exercise was part of the normal workday. Our ancestors were farmers, pioneers, sailors, and so on. Few of our parents, however, made their living by ploughing the land or chopping down trees. Since the early 1900s, the trend in work has been away from physical exertion and toward automation. Today's generation uses technology to reduce physical activity even further: they pick up the phone, ride the elevator, and take the car to the corner store. Modern inactivity has negative consequences that only physical exercise can counter. To sustain good health, sharpen your mental edge, and have fun, you should take up aerobics or sports and use your body in the way it was intended—actively.

6. Challenge a common opinion. Perhaps your readers have also doubted a popular belief. Your thesis statement can assert that an opinion is false, and the body of your paper can contain evidence to support your opposing view.

Physical activity is for kids. Adults don't have time to hit a baseball or run around a field chasing after one, or to do aerobics and lift weights in a gym. They have to earn a living, raise families, and save money for retirement. They can leave exercise to their children. I firmly believed this until one morning when, late for work, I ran after a bus. My heart pounded, my lungs gasped, my head swam. It had been some years since my last stint of exercise, and I realized I wouldn't be around to do my job, support my family, or enjoy retirement unless I got into the habit of doing something physical to maintain my health. Regular exercise can rejuvenate the body, refresh the mind, and broaden one's interests.

7. Begin with a definition. A definition is a good way to begin if you are introducing a key term that you suspect may be unfamiliar to your readers. If the subject of your essay depends on a personal meaning of a term that most people understand in a different way, a definition is essential.

Myocardial infarction—the very term is frightening. It occurs when a person's muscles slacken from disuse, the veins clog up with sticky fats, and the heart has to work too hard to sustain even minor exertion such as raking leaves or shovelling snow. The muscles of the heart become strained to exhaustion or balloon outward because the veins cannot pass blood quickly enough. In plain English, a myocardial infarction is a heart attack. If the victim is lucky enough to survive, physicians prescribe a regimen of less stress, low fat intake, and regular exercise.

8. Describe an interesting incident or tell an anecdote related to your subject. Readers like stories. Keep yours short and to the point by narrating only the highlights. The incident or anecdote you select might be a story from the media, an event involving family or friends, or a personal experience.

Last year, I got a free invitation in the mail to a fitness club. I responded, out of curiosity, but I needed to be convinced. After all, I was 35, had grown a little paunch, and was a bit short of breath on the stairs; 10 years had passed since I had last played sports. My first workout was a nightmare. My joints ached, my muscles throbbed, and my head spun. I was in worse shape than I thought. After a few weeks, those symptoms disappeared, and I began to enjoy myself. My paunch vanished and my muscles toned up. My capacity for concentration increased. Also, I met some new people who have become friends. Obviously, 10 years is too long between workouts, given that exercise not only rejuvenates the body and refreshes the mind but also improves one's social life.

Exercise 7.1

In small groups (four or five people), consider five movies you have all seen within the past year. How did each of these movies begin so that the audience was "locked in"? How do these movie "grabbers" relate to the kinds of attention-getters you have just read?

Exercise 7.2

Each of the following paragraphs is the introductory paragraph of an essay. Work in pairs and, using the strategy given in parentheses, write an appropriate attention-getter for each paragraph.

1. (Significance of subject) _____

_____

TV commercials that portray unrealistic and unattainable lifestyles should be banned. Although I do not support censorship, I believe there is sufficient evidence of the damage done by these advertisements to justify eliminating them in the name of public interest. The objectionable commercials promote sexual stereotyping, set up unrealistic and dangerous expectations, and encourage irresponsible consumerism.

2. (Quotation) _____

_____

Every sport has its strange expressions, just as every sport has its devoted fans, its famous teams, and its legendary heroes. A sport that gets very little attention in Canada but is very popular in many parts of the world, especially Commonwealth countries, is cricket. Like the sports that millions of Canadians follow enthusiastically, cricket is an exciting and fascinating game once you become familiar with its rules and style. In fact, it compares very favourably with baseball in skill, pace, and strategy.

3. (Startling statement) _____

_____

Canadian roads are overrun by drivers who are a danger to themselves, their passengers, and others on the road. Inept drivers demonstrate their inadequacies in so many ways that it would be impossible to list them all in one short paper. Nevertheless, bad drivers can be broadly categorized as traumatized turtles, careening cowboys, and daydreaming dodos.

4. (Question) _____

_____

Arranged marriages are a very important part of my culture. When my family moved to Canada, we left behind many of the traditions and customs that were as natural to us as breathing. However, my parents retained their right to choose a wife for me, even though they are aware that this custom is at odds with the Canadian way of life. Although their decision was at first difficult to accept, I believe there are good reasons that an arranged marriage may be best for me. The decision will be made by mature people in a thoughtful manner, uninfluenced by the enthusiasms of youth; the decision will be made by people who have at heart the best interests of our family, the bride's family, and me; and the decision will be made in accordance with a centuries-old tradition that has proven its success generation after generation.

5. (Generalization) _____

_____

My first project manager was the sort of person that nightmares are made of. It's been a year since she was finally transferred to another department, but I still shudder when I recall our six months together. Denise was rude, bossy, and, worst of all, thoughtless.

6. (Opinion you challenge) _____

_____

There's really no reason to retain the Canadian dollar. We are so closely tied to the U.S. economy that independence is an illusion. If the French could give up the franc, the Italians abandon the lire, and the Germans say auf wiedersehen to the mark in favour of the efficiency, convenience, and savings of a common currency, then we ought to follow their lead and adopt the American dollar.

7. (Definition) _____

_____

Most people have a hobby of some kind, although not everyone knows it. While traditional hobbies like collecting stamps or building models or arranging flowers are easily identified, other activities may not be thought of as hobbies. Collecting tattoos or watching a game in every major league arena or researching your family tree can all be considered hobbies. As long as you aren't being paid, enjoy the activity, and do it obsessively, you are benefiting from a hobby.

8. (Anecdote or incident) _____

_____

Black flies are just one of the pests that make life less than comfortable in Canada during the spring, but they tend to be the most irritating. No method of combatting the pests is foolproof, but there are several methods that can be employed, either singly or together, to repel most of them. The campaign against the black fly begins with protective clothing, follows up with an effective repellent, and goes over the top with the secret weapon: garlic.

Exercise 7.3

With the class divided into four or five teams, consider the following essay topics. Each team will take one of the topics and develop the first sentence of an introductory paragraph for it. The sentence will then be passed in sequence to the next group, who will add a sentence to the paragraph. Continue this exercise until each paragraph contains both an attention-getter and a thesis statement. When each team gets back the paragraph it initiated, it will revise and polish the paragraph, identify the kind of attention-getter that has been developed, and underline the thesis statement. Share the results with the rest of the class. (Keep these paragraphs; you will need them later.)

1. Why I want to be a _____ (fill in your career choice)
2. Why I chose _____ (fill in your school)
3. How not to treat a co-worker (customer, class)
4. My favourite TV show
5. The trouble with roommates (parents, teachers, etc.)

The Concluding Paragraph

Like the introduction, the conclusion of your paper has a special form. Think of your favourite television sitcom. The last section of the show wraps up the plot, explains any details that might still be unresolved, and leaves you with a satisfying sense that all is well, at least until next week. A concluding paragraph works in a similar way.

The last paragraph of your paper has two functions:
1. It summarizes or reinforces the main points of your paper.
2. It ends with an appropriate memorable statement.

Your **summary statement** should be as concise as you can make it, and must be phrased in such a way that it does not repeat word for word the portion of your thesis statement that identifies the main points. (Note that a summary is not needed in a very short essay.)

A **memorable statement** is a sentence designed to leave your readers feeling satisfied with your essay and perhaps taking away with them something for further thought. Never end without a clincher. Don't just quit writing when your main points are covered, or you'll leave your readers hanging, wondering what to make of it all.

Six strategies you can choose from when you write a concluding paragraph are listed below. Each strategy is illustrated by an example paragraph. Identify the summary and the memorable statement in each conclusion.

1. End with a relevant or thought-provoking quotation. You can use this type of ending in two ways: repeat an earlier quotation but give it a new meaning, or place your subject in a larger context by supplying a new quotation from a recognized authority in the field.

Since I began lifting weights every second day, I have lowered my blood pressure, improved my productivity at work, and made some new friends at the fitness club. I will never be Arnold Schwarzenegger, but that isn't my goal. My muscles are pleasantly sore after a good workout, but as Arnold says, "No pain, no gain." As long as the pain is so little and the gain is so great, I will continue to enjoy my regular workouts.

2. Offer a solution to a problem discussed in your paper. You can plan an organization for your paper that will allow you to resolve a problem or neutralize negative consequences in your conclusion.

I've got the best intentions in the world. I know that exercise benefits me physically, mentally, and emotionally—but I still don't have the time. I didn't, that is, until last month, when I was home from work for a week because I sprained my ankle while walking the dog. That never would have happened if I had been in shape. Since then, I have forced myself to manage my time to allow for a fitness program. Four hours of exercise a week is not a very big investment of time compared with four days of lying on the couch with a painfully swollen foot.

3. End with one or more relevant or thought-provoking questions. The advantage of clinching with a question is that readers tend automatically to pause and consider it: questions stimulate thought. Before they know it, readers will begin to formulate answers to your question—and that activity will make them remember your points. Be sure your question relates directly to your subject.

My life has improved considerably since I took up jogging three times a week: I enjoy better health, less brain-fog, and more confidence. And I'm inspired to continue jogging by the fact that coronary disease runs in my family. My father and grandfather both suffered heart attacks in their fifties. If they had done regular exercise, could they have reduced their chances of coronaries? Would they still be alive today?

4. Point out the value or significance of your subject to your readers. If you emphasize your subject matter at the end of your paper, you can stamp its importance on your readers' memory.

Regular exercise is the best way to stay in shape, be sharp, and feel strong; it is the best way to reduce the risk of arthritis, arterial decay, and heart dysfunction. In a country where the most common cause of mortality is coronary disease, everyone needs to consider the value of consistent exercise. It is a small daily inconvenience that pays large and long-term rewards.

5. Make a connection to a statement made in your introduction. This strategy provides your readers with a sense of closure. They will recall your earlier statement and feel satisfied that the loose ends have been tied up.

Having exercised now for six months, I can run for the bus without losing my breath, sweating profusely, or feeling dizzy. My body is in better shape; my endurance and confidence on the job have grown. After a lapse of 20 years, I have even taken up bicycling again: I go riding along local bike trails with my family and friends. And now, when my children are playing baseball in the yard, I don't think, "Baseball is for kids." I'm first at the plate. Batter up!

6. End with a suggestion for change or a prediction about the future. Your suggestion for change will influence your readers if they have been persuaded by your arguments. Your predictions of events that might occur should not be misleading or exaggerated, or your readers will be skeptical. Make predictions that are possible and plausible.

If those of us who still prefer junk food, overwork, and television don't shape up, then the incidence of coronary disease will continue to rise. Moderate exercise will benefit body, mind, and spirit. If we use common sense and change our habits of self-pollution and self-destruction, all of us can lead long, active, and healthy lives.

Exercise 7.4

Each of the following is the concluding paragraph of an essay. Working in pairs, underline the summary statement and write a memorable conclusion. See if you can use a different kind in each paragraph.

1. Both games are enjoyable for spectators and create real enthusiasm among fans. High schools that have chosen soccer have seen no reduction in school spirit or fan support. For educational institutions to make the switch from football is really a "no-lose" proposition because soccer provides dramatic advantages in reducing player injury, increasing player fitness, and shaving thousands of dollars from school expenses.

    _____

    _____

    _____

    _____

2. While there are many machines that will help you to get fit, others you can use for commuting to work, and still others that allow you the thrill of competing, nothing but a bicycle will give you all three of these benefits and many more.

    _____

    _____

_____

_____

3.　　Although the causes of dropout among first-year students are as individual as the students themselves, the effects are easier to categorize.
Conflict with parents and others whose expectations have not been met
comes first, followed by a loss of self-esteem. The determination to succeed
despite this unfair setback is common, but statistics show that low-paying,
dead-end jobs are the norm for the college or university dropout. The situation is much worse, of course, for those who don't complete high school.

_____

_____

_____

_____

4.　　Employers who are looking for skilled young people to replace retiring
workers need to understand the major differences between the Boomers
and the generation that is replacing them. The Internet Generation brings
to the workplace most of the skills and abilities of their predecessors, along
with some new ones, but their attitudes are different. Job satisfaction is not
optional; it is required. Work is not as important as family and personal
considerations. The Internet Generation views the "good life" not as the
accumulation of wealth, but as the achievement of balance and satisfaction
in all aspects of their lives.

_____

_____

_____

_____

5.　　Drinking and driving must be stopped. To stop it will require substantial
commitment from all levels of government, both in terms of money and
in terms of political will. The penalties for driving while under the influence of alcohol must be increased, and more money must be spent for education and publicity. But, more than these measures, it will take the
individual will of every Canadian to make the promise not to drive after
drinking. Nothing will bring my sister back, but there are lots of other sisters out there—and brothers and mothers and fathers—who can be saved.

_____

_____

_____

_____

Exercise 7.5

With the class divided into the same teams as in Exercise 7.3, write concluding paragraphs to complement the introductions you developed. Here's how to proceed:

- Review the paragraph you developed for Exercise 7.3.
- Write the first sentence of a concluding paragraph for this same topic.
- Pass your sentence, together with your introductory paragraph, along to the next team, who will write a second sentence for the conclusion.
- Continue this process until the conclusion contains both a summary or reinforcement and a memorable statement.
- Return the paragraph to the team that initiated it for revising and polishing.
- Share the results with the rest of the class.

8

Keeping Your Readers with You

As you write, remember that it is your responsibility to make it as easy as possible for your readers to follow you through your essay. Unity, coherence, and tone can make the difference between a paper that confuses or annoys your readers and one that enlightens and pleases them.

Unity

Unity means "oneness." The contents of a paragraph must relate to a single main idea. All supporting sentences in the paragraph should clearly and directly relate to the topic sentence of that paragraph.

Achieving unity requires focus. Your job is to develop to your readers' satisfaction the points that you have set out to make. In an ideal world, the time to set down whatever happens to come to mind is in the prewriting stage, but writing is a complex process and new ideas often occur to you as you write. Don't dismiss them; record them and decide when you revise if these new ideas are significant and relevant or if they are whims that should be discarded.

When you've completed your first draft, it's time to revise. This is where real writing begins. Check each paragraph carefully. Any material that does not clearly and directly support the topic sentence should be deleted; if it's directly relevant elsewhere in the essay, insert it there.

Take a look at the following paragraph. It contains several sentences that spoil the unity of the paragraph because they do not clearly relate to the topic.

(1) I knew I wanted to return to school, but did I want to be a full-time or a part-time student? (2) The major consideration was, not surprisingly, money.

(3) If I chose to go to college full-time, then I would have to give up my full-time job. (4) The resulting loss of income would reduce my buying power to zero. (5) Even the tuition fees would be beyond my reach. (6) Also, my choice of program would be a difficult decision, because I still wasn't sure which career path to follow. (7) My other option was part-time education. (8) If I kept my full-time job, I could at least pay for food, rent, and a modest amount of clothing. (9) Also, I could afford the tuition fees. (10) Going to school part-time costs less per year because the expenditure is spread over a longer period of time than it is in the full-time program. (11) Therefore, I chose to educate myself part-time, through continuing education courses. (12) While working, I could learn new skills in my spare time. (13) My career choice would still be in doubt, but I would have a longer time in which to make up my mind. (14) Money is scarce for a full-time, self-supporting student, but as a part-time student I could have the best of both worlds: a steady income and a college education.

Draw a line through the sentences that do not logically and directly support the topic of the paragraph: the writer's decision whether to be a full-time or part-time student.[1]

Exercise 8.1*

The paragraphs below contain some irrelevant sentences that disrupt unity. Read each paragraph through and then, with a partner, find and cross out the sentences that don't belong. Answers for exercises in this chapter begin on page 537.

1. (1) A good pizza consists of a combination of succulent ingredients. (2) First, you prepare the foundation, the crust, which may be thick or thin, depending on your preference. (3) I like my crusts thick and chewy. (4) The crust is spread with a layer of basil- and oregano-flavoured tomato sauce. (5) Next, a rich smorgasbord of toppings—pepperoni, mushrooms, green peppers, bacon, anchovies—should be scattered over the tomato sauce. (6) *Smorgasbord* is a Swedish word meaning a buffet meal; *pizza* is Italian in origin. (7) Last of all, a double-thick blanket of grated mozzarella cheese should be spread over everything. (8) Pizza is simple to make—all you need is dough, tomato sauce, vegetables, sausage, herbs, and cheese—but the combination has an unbeatable taste.

2. (1) Keeping a job is not easy in a tight market in which well-educated job-seekers are plentiful. (2) Here are a couple of hints you will find helpful in maintaining your "employed" status. (3) First, you should not only apply

---

[1]The sentences that you should have crossed out because they do not belong in this paragraph and detract from its unity are 6, 12, and 13.

your specialized knowledge on the job every day, but also continually update it by taking seminars and evening courses to enhance your skills. (4) Doing your job effectively is difficult without becoming burned out. (5) Second, good communication—with the public, your co-workers, and your supervisor—is perhaps the most important factor in keeping you on the payroll. (6) Upgrading your education and improving your communication skills are your best defences against the pink slip.

3.   (1) Comedies are my favourite way to relax. (2) Horror films terrify me, and adventures become tedious after the tenth chase, but comedies entertain and refresh me after a long shift at work. (3) Woody Allen movies, especially the early farces, help me to take my mind off the stress of the day. (4) For example, *Bananas*, a satire about American politics in the 1960s, is more relaxing for me than a double martini. (5) It's also less fattening, and I've been trying to give up drinking. (6) *Sleeper*, a futuristic spoof, has me laughing, on average, twice a minute. (7) Perhaps my favourite, however, is *Annie Hall*. (8) After viewing it, I am so weak with laughter that I can go to sleep within minutes. (9) Now that all of Allen's comedies are available on DVD, I never need to feel tense and worn out for longer than it takes to insert a disc.

4.   (1) My department's job is to produce reports. (2) We research and prepare year-end reports, shareholders' reports, and reports on the competition, on the customers, on the suppliers, and on just about everything else. (3) We think of ourselves as creative rather than technical writers because there is no future in our company for anyone who is critical or who dares to tell the truth if truth isn't what the senior managers want to hear. (4) Instead of fixing the problem, they punish the person who tells them what's wrong; that is, they "shoot the messenger." (5) I believe this saying originated in ancient days, long before there were guns, so presumably the original idea was "knife the messenger" or "behead the messenger." (6) If employees understand this management practice, however, they can protect themselves. (7) For example, our department has developed three rules to help us produce reports that are guaranteed a favourable reception. (8) First, teamwork is essential; without it, you have no one else to blame. (9) Second, when you don't know what you're doing, do it neatly. (10) Third, if at first you don't succeed, destroy all evidence that you ever tried. (11) With these rules to guide us, our department has survived three new managers in the past two-and-a-half years.

5.   (1) The office manager who demands that all employees not only arrive on time but actually get in early to demonstrate their enthusiasm and drive is actually damaging productivity. (2) Such a manager is, of course, always in the office at least an hour early herself, and because she attributes her success to this habit, she demands it of others. (3) Not everyone is suited to an early start. (4) Individual biorhythms vary

widely, and some employees may be better suited to demonstrating their keenness by staying late at night. (5) The old adage "The early bird gets the worm" is based on some truth, but there are many exceptions. (6) Besides, what office worker wants a worm, anyway? (7) For that matter, there are lots of other sayings and aphorisms that can apply just as readily to the situation. (8) If your manager cites this tired old phrase as her justification for demanding unreasonably early hours, you may want to point out that another saying is equally true: "The second mouse gets the cheese."

Coherence

As we have seen, the sentences in the body of a paragraph are individual points that support the controlling idea of the topic sentence. But if that is *all* your paragraph is, then it is little more than a shopping list. Good paragraphs have **coherence**, which means that the sentences "stick together." The sentences within a paragraph should read as a unit, with one sentence flowing smoothly into the next. Sentences are like the pieces of a jigsaw puzzle. Your task is to assemble the pieces so that your reader can see the picture you have drawn. Ignoring coherence is like handing your readers an uncompleted puzzle; you leave them to sort out the pieces and fit them together. Most readers won't bother.

Although coherence is related to unity, they are not the same thing. It is possible for a paragraph to consist of a topic sentence followed by supporting sentences that relate to and develop the controlling idea—and still not make sense. Here's an example:

I knew I wanted to return to school, but did I want to be a full-time or a part-time student? The loss of income would reduce my buying power to zero. The tuition fees would be beyond my reach. If I kept my job, I could at least pay for food, rent, and a modest amount of clothing. If I chose to go to college full-time, then I would have to give up my full-time job. My other option was part-time education. The expenditure would be spread over a longer period of time. Not surprisingly, the major consideration was money. I could afford the books and tuition fees. Money is scarce for a full-time, self-supporting student. I chose to educate myself part-time, through night-school courses. I could have the best of both worlds: a steady income and a college education.

There is no problem with the unity of this paragraph. All the sentences relate directly to the topic: the choice between returning to school as a full-time or a part-time student. But, even so, the paragraph doesn't make sense. The arrangement of ideas isn't clear or even sensible; the sentences don't connect with one another. Now take a look at the same paragraph, written coherently:

I knew I wanted to return to school, but did I want to be a full-time or a part-time student? Not surprisingly, the major consideration was money. If I chose to go to college full-time, then I would have to give up my full-time job. The resulting loss of income would reduce my buying power to zero. Even the tuition fees would be beyond my reach. My other option was part-time education. If I kept my job, I could at least pay for food, rent, and a modest amount of clothing. Also, I could afford the books and tuition fees. Going to school part-time costs less per year because the expenditure is spread over a longer period. Money is scarce for a full-time, self-supporting student, but as a part-time student, I could have the best of both worlds: a steady income and a college education.

This paragraph is easy to read. The arrangement of ideas is logical and easy to follow: the writer first considers full-time study, a choice that for her has many disadvantages, then considers part-time study, which offers enough advantages to clinch her decision. Within the paragraph, the sentences flow smoothly: they relate clearly and logically to each other.

There are two ways to ensure coherence in your writing, and you need to use both:

1. Arrange your ideas in an appropriate order.
2. Use transitions to guide your reader.

Transitions are verbal cues that connect one idea to the next. Whether expressed or implied, transitions are the sparks that jump the gaps between sentences in a paragraph and between paragraphs in an essay. Why do you need transitions? Read the paragraph below and you'll see clearly that something is missing. The paragraph has adequate development and the points are in order, but there are no transitions.

We were bored one day. We didn't know what to do. It was Friday. We thought about going to the library. No one really wanted to do schoolwork. We went to the mall. For a short time we window-shopped. We discussed what to do. It was agreed that we would drive to the American side of the border. We would do our shopping. It was a short drive. We went to a discount mall. The bargains were great. We spent much more money than we intended to. We went home. We discovered that with the American exchange, prices were better at home. We should have gone to the library.

Not very easy to read, is it? Readers are jerked abruptly from point to point until, battered and bruised, they finally reach the end. This kind of writing is unfair to readers. It makes them do too much of the work. The ideas may all be there, but the readers have to figure out for themselves how the ideas fit together. After a couple of paragraphs like the one above, even the most patient readers can become annoyed.

Now read the same paragraph, rewritten with transitions.

Last Friday we were so bored we didn't know what to do. We thought about going to the library, but no one really wanted to study, so we went to the mall and window-shopped for a while. After a long discussion about what to do next, we agreed to drive to the American side of the border for some serious shopping. A short drive later, we arrived at a discount mall, where the bargains were so great that we spent much more money than we had intended. Finally, we returned home, where we discovered that, with the American exchange, prices were better at home after all. We should have gone to the library.

In this paragraph, readers are gently guided from one point to the next. By the time they reach the conclusion, they know not only what thoughts the writer had in mind, but also how they fit together to form a complete idea. The transitions connect the pieces of the puzzle and make the readers' job easy and rewarding.

Five kinds of transition strategies can be used as verbal cues to guide your readers through your writing. Be sure to use a variety of these techniques every time you write. Nothing improves the polish of your prose more than the skilful use of coherence strategies.

1. Repeat a key word. Repetition focuses the reader's attention on an idea and creates a thread of meaning that runs through a paragraph or a paper, tying the whole thing together. (Don't overdo it, though.) In the following example, the student chose to tie his supporting ideas together by beginning them all in the same way:

> *Violence* in prime time is harmful. . . . *Violence* in prime time is hurtful. . . .
> *Violence* in prime time is unnecessary. . . .

2. **Use synonyms.** Frequent repetition of a key word can become monotonous after a while. You can keep the reader both focused and interested by using synonyms—different words that convey the same meaning.

> *Movies* are relying more and more on special effects. . . . *Films* are becoming increasingly expensive. . . . *Motion pictures* now are more dependent on the star system than ever before.

3. **Use pronoun references.** Another way of maintaining the focus but varying the wording is to use appropriate pronouns to refer back to a key noun. (This technique involves pronoun–antecedent agreement, a topic covered in Part 7, Section 7.9.)

> First, smoking is harmful. . . . Second, *it* is both annoying and dangerous.
> . . . And worst of all, *it* creates an addiction. . . .

4. **Use parallel structure.** The three examples above, illustrating the use of repetition, synonyms, and pronoun references, are also examples of parallel structure. Transition strategies are even more powerful when used in combination than when they are used alone.

Phrasing your sentences in parallel form helps to maintain focus, reinforces the unity of your thoughts, and adds emphasis. Parallelism adds "punch" to your writing. (More punch is served in Part 7, Section 7.5.)

5. **Use transitional words and phrases.** Transitional words and phrases show the relationships between sentences in a paragraph as well as between paragraphs in an essay. They act like tape, sticking together the elements of a paragraph or a paper so your reader does not fall between the cracks. Use them the way you use turn signals on a car: to tell the person following you where you're going.

Here are some transitional phrases that will help make your writing read smoothly.

Transitional Function	Words/Phrases Used
1. To show a time relationship between points	• first, second, third • now, simultaneously, concurrently, at this point, while • during, meanwhile, presently, from time to time, sometimes • before, to begin, previously • after, following this, then, later, next • finally, last, subsequently
2. To add an idea or example to the previous point	• and, in addition, also, furthermore, besides, moreover, for the same reason • another, similarly, equally important, likewise • for example, for instance, in fact
3. To show contrast between points	• although, nevertheless, on the other hand, whereas, while • but, however, instead, nonetheless • in contrast, on the contrary, in spite of, despite
4. To show a cause-and-effect relationship between points	• since, because, thus, therefore, hence • as a result, consequently, accordingly
5. To emphasize a significant point	• in fact, indeed, certainly, undoubtedly • in other words, as I have said, that is to say
6. To summarize or conclude	• in brief, on the whole, in summary, in short • therefore, as a result, last, finally

Exercise 8.2*

Working with a partner, identify the transitional words and phrases that create coherence in each of the sentence groups below.

1. The mountain pine beetle threatens British Columbia's forests, killing trees that have resisted all other predators. Therefore, governments at

both the local and provincial levels are pursuing a controlled burn program.

2. The two women spent the whole day tramping from car dealer to car dealer. Finally, they found a used Toyota they could live with, but the price was higher than they had hoped to pay.

3. There are many jokes about cats. Unfortunately, however, in most of them the cat is either very unhappy or dead.

4. There are those who think Quebec would thrive as a separate state. On the other hand, some feel that its economic viability depends on a close relationship with the rest of Canada.

5. Almost 90 percent of Canadians say that they are cooking and eating at home more often than they have in the past. Still, obesity and its related illnesses remain causes for concern in the land of poutine, doughnuts, and beer.

Exercise 8.3

In each of the following sentences, supply transitional words or phrases that help the meaning become clearer and make the sentence more coherent. When you've finished, exchange exercises with another student and check each other's answers. If you disagree with any of your partner's choices, explain why.

1. My first impression of my supervisor was that he was aloof and arrogant; _____, I discovered I was wrong. He was painfully shy.

2. Many bestsellers have become pathetic movies, now long forgotten. _____, many poor novels have been turned into movie classics, such as *Gone with the Wind*, that last forever.

3. Many sports were discovered by accident. _____, one day at England's Rugby School in the 1830s, a schoolboy, during a game of rugby, threw the ball overhand down the field. Football (as we call it in North America) was born.

4. Architecture in the 20th century became more streamlined, geometrical, and uniform. _____, it became monotonous.

5. Vitamin supplements can be useful in ensuring that you get all of the nutrients you need for good health. _____, they are no substitute for a healthy diet.

Now let us see how the five coherence strategies can work together to produce easy-to-follow text. In the following paragraph, examples of repetition and synonyms are highlighted in colour; the one pronoun reference is circled; examples of parallel structure are highlighted in grey; and the transitional phrase is italicized.

> While the Internet can be a useful tool for some businesses, studies have shown that in most workplaces (it) is a time-wasting drain on resources. *As a result of one such study,* Deloitte & Touche have issued a report pointing out the "five Gs": risks of allowing employees unsupervised Internet activity during business hours. A company risks Giving, handing trade or business secrets over to the competition or the general public. A company risks Gawking, time-wasting employee fascination with particular sites, including pornography. A company risks Gambling, an increasingly common and potentially addictive lure for surfers. A company risks Goofing Off, the pointless surfing of sites that are unrelated to the task at hand. A company risks Grabbing, the downloading of virus-loaded material and copyrighted software. To counter the five Gs, Deloitte & Touche recommend that companies establish clear policy on Internet use.

"Owner–Manager Advisor" newsletter. *Globe and Mail* 25 Jan. 1998: B15. Print.

Exercise 8.4*

Read the paragraphs below and identify by number (see pages 102–3) the transitional strategies that contribute to coherence. Both paragraphs contain examples of all five techniques.

1. Finally, developing the proper attitude is the true key to winning tennis. I define winning tennis as playing the game to the best of your ability, hitting the ball as well as you know you can, and enjoying the feeling of practised expertise. Winning tennis has nothing to do with beating an opponent. Naturally, if you play winning tennis by learning the basics, practising sufficiently, and concentrating, you'll win many matches, but that is the reward of playing well, not the reason for playing well. People who swear and throw their racquets when they lose are very useful; they are the most satisfying players to trounce. But I don't understand why they play a game that causes them such pain. Tennis players who enjoy the feel of a well-hit ball and the satisfaction of a long, skilfully played rally are winners, regardless of the score.

2. Travel abroad offers you the best education you can get. For one thing, travel is a course in communication skills. In order to function in a foreign language, you must practise every aspect of the communication process,

from body language to pronunciation. In fact, just making yourself understood is a lesson in creativity, a seminar in sign language, and a lab in communication theory. Another educational aspect of travel is the history, geography, and culture that you learn about almost unconsciously. Everywhere you go, you encounter memorable evidence of historical events you may dimly recall from school, and you are continually confronted by the practical realities of geography as you try to find your way around. As for culture, no book or course of study could provide you with the understanding and appreciation of another society that living in it can. A third way in which travel educates is through teaching you about yourself. Your ability—or inability—to cope with unfamiliar customs, with language difficulties, and with the inevitable problems of finding transportation and accommodation will tell you more than you might want to know about yourself. Without the safety net of family and friends, perhaps without even the security of knowing where you'll spend the night, you develop self-reliance or you go home. Either way, you learn valuable lessons. While you may not get a diploma from Travel U., you'll learn more about the world, about people, and about yourself than you will in any classroom.

Now compare your answers to ours on page 538.

Exercise 8.5

Next, consider the ways coherence strategies can be used to promote the smooth flow of ideas throughout an essay. Working with a partner, identify the techniques used in Bertrand Russell's "What I Have Lived For," on page 6. (*Note:* Russell's essay is famous for his concise phrasing of his message. The author's brevity is due in large part to his mastery of coherence strategies.)

Tone

As you write the paragraphs of your paper, be conscious of your **tone**. Your audience, purpose, and subject will all influence the tone you choose, which must be appropriate to all three. The examples, quotations, other supporting materials, and the words you choose to explain your main points—all these contribute to your tone. (More about words in Chapter 9.)

When you are trying to explain something to someone, particularly if it's something you feel strongly about, you may be tempted to be highly emotional in your discussion. If you allow yourself to get emotional, chances are you won't be convincing. What will be communicated is the strength of your feelings, not the depth of your understanding or the validity of your opinion. To be clear and credible, you need to restrain your enthusiasm or anger and present your points in a calm, reasonable way.

Here are a few suggestions to help you find and maintain the right tone:

- Be tactful. Avoid phrases such as "Any idiot can see," "No sane person could believe," and "It is obvious that. . . . " What is obvious to you isn't necessarily obvious to someone who has a limited understanding of your subject or who disagrees with your opinion.

- Don't talk down to your readers as though they were children or hopelessly ignorant. Never use sarcasm, profanity, or slang.

- Don't apologize for your interpretation of your subject. Have confidence in yourself. You've thought long and hard about your subject, you've found good supporting material to help explain it, and you believe in its significance. Present your subject in a positive manner. If you hang back, using phrases such as "I may be wrong, but . . . " or "I tend to feel that . . . ," your reader won't be inclined to give your points the consideration they deserve. Keep your reader in mind as you write, and your writing will be both clear and convincing.

The following paragraph is an example of inappropriate tone. The writer is passionate about his topic, but his tone is arrogant, bossy, and tactless rather than persuasive.

How dumb can people get? Here's this guy with a bumper sticker reading, "Out of work yet? Keep buying foreign." on his "North American" car parked in a Walmart parking lot. What can you buy in a Walmart that's made in Canada? Zilch. And besides, the car this idiot is driving wasn't made in Canada or even the United States. The engine was imported from Japan, and the transmission was made by Mexicans working for next to nothing. The plastic body moulding came from that model of capitalism and human rights, China, and the interior was made in Taiwan. Not foreign? Give me a break. About the only part of his car that was made here is the bumper that holds his stupid sticker. Meanwhile, parked right next to him was a "Japanese" car that was manufactured in Canada by Ontario workers. Of course, he's obviously too ignorant to get the irony.

Now read the paragraph below, which argues the same point but in a courteous, tactful way.

As the driver pulled into the parking spot beside me, I could hardly help noticing his bumper sticker: "Out of work yet? Keep buying foreign." It was attached to a car produced by one of North America's "Big Three" automakers, of course, but the driver's message lost much of its force because of where we were: in a Walmart parking lot. There is precious little to buy in Walmart that is produced in Canada. However, even that fact is beside the point, given the current internationalization of the auto industry. The car with the sticker on it, while nominally North American in origin, had an engine produced in Japan, a transmission built in Mexico, plastic body moulding made in China, and upholstery imported from Taiwan. One of the few parts actually made in Canada, ironically, was the bumper to which the sticker was attached. Meanwhile, the car next to it, a "Japanese" mid-size, had been built in Ontario.

Exercise 8.6*

The following paragraph is a draft written for a general reader. The writer's purpose is to persuade his audience that fighting should be banned in professional hockey. Revise the paragraph to make it appropriate for its audience and purpose by deleting or rewording any lapses in tone. Then compare your answer with ours on pages 538–39.

We've all heard the arguments: "It's part of the game," "It's what the fans want," "It prevents dangerous, dirty play." What nonsense! Fighting has no place in hockey or any team sport, and people who think differently are Neanderthals. Anyone with half a brain knows that fighting is banned in every other sport. What makes hockey any different? If the fans wanted fighting, they wouldn't watch the Olympics or World Championships. Ever seen the ratings for those events? Through the roof. Meanwhile, NHL ratings are in decline, and the game is treated as a third-rate sport in most of the world. Hockey can be a beautiful, fast, skilful, creative game, but when goons who have no other purpose than to fight are sent onto the ice, it is a joke.

Exercise 8.7

Revise the following paragraph, adding transitions and moderating its tone.

The armed forces of most nations are trained to be psychopaths. Canada's military personnel face a greater challenge: they need to be schizophrenics. The boot-camp training that recruits undergo, together with instruction in combat and weaponry, produces efficient and remorseless killers—psychopaths. The role of Canada's armed forces over the past 50 years has been to keep the peace. When the Nobel Peace Prize was awarded to the United Nations peacekeeping forces, Canada, as the only nation to have participated in every mission, considered the prize largely hers. Canada's elite forces played a traditional military role as hunters and killers in Afghanistan. Is Canada's military adequately trained for these two contradictory roles? Our country needs highly trained units of efficient psychopaths. The majority of armed forces personnel need training in mediation, conflict resolution, cultural sensitivity, basic medical treatment, and infrastructure repair. This is a hard concept for fans of the military to get through their thick skulls: soldiers trained to prevent violence. Peacekeeping is still the Canadian military's primary function. Canada's armed forces have two roles. Both must be prepared for.

9

Choosing the Right Words

The difference between the right word and the almost right word is the difference between lightning and a lightning bug.

Mark Twain, 1835–1910

In this chapter, we provide a brief introduction to language that is accurate and appropriate for your message and your audience. Our assumption is that you are writing for readers in academic and professional environments. Our goals are to help you convey your message clearly and in a way that will leave your readers with a positive impression of you and your ideas.

Before you begin drafting, you need to equip yourself with a few essential resources and some basic knowledge of what kinds of language are inappropriate when you write.

The Writer's Toolkit

In addition to basic skills, all workers need tools. As a general rule, the better their tools, the better their work. Every writer comes equipped with a set of language skills acquired from birth. In most cases, however, these skills are not sufficiently developed to handle the complex task of producing clear, error-free prose in a professional style. Fortunately, tools are available to assist writers in bringing their language skills up to the standards required by professional environments. Collectively, we call these indispensable aids the Writer's Toolkit.

No one expects a writer to write without assistance. In fact, our first recommendation to beginning writers is to GET HELP! Every writer needs three basic tools and to know how to use them.

1. Buy and use a good dictionary.

A dictionary is a writer's best friend. You will need to use it every time you write, so if you don't already own a good dictionary, you need to buy one. For Canadian writers, a good dictionary is one that is Canadian, current, comprehensive (contains at least 75 000 entries), and reliable (published by an established, well-known firm).

A convenient reference is the *Collins Gage Canadian Dictionary*, available in an inexpensive paperback edition. It is the dictionary on which we have based the examples and exercises in this chapter. Also recommended are the *Nelson Canadian Dictionary of the English Language*, the *Canadian Oxford Dictionary* (2nd ed., 2004), and, for those whose native language is not English, the *Oxford Advanced Learner's Dictionary*. Unfortunately, no comprehensive Canadian dictionary is available on the Internet.

Whichever dictionary you choose, begin by reading the information in the front on how to use the dictionary. This information may not be very entertaining, but it is essential if you want to understand how to use your dictionary efficiently. No two dictionaries are alike. You need to be familiar with your dictionary's symbols, abbreviations, and the format of its entries.

Knowing how the dictionary entries are set up will also save you time. For example, you may not need to memorize long lists of irregular plurals, as good dictionaries include irregular plurals in their entries. They also include irregular forms of verbs, adjectives, and adverbs. And if you've forgotten how regular plurals, verbs, adjectives, and adverbs are formed, you'll find that information in the dictionary's front matter as well.

2. Use spelling and grammar checkers responsibly.

Good spell-check programs can find typing errors and common spelling mistakes that distract your readers and make you look careless. They do have limitations, however. As we'll see, they can't tell if you meant to write "your" or "you're" and will not flag either word, even if it's used incorrectly. (You'll learn more about such words in Part 7, Section 7.16, "Hazardous Homonyms.")

Also, since we use Canadian English, our spelling is frequently different from American spelling, which is the standard on which most word-processing spell-check programs are based. Set your program to Canadian spelling if the option exists. If it does not, be aware that words such as *colour*, *honour*, and *metre*—all correct Canadian spellings—will be flagged as errors.

Another useful tool is a hand-held spell checker. Conveniently pocket-sized and not expensive, these devices contain a large bank of words and can provide the correct spelling if the "guess" you key in is not too far off. Some checkers even pronounce the word for you. Ask your instructor if you can use this device (sound turned off, please) when you are writing in class and during exams.

The best advice we can give you about grammar checkers (they announce their presence by producing wavy green lines under words or sentences as you write on your word processor) is to use them with caution. So far, no grammar checker has been able to account for even most, let alone all, of the subtleties of English grammar. A grammar program is as likely to flag a perfectly good sentence, even to suggest a "fix" that is incorrect, as it is to ignore a sentence full of errors. "I done real good on my grammar test," for example, escapes the dreaded wavy green line.

3. Buy and use a good thesaurus.

If you repeat yourself, using the same words again and again, you won't communicate your thoughts interestingly, let alone memorably. Worse, you will bore your reader. A thesaurus is a dictionary of synonyms—words with similar meanings. For any word you need to use repeatedly in a document, a good thesaurus will provide a list of alternatives.

Synonyms are *not* identical in meaning. Your dictionary will help you decide which of the words listed in your thesaurus are suitable for your message and which are not. We do not recommend that you rely on the thesaurus in your word-processing program. For any given word, a word-processing thesaurus provides a list, in alphabetical order, of more-or-less synonyms, with no usage labels or examples. "More-or-less" is not good enough. At the very least, you need to know whether the synonyms offered are nouns or verbs and whether they are in general use or are informal, technical, derogatory, or even obsolete. For this information, buy a good book-form thesaurus and use it in conjunction with your dictionary. Two thesauruses are available in inexpensive paperback editions: the *Oxford Thesaurus of Current English* (2nd ed., 2006) and *Roget's 21st Century Thesaurus in Dictionary Form* (3rd ed., 2005).

Use the information you find in a thesaurus with caution. Inexperienced writers sometimes assume that long, obscure words will impress their readers. In fact, most readers are irritated by unnecessarily "fancy" language. For more information on this topic, see the "Pretentious Language" section on pages 118–19.

NEVER use a word whose meaning you do not know. When you find a potential but unfamiliar synonym, look it up in your dictionary to be sure it's the word you need.

So far, we've introduced you to the tools you'll need as a writer and to the levels of language you can choose from when writing a message for a particular audience. Let's turn now to the writing errors you must not commit, no matter what message you're sending or the audience to which you're sending it: wordiness, slang and jargon, pretentious language, clichés, sexist language, offensive language, and the misused words and phrases that we call "abusages."

The Seven Deadly Sins of Writing

1. WORDINESS

Wordiness—words and phrases that are not essential to the communication of your message—is annoying to readers, no matter what topic you are writing about. Good writing communicates a message as concisely as possible. Wordy messages take up your readers' time and try their patience. If you want to please your audience, be brief.

Sometimes wordiness results from a failure to revise carefully. In the editing stage of writing, you should be looking for the best words to express your meaning. Wordy expressions and awkward phrasing often pop into your mind when you are struggling to express an idea, and they often make their way into a first draft. There is no excuse for them to survive a careful edit and make their way into the second draft, however.

Here's an example of what can happen when a writer fails to prune his or her prose:

> In my personal opinion, the government of this country of ours needs an additional amount of meaningful input from the people of Canada right now.

This wordy sentence could be nicely condensed into "In my opinion, our government needs to hear more from the people." The writer has chosen impressive-sounding phrases (*meaningful input, this country of ours*) and has slipped in unnecessary and meaningless words that should have been caught during editing (*personal opinion, an additional amount*). The result is a sentence that is so hard to read that it isn't worth the effort to decipher.

As you can see from the above example, one of the symptoms of wordiness is redundancy, or saying the same thing twice. Another is using several words where one or two would do.

The following list contains some of the worst offenders we've collected from student writing, corporate memoranda, form letters, and advertisements.

Wordy	Concise
a large number of	many
absolutely nothing (everything/ complete/perfect)	nothing (everything/ complete/perfect)
actual (*or* true) fact	fact
almost always	usually
at that point in time	then
at the present time	now
consensus of opinion	consensus
continue on	continue
could possibly (*or* may possibly, might possibly)	could (*or* may, might)
crisis (*or* emergency) situation	crisis (*or* emergency)
due to the fact that	because
end result	result
equally as good	as good
few and far between	rare
final conclusion	conclusion
for the reason that	because
free gift	gift
I myself (*or* you yourself, *etc.*)	I (*or* you, *etc.*)
I personally think/feel	I think/feel
in actual fact	in fact
in every instance	always
in my opinion, I think	I think
in the near future	soon
in today's society/in this day and age	now (*or* today)
is able to	can
many different kinds	many kinds
mutual agreement/cooperation	agreement/cooperation
my personal opinion	my opinion
no other alternative	no alternative
personal friend	friend
real, genuine leather (*or* real antique, *etc.*)	leather (*or* antique, *etc.*)
red in colour (*or* large in size, *etc.*)	red (*or* large, *etc.*)
repeat again	repeat
return back	return (*or* go back)
really, very	*These words add nothing to your meaning. Leave them out.*
8:00 a.m. in the morning	8:00 a.m.
such as, for example	such as

Wordy	Concise
take active steps	take steps
totally destroyed	destroyed
truly remarkable	remarkable
very (most, quite, almost, rather) unique	unique

Exercise 9.1*

Working with a partner, revise these sentences to make them as concise and clear as possible. Then compare your answers with our suggestions on page 539.

1. I wondered why the baseball seemed to keep getting bigger and bigger and bigger. Then, at that point in time, it hit me.

2. Would you repeat again the instructions about wordiness? In actual fact, I didn't hear them because I was busy texting at the very same time you were speaking.

3. It has come to my attention that our competitor's products, although not equally as good as ours, are, nevertheless, at this point in time, selling better than our products.

4. In my opinion, I believe that my writing is equally as good as Ashley's and deserves equally as good a mark, especially considering that I use a larger number of words to say exactly the same thing.

5. Basically, I myself prefer *Facebook* to *MySpace* because *MySpace* is owned lock, stock, and barrel by Fox, whose politics I find reprehensible, offensive, and abhorrent because they are so far to the right of mine as to be off the charts.

6. I doubt that this particular new innovation will succeed in winning much in the way of market share.

7. In my view, I feel that a really firm understanding of the basic fundamentals of English is an essential prerequisite to a person's success in college or university, the business world, and the community at large.

8. "As a new beginning teacher," we told our English instructor, "you need to understand the fact that the grammar, spelling, and punctuation conventions and rules you insist on are totally stifling our creativity."

9. There are many different kinds of social media we use in today's society, but I think that in the not too distant future, we'll see a convergence with the end result that the electronic world will in actual fact resemble the "real" world so closely that the boundaries between the two will blur and begin to disappear.

10. Due to the fact that the law, not to mention our company's policy, rules, and regulations, absolutely prohibits any mention of race, age, gender, religion, and marital status in official documents such as per-

sonnel documents, we have made sure that all such descriptors have been entirely eliminated from our files. Now, as a result, all our personnel documents are now almost practically identical.

2. SLANG AND JARGON

Slang is "street talk": nonstandard words and phrases used by members of a group—people who share a culture, interest, or lifestyle. The group may be as large as a generation or as small as a high-school clique. Do you know what "amped," "badload," "busting," and "hodger" mean? Probably not. The whole point of slang is its exclusivity. It's a private language and thus not appropriate for a message aimed at a general reader.

Another characteristic of slang is that it changes quickly. Terms that were "in" last month are "out" today. Except for a few expressions that manage to sneak across the line that separates private language from mainstream English, most slang expressions are quickly outdated and sound silly. And finally, slang is an oral language. It is colloquial—that is, characteristic of casual speech—and not appropriate for use in professional or academic writing.

When you aren't sure if a word is appropriate for a written message, consult your print dictionary. The notation *sl.* or *slang* appears after words that are slang or have a slang meaning. (Some words, such as *house*, *cool*, and *bombed*, have both a general and a slang meaning.) If the word you're looking for isn't listed, chances are it's a recent slang term, and you should avoid using it in writing. Taking the time to choose words that are appropriate to written English increases your chances both of communicating clearly and of winning your readers' respect.

Exercise 9.2

- Working in groups of three or four, identify five current slang expressions.
- Now list five slang expressions that are no longer in use among your peers.
- Finally, define each current slang term in language appropriate to a general reader. (If you don't have a clear picture of a "general reader," write each definition in words your parents or teachers would understand.)

Jargon is similar to slang because it, too, is the private language of a subgroup; however, whereas the subgroups for slang are formed by culture or lifestyle, the subgroups who speak jargon are formed by profession or trade. The jargon of some professions is so highly technical and specialized it amounts almost to a private language.

Although jargon is useful, even necessary, in the context of some jobs, it is inappropriate in most writing because it does not communicate to a general reader. Our vocabulary and even the content of our writing are influenced by the contexts within which we work and live. In the following paragraph, D. E. Miller explains the extent to which our individual perceptions are influenced by our life experience.

A group of people witness a car accident. What each person sees, and how he or she describes it, is determined to a large extent by the language each one normally uses. A doctor or nurse would see and describe contusions, lacerations, and hemorrhages. A lawyer would think in terms of civil liabilities and criminal negligence. A mechanic would see crushed fenders, bent axles, and damaged chassis. A psychologist would be concerned about stress reactions, trauma, and guilt. You or I might see and describe the pain and injury caused by a driver's error in judgement or lapse of skill.

Miller, D. E. *The Book of Jargon.* New York: Collier, 1981. 26. Print.

Jargon restricts your audience to those who share your specialized vocabulary and limits or destroys your ability to reach a wider audience. The cure for jargon is simple: unless your readers share your technical background, use nonspecialized language.

Exercise 9.3

Working in small groups, list as many examples of technical jargon as you can for each of the following occupations.

1. Chef (e.g., sauté, braise, sous vide)
2. computer technician (e.g., TWAIN, burn)
3. music (e.g., sample, bridge, axe)
4. financial analyst (e.g., fallen angel, dead cat bounce)
5. filmmaker (e.g., take, MOS)

Choose five technical terms from your own career field and write a general-level equivalent for each one.

3. PRETENTIOUS LANGUAGE

One of the challenges writers face when trying to adapt their style from the familiar to the formal level is a tendency to overcompensate. Many beginning writers try so hard to impress their readers that they forget that the purpose of writing is to communicate. Writing filled with abstract nouns, multi-syllable words, and long, complicated sentences is **pretentious**. All readers hate pretentious writing because they have to take the time to "translate" it into language they can understand. (Most teachers and supervisors won't bother. They'll just return the piece to the student or employee for revision.)

Sometimes called "gobbledygook," pretentious language has sound but no meaning:

> Our aspirational consumer strategy must position the brand's appeal to women shoppers who are seeking emblematic brands that are positively identified with health-oriented and fitness-centred lifestyles, so they can align their personal images with those lifestyle indicators.

This sentence, part of a marketing presentation to senior management, was written by a middle manager for a major yogurt company. What the struggling writer is trying to say is that the company's customers want to be seen as people interested in fitness and health, so the company should advertise its yogurt accordingly.[1]

One symptom of pretentious writing is the use of "buzzwords." These are words and phrases that become popular because they reflect the latest academic or psychological fad. They are often nouns with *-ize* added to them to make them into verbs: *utilize, verbalize, conceptualize.* What's wrong with *use, say,* and *think*?

Every teacher knows this annoying trick, and so do most managers. Instead of impressing readers, pretentious writing makes readers impatient and causes them to lose respect for the writer. If you really want to get your message across, write plainly and clearly in language your readers can understand.

Exercise 9.4*

Rewrite the following sentences, expressing the ideas in a way that allows the reader to grasp your meaning clearly and quickly. Then compare your answers to our suggestions on page 539.

1. We were forced to utilize the moisture-removing apparatus in our motorized personal conveyance when precipitate liquid impacted our windshield.
2. The chronologically less advanced generation sometimes achieves a communication deficit with authority figures and parental units.

---

[1] This anecdote is paraphrased from Doug Saunders, "Aspiration Nation: Life Is but a Brand-name Dream," *Globe and Mail* 3 July 2004: F3. Print.

3. The witness was ethically disoriented truthwise when she claimed that her interface with the accused resulted in his verbalization of an admission of guilt.
4. The parameters of our study vis-à-vis the totality of research in the field demonstrate that surveywise our validity is on a par with that of other instruments.
5. The cancellation of IMF funds to the Pacific Rim countries could lead to negative distortion of mutual interrelationships between developed and developing nations.

---

4. CLICHÉS

Unless you're a career civil servant or a long-time bureaucrat, writing pretentious language is a time-consuming and tiring task. You have to look up practically every word in a thesaurus to find a polysyllabic equivalent. Clichés, on the other hand, are easy to produce: they represent language without thought.

A **cliché** is a phrase that has been used so often it has lost its ability to communicate a meaningful idea to a reader.

> In this day and age, it seems that anything goes in our private lives. But in our professional lives, the name of the game is what it has always been: the bottom line.

In this day and age, anything goes, the name of the game, and *the bottom line* are clichés. Readers know what these phrases are supposed to mean, but they have been used so often they no longer communicate effectively. Cliché-filled writing will not only bore readers, but also affect their reaction to your message: "There's nothing new here. It's all been said before."

Spoken English is full of clichés. In the rush to express an idea, we often take the easy way and use ready-made expressions to put our thoughts into words. There is less excuse to use clichés in writing. Writers have time to think through what they want to say. They also have the opportunity to revise and edit. Writers are expected to communicate with more care, more precision, and more originality than speakers.

Clichés are easy to recognize if you are a native speaker. When you can read the first few words of an expression and automatically fill in the rest, the phrase is a cliché: free as a _____; a pain in the _____; last but not_____; it goes without _____. It is difficult to get rid of *all* clichés in your writing, but you can be aware of them and use them as seldom as possible.

The solution to a cliché problem involves time and thought. Think carefully about what you want to say; then say it in your own words, not everyone else's.

As you read through Exercise 9.5, notice how hard it is to form a mental picture of what the sentences mean and how hard it is to remember what you've read—even when you've just read it!

Exercise 9.5

Working with a partner, rewrite these sentences, expressing the ideas in your own words. When you're finished, exchange papers with another team and compare your results.

1. The classroom was so quiet you could hear a pin drop.
2. At midnight, I didn't think I had a hope, but I managed to finish the assignment at the crack of dawn.
3. All our good intentions fell by the wayside when we passed a fast-food joint and caught the mouth-watering smell of French fries and grilled burgers.
4. When you are playing poker, you must keep your cool; otherwise, you could lose your shirt.
5. The CEO could not find a way to keep her company afloat, so she threw in the towel.
6. In these difficult times, we must all tighten our belts and hope for a silver lining.
7. Their offer is a far cry from what we had hoped for, but let's make the best of it and show them what we're made of!
8. Until he got the sack, he was a legend in his own mind, but once the axe fell, even he had to face the truth: he was only a flash in the pan.
9. Your proposal is as good as they get; however, until the deal is signed, sealed, and delivered, we had better not count our chickens.
10. I hate to eat and run and stick you with the bill, but I'm between a rock and a hard place, so I have to lie low until my ship comes in.

---

5. SEXIST LANGUAGE

Any writing that distracts your readers from your meaning is weak writing. Whether the distraction is caused by grammatical errors, spelling mistakes, slang, or the use of sexist language, your readers' concentration on your message is broken, and communication fails. **Sexist** (or gender-biased) **language** includes the use of words that signify gender (e.g., *waitress*, *sculptress*, *actress*) and the use of the pronouns *he, his, him* to refer to singular antecedents such as *everybody, anyone, no one*. Some readers object to terms that draw attention to gender differences, such as *man and wife* or *host and hostess*, preferring instead gender-neutral, inclusive terms such as *married couple* and *hosts*.

It is easy to dismiss nonsexist writing as "politically correct," but the language we use is a powerful force that influences the way we think. If we consistently refer to a *chairman* or *businessman*, we are perpetuating the idea that only men qualify for these positions. Far from being a politically correct fad, the use of inclusive or neutral words is both accurate and even-handed.

Here are three tips to help you steer clear of sexist writing:

- Avoid using the word *woman* as an adjective. There is an implied condescension to phrases such as *woman athlete* and *woman writer* and *woman engineer*.
- Be conscious of the dangers of stereotyping. Physical descriptions of women are appropriate only where you would offer a similar description if the subject was a man. Just as some men can be excellent cooks, some women can be ruthless, power-hungry executives. It is possible for men to be scatterbrained and gossipy, while women can be decisive, tough, even violent.
- When making pronouns agree with singular antecedents, be careful that your pronouns do not imply bias. For example, "A teacher who discovers plagiarism must report it to *his* supervisor." Either use masculine and feminine pronouns interchangeably, or switch to a plural noun and avoid the problem: "Teachers who discover plagiarism must report it to their supervisors."

Exercise 9.6*

Correct the use of sexist or gender-biased language in the following sentences. Exchange papers with a partner and compare revisions. Then turn to pages 539–40 and compare your answers with our suggestions.

1. The well-known female writer and director Nora Ephron regrets that she cannot go out in public without attracting the attention of fans and photographers.
2. Amy King, an attractive, blonde mother of two, first joined the company as a saleswoman; 10 years later, she was promoted to president.
3. A businessman sitting in the first-class cabin rang for the stewardess, a friendly gal who quickly arrived to assist him.

4. The list of ingredients on food packages contains information that may be important to the housewife, especially if she is the mother of young children.
5. The typical working man with a wife and two children is often hard-pressed to find time for recreation with his bride and the kids.

6. OFFENSIVE LANGUAGE

The last thing you want to do when you write is to offend your reader, even if you are writing a complaint. As we've seen above, some words occasionally used in speech are always inappropriate in writing. Swear words, for example, are unacceptable in a written message. So are obscene words, even "mild" ones. Offensive language appears much stronger in print than in speech and can provoke, shock, or even outrage a reader. Racist language and blasphemy (the use of names or objects that are sacred to any religion) are deeply offensive and always unacceptable.

Many writers have experienced the acute embarrassment of having a message read by people for whom it was not intended. What might have seemed at the time of composition to be an innocent joke may prove hateful to the unintended audience and mortifying to the writer.

It is wise to avoid all questionable, let alone unacceptable, expressions in your writing. Language has power: as many linguists have observed, our language actually shapes as well as reflects our attitudes and values. Those who use racist, blasphemous, sexist, or profane terms not only reinforce the attitudes contained in those terms, but also project a profoundly negative image of themselves to their readers.

7. ABUSAGES

Some words and phrases, even ones we hear in everyday speech, are *always* incorrect in written English. Technically, they are also incorrect in speech, but most people tolerate them in informal conversation. If these expressions appear in your writing, your reader will assume you are uneducated, ignorant, or worse. Even in some conversations, particularly in academic and professional environments, these expressions make a poor impression on your listeners.

Carefully read through the following list and highlight any words or phrases that sound all right to you. These are the ones you need to find and fix when you revise.

allready	A common misspelling of *already.*
alot	There is no such word. Use *much* or *many.* (*A lot* is acceptable in informal usage.)
alright	A common misspelling of *all right.*
anyways (anywheres)	There is no *s* in these words.
between you and I	The correct expression is *between you and me.*
can't hardly couldn't hardly	Use *can hardly* or *could hardly.*
could of (would of, should of)	The helping verb needed is *have,* not *of.* Write *could have, would have, should have.*
didn't do nothing	All double negatives ("couldn't see nothing," "couldn't get nowhere," "wouldn't talk to nobody") are wrong. Write *didn't do anything, couldn't see anything, couldn't get anywhere, wouldn't talk to anyone.*
for free	Use *free* or *at no cost.* (Also "free gift." Is there any other kind of gift?)
in regards to	Use *in* (or *with*) regard to.
irregardless	There is no such word. Use *regardless.*
media used as singular	The word *media* is plural. The singular is *medium.* Newspapers and television are mass *media.* Radio is an electronic *medium.*
most all	Use *most* or *almost all.*
off of	Use *off* alone: "I fell *off* the wagon."
prejudice used as an adjective	It is wrong to write "She is *prejudice* against blondes." Use *prejudiced.*
prejudism	There is no such word. Use *prejudice.* "A judge should show no *prejudice* to either side."
real used as an adverb	"Real good," "real bad," and "real nice" are wrong. You could use *really* or *very,* but such filler words add nothing to your meaning.

reason is because	Use *the reason is that*: "The reason is that my printer blew up."
suppose to	This expression, like *use to*, is nonstandard. Use *supposed to* and *used to*.
themself	Also "theirself," "ourselfs," "yourselfs," and "themselfs." These are all nonstandard words. The plural of *self* is *selves*: *themselves*, *ourselves*, and so on. Don't use "theirselves"; it's another nonstandard word.
try and	Use *try to*.
youse	There is no such word. *You* is both the singular and plural form of the pronoun.

Exercise 9.7*

Correct the following sentences where necessary. Suggested answers are on page 540.

1. Irregardless of what you think, the problem between her and I has nothing to do with you.
2. If you want to be in the office pool, I need $5.00 off of you today because there will be no spots left by tomorrow.
3. If I hadn't of texted you this morning to remind you that you were suppose to write your chemistry exam, you would of missed it.
4. I didn't feel like seeing nobody, so I went home, turned on the TV, and didn't do nothing for the rest of the night.
5. This use to be a real good place to work, but now we are suppose to work a full shift every day, or a penalty is deducted off of our pay.
6. When Barack Obama was elected president, most all U.S. liberals hoped that alot of the prejudism in that country had finally been put to rest.
7. Irregardless of media hype, Barack Obama is not the first person of African descent to head a G8 country; that distinction had allready been won by Canada's Michaëlle Jean.
8. It's unresponsible of us to blame television or any other media for causing violence.
9. Television is partly responsible, however, for the fact that alot of ungrammatical expressions sound alright to us.
10. Between you and I, the reason I didn't speak to no one about Elmo's cheating is because he would of broke my arm.

The Seven Deadly Sins of Writing

1. **Wordiness:** Make every sentence as clear and concise as possible.

2. **Slang and jargon:** When you are writing for a general audience, avoid expressions that may be understood only by specific social or professional groups.

3. **Gobbledygook:** Avoid pretentious language in all of your writing.

4. **Clichés:** As you revise, reword any clichés that have slipped into your prose. (Guarantee: There will be some.)

5. **Sexist language:** Refer to the three tips on page 122 to ensure that your paper is free of gender-biased language.

6. **Offensive language:** Do not use swear words, obscene words, racist expressions, or blasphemy (unless you are quoting from a source).

7. **Abusages:** Check every paper you write to be sure you have excluded all nonstandard words and phrases (see pages 123–25).

Exercise 9.8

The following "update" of a familiar folk tale contains numerous examples of wordiness, jargon, pretentious language, slang (much of it outdated), and clichés. As you read this story, highlight every example of the "seven deadly sins of writing" that you discover. Be prepared to explain your "sinful" selections.

LITTLE RED RIDING HOOD REVISITED

Russell Baker

In an effort to make the classics accessible to contemporary readers, I am translating them into [modern English]. Here is the translation of *Little Red Riding Hood*:

Once upon a point in time, a small person named Little Red Riding Hood initiated plans for the preparation, delivery and transportation of foodstuffs to her grandmother, a senior citizen residing at a place of residence in a wooded area of indeterminate dimension.

In the process of implementing this program, her incursion into the area was in mid-transportation process when it attained interface with an alleged perpetrator. This individual, a wolf, made inquiry as to the whereabouts of Little Red Riding Hood's goal, as well as inferring that he was desirous of ascertaining the contents of Little Red Riding Hood's foodstuffs basket, and all that.

"It would be inappropriate to lie to me," the wolf said, displaying his huge jaw capability. Sensing that he was a mass of repressed hostility intertwined with acute alienation, she indicated.

"I see you indicating," the wolf said, "but what I don't see is whatever it is you're indicating at, you dig?"

Little Red Riding Hood indicated more fully, making one thing perfectly clear—to wit, that it was to her grandmother's residence and with a consignment of foodstuffs that her mission consisted of taking her to and with.

At this point in time, the wolf moderated his rhetoric and proceeded to Grandmother's residence. The elderly person was then subjected to the disadvantages of total consumption and transferred in residence to the perpetrator's stomach.

"That will raise the old woman's consciousness," the wolf said to himself. He was not a bad wolf, but only a victim of an oppressive society, a society that not only denied wolves' rights, but actually boasted of its capacity for keeping the wolf from the door. An interior malaise made itself manifest inside the wolf.

"Is that the national malaise I sense within my digestive tract?" wondered the wolf. "Or is it the old person seeking to retaliate for her consumption by telling wolf jokes to my duodenum?" It was time to make a judgment. The time was now, the hour had struck, the body lupine cried out for decision. The wolf was up to the challenge. He took two stomach powders right away and got into bed.

The wolf had adopted the abdominal distress recovery posture when Little Red Riding Hood achieved his presence.

"Grandmother," she said, "your ocular implements are of an extraordinary order of magnitude."

"The purpose of this enlarged viewing capability," said the wolf, "is to enable your image to register a more precise impression upon my sight systems."

"In reference to your ears," said Little Red Riding Hood, "it is noted with the deepest respect that far from being underprivileged, their elongation and enlargement appear to qualify you for unparalleled distinction."

"I hear you loud and clear, kid," said the wolf, "but what about these new choppers?"

"If it is not inappropriate," said Little Red Riding Hood, "it might be observed that with your new miracle masticating products you may even be able to chew taffy again."

This observation was followed for the adoption of an aggressive posture on the part of the wolf and the assertion that it was also possible for him, due to the high efficiency ratio of his jaw, to consume little persons, plus, as he stated, his firm determination to do so at once without delay and with all due process and propriety, notwithstanding the fact that the ingestion of one entire grandmother had already provided twice his daily recommended cholesterol intake.

There ensued flight by Little Red Riding Hood accompanied by pursuit in respect to the wolf and a subsequent intervention on the part of a third party, heretofore unnoted in the record.

Due to the firmness of the intervention, the wolf's stomach underwent ax-assisted aperture with the result that Little Red Riding Hood's grandmother was enabled to be removed with only minor discomfort.

The wolf's indigestion was immediately alleviated with such effectiveness that he signed a contract with the intervening third party to perform with Grandmother in a television commercial demonstrating the swiftness of this dramatic relief for stomach discontent.

"I'm going to be on television," cried Grandmother.

And they all joined her happily in crying, "What a phenomena!"

PART 3

Revising

I'm sorry this letter is so long; I didn't have time to make it short.
George Bernard Shaw, 1856–1950

Everything should be made as simple as possible—but not simpler.
Albert Einstein, 1879–1955

The best writing is rewriting.
E. B. White, 1899–1985

A sentence should contain no unnecessary words, a paragraph no unnecessary sentences, for the same reason that a drawing should have no unnecessary lines and a machine no unnecessary parts.
William Strunk, Jr., 1869–1946

10

Rewriting, Editing, and Proofreading

Revision means "re-seeing." It does not mean "recopying."

No one can produce in a first draft a document that is effectively organized and developed, let alone one that is free of errors. The purpose of the first draft is to get down on paper something you can work with until it meets your readers' needs and expectations. Planning and drafting should take no more than half the time you devote to writing a paper. The rest should be devoted to revision: rewriting, editing, and proofreading.

The purpose of rewriting is to clarify the message of your essay; the purpose of editing is to polish the style. Proofreading confirms that you have corrected all errors in your earlier drafts and not introduced any new ones. Why bother? Read on, and we will show you how and why revision is essential to a message that communicates clearly and makes a positive impression on your readers.

The three phases of revision are not separate and distinct: you don't march lock step from one to the other. While you are working on rewriting, you'll find errors that we've identified in the section on editing. While you are editing, you'll undoubtedly come across errors that we've listed in the proofreading section. The revision process is not fixed, but fluid, and it is essential to good communication.

Good communication requires that you learn to **revise from your readers' point of view.** Because a first draft reflects the contents of the writer's mind, it often seems all right to the writer. But in order to transfer an idea clearly from the mind of the writer to the mind of the reader, revision is necessary.

It's often difficult to identify muddled thinking and stylistic errors in your own writing. This is why **getting a second reader is the smartest thing you can do as a writer.** Most students can recognize problems in another's writing more easily than they can identify problems in their own. You may not be able to put a name to the problem, but you know when the writing goes off-track, is unconvincing, needs more (or less) detail, or somehow confuses you. Working with a peer reviewer is not easy on the ego: you must be prepared for any criticism you receive. Don't be defensive; if you are, your peer reviewer will soften his or her critique and you won't get the information you need in order to revise effectively. Of course, you don't have to follow every suggestion your reader makes, but the comments will provoke a re-thinking of your paper that you will profit from in the end. And all you're required to do is return the favour.

The second-smartest thing you can do as a writer is to be a second reader. There's no better way to learn how to revise a paper than to help someone else revise hers or his. Because you come to someone else's document without the tangle of ideas that influence your own writing, you can be objective. You can see where holes in the argument exist, where the author has given too little information to develop a point convincingly and where too much information is provided—to the point of boredom. You are also in an ideal position to critique your partner's introduction and conclusion—two critical parts of every essay.

A partnered revision takes time: each of you will need to read the other's essay three times. We don't mean to discourage you—partnered revisions are the best way of getting objective feedback at each stage of the process. But it would be irresponsible of us not to warn you that partners must take into account each other's schedule when they agree to work together. Treat the agreement as a contract. Agree up front on the dates by which you will exchange your essays for the first, second, and third readings. And stick to these dates. Another advantage to a partnered revision is that most students won't let a partner down. So you'll be less likely to procrastinate and more likely to get each stage of the project finished on time.

The Three Steps to Revision

Rewriting, editing, and proofreading: by working carefully through these steps, you can produce a paper that is organized, accurate, and error-free. Each stage of the process requires you to read your essay from start to finish—sometimes more than once.

Here are the steps to follow in revising a paper:

1. **Rewrite:** Improve the whole paper by changing its content, organization, paragraph development, usage, and tone.
2. **Edit:** Refine sentence structure and correct any errors in grammar.
3. **Proofread:** Correct typos and any remaining errors in spelling and punctuation.

Inexperienced writers often skip the first two stages and concentrate on the third, thinking they will save time. In fact, they waste time—both theirs and their readers'—because the result is writing that doesn't communicate clearly and won't make a positive impression.

The best way to begin revising is to let as much time as possible pass between completing your first draft and rereading it. Ten minutes, or even half a day, is not enough. The danger in rereading too soon is that you're likely to "read" what you think you've written—what exists in your head, not on the paper.

There are two other things you can do to help you get some distance from your draft. First, if it is handwritten, key it into a computer. Reading your essay in a different form helps you to "re-see" its content. If you have arranged to revise with a partner, this is the point at which you should exchange papers. (You won't get a useful critique if you expect your partner to struggle with your handwriting while attempting to follow your reasoning.) Most people find it easier to revise on paper rather than on a computer screen, so print your draft double- or triple-spaced. Read it through carefully, making notes for changes in the margins or in the spaces between the lines; then go back to the computer to make the changes.

Second, if you don't have a revision partner, read your paper aloud and try to hear it from the viewpoint of your readers. Listen to the way your explanation unfolds, and mark every place you think your readers might find something unclear, irrelevant, inadequately developed, or out of order.

Step 1: Rewriting

The goal of rewriting is to adjust the logical organization of your message and the quality of your language. There are four kinds of changes you can make at this stage.

1. You can rearrange information. This is the kind of rewriting that is most often needed but least often done. Consider the order in which you've arranged your paragraphs. From your readers' point of view, is this the most effective order in which to present your ideas? Try rearranging your main points in an informal outline. Might this be a better way to get your message across?

2. You can add information. Adding new main ideas or more development is often necessary to make your message interesting and convincing as well as clear. Here is where your revision partner can be especially helpful, by identifying what needs to be expanded or clarified.

3. You can delete information. Now is the time to cut out anything that is repetitious, insignificant, or irrelevant to your subject, your purpose, or your readers. Again, your partner can be invaluable in this evaluation process.

4. You can adjust your level of language and tone. Even a well-organized, logical argument with adequately developed paragraphs will fail to convince a reader if the tone or level of language is inappropriate. See Chapter 9, "Choosing the Right Words," for errors that can trip you up and cause your reader to sigh, stop reading, and toss your paper aside.

Keep your outline beside you and change it as you rearrange, add, and subtract ideas. When you think you've completed the rewriting stage, check your revised outline one last time to be sure your changes have improved the organization and persuasiveness of your essay.

Your thesis statement is your contract with your reader, so it should be the guiding principle of your paper. It should contain nothing that is not developed in the body of the essay, and there should be nothing in the essay that is not directly related to your thesis statement. When you find a mismatch between the thesis statement and the paper, change one or the other—or both—until the two agree.

If you are thinking that this process will probably take two, three, or more passes to complete, you're right. But if the message is important to you (your grade is at stake; your promotion is on the line), you will take the time.

If you are not already using a word-processing program, now is the time to begin. Using a word processor to move blocks of text around is as easy as shuffling a deck of cards. Before you start to revise, change the computer's settings to meet the format requirements of your paper: set the spacing, margins, font style and size, running head, and so on. (See Chapter 14 for instructions and examples.)

Remember to save your work frequently. It takes only a split second to click on "Save," but that split second could save you hours—even days—in the event of a computer disaster. (Most programs have an auto-save function; if so, use it and let the computer remember to save your work every two or three minutes.) Save your work in a systematic and easy-to-find filing system. Give each file a distinctive name (e.g., English essay 3), and save each draft separately (e.g., English essay 3-rev 2) in case you want to go back and use material from a previous version of your document.

Use the checklist that follows to guide you as you review your paper's form and content.

REWRITING CHECKLIST

ACCURACY

- Is your information consistent with your own experience and observations and/or with what you have discovered through research?
- Are all of your facts and evidence up-to-date?

COMPLETENESS

- Have you included enough main ideas and development to explain your subject and convince your reader? (Remember that "enough" means from the reader's point of view, not the writer's.)

SUBJECT

Is your subject

- significant? Does it avoid the trivial and the obvious?
- single? Does it avoid double and combined subjects?
- specific? Is it focused and precise?
- supportable? Have you provided enough evidence to make your meaning clear?

MAIN POINTS

Are your main points

- significant? Have you deleted any unimportant ones?
- distinct? Are they all different from one another, or is there an overlap in content?
- relevant? Do all points relate directly to your subject?
- arranged in the most appropriate order? (Again, "appropriate" means from the reader's perspective. Choose chronological, climactic, logical, or random order, whichever is most likely to help the reader make sense of your information.)

PARAGRAPHS

Does each paragraph

- begin with a clear, identifiable topic sentence?
- develop one—and only one—main idea?
- use one or more kinds of development appropriate to the main idea?
- contain clear and effective transitions to signal the relationship between sentences? Between paragraphs?

WORDS

Usage
- Have you used words to convey meaning rather than to impress?
- Have you eliminated any slang, pretentious language, or offensive language?
- Have you cut out any unnecessary words?
- Have you corrected any "abusages"?

Tone
- Is your tone consistent, reasonable, courteous, and confident throughout your essay?

INTRODUCTION
Does your introduction
- catch the reader's attention and make him or her want to read on?
- contain a clearly identifiable thesis statement?
- identify the main points that your paper will explain?

CONCLUSION
Does your conclusion
- contain a summary or reinforcement of your main points, rephrased to avoid word-for-word repetition?
- contain a statement that effectively clinches your argument and leaves the reader with something to think about?

Exercise 10.1*

Below you will find the first draft of an essay on the "3 Rs" of environmental responsibility. This draft needs to be rewritten and edited. Using the "Rewriting Checklist" as your guide, rewrite the draft to ensure the content is accurate (to the best of your knowledge) and well organized. Improve the introduction and conclusion. Improve the topic sentences and examine the development of the body paragraphs. If you think more support is needed to develop a main point, add some supporting details. Delete any inappropriate, irrelevant, or repetitious material.

When you have finished your rewrite, exchange papers with another student and compare results. Go through the essay one paragraph at a time and discuss any significant differences you find: Whose version is clearer? More logical? More concise?

1   We are having a garbage crisis. There is so much waste being produced in North America, we no longer have any idea of were to put it. Toronto's garbage problem is so great that they are trucking thousands of tonnes of it to Michigan every year. A short-term solution that is just plain stupid and how long can it last? We must act now, and we must act as individuals. We cannot wait for the Government to save us from this crisis. We produce the garbage; we must solve the problem, that much is perfectly obvious to anyone. In very practical, down to earth, concrete terms, here are some things we can do to reduce, recycle, and reuse.

2   First, we must reduce the amount of garbage we produce. We can do this be refusing to buy products that are over packaged, like fast food that comes in styrafoam containers and chocolates that have a paper wrapping, a box, lining paper, a plastic tray for the candies, and foil wrap around each chocolate. By not purchasing such wasteful items, we say to the manufacturer, Either reduce the packaging of your product or lose business to your competition. We can also be less wasteful in our own habits by car-pooling, for example.

3   We must recycle everything we can instead of sending it to the dump. Old cloths can be sent to the Salvation Army, Goodwill, or other charitable organizations. As can furniture, appliances, books, and most other household items. There are dozens of ways to make useful items from things that would otherwise be thrown away, such as quilts from old clothes; bird feeders from plastic jugs, and fire logs from newspapers. We don't need to consume as much as we do, and it won't hurt us to use things longer instead of buying new items before the old ones are completely worn out. Many companies now manufacture products from recycled goods. We should be on the lookout for their products to support their efforts and to

reduce the waste that is dumped into landfills. And whatever we can't use ourselves can be sent to organizations that help others where they will have a life away from a landfill.

4   We can reuse most things. Composting vegetable garbage is a good way to put waste to valuable use. Things we no longer need or want can be offered to others through lawn sales and flea markets.

5   This is an absolute necessity. If we do not stop producing so much waste, we will inevitibly destroy our own enviornment. Unlike most efforts to improve things, the move to recycle, reuse, and reduce has one other advantage, it doesn't cost any money. In fact, it can save every household that practises it hundreds of dollars a year.

Step 2: Editing

Editing is the fine-tuning of sentences, grammar, spelling, and punctuation to ensure clarity and correctness. By now you're probably so tired of refining your paper that you may be tempted to skip this step. Don't. Careful editing is essential if you want your paper to make a positive impression.

Most word-processing programs include a spelling and grammar checker. These programs have some useful features. For example, they will question (but not correct) your use of apostrophes, they will sometimes catch errors in subject–verb agreement, and they will catch obvious misspellings and typos. But don't make the mistake of assuming these programs will do all your editing for you. Many errors slip past them. Only you or a knowledgeable and patient friend can find and correct all errors.

Again, you should allow time—at least a couple of days—between rewriting and editing. If your deadline is tight, see if your partner can take time to review your paper right away. (Your partner may be feeling deadline pressure, too, and might be happy to check your edits in exchange for your checking hers or his.) If not, read your draft aloud and use the following checklist to help you identify and correct errors in sentences, grammar, and mechanics (spelling and punctuation).

EDITING CHECKLIST
SENTENCES
1. Is each sentence clear and complete?
   - Are there any fragments or run-ons?
   - Are there any misplaced or dangling modifiers?
   - Are all lists (whether words, phrases, or clauses) expressed in parallel form?
2. Are your sentences varied in length? Could some be combined to improve the clarity and impact of your message?

GRAMMAR
1. Have you used verbs correctly?
   - Are all verbs in the correct form?
   - Do all verbs agree with their subjects?
   - Are all verbs in the correct tense?
   - Are there any confusing shifts in verb tense within a paragraph?
   - Are all verbs in active voice unless there is a reason to use the passive?
2. Have you used pronouns correctly?
   - Are all pronouns in the correct form?
   - Do all pronouns agree with their antecedents?
   - Have any vague pronoun references been eliminated?

SPELLING
- Are all words spelled correctly?
- Have you double-checked any homonyms?
- Have you used capital letters where they are needed?
- Have you used apostrophes correctly—for contractions, possessive nouns, but NOT for plurals?

PUNCTUATION
Within sentences
- Have you eliminated any unnecessary commas and included commas where needed? (Refer to the comma rules on pages 453–59 as you consider this question.)
- Have you used colons and semicolons where appropriate?
- Are all quotations appropriately marked?

Beginnings and endings
- Does each sentence begin with a capital letter?

- Do all questions—and only questions—end with a question mark?
- Are all quotation marks correctly placed?

When you're sure you've answered these questions satisfactorily, it's time to go to the third and last stage of the revision process.

Exercise 10.2*

Read the following sentences and consider each one against the "Editing Checklist." Correct any errors in sentence structure, grammar, spelling, and punctuation. Then compare your edited sentences with ours on page 543. (Our thanks to *Fortune* magazine [July 21, 1997] for collecting these howlers from real résumés and cover letters.)

1. I demand a salary commiserate with my qualifications, and extensive experience.

2. I have lurnt Microsoft Word and Excell computor and spreadsheet progroms

3. In 2007, I recieved a plague for being salesperson of the year.

4. Reason for leaving last job; maturity leave.

5. You will want me to be Head Honcho in no time!

6. I am a perfectionist and rarely if if ever forget details.

7. Marital status: single. Unmarried. Unengaged. Uninvolved. No comitments.

8. In my previous job I became completely paranoid trusting completely no one and absolutely nothing.

9. As indicted, I have over five years of analyzing investments.

10. I was responsible for ruining the entire operation for a western chain store.

Exercise 10.3*

Turn to the draft of the essay you rewrote for Exercise 10.1. With the "Editing Checklist" beside you, go through it and correct the errors in sentence structure, grammar, spelling, and punctuation. (You may have corrected some of these errors as you were rewriting, but there will be others.)

Step 3: Proofreading

Why proofread? To confirm that you have corrected all errors, and that your paper is ready to be submitted. Misspellings, faulty punctuation, and messiness don't always create misunderstandings, but they do cause the reader to form a poor opinion of you and your work. Careful proofreading will ensure that the appearance of your paper reflects the care you have put into writing it.

By the time you get to this stage, you will have gone over your paper so many times you may have practically memorized it. When you are very familiar with a piece of writing, it's hard to spot the small mistakes that tend to creep in as you produce your final copy. Once again, a dedicated revision partner can be helpful, possibly saving you embarrassment and lost marks. Here are some tips to help you find those tiny, elusive errors both in your paper and in your partner's:

1. Read through the essay line by line, using a ruler to guide you.
2. If you've been keeping a list of your most frequent errors in this course (and you should have), check your essay for the mistakes you're most likely to make. Use the list of correction marks on the inside back cover to check for errors your instructor has identified in your writing.

Your "last" draft may need one more revision after your proofreading review. If so, take the time to rekey or rewrite the paper so that the version you submit is clean and easy to read. If a word processor is available to you, use it. Computers make editing and proofreading almost painless since they make errors so easy to correct.

That's it! At long last, you're ready to submit your paper. If you've conscientiously followed the three steps to revision we've presented in this chapter, you can submit your paper with confidence that the content says what you want it to say, and that its appearance reflects the time and care you put into writing it. One last word of advice:

DON'T FORGET TO KEEP A COPY FOR YOUR FILES!

Exercise 10.4*

Is the following essay ready for submission? Go over it carefully, correcting all errors (there are 20). Then get together with another student and compare your results.

According to a recent survey in Maclean's magazine, only 43 percent of Canadians are satisfied with their jobs. What can you do to ensure that you will not be one of the 57 percent who are unhappy with the work they do. There are three questions to consider when seeking employment that will provide satisfaction as well as a paycheque.

First are you suited to the kind of work you are applying for. If you enjoy the outdoors, for example, and like to be active, your not going to be happy with a nine to five office job, no matter how much it pays.

Second is the job based in a location compatible with your prefered lifestyle. No matter how much you like your work, if you go home every night to an enviorment you are miserable in, it will not be long before you start transfering your disatisfaction to your job. If you like the amenities and conviences of the city, you probably will not enjoy working in a small town. If, on the other hand, you prefer the quiet and security of small-town life, you may find the city a stressful place in which to live.

Finally, is it one that you want to work for. Do you need the security of generous benifits, a good pension plan, and incentives to stay and grow with one company? Or are you an ambitous person who is looking for variety, quick advancement, and a high salary. If so, you may have to forgo security in favour of commissions or cash incentives and be willing to move as quickly and as often as opportunities occur. Some carful self-analysis now, before you start out on your career path, will help you chose a direction that will put you in the 43 percent minority of satisfied Canadian workers.

Exercise 10.5

Turn to the draft you produced for Exercise 10.3. Now go over it, line by line, and proofread it to make it as error-free as you can. No answer is provided for this exercise.

PART 4

The Research Paper

I use not only all the brains that I have, but all that I can borrow.
Woodrow Wilson, 1856–1924

Absorb what is useful, reject what is useless, and add what is specifically your own.
Bruce Lee, 1940–1973

Introduction

A **research paper** is an essay that presents the results of a writer's investigation of a topic in print, electronic, or multimedia formats. The skills involved—finding, evaluating, and assimilating the ideas of other writers— are essential in any field of study. They will also be useful to you in your career. Much of the writing you do on the job, especially if you are in management, requires you to express in your own words the facts, opinions, and ideas of others.

Writing a research paper follows the same process as other kinds of essay writing, from planning through drafting to revising. The difference is that instead of relying exclusively on what you already know about a topic, you are expected to include additional source material—facts, data, examples, or opinions of other writers—to support your thesis. Chapter 11 explains the different kinds of source material you can choose from and tells you the strengths and weaknesses of each. Chapter 12 shows you how to integrate source material into your paper.

A research paper is not simply a collection of what other people have said about a subject. It is your responsibility to set the thesis, determine the focus, and control the discussion. It is *your* paper, *your* subject, *your* main points; ideas from other writers should be included as support for *your* topic sentences.

You must be sure, from the start, that you clearly understand what the instructor will accept as source material to support your thesis. Some instructors will accept information from popular magazines, *Wikipedia*, or social networking sites. Others will not. Generally, instructors look for a range of resources, including primary materials such as eyewitness accounts, historical documents, literary works, personal interviews, or speeches. Instructors will also be looking for secondary sources that contribute supporting ideas or analysis, such as books, government documents, articles in newspapers or journals, and information from reputable websites.

One of the challenges of writing a research paper is differentiating between your ideas and those you took from sources. Readers cannot hear the different "speakers," so you have to indicate who said what. To separate your sources from your own ideas, research papers require **documentation**—a system of acknowledging source materials. Documentation tells your readers that the ideas they are reading have been borrowed from another writer; it also enables your readers to find the source and read the material for themselves. In academic institutions, two widely used documentation styles are the American Psychological Association (APA) style and the Modern Language Association (MLA) style.

Chapters 13 and 14 show you how to provide your readers with appropriate documentation as you write your paper and how to prepare your bibliography (called "References" in APA style and "Works Cited" in MLA style). The bibliography, included at the end of your paper, identifies the sources you used to support your thesis.

Tips on Writing a Research Paper

1. Instructors assign research papers so that they can assess not only your research skills but also your writing skills.
2. Choose a subject that interests you. Define it as precisely as you can before beginning your research, but be prepared to modify, adapt, and revise it as you research and write your paper.
3. Once you have a topic in mind, do some preliminary research and talk to a librarian. Be specific when you discuss your topic and your focus. Every library is unique. In addition to books, journals, and audiovisual sources, there will be library subscriptions to online journals (e-journals) and electronic books (e-books) as well as "best of the Web" collections that have been selected by the librarians for your program of study. Working with the library staff early in the research process will save hours of time.
4. Even though your instructor may be your only reader, think of your potential audience as your classmates—this way, you can count on a certain amount of common or shared knowledge. Assume that your audience wants to learn more about your topic, what conclusions you have reached, and what evidence you have found to support your thesis.

5. Manage your time carefully. Divide the work into a number of tasks, develop a schedule that leaves lots of time for revision, and stick to your schedule. Research papers are usually longer than essays, and the planning process is more complex. You will need all the time you've been given to find the sources you need, decide what you want to say, and then draft, revise, and polish your paper.

6. When making research notes, be diligent. Sources cannot be used unless they are clearly documented. There is nothing worse than having to discard a great quote because you cannot find the original source. Whether it is print, audiovisual, or electronic in format, each resource has specific documentation requirements. For every source you use, record all of the authors' names, the book or document title, publication data, and page numbers. For electronic sources, also record the URL and the date you accessed the website.

7. Document your sources according to whatever style your instructor prefers.

8. Use your source material to support your own ideas, not the other way around.

9. Revise, edit, and proofread carefully. If you omit this step, the hours and weeks you have spent on your assignment will be wasted, not rewarded.

11

Researching Your Subject

Your first step in writing a research paper is the same as your first step in any writing task: select a suitable subject, preferably one you are curious about. Whether you are assigned a topic or choose your own, don't rush off to the library or log onto the Internet right away. A little preparation up front will save you a lot of time and possibly much grief later on.

First of all, if you're not sure what your instructor expects, clarify what is required of you. Next, even if your subject is tentative, check it with the 4-S test: is it significant, single, specific, and supportable (researchable)? If not, refine it by using the techniques discussed in Chapter 2. Finally, consider what approach you might take in presenting your subject. Does it lend itself to a comparison? Process? Cause or effect? If the topic is assigned, often the wording of the assignment will suggest how your instructor wants you to develop it. Deciding up front what kind of paper you are going to write will save you hours of time, both in the library and at your desk.

Exercise 11.1

In the workplace, people rarely have the opportunity to select a research topic without consultation. In some cases, the subject is assigned or approved by a board of directors; in others, a committee is responsible for ensuring that a research project meets the company's needs.

Before you start your own research project, take some time to ensure that your proposed subject is appropriate for the time and space you have been given. For this exercise, the class should be divided into "committees" of four or five people. Each committee should be assigned a colour and each member given a piece of coloured paper. (For example, everyone in the Red group gets a piece of red paper.)

· 147 ·

- Each committee identifies a chairperson and a note-taker. At the direction of the chair, each member of the committee presents an idea for a research paper. After each presentation, discuss the subject in terms of its significance to the target audience (the whole class, including the instructor). If the committee feels a subject requires revision to be significant, make these revisions as a group. It is important that the committee come to a consensus regarding any revisions.
- Once each subject is agreed upon as significant, record it on a slip of the coloured paper assigned to your committee.
- Repeat this procedure until your committee has identified at least one significant subject for each of its members.
- Toss your committee's subjects into the company's think tank (a container), along with the subjects submitted by the other committees in the class.
- The chair of each committee draws out of the think tank four or five proposed research subjects, being sure to have a representative sampling of colours from other committees.
- As a committee, discuss each subject that has been drawn from the think tank. Since each has already been approved as significant by another committee, your task is to determine whether each proposed subject is single and specific.
- For each subject, record any revisions that the committee deems necessary and briefly explain why.
- Return the revised subjects to their appropriate committees according to the corresponding coloured paper.
- When every committee has received its original proposed research subjects, each group discusses the suggested revisions until everyone understands them.
- Next, as a committee, discuss whether each proposed subject is supportable. What sorts of research materials would you look for to help you explain and defend each subject?
- Record the final version of the proposed research subjects on a flipchart, ready to present to a board of directors. (You should have one subject for each member of the committee.)
- Present your committee's proposed research subjects before the board of directors (the whole class). Discuss the revisions and decide whether each proposal now meets the criteria of the 4-S test.

When you're sure your subject is appropriate and you've decided, at least tentatively, on the approach you're going to take, you are ready to focus on the kind of information you need to look for in your research. For example, if you've been asked to apply four theories of conflict to a case study, you won't waste time discussing the major schools of conflict theory or their development over the last few decades. You can restrict your investigation to sources that contain information relevant to your specific subject.

Once you have an idea of the kind of information you need in order to develop your topic, it's time to find the best sources you can. But how will you know if what you've found is "good" information?

Using the Library

Your library website is a powerful online information portal. The library catalogue connects you to collections of books, government documents, audiovisual materials, perhaps even maps, archival works, or music scores. Your library website will have links to specialized online databases and sub-scriptions to e-books, e-journals, and authoritative sites on the Internet that are otherwise inaccessible. It also contains valuable information regarding your library's policies and services.

With new technology, finding information is faster, easier, and more efficient than ever before. In this section, we will explain some of the ter-minology used by library staff, give you tips on how to access electronic information and physical collections, and summarize the strengths and weaknesses of various sources.

THE LIBRARY CATALOGUE

Your library catalogue is the first place you should check when beginning a research paper. It is accessible on computer terminals in the library, as well as on computers outside of the library, through the library's website. Search options include title, author, subject, or keyword. How you search the catalogue will depend on what you are looking for and on what you already know.

A title keyword search is often the fastest way of retrieving material. If the library carries a book, journal, government document, audiovisual item, or even a full-text Internet link, chances are a keyword will appear somewhere in the title. Alternatively, ask a librarian to demonstrate an "advanced search" or "power search" feature that will allow you to cross-search several fields at the same time.

The search will result in a list of "brief records." Click on a brief record for more information. The "full record" will include subjects, notes, descrip-tions, and so on. These descriptions will provide ideas on new subjects to extend your search. The full record may connect you directly to the full text of an online source. In these cases, the linked book, government report, or journal can be reviewed right from the screen, without further searching.

When you find an item that is of interest, be sure to record the author(s)' name(s), book or document title, and the full library call number, location, and status. In many libraries you can use a "shopping cart" feature to create a list of books or other materials that you want to review, and you can e-mail it to yourself.

Most colleges and universities use the **Library of Congress (LC)** system for organizing materials on a topic and filing them together on a shelf. The LC call number system uses a combination of letters and numbers: e.g., RC674.367.2. Every letter and number is essential in the filing scheme.

The **location** is important, especially in a large library, where the book might be on another floor, or in the reference section (where it may not be available for loan), or on reserve (where it may be available for only a short loan period). It could be shelved in an audiovisual collection, a government document collection, or a special collection.

The **status** lets you know if the item is in the library or when it is due back. Many systems allow you to place a hold on a book so that when it is returned it will be set aside for you. In order to find an item on the shelves, you match the call number as it appears in the catalogue list with the call number taped on the item. Guide signs are usually posted on the ends of shelving units.

The image below is taken from the Douglas College Library catalogue. Note the information it includes: author's name, title of book, publisher, city and date of publication, subjects covered, location, call number, and loan status.

LIBRARY SUBSCRIPTION DATABASES

Library subscription databases provide access to millions of articles published in electronic periodicals (publications that are issued at regular intervals, such as magazines, newspapers, scholarly and technical journals) that were formerly available only in a print format. In these e-journals, the articles provided by vendors such as Ebscohost, ProQuest, LexisNexis, and InfoTrac[1] are searchable by keyword and can be downloaded. Access is restricted by licence agreements to the students and staff of institutions that pay to subscribe, so they are not available through normal Google or Yahoo search engines. To access the databases you will need a log-in code or other means of identifying yourself as a student.

Databases often have a subject focus, such as nursing, business, engineering, psychology, communications, environmental issues, or computer science. Before you begin, read the description of the database to determine if it has a focus on your topic. Once you have found a database, you will be presented with a search box similar to those found on Internet search engines. Here you can type in a word or phrase that relates to your research topic. The search mechanism of the database will look for this term, and a list of all articles containing the word or phrase will be displayed on the screen. From the list, you can select those you think may be useful.

Although each database can be searched independently, you should ask if your library has a "federated search" or "aggregator" service, which allows you to search several databases at the same time, providing a variety of viewpoints on your topic.

Note: Most academic libraries will have collections of older printed journals, sometimes available on microfilm or microfiche. If you are doing historical or background research, these resources may be important in supporting your thesis. The collections are not included in the databases, so you should be aware that your library has special indexes that will help you find the information you need.

We recommend that you discuss your project with a librarian early in the research process. The library staff will be helpful in suggesting appropriate indexes or databases. They will also demonstrate advanced features and search strategies that will connect you to images, full-text articles, peer-reviewed sources, and more.

---

[1] Your purchase of *Essay Essentials with Readings*, Fifth Edition, entitles you to free access to InfoTrac.

LIBRARY SERVICES

New technologies have created opportunities for libraries to provide new services. Check your library's blog or website regarding ongoing developments. For example, real-time reference and research assistance using chat and text messaging is becoming increasingly popular. Your library may have its own "Ask a Librarian" service, or it may be part of a larger project to which many libraries contribute time and expertise to support student research questions.

Some libraries provide Web-based "reference manager" programs. Be sure to ask if your library offers this service. These programs help you organize and format your list of potential sources as you search the library catalogue and subscription databases.

You should be aware that college and university librarians (often in collaboration with faculty) regularly scan the Internet for resources. They often organize these "best of the Web" sites by subject, and link them directly through the library's home page, so you can quickly identify reputable websites related to your topic. Some academic libraries link to other libraries that already have this service in place; for example:

Toronto Public Library: http://www.virtualreferencelibrary.ca
Vancouver Public Library: http://www.vpl.vancouver.bc.ca/ research_guides
Librarians' Internet Index: http://www.lii.org

Selecting Your Sources

A good research paper will contain references to material from a variety of sources. Some instructors require a minimum number of references from print or online books, periodicals, encyclopedias, interviews, and so on. Many instructors will allow you to use Internet websites, providing that the websites are reputable and that they are not the only resources listed in your bibliography.

As you conduct your research and think about your paper, keep your reader in mind. Every teacher faced with a pile of papers hopes to find some that are not simply a rehash of known facts. Before anything else, teachers are learners; they like nothing better than discovering something new. If you cannot find new information about your subject, be sure to provide an original interpretation of the evidence you find.

Not all sources are created equal. Evaluating the quality of source material before you use it is a key step in the research process. The information you select must meet three criteria: it must be relevant, current, and reliable.

PRINT AND ONLINE ENCYCLOPEDIAS

A useful source of summary information on a topic is an encyclopedia. You might begin your search with a general encyclopedia such as *Britannica*, and then move on to a specialized encyclopedia such as the *Encyclopedia of Religion*. Encyclopedia publishers hire subject experts to write the entries and use editorial boards to check that the information they provide is reliable. Once a print or online entry is published, it remains fixed until the next update. Online versions are updated fairly frequently. The online encyclopedia *Wikipedia*, while popular and helpful, may not provide the rigour in fact-checking that is required for an academic research paper. Be aware that many instructors will not accept *Wikipedia* as a reliable source.

Strengths	Weaknesses
• Encyclopedias provide a good overview of a subject.	• Information in print versions may be dated.
• They often list titles of major books on the subject.	• Some popular online encyclopedias are not accepted as reliable sources of information.
• Online editions are convenient, easy to use, and updated regularly.	

PRINT AND ONLINE BOOKS, REPORTS, AND DOCUMENTS

Books purchased by the library will have been selected by faculty or subject specialist librarians, so you have a good chance of quickly locating materials to begin your research. To evaluate a print source, scan the table of contents, chapter titles, headings, and index at the back, which can lead to relevant pages within the book for quick review. Information in e-books can be searched by keyword, leading you directly to a page in the book. Be aware that e-books as well as print books may be available only on a short-term basis and may not be available when you are doing your research. Borrow or access them early in your project to avoid disappointment. The government, as one of the country's largest publishers, may have produced documents related to your topic. Many of these documents are available in print format, as well as on the Internet.

Strengths	Weaknesses
• The author may be an authority on the subject.	• Information may not be as current as other sources.
• Books often give an introductory overview of the subject.	• Information may not be applicable to a Canadian context.

Strengths	Weaknesses
• Bibliographies can often lead to other works on the subject. • Information is usually reliable (if published by a respected publisher). • Several key issues of the subject may be covered in the book.	• Copies of the book you need—in print or e-book format—may be limited.

PRINT AND ONLINE ARTICLES

Library subscription databases contain articles published within the past five to ten years or so. They are subject to the same standards of fact-checking and editorial review as the print versions. Peer-reviewed articles are highly respected. Most scholarly or technical articles provide detailed bibliographies that identify sources you may wish to consult. The sources in a bibliography will lead you to the perspectives of other specialists.

Currently, there is no standard on what is meant when a database reference is coded as "full text." In some cases, a full-text entry is simply an abstract, and not the full article. When a full-text article is available, it is usually published with photos, tables, and charts, just as it would appear in print. When an abstract is presented, the full article can generally be purchased for a fee, or it may be acquired on interlibrary loan. Check with your library staff to review the best option.

Strengths	Weaknesses
• Recent print and online articles contain current information, with a good degree of fact-checking and reliability. • Articles in databases are easy to retrieve, and often can be searched back in time 5–10 years. • Articles in databases are accessible 24/7. • Articles in peer-reviewed journals are well respected, and most contain detailed bibliographies.	• Articles may not contain background information required to establish historical context. • Some articles may be opinion pieces but presented as factual. • Not all "full-text" references will contain the full article; they may be abstracts that don't provide the required information. • Many articles may not be applicable to a Canadian context.

INTERNET RESOURCES

If you do not have a subject guide to the "best of the Web" on your library website, there are two important steps to locate current and reliable information on the Internet: develop a good search strategy, and critically evaluate the results of your search. We recommend that you use more than one search engine to get the best results. Many search engines offer advice on effective searching, including the following four ways in which you can limit and focus the results of an initial query:

1. Use one or more of the shortcuts available on most search engines (select the "Canada" option, for example).
2. Use the "advanced search" option that allows you to combine concepts. For example, Google's advanced search option allows you to search for an exact phrase such as "breast cancer" and include the word "treatment" without the word "chemotherapy." You can also limit the type of domain you'd like to search (e.g., ".edu"—indicating a university site), choose the language you'd like for your results, and decide where you'd like the search engine to look for your terms (in the title only, for example). If you decide to use the basic search option, you can do the same search, but it takes a bit more thinking as you won't have all the prompts provided for an advanced search.
3. Put quotation marks around your search term(s). Doing so turns your keyword search into a search for a specific phrase ("breast cancer treatment," for example).
4. Use the tilde sign (~) or plus and minus signs to add or eliminate concepts. Plus and minus signs add or subtract words from your search word or phrase (e.g., "breast cancer" + treatment – chemotherapy). Google interprets the tilde as a signal to search for variations of a word. For example, "~treatment" would include the plural "treatments" in your results list.

Evaluating the reliability of Internet information is not a simple matter, and Canadian sources are not easily identified. An excellent guide for evaluating websites can be found at http://www.lib.berkeley.edu/TeachingLib/Guides/Internet/Evaluate.html.

For electronic sources that have no hard-copy equivalent, the domain name is one place to begin your evaluation. Does the source's URL end with .com (commercial), .gov (government), or .edu (educational institution)? Links provided by these different sources will present data on a topic in different ways. A commercial site will probably attempt to influence consumers as well as to inform them. The .edu suffix suggests the credibility of a recognized college or university, but offbeat student Web pages or the informal musings of faculty members at the institution may share the suffix as well.

For Canadian sources, look for provincial domain names such as ab.ca (Alberta), on.ca (Ontario), or gc.ca for federal government sites. Professional associations normally include the association's name or initials as part of the domain name; for example, the Canadian Medical Association (cma.ca).

There is seldom any doubt about who wrote a particular print book or article. In online material, however, often no author or date is identified. Sometimes the person who compiles ("comp") or maintains ("maint") the website is the only one named. For academic research, it's wise to be cautious of "no-name" sources. If you want to use information from one of these sources, be sure that the organization or institution that originated it is reliable. You wouldn't want to be researching the history of discrimination in Canada, for example, and find yourself quoting from the disguised website of a hate organization.

Much online work is collaborative: several writers may have contributed to an online document, so it is a good idea to check out the people involved in producing it. Online search engines make checking the author's reliability easier for electronic sources than it is for print sources. Simply key the author's name into a search engine such as Google, and then evaluate the results to see if the author is a credible person in the field. Often you'll be able to check the author's biography, credentials, other publications, and business or academic affiliation. If no author's name is given, you can check on the company, organization, or institution in the same way. Cyber-sleuthing is a useful skill to learn!

Strengths

- Internet resources are fast and convenient.
- They efficiently provide directory-type information.
- The websites of leading experts are sometimes available.
- Increasingly, authoritative information is posted on the Net (e.g., government documents, databases of scholarly journals).

Weaknesses

- The reliability and authority of Internet resources can be difficult to determine.
- The amount of information provided is staggering (most users will not browse past the first two or three pages of results, so valuable information may be missed).
- Questionable content may appear to be valid.

OTHER SOURCES

Most libraries contain other collections that may help you in your research. Don't overlook the possibility of finding useful information in the audio-visual collection, which normally includes videotapes, films, audiotapes, and DVDs.

Finally, the library is not the only source of information you can use. Interviews with people familiar with your subject are excellent sources because they provide a personal view, and they ensure that your paper will contain information not found in any other paper the instructor will read. It is perfectly acceptable to e-mail a question or set of questions to an expert in a field of study. (But don't send your e-mail two days before your assignment is due. Allow at least a month between your request and a reply.)

Original research, such as surveys or questionnaires that you design, distribute, and analyze can also enhance your paper. Doing your own research is time-consuming and requires some knowledge of survey design and interpretation, but it has the desirable advantage of being original and current.

Strengths	Weakness
• Experts in the field and original research provide information not found elsewhere. • Such sources can be specific and current.	• Surveys may be difficult to organize, develop, and administer.

Taking Good Research Notes

When taking notes from print and electronic sources, you must apply your own critical intelligence. Is the information reliable, relevant, and current? Is there evidence of any inherent bias? How can you best make use of the findings to support and enhance your own ideas? The answers to these questions are critical to producing a good research paper.

Once you've found a useful source, record the information you need. You'll save time and money by taking notes directly from your sources rather than photocopying everything. Most often, you will need a summary of the information. Follow the instructions on summarizing given on pages 164–65. Alternatively, you can paraphrase (see pages 167–70).

Sometimes a quotation is appropriate. Whether you eventually decide to summarize, paraphrase, or quote, you will need a record of all of the publication details related to your source.

Some word-processing programs, such as Microsoft Word, provide templates to assist in citing sources and formatting information to create a bibliography. As you key in your draft and make reference to source material, you will be prompted to choose a documentation style such as APA or MLA and a source type—book, article, website, broadcast, and so on.

While documentation styles differ in the information and format they require in a bibliography, the following guidelines provide an overview of the information you are most likely to require in preparing your research paper.

For each published source that you use in your paper, you should record the following information.

For books, reports, documents:
1. Author(s)' or editor(s)' full name(s)
2. Title of book, report, or document
3. Edition number (if any)
4. City of publication (for printed works)
5. Name of publisher (for printed works)
6. Year of publication
7. Page(s) from which you took notes
8. Library database (for online works)
9. Full electronic address or URL (for online works)
10. Date you accessed the work (for online works)

For articles in journals, magazines, newspapers:
1. Author(s)' full name(s)
2. Title of article
3. Name of the journal, magazine, or newspaper
4. Volume and issue number (if any)
5. Date of publication
6. Inclusive page numbers of the article
7. Page(s) from which you took notes
8. Library database (for online articles)
9. Digital Object Identifier (if any)
10. Date you accessed the article (for online articles)

For Internet sources:
1. Full names of important contributors (such as author, editor, writer, compiler, director)
2. Title of the document
3. Name of the website

4. Name of the institution or organization sponsoring the site (if any)
5. Date of publication, edition, or last update
6. URL for the document (more information is provided in Chapter 13)
7. Date you accessed the source

For audiovisual sources:

1. Full names of important contributors (e.g., director, producer, writer, performer)
2. Title of the work
3. Date of the work
4. Format of the work, CD, film, etc.

Some researchers record each piece of information on a separate index card. Others write their notes on sheets of paper, being careful to keep their own ideas separate from the ideas and words taken from sources. (Using a highlighter or a different colour of ink will help you to tell at a glance which ideas you have taken from a source.) Use the technology available to help you record, sort, and file your notes. You can record and file information by creating a database, and you can use a photocopier to copy relevant pages of sources for later use. Whatever system you use, be sure to keep a separate record for each source and to include the documentation information. If you don't, you'll easily get your sources confused. The result of this confusion could be inaccurate documentation, which could lead your reader to suspect you of plagiarism.

$\overline{}$ (**Exercise 11.2**)

This exercise will quickly familiarize you with your school's library, the variety and extent of its holdings, the different ways you and the library staff can communicate with each other, and basic library policies you should know about.

1. What is the URL for your library's website? What are the library hours?
2. What is the loan period for books? Is there a fine for an overdue book?
3. Does your library have a reserve collection? What does it mean if an item is on reserve?
4. Use a title keyword search in the library catalogue. Does your library have the following books? If so, give the call number and location for each.
   • *MLA Handbook for Writers of Research Papers*. 7th ed. New York: MLA, 2009. Print.
   • *Publication Manual of the American Psychological Association*. 6th ed. Washington: APA, 2009. Print.
5. Use an advanced search feature in the library catalogue and find a video or DVD that deals with study skills. Note the title, full call number, location, and status.

6. Does your library provide subject guides that provide links to reputable websites?
7. Use one of your library's subscription databases. Search for an article on a topic of your choice. Document the article using the guidelines listed on pages 158–59 ("Taking Good Research Notes," "For articles in journals . . .").
8. Can you access your library's databases from home? If so, what procedure do you follow?
9. Is it possible to contact the library staff by chat and text messaging or by e-mail?

Summarizing, Paraphrasing, and Quoting

Once you have identified and evaluated your research sources, you need to make accurate notes of the information you think you might use in your paper. There are many ways to take notes, ranging from jotting down single words or phrases to photocopying entire articles. You will save time if you remember that there are three ways of incorporating source information into your own writing: **summary**, **paraphrase**, and **direct quotation**. When you summarize or paraphrase, you restate in your own words the idea(s) of another speaker or writer. When you quote, you reproduce the exact words of another speaker or writer. Before we examine these three techniques, it is worthwhile to review what plagiarism is and how to avoid it.

Plagiarism is presenting someone else's ideas as your own. It is a form of stealing (the word comes from the Latin word *plagiarius*, which means "kidnapper"). In the professional world, suspected plagiarists who are found guilty often lose their jobs. Sometimes the accusation alone is enough to compromise an author's reputation and thus prevent him or her from continuing to work as a scholar or writer.

Students who copy essays or parts of essays from source material, download them from the Internet, or pay someone else to write them are cheating, and cheating is a serious academic offence. Sometimes, however, academic plagiarism is accidental. It can result from careless note-taking or an incomplete understanding of the conventions of documentation. If, after you have finished your first draft, you are not sure which ideas need documenting and which don't, take your research notes and your outline to your instructor and ask. It's better to ask before submitting a paper than to try to explain a problem afterward. Asking saves you potential embarrassment as well as time.

Preventing Plagiarism

You can avoid plagiarism by acknowledging (citing) all information you found in the sources you used for your paper. Cite your sources in an approved documentation style (usually MLA or APA).

Here are some guidelines to follow:

- Facts or sayings that are common knowledge do not have to be attributed; that is, you need not give sources for them. Examples: "Quebec City is the capital of Quebec"; "Sir John A. Macdonald was Canada's first prime minister"; "Beauty is in the eye of the beholder."
- Any passage, long or short, taken word for word from a source must be marked as a quotation, and you must cite its source. (See below, pages 170–77, and Chapter 13.)
- Facts, opinions, or ideas that you discovered on the Internet, found in a book or article, or learned from any other source—even if you express the information in your own words—must be acknowledged. (See below, pages 170–77, and Chapter 13.)
- Always provide source information for statistics. The meaning of numbers is variable, depending on who is using them and for what purpose.
- Facts, opinions, or ideas that you remember reading or hearing somewhere cannot be presented as your own. If you cannot find and acknowledge the source, you should not use the information.
- If you are not sure whether a fact, opinion, or idea should be acknowledged, err on the side of caution and provide the source information for it. It's better to be safe than sorry.

Summarizing

When you summarize information, you find ideas in an article, essay, report, or other document, and rephrase them. You shorten (condense) the most important idea or ideas in the source material and express your understanding of them in your own words. The purpose of summarizing is to give the reader an overview of the source article, report, or chapter. If the reader is interested in the details, he or she will read the original.

It's hard to overstate how valuable the ability to summarize is. Note-taking in college or university is one form of summarizing. Abstracts of articles, executive summaries of reports, market surveys, legal decisions, research findings, and records of meetings (called "minutes"), to name only a few kinds of formal documents, are all summaries. Thesis statements and topic sentences are essentially summaries; so, often, are conclusions. In committee, group, or teamwork, imagination and creativity are valuable, but the ability to summarize is even more so. There is no communication skill that you will need or use more than summarizing.

As a matter of fact, you summarize for yourself and others in every conversation you have. With friends, you may summarize the plot of a movie you've just seen or what happened in class this morning. When your mother calls, you'll summarize the events of the past week that you want her to know about. But most of us are not very good at summarizing effectively, especially in writing. It is a skill that doesn't come naturally. *You need to practise it.* You'll improve quickly, however, if you think about what you're doing—that is, if you are conscious of the times and circumstances in which you are called on to summarize. The following exercise will get you started.

Exercise 12.1

1. In groups of three or four, choose a movie you have all seen, a course you have all taken, a party or concert you have all attended, or a book you have all read. Without discussing your topic first, spend five minutes each writing a one-paragraph summary. After you have written your summary, read it over and highlight your main points.
2. Read and compare the group's summaries. What similarities and differences do you notice? Can you all agree that one summary is both complete and accurate? If not, spend another five or ten minutes discussing which are the main ideas and which are secondary to a discussion of your topic.
3. Now revise your one-paragraph summary to include all the main ideas and no secondary details.
4. Once again, read and compare each other's paragraphs. Which paragraph summarizes the topic best? What features does this paragraph have that the others lack?

HOW TO WRITE A SUMMARY

The work you summarize can be as short as a paragraph or as long as a book, as the following passage demonstrates:

> One of Edward de Bono's books is called *Six Thinking Hats*. [In it] he proposes that you adopt six different mind sets by mentally putting on six different coloured hats. Each hat stands for a certain way of thinking about a problem.

By "putting on the hat" and adopting a certain role, we can think more clearly about the issues at hand. Because we're only "playing a role," there is little ego riding on what we say, so we are more free to say what we really want to say. De Bono likens the process of putting on the six hats one at a time to that of printing on a multicoloured map. Each colour is not a complete picture in itself. The map must go through the printing press six times, each time receiving a new colour, until we have the total picture.

Perrin, Timothy. "Positive Invention." *Better Writing for Lawyers.* Toronto: Law Society of Upper Canada, 1990. 51. Print.

Notice that Perrin is careful to tell his readers the source of the ideas he is summarizing: both the author and the book are identified up front.

Before you can summarize anything, you must *read* and *understand* it. The material you need to summarize is usually an article, essay, or chapter (or some portion of it). Depending on how much of the piece you need, your summary will range from a few sentences to one or two paragraphs.[1] Here's how to proceed:

1. Read through the piece carefully, looking up any words you don't understand. Write their meanings between the lines, above the words they apply to.
2. Now read the article or essay again. Keep rereading it until you have grasped the main ideas and formed a mental picture of their arrangement. Highlight the title, subtitle, and headings (if there are any). The title often identifies the subject of the piece, and a subtitle usually indicates its focus. If the article is long, the writer will often divide it into a number of smaller sections, each with its own heading. These headings usually identify the main points. If there are no headings, pay particular attention to the introduction—you should find an overview of the subject and a statement of the thesis—and the conclusion, which often summarizes the information and points to the significance of the topic.
3. In point form, and in your own words, write a bare-bones outline of the piece. Your outline should consist of the controlling idea (thesis) of the article and the main ideas, in the order in which they appear. Do not include any supporting details (statistics, specific facts, examples, etc.).

---

[1]This restriction applies only to the kind of research paper we are discussing in this part: one prepared for a college or university course. Other kinds of summaries are longer. A précis, for example, is one-third the length of the source document. An abstract, which is a summary of a dissertation, academic paper, or public presentation, can be several paragraphs long.

4. Working from your outline, draft the summary. In the first sentence, identify the article or essay you are summarizing (by title, enclosed in quotation marks) and the author (by name, if known). Complete the sentence by stating the author's controlling idea. Here's an example:

> In his essay "The Canadian Climate," D'Arcy McHayle divides Canadians into two types: warm and cool.

Then state, in order, the author's main points. After each sentence in which you identify a main point, include any necessary explanation or clarification of that point. (The author, remember, developed each idea in the supporting details.) Try to resist going back to the article for your explanation. If you have truly understood the article, you should be able to explain each point from memory. If the author's conclusion contains any new information (i.e., is more than a summary and memorable statement), briefly state that information in your conclusion.

5. Revise your draft until it is coherent, concise, and makes sense to someone who is unfamiliar with the original work. It's a good idea to get someone to read through your summary to check it for clarity and completeness.

6. Don't forget to acknowledge your source. (Chapter 13 will show you how.)

The paragraph below summarizes the essay found on pages 252–53. Read the essay first, then read the summary that follows.

> In his essay "The Canadian Climate," D'Arcy McHayle divides Canadians into two types: "warm" and "cool." The first category includes people who are enthusiastic about Canada's scenery, climate, and recreational activities, which they encourage newcomers to enjoy. Warm Canadians are also sincerely interested in learning about what life is like in the visitor's country of origin. In contrast, Cool Canadians are negative about their country and find it hard to believe that anyone from a warm climate would choose to endure the cold, bleak Canadian winters. Cool Canadians are not interested in detailed information about the visitor's country of origin, either; they are comfortable with their stereotypes. Finally, McHayle acknowledges that the two types are mixed: each can at times behave like the other. Canadians, like the weather, are unpredictable, and newcomers are encouraged to accept them as they are and for themselves.

This seven-sentence paragraph (140 words) captures the gist of McHayle's 600-word essay. Admittedly, it isn't very interesting. It lacks the flavour of the original. Summaries are useful for conveying an outline or a brief overview of someone else's ideas, but by themselves they are not very memorable. Details and specifics are what stick in a reader's mind; these are what your own writing should provide.

A summary should be entirely in your own words. Your ability to identify and interpret the author's meaning is evidence of your understanding of the article or essay. If you must include a short phrase from the source because there is no other way to word it, enclose the quoted material in quotation marks.

When writing a summary, do not

- introduce any ideas not found in the original
- change the proportion or emphasis of the original
- introduce your own opinion of the material

Exercise 12.2

Following the first five steps of the process outlined above, summarize "Ready, Willing . . . and Employable," which appears on pages 62–63. When you have completed your work, exchange papers with a partner. Use the following checklist to critique each other's summary.

	Good	Adequate	Try Again
1. The first sentence gives the title and the author's name.			
2. The essay's thesis is clearly and concisely reworded.			
3. Each main point (topic sentence) is restated in a single sentence.			
4. Each main point is briefly explained.			
5. The summary includes no secondary details that could be eliminated without diminishing the reader's understanding.			
6. The summary is balanced and objective.			
7. The paragraph flows smoothly; there are no obvious errors in sentence structure, grammar, spelling, or punctuation.			

Exercise 12.3

Select an article from a professional journal in your field. Summarize it by following the six steps given on pages 164–65. Assume your reader is a professional in the field.

Exercise 12.4

Choose an article that interests you from one of the regular sections (e.g., business, health, sports, the arts) of a general news magazine such as *Maclean's*, *Time*, *Newsweek*, or *The Economist*. Summarize the article for a friend who is not an expert in the field and who has not read it. Do not evaluate the article or give your opinion about it. In a paragraph of approximately 100–150 words, simply inform your friend of its contents. And don't forget to cite your source.

Paraphrasing

When you paraphrase, you restate someone else's ideas in your own words. Unlike a summary, a paraphrase includes both the main and the supporting ideas of your source. The usual purpose of a paraphrase is to express someone else's ideas more clearly and more simply—to translate what may be complex in the original into easily understandable prose. A paraphrase may be longer than the original, it may be about the same length, or it may be shorter. Whatever its length, a good paraphrase satisfies three criteria:

1. It is clear, concise, and easy to understand.
2. It communicates the idea(s) of the original passage.
3. It doesn't contain any idea(s) not found in the original passage.

Occasionally, you may need to clarify technical language or explain an aphorism, a proverb, or other saying that states a principle, offers an insight, or teaches a point. Statements that pack a lot of meaning into few words can be explained only at greater length. For example, one of the principal tenets of modern biology is "ontogeny recapitulates phylogeny." It simply isn't possible to paraphrase this principle in three words. (It means that as an embryo grows, it follows the same pattern of development that the animal did in the evolutionary process.)

Exercise 12.5

Working with a partner or a small group, discuss the meaning of the following expressions. When you are sure you understand them, write a paraphrase of each one.

1. A closed mouth catches no flies. (Italian proverb)
2. Love makes time pass. Time makes love pass. (French proverb)
3. Better wear out shoes than sheets. (Scottish proverb)
4. Better light a candle than curse the darkness. (Chinese proverb)
5. It is hard to pray for bread that has been eaten. (Danish proverb)

To paraphrase a passage, you need to dig down through your source's words to the underlying ideas and then reword those ideas as clearly and simply as you can. Like summarizing, the ability to paraphrase is not an inborn talent; it takes patience and much practice to perfect it. But the rewards are worth your time and effort. First, paraphrasing improves your reading skill as well as your writing skill. Second, it improves your memory. In order to paraphrase accurately, you must thoroughly understand what you've read—and once you understand something, you're not likely to forget it.

First, let's look at how not to paraphrase. Assume we are writing an essay about the loss of jobs in the Canadian clothing industry, and we want to use the information given in the following paragraph, found in "No Sweat?" by Rubi Garyfalakis, on pages 337–38.

If only the problem were that simple. For those who like tidy problems with clear solutions, it is disturbing to find that there is another side to the sweat-shop debate. To begin with, sweatshops are "the first rung on the ladder out of extreme poverty" (Sachs 11). They allow developing countries to expand their exports and consequently to improve their economies (Arnold and Hartman 2). Workers (usually women) choose to work in sweatshops because they are often the only means by which women can further their own ends. By working in a sweatshop, women make a small income, learn about business practices, and benefit from the improved social and economic conditions that come with economic growth. Arnold and Hartman explain that as the economy grows, more jobs are created, so the labour market tightens, and companies are forced to improve their working conditions in order to attract employees (2–3). Theoretically, this analysis makes sense, but does it apply in practice? Do employees really benefit from working in sweatshops?

There are three pieces of information in this paragraph that we want to include in our essay:

1. Sweatshops do improve the economies of Third World nations.
2. Sweatshops are a means for individuals to improve their own circum-stances.

3. Sweatshops lead to job growth, and force companies to improve conditions to attract workers.

If we are not careful, or if we don't have much experience with paraphrasing, our paragraph might look something like this:

> In her essay, "No Sweat?" Rubi Garyfalakis suggests that sweatshops permit developing nations to increase their exports and so improve their economies. She goes on to say that workers in those countries choose to work in sweatshops in order to improve their lives by making a small income and learning about employer–employee relations; they also benefit from the higher standard of living that results from an improved economy. In addition, successful sweatshops increase the demand for workers and as the labour market tightens, companies are forced to improve conditions in order to attract workers.

This is plagiarism. Although we have indicated the source of the information, we have not indicated that the wording is almost identical to that of the original. Of the total 95 words, more than half come from the source. There are no visual or verbal cues to alert the reader that these are the author's words, not ours. Let's try again.

> In her essay, "No Sweat?" Rubi Garyfalakis suggests that sweatshops can have several benefits, including allowing developing nations to improve their economies by increasing their exports. Another benefit is that people who decide to work in sweatshops do improve their lives by gaining a small income, learning about business relations, and benefiting from the improved standard of living that is part of economic advancement. In addition, an improved economy creates more jobs, thereby forcing companies to compete for workers by improving wages and conditions.

Although this draft is technically a paraphrase rather than plagiarism, it doesn't demonstrate very much work on our part. We have replaced the author's words with synonyms and simplified the argument, but our paragraph still follows the original too closely. A paraphrase should not be used to pass off someone else's ideas as your own by changing a few words and sentences. A good paraphrase goes further. It uses source information but rearranges it, rephrases it, and combines it with the writer's own ideas to create something new.

Let's try once more. Remember that this paraphrase is an illustration for a point we want to make in an essay about the loss of jobs in the Canadian clothing industry. The italicized sections are original ideas, part of the essay, while the nonitalicized part is the paraphrase.

From the point of view of Canadian manufacturers and their workers, sweatshops are economic poison, but for the countries (and their workers) where sweatshops exist, there are reasons for their appeal. Countries that house sweatshops benefit from increased exports, and the standard of living in those countries increases as a result. While earning pitifully small wages by our standards, the workers do at least make something, and they benefit from exposure to business experience and from the higher standard of living (Garyfalakis 338). *This may be small comfort to Canadians, but it makes the existence of sweatshops in Third World nations understandable.*

Here we have used paraphrase to incorporate information from a published source into a paragraph whose topic and structure are our own. This is how paraphrase can be used both responsibly and effectively. If you want to take ideas more directly from a source, retaining the original arrangement and some of the wording, you should use quotation marks, as discussed in the next section.

Quoting

Of the three ways to introduce ideas from a source into your research paper, direct quotation is the one you should use least. (The exception is the literary essay, in which quotations from the original work are the evidence in your argument.) If you use too many quotations, your paper will be a patchwork of the ideas of others, in their words, and very little of your own thinking will be communicated to the reader. Remember that the main reason teachers assign research papers is to test your ability to find, digest, and make sense of specific information about a topic. If what you hand in consists of a string of quotations, your paper will demonstrate only one of these three capabilities.

In most research papers, the ideas, facts, and statistics are the important things, not the wording of an idea or the explanation of facts or statistics. Occasionally, however, you will find that someone else—an expert in a particular field, a well-known author, or a respected public figure—has said what you want to say eloquently, vividly, more memorably than you could ever hope to say it. In such cases, quotations, *as long as they are short and not used too frequently*, are useful in developing your topic. Carefully woven into your paragraphs, they help convince the reader of the validity of what you have to say. Use quotations in writing the way you use salt in cooking: sparingly.

You can quote from two kinds of sources—

- people you know, have interviewed, or have heard speak
- print, electronic, or recorded materials (e.g., books, articles, CD-ROMs, DVDs, websites, films, tapes)

—and your quotation may be long or short.

BLOCK AND SPOT QUOTATIONS

If the material you are quoting is more than 40 words or four typed lines, it is a long—or **block**—quotation. After you have introduced it, you begin the quoted passage on a new line and indent all lines of the quotation 10 spaces or 2.5 cm from the left margin. *Do not put quotation marks around a block quotation.* The 10-space indentation is the reader's visual cue that this portion of the paragraph is someone else's words, not yours. Here's an example:

Committees put a lot of thought into the design of fast foods. As David Bodanis points out with such good humour in *The Secret House*, potato chips are

. . . an example of total destruction foods. The wild attack on the plastic wrap, the slashing and tearing you have to go through is exactly what the manufacturers wish. For the thing about crisp foods is that they're louder than non-crisp ones. . . . Destructo-packaging sets a favourable mood. . . . Crisp foods have to be loud in the upper register. They have to produce a high-frequency shattering; foods which generate low-frequency rumblings are crunchy, or slurpy but not crisp. . . . (142)

Companies design potato chips to be too large to fit into the mouth, because in order to hear the high-frequency crackling, you need to keep your mouth open. Chips are 80 percent air, and each time we bite one we break open the air-packed cells of the chip, making that noise we call "crispy." Bodanis asks:

How to get sufficiently rigid cell walls to twang at these squeaking harmonics? Starch them. The starch granules in potatoes are identical to the starch in stiff shirt collars. . . . [In addition to starch,] all chips are soaked in fat. . . . So it's a shrapnel of flying starch and fat that produces the conical air-pressure wave when our determined chip-muncher finally gets to finish her chomp. (143)

Ackerman, Diane. *A Natural History of the Senses.* New York: Random House, 1990. 142-43. Print.

Notice that Ackerman is careful to tell her readers the source of her quotations. To introduce the first one, she gives the author's full name and the title of his book. To introduce the second quotation, which is from the same book, she simply identifies the author by surname. Thus, she doesn't waste words by repeating information, nor does she leave readers wondering where the quotation came from. (The only information missing is the publication data—city, publisher, and date—which is provided in the list of sources. See Chapter 13 for information on how to document your sources.)

A **spot quotation** is a word, a phrase, or a short sentence that is incorporated into one of your own sentences. *Put quotation marks before and after a spot quotation.* The quotation marks are a signal to the reader that these aren't your words; a new voice is speaking. The following paragraph contains several spot quotations.

"You are what you quote," in the words of the American essayist Joseph Epstein, himself a heavy user of quotations and the writer who introduced "quotatious" into my vocabulary. Winston Churchill understood the value of a well-aimed quotation: as a young man he read a few pages of *Bartlett's Familiar Quotations* every day to spruce up his style and compensate for his lack of a university education. [Gradually,] he transformed himself from a quotatious writer into the most quoted politician of the western world. . . . Fowler's *Modern English Usage* warns against quoting simply to demonstrate knowledge: "the discerning reader detects it and is contemptuous," while the undiscerning reader finds it tedious. A few years ago Garry Trudeau made fun of George Will's compulsive quoting by inventing a researcher who served as "quote boy" in Will's office: "'Quote boy! Need something on the banality of contemporary society.' 'Right away, Dr. Will!'" . . . As for me, I say don't judge, because you might get judged, too. That's how the quotation goes, right?

Fulford, Robert. "The Use and Abuse of Quotations." *Globe and Mail* 11 Nov. 1992: C1. Print.

HOW TO MODIFY A QUOTATION

In addition to illustrating how to introduce and format block quotations and how to punctuate spot quotations, the examples above also show how to modify a quotation to fit your space and suit your purpose. Although *you must quote exactly and never misrepresent or distort your source's intention*, you may, for reasons of conciseness or smoothness, omit or add a word or phrase or even a sentence or two.

- To leave out a word or words, indicate the omission by replacing the word(s) you've omitted with three spaced dots called **ellipses** (. . .). Place the first dot one space after the last word of the quotation. If the omission comes at the end of your sentence, add a fourth dot as the period.
- If you need to add or change a word or words to make the quoted passage more readable within your paragraph, use **square brackets** around your own words, as we did when we added "[In addition to starch,]" in Ackerman's second block quotation from Bodanis and "[Gradually,]" to Fulford's paragraph.

    If you have omitted some words from a source, you may need to add a transitional phrase or change the first letter of a word to a capital: [T]hus. Another reason for changing words in a quoted passage is to keep the verb tenses consistent throughout your paragraph. If you are writing in the present tense and the passage you are quoting is in the past tense, you can change the verbs to present tense (so long as the change doesn't distort the meaning) and put square brackets around them so the reader knows you have made these changes.

Modifying short quotations to make them fit smoothly into your own sentences without altering the source's meaning takes practice. Reread the paragraph that we have quoted on page 172. Notice that to make Fulford's original slightly shorter and easier to read, we made a couple of minor alterations to the original. The signals to the reader that something has been added or left out are the same as those used in a block quotation: square brackets and ellipses.

HOW TO INTEGRATE QUOTATIONS INTO YOUR WRITING

When you decide to quote source material, you should introduce it so that it will blend as seamlessly as possible into your writing. Don't simply park someone else's words in the middle of your paragraph; you'll disrupt the flow of thought. If Diane Ackerman were not so skilful a writer, she might have "dumped" quotations into her paragraph instead of integrating them. Contrast the readability of the paragraph below with that of Ackerman's second paragraph (on page 171).

Companies design potato chips to be too large to fit into the mouth because, in order to hear the high-frequency crackling, you need to keep your mouth open. Chips are 80 percent air, and each time we bite one, we break open the air-packed cells of the chip, making that crispy noise. "The starch granules in potatoes are identical to the starch in stiff shirt collars." Starch is just one of the ingredients that contribute to the crispiness of potato chips. "All chips are soaked in fat. . . ." "So it's a shrapnel of flying starch and fat that produces the conical air-pressure wave when our determined chip-muncher finally gets to finish her chomp."

Without transitional phrases to introduce the quotations, the paragraph lacks coherence and doesn't make sense. Not convinced? Try reading the two paragraphs aloud.

Every quotation should be introduced and integrated into an essay in a way that makes clear the relationship between the quotation and your own argument. These introductions are called **signal phrases**. There are four ways to signal a spot quotation.

1. You can introduce it with a phrase such as "According to X," or "Y states" (or *observes*, or *comments*, or *writes*), followed by a comma. Different verbs suggest different attitudes toward the quoted material. For example, "Fulford *suggests* that writers should not overuse quotations" is more tentative than "Fulford *warns* that writers should not overuse quotations." Other verbs you can use to introduce quotations are *asserts*, *notes*, *points out*, *maintains*, *shows*, *reports*, and *claims*. Choose your introductory verbs carefully, and be sure to use a variety of phrases. The repetitive "X says," "Y says," and "Z says" is a sure way to put your reader to sleep.

2. If your introductory words form a complete sentence, use a colon (:) to introduce the quotation.

   George Bernard Shaw's poor opinion of teachers is well known: "Those who can, do; those who can't, teach."

   Oscar Wilde's opinion of teachers is less famous than Shaw's but even more cynical: "Everybody who is incapable of learning has taken to teaching."

3. If the passage you are quoting is a couple of words, a phrase, or anything less than a complete sentence, do not use any punctuation to introduce it.

   Oscar Wilde defined fox hunters as "the unspeakable in full pursuit of the uneatable."

   Wilde believed that people "take no interest in a work of art until they are told that the work in question is immoral."

4. If you insert your own words into the middle of a quotation, use commas to separate the source's words from yours.

> "It is a truth universally acknowledged," writes Jane Austen at the beginning of *Pride and Prejudice*, "that a single man in possession of a good fortune must be in want of a wife."

In general, periods and commas are placed inside the quotation marks (see the examples above). Unless they are part of the quoted material, colons, semicolons, question marks, exclamation marks, and dashes are placed outside the quotation marks. Use single quotation marks to mark off a quotation within a quotation.

> According to John Robert Colombo, "The most widely quoted Canadian aphorism of all time is Marshall McLuhan's 'The medium is the message.'"

Block quotations are normally introduced by a complete sentence followed by a colon (for example, "X writes as follows:"). Then you copy the quotation, beginning on a new line and indenting 10 spaces or 2.5 cm. If your introductory statement is not a complete sentence, use a comma or no punctuation, whichever is appropriate. The passage by Diane Ackerman on page 171 contains examples of both ways to introduce block quotations. Turn to it now. Can you explain why Ackerman has used no punctuation to introduce the first block quotation and a colon to introduce the second one?

Exercise 12.6

For each of the following quotations, make up three different sentences using different signal phrases, as follows:

a. Introduce the complete quotation with a phrase followed by a comma.
b. Introduce the complete quotation with an independent clause followed by a colon.
c. Introduce a portion of the quotation with a phrase or statement that requires no punctuation between it and the quotation. Use ellipses and square brackets, if necessary, to indicate any changes you make in the original wording.

Example: Education is the ability to listen to almost anything without losing your temper or your self-confidence. (Robert Frost)

a. According to Robert Frost, "Education is the ability to listen to almost any-thing without losing your temper or your self-confidence." (complete quotation introduced by phrase + comma)

b. Robert Frost had a peculiar notion of higher learning: "Education is the ability to listen to almost anything without losing your temper or your self-confidence." (complete quotation introduced by independent clause + colon)

c. Robert Frost defined education as "the ability to listen to . . . anything without losing [one's] temper or [one's] self-confidence." (partial quotation introduced by phrase requiring no punctuation; changes indicated with ellipses and square brackets)

1. I find the three major administrative problems on a campus are sex for the students, athletics for the alumni, and parking for the faculty. (Clark Kerr, former president of the University of California)

2. Education is not a *product*: marks, diploma, job, money—in that order; it is a *process*, a never-ending one. (Bel Kaufman, author of *Up the Down Staircase*)

3. School days, I believe, are the unhappiest in the whole span of human existence. (H. L. Mencken, American humorist)

4. In the first place, God made idiots. This was for practice. Then he made school boards. (Mark Twain)

5. Education makes a people easy to lead, but difficult to drive; easy to govern, but impossible to enslave. (Lord Brougham, founder of the University of London, 1825)

TIPS ON USING QUOTATIONS IN YOUR WRITING

1. **Use quotations sparingly and for a specific purpose**, such as *for emphasis* or *to reinforce an important point.* Avoid the temptation to produce a patchwork paper—one that consists of bits and pieces of other people's writing stuck together to look like an original work. Far from impressing your readers, overuse of quotations will give them the impression you have nothing of your own to say.

2. **Be sure every quotation is an accurate reproduction of the original passage.** If you need to change or omit words, indicate those changes with square brackets or ellipses, as appropriate.

3. **Be sure every quotation is relevant.** No matter how interesting or well worded, a quotation that does not clearly and directly relate to your subject does not belong in your essay. An irrelevant quotation will either confuse readers or annoy them (they'll think it's padding), or both.

4. **Make clear the link between the quotation and your controlling idea.** Don't assume readers will automatically see the connection you see between the quotation and your topic sentence. Comment on the quotation so they will be sure to make the connection you intend. If you have used a block quotation, your explanatory comment can sometimes form the conclusion of your paragraph.

5. **Always identify the source of a quotation.** This can be done by mentioning in your paragraph the name of the author and, if appropriate, the title of the source of the quotation. Include the page number(s) in a parenthetical citation. See Chapter 13 for details, and follow the format your instructor prefers.

Exercise 12.7

Read the passages below and then, with your partner, discuss and answer the questions that follow.

1.　　　Whenever college teachers get together informally, sooner or later the conversation turns to students' excuses. The stories students tell to justify absences or late assignments are a source of endless amusement among faculty. These stories tend to fall into three broad thematic categories.

　　　Accident, illness, and death are at the top of the list. If the stories were true, such incidents would be tragic, not funny. But how could any instructor be expected to keep a straight face at being told, "I can't take the test on Friday because my mother is having a vasectomy"? Or "I need a week's extension because my friend's aunt died"? Or—my personal favourite—"The reason I didn't show up for the final exam was because I have inverse testosterone"?

　　　Problems with pets rank second in the catalogue of student excuses. Animals take precedence over tests: "I can't be at the exam because my cat is having kittens and I'm her coach"; and they are often responsible for a student's having to hand in an assignment late. The age-old excuse "My dog ate my homework" gets no more marks for humour than it does for originality, but occasionally a student puts a creative spin on this old chestnut. Would you believe "My paper is late because my parrot crapped in my computer"?

　　　In third place on the list of students' tales of extenuating circumstances are social commitments of various sorts. "I was being arraigned in Chicago for arms dealing"; "I had to see my fence to pick out a ring for my fiancée"; and "I can't take the exam on Monday because my Mom is getting married on Sunday and I'll be too drunk to drive back to school" are just three excuses collected by one college teacher in a single semester.

　　　An enterprising computer programmer could easily compile an "excuse bank" that would allow students to type in the code number of a standard explanation and zap it to their professors. I suspect, however, that there would be little faculty support for such a project. Electronic excuses would lack the humour potential of live ones. Part of the fun comes from watching the student confront you, face to face, shamelessly telling a tale that would make Paul Bunyan blush.

1. Are all the quotations relevant to the subject of this brief essay? Are they sufficiently limited, or could the essay be improved by leaving any out?
2. Underline the specific connections the writer makes between her quotations and her controlling idea.
3. What purpose does the concluding sentence serve? Would the essay be equally effective without it? Why?

2.   U.S. federal drug policy, especially the mandatory minimum sentences for drug offenders enacted by Congress in 1987, has so distressed federal judges that approximately 10 percent of them will not hear drug trials. Judge Jack B. Weinstein of Brooklyn, N.Y., is a case in point. In an April 1993 memo to all the judges in his district, he announced that he would no longer preside over trials of defendants charged with drug crimes:

> One day last week I had to sentence a peasant woman from West Africa [with four dependent children] to forty-six months. . . . On the same day I sentenced a man to thirty years as a second drug offender—a heavy sentence mandated by the Guidelines and statute. These two cases confirm my sense of frustration about much of the cruelty I have been party to in connection with the "war on drugs" that is being fought by the military, police, and courts rather than by our medical and social institutions.
>
> I myself am unsure how this drug problem should be handled, but I need a rest from the oppressive sense of futility that these cases leave. Accordingly, I have taken my name out of the wheel for drug cases. This resolution leaves me uncomfortable since it shifts the "dirty work" to other judges. At the moment, however, I simply cannot sentence another impoverished person whose destruction can have no discernible effect on the drug trade. I wish I were in a position to propose a solution, but I am not. I'm just a tired old judge who has temporarily filled his quota of remorselessness.

The sentencing guidelines that Congress requires judges to follow are so harsh they cause, in Weinstein's words, "overfilling [of] our jails and . . . unneccessary havoc to families, society, and prisons." As a senior judge, Weinstein can choose the cases he hears. But 90 percent of judges are not so fortunate. After they have imposed on a low-level smuggler or a poverty-stricken "mule" a sentence far harsher than those mandated for someone convicted of rape or manslaughter, one wonders how—or if—judges can sleep at night.

Quotations from a speech by J. B. Weinstein. "The War on Drugs: A Judge Goes AWOL." *Harper's Magazine* July 1993: 18. Print.

1. This writer uses both block and spot quotations to develop her point. Where does she make clear the connection between the block quotation and her topic?
2. The original passage from which the writer extracted her spot quotation reads as follow: "Most judges today take it for granted, as I do, that the applicable guideline for the defendant before them will represent an excessive sentence. The sentencing guidelines result, in the main, in the cruel imposition of excessive sentences, overfilling our jails and causing unnecessary havoc to families, society, and prisons." Why did the writer modify the quotation the way she did?
3. In Tip 4 (see page 177), we advise you not to introduce a quotation and just leave it hanging but to comment on it. Where does this writer comment on the quotations she has used?

Additional Suggestions for Writing

1. Interview someone two generations removed from you (e.g., a grandparent, an elderly neighbour) about his or her life as a young person. What were the sources of entertainment? Leisure activities? Work? Family responsibilities? Major challenge or concerns? Goals? Write an essay in which you tell this person's story, using summary, paraphrase, and quotation to develop your main points.
2. Interview a friend, classmate, or relative on one of the following topics. Then write an essay using summary, paraphrase, and quotation to help tell your reader how your interviewee responded.
   a. If you were to live your life over knowing what you know now, what would you do differently?
   b. Explain what being a Canadian (or a parent, or childless, or unemployed, or successful, or a member of a particular religious group) means to you.
   c. "Once I was _____; now I am _____."
3. Research a topic of particular interest to you and write an essay using summary, paraphrase, and quotation to develop your main points.
4. Select a news article or a group of articles dealing with a current issue in your career field. In a paragraph of approximately 200 to 300 words, summarize the issue for your instructor, who has just returned from spending six months in the wilderness without access to either print or electronic media.

13

Documenting Your Sources

Documentation is the process of acknowledging source material. When you document a source, you provide information that

1. tells your readers that the ideas they are reading have been borrowed from another writer
2. enables your readers to find the source and read the material for themselves

When acknowledging your sources in a research paper, you need to follow a system of documentation. There are many different systems, but two of the most widely used are that of the Modern Language Association (MLA) and that of the American Psychological Association (APA). The instructions and examples provided in this chapter include slightly simplified versions of both styles. For examples not covered in this book, see the source documents:

MLA Handbook for Writers of Research Papers. 7th ed. New York: MLA, 2009. <http://www.mla.org>.

Publication Manual of the American Psychological Association. 6th ed. Washington: APA, 2009. An updated PDF guide to APA electronic style is on the APA website: *APA Style Guide to Electronic References*. Washington: APA, 2007. <http://www.apa.org>.

For research papers in the biological sciences, your instructor may require the Council of Biology Editors (CBE) style, presented in *Scientific Style and Format: The CBE Manual for Authors, Editors, and Publishers* <http://www.councilscienceeditors.org>.

For research papers in the engineering sciences, your instructor may require the Institute of Electrical and Electronics Engineers (IEEE) style, presented in the *IEEE Standards Style Manual* <http://www.standards.ieee.org>.

Most instructors in English and the humanities require students to use the MLA style. Instructors in the social sciences (e.g., psychology, sociology, political science, and economics) usually expect papers to conform to the principles of the APA style.

Fortunately, technology is available to help you make the task of documenting much less onerous than it once was. Some word-processing packages, such as Microsoft Word, have built-in templates to assist writers in preparing citations and generating bibliographies. Some academic libraries have licensed "reference manager" programs for their students. Programs such as RefWorks, EndNote, and ProCite help you store and organize sources during the research process. These programs also format citations and bibliographies as you write your paper. If your library does not have a site licence, check your bookstore or search online and decide if you are interested in obtaining a personal copy. Some programs offer a 30-day free trial. Different programs have different features, but most will help you keep track of the notes you've taken from various sources, and all will format your Works Cited (MLA) or References (APA) list for you.

Many academic institutions publish their own style guides, which are available in college and university libraries and bookstores. Be sure to ask your instructor which documentation style he or she prefers.

Introduction: The Two-Part Principle of Documentation

Documentation styles vary in their details, but all styles require authors to

1. identify in a parenthetical reference in the text any information taken from a source
2. list all sources for the paper on a separate page at the end

A **parenthetical reference** (MLA) or a **parenthetical reference citation** (APA) tells the reader that the information preceding the parentheses[1] is borrowed from a source and provides a key to the full identification of that source. For the most part, footnotes are no longer used to document source material; they are used to give additional information that cannot be conveniently worked into the body of your paragraph. (Note the example in this paragraph.)

A **Works Cited** (MLA) or **References** list (APA) is a list of all the sources from which you have borrowed words, ideas, data, or other material in

---

[1] A punctuation note: *Parentheses* means the pair of curved punctuation marks: ( ). *Brackets* are the pair of square marks that surround altered words or phrases in a quotation: [ ].

your paper.[2] Preparing and presenting a Works Cited or References list requires paying close attention to the details of presenting the information required in each entry. The format—including the order of information, capitalization, and punctuation—prescribed by your style guide must be followed *exactly*. This requirement may sound picky, but there is a good reason to abide by it.

Every kind of source you use requires a particular format. If entries are formatted correctly, an experienced reader can tell by glancing at them what kinds of sources you have used: books, journal articles, newspaper articles, Web documents, etc. If you use the wrong style, or leave something out, or scramble the elements in a citation, you will mislead or confuse your reader.

The MLA Style

PARENTHETICAL REFERENCES

Every time you include in your paper a quotation, paraphrase, summary, fact, or idea you have borrowed from another writer, you must identify the source in parentheses immediately following the borrowed material. The parenthetical reference tells your reader that what he or she has just read comes from somewhere else, and it points your reader to the complete information about the source in your Works Cited list. Parenthetical references should be as short and simple as possible while still fulfilling these two purposes. (For an example of an essay that has been prepared in the MLA style, see "No Sweat?" on pages 336–41.)

The standard practice in MLA style is to provide the surname of the author of the source material and the page number where the material was taken from. Once your reader has the author's name and page number, he or she can find complete bibliographic information about the source in your Works Cited list at the end of your paper. Of course, electronic sources present a challenge to this author-based citation method because they often lack an identifiable author, and they rarely include page numbers. More on this later.

You need to include a piece of source information only once; don't repeat information unnecessarily. For example, if you've already mentioned the author's name in your paragraph, you need to give only the page number in parentheses following subsequent references to the author's work.

---

[2] Formerly, this list was called a *bibliography*.

On page 184 is an excerpt from a research paper. The writer uses summary, paraphrase, and quotation, and gives the necessary source information in parentheses immediately following each borrowing. This excerpt also demonstrates how to omit a word or words from a source, using ellipses, and how to add or change a word or words, using square brackets.

The Works Cited list that follows the excerpt gives the reader full bibliographic information about each source. Note the following word-treatment rules for the entries in a Works Cited list.

1. *Italicize* titles and subtitles of any work that is published as a whole— e.g., the names of books, plays, periodicals (newspapers, magazines, and journals), films, radio and television programs, compact discs, DVDs— or underline them if you are using a pen.

2. Put quotation marks around the titles of works published within larger works—e.g., the names of articles, essays, poems, songs, and individual episodes of television or radio programs. Also put quotation marks around the titles of unpublished works, such as lectures and speeches.

3. Use capital letters for the first, the last, and all main words in a title and subtitle even if your source capitalizes only the first word in a title.

Smith 3

Until the passage of the Tobacco Act in 2003, cigarette companies were able to exercise the full talents of their advertising and marketing divisions. The attractive young people who were portrayed in tobacco advertising made it easy for viewers to forget the terrible consequences of tobacco addiction. Cigarette advertisements routinely portrayed happy, energetic young people engaging in athletic activities under invariably sunny skies. The implication of these ads was that smoking was not a deterrent to an active lifestyle; in fact, it may even have been a prerequisite (Cunningham 67).

It is difficult to overstate the impact of tobacco advertising on young people. As Cunningham pointed out,

> Few teenagers begin smoking for cigarettes' inherent physical qualities. Instead, teens are attracted to smoking for its image attributes, such as the five Ss: sophistication, slimness, social acceptability, sexual attractiveness, and status. Marketing gives a cigarette a false "personality." (66)

Is it any wonder that young people continued to take up the habit?

In an effort to reverse the trend of teenage tobacco addiction, the federal government sponsored awareness campaigns in the 1980s and 1990s to demonstrate how the tobacco industry duped and manipulated young people. This was a progressive campaign that was supported by increasingly restrictive legislation, to which the tobacco companies responded by becoming increasingly creative. In the late 1990s, Robert Sheppard wrote, "the industry plays on teenagers' need [for] something to rebel against . . . [which] is exactly how cigarette manufacturers market their wares" (20). To counteract the image of smoking as a symbol of rebellion, government anti-tobacco campaigns presented smoking as a symbol of conformity.

Finally yielding to pressure from the government and the community, the tobacco industry began to sponsor programs aimed at restricting youth access to tobacco products. In a comprehensive review, however, the Ontario Medical Association concluded that these programs were ineffective and made several recommendations to strengthen youth smoking-reduction initiatives (Ontario Medical Association).

The OMA recommended that all parties interested in reducing tobacco use endorse a comprehensive tobacco control program and that all tobacco industry-sponsored programs be carefully monitored in the future (Ontario Medical Association). These recommendations culminated in 2003 with the passage of the Tobacco Act, which prohibited all advertising and sponsorship aimed at young people.

Full parenthetical citation for paraphrase; see the first item in Works Cited

Block quotation

Abbreviated parenthetical citation

See third item in Works Cited

Short quotation with
- *words left out (ellipses)*
- *words changed (square brackets)*

Paraphrase; see second item in Works Cited

Parenthetical citation; Web, no page number

Summary

Parenthetical citation; Web, no page number

Smith 6

Works Cited

Cunningham, Rob. *Smoke and Mirrors: The Canadian Tobacco War*. Ottawa: IDRC, 1996. Print.

Ontario Medical Association. *More Smoke and Mirrors: Tobacco Industry-Sponsored Youth Prevention Programs in the Context of Comprehensive Tobacco Control Programs in Canada*. Feb. 2002. n. pag. Web. 3 Feb. 2009. <http://www.oma.org/phealth/smokeandmirrors.htm>.

Sheppard, Robert. "Ottawa Butts Up against Big Tobacco." *Maclean's* 6 Dec. 1990: 20-24. Print. *eLibrary Canada*. n. pag. Web. 4 Feb. 2009.

Study the way the excerpt on page 184 uses parenthetical references to identify information sources. The introductory paragraph ends with a paraphrase, which is immediately followed by a full parenthetical reference. Because the author's name is not mentioned in the writer's paragraph, it is given in parentheses, together with the number of the page on which the information was found. For more details, the reader would turn to the Works Cited list, reproduced at the top of this page.

The second paragraph includes a block quotation from the same source. The author's name is given in the statement that introduces the quotation, so the parentheses contain only the page number on which the quotation can be found.

The third paragraph includes a short quotation integrated into the writer's own sentence. The introductory phrase gives the author's name, so the parenthetical reference provides only the page number of the article on which this partial quotation is found. Complete bibliographic information for this source appears in the Works Cited list.

In the fourth and fifth paragraphs, the writer includes a paraphrase and a summary of information found in an unsigned article posted on the website of the Ontario Medical Association. The source document is not paginated, so no page number is given. Complete information about this source appears in the alphabetical list of Works Cited under "Ontario Medical Association," the sponsor of the site.

Examples of Parenthetical References: Traditional Print Sources

1. If you name the source author in your paragraph, give just the page number in parentheses.

Isajiw asserts that the twentieth century "has produced more refugees and exiles than any other preceding period since the fall of the Roman Empire" (66).

The Works Cited entry for this book is on page 199.

2. If you do not name the source author in your paragraph, give the author's surname and the page number.

The effect of "status drop" on the psychological well-being of immigrants can be substantial: "Especially among those more highly educated, this experience can cause feelings of bitterness or hostility. . . ." (Isajiw 97).

3. If no author is named in the source, give the first few words of the title as it appears in the Works Cited entry.

Legislation to reduce the amount of pollution generated by large-scale vehicles has been on the federal agenda for some time: "Canada has said it will toughen pollution-emission rules for all new vehicles, ending a loophole that allowed less stringent standards for popular sport-utility vehicles and minivans" ("Canada to Toughen" A6).

The Works Cited entry for this source is on page 199.

4. If your source was published in more than one volume, give the volume number before the page reference.

Only once in his two-volume work does Erickson suggest conspiracy (2: 184).

The Works Cited entry for this source is on page 199.

5. If you are quoting from a literary classic or the Bible, use Arabic numerals separated by periods to identify act, scene, and lines from a play or a biblical chapter and verse.

In Shakespeare's play, the duke's threat to give "measure for measure" (5.1.414) echoes the familiar passage in the Bible (Matthew 7.1–2).

Examples of Parenthetical References: Electronic Sources

Parenthetical references for print sources in MLA style usually include the author's surname and the page number of the source. This principle is problematic for electronic sources since many of them lack one or both of these elements. Give enough information to guide your reader to the source listed in your Works Cited list.

1. If the electronic source lists an author, give the surname in your parenthetical reference.

Science is about immersing ourselves in piercing uncertainty while struggling with the deepest of mysteries. It is the ultimate adventure. . . . Einstein captured it best when he wrote, "the years of anxious searching in the dark for a truth that one feels but cannot express." *That's* what science is about (Greene).

This quotation comes from *Wired*, an online magazine. The Works Cited entry for this quotation is on page 199.

2. If the electronic source does not list an author, give the document title (or a shortened version of the title) in italics or quotation marks as appropriate, instead of the author's name.

New websites are available to help students navigate their way through the challenging works of William Shakespeare:

> There are some people who don't even attempt to learn Shakespeare because they think that Shakespeare is . . . only for English scholars. But that's not true! Shakespeare can be FUN. That's right—Shakespeare can actually be something you want to learn about. ("William Shakespeare")

This quotation comes from a website called *Shakespeare: Chill with Will*. The Works Cited entry for this quotation is on page 199.

3. You do not usually find page numbers or other navigation devices in an electronic source. If there are page, paragraph, or section numbers that could guide your reader to the specific material being quoted, include them. If the author's name is included in the parenthetical reference, put a comma after it and include the section or paragraph numbers. Use the abbreviations *sec.* and *par.*

Even Margaret Atwood must endure the editing process before her books are published:

> Being edited is like falling face down into a threshing machine. Every page gets fought over, back and forth, like WWI. Unless the editor and the writer both have in mind the greater glory of the work, . . . blood will flow and the work will suffer. Every comma, every page break, may be a ground for slaughter. (sec. 6)

This quotation comes from an article posted on Atwood's website. The Works Cited entry is found on page 199.

If there are no page, paragraph, or section numbers to identify the quotation, simply give the author's name or the title in parentheses. If your reader wants to locate the information, Web search engines can often find it through a keyword search.

THE MLA WORKS CITED LIST

A Works Cited list is required on a separate page at the end of your essay. It includes detailed bibliographical information for all the sources you have summarized, paraphrased, or quoted in your paper. The information in the Works Cited list enables your reader to assess the extent of your research and to find and check every source you used. The sample Works Cited list on page 199 illustrates the information given in the following bulleted list.

- Begin the list on a new page and number each page, continuing the page numbers of your paper. Your last name and the page number appear in the upper right-hand corner, 1.25 cm from the top and lined up with the right margin. (*Note:* Use the automatic function of your word-processing program to create the running head.)
- Centre the heading, Works Cited, 2.50 cm from the top of the page.
- Double-space the entire list, including the title and the first entry.
- Begin each entry at the left margin. If an entry runs more than one line (and most do), indent the subsequent line or lines five spaces or 1.25 cm. This format is called a "hanging indent"[3] and can be found in most word-processing packages.
- Arrange the entries alphabetically, beginning with the first word of the entry, which is often the author's surname. Do not number your entries.

---

[3] Hanging indents help readers locate authors' names in the alphabetical listing. If you have only one source to acknowledge, you do not need to indent the second line. For example, see the source citation for the excerpt from Judge J. B. Weinstein's speech on page 178.

- If there are several works by the same author, put the author's name in the first entry only. In the subsequent entries, type three hyphens and a period to represent the author's name.
- If no author is identified in your source, alphabetize by the first word in the title, ignoring *A*, *An*, and *The*. For example, *The Canadian Encyclopedia* would be listed under *C*, for *Canadian*.

Below you will find examples for Works Cited entries commonly found in research papers, including print, broadcast, and electronic sources.

Books, Encyclopedias, Reports, Government Publications

Here is the basic model for a book entry in a Works Cited list. Note the spacing, capitalization, punctuation, and order of the information.

> Last name of author, First name and/or initials. *Title of Book: Subtitle of Book.* City of publication: Publisher, Year of publication. Medium of publication.

- Leave only one space between the comma that follows the author's surname and the author's first name and/or initials, as well as after other commas, colons, semicolons, and periods that separate parts of the citation.
- Capitalize all proper names and significant words in the title and subtitle, if any. *Italicize* title and subtitle.
- In the publication data:
  - If several cities are listed for a publisher, use the first one.
  - Shorten the publisher's name. For example, McGraw-Hill, Inc. is abbreviated to McGraw. If the publisher is a well-known university press, use the abbreviation UP—e.g., Oxford UP, U of Toronto P. Write out the names of associations and corporations.
  - The year the book was published is usually found on the back of the title page (the copyright page); if it is not given, use the latest copyright date.
- Include the medium of publication—e.g., Print. (See the sections below on audiovisual sources and electronic sources.)

Book with One or More Authors

> Barlow, Maude. *Blue Covenant: The Global Water Crisis and the Fight for the Right to Water.* Toronto: McClelland, 2007. Print.

> O'Neil, John, Alan Holland, and Andrew Light. *Environmental Values.* New York: Routledge, 2008. Print.

If there are more than three authors, you may give the first author's name only, followed by a comma and the abbreviation *et al.* (meaning "and others").

> Morgan, Sarah E., et al. *Cosmetic Nanotechnology: Polymers and Colloids in Cosmetics*. Washington: American Chemical Society, 2007. Print.

Book with More Than One Edition

> Peak, Kenneth J., and Ronald W. Glesnor. *Community Policing and Problem Solving: Strategies and Practices*. 5th ed. Upper Saddle River: Prentice, 2008. Print.

Book with No Author

> *Webster's New College Dictionary*. 3rd ed. Boston: Houghton, 2008. Print.

Book with One or More Editors

> Bhushan, Bharat, ed. *Springer Handbook of Nanotechnology*. 2nd ed. New York: Springer, 2007. Print.

> Baum, J. Robert, Michael Frese, and Robert A. Baron, eds. *The Psychology of Entrepreneurship*. Mahwah: Erlbaum, 2007. Print.

If there are more than three editors, you may give the first editor's name only, followed by a comma and the abbreviation *et al.*

> Massat, Carol R., et al., eds. *School Social Work: Practice, Policy and Research*. 7th ed. Chicago: Lyceum, 2009. Print.

Recent Edition of a Classic Work

> Shakespeare, William. *The Tempest*. Ed. Stephen Orgel. Oxford: Oxford UP, 1994. Print.

Multivolume Work

> Yates, Arthur. *The Trooper: Memoirs of Arthur Yates*. 2 vols. Victoria: Trafford, 2001. Print.

Book with Introduction, Preface, Foreword, or Afterword (to which you refer in your paper)

Willmott, Glenn. Introduction. *Think of the Earth*. By Bertrand Brooker.
1936. Toronto: Brown Bear Press, 2000. 1-6. Print.

Article, Essay, Story, or Poem in a Collection

Mistry, Rohinton. "Journey to Dharmsala." *The Reader: Contemporary
Essays and Writing Strategies*. Ed. Carolyn Meyer and Bruce Meyer.
Toronto: Prentice, 2001. 38-51. Print.

Encyclopedia Reference

Driedger, Leo. "Ethnic Identity." *Canadian Encyclopedia*. 2000 ed. Print.

Book Published by a Corporation (Company, Commission, Agency)

International Joint Commission. *Protection of the Waters of the Great
Lakes: Final Report to the Governments of Canada and the United
States*. Ottawa: International Joint Commission, 2000. Print.

United Nations Environment Programme. *Beijing 2008 Olympic Games:
An Environmental Review*. Nairobi: UNEP, 2007. Print.

Government Publication

If the author is not named, identify the government first, then the agency,
then the title, city of publication, publisher, date, and publication medium.

Alberta. Environmental Protection Commission. *A Review of Alberta's
Environmental and Emergency Response Capacity: Learning the
Lessons and Building Change*. Edmonton: Alberta Environment,
2005. Print.

Canada. Canadian Heritage. *Canadian Content in the 21st Century: A
Discussion Paper about Canadian Content in Film and Television
Productions*. Hull: Canadian Heritage, 2002. Print.

Brochure or Pamphlet

Council of Canadians. *Not Counting Canadians: The Security and
Prosperity Partnership and Public Opinion*. Ottawa: Council of
Canadians, 2008. Print.

Articles in Magazines, Newspapers, and Journals

The MLA provides different sets of guidelines for articles published in magazines and for those published in what it calls "scholarly journals." Both sets of guidelines are given below. If you are not sure whether a source should be treated as a magazine or as a scholarly journal, consult your instructor.

Article in a Magazine or Newspaper

Note the spacing, capitalization, punctuation, and order of the information required in a Works Cited entry for a magazine or newspaper.

> Last name of author, First name and/or initials. "Title of Article." *Title of Periodical* Volume no. [if any] Issue no. [if any] Date: pages. Medium of publication.

- If the writer's name does not appear with the newspaper article, simply give the article's full title (in your in-text parenthetical reference for the article identified below, it would appear as "Ottawa Recalls"):

> "Ottawa Recalls Sensitive Data." *Toronto Star* 16 Feb. 2009: A2. Print.

Use the same format for a magazine article, although sometimes the date consists of only a month (or two months) and the year, or a season and the year:

> Bidini, David. "Iqaluit in the Groove." *Canadian Geographic* July/Aug. 2009: 57-64. Print.

- Volume number and issue number (if any): These are rare in magazines and newspapers, but are expressed as, for example: 13.6 (Volume 13, Issue 6)
- Date of publication: day [if applicable] month year (e.g., 13 Mar. 2010)
- Inclusive page numbers of the article (see details below)
- Medium of publication: Print, Web, CD, etc.

Give the magazine's or newspaper's name as it appears on the masthead (at the top of the front page of the magazine or newspaper) but omit *The* (e.g., *Globe and Mail*) even if *The* is an official part of the name. If the name of the city is not included in a locally published newspaper, add it in square brackets after the name of the paper so that readers will know where it was published; for instance, *Comox Valley Record* [Campbell River].

For a magazine or newspaper that is published weekly or every two weeks, provide the day, month, and year, in that order. Abbreviate all months except May, June, and July (Jan., Feb., Mar., Apr., Aug., Sept., Oct., Nov., Dec.). If the periodical is published monthly, provide month and year.

Give the complete page span for each article in your Works Cited list. For example, if an article begins on page 14 and concludes on page 16, put a colon and the page numbers after the date: 5 June 2009: 14-16. If the article begins on page 36, then skips to page 40 and concludes on page 41, give only the first page number and a plus sign: 36+. In a newspaper, the sections are usually numbered separately, so include the section identifier as well as the page number.

> Bradford, Keith. "The Obscurity of a World Champ." *Calgary Herald* 2 Aug. 2009: B1+. Print.

Article in a Scholarly Journal

The major differences between a magazine article and one in a scholarly journal are that a volume number and an issue number are often included in the publication information, and the year of publication is enclosed in parentheses. In the following entry, only a volume number ("19") is given because this journal does not use issue numbers:

> Chen, Gary K., Paul Marjoram, and Jeffery D. Wall. "Fast and Flexible Simulation of DNA Sequence Data." *Genome Research* 19 (2008): 136-42. Print.

The journal cited below publishes in issues within (annual) volumes, so both volume (34) and issue number (7) are required.

> Matzo, Marianne. "The Universal Nursing Obligation: All Gerontological Care Is Palliative Care." *Journal of Gerontological Nursing* 34.7 (2008): 3-4. Print.

Published Review—Books, Plays, Films, Etc.

> Dixon, Guy. "Mash-Up Doc Argues That Creativity Begins Where Copyright Ends." Rev. of *RiP: A Remix Manifesto*, dir. Brett Gaylor. *Globe and Mail* 14 Mar. 2009: R11. Print.

> Bland, Jared. Rev. of *The $12 Million Stuffed Shark: The Curious Economics of Contemporary Art* by Don Thompson. *Walrus* Oct./Nov. 2009: 94. Print.

Other Sources
Published Interview

> Monahan, Patrick. Interview. "Where Angels Fear to Tread." *Globe and Mail* 21 Mar. 2009: M3. Print.

Unpublished Personal Interview

> Carpenter, Carole. Personal interview. 22 Mar. 2009.

Personal Communication

> Green, Brian. "Re: The Musical Brain." Message to the author. 16 Mar. 2009. E-mail.

In the following entry, "MS" (stands for "manuscript") at the end of the entry indicates that a document was handwritten. "TS" ("transcript") would indicate that a document was prepared using a machine.

> Mason, Marie. Letter to the author. 5 Aug. 2009. MS.

Audiovisual Sources
Television/Radio Broadcast

> "Elton John." Interview by Elvis Costello. *Spectacle: Elvis Costello with . . .* CTV, Toronto, 3 Apr. 2009. Television.

> "Recession Marketing." Narr. Terry O'Reilly. *The Age of Persuasion.* CBC Radio One, Toronto, 20 Apr. 2009. Radio.

Film, Video, CD, DVD

> Nickelback. *Dark Horse.* Road Runner Records, 2009. CD.

> *Bowling for Columbine.* Dir. Michael Moore. United Artists/Alliance Atlantis, 2002. Film.

> *Delmar's Community Health Nursing: A Case Study.* Clifton Park: Delmar, 2003. CD.

> Ward, Al. *Photoshop for Right-Brainers: The Art of Photo Manipulation.* San Francisco: Sybex, 2009. DVD.

If you want to acknowledge a specific individual's contribution to a film or recording, begin with that person's name. (This format is useful when you are writing about the work of a particular artist—in this case, Alfred Hitchcock.)

> Hitchcock, Alfred, dir. *Rear Window*. Perf. Jimmy Stewart, Grace Kelly, and Raymond Burr. 1954. Universal, 2001. DVD.

Electronic Sources

The rules for citing electronic sources are essentially the same as for print or broadcast sources. The reference should provide enough information to enable a reader to locate the source quickly—author, title, date, and publishing information. In the case of electronic sources, the latter includes the name of the website or library subscription database. Always include "Web" as the medium of publication, and always include the date that you, as the researcher, accessed the information. The access date is important because online documents can be altered at any time. We recommend that you download and print online material so that you can verify it if, at a later date, it is revised, unavailable, or inaccessible.

The URL (Uniform Resource Locator) is the electronic address for a document on the Web. MLA no longer requires the URL to be included in a citation unless readers would be unlikely to find the source using a simple keyword or title search. However, you have the option to include the full URL as supplemental information or if your instructor requires it. If the URL is required, place it in angle brackets at the end of the citation, followed by a period.

Capitalization, punctuation, and the order in which the information is provided are very important when citing electronic sources. Here are the elements to look for:

- Full name of author (or compiler, director, editor, narrator, performer, translator)
- Title of the document (in italics if it is independent, in quotes if it is part of a larger website)
- Title of the overall website in italics
- Version or edition statement, if available
- Publisher or sponsor of the site. If unavailable use the notation "n.p."
- Library database, if applicable
- Date of the publication. If unavailable use "n.d."
- Medium of publication (Web)
- Day, month, year on which you found and read the source
- The URL, if required, or helpful to the reader

Online Book from a Library Subscription Database

Kay, Melvyn. *Practical Hydraulics.* 2nd ed. New York: Routledge, 2008. *Netlibrary.* Web. 12 Mar. 2009.

Online Book from a Public Internet Site

Canada. Health Canada. *Regulation and Beyond: Progress on Health Canada's Therapeutics Access Strategy.* Ottawa: Health Canada, 2005. Web. 23 Mar. 2009.

Wollstonecraft, Mary. *A Vindication of the Rights of Women.* Boston, 1792. *Bartleby.com.* 2000. Web. 4 Mar. 2009.

Chapter, Essay, Story, or Poem in an Online Book

de Maupassant, Guy. "The Necklace." *The Short Story: Specimens Illustrating Its Development.* Ed. Brander Matthews. New York: American Book Company, 1907. *Bartleby.com.* 2000. Web. 15 Mar. 2009.

Mallett, Dan. "Sampling and Weighting." *The Handbook of Marketing Research: Uses, Misuses and Future Advances.* Ed. Rajiv Grover and Marco Vriens. Thousand Oaks: Sage, 2006. 159-77. *Google Book Search.* Web. 28 Apr. 2009.

Online Encyclopedia, Dictionary

Falco, Charles. M. "Use of Optics by Renaissance Artists." *AccessScience@McGraw-Hill.* McGraw, 2009. Web. 5 May 2009.

"Canadian Literature." *Encyclopaedia Britannica Online.* Encyclopaedia Britannica, 2009. Web. 5 May 2009.

"Capricious." *Merriam-Webster Online Dictionary.* Merriam-Webster, 2009. Web. 30 Mar. 2009.

Web Document

This sample includes the URL, which is optional.

"Michael Ondaatje." *The Canadian Literature Archive.* 20 Mar. 2006. Web. 2 Apr. 2009. <http://www.umanitoba.ca/canlit/ michael_ondaatje.shtml>.

Journal Article from a Library Subscription Database

Vassanji, M. G. "Am I a Canadian Writer?" *Canadian Literature* 190
(2006): 7. *eLibrary Canada.* Web. 12 Mar. 2009.

Journal Article from Public Internet Journal

Herman, Deborah. "Wonderland." *Rhythm* 2.2 (2009). Web. 13 May
2009. <http://rhythmpoetrymagazine.english.dal.ca/i2v2/
rhythm.html>.

Cimolai, N. "Streptococcus Pyogenes Is Alive and Well." *BCMJ* 51.3
(2009): 122-27. Web. 2 May 2009.

Newspaper Article from a Public Internet Site

Brooymans, Hanneke. "Duck Death Toll Triples at Alberta Oilsands
Pond." *edmontonjournal.com.* Edmonton Journal, 31 Mar. 2009.
Web. 1 Apr. 2009.

Online News Service Article

"Ontario Set to Allow Medication Vending Machines." *MSN.com.* CTV
News Services, 6 May 2009. Web. 7 May 2009.

Online Image

Carr, Emily. *A Rushing Sea of Undergrowth.* 1935. Oil on canvas. *Google
Image Search.* Web. 20 Apr. 2009.

Online Course Materials

Madar, Jason, and Margaret Dulat. "Lecture Slides: Artificial Intelligence
and Robotics: An Exploration." *Capilano University*.
OpenCourseWare, 2007. Web. 30 Mar. 2009.

Wurfel, Marlene. "Canadian Writers: Alice Munro." *Athabasca University*,
n.d. Web. 2 May 2009.

Personal Website

Atwood, Margaret. "The Rocky Road to Paper Heaven." *O.W.Toad:
Margaret Atwood Reference Site*, n.d. Web. 7 Apr. 2009.

Television Show (Episode of a Continuing Series)

"Shock Wave." Dir. Jerry Thompson. Prod. Brian Hamilton. *Doc Zone.* *CBC.ca.* CBC, 22 Mar. 2009. Web. 29 Mar. 2009.

Audio Podcast

Campbell, G. "Building a Strong Economic Future." *BC Government Media Room*, 8 Nov. 2008. MP3 file.

There are no examples in the *MLA Handbook for Writers of Research Papers* that illustrate citations for social networking sites on the Internet. However, the MLA style is intended to be a simple, flexible system of documentation that lends itself to several options for citing a source. Since consistency of presentation is important, we suggest the following formats. You can always add the full URL, in angle brackets, at the end of the citation, for quick retrieval. (*Note:* Some instructors may not accept the following formats, or indeed, the following sources, as reputable or reliable. Check with your instructor before including them in your work.)

Full name of author/presenter. "Title of Item." *Website name*. Website sponsor, Date of item (or "n.d."). Web. Date of retrieval.

Video Web Post

Utko, Jacek. "Can Design Save the Newspaper?" *Youtube.com.* Mar. 2008. Web. 15 Apr. 2009.

Blog, Social Network Post

"Young Drivers against New Ontario Laws." *Facebook.com.* Facebook, n.d. Web. 16 Apr. 2009.

Edward. Online posting. "Q Blog." *CBC Radio.* CBC, 9 Jan. 2009. Web. 18 Apr. 2009. <http://www.cbc .ca/q/blog/2009/01/ where_do_you_stand_on_illegal.html>.

SAMPLE MLA WORKS CITED LIST

On the next page, you will find a sample MLA Works Cited list to show you what the final page of your paper should look like. A description of the type of source used appears to the right of each entry.

Author Name 15

Works Cited

Atwood, Margaret. "The Rocky Road to Paper Heaven." *O.W.Toad: Margaret*
 Atwood Reference Site. Margaret Atwood, n.d. Web. 7 Apr. 2009. ← *Personal website*

Bowling for Columbine. Dir. Michael Moore. United Artists/Alliance Atlantis, ← *Audiovisual item*
 2002. DVD.

"Canada to Toughen Auto-Emissions Rules." *Wall Street Journal* 5 Apr. 2002: ← *Article in a daily*
 A6. Print.   *print newspaper*

Erickson, Edward W., and Leonard Waverman, eds. *The Energy Question: An*
 International Failure of Policy. 2 vols. Toronto: U of Toronto P, 1974. ← *Multivolume*
 Print.   *book by two*
                                                                           authors

Greene, Brian. "Questions, Not Answers, Make Science the Ultimate
 Adventure." *Wired* 20 Apr. 2009. Web. 26 May 2009. ← *Article in an*
                                                       online magazine

Isajiw, Wsevolod W. *Understanding Diversity: Ethnicity and Race in the*
 Canadian Context. Toronto: Thompson, 1999. Print. ← *Book by one*
                                                       author

"Shakespeare: Chill with Will." *ThinkQuest*. Oracle Education Foundation, n.d.
 Web. 1 May 2009. ← *Educational*
                     website

Exercise 13.1

For each of the following quotations, write a short paragraph in which you use
all or a portion of the quotation and credit it in a parenthetical citation.

1. From a book entitled Getting it done: the transforming power of self-
   discipline by Andrew J. Dubrin, published by Pacesetter Books in
   Princeton in 1995. This sentence appears on page 182: "Stress usually
   stems from your interpretation and perception of an event, not from
   the event itself."

2. From a journal article by Linda A. White that appeared on pages 385 to
   405 of Canadian Public Policy, a journal with continuous paging: "If a
   clear connection exists between the presence of child care and high
   levels of women's labour market participation, that would provide
   good reasons for governments and employers to regard child care as
   part of an active labour market policy." White's article is entitled Child
   Care, Women's Labour Market Participation, and Labour Market Policy
   Effectiveness in Canada. The quotation appears on page 389 of the
   fourth issue of the 27th volume, published in 2001.

3. From the article entitled "Stress, Definition of Stress, Stressor, What Is
   Stress? Eustress?" on the American Institute of Stress website, found on

May 2, 2009, at http://www.stress.org: "Increased stress results in increased productivity—up to a point." The article has no publication date.

4. From a newspaper article written by Nancy Cleeland that appeared on page A2 in the March 30, 2005, issue of The Vancouver Sun. You found it on the e-Library Canada database on April 26, 2009, at your college library. The article is entitled As jobs heat up, workers' hearts take a beating: "For years, occupational health researchers have struggled to come up with formulas for measuring job stress and determining its effect on health."

5. During the February 3, 2009, CBC broadcast of the Mercer Report, Rick Mercer says, "According to a recent Dominion Institute poll, a majority of Canadians have no idea how Parliament works." You watched the broadcast on *YouTube* on February 6, 2009. The segment is entitled Everything you wanted to know about Canada but were afraid to ask. It was located at the following *YouTube* URL: http://www.youtube.com/watch?v=yi1yhp-_x7A.

6. From an e-mail message on the subject of time management from your friend, Janet Ford, on June 5, 2009: "Using a daily planner and checking e-mail only once a day are two ways I've found to manage my stress during the school year."

Exercise 13.2*

Prepare a Works Cited list in the MLA style for the sources provided in Exercise 13.1. Pay particular attention to punctuation.

The APA Style

PARENTHETICAL REFERENCES

A parenthetical reference in the text of your paper serves two functions: (1) it tells your reader that the information comes from somewhere else, and (2) it points the reader to full details about the source in the References list at the end of your paper. (For an example of an essay that has been prepared in the APA style, see "A City for Students" on pages 273–74.)

One way to acknowledge another author's work is to name the author of the source in your own sentence and include the date of publication in parentheses immediately after the author's name: e.g., Smith (2009) reported . . . . If you do not name the author in your sentence, put the author's surname + a comma + the date in parentheses—(Smith, 2009)—right after your quotation, summary, or paraphrase. (See the examples on the next page.)

If you are quoting from a source, you must include in your parenthetical reference the page number(s) on which the quotation appears, using the abbreviation *p.* (page) or *pp.* (pages)—(Smith & Dolittle, 2010, p. 32). APA style encourages, but does not require, page references in citations for paraphrases or summaries. We strongly encourage you to provide page references for all source citations.

Sometimes, no author's name is provided in the source information, so the in-text reference should include the first few words of the title of the publication or article. The title of a publication is italicized in the in-text reference (e.g., *Essay Essentials*, 2010), while quotation marks are used for the shortened title of an article and capitals are used for the major words (e.g., "Questions, not Answers," 2009). Note that in the sample References list provided later in this chapter, the full title of the article cited in the preceding example is not enclosed in quotation marks, and a capital letter is used for only the first word: Questions, not answers, make science the ultimate adventure.

Electronic sources (discussed below) do not always follow the author-date in-text reference method because they often do not have an identifiable author, rarely include page numbers, and often are not dated. Usually, an abbreviated version of the website name or of the title of the document is used for an in-text reference: (*Purdue OWL*)—the abbreviated version of *The Purdue Online Writing Lab (OWL)* website name—and ("Literary Theory")—the abbreviated version of the article "Literary Theory and Schools of Criticism" that appears on *Purdue OWL* website.

Italics or Quotation Marks?

Italicize the titles and subtitles of any work that is published as a whole—e.g., names of books, plays, periodicals (newspapers, magazines, and journals), films, radio and television programs, DVDs. Also italicize the titles of published and unpublished doctoral dissertations and master's theses (unless they are part of a larger work), and the titles of speeches and lectures. (If you are using a pen, underline these titles.)

In all in-text references, whether parenthetical or not, put quotation marks around the titles of works published within larger works—e.g., the names of articles, essays, poems, songs, and individual episodes of television and radio programs. Use capital letters for the first, the last, and all main words in a title and subtitle. (*Note:* These rules are different for the References list; see pages 205–16.)

On page 202 is an excerpt from a research paper. The writer uses summary, paraphrase, and quotation, and gives the necessary source citations in parentheses.

UP IN SMOKE   3

     Until the passage of the Tobacco Act in 2003, cigarette companies were able to exercise the full talents of their advertising and marketing divisions. The attractive young people who were portrayed in tobacco advertising made it easy for viewers to forget the terrible consequences of tobacco addiction. Cigarette advertisements routinely portrayed happy, energetic young people engaging in athletic activities under invariably sunny skies. The implication of these ads was that smoking was not a deterrent to an active lifestyle; in fact, it may even have been a prerequisite (Cunningham, 1996, p. 67).

     It is difficult to overstate the impact of tobacco advertising on young people. As Cunningham pointed out,

> Few teenagers begin smoking for cigarettes' inherent physical qualities. Instead, teens are attracted to smoking for its image attributes, such as the five Ss: sophistication, slimness, social acceptability, sexual attractiveness, and status. Marketing gives a cigarette a false "personality." (p. 66)

Is it any wonder that young people continued to take up the habit?

     In an effort to reverse the trend of teenage tobacco addiction, the federal government sponsored awareness campaigns in the 1980s and 1990s to demonstrate how the tobacco industry duped and manipulated young people. This was a progressive campaign that was supported by increasingly restrictive legislation, to which the tobacco companies responded by becoming increasingly creative. As Robert Sheppard (1990, p. 20) observed, "the industry plays on teenagers' need [for] something to rebel against . . . [which] is exactly how cigarette manufacturers market their wares." To counteract the image of smoking as a symbol of rebellion, government anti-tobacco campaigns presented smoking as a symbol of conformity.

     Finally yielding to pressure from the government and the community, the tobacco industry began to sponsor programs aimed at restricting youth access to tobacco products. In a comprehensive review, however, the Ontario Medical Association concluded that these programs were ineffective and made several recommendations to strengthen youth smoking-reduction initiatives (Ontario Medical Association, 2002, Recommendations section).

     The OMA recommended that all parties interested in reducing tobacco use endorse a comprehensive tobacco control program and that all tobacco industry-sponsored programs be carefully monitored in the future (Ontario Medical Association, 2002, Recommendations section). These recommendations culminated in 2003 with the passage of the Tobacco Act, which prohibited all advertising and sponsorship aimed at young people.

Full parenthetical citation for paraphrase; see the first item in References

Block quotation

Abbreviated parenthetical citation

See third item in References

Short quotation with
- *words changed (square brackets)*
- *words left out (ellipses)*

Paraphrase; see second item in References

Parenthetical citation; Web, no page number

Parenthetical citation; Web, no page number

UP IN SMOKE   6

References

Cunningham, R. (1996). *Smoke and mirrors: The Canadian tobacco war.*
    Ottawa: IDRC.

Ontario Medical Association. (2002, February). *More smoke and mirrors:*
    Tobacco industry-sponsored youth prevention programs in the context of
    comprehensive tobacco control programs in Canada. Retrieved from
    http://www.oma.org/phealth/smokeandmirrors.htm

Sheppard, R. (1990, December 6). "Ottawa butts up against Big Tobacco."
    Maclean's, 20–24. Retrieved from *eLibrary Canada* at http://www
    .proquestk12.com

Examples of Parenthetical References: Traditional Print Sources

Author's Name Given in Your Text

Kevin Patterson (2000) writes about his sailing journey from British Columbia to the South Pacific and back: "Suffused with optimism and rum, I told Peter I wanted to sail to Tahiti" (p. 6).

For the format of a References entry for this type of source, see the sample References list on page 216.

Author's Name Not Given in Your Text

Long voyages by sea, especially in small boats, present obvious dangers depending on the ocean and the season of crossing: "The North Pacific is cold and volatile in the autumn and anyone who knew enough about the sea to consider sailing to Canada knew that much" (Patterson, 2000, p. 249).

No Author Named in Source

When no author is named, give the first two or three words of the title of the publication or article in which the quotation appeared. For the References entry for this source, see the sample References list on page 216.

Legislation to reduce the amount of pollution generated by large-scale vehicles has been on the federal agenda for some time: "Canada has said it will toughen pollution-emission rules for all new vehicles, ending a loophole that allowed less stringent standards for popular sport-utility vehicles and minivans" ("Canada to Toughen," 2002, p. A6).

Source with Two Authors

Name both authors in the order in which their names appear on the work.

> Norton and Green (2005) observe that inexperienced writers achieved superior results when they spent half the allotted time on planning and drafting, and the other half on revising.

If you do not name the authors in your own sentence, use an ampersand (&) instead of *and* in the parenthetical reference.

> One approach to writing recommends that students spend half the allotted time on planning and drafting, and the other half on revising (Norton & Green, 2005).

Classical Works

The first time you quote or paraphrase from a classical work of literature (such as the Bible or a Shakespearean play), give the book, chapter, canto, act, scene, verse, and/or line numbers, as relevant, and identify the version, edition, or translation that you are using. Do not include this kind of source in your References list.

> In the Bible, it is clear that people who have suffered exile from their land are not allowed to subjugate others because they themselves have suffered and understand the suffering of the oppressed: "Also thou shalt not oppress a stranger, seeing ye were strangers in the land of Egypt" Exodus 23:8 (King James Version).

Further information on APA parenthetical citations (e.g., two or more books by the same author, a work in an edited anthology, a work cited in a secondary source) can be found on the APA website (http://www.apa.org).

Examples of Parenthetical References: Electronic Sources

If the electronic source includes the author's name, give the surname and the publication date (if provided) in your parenthetical reference. If no date is provided and your References list includes another author with the same surname, give the author's first name and/or initial(s) in your in-text reference. This is all the information your reader needs in order to find the full bibliographical data in your References list. Example:

"Science is about immersing ourselves in piercing uncertainty while struggling with the deepest of mysteries. It is the ultimate adventure. . . .
Einstein captured it best when he wrote, 'the years of anxious searching
in the dark for a truth that one feels but cannot express.' *That's* what science is about" (Greene, 2009).

The quotation in the example above comes from *Wired,* an online magazine. (The sample References list on page 216 shows you how to format this
kind of source.)

If the electronic source does not list an author, use the document title
(or a shortened version of the title) instead of the author's name.

Statistics Canada calculates that the nation's infant mortality rate in 1997
was 5.5 for every 1000 live births (*Infant Mortality*, 2002).

(See the sample References list on page 216 for the bibliographic format for
this source.)

Electronic sources don't usually include page numbers or other navigation devices, but if there are page, paragraph, or section numbers that could
guide your reader to the specific material being quoted, include them. Use
the abbreviation *par.* or *pars.* for paragraph numbers, as shown in the following example from an online edition of a Guy de Maupassant story:

In the short story "The Necklace" (de Maupassant, 1907), Mme.
Loisel undergoes a dramatic change after she loses her friend's jewels:

The frightful debt must be paid. She would pay it. They dismissed the servant; they changed their rooms; they took an attic
under the roof.

She learned the rough work of the household, the odious labors
of the kitchen. She washed the dishes, wearing out her pink nails on
the greasy pots and the bottoms of the pans. (pars. 98–99)

(The sample References list on page 216 illustrates the correct bibliographic
format for this source.)

More information on the treatment of electronic sources can be found
on the APA website (http://www.apa.org).

THE APA REFERENCES LIST

The References list at the end of your essay must include detailed documentation of all the sources you have summarized, paraphrased, quoted, or
referred to in any way in your paper. This information enables your reader
to assess the extent of your research and to find every source you used. As

you read through the bulleted list below, check each item against the sample References list on page 216.

- Begin the References list on a new page.
- Centre the word "References" on the page, two spaces below your running head (the title of your paper in all upper-case letters, abbreviated if necessary). (*Note:* Use the automatic function of your word-processing program to create the running head.)
- Leave a double space between the title "References" and the first entry, and double-space all of the entries.
- Begin each entry at the left margin. If the entry runs more than a single line—and most do—indent the second and subsequent lines 1.25 cm. (Use the five-space tab that you use for paragraph indentation.) This format is called a "hanging indent" and can be set automatically in most word-processing packages.
- Arrange the entries alphabetically, beginning with the first word of the entry, which is often the author's surname. Do not number your entries.
- If there are several works by the same author, arrange by year of publication, earliest first.
- If no author is identified in your source, alphabetize by the first word in the title, ignoring *A*, *An*, and *The*. For example, *The Canadian Encyclopedia* would be listed under *C*, for *Canadian* (but would still retain "*The*" in the title).

Below you will find examples of References entries for the types of sources commonly used in research papers, including print, broadcast, and electronic sources.

Books, Encyclopedia, Reports, Government Publications

Here is the basic model for a book entry in a References list.

> Last name of author or editor, and Initials. (Year of publication). *Title of book: Subtitle of book*. Place of publication: Publisher.

Note the capitalization, punctuation, and order of the information. Leave one space between the initials in authors' names as well as after commas, colons, semicolons, and periods that separate the parts of the reference citation.

- Give each author's or editor's surname, a comma, and initials.
- In parentheses, give the year the book was published. This is usually found on the back of the title page (the copyright page); if it is not, use the latest copyright date.

- Capitalize only proper names and the first word of the title and first word of the subtitle, if any. *Italicize* the title and subtitle.
- For the place of publication, if several locations are listed, use the first one. Add the province or state if the city is not well known.
- Shorten the publisher's name. For example, Prentice Hall, Inc., is abbreviated to Prentice. Write out the names of associations, corporations, and university presses: e.g., University of Toronto Press.

Book with One or More Authors

Barlow, M. (2007). *Blue covenant: The global water crisis and the fight for the right to water.* Toronto: McClelland.

O'Neil, J., Holland, A., & Light, A. (2008). *Environmental values.* New York: Routledge.

(*Note:* List up to six authors or editors. Place an ampersand before the last author's name. If there are seven or more authors, use the Latin abbreviation *et al.* [meaning "and others"] in the position of the seventh author and do not use the ampersand.)

Book with More Than One Edition

Peak, K. J., & Glesnor, R. W. (2008). *Community policing and problem solving: Strategies and practices.* (5th ed.). Upper Saddle River, NJ: Prentice.

A Book with No Author

Webster's new college dictionary. (2008). (3rd ed.). Boston: Houghton.

Book with One or More Editors

Baum, J. R., Frese, M., & Baron, R. A. (Eds.). (2007). *The psychology of entrepreneurship.* Mahwah, NJ: Erlbaum.

Bhushan, B. (Ed.). (2007). *Springer handbook of nanotechnology* (2nd ed.). New York: Springer.

See authors' note above for information on citing a book with more than six editors.

Recent Edition of a Classic Work

Shakespeare, W. (1998). *The tempest.* Orgel, S. (Ed.). Oxford: Oxford University Press. (Original work published 1623)

Multivolume Work

Yates, A. (2001). *The trooper: Memoirs of Arthur Yates* (Vols. 1–2). Victoria, BC: Trafford.

Chapter, Article, Essay, Story, or Poem in an Edited Book or Collection

Mistry, R. (2001). Journey to Dharmsala. In C. Meyer & B. Meyer (Eds.), *The reader: Contemporary essays and writing strategies* (pp. 38–51). Toronto: Prentice.

Presentation at a Conference

Long, R. J. (2005, September). *Group-based pay, participatory practices, and workplace performance.* Paper presented at the Conference on the Evolving Workplace, Ottawa.

If the conference proceedings are numbered or published regularly, use the following format:

Toorman, E. A. (2002). Modelling of turbulent flow with suspended cohesive sediment. In J. C. Winterwerp & C. Kranenburg (Eds.), *Fine sediment dynamics in the marine environment: Proceedings in Marine Science 5,* 155–169.

Reference Book

Newland, T. E. (2004). Intelligence tests. In *Compton's encyclopedia & fact index* (Vol. 11, pp. 245–249). Chicago: Britannica.

Book Published by a Corporation (Company, Commission, Agency)

International Joint Commission. (2000). *Protection of the waters of the Great Lakes: Final report to the governments of Canada and the United States.* Ottawa: Author.

Government Document

If the author is not named, identify the government first, then the agency, then the date, title, city of publication, and publisher. Include specific information such as report or catalogue number after the title.

Alberta. Environmental Protection Commission. (2005). *A review of Alberta's environmental and emergency response capacity: Learning the lessons and building change.* Edmonton: Alberta Environment.

Canada. Statistics Canada. (2006). *How to cite Statistics Canada products* (Catalogue No. 12-591-XWE). Ottawa: Statistics Canada.

Brochure or Pamphlet

Council of Canadians. (2008, April). *Not counting Canadians: The security and prosperity partnership and public opinion* (brochure). Ottawa: Author.

Articles in Magazines, Newspapers, and Journals

Note the spacing, capitalization, punctuation, and order of the information required in a References entry for a magazine, newspaper, or journal.

- Each author's last name and initials
- Date of publication in parentheses and in year–month–day order; do not abbreviate the names of months: (2009, September 30) or (2010, January–February)
- Title of the article with no quotation marks and with an initial capital letter only; a capital letter is also required after the colon that introduces an article's subtitle
- Name of the magazine, newspaper, or journal as it appears on the front page, in italics, with capital letters for all major words; include *A, An,* or *The* if it is part of the official name of the publication: *The Globe and Mail*
- Volume number and issue number (if any); these are rare in magazines and newspapers, but often appear in journal entries and are expressed as, for example: *13*(6), which means Volume 13, Issue 6. (Note that the volume number is italicized.)
- Inclusive page numbers of the article

If the name of the city is not included in the name of a newspaper with which the reader might not be familiar, add the name of the city in square brackets—not in italics or underlined—after the name so that readers will know where it was published; for instance, *Comox Valley Record* [Campbell River].

Give the complete page span for each magazine and newspaper article in your References list. For magazines, if an article begins on page 14 and concludes on page 16, put a comma after the magazine's name (or after the volume and issue numbers, if these are included) and show this span: *Maclean's*, 14–16. (*Note:* Do not use "p." or "pp." when citing magazines or journals.) If the article begins, for example, on page 36, then skips to page 40 and concludes on page 41, give all three numbers: 36, 40, 41.

In a newspaper, the sections are usually numbered separately, so include the section identifier as well as the page number, which in this case is preceded by "p." or "pp.": *The Vancouver Sun,* pp. B1–B2. As in the case of magazines, if the article begins on one page and is continued on another page or pages, give all of the page numbers: pp. C1, C3, C6, C9–C11.

Article in a Monthly/Seasonal Magazine

Wood, C. (2008, October/November). The business of saving the earth. *The Walrus,* 37–45.

Article in a Weekly Magazine

Campbell, C. (2009, February 9). The vanishing middle ground. *Maclean's,* 38–40, 42.

Article in a Daily Newspaper

Honderich, J. (2009, February 1). All the news that's fit to fund. *Toronto Star,* pp. IN1, IN5.

Article in a Scholarly Journal

Matzo, M. (2008, July). The universal nursing obligation: All gerontological care is palliative care. *Journal of Gerontological Nursing, 34*(7), 1, 3–4.

Danes, S. M., Lee, J., Stafford, K., & Heck, R. K. Z. (2008, September). The effects of ethnicity, families and culture on entrepreneurial experience: An extension of sustainable family business theory. *Journal of Developmental Entrepreneurship, 13,* 229–268.

List up to seven authors. Place an ampersand before the last author's name, as shown in the second entry directly above. If there are eight or more authors, give the names of the first six authors, insert three ellipsis points (. . .), and add the last author's name.

If each issue of a journal begins with page 1, include the issue number. If the journal is paged continuously throughout the year, do not include the issue number.

No Author Named in Source

Clear as glass; warm as toast. (2009, Summer). *Yukon, North of Ordinary,* 38.

Ottawa recalls sensitive data. (2009, February 16). *Toronto Star*, p. A2.

Carbon credit transfer. (2009). *Alternatives Journal, 35*(2), 5.

Published Review: Books, Plays, Films, Etc.

Bland, J. (2008, October/November). [Review of the book *The $12 million stuffed shark: The curious economics of contemporary art*, by D. Thompson]. *The Walrus*, 94.

Dixon, G. (2009, March 14). Mash-up doc argues that creativity begins where copyright ends [Review of the film *RiP: A remix manifesto*]. *The Globe and Mail*, p. R11.

Published Interview

Radwanski, A. (2009, March 21). Where angels fear to tread [Interview with Patrick Monahan]. *The Globe and Mail*, p. M3.

Unpublished Personal Interview

Personal interviews are not included in the References list. Instead, use a parenthetical citation in the body of your essay:

(A. Breen, personal interview, February 12, 2010)

Personal Communications

As in the case of personal interviews, memos, letters, telephone conversations, and e-mail messages from non-archived sources are not included in the References list. Instead, use a parenthetical citation in the body of your essay. Never provide your source's e-mail address or telephone number.

(B. Green, personal communication, February 2, 2009)

Audiovisual Sources
Television/Radio Broadcast

Costello, E. (Writer/host). (2009). Elton John [Television series episode]. In J. Jacobs (Executive producer), *Spectacle: Elvis Costello with . . .* Toronto: CTV.

Anniko, T. (Executive producer). (2008). *Monsoon House* [Radio series]. Toronto: CBC.

Motion Picture, Music Recording, Video

Jaiko, C. (Producer), & Barczewska, A. (Writer/director). (2005). *A child unlike any other* [Motion picture]. Montreal: National Film Board.

Nickelback. (2009). *Dark horse* [CD]. New York: Road Runner Records.

Delmar's community health nursing: A case study. (2003). [CD]. Clifton Park, NJ: Delmar.

Ward, Al. (2009). *Photoshop for right-brainers: The art of photo manipulation* [DVD]. San Francisco: Sybex.

ELECTRONIC SOURCES

The rules for citing APA electronic sources are essentially the same as for print and broadcast sources. The reference should provide enough information to enable a reader to locate the source quickly—author, date, title, publisher or sponsor of the site, the date you retrieved the material from the Internet source, and the URL (uniform resource locator) or a DOI (digital object identifier).

The URL is an addressing system that links you to a host server and identifies the path to a specific file location. The DOI is an added, unique code. If a DOI is listed in a publication and the link is not working, you will be directed to a "DOI resolver" to access the material. This practice ensures that the document is always available, even if there are changes to a host server or file location. If a document has a DOI, it is the only address that you need to use. For items accessed through library subscription databases, you use the database name instead of the URL.

Retrieval dates are not necessary for electronic sources.

Consistency in capitalization, punctuation, and the order of the information are important when you cite electronic sources. Here are a few guidelines:

- Do not use a hyphen to divide a URL over two lines; if you do, you will make the URL invalid.
- URL and DOI address strings can be long and prone to mistakes if retyped. Copy and paste for best results.
- Download and print online material so that you can verify it if, at a later date, it is revised, unavailable, or inaccessible.

Online Book from a Library Subscription Database

Kay, M. (2008). *Practical hydraulics.* (2nd ed.). Retrieved from NetLibrary database.

Online Book from a Public Internet Site

Canada. Health Canada. (2005). *Regulation and beyond: Progress on Health Canada's therapeutics access strategy*. Retrieved from http://www.hc-sc.gc.ca/hcs-sss/pubs/pharma/2005-therap-strateg/index-eng.php

Wollstonecraft, M. (1792). *A vindication of the rights of women*. Retrieved from http://www.bartleby.com/144

Chapter, Essay, Story, or Poem in an Online Book

de Maupassant, G. de (1907). The necklace. In B. Matthews (Ed.), *The short story: Specimens illustrating its development*. Retrieved from http://www.bartleby.com/195

Mallett, D. (2006). Sampling and weighting. In R. Grover & M. Vriens (Eds.), *The handbook of marketing research: Uses, misuses and future advance*s (pp. 159–177). Retrieved from http://books.google.ca/books?id=RymGgxN3zD4C&printsec=frontcover&source=gbs_summary_r&cad=0#PPA177,M1

Online Encyclopedia, Dictionary

Falco, C. M. (2009). Use of optics by Renaissance artists. In *AccessScience@McGraw-Hill Online*. doi: 10.1036/1097-8542.YB084340

Canadian literature. (2009). In *Encyclopaedia Britannica*. Retrieved from Encyclopaedia Britannica Online database.

Capricious. (2009). In *Merriam-Webster online dictionary*. Retrieved from http://www.merriam-webster.com/dictionary/

Journal Article from a Library Subscription Database

Engardio, P., Hall, K., Rowley, I., Welch, D., & Balfour, F. (2009, February 23). The electric car battery war. *BusinessWeek*, 52. Retrieved from Academic Search Complete database.

Journal Article from a Public Internet Journal

Herman, D. (2009, Spring/Summer). Wonderland. *Rhythm*. Retrieved from http://rhythmpoetrymagazine.english.dal.ca/i2v2/poet10.html

Chen, G. K., Marjoram, P., & Wall, J. D. (2009). Fast and flexible simulation of DNA sequence data. *Genome Research*, *19*, 136–142. doi:10.1101/gr.083634.108

Newspaper Article from a Public Internet Site

Brooymans, H. (2009, March 31). Duck death toll triples at Alberta oilsands pond. *Edmonton Journal*. Retrieved from http://www.edmontonjournal.com

Online News Service Article

CTV News Services. (2009, May 6). *Ontario set to allow medication vending machines*. Retrieved from http://news.sympatico.msn.ctv.ca

Online Image

Carr, E. (1935). *A rushing sea of undergrowth*. Retrieved from www.virtualmuseum.ca/Exhibitions/EmilyCarr

Online Course Materials

Madar, J., & Dulat, M. (2007). *Lecture: Artificial intelligence and robotics: An exploration* [PowerPoint slides]. Capilano University. OpenCourseWare project. Retrieved from http://ocw.capcollege.bc .ca/computing-science/comp-106-programming-with-robots/COMP106-Course-Files/lectures/18AI-robotics.pdf

Wurfel, Marlene. (n.d.). *Canadian writers: Alice Munro* [Course materials]. Athabasca University. Retrieved from http://www.athabascau.ca/writers/munro.html

Personal Website

Atwood, M. (n.d.). *The rocky road to paper heaven*. Retrieved from http://www.owtoad.com

Television Show (Episode of a Continuing Series)

Thompson, J. (Writer/director). (2008). Shock wave [Television series episode]. In B. Hamilton (Executive producer), *Doc zone* [Television podcast]. Retrieved from http://www.cbc.ca/documentaries/doczone

Audio Podcast

> Campbell, G. (2008, November 8). *Building a strong economic future.*
>   [Audio podcast]. Retrieved from http://www.mediaroom.gov.bc.ca/
>   podcasts/Premier_audio_podcasts.xml

Blog, Social Network Post

Video or message posts on social network sites include the date of the posting. Titles are not italicized. Some instructors do not accept these sources as valid or reliable, so be sure to check with your instructor before including them in your work.

> Utko, J. (2009, February). Can design save the newspaper? [Video file].
>   Retrieved from http://www.youtube.com/watch?v=zHuH8P_Vqc0

> Young drivers against new Ontario laws. (n.d). [Discussion group]. Retrieved
>   from http://www.facebook.com/group.php?gid=35271482979

> Edward. (2009, January 9). Re: Where do you stand on illegal movie
>   downloading? [Blog]. Retrieved from http://www.cbc.ca/q/blog

SAMPLE APA REFERENCES LIST

Entries in a References list are arranged alphabetically according to the first word in the entry and are not numbered. On the next page you will find a sample References list made up of different kinds of sources.

TITLE OF PAPER   29

References

Article in a newspaper

Canada to toughen auto-emissions rules. (2002, April 5). *The Wall Street Journal*, p. A6.

Selection from an online anthology

de Maupassant, G. (1907). The necklace. In B. Matthews (Ed.). *The short story: Specimens illustrating its development.* Retrieved from http://www.bartleby.com/195/20/html

Article in an online periodical

Greene, B. (2009, April 20). Questions, not answers, make science the ultimate adventure. *Wired Magazine.* Retrieved from http://www.wired.com/culture/culturereviews/magazine/17-05/st_essay

Book by three authors

France, H., Rodriguez, M., & Hett, G. (2004). *Diversity, culture and counselling: A Canadian perspective.* Calgary: Detselig.

Article in a scholarly journal

Helson, R., & Pals, J. (2000). Creative potential, creative achievement, and personal growth. *Journal of Personality, 68*(2)*,* 39–44.

Selection from a print anthology

Mistry, R. (2001). Journey to Dharmsala. In C. Meyer & B. Meyer (Eds.), *The reader: Contemporary essays and writing strategies* (pp. 38–51). Toronto: Prentice.

Movie

Moore, M. (Writer, producer, director). (2002). *Bowling for Columbine* [Motion picture]. United States: United Artists, Alliance Atlantis, and Dog Eat Dog Films.

Book by one author

Patterson, K. (2000). *The water in between: A journey at sea.* Toronto: Vintage Canada.

Article in a monthly magazine

Sreenivasan, A. (2002, February). Keeping up with the cones. *Natural History,* 40–46.

Online government publication

Statistics Canada. (2002, October 11). *Infant mortality rates.* Retrieved from http://www.statcan.ca/english/Pgdb/health21.htm

Magazine article from an online library subscription database

Wahl, A. (2005, February 28). Emission impossible. *Canadian Business, 24.* Retrieved from eLibrary Canada database.

Exercise 13.3

For each of the following quotations, write a short paragraph in which you use all or a portion of the quotation and credit it in an APA-style parenthetical reference. Be sure to use capital letters as required and to punctuate titles correctly.

1. From a book entitled Getting it done: the transforming power of self-discipline by Andrew J. Dubrin, published by Pacesetter Books in Princeton in 1995. This sentence appears on page 182: "Stress usually stems from your interpretation and perception of an event, not from the event itself."

2. From a journal article by Linda A. White that appeared on pages 385 to 405 of Canadian Public Policy, a journal with continuous paging: "If a clear connection exists between the presence of child care and high levels of women's labour market participation, that would provide good reasons for governments and employers to regard child care as part of an active labour market policy." White's article is entitled Child Care, Women's Labour Market Participation and Labour Market Policy Effectiveness in Canada. The quotation appears on page 389 of the fourth issue of the 27th volume, published in 2001.

3. From the article entitled "Stress, Definition of Stress, Stressor, What is Stress? Eustress?" on the American Institute of Stress website, found at http://www.stress.org: "Increased stress results in increased productivity—up to a point." The article has no date of publication.

4. From a newspaper article that appeared on page A2 in the March 30, 2005, issue of The Vancouver Sun, written by Nancy Cleeland, found on the eLibrary Canada database at your school library. The article is entitled As jobs heat up, workers' hearts take a beating. "For years, occupational health researchers have struggled to come up with formulas for measuring job stress and determining its effect on health."

5. During the February 3, 2009, CBC broadcast of the Mercer Report, Rick Mercer says, "According to a recent Dominion Institute poll, a majority of Canadians have no idea how Parliament works." The segment was entitled Everything you wanted to know about Canada but were afraid to ask. You watched the broadcast on *YouTube* at http://www.youtube.com/watch?v=yi1yhp-_x7A

6. From an e-mail message on the subject of time management from your friend, Janet Ford, on June 5, 2009: "Using a daily planner and checking e-mail only once a day are two ways I've found to manage my stress during the school year."

Exercise 13.4

Prepare a References list for the sources listed in Exercise 13.3.

14

Formatting a Research Paper

The appearance of your paper makes an impression on your reader. A correctly formatted paper reflects the care and attention to detail that instructors value in students' work.

Ask your instructor if he or she has any special requirements for the format of your research assignment. If so, follow them carefully. Otherwise, follow the guidelines in this chapter to prepare your paper for submission.

Basic Formatting Guidelines

PAPER

Compose your final draft on 22 × 28 cm (8.5 × 11 inch) white bond paper. Be sure to use a fresh cartridge in your printer. If your instructor will accept a handwritten document, make sure it adheres to all of the guidelines that follow, including those regarding ink colour, margins, and spacing. Print out or write your research paper on *one side* of the paper only.

Fasten your paper together with a paper clip or a single staple in the upper left-hand corner. Unless your instructor specifically requests, don't bother with plastic or paper covers; most teachers find it annoying to disentangle your essay for marking.

PRINTING/TYPING

Choose a standard, easily readable typeface, such as Times New Roman, in a 12-point font. Use black ink (or dark blue, if you are writing by hand).

SPACING AND MARGINS

Unless you are instructed otherwise, double-space throughout your essay, including quotations and the Works Cited list or References. In a hand-written paper, write on every other line of a ruled sheet of white paper.

Adequate white space on your pages makes your paper more attractive and easier to read. It also allows room for instructors' comments. Leave margins of 2.5 cm at the top, bottom, and both sides of your paper. If you are using a word processor, click on the "align left" formatting command.

Indent the first line of every paragraph five spaces or 1.25 cm; use the tab default setting in your word-processing program. Indent all lines of a block quotation 10 spaces or 2.5 cm from the left margin.

Always keep a copy of your paper for your files!

Formatting an MLA-Style Research Paper

TITLE PAGE

Do not prepare a separate title page unless your instructor requires it. Instead, at the top of the left margin of the first page of your essay, on separate lines, type your name, your instructor's name, the course number, and the date. Leave a double space and centre the title of your essay. Capitalize main words (see Part 7, Section 7.19, page 511), but do not underline, italicize, or put quotation marks around your title (unless it contains the title of another author's work, which you should treat in the usual way).

HEADER AND PAGE NUMBERS

Number your pages consecutively throughout the paper, including the Works Cited list, in the upper right-hand corner, 1.25 cm from the top and 2.5 cm from the right edge of the page. Type your last name before the page number. Use a word processor to create a running head consisting of your last name, a single space, and the page number—no punctuation or *p*.

A sample first page of an MLA-style paper follows.

Remember, double-space your paper throughout unless instructed otherwise.

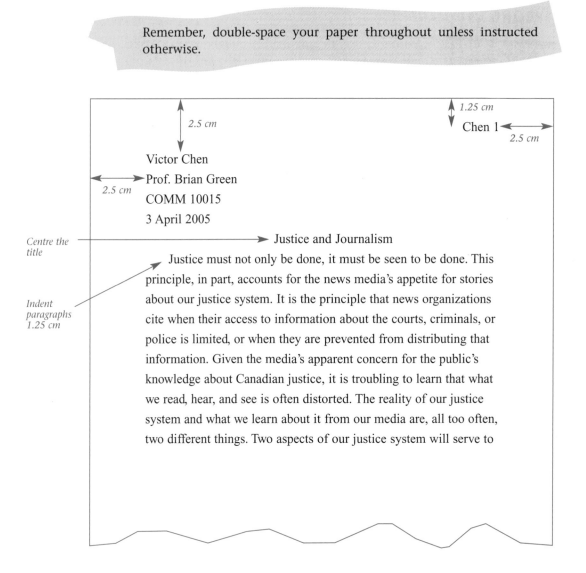

2.5 cm

1.25 cm

Chen 1

2.5 cm

Victor Chen

2.5 cm

Prof. Brian Green

COMM 10015

3 April 2005

Centre the title

Justice and Journalism

Indent paragraphs 1.25 cm

Justice must not only be done, it must be seen to be done. This principle, in part, accounts for the news media's appetite for stories about our justice system. It is the principle that news organizations cite when their access to information about the courts, criminals, or police is limited, or when they are prevented from distributing that information. Given the media's apparent concern for the public's knowledge about Canadian justice, it is troubling to learn that what we read, hear, and see is often distorted. The reality of our justice system and what we learn about it from our media are, all too often, two different things. Two aspects of our justice system will serve to

Formatting an APA-Style Research Paper

TITLE PAGE

In APA style, a research paper or essay requires a separate title page. On the title page, include a running head as follows: "Running head: NAME OF PAPER" and set it flush left; the page number goes flush right. Choose a concise title that identifies the subject of your paper, and then shorten it for the running head, if necessary. Capitalize main words, but don't underline, italicize, or put quotation marks around your title. Centre the title in the upper half of the page (quadruple-space it from the top of the page). If the title is more than one line, double-space between the lines.

After the title, centre your name, the name of your college or university, the name of the course you are preparing the paper for, the professor's name, and the date of submission. Double-space between each of these elements. A sample APA-style title page follows. The italicized words to the left of the page identify the components of the title page.

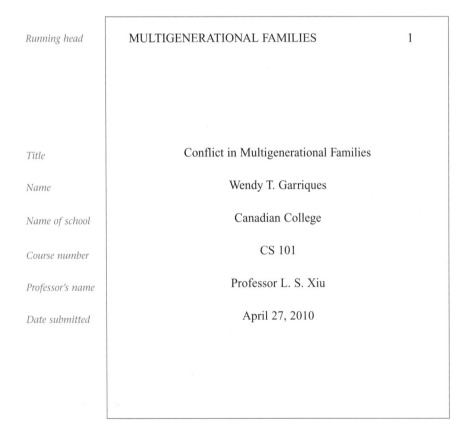

| *Running head* | MULTIGENERATIONAL FAMILIES | 1 |

Title — Conflict in Multigenerational Families

Name — Wendy T. Garriques

Name of school — Canadian College

Course number — CS 101

Professor's name — Professor L. S. Xiu

Date submitted — April 27, 2010

HEAD, PAGE NUMBERS, AND SPACING

Number your pages consecutively throughout the paper, beginning with the title page and ending with the last page of the References list. Using the automatic running head function of your word processor, key in the title and the page number. As on the title page, the title of your paper should appear in upper-case letters flush left, this time without the words "Running head," while the page number appears flush right. There is no punctuation or use of *p.*

Double-space between all lines of your paper, including the title page, abstract, headings (if any), pages of the text itself, quotations, and References list. Indent the first line of every paragraph 1.25 cm.

ABSTRACT

Some assignments require you to provide an abstract—a short summary of the contents of your whole paper. It should give the purpose of your paper and the key ideas; that is, it should give your reader a preview of your paper. An abstract is usually one paragraph long. It must be well organized and carefully written.

Type the abstract on a separate page that includes the running head and the page number (2). Centre the word "Abstract" a double space under the running head. Type the abstract paragraph itself in block format (without indentation).

FIRST PAGE OF TEXT

On page 3 (following the title page and abstract), centre the full title of your research paper (in upper- and lower-case letters). Double-space, and begin the text of your essay.

Projecting an Image

As well as presenting your understanding of the topic, a research paper demonstrates your writing skills and your ability to follow the specific requirements of documentation and format. Meeting your instructor's submission requirements is as important as any other aspect of the preparation of your paper. This may be the last stage of your writing task, but it is the first impression your reader will have of your work. Make it a good one!

Patterns of Development

To understand is to perceive patterns.
Sir Isaiah Berlin, 1909–1997

Introduction

In school and on the job, you will be required to write **nonfiction prose**—essays, papers, reports, summaries, and proposals that are based on verifiable, factual evidence. Traditionally, journalists, whose job it is to report events as objectively as possible, have relied on six questions to help them discover what they can say about an incident: *where, when, who, how, what,* and *why*. Each of these questions produces one or more answers that should be structured according to specific patterns of development. We will explore five of these patterns in this unit, together with three basic writing techniques that can be used as paragraph-level support for the main points of any subject.

1. To answer the questions *where, when, and who,* you describe, narrate, and provide examples. (See Chapter 15.) These questions do not call for specific structural patterns—we cannot offer you diagrams or blueprints that you could follow to produce answers to them. Description, narration, and example can be used alone or in combination to produce an essay or report, but more often they are used as paragraph-level strategies to provide supporting evidence in papers with broader purposes.

2. To answer the question *how,* you explain the process by which something is made or happened or works. The answer should follow a pattern called **process analysis**. (See Chapter 16.) It's almost impossible to explain a process without providing details of where and how it occurs and what equipment or personnel are involved (description), explaining the order in which the process takes place (narration), and adding examples of acceptable (and possibly unacceptable) outcomes.

3. Before you can answer the question *what,* you must first choose the angle or viewpoint of your subject that you want to explore in your paper. You have three main choices:

   • If you want to explain the kinds, or parts, or important features of your subject, you should frame your answer in a **classification/division** pattern (see Chapter 17).
   • If you want to explain the similarities or differences between your subject and something else, your answer should follow the pattern of **comparison** or **contrast** (see Chapter 18).
   • If you want to explain what caused some event or circumstance, or what the consequences were (or might be), you should organize your paper according to the pattern of **causal analysis** (see Chapter 19).

   As you develop the main points of any of these *what?* structures, you may find it useful to employ the three basic strategies discussed in Chapter 15: description, narration, and example.

4. To answer the question *why,* you need to develop an **argument**, and there are several ways you can structure your answer. There are two kinds of argumentation: one is intended to convince the reader that your opinion is valid and worthwhile; the other is intended to change the reader's beliefs or behaviour in some way. Fortunately, both kinds rely on the same patterns of development (see Chapter 20). The nature of the evidence you provide differs slightly, but again, description, narration, and example are strategies you can use to help build your case.

With the exception of Chapter 15, each chapter in this unit begins with a definition of a prose pattern, followed by some suggested practical applications. Next, we offer tips on how to structure your essay to follow the pattern discussed in the chapter. Finally, we provide two short essays to illustrate each pattern. We have annotated the first essay in each case, and we ask you to annotate the second in similar fashion.

When you have finished this unit, you should be able to decide which pattern of development to choose for an essay, research paper, or professional report so that your document provides your readers with a clearly structured presentation of the information they require.

Three Basic Strategies: Description, Narration, and Example

Description, narration, and example are basic to all writing. It would be difficult to write any essay or report without using at least one of these strategies. In this chapter, we use examples from essays in this book to illustrate what the three strategies are, why we use them, and how to write them.

Description

The goal of descriptive writing is to create a picture in words—to tell readers what something or someone looks or looked like. Effective description appeals not only to the reader's visual sense, but also to the senses of hearing, taste, smell, and touch. The more senses your description involves, the better your reader will be able to experience the person, object, or scene you are describing. For example, in "Stupid Jobs Are Good to Relax With" (see pages 346–50), Hal Niedzviecki creates a vivid picture of a concert hall during a Bruce Springsteen performance at which Niedzviecki was working as an usher:

> For an usher, danger takes many forms, including vomiting teens and the usher's nemesis: the disruptive patron. And yes, . . . there she was: well-dressed, blonde, drunk and doped up, swaying in her seat and . . . clapping. Clapping. In the middle of Springsteen's solo dirge about Pancho or Pedro or Luisa, she was clapping.
> Sweat beaded on my forehead. The worst was happening. She was in my section. Her clapping echoed through the hall, renowned for its acoustics. The Boss glared from the stage, his finger-picking folksiness no match for the

drunken rhythm of this fan. Then, miracle of miracles, the song ended. The woman slumped back into her seat. Bruce muttered something about how he didn't need a rhythm section. Placated by the adoring silence of the well-to-do, he launched into an even quieter song about an even more desperate migrant worker.

I lurked in the shadows, relaxed the grip I had on my flashlight (the usher's only weapon). Springsteen crooned. His guitar twanged. . . . The woman roused herself from her slumber. She leaned forward in her seat, as if suddenly appreciating the import of her hero's message. I wiped the sweat off my brow, relieved. But slowly, almost imperceptibly, she brought her arms up above her head. I stared, disbelieving. Her hands waved around in the air until . . . boom! Another song ruined, New York record execs and L.A. journalists distracted from their calculations of Bruce's net worth, the faint cry of someone calling, "Usher! Do something!"

The descriptive details in this excerpt recreate an experience for the reader: we see the darkened concert hall and the drunken fan; we hear the woman clapping loudly; we sense the singer's frustration; and we feel the tension the usher feels, knowing he is expected to put a stop to the woman's disruptive behaviour.

Things—inanimate objects—can also be described in convincing detail. Consider the following passage and see if you can figure out what common substance David Bodanis is describing:

To keep the glop from drying out, a mixture including glycerine glycol—related to the most common car anti-freeze ingredient—is whipped in with the chalk and water, and to give *that* concoction a bit of substance, . . . a large helping is added of gummy molecules from the seaweed *Chondrus crispus*. This seaweed ooze spreads in among the chalk, paint and anti-freeze, then stretches itself in all directions to hold the mass together. A bit of paraffin oil (the fuel that flickers in camping lamps) is pumped in with it to help the moss ooze keep the whole substance smooth. . . .

The only problem is that by itself this ingredient tastes, well, too like detergent. It's horribly bitter and harsh. . . . It's to get around that gustatory discomfort that the manufacturers put in the ingredient they tout perhaps the most of all. This is the flavoring, and it has to be strong. Double rectified peppermint oil is used—a flavorer so powerful that chemists know better than to sniff it in the raw state in the laboratory.

Did you guess that this disgusting-sounding substance is toothpaste? (See Bodanis's essay on pages 308–10.)

TIPS ON WRITING DESCRIPTION

1. Decide whether your description should be purely factual and objective, or if you want to convey an emotional attitude along with the facts. Select your words according to your purpose. For example, consider the difference between these two sentences:

   The woman sat back in her seat.
   The woman slumped back into her seat.

   The verb *sat* is objective; the verb *slumped* communicates the writer's attitude toward the woman as well as the way she was sitting.

2. Select the most important physical details. You cannot describe every detail about a topic without losing your focus and that of your reader.

3. Always choose a specific, concrete word in favour of an abstract, general one. Readers can't "see" an abstraction, so you must choose words that they *can* visualize. If you try to create a mental image of the word "substance," you'll see why Bodanis chose the word "glop" instead.

Exercise 15.1

In pairs, select a site or a building or a space that is associated with your career. Then, working alone, write a paragraph describing its physical appearance. When you have finished, exchange papers with your partner and critique each other's descriptions. What similarities do you find in your paragraphs? What differences? What accounts for these similarities and differences?

Finally, highlight three or four descriptive details in each paragraph that you agree would help a reader visualize your topic.

Narration

Narration is story-telling, and we all love stories that are well told and appropriate for the occasion. A good story tells a sequence of events in a way that captures the reader's interest and imagination. In the kinds of writing most often demanded in school and professional circumstances, narration often takes the form of an anecdote that exemplifies and adds an emotional element to an abstract concept. Providing a short, illustrative story is often a good way to develop a key idea or to introduce an essay, as in the following example, in which Maria Amuchastegui uses a story to draw the reader into her essay on one of the problems facing Canada's migrant agricultural workers (you can read the full essay on pages 351–58):

> It was the Thursday before Easter that Henk Sikking Jr. got the doctor's call. The 28-year-old tulip farmer was getting ready to take his crew of Mexican migrant workers grocery shopping. The workers live on his property and get around with bicycles but rely on their boss to take them on major shopping trips. He had arranged for a bus to take the workers into town.
>
> Sikking's best worker, Hermelindo Gutiérrez, had gone to see the doctor earlier in the week, complaining of swollen feet and ankles. Sikking assumed that Gutiérrez had injured himself while driving one of the carts used to navigate the sprawling complex of greenhouses. The doctor was blunt. The blood work revealed that both of Gutiérrez's kidneys had failed. If Gutiérrez did not go to the hospital, he was going to die.

Now that the writer has your attention, she'll go on to develop her argument, and she will use other events and details of Gutiérrez's experience as support for her key ideas.

TIPS ON WRITING NARRATION

1. Decide on your purpose. Every narrative you use should contribute to your thesis by developing one of your main ideas, or should serve as an attention-getter or a memorable conclusion.
2. Select events that are clearly and directly related to your thesis. Your story should be long enough to accomplish its purpose, whether that is to illustrate a main point or to add a personal touch to your argument, but not so long that it diverts the reader from the message of your essay.
3. Arrange the events of the story in an effective order. Usually, a story unfolds in chronological (time) order: first this happened, then this, and finally that. This is the order in which Amuchastegui lays out Hermelindo Gutiérrez's story for her readers. But sometimes a narrative is more effective if the writer begins at the end and then goes back to tell how the story began. Kevin Myers' essay, "The Country the World Forgot—Again," on pages 334–36, is an example of this narrative structure, which is called **flashback**. There are other ways to tell a story effectively: think of movies you've seen in which the narrative line begins at the beginning, or in the middle, or close to the end of the series of events.

Exercise 15.2

With a partner, identify a movie you have both seen and remember clearly. It's not important that you both liked it; in fact, you may get better results if you disagree on the movie's merits. Working independently, write a paragraph narrating the plot of that movie. Include important events, not every detail of the story. This task is not as easy as it sounds: you'd be wise to begin with an outline.

When you have finished, exchange papers and critique each other's work. How closely do your versions of the story resemble each other? Did you both tell the story in the same order? Does the order you chose reflect the order of the film, or did you realign events, if necessary, so that you could discuss them chronologically? What do you think might account for any differences between your versions of the movie's plot?

Example

An example, or a series of examples, is used to give concrete form to abstract ideas. In "What I Have Lived For" (page 6), Bertrand Russell writes that he "feels unbearable pity for the suffering of mankind." We don't know what he means by the suffering of mankind until he provides examples: "Children in famine, victims tortured by oppressors, helpless old people a hated burden to their sons, and the whole world of loneliness, poverty, and pain make a mockery of what human life should be." In a single sentence, Russell gives us three concrete examples that *show* us what he means by human suffering. If he had not provided us with examples, most of us would have read on, no better informed, or perhaps filled in the conceptual blank with our own favourite examples of human suffering and thus missed Russell's point.

Examples can be taken from research sources, personal experience, or the experience of others. You can choose to use a number of examples to support an idea, as Richard Lederer does in his essay on pages 285–87, "How I Write":

For stimulation, Honoré de Balzac wrote in a monk's costume and drank at least twenty cups of coffee a day, eventually dying of caffeine poisoning. As his vision failed, James Joyce took to wearing a milkman's uniform when he wrote, believing that its whiteness caught the sunlight and reflected it onto his pages. Victor Hugo went to the opposite lengths to ensure his daily output of words on paper. He gave all his clothes to his servant with orders that they be returned only after he had finished his day's quota.

Or you can choose to develop one example in detail (called an **illustration**), as Gabor Maté does in the following paragraph:

Carl, a 36-year-old native, was banished from one foster home after another, had dishwashing liquid poured down his throat for using foul language at age 5, and was tied to a chair in a dark room to control his hyperactivity. When angry at himself—as he was recently, for using cocaine—he gouges his foot with a knife as punishment. His facial expression was that of a terrorized urchin. . . .

Carl's story serves to humanize Maté's factual account of drug addiction and its causes in "Embraced by the Needle" (see pages 320–22).

TIPS ON USING EXAMPLES

1. Be sure that any example you use is representative of your topic. Choose typical examples, not rare or extraordinary ones. If your examples are so wacky that readers cannot relate to them, they will dismiss your argument or discussion.
2. Remember that examples should *illustrate,* not *be,* the point. Your job as the writer is to explain the point to your readers in your own words, using credible examples as support.
3. Include only examples that directly and effectively support your main ideas. Too many or too-long examples will weaken rather than strengthen your argument. Readers need the highlights, not the whole catalogue.

Exercise 15.3

Using examples as your developmental strategy, write a paragraph of about 150 words on the following topic: "Movies (*or* TV shows/popular music/fashion) reveal significant insights into _____ culture. (Fill in the blank by applying one of the limiting factors to make the general term *culture* more specific: *kind* (e.g., *teen*), *time* (e.g., *1970s*), *place* (e.g., *Quebec*).

Putting Description, Narration, and Example to Use

To see how these three basic strategies can be used together to convey a thesis, read the essay on the next page. We have annotated the essay for you; that is, we have indicated in the right margin where the writer uses description, narration, and example to help develop her ideas.

LOOKING BOTH WAYS

Amanda van der Heiden

1   I'm perched on a swing, moving my legs forward and back, forward and back, moving my body forward and back, forward and back. I won't gain any ground. I won't accomplish anything. But I'm swinging and it's relaxing. I love the feeling of jumping off the swing, flinging myself into the air. I look forward to the brief moment of freefall before I land hard on the ground. Sometimes, though, I drag my feet and kick up stones. I slow down only a little at a time and jump only when I know it is finally safe.

Introduction developed by descriptive details

Topic sentence

2   We do a lot of things to ensure safety. We wear seatbelts and drive cars with airbags. We learn to ride our bikes with training wheels and we wear helmets and elbow-pads. We hire health and safety inspectors and spend money to keep everything running properly. We post signs along busy highways, reminding us to make safe choices. We volunteer to wear reflective clothing and carry stop signs so others get home in safety.

Paragraph 2 developed by examples

3   I'm thinking about crossing guards as I breeze through the air on my swing. I have never really liked them. They come to the street corners, advertising their good works with their orange vests and big, bold stop signs. There are two crosswalks on my way home from school, and both are well equipped with crossing guards and Children Crossing signs. The intersection nearest my house is a four-way stop and it has sixteen of these signs—one double-sided sign on each side of each street. Excessive, I know.

Topic sentence

Paragraph 3 developed by descriptive details

4   Each day, as I near the first intersection, a three-way stop, I do my best to avoid eye contact with the crossing guard. I suppose I think that if we don't make eye contact, I can cross the street on my own. Each day this proves to be faulty logic. I wait at the corner for the orange-clad man to walk out into the middle of the street and put the world on hold as I make my way across. I am seventeen years old and I should be able to make it safely on my own.

Paragraph 4 introduces the narrative portion of the essay

5   I always dare myself to cross the street on my own before I reach the designated crosswalk. One day I will do it. I will look the crossing guard in the eye and smile. And then I will look both ways and make my way to the other side. I always wonder if he would consider that a failure, a safety breach, a reason to call the police. To be sure, I would survive the incident, but maybe I would feel just a little bit bad inside. He is probably a lonely old man whose only joy is helping children and young people avoid danger.

Topic sentence

6   But I continue my daily walk, all the while making sure I avoid any cracks in the sidewalk. I wouldn't want to fall and break my mother's back or cause her some other harm. The sidewalk ends at the next intersection and again I awkwardly wait for the woman with the sign to signal safety. I could ask her to fulfill her duties one more time, allowing me to walk on the sidewalk, but I would just have to cross the street again. Instead, I crush the hard work of my neighbours as I trample their immaculate lawns.

Paragraph 6 developed by descriptive details

Transition

Climax of the story

7   Today, though, was a little bit different. Today I watched a little boy race across a busy street to reach his friends who were waiting on the other side. A large green van was barreling down the road and its tires squealed loudly, stopping just in time. I wonder about the boy. Did he realize how horrible that could have been? Or would he laugh it off with his friends? Would he tell his parents? I think about what might have been racing through the mind of the driver. Will he tell his wife? Will he remind his children about the importance of crossing guards and looking both ways? Will he drive more cautiously?

Narrator reflects on how a near-accident affects others.

8   The streets are full of cars and they can go fast—faster than they can stop. The sidewalks are full of children who are laughing and talking with their friends. Often, neither party pays a lot of attention or realizes the risks. Drivers do not always focus on the road, and neither do children.

Topic sentence

Summary

9   We value safety, but we easily forget about it too. So today as I swing through the air, I am not going to jump, enjoy the freefall, or land hard. I am going to kick up the stones as I slow to a stop. And I might just wait there for a moment longer. As I walk home, I think I will look the crossing guard in the eye and smile. And then I will wait patiently until he summons me to cross. I will be his best customer and tell him that I appreciate what he is doing, even thank him for being a reminder of safety.

Memorable statement

Questions for Discussion

1. What is the meaning of the title? How does it prepare the reader for the essay?
2. In your own words, state the thesis of this essay.
3. How does the first paragraph contribute to the thesis of this essay?
4. How does the conclusion contribute to the unity of the piece?

Suggestions for Writing

1. From the point of view of the little boy, write a paragraph describing the incident that occurs in paragraph 7.
2. From the point of view of the truck driver, write a paragraph narrating the story of the incident that occurs in paragraph 7.
3. From the point of view of the crossing guard, write a paragraph using the incident in paragraph 7 as an illustration of your topic sentence.
4. Using the first person and the present tense, as the writer of "Looking Both Ways" has done, write a short essay that uses description, narration, and example to convey a clear impression of one of the following experiences:

a. the daily trip you take from home to school
b. the time from your arrival at school to the end of your first class
c. an embarrassing (or surprising/joyful/unexpected) incident during your day

When you've completed your essay, exchange papers with a partner and find the descriptive, narrative, and example passages your partner has used to develop his or her main points. Note them in the margin. Then exchange papers again and see if your partner has correctly identified your methods of development. Discuss any differences between your intentions and your partner's perceptions.

5. Write a short essay in which you respond to one of the aphorisms that appear on the openers for Part 1 (page 7) and Part 2 (page 65). Leave a wide margin (about 5 cm) on the left side of your pages. Use at least one description, one narration, and one paragraph developed by example or illustration to support your main points. When you have finished your essay, exchange papers with a partner. Using the outline format on page 60, identify in the margin the main parts of your partner's essay. Then identify the kind of support used to develop each paragraph.

Finally, exchange papers once more and see if your partner has been able to identify the main parts of your essay and the kind of development you used in each paragraph.

16

Process Analysis

Like narration, **process analysis** explains events that follow one another in time. There are two kinds of process analysis: one instructs or directs the reader how to perform a task; the other informs the reader how something is done, is made, or works.

1. **Instructional/directional process:** When you explain how to get from the registrar's office to the resource centre, how to start a wet motor, how to make perfect pastry, or any other how-to topic, your purpose is to enable your readers to perform the process themselves. Giving instructions or directions is often done in point form: think of a recipe, for example, or the instructions that come with a child's toy, a barbecue, or a piece of furniture from Ikea. Instructions are usually written in the second person (*you*) and include commands (e.g., "Allow to dry for 10 minutes," "Leave yourself time to revise").

2. **Informational process:** This type of process analysis describes how something is done, or is made, or works. In explaining how a hamburger gets from the farm to McDonald's, how snowflakes form, or how the stock market operates, you do not expect your readers to be able to reproduce the process. Your purpose is simply to inform them about it.

Process analysis is usually written in the third person (e.g., "Wise writers leave plenty of time for revision") and often includes the passive voice ("When the paper has been proofread, it is ready for submission"). The tone of your essay, and the amount and kind of detail you include, will vary depending on your audience and purpose.

Whether you are writing instructions or providing details about a process, keep your language simple and clear. Remember that your readers probably do not share your expertise on the subject (if they did, they wouldn't be reading your explanation). If you use highly technical language or skip over steps that are obvious only to an expert, you will confuse or mislead your readers.

Consider the following instructions, written for inexperienced anglers who want to learn how to cast a fly:

> To execute the cast, play out about 10 metres of fly line in front of you. Ensure that there is no slack in the line, and begin your back cast. As the rod tip reaches about one o'clock, stop the backward motion and begin a crisp forward motion, loading the rod. On the back cast, the line must straighten behind you, parallel to the ground, before the forward motion begins.
>
> The quick forward thrust, stopping abruptly at about ten o'clock, will result in an aerodynamic loop that will travel the length of the fly line, straightening the line in front of you, and resulting in the perfect cast.

These directions break the process of fly-casting down into chronologically arranged steps, but the writer has forgotten the most basic rule of good writing: Remember the reader. Only someone who already knows what the writer is talking about would be able to follow these instructions.

An effective process analysis paper takes into account the readers' familiarity—or lack of it—with the process, their experience, and their level of vocabulary. Finally, it communicates the steps of the process in a way that holds the readers' interest.

One of the most challenging aspects of process analysis is making sure that you have included all the necessary steps. Only an expert, someone who knows what the result should look like, can leave out a step or two, or combine steps, or take shortcuts. As you write, try to imagine yourself in the reader's position: someone with little or no experience who is reading the instructions or description for the first time.

Tips on Writing Process Analysis Papers

1. Plan carefully. Prepare an outline listing all the steps of the process. Include everything that your readers need to know, and use language they can understand. Now put the steps in chronological or logical order. (See pages 44–46 for definitions and examples.) Be prepared to revise your list several times before your steps are arranged correctly. Too much detail can be as confusing as too little, so if there are many small steps, group them into a number of more easily manageable stages.
2. Write the introduction. State your purpose, and include any background information or theory (for example, identify any necessary equipment).
3. Write a thesis statement that makes it clear what your readers are about to learn. If it is appropriate, include a preview of the major steps you

will describe. The examples of thesis statements below illustrate the three ways you can preview main steps: as nouns, phrases, or clauses.

The steps involved in becoming a winning tennis player can be summed up in four words: basics, practice, concentration, and attitude. (nouns)

Getting married is a process that involves fulfilling arcane legal requirements, enduring an official ceremony, and surviving the abuse of one's in-laws. (phrases)

According to the Niagara Culinary Institute, creating a signature dish is a process that involves selecting fresh, local ingredients; preparing them to bring out the best of their flavours in combination; and presenting the finished product with imagination and flair. (clauses)

4. Develop each step in a paragraph. Be sure to use transitions both within paragraphs and between paragraphs. Transitions help your reader follow the sequence of the process; they also make your writing easier to read. Review the list of transition techniques on pages 102–4 before you begin your essay.

5. Avoid shifts in person. Inexperienced writers often start with the third person and then switch to *you* and give commands. If you focus on your purpose—either to instruct or to inform—as you write, you will be less likely to use pronouns inconsistently.

6. Write the conclusion. Sometimes a brief summary is useful, especially if the process is a complex one. Alternatively, you could end your paper with an evaluation of the results, or remind your readers of the importance or usefulness of the process.

7. When revising, put yourself in the position of someone who knows nothing about the process and see if you can follow the instructions or description with ease. Have you included all the steps or stages? Have you defined any technical terms? Better yet, ask someone who really is a novice to read your paper and try to follow your directions or understand your description.

The essays that follow illustrate the two kinds of process analysis.

HOW TO PLAY WINNING TENNIS

Brian Green

Attention-getter (establishes writer's credentials)

1   As a tennis instructor for the past three summers, I have watched many people waste their money on hi-tech racquets, designer outfits, and professional lessons, and then complain loudly that in spite of all the expense they

still can't play the game. Unfortunately for them, a decent backhand is one thing that money can't buy. No matter what level of player you are or what level you wish to be, there are four steps to achieving the goal of winning tennis. They can be summed up in four words: basics, practice, concentration, and attitude.

Thesis statement

2   All sports may be reduced to a few basic skills, which, if learned properly at the outset and drilled until they are instinctive, lead to success. Tennis is no exception; however, few people seem willing to spend the time needed to master the basics. Having been shown the proper grip and swing for a forehand, backhand, and serve, my students seem to feel they can qualify for Wimbledon. The basics are not learned that easily. Many tennis schools are now using a system developed in Spain that helps new players establish the correct stroke. For the first month of lessons, they aren't allowed to use a tennis ball. For that first month, correct positioning, proper swing, footwork, and technique are drilled without any of the distractions of keeping score, winning or losing, or chasing errant balls. That's how important the basics are to winning tennis.

Topic sentence

First step (developed by examples)

Paragraph conclusion

Transition phrase and topic sentence

3   Having acquired the basics, a beginning player must now practise and practise and practise to remember and refine those important skills. It isn't very much fun sometimes to play against a ball machine that never swears or sweats and doesn't care whether you hit a winning return. Drills and exercises won't do much for your social life while your friends are on the next court playing "pat-a-ball" with a couple of good-looking novices. Those basic strokes that you must keep hitting correctly hundreds of times a day aren't as impressive as the sexy spins and tricky between-the-legs shots the club players are perfecting . . . but if you're going to play winning tennis, practice is vital. Your feet must move instinctively to get you to the ball properly positioned for an effective stroke; a smooth backhand must become automatic from everywhere on the court; a crisp forehand, hit with accuracy, must be as natural as breathing.

Second step (developed by description and examples)

Paragraph conclusion

Transition sentence

4   When you're finally ready for competition, everything seems calculated to make you forget all you've learned. It requires enormous concentration to shut out distractions and continue to practise the basics that are essential to your game: watch the ball, keep your head down, turn 90 degrees from the path of the ball, keep your feet moving, and so on and so on. With an opponent opposite you, people watching, and your own self-esteem on the line, it's difficult to keep your mind from wandering. Tennis is about 50 percent mental effort. Successful players are those who are able to block out distractions and concentrate on making the racquet meet the ball with precision.

Third step (developed by factual details)

Topic sentence

Topic sentence

5   Finally, developing the proper attitude is the key to winning tennis. I define winning tennis as playing the game to the best of your ability, hitting the ball as well as you know you can, and enjoying the feeling of practised expertise.

Summary of main points

Winning tennis has little to do with beating an opponent. Naturally, if you learn the basics, practise sufficiently, and concentrate, you'll win many matches, but that is the reward of playing well, not the reason for playing well. People who swear and throw their racquets when they lose are very useful; they are the most satisfying players to trounce. I don't understand why they play a game that gives them such pain. Tennis players who enjoy the feel of a well-hit ball and the satisfaction of a long, skillfully played rally are winners, regardless of the score.

Memorable statement

Questions for Discussion

1. What audience did the author have in mind when he wrote this essay? Consider their interests and goals.
2. What is the role of the author?
3. The author divides the process into three main steps, each identified and developed in a paragraph. Why does he leave his fourth main point, attitude, for the conclusion?
4. What functions does the introductory paragraph serve in this essay?
5. Discuss the final paragraph as an effective conclusion to the essay.

FORGING: THE BLACK ART

Paul Allen

1   The art of shaping metal by forging is as old as civilization itself. Its significance to human progress is evident in the names we give to historical periods: the Bronze Age, the Iron Age. Forging is the working of metals by heating them until they are pliable and then hammering or pressing them into shapes. The process can be used to produce objects ranging from giant propellers to tiny manicure scissors. Whether the end product weighs tonnes or grams, the procedure is the same: the metal to be forged must be prepared, processed, and finished.

2   The first step in the process is to identify precisely the material to be forged and to determine its weight and grade. The carbon content and the presence of any alloying elements, such as nickel or molybdenum, will determine the temperature and duration of the heating process. Once the calculations are complete, the metal can be heated. While it heats to forging temperature (1200°C), any tools that are required for shaping should be prepared. Punches are needed if rings are being forged; blocks of varying thicknesses are required if bars or shafts are being formed.

3   Forging begins when all the preparations have been completed and the material has reached forging temperature. The part is removed from the furnace and taken to the forging hammer or press. Hammer forging involves shaping the metal by a series of swift blows; press forging squeezes the metal into shape. Press forging is slower than hammer forging, but it can produce closer tolerances in shape and size.

4   Finishing is the final stage of the process. When a part has been forged, it must be inspected to ensure that it is precisely the right size and configuration. Inspection is crucial because if required tolerances are not met, the part may need to be forged again or scrapped. Manufacturers have good reasons for wanting to get the piece right the first time: the materials range from a few cents to $150 a kilogram, and labour costs are as high as $15 a minute. Once the forging has passed inspection, each piece is stamped with an identification mark such as the customer's name and order number. The part can now be allowed to cool before any finishing or fine shaping. Materials that may crack if they lose heat too quickly require slow cooling in a specially prepared furnace.

5   Forging is not just "metal beating," as some have described it; it is a complex operation requiring highly skilled workers. Metalworking is sometimes called "the black art," and the descriptor is apt. There is something magical about the transformation of a cold lump of steel into parts for a jet engine, a submarine, or a nuclear generator. To produce a high-quality forged part requires considerable skill and careful judgment. Neglect or carelessness in preparing, processing, or finishing means the loss of time, effort, and money.

Reprinted by permission of the author.

Questions for Discussion

1. Using the outline format on page 60 as your guide, write in the margin the main parts of this essay. For each main point, identify the kind(s) of support used, as we have done above for "How to Play Winning Tennis."

2. What is the purpose of this essay? Is it intended to teach readers how to perform the process themselves? How do you know?

3. Study the introductory and concluding paragraphs. If you have not already done so, identify the attention-getter, the thesis statement, the summary, and the memorable statement. Are these clear? Effective? Why?

   How does the concluding paragraph contribute to the unity of the essay?

4. Not many readers are likely to be familiar with the process described in this essay. How has the author made his subject accessible to general readers?

Exercise 16.1

You have some expertise that is not shared by others. Your skill may be restoring old cars, serving customers, eating spaghetti, or designing Web pages. Choose an activity at which you excel and write a short instructional process essay that describes how to do what you do so well.

Exercise 16.2

The "Dummies" books (*Poker for Dummies, Computers for Dummies, Office 2008 for Mac for Dummies*) have become bestsellers by explaining how something works or how to do something in simple, easy-to-understand steps. Write a short chapter for the soon-to-be-published book *College for Dummies* entitled "Surviving Your First Day," or "College Clothing," or "How to Eat School Cafeteria Food and Not Gain 5 kg a Term" (or any other similar topic).

Exercise 16.3

Write a process essay on one of the following topics or on any topic of your choice, as long as it requires an explanation of *how* to do something or *how* something is done, is made, or works. Review the tips on pages 235–36 before you begin.

How my family came to Canada
How to build an iTunes library
How to break up with a boyfriend (girlfriend) and still remain friends
How to create a great *Facebook* page
How to find time for everything you have to do in a single day
How to apologize
How to get a bargain
How a biological process works (e.g., how skin heals, how the lungs function)
How a fuel cell works (or any other mechanical, chemical, or electronic device)

17

Classification and Division

Classification and **division** are structural patterns based on our instinct to arrange and analyze our experiences. We group like things into categories or classes, and we separate the component parts of something in order to understand them better. For example:

- College and university students can be grouped into undergraduates and graduates, or by year, or by political affiliation, or by where they reside during the term (classification).
- An undergraduate class might be divided by programs or majors, such as engineering, nursing, arts and science, and so on (division).
- Items on a restaurant menu are listed in categories such as appetizers, entrées, desserts, and beverages (classification).
- A meal is divided into courses: soup, salad, entrée, dessert (division).
- Plants can be grouped into three categories, based on their effect on humans: edible, inedible, poisonous (classification).
- An individual plant can be divided into its parts: flower, stalk, leaf, and root (division).
- A flower can be further divided into petals, pistils, and stamen (division).

The process of **definition** involves both classification and division. We define a concept (e.g., a good student) by identifying the features or characteristics that are shared by all members of the class. That is, having mentally grouped students into three classes (good, poor, and average), we focus on the unique qualities or distinctive features shared by the group (good students) we want to define: a good student is one who is motivated, hardworking, and creative.

Writing a classification paper involves grouping similar things (people, ideas, whatever) to place them into one of several categories. For example, in the first bulleted point above, we classify college and university students according to four different principles: degree status, year of study, political inclination, and place of residence. There are many more ways in which we could classify college students; for example, how they use their leisure time; whether they smoke, drink, get along with their parents; number of hours they work each week; extracurricular activities—and the list goes on. There are numerous ways to group a number of entities into subgroups.

Writing a division paper requires examining a single entity (a person, place, thing, concept) and breaking it down into its constituent parts, features, or characteristics. You are writing a division paper whenever you write about the accomplishments of someone (whether that person is historically real or fictional), the parts of a work of fiction or nonfiction, the qualities of a good leader, the strengths or weaknesses of a particular team, and so on—the possibilities for division are infinite.

Here are some examples of classification and division topics, paired according to three subjects: television programming, patients, parents.

Classification		Division	
Saturday a.m. TV programs	• cartoons • sports shows • interview programs	Saturday a.m. TV programming	• infantile • infuriating • informative
Patients doctors hate to treat	• clingers • deniers • demanders	The ideal patient	• cooperative • knowledgeable • self-disciplined
Types of bad parents	• overprotective • uninterested • disengaged	A good parent	• supportive • firm • consistent

Tips on Writing Classification and Division Essays

1. The key to a good paper is choosing your main points carefully. Make sure that all points are of approximately equal significance and that the points do not overlap.
2. If you have deliberately left out some aspects of the subject, briefly let your readers know this and why you have limited your discussion. Some topics are too complex to discuss exhaustively in a short paper.

You are better off discussing a few representative points in detail than skimming over all the categories or components.

3. Your thesis statement should set out your subject and its main points, as in the following examples.

Inanimate objects can be classified into three major categories—those that don't work, those that break down, and those that get lost.

An appropriate wardrobe for work consists of outfits that are comfortable, easy to maintain, and, within limits, distinctive.

Our softball team is made up of has-beens, might-have-beens, and never-weres.

The two essays that follow illustrate classification and division. In the first essay, the writer explains her subject by dividing it into its main features. The second essay shows how subjects (here, methods of conflict resolution) can be classified into categories. Read the essays and then answer the questions that follow.

ON-THE-JOB TRAINING
Alice Tam

1   What can you expect from your first job after you leave college? As a recent graduate from a technical program, I entered the workforce fully prepared to do the job I was hired to perform. What I was *not* prepared for were some of the expectations and challenges posed by my employer, my co-workers, and—surprisingly—myself.

Attention-getter

Thesis statement

2   During the hiring process, the employer makes sure that you have the knowledge and skills that the position calls for. However, once you are on the job, you will discover that he or she has many other expectations of you as well. Basic job requirements such as being on time should come as no surprise, but volunteering for tasks outside working hours, cheerfully taking on additional responsibilities, and demonstrating work habits that go beyond the basic requirements of the job are all unspoken expectations that employers have of new employees. In my first month on the job, I attended a managers' weekend retreat; joined the company's health and safety committee and United Way campaign; and, on the advice of my supervisor, accepted an offer to serve on my college program's advisory board. My social life suffered, but I felt that I was becoming a valued member of the company's management team.

1. Topic sentence

Main point developed by examples

Paragraph conclusion

2. Topic sentence

3   Co-workers present a different challenge. Those who did not attend college may question the value of your diploma or degree; they learned the business the hard way, on the job, and they want you to know that your "book learning" will carry you only so far. You will cope with this hostility more easily if you understand that it is caused by insecurity. Many employees feel intimidated by colleagues who have qualifications they lack; their aggressive stance is their defence. Even those whose college or university days are long behind them may display this attitude. If you show them that you are willing to learn from their experience, you will prove to them that you have the skills and attitude the job requires. One of the unwritten responsibilities of any job is earning the respect of your colleagues. This is not an easy task. It requires time and humility, but, in the long run, it is critical to be an accepted part of the team. Outsiders don't get past the first or second rung on the long ladder to career success.

Main point developed by contrast and examples

Paragraph conclusion

3. Topic sentence

4   Finally, your expectations of yourself may surprise you. In your first job out of college, the stakes are higher than any you have ever experienced. The pressure to succeed can create real stress and even hamper your performance. One of the grads who was hired the same month that I was became so nervous about doing well that he couldn't make decisions in case he was wrong, wouldn't take on extra jobs in case he couldn't handle them, and drove himself (and those around him) crazy by compulsively checking and rechecking everything he did to be sure he hadn't made a mistake. As a new employee, you should expect some performance anxiety. The best way to deal with it is to channel it productively by working extra hours or volunteering for charity work until you develop the confidence to be satisfied with just doing your best at your job.

Main point developed by extended example (illustration)

Paragraph conclusion

Transition

5   I celebrated my first year as a full-time employee just a month ago, and when I look back on the past year, I can't believe how fast it has gone or how much I have learned. Because of my college training, I certainly had the ability to do the job, but it has taken me almost the full year to become comfortable with the culture and attitudes of the workplace and to get my own expectations under control. I wish I'd been given this essay to read while I was in school, and I hope it will be helpful to you!

Summary of main points

Memorable statement

Questions for Discussion

1. Drawing on your own work experience, do you agree that a critical part of on-the-job training is learning how to fit in with your colleagues, even if it means extra time (e.g., volunteering for community or charity work) and extraordinary patience (e.g., holding your tongue when co-workers belittle your education)?

2. The author uses all three pronoun "persons" in this essay. She writes about her own experience in the first person ("I"); addresses the reader in the second person ("you"); and describes the behaviour of a colleague in the third person ("he"). Why do you think Tam has chosen to vary her point of view in this way? Would her essay be more effective if she had told her story as a first-person narrative, or as a second-person instructional process, or as a third-person division analysis? Support your opinion with evidence from the essay.

3. Use InfoTrac to find at least one article that supports the author's view of her first year on the job and at least one article that contradicts this view. Briefly summarize the main points of each article.

METHODS OF CONFLICT RESOLUTION
Eva Tihanyi

1   Imagine you are the supervisor of a call centre that employs a full-time staff of 40 telephone sales representatives. During the past few months, there has been an increase in employee requests for schedule changes in order to accommodate personal needs. These employees, of course, would prefer not to lose pay, so they want to make sure they work their regular number of weekly hours. Unfortunately, the growing number of schedule changes is having an adverse effect, creating confusion and inconvenience for you, the payroll department, and the employees in general. You, as the person in charge, recognize that you must deal with this situation quickly and fairly—before it escalates. There are four methods of conflict resolution to consider: deference, competition, compromise, or co-operation.

2   If the scheduling issue is not a major one, you might opt to defer; in other words, "let the other side win." Employees could continue to ask for schedule changes as they saw fit, and you would do your best to accommodate them and ignore the inconvenience. Maintaining employee morale would be more important than enforcing a smooth scheduling process.

3   If, on the other hand, you view the scheduling issue as so important that it must be resolved to the company's advantage, you will want to exercise your authority and insist on a no-change policy. Employees would be assigned to particular shifts, and if they wanted time off, they would have to take it without pay. There would be no rescheduling. This is a competitive approach, one which ensures that you "win" while the other side "loses"—and one that also ensures that your relationship with the "losers" will be tarnished.

4   A more empathetic way of managing the situation would be to compromise. You could circulate a memo in which you laid out parameters, specific guidelines for how and when schedule changes could occur. This would allow some flexibility, but would at the same time limit the frequency and nature of schedule change requests. In this way, both you (i.e., the company) and the employees would "win"—partially. Both sides would get a part of what they wanted, but both would also lose a part. And so long as both sides were satisfied, this could be an effective solution.

5   Finally, if you're a supervisor who believes in the concept of mutual benefit, the notion that it's possible for both sides to "win," you will choose the method of co-operation. You and the employees might brainstorm the scheduling issue together and in the process discover new ways in which it might be settled to the satisfaction of both sides—not compromise, but resolution. Because co-operation produces no "loser," it fosters an atmosphere of trust and respect and, although certainly more time-consuming than the other three methods, it is generally the best way to encourage goodwill in the workplace.

6   Deference, competition, compromise, and co-operation are all viable ways of handling conflict. The one you choose will most likely depend on how significant the issue is, how much time you have to deal with it, to what extent you value employee morale, and what the word "winning" means to you.

Questions for Discussion

1. Using the outline format on page 60 as your guide, identify in the margin the main parts of this essay.
2. What introductory strategy does the author use to set up her thesis? (See pages 86–89 for a review of eight different ways to introduce an essay.) A good introduction intrigues readers, involves them in the subject, and makes them want to read on. How does Tihanyi's introductory paragraph accomplish these goals?
3. One reason this essay is easy to read is that the author has made skilful use of transitional devices. Turn to pages 102–4 to review the five transitional techniques that an author can use. Which ones does Tihanyi employ in this essay? Identify one example of each technique.
4. In Chapter 7, you learned that a good conclusion should (a) summarize or reinforce the main points of the paper and (b) end with a memorable statement. Does Tihanyi's conclusion satisfy these criteria?

Exercise 17.1

This exercise is designed to improve your skill in identifying *unity* within classification and division. In each of the following thesis statements, cross out any irrelevant, insignificant, or overlapping points.

1. A good teacher doesn't bark at the students, give last-minute assignments, study for a test the night before, or grade unfairly.
2. The most important computer interfaces are the keyboard, webcam, voice recognition, mouse, and memory card.
3. A journalist has four major tasks: to report news accurately, to entertain with social information, to collect a big salary, and to resist government control of information.
4. Finding the right career depends on careful planning: getting all the education you can, continually monitoring your enthusiasms and interests, being flexible enough to shift focus as circumstances change, and having luck on your side.
5. The music I enjoy can be divided into five distinct categories: blues, jazz, light rock, vocal, hip hop, and rap.
6. Online newspapers are my main source of information. At least twice a week I read the *Montreal Gazette*, *Winnipeg Free Press*, *The Globe and Mail*, and *Wired* magazine.
7. It's not easy to work for a perfectionist. She wants perfect results, twice the work in half the time, unpaid overtime, and memos for everything.

Exercise 17.2

Humans have a strong instinct to classify everything including themselves. List at least seven classifications (groups or categories) to which you belong.

Exercise 17.3

To help explain what things are, we often divide them into their constituent parts. For each of the following terms, list four or five characteristics that would help to define it. After discussion, agree on the best three.

- a good manager/team leader/coach
- a good friend
- an ideal summer
- a worthwhile college or university course
- a great TV drama (or comedy)

Exercise 17.4

Select one of the terms you used in Exercise 17.3 and expand your list of characteristics into an essay.

Exercise 17.5

Sports analogies are very common ("He can't get to first base," or "Just when she was making the right moves, she dropped the ball"). For each of the following subjects, give an analogy and an example that would enhance your readers' understanding in a classification or division essay.

Subject	Analogy	Example
Overwork	electronics	When the brain's circuits are overloaded, a fuse can blow, resulting in a nervous breakdown.
Physical fitness	auto mechanics	_____ _____ _____
Marriage	a journey	_____ _____ _____
The aging process	_____	_____ _____ _____

Exercise 17.6

Focus each of the following general topics into a specific subject suited to a classification or division paper. For each, identify three types or categories; or three parts, characteristics, functions, or features.

Restaurants   Subject _____
- _____
- _____
- _____

Health care providers   Subject _____
- _____
- _____
- _____

Television commercials	Subject _____
	• _____
	• _____
	• _____

Drivers	Subject _____
	• _____
	• _____
	• _____

Computer experts	Subject _____
	• _____
	• _____
	• _____

Exercise 17.7

Write an essay on one of the following subjects.

The main kinds, types, or categories of
- co-workers
- salespeople
- small businesses
- social media
- employers

The characteristics of
- a star player (hockey, football, basketball, soccer)
- a bad movie
- a successful interview
- great art
- a good Web page

The component parts of
- a citizenship hearing
- a love affair
- a golf swing (or slap shot, or save, etc.)
- a healthy lifestyle
- a religious service or ceremony

18

Comparison and Contrast

If you are focusing on the similarities between two things (or ideas or concepts or points of view), you are writing a **comparison**. If you are focusing on the differences, you are writing a **contrast**. Most people, however, use the term "comparison" to cover both (as in "comparison shopping"), and similarities *and* differences are often discussed together in a paper.

You can choose from two approaches when you are organizing a comparison. In the first option, you discuss one item fully and then turn to the other item. This approach is called the **block method** of organizing. The alternative option is to compare your two items **point by point**. For example, suppose you decided to compare Russell Crowe and Brad Pitt. You might identify the following three points:

- physical appearance
- acting technique
- on-camera heroics

Using the block method, you would first consider Crowe in terms of these three points; then you would do the same for Pitt. You would need to outline only four paragraphs for your essay:

1. Introduction
2. Crowe's physical appearance, acting technique, and on-camera heroics
3. Pitt's physical appearance, acting technique, and on-camera heroics
4. Conclusion

The block method works best in short papers, where the points of comparison are easy to understand and remember. As comparisons get more complex, your readers will be able to understand your points better if you present them point by point. You would then need to write an outline of five paragraphs for your essay:

1. Introduction
2. Physical appearance of Crowe and Pitt
3. Acting technique of Crowe and Pitt
4. On-camera heroics of Crowe and Pitt
5. Conclusion

The introductory paragraph in the comparison essay usually tells readers what two things are to be assessed and what criteria will be used to assess them. The concluding paragraph may (or may not) reveal a preference for one over the other.

Tips on Writing a Comparison or Contrast

1. Make sure that the two items you have chosen are appropriately paired; to make a satisfactory comparison, they must have something in common. Both might be baseball teams or world leaders, but to compare the Toronto Blue Jays and the Calgary Stampeders or to contrast Queen Elizabeth and your Aunt Agatha would be futile and meaningless.
2. Your main points must apply equally to both items. Reject main points that apply to one and have only limited application to the other. For example, in a comparison of digital and analogue instruments, a category for dial configuration would be pointless.
3. Your thesis statement should clearly present the two items to be compared and the basis for their comparison. Consider these examples.

   E-mail and interoffice memos differ not only in format but also in style and purpose.

   The major points of comparison in automobiles are performance, comfort, and economy, so I applied these factors to the two cars in the running for my dollars: the Ford Focus and the Mazda 3.

4. Use transitional words and phrases within and between paragraphs to provide coherence. (See pages 102–4.)

The essays that follow demonstrate the two approaches to writing comparisons and contrasts. Read each essay and answer the questions that follow it.

THE CANADIAN CLIMATE

D'Arcy McHayle

1   The student who comes to Canada from a tropical country is usually prepared for cold Canadian winters, a sharp contrast to our hot northern summers. What the student may not be prepared for is the fact that Canadian personalities reflect the country's temperature range but are less extreme. Canadian personalities fall into two categories: warm and cool. The two groups share the Canadian traits of restraint and willingness to compromise, but they are dissimilar in their attitudes both to their own country and to the foreign student's country of origin.

2   Warm Canadians are, first of all, warm about Canada and will, at the first sound of a foreign accent, describe with rapture the magnificence of the country from the Maritimes to the West Coast, praising the beauty of the Prairies, the Rockies, and even the "unique climate of the Far North." Canadian leisure activities are enthusiastically described with a special place reserved for hockey. "So you've never skated? You'll learn. Come with us; you'll have a great time." The Warm Canadian wants the newcomer to share in the pleasures of life in Canada. When she turns her attention to the foreign student's homeland, she seeks enlightenment, asking questions about its geography, social and economic conditions, and other concerns not usually addressed in travel and tourism brochures. The Warm Canadian understands that the residents of tropical countries are not exotic flower children who sing and dance with natural rhythm but are individuals who, like Canadians, face the problems of earning a living and raising a family.

3   Compared to the Warm Canadian, who exudes a springlike optimism, the Cool Canadian is like November. Conditions may not be unbearable for the moment, but they are bound to get much colder before there is any sign of a thaw. The Cool Canadian's first words on hearing that the foreign student is from a warm country are, "How could you leave such a lovely climate to come to a place like this?" Not from him will one hear of Banff, or Niagara Falls, or anything except how cold and dark and dreary it gets in the winter. It sometimes seems that the Cool Canadian's description of his own country is designed to encourage foreign students to pack their bags and return home at once. As for the foreign student's country of origin, the Cool Canadian is not really interested, although he may declare, "I hear it's beautiful. I'd love to go there." Beyond that, however, he has no interest in information that may shake the foundations of his collection of myths, half-truths, and geographic inaccuracies. This type of Canadian, if he does travel to a tropical country, will ensure that he remains at all times within the safe confines of his hotel and that he returns to Canada with all his preconceived ideas intact.

4   Foreign students should not be upset by the Cool Canadian; they should ignore his chilliness. Besides, like a heat wave in March, an unexpected thaw can occur and create extraordinary warmth. Likewise, a Warm Canadian may become a little frosty sometimes, but, like a cold spell in June, this condition won't last. And when the weather changes, foreign students will find an opportunity to display their own qualities of understanding, tolerance, and acceptance of others as they are.

Concluding paragraph (developed by analogy)

Memorable statement

Questions for Discussion

1. What are the main points of contrast in "The Canadian Climate"?
2. Which method of contrast has the author chosen for the subject, block or point by point?
3. Why did the author choose this approach? Would the essay work as well if it were organized the other way? Outline the main points of contrast as they would look in the other format.
4. What other points of contrast between the two kinds of Canadians can you think of?
5. What audience does the author have in mind? How do you think Canadians would respond to this essay? Foreign students?

SHOPPING AROUND

Aniko Hencz

1   The word "shopping" inspires visions of crowded, airless malls, aggressive salespeople, whining children, and weary feet. Some consumers embrace the ritual chaos while others recoil in horror. For the mall-weary shopper, help has arrived in the form of the Internet. Online shopping has exploded in recent years and now offers a viable alternative to the bricks-and-mortar experience. However, as my partner and I discovered recently, when it comes to selection, service, pricing, and convenience, there are significant differences between the two options. Which should you choose? It depends on your priorities.

2   Sometimes too much choice leads to confusion, but having a wide selection to choose from is generally considered a good thing. Online shopping makes available millions of products at the click of a mouse. When we explored dozens of sites in our search for a digital video camera, national borders didn't limit us, and we found models with all the latest features and functions. In contrast, when we visited a number of electronics stores—after wasting half an hour looking for a parking space—we found a limited selection of models and options in our price range.

3   While we are not exactly Luddites, we needed the intricacies and features of the latest generation of video cameras explained to us. Most electronics stores are staffed with knowledgeable salespeople who are only too happy to explain technical jargon, demonstrate a product's features, and offer an opinion on its relative merits. On the other hand, if you are willing to spend time on your computer, online information may well serve your needs. You can do all your research and decision-making electronically by visiting manufacturers' and retail outlets' websites, and even by consulting the opinions of other consumers at product comparison and review sites.

4   "Where can I get the best deal?" is something every consumer wants to know. Ask happy customers the reason for their satisfaction, and the answer invariably involves price. Online merchants can often offer lower prices because they can avoid the overhead (rent, inventory, heat and light, wages, etc.) of conventional stores. Not surprisingly, we found that in-store prices for digital video cameras were routinely higher than those posted by online merchants. Electronics stores have responded to the online competition by routinely offering coupons and special discounts.

5   Shopping online is undoubtedly convenient. As long as you have a credit card, you can shop anywhere, anytime. There are no salespeople to pressure you, and you never have to deal with parking or crowds. However, these advantages are countered by the major inconvenience of returning a damaged or unsatisfactory product, especially if you have to repackage the item and ship it across borders. We were disconcerted by the possibility that we would have to return our video camera, a fragile item that could be easily damaged during shipping. Offsetting the limitations of the bricks-and-mortar experience is the relative speed with which items can be returned or exchanged.

6   So where did we buy our camera? We weighed the pros and cons of the alternative selections, services, prices, and convenience of the two shopping environments, and decided that service—both before and after our purchase—was more important to us than saving money and time by shopping online. While we chose the local electronics store as the supplier that best met our needs, other consumers have different priorities, as the increasing popularity of online shopping demonstrates. Bricks and mortar or mouse and monitor? North Americans should consider themselves fortunate to enjoy the advantages of both—for now.

Questions for Discussion

1. Using the outline format on page 60 as your guide, identify the main parts of this essay. Indicate them in the margins, as we have done with "The Canadian Climate." How is the information organized: in blocks

or point by point? Why do you think the author chose this organizational pattern?

2. In your own words, combine the thesis and the main points of this essay in a single sentence. Is it an effective thesis statement? Why?

3. This piece is told from the first-person plural point of view. Consider how the effect on the reader would change if it had been written from either the first-person singular point of view (personal) or from the third-person point of view (impersonal). Did the author choose her point of view wisely? Why?

4. Identify three or four transitional techniques the author has used to enhance her essay's coherence. (See pages 102–4 for a review of transition strategies.)

5. Early in the essay, the author provides clues as to which shopping option she and her partner eventually chose. Do these hints spoil the conclusion for the reader? Why?

6. Search InfoTrac to find two or three articles that present evidence of the rapid growth of online shopping and its negative effects on the profitability of bricks-and-mortar stores.

7. Does it matter to you who wins the battle of the shopping options? Why?

Exercise 18.1

List eight to ten characteristics of two people, or jobs, or courses. Examine your lists and choose two or three characteristics of each that would make a good basis for a comparison of the two. Then go back over your lists and choose two or three characteristics that would make a good basis for contrasting them.

Exercise 18.2

Write a comparison or contrast essay on one of the following subjects. Be sure to follow the guidelines for essay development, from selecting a subject, through managing your main points, to outlining your paper and writing your paragraphs.

Two magazines with the same target audience (e.g., *Maclean's* and *Time*, *People* and *Us*, *Shift* and *Wired*)
Two bands (or singers or musicians)
A movie and the book it was based on
Two pop stars (music, film, TV, etc.)
Two Canadian writers (or filmmakers)
Your generation and that of your parents (or grandparents)
Two fast-food restaurants

Exercise 18.3

Contrast papers tend to become persuasive, but they don't have to. When you are presenting a contrast, try not to be influenced by your own opinion. List the arguments on both sides of three of these controversial issues.

Single-sex schools
Gay marriage
The use of animals in medical research
Nuclear power
Physician-assisted suicide

Exercise 18.4

For one of the topics you worked on in Exercise 18.3, write an essay contrasting the views held by the two sides. Some research may be necessary to find out exactly what the opposing arguments are and to explain those arguments to your reader.

Exercise 18.5

Construct a comparison essay or a contrast essay, using one of the suggestions given below. Develop a thesis statement that reflects the relationship of the two subjects. Before you begin, write an outline of your thoughts, using either the block or the point-by-point method.

Quebec (or the west—British Columbia and Alberta) and TROC (the rest of Canada)
Your spouse and the fantasy you had of a spouse before you were married
Coverage of a specific news event by a newspaper and a TV channel
Your life now with your life five (or ten or twenty) years ago
Working in an office and working at home
Television advertisements for one of these pairs of consumer products: new cars and beer; home cleaning/maintenance and personal care products; financial services and travel services; a fast-food chain and muffler repairs

19

Causal Analysis

- What are the consequences of dropping out of school?
- What are some of the effects of low interest rates?
- What are the causes of addiction?
- Why is interest in alternative medicine growing so rapidly?

These are the kinds of subjects often discussed in **causal analysis**. In some instances, cause and effect may be combined in one paper or report, but its length and complexity would put it out of the range of our introductory discussions here. In short papers, writers usually concentrate either on causes or on effects.

The most common problem found in causal analysis is oversimplification. Without solid facts, figures, or evidence, inexperienced writers have a tendency to generalize and to substitute unsupported opinions for reasons. One cause of this problem is choosing a topic that is too large for the prescribed length of the paper. For example, one student decided to analyze the effects of Canada's immigration policy, a subject so big and so complicated that he could do nothing more than give vague and unsupported opinions. The result made him seem not only ignorant but also racist. You can avoid this pitfall by choosing your subject carefully, focusing it into a limited topic, and supporting each main point with lots of evidence.

Tips on Writing Causal Analysis

1. Your thesis statement should clearly indicate whether you are tackling cause or effect, and it should present your main points in order. Consider these examples:

The benefits of a long canoe trip include reduced stress and increased fitness.

"Trashy" novels educate, relax, and entertain me in ways that "intellectual" novels do not.

The main complaints of the workers in this office are pay, safety, and boredom.

2. Avoid three common logical fallacies: oversimplification, faulty causal relation, and leaping to a conclusion.
   - An oversimplified analysis is one that ignores the complexities of an issue. If, for example, you claim that "men deliberately keep women down" and base this conclusion on the fact that, on average, the annual salary of women is lower than that of men, you are oversimplifying because the two groups are not identical. To take just one difference, there are more part-time workers among females than among males, and the salaries of part-timers cannot be compared to the earnings of full-time workers. (And even if the two wage groups were identical in all respects except one—annual income— that one difference is not proof of a male conspiracy.)
   - Just because one event occurs along with or after another event does not mean that the first *caused* the second. For example: On Tuesday, your little brother swallowed a nickel. On Wednesday, he broke out in a rash. To conclude that the nickel caused the rash is a faulty causal relation. He may be allergic to something; he may have measles. As a writer, you must carefully examine all possible causes before determining that Y is the result of X.
   - Leaping to a conclusion (sometimes called *hasty generalization*) results when you do not consider enough data before forming a judgment. This is a common error: We commit it every time we form an opinion based on one or two instances. For example, the sponsorship scandal that occurred during Jean Chrétien's final years in office is not proof of the assertion, "the Liberal government was full of crooks."

3. Fully support your statements. You must provide proof of what you say in the form of examples, facts, statistics, quotations, anecdotes, and so on (see Chapter 6). If you begin with the assumption that your reader disagrees with you, you will be more likely to provide adequate support for your points.

The essays that follow demonstrate writing that discusses causes and effects. Both writers use a variety of supporting evidence to develop their points.

THE ENEMY IN THE MIRROR
Brian Green

1   Our planet is under attack. If the source of the attack were some external force, such as aliens from another galaxy or a rogue comet, then we humans would band together and fight the threat with every resource at our disposal. We wouldn't count the cost in lives, effort, or money; we would throw every *Attention-getter* gram of our strength, ingenuity, and will into the effort. However, while the threat we face is just as real as if it came from marauding space ships bombarding us with poison rays, we are doing little to save ourselves from destruction because the evil-doers are much closer to home. We see them daily in our mirrors. Motivated by greed and enabled by indolence, we are wrecking our ← *Thesis statement* own environment with ruthless efficiency.

2   Greed—industrial, commercial, and personal—has impelled us to plunder ← *Topic sentence* the earth's resources without giving a thought to the consequences. We can no longer claim ignorance of our peril as an excuse, since the "Green Movement" is a well-publicized catch phrase. Regrettably, it is little more than that. Canada's record of curbing greenhouse emissions is the worst among *First main point* the top eight industrial nations, and predictions suggest that we are on course *(developed by* to continue in that shameful position for the foreseeable future. Mining emis- *facts, statistics,* sions are the biggest culprit, with oil sands extraction leading the way, but *and specific* coal-powered electrical generation and vehicle emissions are also up (in spite *details)* of the much-ballyhooed trend toward less-polluting cars and trucks). Our overall greenhouse emissions rose by 30 million tonnes in 2007 over the previous year. Globally, since the Industrial Revolution, two-thirds of the world's rainforest, the largest single source of the Earth's oxygen supply and a resource that Canada is fortunate enough to share in, has been cut or burned. Currently it is being destroyed at a rate of almost one hectare per second to produce highly profitable but resource-intensive timber and beef. We fill our *Paragraph* rivers and shorelines with chemicals and sewage, kill our lakes and forests with *conclusion* industrial pollutants, poison our soil and water table with waste—all in the name of industrial growth and the jobs it creates. *Transition and topic sentence*

3   While greed is the motivator, indolence is the enabler. We can no longer claim ignorance, so if we continue to destroy the planet (and we do), then our own inaction is to blame. Emissions from SUVs were up 117 percent in 2007, thanks to aggressive marketing (which even called some of these gas guzzlers "green") and lower fuel prices. Canadians throw away about 275 000 tonnes *Second main* of disposable (but not biodegradable) diapers every year. We munch our fast *point (developed* food and sip our coffee in its environmentally harmful containers; demand *by numerical* that our paper products be thick, soft, and pure white (bleached at huge cost *facts, examples,* to our rivers and soil); and cheerfully accept—even demand—the overpack- *and specific* aged goods that our stores and supermarkets peddle. Canadians are by far the *details)*

*Paragraph
conclusion*

world's biggest per capita users of fresh water in our homes, consuming an average of 330 litres per person per day (*double* the usage in EU countries). Despite the hand-wringing and well-publicized efforts of a few, the majority of us just can't be bothered to make the effort required to contribute effectively to a reduction in our destructive behaviour.

Topic sentence

4   Is there any reason for optimism? There is some evidence that Canadians are becoming more conscious of the environment, and consciousness can only lead to changes for the better. An international poll in 2008 indicated that the environment was Canadians' number one concern, even topping the economy, for a majority of the respondents. Twenty years ago, similar polls revealed that only one in ten felt the environment was the most important issue facing the world. This is progress of a sort. A clear majority of Canadians now favour tougher action against polluters, even if that action means higher taxes, higher prices, and fewer jobs. Sadly, our governments, federal, provincial, and local, have done little if anything of significance to respond to these trends. And even this heightening of Canadian consumer concern is far from the concerted, all-out effort to save the planet that would result if we were threatened by some external catastrophe. How much more difficult it is to mobilize resources and will when the enemy lies within.

*Main point
(developed by
examples and
statistics)*

*Memorable
statement*

Questions for Discussion

1. What is the main problem the author identifies in this essay, and what are its two causes?
2. What is the purpose of the author's description in the first paragraph of a catastrophic attack from outer space? What effect is this description intended to have on the reader?
3. What is the author's attitude toward Canadians? Highlight at least three words or phrases that led you to this conclusion. What effect is the author's attitude likely to have on Canadian readers?
4. Study the concluding paragraph of this essay. How does it affect you as a reader? What purpose does the writer hope to achieve in this paragraph?
5. What evidence have you observed that Canadians are changing in their attitudes and actions with respect to the environment? List at least five specific behaviours, actions, or policies that you have witnessed in the last five years that suggest Canadians are becoming more aware of environmental issues or are making an effort to change their wasteful habits.

THE SLENDER TRAP
Trina Piscatelli

> Starvation is not a pleasant way to expire. In advanced stages of famine, as the body begins to consume itself, the victim suffers muscle pain, heart disturbances, loss of hair, dizziness, shortness of breath, extreme sensitivity to cold, physical and mental exhaustion. The skin becomes discoloured. In the absence of key nutrients, a severe chemical imbalance develops in the brain, inducing convulsions and hallucinations. (Krakauer 198)

1   Every day, millions die of hunger. The symptoms of starvation are so horrific that it seems unthinkable anyone would choose this way of death. How is it possible that in the Western world, one in two hundred young women from upper- and middle-class families practises starvation as a method of weight control? How do young women become so obsessed with being thin that they develop anorexia nervosa? To cause such a fearsome and potentially fatal condition, the influencing factors must be powerful indeed. And they are powerful: the psychological pressures of adolescence, the inescapable expectations of family and peers, and the potent influence of the media.

2   A tendency to perfectionism, lack of identity, and feelings of helplessness are three aspects of a young woman's psychology that can contribute to the development of anorexia nervosa. Young women who exhibit perfectionism are particularly susceptible to the disease because they often have unrealistic expectations about their physical appearance. These expectations can lead to feelings of helplessness and powerlessness, and some young women with these feelings see starving themselves as a means to empowerment. Their diet is often the only thing they can control, and they control it with a single-mindedness that astonishes and horrifies their families and friends. As well as the need for control, anorexia in young women can be caused by a weak or unformed identity. Confused about who they are, many young women define themselves by how closely they approximate our society's notion of the ideal woman. Unfortunately, for the past half-century, Western society's ideal female image has been that of an unrealistically thin young woman. When women focus on this impossible image as the ideal and strive to starve their bodies into submission, they suffer emotional and physical damage.

3   In addition to an unstable psychological state, family and peer pressure can contribute to a fragile young woman's development of anorexia nervosa. By emphasizing physical appearance, by criticizing physical features, and even by

restricting junk food, family members can push a young woman over the cliff edge that separates health from illness. A home environment in which physical appearance is overvalued can be destructive for young women. Surrounded by family members and friends who seem to be concerned primarily about appearance, a young woman can begin to feel insecure about how she looks. This uncertainty can produce the desire—and then the need—to look better. And better means thinner. This flawed logic underlies the disease in many young women. A family or peer group that overvalues physical appearance is often also critical of physical flaws. Critical comments about weight and general appearance, even when spoken jokingly, can be instrumental in a young woman's desire to be thin. Ironically, food restrictions imposed by parents can also contribute to anorexia in young women. Restricting the consumption of junk food, for example, has been known to cause bingeing and purging, a condition associated with anorexia.

4   While a young woman's developing psyche and the pressures of those close to her can exert tremendous influence, the root cause of the "thin is beautiful" trap is a media-inspired body image. Television, fashion magazines, and stereotypical Hollywood images of popular stars provide young women with an unrealistic image of the ideal female body. While only 5 percent of North American females are actually underweight, 32 percent of female television and movie personalities are unhealthily thin (ANRED sec. 6). The media's unrealistic portrayal of a woman's ideal body can cause a young woman to develop a sense of inadequacy. To be considered attractive, she feels she must be ultra-thin. Television's unrealistic portrayal of the way young women should look is reinforced on the pages of fashion magazines. Magazine ads feature tall, beautiful, *thin* women. Media images also perpetuate the stereotype that a woman must be thin in order to be successful. Thanks to television and movies, when we think of a successful woman, the image that comes to mind is that of a tall, well-dressed, *thin* woman. This stereotypical image leads impressionable young women to associate success with body weight and image. When internalized by young women, these artificial standards can result in the development of anorexia nervosa.

5   If the media do not begin to provide young women with a positive and healthy image of femininity, we will see no lessening in the numbers of anorexia victims. If our cultural ideal of female beauty does not change to reflect a range of healthy body types, the pressures to realize idealized and unhealthy physical standards will continue, and young women's feelings of helplessness and inadequacy will persist. In order for anorexia to become less prominent among young women, healthier associations must replace the existing connections among beauty, success, and thinness. Young women must realize that self-inflicted starvation is not a means to empowerment, but a process of self-destruction.

Works Cited

ANRED: Anorexia Nervosa and Related Eating Disorders Inc. 2004. Web. 13
June 2004. <http://www.anred.com/causes.html>.
Krakauer, Jon. *Into the Wild.* New York: Villard, 1996. Print.

Questions for Discussion

1. Using the outline format on page 60 as your guide, identify the main parts of this essay. Indicate them in the margin, as we have done in the previous essay.
2. Compose a single sentence combining the thesis and the main points that Piscatelli uses to develop her thesis. Which version do you prefer? Why?
3. What two supporting points does the author use to develop the main point of paragraph 2? (See sentence 5, which serves as a transition between the two supporting ideas.)
4. What kind of development does Piscatelli use in paragraph 3?
5. Study the concluding paragraph carefully. The author's treatment of her summary and memorable statement is unusual and interesting. Sentence 2 of the conclusion summarizes the three main points that have been developed in the essay, but in an original, unpredictable way. Underline the clauses of this sentence, and write above each clause the number of the main point it reinforces.

Exercise 19.1

Develop each of the following thesis statements by adding three good main points.

1. Obesity, a common problem in North America, is the result of three

   major factors: _____

   _____,

   _____, and

   _____.

2. The positive effects of professional day care upon preschool children are

   _____,

   _____, and

   _____.

3. The interest in eating locally grown food is a result of _____

_____,

_____, and

_____.

4. There are several causes for the increase in numbers of full-time workers returning to college or university for part-time study: _____

_____,

_____, and

_____.

5. Three common effects of emotional stress are _____

_____,

_____, and

_____.

Exercise 19.2

Begin with the question "What are the causes of _____?" and fill in five career-related topics that you know enough about to identify at least three causes. If possible, work with a partner who shares your career interests.

Examples: What are the causes of the widespread frustration among nurses?
What are the causes of public school teachers' unhappiness with their jobs?
What are the causes of strikes by unionized public workers?

Exercise 19.3

Repeat Exercise 19.2, using the question "What are the effects of _____?"

Examples: What are the effects of understaffing in our hospitals?
What are the effects of large classes (30–35 children) in Grades 1 to 3?
What are the effects of strikes by unionized public workers?

Exercise 19.4

Choose one of the topics that you have developed in either Exercise 19.2 or Exercise 19.3 and work that topic into a full essay, taking care to select a subject about which you know enough to support your ideas.

Exercise 19.5

Write a cause essay or an effect essay on one of the following subjects. If you don't know enough to fully support your ideas, be prepared to do some research.

Causes
Adjusting to college (or university) was not as easy as I'd thought it would be.
I doubt I will ever be able to retire.
My first job was a good (or bad) experience.
Vandalism is a symptom of adolescent frustration.
Self-employment is the best option for many college and university grads.
Many workers have unrealistic expectations of their employers.
Eating a balanced diet is a challenge for many young people.
Homelessness is increasingly widespread in large cities.
Many runaways prefer the street to a dysfunctional home life.

Effects
Technology is making us lazy.
A poor manager can have a devastating influence on morale.
Credit cards can be dangerous.
Being an only child is a difficult way to grow up.
Poor driving skills are a hazard to everyone.
Caffeine is a harmful substance.
Injuries resulting from overtraining are common among athletes.
Worrying can age you prematurely.
Losing your job can be a positive experience.

20

Argumentation

How many times have you won an argument? If you're like most of us, not very often. Getting people to understand what you say is hard enough; getting them to agree with you is the most difficult task any writer faces.

Argumentation can be divided into two kinds: *argument* and *persuasion*. In the context of writing, these terms have specific meanings, slightly different from their meanings in general conversation.

- An **argument** is a piece of writing that is intended to convince readers that the writer's opinion about an issue is reasonable and valid. An **issue** is an opinion or belief, something that not all people agree on; it is *controversial*, a word that literally means "having two sides."

  Factual reports, memos, and analyses are not likely to be arguments, although some writing intended primarily to inform may also be intended to influence the reader's thinking: "How to Play Winning Tennis" (pages 236–38), "The Enemy in the Mirror" (pages 259–60) and "The Slender Trap" (pages 261–63) are just three examples.
- **Persuasion** is intended to change the way readers think or feel about an issue, perhaps even to act in some way that supports the writer's point of view (e.g., buy a product, donate to a charity, vote for a particular candidate).

Drafting, rewriting, and editing argument and persuasion are much the same as for other kinds of writing. Planning, however, requires a slightly different approach.

Choose Your Issue Carefully

If you have not been assigned a topic, you will need to choose one. Your choice is even more critical for an argumentation essay than it is for a factual analysis. You can argue only matters of opinion, not fact. Facts can be interpreted in different ways—that's what an argument is: an interpretation of a set of facts. No one can dispute the fact that Canada has ten provinces and three territories. An appropriate subject for your paper is one that can be disputed. Someone has to be able to say, "No. I disagree. That's not what these facts mean." For example, "Canada should be reorganized into five regional provinces and one territory."

You cannot argue matters of taste, either. Taste is personal preference: there is no point in arguing that Thai food is better than pizza, or that green is more flattering than blue. Even if you could argue these assertions, they are not significant enough to bother with. Choose your subject carefully. It must pass the 4-S test (see page 25), and it should be one you know and care about. Ideally, it should be one your reader cares about, too.

Next, consider the scope of your subject. How much time do you have to prepare? How long is your paper expected to be? Throughout this book, we have recommended that when you choose a subject, you should limit your focus. This recommendation is even more important when you are preparing an argument than when you are proposing to explain something. Even subjects that look narrowly focused can require surprising amounts of development when you are composing an argument for or against them.

Stay away from large, controversial issues: abortion, for example; or capital punishment; or religious faith. There are two reasons for this caution. First, they are hugely complex issues; and, second, they are issues on which virtually everyone already has an opinion. It is difficult enough to convince readers about an issue on which they have not already formed an opinion. It's practically impossible to get them to change their minds when they hold an entrenched belief.

Consider Your Audience

When you are trying to get readers to agree with you, you must know (or be able to make an educated guess about) what opinions they already hold and how likely they are to disagree with your views. If, for example, you want to convince your readers that television broadcasters should be required to adhere strictly to Canadian content regulations, the approach you take will depend on your readers' level of knowledge, their interest in the subject, even their age. What do they think about the issue? Do they care about it, one way or the other? What beliefs do they hold that would make them inclined to agree or disagree with you? If you know the answers to these questions, you'll know how to approach your subject: what points to argue, which to emphasize, and which to downplay.

Identify Your Purpose

Do you want your readers simply to understand and respect your opinion on an issue? Or do you want to change their thinking or their behaviour in some way? If your primary purpose is to get them to agree with you, your argument will rely on solid evidence and sound, logical reasoning.

If your primary purpose is to get your readers to change in some way, your argument will need to appeal not only to their sense of what is reasonable, but also to their feelings, loyalties, ambitions, or desires.

State Your Thesis

Before you begin your first draft, write out your opinion in the form of a proposition (opinion statement). You may or may not use this statement in your paper, but you need it in front of you as you (1) identify your reasons for holding the opinion you do, (2) list the evidence you intend to use, and (3) decide on the order of presentation. If you have ever heard a formal debate, you know what a proposition is. It is the statement of opinion that one side argues in favour of and the other side argues against. Here are three examples:

> Few cities in the world offer the affordable living, student amenities, and cultural dynamism that Montreal does. (Thesis of "A City for Students," pages 273–74)

> A liberal arts education is a sound investment of time and money. (Thesis of "Arts Education Does Pay Off," pages 329–31)

> Rather than promoting community engagement, *Facebook* encourages self-obsession. (Thesis of "Fleeing *Facebook*," pages 332–34)

The test of a satisfactory proposition is that it is debatable—that is, someone could defend the contrary point of view. (A statement that includes the word *should* or *must* is likely to be a proposition.) You could argue that fishing is a cruel, unjustifiable sport; or that a liberal arts education is a waste of time and money; or that to anglophone students, Montreal offers decrepit housing, poor amenities, and few cultural opportunities.

Once you have a clear statement of a specific opinion, you are ready to identify your reasons for holding it and present evidence to support your reasons. It is possible to support an argument entirely from personal experience, but you are more likely to convince your readers if you provide a variety of kinds of evidence (see Chapters 6 and 11).

Identify Your Reasons and Evidence

You will not convince your readers of anything unless they understand your proposition. Whether your purpose is to argue or to persuade, you need to provide reasons for believing your opinion. Your reasons, which are your main points, must be significant, distinct, and relevant (see Chapter 3). To support each reason, you need to provide accurate evidence: facts, concrete details, statistics, events, or experiences with which your readers are familiar or can relate to, and/or authorities you can refer to or quote. When you attempt to persuade, you must engage your readers' hearts as well as their minds, so at least some of your evidence should be emotionally "loaded." That is, it should arouse your readers' compassion, or anger, or sense of justice, or any other emotion that might tend to bring your reader over to your side.

Decide on an Approach: Direct or Indirect?

If you think your readers are likely to argue with your view or even slightly inclined to oppose it, it is best to build your case with examples, definitions, and other evidence before stating your own opinion. Readers who are confronted early by a statement they disagree with are often not open to argument or persuasion. Instead, they are inclined to read the rest of the paper while trying to pick holes in the argument and thinking of rebuttals. A potentially hostile audience would respond best to an indirect, or inductive, approach:

> Before we decide how to vote, we should consider the candidates' records, their platforms, and their characters.

On the other hand, if your readers are sympathetic to your point of view, you can state your opinion up front and then identify your reasons and the evidence that supports those reasons. This is the direct, or deductive, approach:

> Based on her record, her platform, and her character, Julie Kovac is the candidate who deserves your vote.

For an explanation of inductive and deductive reasoning, together with a discussion of some of the common logical fallacies that can damage your argument, see "Making the Argument" on the *Essay Essentials* website (http://www.essayessentials5e.nelson.com).

Arrange Your Reasons and Evidence

An argument or a persuasive essay can be developed in several ways. It is possible, as you will see in the essays at the end of this chapter, to use a number of different structural patterns to convince your readers. A cause–effect analysis might be an effective way to urge action to lower the carbon monoxide and carbon dioxide emissions that contribute to global warming. You might choose comparison to discuss the efficiency of Canada's regulated airline industry as opposed to the deregulated industry in the United States and to argue in favour of one approach over the other.

Two patterns are specific to argument and persuasion. One is the classic "their side–my side" strategy, which is particularly useful when you are arguing a controversial position that may provoke serious dispute. This pattern involves your presenting the "con" (or "against") points of an argument, then refuting them with the "pro" (or "for") side of the argument. For instance, if a writer was to argue that women in the Canadian Forces should participate in combat, she might choose to present the opposing position and then counter each point with well-reasoned arguments of her own.

Like a comparison, the "their side–my side" strategy can be presented either in block form or in point-by-point form, depending on how many points there are to discuss. Be sure to arrange your points in the order in which they will be most effective (see the list of possible arrangements discussed in Chapter 3).

If you are a skilled debater, you can often dismiss the opposing side's argument by identifying and exposing flaws in their reasoning or evidence. If you are an inexperienced writer, however, you will probably find it easier to use one or more of the following techniques:

- Identify any irrelevant or trivial points.
- Show that a point covers only part of the issue.
- Show that a point is valid only some of the time.
- Show that a point may have immediate advantages, but that its long-term results will be negative.
- Acknowledge the validity of the opposition's point(s), but provide a better alternative.

Carefully presented, the "their side–my side" pattern impresses readers with its fairness and tends to neutralize opposition.

The second structural pattern specific to argument and persuasion makes use of the familiar thesis statement. Add carefully worded reasons to your proposition, and you have a thesis statement that can appear in the introduction of your paper, in a direct approach, or near the end, if you are treating your subject indirectly. Be sure you have arranged your reasons in the most effective order. Usually, writers present their reasons in climactic order, saving their most compelling reason for the end of the paper.

The keys to good argumentation are to think carefully about your opinion and to present objectively your reasons for believing it—*after* you have analyzed your reader's possible biases or prejudices and degree of commitment to one side or the other.

To argue or persuade successfully, you need to be not only well organized, informative, and thorough, but also honest and tactful, especially if your readers are not already inclined to agree with you.

Tips on Writing Argumentation

1. Choose an issue that you know and care about and can present with enthusiasm.
2. Select your reasons and evidence with your audience in mind. You are already convinced; now you have to convince your readers.
3. Decide whether your audience can be approached directly or if they should be approached indirectly—gently and with plenty of evidence before receiving your "pitch."
4. Arrange your argument in whatever structural pattern is most appropriate for your issue and your audience.
5. Remember that there is another side to the issue. You can help your own cause by presenting the opposing viewpoint and refuting it. Present the other side tactfully and fairly. You will only antagonize readers by unfairly stating or belittling the case for the opposition. Opinions are as sensitive as toes: tread carefully to avoid causing pain.

The essays that follow illustrate two approaches to argumentation. Read them carefully so you can answer the questions that follow each one. (*Note:* The first essay is a research paper with APA-style documentation.)

A CITY FOR STUDENTS

Aliki Tryphonopoulos

Attention-getter

1   It is hard to think of a city more exhilarating for a student to live in than Montreal. Where else can you hear a conversation shift between two or even three languages with ease and playfulness at the local coffee shop?

Definition

Cosmopolitan and cultured, *la belle ville* is unique in North America for its intersection of two historically established language groups with a large and growing immigrant population. Montrealers have translated this rich cultural diversity into a vibrant civic life with world-renowned festivals, a well-established art scene, lively café culture, and acclaimed international cuisine

Thesis statement

and fashion. Few cities in the world offer the affordable living, accessible arts scene, and cultural dynamism that Montreal does.

Topic sentence

2   Long-standing socioeconomic factors make Montreal an affordable city for students—no small consideration given that Canadian undergraduate tuition has risen by 111 percent since 1990 ("Bottom Line," 2004). Naysayers point

First main point (developed by numerical facts)

out that although Quebec has the lowest tuition rates in Canada (frozen since 1994), out-of-province students must pay roughly twice as much as Quebec residents, placing them in the higher bracket of national tuition payers. Some students get around this disadvantage by working and taking part-time classes for a year in order to qualify for the in-province tuition rates. For those who are required to pay the higher rates, however, the financial burden is more than offset by the relatively low cost of rental housing in Montreal

Paragraph conclusion

(Canada Mortgage, 2004, Table 2). One of the best ways for students to economize is by living close to the university. Montreal is a walking city, so it is possible for students to conduct all of their business within a five-block radius.

Transition and topic sentence

3   Pedestrian-friendly urban planning plays a large part in Montreal's reputation as a festival city that hosts over 40 events annually. In the sultry summer months, streets shut down for the Jazz Festival, the Montreal Grand Prix, and Just for Laughs, while the Fête des Neiges and the Montreal High Lights Festival provide outdoor activities and culinary delights in the winter. Students

Second main point (developed by examples)

find plenty of ways to keep active—cycling, jogging, skating, skiing, dancing and drumming at Montreal's sexy Tam-Tams in Mount Royal Park—and gain an appreciation of the city's vibrant arts scene, from the numerous galleries in Old Montreal to fine art cinemas such as Cinema du Parc and Ex-Centris. Students can argue the merits of the latest Denys Arcand film in one of the many cafés along St. Denis frequented by their compatriots from Concordia, McGill, Université de Montréal, and Université du Québec à Montréal. As for ambience, the eclectic mix of old European limestone mansions and North

Paragraph conclusion

American glass towers lends this oldest of Canadian cities a unique architectural allure.

Topic sentence

4   Montreal's cultural dynamism, whose historic roots draw comparisons to such international cities as Barcelona and Brussels, is not only the city's most attractive attribute, but sadly, what scares many students away. Bill 101, meant to protect the French language in Quebec, contributed to the exodus of nonfrancophones from Montreal during the 1980s and 1990s. That trend is slowly reversing (DeWolf, 2003). A recent study reveals what Montrealers already know: the unique interaction of francophone, anglophone, and allo-phone (languages other than French or English) cultures in Montreal is char-acterized by mutual respect, accommodation, and even a sense of fun (Lamarre, 2002). Students can absorb and appreciate the international flavour of the various boroughs and contribute to the daily cultural exchange. With the city's high rates of bilingualism and trilingualism, anglophone students do not need to know French in order to function, but their social and cultural life will be far richer if they do. And what better place to learn *la langue française* than in the second-largest French-speaking city in the world!

Acknowledg-ment of the opposition's point of view

Third main point (developed by examples)

Paragraph conclusion

5   Education is as much about what goes on outside the classroom as in it. Those students who are willing to embrace Montreal's vibrant cultural milieu will find their worldviews challenged and broadened. In a global environment fraught with the dangers of intercultural miscommunication and ignorance, that kind of education is vital.

Summary

Memorable statement

References

The bottom line. (2004, November 15). *Maclean's*, 72.

Canada Mortgage and Housing Corporation. (2004, December 1). *Average rents in privately initiated apartment structures of three units and over in metropolitan areas* (Table 2). Retrieved from http://www.cmhc.ca/en/News/nere/2004/2004-12-21-0715.cfm

DeWolf, C. (2003, May 25). The road to Montreal. *The Gazette* [Montreal]. Retrieved from http://maisonneuve.org/about_media.php?press_media_id=21

Lamarre, P. (2002). Multilingual Montreal: Listening in on the language prac-tices of young Montrealers. *Canadian Ethnic Studies, 34*(3), 47–75.

Questions for Discussion

1. This essay's introduction establishes the author's thesis and previews her main points. What other purposes does it serve?
2. In an argument, it is often necessary to address the opposition's point of view. The writer can choose either to turn a negative into a positive, or to present the opposition's arguments and then refute them. Find examples of both techniques in this essay.

3. Use InfoTrac to do a keyword search of "Montreal." How many hits did you get? Narrow your search to find information that supports the key points of this essay. What keyword gave you the best results?

OF PAIN, PREDATORS, AND PLEASURE
Walter Isaacs

1   The issue of whether fish feel pain when hooked by an angler has recently been a topic of heated debate. Published scientific studies arguing that the fish's mouth does or does not have pain receptors have supported both sides of the argument. It seems to me that this squabble is as irrelevant as the medieval debates about how many angels can dance on the head of a pin. Of course we cause the fish distress—mortal distress! Like any animal, the fish is programmed to survive and procreate. Any predatory threat to that primal function (from a bear, an osprey, a bigger fish, or an angler) must cause extreme stress. Whether that stress can be called "pain" through anthropomorphism, it's certainly more dire to the fish than the prick of a hook in its jaw (felt as "pain" or not). To argue that we aren't distressing a fish by catching it is to hand opponents of fishing proof that fishers are either ignorant or in denial.

2   I admit that I love tricking fish. I take as much pleasure as anyone in catching them, and my pleasure is increased when I've been especially clever or skillful in fooling one of these cunning creatures into taking my fly. I do everything that I can to minimize the pain and stress on any fish I catch, but I cannot deny that by catching the fish, I am in a sense torturing it for my pleasure. How can I justify my actions?

3   First, I acknowledge that I am a predator and something somewhere in me loves the idea of capturing a wild animal through stealth or guile, even when (as I almost always do) I release it unharmed. Whether this instinct comes from a gene somewhere in my DNA or a gland buried in the folds of my brain, there's no denying that it's there. Just as I enjoy laughter, anchovies on pizza, warm fall days, sex, a Bach concerto, and a good Riesling, I enjoy catching fish on a fly. Some pleasures are instinctive, some are learned, but the fact that they are pleasures cannot be denied. Yes, I could give up these pleasures if the motivation were sufficient, but so far I haven't heard any arguments strong enough to convince me to relinquish any of them.

4   Second, let's acknowledge that, as predators go, anglers are relatively benign. When you compare the millions of fish that are hatched to the number that live long enough to be the prey of anglers, it's clear that other predators are more efficient and more dangerous than fly fishers. I suppose the case could be made that for every salmon killed by an angler, thousands

of eels and other sea creatures are saved. If we can anthropomorphize the fish's pain, let's go another step and ask the fish which predator it would rather be caught by: that female osprey gliding over the river, or Walter Isaacs. Both predators will cause it the immediate stress of being caught, but in the first case, the osprey will feed its catch alive to its chicks; in the second, the fish will survive to procreate.

5   Finally, because of my love of fishing, I contribute both time and money to support such activities as the restoration and maintenance of stream habitats, stocking programs, and the development of a cleaner, wilder environment in which fish can thrive. In other words, my conservation efforts help to produce more and healthier fish at the end of each season than there would be if I didn't enjoy fishing so much.

6   If I could fish without harming the creatures in any way, I'd do it in a heartbeat. But since I must hurt the fish somewhat to pursue an activity that gives me such pleasure, these justifications serve to let me do it in good conscience, while recognizing and respecting the stress I cause. I know that what I've said won't convince those who are fundamentally opposed to angling, and I understand their viewpoint. But such people just don't seem to have that gene or gland that makes fishing such a pleasure for me. Heck, I even know people who don't like sex.

Questions for Discussion

1. In the margin, identify the main parts of this essay (see the outline format on page 60).
2. The argument that is the basis for this essay is supported by three points. What are they? In what order has the author arranged his supporting evidence?
3. This essay was first published in a fly-fishing magazine. Identify three or four clues that indicate the piece was written for a sympathetic audience.
4. How would the essay differ if it had been written for an audience of animal-rights activists? Draft a rough outline for such an essay.
5. The essay's concluding sentence seems to have been tossed off for the purpose of ending on a light note. What more serious purpose does it serve in supporting the author's argument?
6. This essay is the author's response to contradictory findings about whether or not fish feel pain the way humans do. Use InfoTrac to find articles on this subject. Be sure to choose articles that reflect both sides of the argument. After reading a few of these articles, decide which side of the debate you support. In a sentence or two, summarize your opinion and identify three or four reasons that support it.

Exercise 20.1

Read through the following list of propositions. With a partner, select one that you are both interested in, but do not discuss it. Working individually, write down two or three points both for and against the issue. Then exchange papers and read each other's work. Which points appear on both lists? Why? Can you tell from the points your partner presented whether he or she is for or against the issue?

> Canada should (should not) increase its level of immigration.
> The salaries of professional athletes should (should not) be capped.
> Professional athletes should (should not) be allowed to use performance enhancing drugs.
> Courses in physical education should (should not) be required throughout high school.
> Smartphones should (should not) be allowed in classrooms.
> Canadians should (should not) be required by law to vote in national elections (as is done in Australia).

Exercise 20.2

Most people have firm convictions, yet few are willing to take action to uphold them. Everyone agrees, for example, that a cure for cancer should be found, but not everyone participates in fundraising events or supports the Cancer Society. With a partner, choose a charitable cause in which you believe and list all the reasons why people should give money to support it. Then list all the reasons people might give for not donating.

Decide which of you will take the "pro" side and which the "con," and write a short essay arguing your position. You will know from your discussion whether your partner is sympathetic or hostile, so you will know whether you should approach your subject directly or indirectly. Then exchange papers and critique each other's work.

Exercise 20.3

Together with a partner, select a *small*, controversial, local issue (one involving your community, school, or profession, for example). Choose sides, and write an argument using the "their side–my side" pattern of organization.

With a partner, develop a questionnaire and survey at least 20 students in your school, from different programs and different years, to determine their attitude toward one of the following:

food services
class sizes
professors' teaching ability
required (or general education) courses
tutorial (or counselling) services

Both of you should take notes during these interviews.

When you and your partner have gathered enough information, it's time to work independently. Compose an indirect argument that arrives at a conclusion about the issue and makes a recommendation based on the evidence you have gathered. Compare your paper with your partner's. What are the main similarities and differences between your two compositions? What conclusions can you draw from your comparative analysis?

Choose an issue with which you are familiar and about which you feel strongly. If you don't feel strongly about anything, choose a proposition from the list below. Draft a thesis statement and outline your reasons and evidence. Then write a persuasive paper, making sure that your points are well supported and that the paper is clearly structured. Assume that your reader is not hostile, but is not enthusiastically supportive, either.

Grades in college and university courses should (should not) reflect a students' effort as well as achievement.

Our college should (should not) permit the use of computers during exams.

Self-inflicted health problems like smoking and obesity should (should not) be covered by taxpayer-funded health care.

Facebook and other social media should (should not) be monitored for unacceptable content such as bullying, racism, and bigotry.

Parents should (should not) be held liable for acts of theft or vandalism committed by their minor children.

PART 6

Readings

The mark of an educated mind is the ability to consider a thought without necessarily accepting it.
Aristotle, 384–322 BCE

Easy reading is damned hard writing.
Nathaniel Hawthorne, 1804–1864

The man who does not read has no advantage over the man who cannot read.
Mark Twain, 1835–1910

Reading . . . offers us the ultimate website, where attention, awareness, reflection, understanding, clarity, and civility come together in a transformative experience.
Carol Shields, 1936–2003

I took a speed-reading course and read War and Peace *in twenty minutes. It involves Russia.*
Woody Allen, 1935–

THINKING UNBOUND
Joseph Scheppach

1 "Tie these two ropes together," they were told at the creativity seminar, and each participant took a turn. Easy as pie? Unfortunately not. Two ropes hung from the ceiling to about a metre above the floor. But they hung so far apart that a person holding onto one rope couldn't reach the other. On the floor were two objects to help participants with their task: a pair of scissors and a stapler. The rule: No other objects were allowed. Not one of the participants fulfilled the task.

2 The reason for their failure can be explained by a human attribute that psychoanalysts call "functional constraint." This phenomenon causes us to view a chair primarily as something to sit on, and a bicycle as an object on which to propel yourself forward by pedaling. We consider each object to be useful for just one thing and are often incapable of allowing for further functions. But when dealing with trickier questions, it is important to move on from direct association and imagine objects in a more unusual context. Then a chair becomes a ladder and a bicycle, for instance, a piece of art. Where ordinary observers saw an old bike, the painter Pablo Picasso saw something entirely different. He assembled a pair of handlebars and a seat to create his now famous Bull's Head sculpture.

3 Picasso applied a method that can help overcome functional restraint: free association. All thought combinations that relate in any way to the object are allowed, no matter how far-fetched. This often leads to "inner images" which then point the way for a creative solution when, for instance, you want to write a letter but your paper threatens to stay blank, or a successful inventor runs out of ideas . . . or when you can't, for the life of you, figure out how to tie together two rope ends that hang so far apart.

4 The answer: tie a weight, like the scissors or the stapler, to the first rope. Set it swinging. Then, holding the second rope, grab the first one as it swings into reach.

5 It's quite simple, really—all you have to do is let your mind run free.

Questions for Discussion

1. Why do you think the author tells the story of the ropes in two parts, separated by the body of his essay?
2. The title, "Thinking Unbound," is a pun. Interpret it and explain why you think it is (or is not) an effective title for this short piece.

3. This essay is developed by description, narration, example, and definition. Identify two examples of each.

4. Provide an example from the field you are studying where "thinking outside the box" might help solve a problem. Alternatively, provide an example from the history of your field that illustrates the practical application of free association.

BEAUTY TIPS FROM MOOSE JAW
Will Ferguson

1 The Moose Jaw hot springs were discovered by happenstance back in 1910, and not without a certain rueful disappointment; they were drilling for natural gas, you see, when up pumped a flood of geothermal water. In the 1930s, a "natatorium" was built, and people came from across the prairies to bathe in its salubrious waters, in a pool lined with white marble and illuminated by underwater lights. The natatorium was a fixture in Moose Jaw for twenty-five years, but by the 1950s the original wooden shafts had rotted away and the baths eventually closed. Today's Temple Gardens spa, opened in 1995, represents a revival.

2 For the record, I am a health spa neophyte. I have never had my cuticles buffed or my eyebrows plucked. I have never been wrapped in seaweed or dunked in herbal tea, and the last time I had mousse in my hair was when I passed out in the Denny's dessert tray at two in the morning. I always thought toner was something you put into a Xerox machine.

3 Normally, this wouldn't matter. There are many things I still haven't done: skydive, learn to whistle a recognizable tune, snorkel, pay my 1989 taxes. But I have made the mistake of mentioning my lack of beauty spa experience, my virginability, if you will, to Kim Izzo, an editor at *Flare* magazine. And Kim, in her gleeful way, has decided it would be an absolute riot to send someone as clued out as me to a spa.

4 I've told [my wife] Terumi about this in the faint hope that she may veto the idea. Instead, she all but pushes me through the spa's doors the next morning (assuming, I suppose, that I will emerge from the other end squeaky clean and looking not unlike, say, a young Pierce Brosnan. Talk about yer faint hopes).

5 "But I've never been to a spa before," I protest. "I don't know what to do—I don't know the etiquette involved."

6 "Nothing to worry about," she says. "Just relax and you'll be fine." I've heard that before—usually prior to a bungee jump or a dentist's drill.

7 So I slink into the Temple Gardens spa, bathrobe pulled tight, eyes darting, and am taken to a small room where a reclining chair awaits.

They are going to start at my feet and presumably work their way up. My reflexologist, I am told, will be with me shortly. A few minutes later the door opens and in walks . . . a guy.

8 This is not exactly what I'd expected. If anyone is going to fondle my feet, I'd prefer it wasn't someone with a moustache.

9 "Brad Moffatt," he says. I shake his hand in a gruff but friendly fashion. My voice has mysteriously dropped a few octaves.

10 "How about them Leafs?" I say.

11 Brad dims the lights and puts on soft music. It's like being on a date. He begins rubbing mint lavender oil onto my feet, at which point I start dropping subtle hints that I am married. To a woman.

12 "I'm married," I say. "To a woman."

13 He nods and continues to rub. "You seem tense," he says.

14 You don't know the half of it.

15 As he works on my feet, Brad speaks in a calm, scientific manner about "energy meridians" and "ancient Chinese techniques" and the importance of "removing toxins from your system." I have always been dubious about reflexology, and the notion that your liver and pancreas can be "cleansed" by tweaking your big toe. What if your problem is not your pancreas? What if you have a sore foot? How does reflexology deal with *that?* Do they have to massage your liver?

16 Still, there's no denying that Mr. Moffatt has worked magic on my toes, and the soles of my feet are still tingling as I'm taken to another room to receive my first-ever facial. The aesthetician who's been asked to take care of me (I'm assuming she drew the short straw) is a young woman named Jackie Hill, who examines my skin like an Amsterdam diamond dealer. Having trained a magnifying glass on me at close range, she begins to speak, not coincidentally perhaps, about clogged pores and damaged capillaries. And what would cause such things? "Oh," she says. "Too much alcohol or caffeine, or too much sun and not enough sunscreen."

17 Guilty on all counts.

18 Who knew that beauty was so complicated? When I heard the word "facial" I imagined some sort of mud pack, maybe, with cucumbers over the eyes, like you see in the movies. It turns out to be far more complex than that. Ms. Hill goes through a dozen steps at least: cleanser, toner, moisturizer, "enzyme peel" (who knew I had enzymes, let alone that they needed peeling?), more cleanser, more goop, more moisturizer, lots of gel under the eyes and finally a Zorro-style eye mask to help "reduce wrinkles."

19 The focus on wrinkles around the eyes—at least three of the steps seem to deal with these—is revealing. Temple Gardens, like spas everywhere, is aimed primarily at women. When it comes to aging, wrinkles aren't something men worry about. Baldness, love handles, rampant and inexplicable ear hair: *Yes.* But wrinkles? It's one of the few remaining advantages of

being a man that the creases around your eyes make you look distinguished, not old.

20 Jackie massages my scalp and temples, and even my earlobes (which is nice, but honestly, my earlobes hardly ever get fatigued). She then works on my arms and fingers until they become jellied boneless limbs.

21 It's not over yet. I am passed on next to a soft-spoken but determined young masseuse named Damara Brown, who has powerfully strong hands for someone so small. A couple of times I glance over my shoulder to make sure it isn't a trick, half-expecting to discover that Damara has tiptoed away and I am now being kneaded by a burly lumberjack named Carl.

22 The only memories I have of sore-muscle treatments prior to visiting Moose Jaw involve no-neck coaches knuckling out charley horses and telling us to "Walk it off. It's just a bruise." *But there's a bone protruding from the—*" "*It's just a bruise, walk it off!*" As a result, I suppose, I have always associated massages with twisted ankles and cruel sporting events. This, however, is different.

23 The full-body massage Damara gives me is almost hypnotic. At one point, as she unravels knots I didn't even know I had, I nod off and end up snoring in that "strangled seagull" fashion of mine that women find so appealing. I wake with a start—tongue lolling, eyes unfocused, a large pool of saliva spreading across the table—and immediately ask Damara to marry me.

24 Well, not quite. But I want to. I want to ask Jackie to marry me, as well. Hell, after the way he worked on my feet, I wanted to ask Brad to marry me.

25 My session ends with a rosehip body wrap. Oiled down and bound in layers of plastic, I soon discover how much heat the human body generates. It is prickly and itchy under there, and a tad claustrophobic, but the wrap does make my skin supple and soft. Why, I am positively glowing afterwards! Not Pierce Brosnan, exactly, but still, the difference is remarkable, and Terumi is pleased. Indeed, I will now be able to speak knowledgeably, and at great length if you let me, about the state of my pores and the maintenance said pores require.

26 I am pleased, also, to think I pulled it off. I didn't do anything too stupid or gauche, and even though it was my first time at a spa, I managed to bluff my way through in a suitably suave, urbane fashion without any embarrassing social gaffes.

27 "So," Terumi asks. "How much did you tip?"

28 "Tip?" I say. "You're supposed to *tip?*"

Questions for Discussion

1. The first paragraph of this article describes the discovery of the Moose Jaw hot springs. Other than providing background information, does this paragraph have any connection to the author's experience at the Temple Gardens spa?
2. Ferguson's article is developed by description, narration, and example. For each of these developmental strategies, find two or three passages that you think are particularly effective. What appeals to you about each one?
3. The author's level of language in this piece ranges from highly colloquial, even ungrammatical, (see paragraphs 3, 4, and 10) to sophisticated ("salubrious," "neophyte"). Ferguson even tosses a made-up word into the mix: "virginability." Why do you think he uses such varied diction? What is his purpose?
4. Paragraphs 26 through 28 form the conclusion of this article. What makes it funny?
5. Humour is particular to individuals. What one person finds hilarious, another may not find at all funny. Choose two paragraphs in Ferguson's article that made you laugh (or at least smile). Why? Did others in the class choose the same ones?

HOW I WRITE

Richard Lederer

1 Ernest Hemingway's first rule for writers was to apply the seat of the pants to the seat of the chair. But not all authors are able to survive with such a simple approach.

2 Emile Zola pulled the shades and composed by artificial light. Francis Bacon, we are told, knelt each day before creating his greatest works. Martin Luther could not write unless his dog was lying at his feet, while Ben Jonson needed to hear his cat purring. Marcel Proust sealed out the world by lining the walls of his study with cork. Gertrude Stein and Raymond Carver wrote in their cars, while Edmond Rostand preferred to write in his bathtub. Emily Dickinson hardly ever left her home and garden. Wallace Stevens composed poetry while walking to and from work each day at a Hartford insurance company. Alexander Pope and Jean Racine could not write without first declaiming at the top of their

voices. Jack Kerouac began each night of writing by kneeling in prayer and composing by candlelight. Dan Brown arises at 4 a.m., seven days a week, to write. As an antidote to the dreaded writer's block, he hangs upside down like a bat until the creative juices begin flowing. Friedrich Schiller started each of his writing sessions by opening the drawer of his desk and breathing in the fumes of the rotten apples he had stashed there.

3   Some writers have donned and doffed gay apparel. Early in his career, John Cheever wore a business suit as he traveled from his apartment to a room in his basement. Then he hung the suit on a hanger and wrote in his underwear. Jessamyn West wrote in bed without getting dressed, as, from time to time, did Eudora Welty, Edith Wharton, Mark Twain, and Truman Capote. John McPhee worked in his bathrobe and tied its sash to the arms of his chair to keep from even thinking about deserting his writing room.

4   For stimulation, Honoré de Balzac wrote in a monk's costume and drank at least twenty cups of coffee a day, eventually dying of caffeine poisoning. As his vision failed, James Joyce took to wearing a milkman's uniform when he wrote, believing that its whiteness caught the sunlight and reflected it onto his pages. Victor Hugo went to the opposite lengths to ensure his daily output of words on paper. He gave all his clothes to his servant with orders that they be returned only after he had finished his day's quota.

5   Compared to such strategies, my daily writing regimen is drearily normal. Perhaps that's because I'm a nonfictionalist—a hunter–gatherer of language who records the sounds that escape from the holes in people's faces, leak from their pens, and luminesce upon their computer screens. I don't drink coffee. Rotten fruit doesn't inspire (literally "breathe into") me. My lifelong, heels-over-head love affair with language is my natural caffeine and fructose.

6   To be a writer, one must behave as writers behave. They write. And write. And write. The difference between a writer and a wannabe is that a writer is someone who can't *not* write, while a wannabe says, "One of these days when . . ., then I'll. . . ." Unable not to write, I write every day that I'm home.

7   A grocer doesn't wait to be inspired to go to the store and a banker to go to the bank. I can't afford the luxury of waiting to be inspired before I go to work. Writing is my job, and it happens to be a job that almost nobody gives up on purpose. I love my job as a writer, so I write. Every day that I can.

8   Long ago, I discovered that I would never become the Great American Novelist. I stink at cobbling characters, dialogue, episode, and setting.

You won't find much of that fictional stuff in my books, unless the story serves the ideas I am trying to communicate. A writer has to find out what kind of writer he or she is, and I somehow got born an English teacher with an ability to illuminate ideas about language and literature.

9   Jean-Jacques Rousseau wrote only in the early morning, Alain-Rene Lesage at midday, and Lord Byron at midnight. Early on, I also discovered that I am more lark than owl—more a morning person than a night person—and certainly not a bat, one who writes through the night. I usually hit the ground punning at around 7:30 a.m., and I'm banging away at the keyboard within an hour.

10   I write very little on paper, almost everything on my computer. Theodore Sturgeon once wrote, "Nine-tenths of everything is crap." The computer allows me to dump crap into the hard drive without the sense of permanence that handwriting or type on paper used to signify to me. I'm visual and shape my sentences and paragraphs most dexterously on a screen. The computer has not only trebled my output. It has made me a more joyful, liberated, and better writer.

11   Genetic and environmental roulette has allowed me to work in either a silent or a noisy environment. I'm a speaker as well as a writer, so phone calls and faxes and e-messages chirp and hum and buzz in my writing room, and I often have to answer them during those precious morning hours. That's all right with me. Fictionalists shut the world out. Fictionalists live with their imaginary characters, who get skittish and may flee a noisy room. As I cobble my essays, my readers are my companions, and they will usually stay with me in my writing space through outerworldly alarms and excursions.

12   Besides, the business of the writing business gives me the privilege of being a writer. In fact, I consider the writing only about half my job. Writers don't make a living writing books. They make a living selling books. After all, I do have to support my writing habit.

13   When you are heels over head in love with what you do, you never work a day. That's me: butt over teakettle in love with being a writer—a job that nobody who works it would give up on purpose.

Questions for Discussion

1. This essay is developed almost exclusively by examples. The author has grouped his examples not randomly, but carefully. Study paragraphs 2, 3, and 4 and identify the organizing principle behind each one. That is, what do the examples in each paragraph have in common? What are they examples *of*?

2. What level of language does Lederer use in this essay? Support your answer with examples of words and phrases taken from the piece.

3. Review paragraphs 6 to 13 and, in a sentence or two, describe Lederer's writing habits. That is, what, where, when, how, and why does he write?

4. Richard Lederer is a well-known American writer, teacher, speaker, newspaper columnist, and the father of two world-class poker players. He has written more than 30 books on the English language. Obviously, he is no slacker. What do you think he means by his claim, "When you are heels over head in love with what you do, you never work a day." Can you think of other examples of people who fit this description?

HOW TO BE A SUCCESS
Malcolm Gladwell

1   In 1971 the University of Michigan had one of the most advanced computer science programs in the world, and thousands of students passed through it, the most famous of whom was a gawky teenager named Bill Joy, who came to the university the year the Computer Center opened. He was 16. He was tall and very thin, with a mop of unruly hair. He had been voted "Most Studious Student" by his graduating class at North Farmington High School, outside Detroit, which, as he puts it, meant that he was a "no-date nerd." He had thought he might end up as a biologist or a mathematician. But late in his freshman year, he stumbled across the Computer Center and he was hooked.

2   From that point on, the Computer Center was his life. He programmed whenever he could. Joy got a job with a computer science professor so he could program over the summer. In 1975, he enrolled in graduate school at the University of California at Berkeley. There, he buried himself even deeper in the world of computer software. During the oral exams for his Ph.D., he made up a particularly complicated algorithm on the fly that, as one of his many admirers has written, "so stunned his examiners [that] one of them later compared the experience to 'Jesus confounding his elders.'"

3   Working in collaboration with a small group of programmers, Joy took on the task of rewriting UNIX, a software system developed by AT&T for mainframe computers. Joy's version was very good. It was so good, in fact, that it became—and remains—the operating system on which literally millions of computers around the world run. "If you put your Mac

in that funny mode where you can see the code," Joy says, "I see things that I remember typing in 25 years ago." And do you know who wrote much of the software that allows you to access the Internet? Bill Joy. He later went on to co-found Sun Microsystems and rewrite another computer language—Java.

4   Joy's story looks like the triumph of pure genius. But the problem with this view is that the closer psychologists look at the careers of the gifted, the smaller the role innate talent seems to play and the bigger the role preparation seems to play.

5   Exhibit A in the talent argument is a study done in the early 1990s by the psychologist K. Anders Ericsson and two colleagues at Berlin's elite Academy of Music. With the help of the academy's professors, they divided the school's violinists into three groups. In the first group were the stars, the students with the potential to become world-class soloists. In the second were those judged to be merely "good." In the third were students who were unlikely to ever play professionally and who intended to be music teachers in the public school system. All of the violinists were then asked the same question: Over the course of your entire career, ever since you first picked up the violin, how many hours have you practised?

6   Everyone from all three groups started playing at roughly the same age, around five years old. In those first few years, everyone practised roughly the same amount, about two or three hours a week. But when the students were around the age of eight, real differences started to emerge. The students who would end up the best in their class began to practise more than everyone else: six hours a week by age nine, eight hours a week by age 12, 16 hours a week by age 14, and up and up, until by the age of 20 they were practising—that is, purposefully and single-mindedly playing their instruments with the intent to get better—well over 30 hours a week. In fact, by the age of 20, the elite performers had each totalled 10,000 hours of practice. By contrast, the merely good students had totalled 8,000 hours, and the future music teachers had totalled just over 4,000 hours.

7   The striking thing about Ericsson's study is that he and his colleagues couldn't find any "naturals," musicians who floated effortlessly to the top while practising a fraction of the time their peers did. Nor could they find any "grinds," people who worked harder than everyone else, yet just didn't have what it takes to break the top ranks. Their research suggests that once a musician has enough ability to get into a top music school, the thing that distinguishes one performer from another is how hard he or she works. That's it. And what's more, the people at the very top don't work just harder or even much harder than everyone else. They work much, *much* harder.

8   The idea that excellence at performing a complex task requires a critical minimum level of practice surfaces again and again in studies of expertise. In fact, researchers have settled on what they believe is the magic number for true expertise: 10,000 hours.

9   "The emerging picture from such studies is that 10,000 hours of practice is required to achieve the level of mastery associated with being a world-class expert—in anything," writes the neurologist Daniel Levitin. "In study after study, of composers, basketball players, fiction writers, ice skaters, concert pianists, chess players, master criminals, and what have you, this number comes up again and again. No one has yet found a case in which true world-class expertise was accomplished in less time. It seems that it takes the brain this long to assimilate all that it needs to know to achieve true mastery."

10   And that's why elite athletic squads have practically no one on their rosters born after September 1. A late-born hockey prodigy doesn't get chosen for the all-star team as an eight-year-old because he's too small, compared to his January- and February-born peers. So he doesn't get the extra practice. And without that extra practice, he has no chance at hitting 10,000 hours by the time professional hockey teams start looking for players. And without 10,000 hours under his belt, there is no way he can ever master the skills necessary to play at the top level. Practice isn't the thing you do once you're good. It's the thing you do that makes you good.

11   The other interesting thing about 10,000 hours, of course, is that 10,000 hours is an enormous amount of time. It's all but impossible to reach that number all by yourself by the time you're a young adult. You have to have parents who encourage and support you. You can't be poor, because if you have to hold down a part-time job on the side to help make ends meet, there won't be time left in the day to practise enough. In fact, most people can reach that number only if they get into some kind of special program—like a hockey all-star squad—or if they get some kind of extraordinary opportunity that gives them a chance to put in those hours.

12   So, back to Bill Joy. It's 1971. He's tall and gawky and 16 years old. He's the math whiz, the kind of student that schools like MIT and Caltech and the University of Waterloo attract by the hundreds. He has talent by the truckload. But that's not the only consideration. It never is. Just look at the stream of opportunities that came Bill Joy's way. Because he happened to go to a far-sighted school like the University of Michigan, he was able to practise on a computer system that operated by time-sharing instead of punch cards; because the university was willing to spend the money to keep the Computer Center open 24 hours, he could stay up all night; and because he was able to put in so many hours, by the time he happened to be presented with the opportunity to rewrite UNIX, he was

up to the task. Bill Joy was brilliant. He wanted to learn. That was a big part of it. But before he could become an expert, someone had to give him the opportunity to learn how to be an expert.

13 "At Michigan, I was probably programming eight or ten hours a day," he went on. "By the time I was at Berkeley I was doing it day and night. I was proficient by my second year there. That's when I wrote programs that are still in use today, 30 years later." He paused for a moment to do the math in his head—which for Bill Joy doesn't take very long. Michigan in 1971. Programming in earnest by sophomore year. Add in the summers, then the days and nights in his first year at Berkeley. "So, so maybe . . . 10,000 hours?" he said, finally. "That's about right."

14 Is the 10,000-hour rule a general rule of success? If we scratch below the surface of every great achiever, do we always find the equivalent of the Michigan Computer Center or the hockey all-star team—some sort of special opportunity for practice?

15 Consider the Beatles. John Lennon and Paul McCartney first started playing together in 1957, seven years prior to landing in America. And if you look more closely at those years of preparation, you'll find an experience that, in the context of hockey players and Bill Joy and world-class violinists, sounds awfully familiar. In 1960, while they were still just a struggling high-school rock band, they were invited to play in Hamburg, Germany.

16 "Hamburg in those days did not have rock 'n' roll music clubs. It had strip clubs," says Philip Norman, who wrote the Beatles biography *Shout!* "There was one particular club owner called Bruno, who had the idea of bringing in rock groups. They had this formula: a huge non-stop show, hour after hour. Many of the bands that played in Hamburg were from Liverpool," Norman went on. "It was an accident. Bruno went to London to look for bands. But he happened to meet an entrepreneur from Liverpool, and he arranged to send some bands over. Eventually the Beatles made a connection not just with Bruno but with other club owners as well. They kept going back because they got a lot of alcohol and a lot of sex."

17 And what was so special about Hamburg? The sheer amount of time the band was forced to play. Here is John Lennon, in an interview after the Beatles disbanded, talking about the band's performances at a Hamburg strip club called the Indra: "We got better and got more confidence. We couldn't help it with all the experience of playing all night long. It was handy them being foreign. We had to try even harder, put our heart and soul into it, to get ourselves over. In Liverpool, we'd only ever done one-hour sessions, and we just used to do our best numbers, the same ones, at every one. In Hamburg, we had to play for eight hours, so we really had to find a new way of playing."

18   The Beatles ended up travelling to Hamburg five times between 1960 and the end of 1962. On the first trip, they played 106 nights, five or more hours a night. On their second trip, they played 92 times. On their third trip, they played 48 times, for a total of 172 hours on stage. The last two Hamburg gigs, in November and December of 1962, involved 90 hours of performing. All told, they performed 270 nights in just over a year and a half. By the time they had their first burst of success in 1964, in fact, they had performed live an estimated 1,200 times. Do you know how extraordinary that is? Most bands today don't perform 1,200 times in their entire careers. The Hamburg crucible is one of the things that set the Beatles apart.

19   Let's now turn to the story of a Seattle kid in an elite private school. Bill Gates was midway through Grade 8 at Lakeside School when the Mothers' Club started a computer club. "[They] did a rummage sale every year, and there was always the question of what the money would go to," Gates remembers. "Some went to the summer program, where inner-city kids would come up to the campus. Some of it would go for teachers. That year, they put $3,000 into a computer terminal down in this funny little room that we subsequently took control of. It was kind of an amazing thing." It was an "amazing thing," of course, because this was 1968. Most *colleges* didn't have computer clubs in the 1960s. From that moment forward, Gates lived in the computer room. He and a number of others began to teach themselves how to use this strange new device.

20   Then a group of programmers at the University of Washington formed an outfit called Computer Center Corporation (or C-Cubed). As luck would have it, one of the founders of the firm—Monique Rona—had a son at Lakeside, a year ahead of Gates. Would the Lakeside computer club, Rona wondered, like to test out the company's software programs on the weekends in exchange for free programming time? Absolutely! After school Gates took the bus to the C-Cubed offices and programmed long into the evening.

21   C-Cubed eventually went bankrupt, so Gates and his friends began hanging around the computer centre at the University of Washington. Before long, they latched on to an outfit called ISI (Information Sciences Inc.), which agreed to let them have free computer time in exchange for working on a piece of software that could be used to automate company payrolls. In one seven-month period in 1971, Gates and his cohorts ran up 1,575 hours of computer time on the ISI mainframe, which averages out to eight hours a day, seven days a week.

22   "It was my obsession," Gates says of his early high-school years. "I'd leave at night, after my bedtime. I could walk to the University of Washington from my house. Or I'd take the bus. That's why I'm always generous to the university, because they let me steal so much computer

time." (Years later, Gates's mother said, "We always wondered why it was so hard for him to get up in the morning.") The five years from eighth grade through the end of high school were Bill Gates's Hamburg, and by any measure, he was presented with an even more extraordinary series of opportunities than Bill Joy.

23   And what did virtually all of those opportunities have in common? They all gave Bill Gates extra time to practise. By the time Gates dropped out of Harvard after his sophomore year to try his hand at his own software company, he'd been programming practically non-stop for seven consecutive years. He was *way* past 10,000 hours. How many teenagers in the world had the kind of experience Gates had? "If there were 50 in the world, I'd be stunned," he says. "I had a better exposure to software development at a young age than I think anyone did in that period of time, and all because of an incredibly lucky series of events."

Questions for Discussion

1. "How to Be a Success" is an excerpt from a book. Nevertheless, it has a number of structural components in common with an essay. Identify the introduction, the thesis, and the main examples Gladwell uses to develop his thesis.
2. Paragraphs 4, 8, and 14 are very short (two sentences each). Why do you think Gladwell made these paragraphs so short in contrast to the rest of the excerpt?
3. In addition to examples, Gladwell uses direct quotation extensively to support his thesis. Why?
4. There are many implications to Gladwell's thesis that practice is more important than talent in producing extraordinarily high achievement. He mentions two: you can't be born after September 1 and become a star athlete, and you must be wealthy enough that you don't have to work part-time. Identify three or four other implications that follow from Gladwell's thesis.

GETTING PANCAKE SAUCE FROM TREES
Geoffrey Rowan

1   [1]Soon the sap will be running—which is not a comment on the base-stealing abilities of any specific Toronto Blue Jay. [2]It's maple sap we're talking about, for maple-syrup season is upon us. [3]For centuries, people have been tapping maple trees, drawing off sap, and boiling it down into sweet, sticky, amber syrup that's a perfect sauce for pancakes, French

toast, and waffles. [4]Making maple syrup can be extremely low-tech, requiring little more than a bucket, a pan, a wood fire, and, of course, a maple tree or two. [5]Making lots of maple syrup takes a bit more technical sophistication.

2 [6]First, something about the trees. [7]Most maple syrup comes from the sugar or rock maple (*acer saccharum*), found only in North America, and the black maple (*acer nigrum*). [8]It takes a maple 20 to 80 years to grow to a tappable diameter of 25 centimetres. [9]The sap, which is mostly water and about 2 to 4 per cent maple syrup, is formed through the process of photosynthesis: the tree draws water from the ground and carbon dioxide from the air, and uses the energy of sunlight, absorbed through its leaves, to manufacture organic compounds, including sugar, from the water and carbon dioxide. [10]In winter, the sap retreats to the tree's roots. [11]When the temperature gets above freezing, the sap starts to rise. [12]Maple-syrup producers say the optimum conditions for drawing sap are below-freezing nights and above-freezing days, which create a sort of pump action over the 4- to 6-week-long sap season. [13]Worst is a warm spell, which produces a gush of sap for a few days and then nothing for the rest of the season. [14]It can also give the sap a bad taste. [15]Sap production varies greatly from tree to tree, but producers say they like to get 1 to 2.5 litres of syrup per tap. [16]It takes about 40 litres of sap to make 1 litre of syrup.

3 [17]Once a tappable tree has been identified, [the collection process can begin]. [18]A tap—called a spile—is driven 3.5 centimetres into the tree. [19]A spile is simply a small tube, tapered at one end. [20]Some have a little hook hanging below the lip of the exposed end for hanging a bucket. [21]But big syrup producers don't use buckets anymore. [22]They run plastic tubing from trees to feeder lines to main lines and back to a collection centre, creating a bizarre cat's cradle in the woods. [23]The problems with tube collection are deer, elk, and moose, which can pull tubing down as they wander among the trees, and squirrels, which chew holes in it. [24]Some producers arrange the lines so gravity will pull the sap through the tubes to storage tanks. [25]Others use pumps to create a vacuum that draws the sap along the lines. [26]Vacuum power can suck about 50 percent more sap out of a tree than gravity.

4 [27]From a holding tank in the sugar house, the sap flows into an evaporator, which is basically a pan with a corrugated bottom. [28]The ridges on the bottom create more surface area, making it more efficient to apply heat to boil away the water. [29]The most sophisticated evaporators have automatic draw-off systems. [30]Sensors monitor the density and temperature of the syrup and start the draw-off at the proper time. [31]Less sophisticated systems rely on producers paying careful attention to their thermometers and density metres. [32]Some large producers have intro-

duced a step between the storage tank and the evaporator. [33]They pump the sap through a reverse-osmosis unit, which contains a semi-permeable membrane that can remove up to 75 percent of the sap's water. [34]Once in the evaporator, the sap is kept over the fire until enough water has boiled off to make it 66 percent sugar. [35]At this point it has become maple syrup and is drained off, filtered through felt, and poured into hot bottles.

5   [36]Then there are the really unsophisticated systems for small-scale hobbyists, systems that are closer to the time-honoured process involving buckets and pans and hardwood fires than to the high-tech procedures today's producers employ. [37]Maple-syrup kits are available that include spiles and an evaporator that will fit on a gas barbecue. [38]All you need is a couple of productive, healthy maple trees. [39]A word of caution: don't try to boil down your sap on the stove or in the oven unless you want a sticky, sugary coating over everything in the house.

Questions for Discussion

1. What is the author's purpose in this article: to tell readers how to make maple syrup or to tell readers how syrup is made?
2. Where in the article does Rowan clearly identify his subject? Where does he outline the major steps of the process?
3. What do you think of the author's attention-getter? Is it effective?
4. Outline the main points of the process described in this piece. In what order are the points arranged?
5. What purpose does the second paragraph serve? Would the article be equally effective if this paragraph had been omitted?
6. Consider the concluding paragraph: How does it bring the article to a satisfying close?

THE MAGIC OF MOVIEGOING

Rick Groen

1   What movies to watch; with whom to watch; where, when and why to watch. Of course, we got it covered, and so does everyone else. Turn to your favourite newspaper or magazine and, on any given week, these cinematic five Ws will all be lined up and duly addressed. In the arts no less than the news, they're the standard quintet of queries, forming the foundation for most critical commentary. But there's another question, equally interesting, that seldom gets examined or even asked. It's not the

What but the How of the matter: How do we behave during this pop rite of going to the picture show?

2   Let's confine our little inquiry to theatres proper, and exclude living rooms. Obviously, it's a very different experience viewing a film in the bright confines of your home and through the tiny frame of a TV set. There, we tend to watch more forgivingly, more tolerantly. For every majestic opus, every *Lawrence of Arabia*, that suffers when removed from the big screen, there are a myriad humdrum flicks—tepid thrillers, formula comedies—that actually seem more palatable on the tube. They get better because our expectations get lowered—our investment (of time and money) is just smaller.

3   Clearly, the stakes are raised when the setting shifts to a real movie house. So how do we watch there? Well, indulge me for a second while I pick up a popular line of thought about film theatres, the one that insists on a connection between Where and What. This theory suggests that the architecture of the movie theatre is somehow intrinsically linked to the makeup of the movies. Back in the era of the single-screen theatre, the films neatly fit their abodes—a charming Fred Astaire musical felt right at home in an art-deco palace. And now, with the switch from unique local cinemas to multiplex malls, these vast generic structures are attracting the product they deserve—loud look-alike films for loud, look-alike boxes. There, the argument continues, the patrons pick out a movie as they would a channel, and with about as much optimism—18 screens yet nothing to watch.

4   I don't think so. Although no fan of the multiplex, I'm leery of such rear-view mirror reasoning, the nostalgic yearning for an illusory past where every screen was silver and every movie golden. Anyway, nostalgia just keeps getting updated. No doubt, a few decades from now, some savage modernist will be tearing down some vintage multiplex, and today's 20-year-olds will be penning tearful odes to the passing of an aesthetic landmark. And they'[ll] be doing so for a good reason. Although where we watch and what we watch have changed radically over time, how we watch has stayed relatively constant. Indeed, for many, the ritual of moviegoing is a large part of the allure, every bit as appealing as the movies themselves.

5   That ritual begins at the box office. Movies were invented as a form of mass entertainment, and there's a nicely democratic quality to the very act of entering a theatre. What you buy is a general admission ticket, not an assigned seat, which invariably leads to that through-the-foyer-into-the-aisle scramble for your preferred location—way up front where actors look like giant celluloid idols, mid-range for a less infantilizing perspective, deep in the far reaches for those with extracinematic pursuits in mind.

6   Yes, that's part of the ritual. Moviegoing is a social experience. People tend to go in couples or groups. Always, they want to sit together. Too often, they want to talk together. And usually, they want to eat and drink together. In fact, given the wider variety of fare—the hot dogs, the nachos, the pastries—available at the multiplex, "dinner and a movie" has been replaced by "dinner at the movie." (Thanks to the concessions' inflated prices, the hit to the wallet is about the same.) Last, but hardly least, don't forget to add sex to the social equation. A movie is frequently a date; it's foreplay.

7   But now the picture starts, and a tension immediately develops between two competing interests—between moviegoing, which is primarily a social experience, and movie-watching, which is essentially an individual experience. A film projected onto a screen in a darkened theatre approximates the state of dreaming, and is intensely personal. So when the lights go down, these duelling impulses—to socialize or to watch, to talk with others or to dream alone—begin to meld. As they do, the theatre becomes simultaneously a public and a private space, with people striving to get the balance right and to keep the boundaries straight.

8   We strive for a similar balance inside our automobiles—another hybrid of public and private space. Of course, the car and the motion picture enjoy a shared history. Both came of age through the early part of the last century; both are transporting devices in their separate fashions; and both serve as havens for our sexual desires, either symbolically or otherwise. Inevitably, their twin paths intersected in the steamy atmosphere of the drive-in theatre, a place that typically specialized in showing B-pictures—the kind that weren't too distracting, that prevented the private experience of movie-watching from infringing on the social experience of moviegoing.

9   Which brings us to a conclusion less obvious than it might seem at first glance: How we behave at a movie is directly influenced by what we're viewing. The more engrossing the film, the more that moviegoing gives way to movie-watching. We've all observed, even felt this transition—it's almost palpable. Suddenly, popcorn stops being munched, words stop being exchanged, passes stop being made. As we get lost in the movie, we get lost to our companions. But there's a paradox at work here too. This convergence of disparate people turns into an audience, becomes one, only when the various social groupings have disintegrated and its members have splintered off into their private selves. The irony is bald but delicious: When we are most truly alone, we are most truly an audience.

10   That's how we watch movies at our best. And, for me, that's the recurring magic of movies, the alchemical wizardry that can break down a buzzing crowd into islands of attentive individuals, then re-assemble those islands into an archipelago of a rapt audience. Funny thing about

this wizardry. Disdainful of borders and blind to class, the stuff can pop up anywhere folks gather to find it—at a sprawling multiplex in Dolby surround-sound, or on a white sheet strung between tent poles in the thin open air. The magic may come, or not, but one thing is sure—it's always worth the wait.

Questions for Discussion

1. What stages in the ritual of moviegoing does the author identify? Which paragraphs describe each stage? Have any stages been left out?
2. Paragraphs 7 and 8 are developed by means of comparison. What two things are compared in paragraph 7? In paragraph 8? Did you find these comparisons helpful in understanding Groen's thesis? Why?
3. Identify the elements of the "social experience" (paragraph 6) of going to a movie.
4. According to paragraph 9, what is the connection between people's behaviour at a movie and the movie itself?
5. Analyze the first and last paragraphs of this essay: identify the attention-getter, the statement of thesis, the summary/reinforcement, and the memorable statement.
6. Much of this essay is written in first-person plural: *we* and *us*. How would the effect of the essay change if it was written in the third person (*he*, *she*, *they*)? To demonstrate the change, rewrite paragraph 9 in the third person, beginning with the sentence, "How people behave at a movie is directly influenced by what they're viewing." When you've finished your revision, exchange papers with another student. Check your partner's paper for pronoun consistency. Then decide which version (first person or third person) you prefer and why.
7. What, in your own words, is the magic of moviegoing according to Groen?

GET RADICAL. GET SOME REST.

Matt Carmichael

1   In *Prozac Nation*, a memoir that struck a chord with millions of readers, Elizabeth Wurtzel writes, "I don't want any more of this try, try again stuff. I just want out. I've had it. I am so tired. I am 20 and I am already exhausted." Despite the fact that we are surrounded by labor-saving devices, despite the elevation of convenience and comfort above almost all other values, a profound sense of tiredness seems to be one of the

defining features of modern life. And our world is as exhausted as we are. Our ecosystems are stretched far beyond their limits, and social structures like families and communities battle for survival.

2   The natural response to tiredness is to rest. Modern consumer culture, however, doesn't like rest; "time is money," we are told. Every second saved by a dishwasher or a car must be paid back double in longer working hours. In the gym, exercise (which is freely available in the nearest park) is sold at exclusive rates so that we can do it while we're watching television. Even rest itself is commercialized and repackaged as "leisure."

3   Returning to truly replenishing forms of rest would demand a reevaluation of tiredness—all the different kinds, each of which leads to negative personal, social, and ecological consequences. In doing so, we would address the problem of unsustainability, which is, after all, the essence of tiredness. When we are tired, we know we cannot carry on in the same way for long. In evaluating all the ways we're tired, we confront what makes life unsustainable. For us, and for our world.

4   First, there's *sleepiness*. When we do not sleep properly, our brains run on depleted energy; compassion, creativity, imagination, and reason are lost, and the reptilian fight-or-flight brain takes over. Some psychiatrists have suggested that depression is a symptom of sleep loss, rather than the other way around. A shortage of sleep is associated with obesity, road accidents, torture, and war. In ecological terms, 24-hour culture means more emissions and more consumption of the earth's limited resources; we find ways to justify new runways, new wars, space tourism, and drilling for oil under melting arctic ice. The solution, of course, is sleep. When the emperor of Persia asked his Sufi master how best to renew his soul, he was told to sleep as much as possible because "The longer you sleep, the less you will oppress!" We sacrifice sleep for time, but that time becomes less fulfilling—and robs the earth of resources.

5   Another kind of tiredness is *fatigue*: a tiredness of activity. We live in a hyperactive culture where more is continually demanded of us. Unions have to fight to maintain vacation allowances and workday limits. Life proceeds at a pace that belongs not to the human scale, but to the industrial scale. Fossil fuels allow us to travel great distances at inhuman speeds without feeling tired. The tiredness we would have felt does not disappear, but is displaced onto the ecosystems that support our existence. It turns out that the toddler who observed the airplane "scratching the sky" was right. I used to look askance at evangelical Christian athletes who would not compete on a Sunday. Now I think we should follow their example. We are tempted to avoid rest because we think we will produce more, but what we produce is less wonderful.

6   We should also consider *ennui*, which is tiredness of stasis. Ennui is all about that feeling of being stuck in a rut, of going nowhere. It is extraordinary that in our hyperactive society so many people are bored. Bored young people hang around the streets causing trouble. Bored soldiers commit acts of atrocity in military prisons. Workers are forced to choose between the boredom of the production line and the boredom of unemployment. Television, computer games, and prescription drugs temporarily screen us from the effects of boredom, but it comes back to haunt us in poor mental health, addiction, crime, and disease.

7   It seems logical that the antidote to ennui is activity. However, as we have seen, we are very active—even hyperactive. We need to replace activities that isolate mind from body with activities that involve the whole person in a valuable process. There are many sources of wisdom to help us here. Gandhi viewed work as sacred. Dutch historian Johan Huizinga showed how play is fundamental to human welfare, and the *Kama Sutra* explores the spiritual significance of sex. Martial arts generally developed as forms of meditation, ritualizing movement in order to replenish body and mind. In agriculture, one alternative to a static monoculture is crop rotation: Moving the crop replenishes the soil.

8   Perhaps the most prevalent form of tiredness in our society is *satiation*, tiredness of consumption. Our society has an obesity problem that extends far beyond the body mass index. Shopping is a chief "leisure activity." We continue to consume rapaciously because we are wedded to ownership, but the real effects of satiation are unwelcome. They first show up in the environment, where the raw materials for all this consumption must be found. Then they appear in unequal societies and unjust legislation that favors the obscenely wealthy.

9   The answer is sacrifice. Every year Muslims fast during daylight hours for the month of Ramadan. This is a striking example of the use of sacrifice for the benefit of an entire community. Christians and Jews tithe. Sikhs practice hospitality and share food; monks take vows of poverty; vegetarians and vegans refrain from eating meat; ethical consumers refuse to buy the shiny trinkets that are constantly advertised.

10   We are increasingly aware that capitalism is failing to make sense for our lives; money is not making us happy. But many of us who are ready to change are not aware of any alternative. So we carry on rushing around, making money, buying temporary happiness. In a culture so dependent on activity—on consuming, producing, and achieving—rest becomes a radical form of protest and a catalyst for change.

Questions for Discussion

1. In this essay, Carmichael classifies four kinds of tiredness that afflict us. Name them, define them, and identify the consequences associated with each one.
2. What is the primary method of development that the writer uses to support his main points? Identify five or six instances of this technique.
3. Identify the attention-getter and thesis statement in paragraph 1.
4. Now consider the conclusion (paragraph 10). There is no summary or reinforcement of the writer's main points. Why not? As a reader, do you think paragraph 10 brings the essay to a satisfactory conclusion?
5. What is the purpose of this essay? Is the author really suggesting that we should sleep more because while we are asleep we do less harm? How does the author want to affect us?

SIT DOWN AND SHUT UP OR DON'T SIT BY ME
Dennis Dermody

1 All right, I admit it: I'm a tad neurotic when it comes to making it to the movies on time. I have to be there at least a half hour before the feature begins. Not that I'm worried about long lines at the box office, either. The movies I rush off to see are generally so sparsely attended you can hear crickets in the audience. It's just a thing I do.

2 Of course, sitting for 30 minutes watching a theater fill up is pretty boring, but through the years I've amused myself with a Margaret Mead-like study of the way people come in and take their seats and their antics during a movie. I felt I should share my impressions lest you find yourself succumbing to these annoying traits.

3 Right off the bat: Leave the kids at home. We're not talking about *Aladdin* or *Home Alone 2*—that I understand—but recently I went to see *Body of Evidence*, and it looked like a day-care center in the theater. Strollers were flying down the aisle, children were whining for candy, restless and audibly bored (especially during the hot-wax-dripping sequence), and eventually the day-care atmosphere caused fights among the adults. "Shut your kid up!" prompted a proud parent to slug a fellow patron, and before you knew it there were angry skirmishes all over the theater and the police had to be brought in. So either leave them at home with a sitter or tie them up to a fire hydrant outside the theater.

4   For some people, choosing a seat takes on moral and philosophical implications. Sometimes they stand in the middle of the aisle juggling coats, popcorn, and Cokes, seemingly overwhelmed by the prospect of choice. Should I sit down front, or will that be too close? Is this too far back? That man seems awfully tall, I bet I couldn't see the movie if I sat behind him. I'd love to sit somewhere in the middle but would I be too close to that group of teenagers shooting heroin into their necks? If I sit on this side, will the angle be too weird to watch the movie? Is that seat unoccupied because it's broken? Good Lord, the lights are dimming and I haven't made up my mind and now I won't be able to see where I am going.

5   Many, upon choosing their seats, find they are unsatisfied and have to move. I've watched many couples go from one spot to another more than a dozen times before settling down—it's like watching a bird testing different spots to build a nest.

6   As the lights begin to dim and the annoying theater-chain logo streaks across the screen, lo and behold, here come the *latecomers*! Their eyes unaccustomed to the dark, in a panic they search for friends, for assistance, for a lonely seat. Just the other day, I watched an elderly woman come into the darkened theater 20 minutes after the movie had begun and say out loud, "I can't see anything!" She then proceeded to inch her way down the aisle, grabbing onto what she thought were seats but were actually people's heads. I saw her sit down right in the lap of someone who shrieked in shock. After the woman stumbled back into the aisle, chattering wildly, someone mercifully directed her to an empty seat. Then, after a great flourish of getting out of her bulky coat, she asked spiritedly of the grumbling souls around her, "What did I miss?"

7   I also must address the behavior of people *during* the movie. The *chatterers* comment blithely on everything that is happening on the screen. Like Tourette's syndrome sufferers unable to control what they blurt out, these people say anything that comes into their heads. "What a cute puppy," they say when they spy an animal ambling off to the side of the frame. "I have that lamp at home," they exclaim. And add, five minutes later, "But mine is red."

8   The *krinklers* wander down the aisle with a million shopping bags and wait for a key sequence and then begin to forage in their bags for the perfect and most annoying plastic wrap, which they use to make noise with sadistic relish. You try to focus on the screen but the racket starts up again with a wild flourish. I've seen grown men leap to their feet with tears streaming down their face and scream, "Will you stop shaking that motherfucking bag!"

9   The *unending box of popcorn* people sit directly behind you and start masticating during the opening credits. It's bad enough having the smell

of cooked corn wafting around you, but the sound is enough to drive you mad. You tell yourself that eventually they'll finish, but they never do. They keep chewing and chewing and chewing and you're deathly afraid that next they'll start on a four-pound box of malted milk balls.

10 So in summary: Get to the movie theater early and scout out the territory. It's a jungle in there, filled with a lot of really stupid animals. Know the telltale signs and act accordingly. And then sit down and shut up.

Questions for Discussion

1. What does Dermody mean when he admits, in his opening sentence, that he is a "tad neurotic"? How does this confession affect the reader's response to the judgments that follow?
2. What is the author's purpose in this essay (see paragraph 2)? Do you think he achieves it?
3. This essay classifies moviegoers according to their pre-movie and during-movie behaviours. Identify the six categories of the author's classification system.
4. When Dermody uses phrases such as "tie them up to a fire hydrant" (paragraph 3) or "teenagers shooting heroin into their necks" (paragraph 4), he obviously does not mean to be taken seriously. Identify two or three other examples of this kind of exaggeration and consider how it affects the tone of the essay.
5. What metaphor does Dermody use in the conclusion of this piece? How does it contribute to the unity of the essay?
6. Would you like to go to a movie with the author? Why or why not?

THE TERM PAPER ARTIST
Nick Mamatas

1 One great way to briefly turn the conversation toward myself at a party is to answer the question, "So, what do you do?" with, "I'm a writer." Not that most of the people I've met at parties have read my novels or short stories or feature articles; when they ask, "Have I seen any of your stuff?" I shrug and the conversation moves on. If I want attention for an hour or so, however, I'll tell them my horrible secret—for several years I made much of my freelance income writing term papers.

2 I always wanted to be writer, but was told from an early age that such a dream was futile. After all, nobody ever puts a classified ad in the paper that reads "Writers Wanted." Then, in the *Village Voice*, I saw just such an ad. Writers wanted, to write short pieces on business, economics, and

literature. It was from a term paper mill, and they ran the ad at the beginning of each semester.

3   Writing model term papers is above-board and perfectly legal. Thanks to the First Amendment, it's protected speech, right up there with neo-Nazi rallies, tobacco company press releases, and those "9/11 Was an Inside Job" bumper stickers. It's custom-made Cliff Notes. Virtually any subject, almost any length, all levels of education—indulgent parents even buy papers for children too young for credit cards of their own. You name it, I've done it. Perhaps unsurprisingly, the plurality of clients was business administration majors, but both elementary education majors and would-be social workers showed up aplenty. Even the assignments for what in my college days were the obvious gut courses crossed my desk. "Race in *The Matrix*" was a fashionable subject.

4   The term paper biz is managed by brokers who take financial risks by accepting credit card payments and psychological risks by actually talking to the clients. Most of the customers just aren't very bright. One of my brokers would even mark assignments with the code words DUMB CLIENT. That meant to use simple English; nothing's worse than a client calling back to ask a broker—most of whom had no particular academic training—what certain words in the paper meant. One time a client actually asked to talk to me personally and lamented that he just didn't "know a lot about Plah-toe." Distance learning meant that he'd never heard anyone say the name.

5   In broad strokes, there are three types of term paper clients. DUMB CLIENTS predominate. They should not be in college. They *must* buy model papers simply because they do not understand what a term paper is, much less anything going on in their assignments. I don't believe that most of them even handed the papers in as their own, as it would have been obvious that they didn't write them. Frequently I was asked to underline the thesis statement because locating it otherwise would have been too difficult. But that sort of thing was just average for the bottom of the barrel student-client. To really understand how low the standards are these days, we must lift up the barrel and see what squirms beneath. One time, I got an e-mail from the broker with some last-minute instructions for a term paper—"I told her that it is up to the writer whether or not he includes this because it was sent to me at the last minute. So if you can take a look at this, that is fine, if not I understand." The last-minute addition was to produce a section called "BODY OF PAPER" (capitals *sic*). I was also asked to underline this section so that the client could identify it. Of course, I underlined everything but the first and last paragraphs of the three-page paper.

6   The second type of client is the one-timer. A chemistry major trapped in a poetry class thanks to the vagaries of schedule and distribution

requirements, or worse, the poet trapped in a chemistry class. These clients were generally lost and really did simply need a decent summary of their class readings—I once boiled the 1000-page *New Testament Theology* by Donald Guthrie into a 30-page précis over the course of a weekend for a quick $600.

7   Others are stuck on their personal statements for college applications, and turn to their parents, who then turn to a term paper mill. One mother unashamedly summarized her boy and his goals like so: "[My son] is a very kind hearted young man. One who will make a difference in whatever he does. Barely can go unnoticed because of his vivacious character, happiness, and joy in life. He is very much in tune with his fortune and often helps the less fortunate." The kid planned to be a pre-med major if accepted, but was applying to a competitive college as a Women's Studies major because Mother was "told the chances of him getting into [prominent college] under less desirable subjects (as opposed to Business) was better." Finally, she explained to me the family philosophy—"Since our family places great emphasis on education, [boy] fully accepts that the only guarantee for a good and stable future can be only achieved through outstanding education."

8   The third group is perhaps the most tragic: They are well-educated professionals who simply lack English-language skills. Often they come from the former Soviet Union, and in their home countries were engineers, medical professionals, and scientists. In the United States, they drive cabs and have to pretend to care about "Gothicism in 'A Rose for Emily'" for the sake of another degree. For the most part, these clients actually send in their own papers and they get an edit from a native speaker. Sometimes they even pinch-hit for the brokers, doing papers on graduate-level physics and nursing themselves.

9   Term paper writing was never good money, but it was certainly fast money. For a freelancer, where any moment of slack time is unpaid time, term papers are just too tempting. Need $100 by Friday to keep the lights on? No sweat. Plenty of kids need 10 pages on *Hamlet* by Thursday. Finals week is a gold mine. More than once the phone rang at midnight and the broker had an assignment. Six pages by 6 a.m.—the kid needs three hours to rewrite and hand in the paper by 9 or he won't graduate. "Cool," I'd say. "A hundred bucks a page." I'd get it, too, and when I didn't get it, I slept well anyway. Even DUMB CLIENTS could figure out that they'd be better off spending $600 on the model paper instead of $2,500 to repeat a course. Back in the days when a pulse and pay stub was sufficient to qualify for a mortgage, term papers—along with gigs for dot.com-era business magazines—helped me buy my first house.

10   Term paper work is also extremely easy, once you get the hang of it. It's like an old dance routine buried in one's muscle memory. You hear the

tune—say, "Unlike the ancient Greek tragic playwrights, Shakespeare likes to insert humor in his tragedies"—and your body does the rest automatically. I'd just scan Google or databases like Questia.com for a few quotes from primary and secondary sources, create an argument based on whatever popped up from my search, write the introduction and <u>underline the thesis statement</u>, then fill in the empty spaces between quotes with whatever came to mind.

11 Getting the hang of it is tricky, though. Over the years, several of my friends wanted in on the term paper racket, and most of them couldn't handle it. They generally made the same fundamental error—they tried to write term papers. In the paper mill biz, the paper isn't important. The deadline, page count, and number of sources are. DUMB CLIENTS make up much of the trade. They have no idea whether or not Ophelia committed suicide or was secretly offed by Gertrude, but they know how to count to seven if they ordered seven pages.

12 The secret to the gig is to amuse yourself. I have to, really, as most paper topics are deadly boring. Once, I was asked to summarize in three pages the causes of the First World War (page one), the major battles and technological innovations of the war (page two), and to explain the aftermath of the war, including how it led to the Second World War (page three). Then there was this assignment for a composition class: six pages on why "apples [the fruit] are the best." You have to make your own fun. In business papers, I'd often cite Marxist sources. When given an open topic assignment on ethics, I'd write on the ethics of buying term papers, and even include the broker's Web site as a source. My own novels and short stories were the topic of many papers—several DUMB CLIENTS rate me as their favorite author and they've never even read me, or anyone else. Whenever papers needed to refer to a client's own life experiences, I'd give the student various sexual hang-ups.

13 It's not that I never felt a little skeevy writing papers. Mostly it was a game, and a way to subsidize my more interesting writing. Also, I've developed a few ideas of my own over the years. I don't have the academic credentials of composition experts, but I doubt many experts spent most of a decade writing between one and five term papers a day on virtually every subject. I know something they don't know; I know why students don't understand thesis statements, argumentative writing, or proper citations.

14 It's because students have never read term papers.

15 Imagine trying to write a novel, for a grade, under a tight deadline, without ever having read a novel. Instead, you meet once or twice a week

with someone who is an expert in *describing* what novels are like. Novels are long stories, you see, that depict a "slice of life" featuring a middle-class protagonist. Psychological realism is prized in novels. Moral instruction was once fairly common in novels, but is now considered gauche. Novels end when the protagonist has an epiphany, such as "I am not happy. Also, neither is anybody else." Further, many long fictions are called novels even though they are really adventures, and these ersatz novels may take place in a fantastical setting and often depict wild criminal behaviors and simplified versions of international intrigues instead of middle-class quandaries. Sometimes there are pirates, but only so that a female character may swoon at their well-developed abdominal muscles. That's a novel. What are you waiting for? Start writing! Underline your epiphany.

16 There's another reason I never felt too badly about the job, though I am pleased to be done with papers. The students aren't only cheating themselves. They are being cheated by the schools that take tuition and give nothing in exchange. Last year, I was hired to write two one-page summaries of two short stories. Here are the client's instructions: "i need you to write me two different story in all these listed under. The introduction of the story, the themes, topic and character, please not from internet, Or any posted web sites, because my professor will know if from internet this is the reason why i'm spending money on it. Not two much words, because i will still write it back in clsss go straight to the point and write me the conclution at end of the two story, the second story different introduction, themes, topic and character. Thank you God Bless."

17 At the parties I go to, people start off laughing, but then they stop.

Questions for Discussion

1. What is the purpose of the last line of this essay? What effect did it have on you when you read it?
2. There are three main parts to this essay. The first classifies the types of term paper clients. Identify the other two sections and the paragraphs that contain them.
3. Does the author have a point to make beyond telling his amusing story? What serious conclusions can be drawn from his experiences?
4. Why does the author use capital letters and underlining to emphasize certain phrases? What effect does his typographical emphasis have on the reader?
5. Who, other than the students, does the author hold responsible for the existence of term paper mills? Do you agree with him? Why?

TOOTHPASTE
David Bodanis

1 Into the bathroom [we go], and after the most pressing need is satisfied it's time to brush the teeth. The tube of toothpaste is squeezed, its pinched metal seams are splayed, pressure waves are generated inside, and the paste begins to flow. But what's in this toothpaste, so carefully being extruded out?

2 Water mostly, 30 to 45 per cent of most brands: ordinary, everyday simple tap water. It's there because people like to have a big gob of toothpaste to spread on the brush, and water is the cheapest stuff there is when it comes to making big gobs. Dripping a bit from the tap onto your brush would cost virtually nothing; whipped in with the rest of the toothpaste the manufacturers can sell it at a neat and accountant-pleasing $2 per pound equivalent. Toothpaste manufacture is a very lucrative occupation.

3 Second to water in quantity is chalk: exactly the same material that schoolteachers use to write on blackboards. It is collected from the crushed remains of long-dead ocean creatures. In the Cretaceous Seas chalk particles served as part of the wickedly sharp outer skeleton that these creatures had to wrap around themselves to keep from getting chomped by all the slightly larger other ocean creatures they met. Their massed graves are our present chalk deposits.

4 The individual chalk particles—the size of the smallest mud particles in your garden—have kept their toughness over the aeons, and now on the toothbrush they'll need it. The enamel outer coating of the tooth they'll have to face is the hardest substance in the body—tougher than skull, or bone, or nail. Only the chalk particles in toothpaste can successfully grind into the teeth during brushing, ripping off the surface layers like an abrading wheel grinding down a boulder in a quarry.

5 The craters, slashes, and channels that the chalk tears into the teeth will also remove a certain amount of built-up yellow in the carnage, and it is for that polishing function that it's there. A certain amount of unduly enlarged extra-abrasive chalk fragments tear such cavernous pits into the teeth that future decay bacteria will be able to bunker down there and thrive; the quality control people find it almost impossible to screen out these errant super-chalk pieces, and government regulations allow them to stay in.

6 In case even the gouging doesn't get all the yellow off, another substance is worked into the toothpaste cream. This is titanium dioxide. It comes in tiny spheres, and it's the stuff bobbing around in white wall paint to make it come out white. Splashed around onto your teeth during

the brushing coats much of the yellow that remains. Being water soluble it leaks off in the next few hours and is swallowed, but at least for the quick glance up in the mirror after finishing it will make the user think his teeth are truly white. Some manufacturers add optical whitening dyes—the stuff more commonly found in washing machine bleach—to make extra sure that the glance in the mirror shows reassuring white.

7   These ingredients alone would not make a very attractive concoction. They would stick in the tube like a sloppy white plastic lump, hard to squeeze out as well as revolting to the touch. Few consumers would savor rubbing in a mixture of water, ground-up blackboard chalk and the whitener from latex paint first thing in the morning. To get around that finicky distaste the manufacturers have mixed in a host of other goodies.

8   To keep the glop from drying out, a mixture including glycerine glycol—related to the most common car anti-freeze ingredient—is whipped in with the chalk and water, and to give *that* concoction a bit of substance (all we really have so far is wet colored chalk) a large helping is added of gummy molecules from the seaweed *Chondrus crispus*. This seaweed ooze spreads in among the chalk, paint and anti-freeze, then stretches itself in all directions to hold the whole mass together. A bit of paraffin oil (the fuel that flickers in camping lamps) is pumped in with it to help the moss ooze keep the whole substance smooth.

9   With the glycol, ooze and paraffin we're almost there. Only two major chemicals are left to make the refreshing, cleansing substance we know as toothpaste. The ingredients so far are fine for cleaning, but they wouldn't make much of the satisfying foam we have come to expect in the morning brushing.

10   To remedy that, every toothpaste on the market has a big dollop of detergent added, too. You've seen the suds detergent will make in a washing machine. The same substance added here will duplicate that inside the mouth. It's not particularly necessary, but it sells.

11   The only problem is that by itself this ingredient tastes, well, too like detergent. It's horribly bitter and harsh. The chalk put in toothpaste is pretty foul-tasting too for that matter. It's to get around that gustatory discomfort that the manufacturers put in the ingredient they tout perhaps the most of all. This is the flavoring, and it has to be strong. Double rectified peppermint oil is used—a flavorer so powerful that chemists know better than to sniff it in the raw state in the laboratory. Menthol crystals and saccharin or other sugar simulators are added to complete the camouflage operation.

12   Is that it? Chalk, water, paint, seaweed, anti-freeze, paraffin oil, detergent and peppermint? Not quite. A mix like that would be irresistible to the hundreds of thousands of individual bacteria lying on the surface of even an immaculately cleaned bathroom sink. They would get in, float

in the water bubbles, ingest the ooze and paraffin, maybe even spray out enzymes to break down the chalk. The result would be an uninviting mess. The way manufacturers avoid that final obstacle is by putting something in to kill the bacteria. Something good and strong is needed, something that will zap any accidentally intrudant bacteria into oblivion. And that something is formaldehyde—the disinfectant used in anatomy labs.

13   So it's chalk, water, paint, seaweed, anti-freeze, paraffin oil, detergent, peppermint, formaldehyde and fluoride (which can go some way toward preserving children's teeth)—that's the usual mixture raised to the mouth on the toothbrush for a fresh morning's clean. If it sounds too unfortunate, take heart. Studies show that thorough brushing with just plain water will often do as good a job.

Questions for Discussion

1. This essay analyzes toothpaste by dividing it into its component parts. Identify each ingredient and the paragraph(s) in which it is described.
2. What is the function of paragraph 7? Paragraph 9? Paragraph 13?
3. Highlight six or seven examples of the author's use of vivid description to communicate his analysis and his attitude toward toothpaste.
4. Part of the effect of this essay depends on Bodanis's descriptive details. He uses words that are very different from those we are familiar with in television commercials for the same product. Highlight three or four examples of Bodanis's use of language that you would never hear in a product advertisement. What effect does the author's choice of words have on the reader?
5. Why is Bodanis so harsh on toothpaste manufacturers? (See paragraph 2.) Do you agree with him? What makes you choose a particular brand of toothpaste?

THE GAS–ELECTRIC HYBRID DEMYSTIFIED

Sara R. Howerth

1   A hybrid is a cross between two established varieties of plant, animal, . . . or technology. The hybrid bicycle, for example, combines the features of a road bike with those of an off-road bike to produce a comfortable and efficient bicycle for short-distance cycling. For most people today, the word "hybrid" signifies a fuel-efficient, low-emission automobile. Hybrid car technology combines a gasoline or diesel internal combustion engine

with a battery-powered electric motor. Its objective is to maximize the best properties of both the gas engine and the electric motor.

2   A gasoline engine is powerful enough for the pickup, torque, and speed any driver requires. Because of the petroleum infrastructure that has developed over the past 100 years, gas-powered vehicles are also easy to refuel and can travel 400 km to 800 km between fill-ups. On the other hand, they are expensive to operate and will become even more so as fuel prices rise. More importantly, they are a major cause of the pollution that contributes to smog, environmental degradation, and global warming.

3   Battery-powered electric motors are quiet, efficient, and relatively clean—depending, of course, on how the electricity that charges them is produced. However, they cannot yet travel very far on a charge (some can go 200 km), and most need to be recharged 12 hours or overnight. The technology is evolving rapidly, however, and these limitations of distance and time will probably be significantly reduced in the coming years.

4   The hybrid vehicle uses both types of motors and exploits the advantages of each. A gasoline engine provides the power and torque, while an electric engine adds power and thus reduces the amount of gasoline required. There are two types of hybrid vehicle; the difference between them consists of their approach to the twinning of the two engines.

5   The "mild hybrid" uses a small electric motor that boosts the capability of the gas engine, thus enabling a smaller gas engine to get the same performance as a larger power plant. Small engines consume less gas and produce fewer emissions, so the smaller the gas engine, the more cost and environmental benefit, as long as the electric motor can deliver the performance equivalent of a more powerful engine. Another way the mild hybrid saves fuel is by allowing the gas engine to shut down when the vehicle is stopped, even for a few seconds at a stoplight. The electric engine starts instantly when the accelerator is touched, and it acts as a starter for the gas motor.

6   The "full hybrid" uses the two motors quite differently. Like the mild hybrid, the full hybrid allows the gas engine to shut down when the vehicle is stopped, but it stays off at low speeds (under about 40 km/h), since the vehicle is powered only by the electric motor until more power is required. As speed increases, the gas or diesel motor kicks in automatically and the two work in tandem to provide the power needed for highway driving, acceleration, and climbing. This arrangement means that cars equipped with full-hybrid engines get better mileage in stop-and-start city driving than they do in long-distance highway conditions.

7   Both hybrid models use the power produced by the gas engine to recharge the onboard batteries, so they never need to be recharged by

plugging the vehicle into an outlet. In addition, both models use the electric motor as a generator during deceleration; therefore, power that is normally lost as heat when a conventional car brakes is recaptured and sent to the batteries, keeping them charged. This process is called "regenerative braking."

8   Each year, the marketplace offers more hybrid technology models to cost-conscious and environmentally aware consumers. This trend will continue as long as gas prices rise (which they must do as oil resources decline), and as long as people and governments are concerned about the pollution caused by petroleum-powered vehicles. The hybrid will no doubt be a stepping stone to even more efficient, less polluting technologies, such as fully electric or hydrogen fuel-cell powered cars. But for now and in the immediate future, the hybrid automobile is a technology whose time has arrived.

Questions for Discussion

1. The structure of this essay is more complex than that of the two essays we used to illustrate comparison and contrast in Chapter 18. To understand how this piece is put together, write an outline for it.
2. What audience did the author have in mind when she wrote this essay? Car enthusiasts? Auto mechanics? The general reader? Identify at least three examples from the essay to support your answer.
3. What methods of paragraph development does Howerth use to help her readers understand her explanation of her subject? Support your answer with specific examples in the essay.
4. Search InfoTrac to find another article that discusses the differences between the "full hybrid" and the "mild hybrid." Compare that article to Howerth's essay. Consider target audience, level of language, and the purpose of the two pieces. Which was easier for you to understand? Why?

[*Note:* The following essay is documented in MLA style.]

JUSTICE AND JOURNALISM
Victor Chen

1   "Justice must not only be done, it must be seen to be done." This principle, in part, accounts for the news media's appetite for stories about our justice system. It is the principle that news organizations always cite when their access to information about the courts, criminals, or police is limited, or when they are prevented from distributing that information. Given the media's apparent concern for the public's knowledge about

Canadian justice, it is troubling to learn that what we read, hear, and see is often distorted. The reality of our justice system and what we learn about it from our media are, all too often, two different things. Two aspects of our justice system will serve to illustrate this contrast: the incidence of violent crime and the sentencing of criminals.

2   Occurrences of violent crime have declined steadily in Canada over the past decade. While this fact has occasionally been reported, it doesn't sell newspapers or advertising nearly as well as juicy stories about murder, mayhem, assault, or aggression. The news media are in business to attract an audience, and the pressure to sensationalize is relentless. Hence, while murders constitute about 1% of violent crime committed in Canada, in our news media more than 25% of crime stories are about killings. Since virtually all of our information about crime comes to us from newspapers and news broadcasts, is it any wonder that we have the impression that murders are far more common than they really are? Furthermore, violent crime represents only about 12% of all crime that is dealt with by our police and courts. Yet, in the media, 50% of the coverage of criminal activity is devoted to violent crime. We have two societies: an imaginary one, created by the news media, that most of us think we live in, and the real, less violent one that few of us know about.

3   As well as a distorted view of violent crime, the media give us false impressions about proceedings in the criminal courts. Except in a few notable cases, reporters are not assigned to cover an entire trial; instead, they attend the courtroom only for the sensational opening addresses and for the verdict and sentencing. Very little of what goes on for most of the trial—the evidence, the arguments, the painstaking detail, and the finer points of courtroom procedure—ever appears in the news. What effect does this omission have on our understanding of law and order? In a recent study, J. Roberts and A. Doob demonstrate that the public's understanding of the justice system is distorted. Half of the participants in the study read the newspaper accounts of a trial. The other half read the court documents—transcripts of what had actually taken place during the trial. Of those who read the newspapers, the vast majority (over 60%) thought that the sentence handed down by the judge was too lenient. Less than 15% felt the sentence was too harsh. However, of those who read the court proceedings without the slant provided by reporters and editors, the majority felt the punishment was too harsh. Less than 20% believed that a more severe sentence was warranted, while more than 50% thought the sentence given for the crime was too long (508–12). What does this experiment tell us about how Canadians form their often strongly held opinions about the justice system?

4   The contrast between what our news media tell us about our justice system and the reality of what is going on in the police departments and

courtrooms of the nation is an indictment of the sensationalist media. Even more important, this contrast is a sobering reminder that our opinions are often based on a superficial understanding of the issues. The news media will not change; the pressures for sensational reporting are too great. Public opinion, therefore, will continue to be based on distorted impressions. We can only hope that our lawmakers will form their opinions and base their decisions not on media reports and not on the popular opinion created by those accounts and reported by the polls, but on a careful, researched study of the reality behind the headlines.

Work Cited

Roberts, Julian, and Anthony Doob. "Sentencing and Public Opinion: Taking False Shadows for True Substances." *Osgoode Hall Law Journal* 27.3 (1989): 491–515. Print.

Questions for Discussion

1. Using the outline format on page 60 and the information that introduces Chapter 18, write an outline that displays the main elements of this essay. How has the author organized his contrast: by the block method or by the point-by-point method? Why?
2. What purpose—other than contrasting the image and reality of our justice system—does the author of this piece have in mind? Does he achieve his purpose?
3. Statistics do not often make very interesting reading. How has the author tried to make the statistics in this essay readable as well as meaningful? Is he successful?
4. As long as they are not overused, rhetorical questions (questions asked for effect rather than to elicit an answer) can be effective in capturing and holding readers' attention. Identify two rhetorical questions in this essay and rephrase them as statements. Which version—question or statement—has more impact on the reader? Why?
5. Parallelism (see Part 7, Section 7.5) is often used by writers to reinforce the seriousness of a subject or the weight of an argument. Identify four examples of parallel structure that you think contribute effectively to the solemn tone of this essay.

FOR MINORITIES, TIMING IS EVERYTHING
Olive Skene Johnson

1   Left-handedness and homosexuality both tend to run in families. As my husband's family and mine have some of each, it is not surprising that one of our children is left-handed and another homosexual. Both my left-handed daughter and my homosexual son turned out to be bright, funny, talented people with loving friends and family. But their experience of growing up in different minority groups was a striking contrast and an interesting illustration of how societal attitudes change as sufficient knowledge accumulates to make old beliefs untenable.

2   By the time my daughter was growing up, left-handedness was no longer regarded as a sign of immorality or mental deficiency. Almost everybody knew "openly" left-handed friends, teachers and relatives and viewed them as normal people who wrote differently. Except for a little awkwardness in learning to write at school, my daughter's hand preference was simply never an issue. If people noticed it at all, they did so with a shrug. Nobody called her nasty names or banned school library books about left-handed families, as school trustees in Surrey, B.C., recently banned books about gay families. Nobody criticized her left-handed "lifestyle" or suggested that she might be an unfit role model for young children. Nobody claimed that she *chose* to be left-handed and should suffer the consequences.

3   My gay son did not choose to be different either, but when he was growing up, homosexuality was still too misunderstood to be accepted as just another variant of human sexuality. Because gay people still felt unsafe revealing their sexual orientation, he was deprived of the opportunity of knowing openly gay teachers, friends and relatives. He grew up hearing crude jokes and nasty names for people like him, and he entered adulthood knowing that being openly gay could prevent you from getting a job or renting an apartment. It could also get you assaulted.

4   Bigotry has never been reserved for homosexuality, of course. I am old enough to remember the time when bigotry directed toward other minorities in Canada was similar to that which is still sometimes aimed at homosexuals. In my Vancouver childhood, Chinese were regularly called "Chinks" (the boys in my high school wore black denim "Chink pants" tailored for them in Chinatown). Black people were "niggers," prohibited from staying in most Vancouver hotels. Kids in the special

class were "retards" or "morons." Jews were suspected of all sorts of crazy things, and physically disabled people were often regarded as mental defectives.

5   Left-handed children were still being punished for writing with their left hand, particularly in the more religious parts of Canada. (When I was a graduate psychology student in Newfoundland doing research on handedness, I discovered that several of my "right-handed" subjects were actually left-handers; at school their left hands had been tied behind their backs by zealous nuns.)

6   The gay children and teachers of my childhood were simply invisible. Two female teachers could live together without raising eyebrows, chiefly because women in those days (especially women *teachers*) were not generally thought of as sexual persons. Two male "bachelors" living together did tend to be suspect, and so gay men brave enough to live together usually kept their living arrangements quiet. "Sissy" boys and "boyish" girls took a lot of teasing, but most people knew too little about homosexuality to draw any conclusions. These boys and girls were expected to grow up and marry people of the opposite sex. Some of them did, divorcing years later to live with one of their own.

7   Many of the teachers and parents of my childhood who tried to convert left-handed children into right-handers probably believed they were helping children avoid the stigma of being left-handed, just as many misguided therapists tried to "cure" patients of their homosexuality to enable them to avoid the stigma of being gay in a heterosexual world.

8   Thanks to advances in our understanding, left-handedness gradually came to be seen as a natural and innate trait. We know now that people do not *choose* to be more skillful with one hand than the other; they simply are. While researchers are still debating the precise mechanisms that determine hand preference, there is general agreement that left- and right-handedness are just two different (and valid) ways of being. Left-handers are a minority in their own right, not "deviants" from normal right-handedness.

9   The same is true for sexual orientation. Although we do not yet clearly understand the mechanisms that determine sexual orientation, all indicators point to the conclusion that it results from interactions between genetic, hormonal and possibly other factors, all beyond the individual's control. Like left-handedness, sexual orientation is an innate trait, not a choice or "lifestyle." Like left-handedness, homosexuality is a valid alternative sexuality, not a deviance from "normal" heterosexuality.

10   As with other minorities, attitudes toward homosexuality are inevitably becoming more liberal, at least in Canada. A recent poll, commissioned by the B.C. Teachers' Federation, found that almost 70 per cent of B.C. residents think students should be taught in school to accept

homosexuals and treat them as they would other people. (Twenty per cent said homosexuality should be discouraged, 9 per cent said they didn't know and 3 per cent refused to answer.) These results indicate that overt bigotry toward homosexuality is increasingly limited to religious extremists. The Surrey school trustees who voted against having gay and lesbian resource materials in schools are probably at about the same stage of cultural evolution as were the Newfoundland nuns who tied children's left hands behind their backs 40 years ago.

11   Even so, I'm grateful that they're further along the path of enlightenment than their predecessors in medieval Europe, who burned many left-handers and homosexuals at the stake. Being born in the late 20th century was a wise move on the part of my son and daughter. In some things, timing is everything.

Questions for Discussion

1. To develop the main points of this essay, the author uses her own children as examples. Would the essay have been more effective had she supported her argument with less personal examples? Why?
2. Under what points does the author compare the treatment of left-handedness and homosexuality in Canada in the last century?
3. Comparing two groups is not the purpose of this essay; it is the means the author has chosen to accomplish her purpose. What is the main purpose of this piece? How effective do you think the author is in achieving it?
4. What is the topic sentence of paragraph 10? How is the topic developed? Do you agree with the statement the author makes in the fourth sentence of that paragraph? Why?
5. Consider the final paragraph of this essay. What function does it serve, other than to conclude the piece? What is its effect on readers?

[*Note:* The following research paper has been documented in APA style.]

LABOURING THE WALMART WAY

Deenu Parmar

1   *Always low prices. Always.* This is the slogan of the world's largest corporation, a U.S.-based retailer whose big-box stores offer a one-stop shop, from groceries to garments to garden hoses. The secret of Walmart's success is to give consumers the lowest prices—14 percent lower than its competitors (Greenhouse, 2003)—by increasing the efficiency of the

supply chain, the productivity of the labour force, and the use of labour-saving technology. Competitors must adopt a similar business plan, offer something Walmart does not, or go out of business—as Woolco, Eaton's, Simpsons, and Woodwards have in Canada (Moore & Pareek, 2004). The influence of the Walmart model is not likely to wane in the near future. With over 235 stores in Canada and plans for rapid expansion, Walmart and its effects on labour are worth considering. Are its offers of jobs, its attitude toward unionization, and its influence on industry labour practices worth the low price on the shelf?

2   One of the most frequent complaints about Walmart, which employs 1.4 million people worldwide, is its failure to pay workers a living wage. Store employees are paid 20–30 percent less than the industry average, making many of them eligible for social assistance. It is estimated that American taxpayers fork out $2.5 billion a year in welfare payments to Walmart employees (Head, 2004). Because the retailer hires hard-to-place workers, like recent immigrants, seniors, and single mothers, its employees are often afraid they will not find work elsewhere. The kind of work Walmart does offer is gruelling: stores are intentionally understaffed—the strategy behind the company's legendary productivity gains—so that existing employees will work harder (Head, 2004). It is alleged that systemic discrimination against women within the corporation has denied the majority of Walmart workers the chance at promotion, a charge that is now the subject of the largest civil-rights suit in U.S. history.

3   The corporation's staunch anti-unionism is its main defence in keeping workers' wages down and profits up. Without a union to give them collective clout, the store's employees suffer not only lower wages and benefits but abuses like being forced to work overtime without pay. The hiring process is designed to weed out union sympathizers; however, if organizing activity is reported in the store, an anti-union team is flown out from the headquarters in Bentonville, Arkansas, to break it up (Featherstone, 2004). The unionizing of the first Walmart store in Canada (Jonquière, Quebec) exposed the company's strategy in the event that its anti-union efforts fail: condemn the store as unprofitable and announce a closing date. Although Walmart's methods of keeping its workforce union-free have been ruled illegal in the United States, the company often finds it cheaper to pay labour violations than abide by labour rules (Featherstone, 2004). As a result, litigation is a common but costly form of redress for Walmart workers whose rights have been violated.

4   One of the main reasons retail workers at other stores want to see Walmart unionized is to preserve the gains their own unions have made. The necessity of competing with Walmart has already been used as an excuse for supermarkets all over the United States to lower the wages and benefits of their employees (Featherstone, 2004). In early 2004, unionized

grocery workers in southern California were forced to accept cuts to their benefits so their employers could compete with a soon-to-open Walmart Supercenter. Walmart's reputation for putting local stores out of business also means that employees of the competition may find themselves working at Walmart for less.

5   Although Walmart's record of paying low wages, crushing unionizing efforts, and lowering industry employment standards bodes ill for Canadian labour, it is unlikely that Canadians will refrain from shopping there. The lure of good prices is hard to resist, and the company's widely admired business model would continue to thrive, even if Walmart were to vanish tomorrow. In the interest of justice and fairness—and in avoiding pitting the customer's savings against the worker's ability to make a living—it falls on the government to pass laws that balance the interests of big business with the protection of labour, environmental, and community rights (Golden, 2004). This kind of legislation will require pressure from organized citizens acting not as consumers but as workers and concerned members of a community. The price on the shelf might rise as a result, causing Walmart supporters to point out that the poor can no longer afford to shop there. However, the ability to buy at rock-bottom prices does not address the systemic causes of poverty—though it may contribute to them.

References

Featherstone, L. (2004, June 28). Will labor take the Wal-Mart challenge? *The Nation.* Retrieved from http://www.thenation.com/doc.mhtml?i= 20040628&s=featherstone

Golden, A. (2004, October 7). Productivity, but not at any price [Comment section]. *The Globe and Mail,* p. A23.

Greenhouse, S. (2003, October 19). Wal-Mart, driving workers and super-markets crazy. *The New York Times,* p. D3.

Head, S. (2004, December 16). Inside the leviathan. *The New York Review of Books, 51*(20). Retrieved from http://www.nybooks.com/articles/ 17647

Moore, K., & Pareek, N. (2004, August 19). A whole new take on shock and AWE: There's BWE (before Wal-Mart entered), and there's AWE (after Wal-Mart entered). *The Globe and Mail,* p. A17.

Questions for Discussion

1. In this essay, is the author addressing general readers, Walmart's customers, or Walmart itself? What effect does she hope the essay will have on her target audience?

2. Consider the essay's attention-getter and memorable statement. Given the author's purpose and target audience, are they effective? Why?

3. What are the main kinds of evidence the author uses to support her causal analysis?

4. Why do you think the author uses documented sources to support her thesis? How would the effect of the essay change if the sources were omitted?

5. The author says that even if Canadians are aware of the effects of Walmart's policies and practices, they will continue to shop there. Has this essay reduced your desire to shop at Walmart?

6. Use InfoTrac to do a keyword search of "Walmart." Limit your search to three business journals. Note the kind of article that InfoTrac lists in these journals. Now do the search again, looking for articles from general-interest magazines such as *Maclean's, Time, The New York Times*, and *The Walrus*. What are the main differences between the articles taken from the two categories of print sources?

EMBRACED BY THE NEEDLE

Gabor Maté

1   Addictions always originate in unhappiness, even if hidden. They are emotional anesthetics; they numb pain. The first question—always—is not "Why the addiction?" but "Why the pain?" The answer, ever the same, is scrawled with crude eloquence on the wall of my patient Anna's room at the Portland Hotel in the heart of Vancouver's Downtown Eastside: "Any place I went to, I wasn't wanted. And that bites large."

2   The Downtown Eastside is considered to be Canada's drug capital, with an addict population of 3,000 to 5,000 individuals. I am a staff physician at the Portland, a non-profit harm-reduction facility where most of the clients are addicted to cocaine, to alcohol, to opiates like heroin, or to tranquilizers—or to any combination of these things. Many also suffer from mental illness. Like Anna, a 32-year-old poet, many are HIV positive or have full-blown AIDS. The methadone I prescribe for their opiate dependence does little for the emotional anguish compressed in every heartbeat of these driven souls.

3   Methadone staves off the torment of opiate withdrawal, but, unlike heroin, it does not create a "high" for regular users. The essence of that high was best expressed by a 27-year-old sex-trade worker. "The first time I did heroin," she said, "it felt like a warm, soft hug." In a phrase, she summed up the psychological and chemical cravings that make some people vulnerable to substance dependence.

4   No drug is, in itself, addictive. Only about 8 per cent to 15 per cent of people who try, say alcohol or marijuana, go on to addictive use. What makes them vulnerable? Neither physiological predispositions nor individual moral failures explain drug addictions. Chemical and emotional vulnerability are the products of life experience, according to current brain research and developmental psychology.

5   Most human brain growth occurs [immediately] following birth; physical and emotional interactions determine much of our brain development. Each brain's circuitry and chemistry reflects individual life experiences as much as inherited tendencies.

6   For any drug to work in the brain, the nerve cells have to have receptors— sites where the drug can bind. We have opiate receptors because our brain has natural opiate-like substances, called endorphins, chemicals that participate in many functions, including the regulation of pain and mood. Similarly, tranquilizers of the benzodiazepine class, such as Valium, exert their effect at the brain's natural benzodiazepine receptors.

7   Infant rats who get less grooming from their mothers have fewer natural benzo receptors in the part of the brain that controls anxiety. Brains of infant monkeys separated from their mothers for only a few days are measurably deficient in the key neuro-chemical, dopamine.

8   It is the same with human beings. Endorphins are released in the infant's brain when there are warm, non-stressed, calm interactions with the parenting figures. Endorphins, in turn, promote the growth of receptors and nerve cells, and the discharge of other important brain chemicals. The fewer endorphin-enhancing experiences in infancy and early childhood, the greater the need for external sources. Hence, the greater vulnerability to addictions.

9   Distinguishing skid row addicts is the extreme degree of stress they had to endure early in life. Almost all women now inhabiting Canada's addiction capital suffered sexual assaults in childhood, as did many of the males. Childhood memories of serial abandonment or severe physical and psychological abuse are common. The histories of my Portland patients tell of pain upon pain.

10   Carl, a 36-year-old native, was banished from one foster home after another, had dishwashing liquid poured down his throat for using foul language at age 5, and was tied to a chair in a dark room to control his hyperactivity. When angry at himself—as he was recently, for using cocaine—he gouges his foot with a knife as punishment. His facial expression was that of a terrorized urchin who had just broken some family law and feared Draconian retribution. I reassured him I wasn't his foster parent, and that he didn't owe it to me not to screw up.

11   But what of families where there was not abuse, but love, where parents did their best to provide their children with a secure nurturing

home? One also sees addictions arising in such families. The unseen factor here is the stress the parents themselves lived under even if they did not recognize it. That stress could come from relationship problems, or from outside circumstances such as economic pressure or political disruption. The most frequent source of hidden stress is the parents' own childhood histories that saddled them with emotional baggage they had never become conscious of. What we are not aware of in ourselves, we pass on to our children.

12   Stressed, anxious, or depressed parents have great difficulty initiating enough of those emotionally rewarding, endorphin-liberating interactions with their children. Later in life such children may experience a hit of heroin as the "warm, soft hug" my patient described: What they didn't get enough of before, they can now inject.

13   Feeling alone, feeling there has never been anyone with whom to share their deepest emotions, is universal among drug addicts. That is what Anna had lamented on her wall. No matter how much love a parent has, the child does not experience being wanted unless he or she is made absolutely safe to express exactly how unhappy or angry or hate-filled he or she may feel at times. The sense of unconditional love, of being fully accepted even when most ornery, is what no addict ever experienced in childhood—often not because the parents did not have it to give, simply because they did not know how to transmit it to the child.

14   Addicts rarely make the connection between troubled childhood experiences and self-harming habits. They blame themselves—and that is the greatest wound of all, being cut off from their natural self-compassion. "I was hit a lot," 40-year-old Wayne says, "but I asked for it. Then I made some stupid decisions." And would he hit a child, no matter how much that child "asked for it"? Would he blame that child for "stupid decisions"?

15   Wayne looks away. "I don't want to talk about that crap," says this tough man, who has worked on oil rigs and construction sites and served 15 years in jail for robbery. He looks away and wipes tears from his eyes.

Questions for Discussion

Maté wrote "Embraced by the Needle" for *The Globe and Mail*, a newspaper distributed across Canada. Keeping his audience in mind, answer the following questions.

1. The author's introduction (paragraph 1) and conclusion (paragraphs 14 and 15) are structured the same way: he makes a general statement and then supports it with a specific example or illustration. Identify the generalization and the example/illustration the author has used in each case. Why do you think the author chose this structure rather

than the introduction and conclusion patterns we recommended in
Chapters 5 and 7?

2. Why does the author insert himself into his writing? Identify the four
   times he uses first-person pronouns. Would the piece be as effective if
   he did not mention his personal involvement with the issue? Why?

3. In point form, summarize the causes that Maté thinks lead to addiction.

4. What is the author's attitude toward drug addicts? Highlight words,
   phrases, and examples that reveal how he feels about them.

THE TELEPHONE

Anwar F. Accawi

1   When I was growing up in Magdaluna, a small Lebanese village in the
terraced, rocky mountains east of Sidon, time didn't mean much to anybody, except maybe to those who were dying, or those waiting to appear
in court because they had tampered with the boundary markers on their
land. In those days, there was no real need for a calendar or a watch to
keep track of the hours, days, months, and years. We knew what to do
and when to do it, just as the Iraqi geese knew when to fly north, driven
by the hot wind that flew in from the desert, and the ewes knew when
to give birth to wet lambs that stood on long, shaky legs in the chilly
March wind and baaed hesitantly, because they were small and cold and
did not know where they were or what to do now that they were here.
The only timepiece we had need of then was the sun. It rose and set, and
the seasons rolled by, and we sowed seed and harvested and ate and
played and married our cousins and had babies who got whooping cough
and chickenpox—and those children who survived grew up and married
their cousins and had babies who got whooping cough and chickenpox.
We lived and loved and toiled and died without ever needing to know
what year it was, or even the time of day.

2   It wasn't that we had no system for keeping track of time and of the
important events in our lives. But ours was a natural—or, rather, a
divine—calendar, because it was framed by acts of God. Allah himself set
down the milestones with earthquakes and droughts and floods and
locusts and pestilences. Simple as our calendar was, it worked just fine for
us.

3   Take, for example, the birth date of Teta Im Khalil, the oldest woman
in Magdaluna and all the surrounding villages. When I first met her, we
had just returned home from Syria at the end of the Big War and were
living with Grandma Mariam. Im Khalil came by to welcome my father

home and to take a long myopic look at his foreign-born wife, my mother. Im Khalil was so old that the skin of her cheeks looked like my father's grimy tobacco pouch, and when I kissed her (because Grandma insisted that I show her old friend affection), it was like kissing a soft suede glove that had been soaked with sweat and then left in a dark closet for a season. Im Khalil's face got me to wondering how old one had to be to look and taste the way she did. So, as soon as she had hobbled off on her cane, I asked Grandma, "How old is Teta Im Khalil?"

4 Grandma had to think for a moment; then she said, "I've been told that Teta was born shortly after the big snow that caused the roof on the mayor's house to cave in."

5 "And when was that?" I asked.

6 "Oh, about the time we had the big earthquake that cracked the wall in the east room."

7 Well, that was enough for me. You couldn't be more accurate than that, now, could you? Satisfied with her answer, I went back to playing with a ball made from an old sock stuffed with other, much older socks.

8 And that's the way it was in our little village for as far back as anybody could remember: people were born so many years before or after an earthquake or a flood; they got married or died so many years before or after a long drought or a big snow or some other disaster. One of the most unusual of these dates was when Antoinette the seamstress and Saeed the barber (and tooth puller) got married. That was the year of the whirlwind during which fish and oranges fell from the sky. Incredible as it may sound, the story of the fish and oranges was true, because men— respectable men, like Abu George the blacksmith and Abu Asaad the mule skinner, men who would not lie even to save their own souls—told and retold that story until it was incorporated into Magdaluna's calendar, just like the year of the black moon and the year of the locusts before it. My father, too, confirmed the story for me. He told me that he had been a small boy himself when it rained fish and oranges from heaven. He'd gotten up one morning after a stormy night and walked out into the yard to find fish as long as his forearm still flopping here and there among the wet navel oranges.

9 The year of the fish-bearing twister, however, was not the last remarkable year. Many others followed in which strange and wonderful things happened: milestones added by the hand of Allah to Magdaluna's calendar. There was, for instance, the year of the drought, when the heavens were shut for months and the spring from which the entire village got its drinking water slowed to a trickle. The spring was about a mile from the village, in a ravine that opened at one end into a small, flat clearing covered with fine gray dust and hard, marble-sized goat droppings, because every afternoon the goatherds brought their flocks there to water them. In

the year of the drought, that little clearing was always packed full of noisy kids with big brown eyes and sticky hands, and their mothers—sinewy, overworked young women with protruding collarbones and cracked, callused brown heels. The children ran around playing tag or hide-and-seek while the women talked, shooed flies, and awaited their turns to fill up their jars with drinking water to bring home to their napping men and wet babies. There were days when we had to wait from sunup until late afternoon just to fill a small clay jar with precious, cool water.

10   Sometimes, amid the long wait and the heat and the flies and the smell of goat dung, tempers flared, and the younger women, anxious about their babies, argued over whose turn it was to fill up her jar. And sometimes the arguments escalated into full-blown, knockdown-dragout fights; the women would grab each other by the hair and curse and scream and spit and call each other names that made my ears tingle. We little brown boys who went with our mothers to fetch water loved these fights, because we got to see the women's legs and their colored panties as they grappled and rolled around in the dust. Once in a while, we got lucky and saw much more, because some of the women wore nothing at all under their long dresses. God, how I used to look forward to those fights. I remember the rush, the excitement, the sun dancing on the dust clouds as a dress ripped and a young white breast was revealed, then quickly hidden. In my calendar, that year of drought will always be one of the best years of my childhood, because it was then, in a dusty clearing by a trickling mountain spring, I got my first glimpses of the wonders, the mysteries, and the promises hidden beneath the folds of a woman's dress. Fish and oranges from heaven . . . you can get over that.

11   But, in another way, the year of the drought was also one of the worst in my life, because that was the year that Abu Raja, the retired cook who used to entertain us kids by cracking walnuts on his forehead, decided it was time Magdaluna got its own telephone. Every civilized village needed a telephone, he said, and Magdaluna was not going to get anywhere until it had one. A telephone would link us with the outside world. At the time, I was too young to understand the debate, but a few men—like Shukri, the retired Turkish-army drill sergeant, and Abu Hanna the vineyard keeper—did all they could to talk Abu Raja out of having a telephone brought to the village. But they were outshouted and ignored and finally shunned by the other villagers for resisting progress and trying to keep a good thing from coming to Magdaluna.

12   One warm day in early fall, many of the villagers were out in their fields repairing walls or gathering wood for the winter when the shout went out that the telephone company truck had arrived at Abu Raja's *dikkan*, or country store. There were no roads in those days, only footpaths and dry steambeds, so it took the telephone-company truck

almost a day to work its way up the rocky terrain from Sidon—about the same time it took to walk. When the truck came into view, Abu George, who had a huge voice and, before the telephone, was Magdaluna's only long-distance communication system, bellowed the news from his front porch. Everybody dropped what they were doing and ran to Abu Raja's house to see what was happening. Some of the more dignified villagers, however, like Abu Habeeb and Abu Nazim, who had been to big cities like Beirut and Damascus and had seen things like telephones and telegraphs, did not run the way the rest did; they walked with their canes hanging from the crooks of their arms, as if on a Sunday afternoon stroll.

13   It did not take long for the whole village to assemble at Abu Raja's *dikkan*. Some of the rich villagers, like the widow Farha and the gendarme Abu Nadeem, walked right into the store and stood at the elbows of the two important-looking men from the telephone company, who proceeded with utmost gravity, like priests at Communion, to wire up the telephone. The poorer villagers stood outside and listened carefully to the details relayed to them by the not-so-poor people who stood in the doorway and could see inside.

14   "The bald man is cutting the blue wire," someone said.

15   "He is sticking the wire into the hole in the bottom of the black box," someone else added.

16   "The telephone man with the mustache is connecting two pieces of wire. Now he is twisting the ends together," a third voice chimed in.

17   Because I was small and unaware that I should have stood outside with the other poor folk to give the rich people inside more room (they seemed to need more of it than poor people did), I wriggled my way through the dense forest of legs to get a first-hand look at the action. I felt like a barefoot Moses, sandals in hand, staring at the burning bush on Mount Sinai. Breathless, I watched as the men in blue, their shirt pockets adorned with fancy lettering in a foreign language, put together a black machine that supposedly would make it possible to talk with uncles, aunts, and cousins who lived more than two days' ride away.

18   It was shortly after sunset when the man with the mustache announced that the telephone was ready to use. He explained that all Abu Raja had to do was lift the receiver, turn the crank on the black box a few times, and wait for an operator to take his call. Abu Raja, who had once lived and worked in Sidon, was impatient with the telephone man for assuming that he was ignorant. He grabbed the receiver and turned the crank forcefully, as if trying to start a Model T Ford. Everybody was impressed that he knew what to do. He even called the operator by her first name: "Centralist." Within moments, Abu Raja was talking with his brother, a concierge in Beirut. He didn't even have to raise his voice or shout to be heard.

19   If I hadn't seen it with my own two eyes and heard it with my own two ears, I would not have believed it—and my friend Kameel didn't. He was away that day watching his father's goats, and when he came back to the village that evening, his cousin Habeeb and I told him about the telephone and how Abu Raja had used it to speak with his brother in Beirut. After he heard our report, Kameel made the sign of the cross, kissed his thumbnail, and warned us that lying was a bad sin and would surely land us in purgatory. Kameel believed in Jesus and Mary, and wanted to be a priest when he grew up. He always crossed himself when Habeeb, who was irreverent, and I, who was Presbyterian, were around, even when we were not bearing bad news.

20   And the telephone, as it turned out, was bad news. With its coming, the face of the village began to change. One of the first effects was the shifting of the village's center. Before the telephone's arrival, the men of the village used to gather regularly at the house of Im Kaleem, a short, middle-aged widow with jet-black hair and a raspy voice that could be heard all over the village, even when she was only whispering. She was a devout Catholic and also the village *shlikki*—whore. The men met at her house to argue about politics and drink coffee and play cards or backgammon. Im Kaleem was not a true prostitute, however, because she did not charge for her services—not even for the coffee and tea (and, occasionally, the strong liquor called arrack) that she served the men. She did not need the money; her son, who was overseas in Africa, sent her money regularly. (I knew this because my father used to read her son's letters to her and take down her replies, as Im Kaleem could not read and write.) Im Kaleem was no slut either—unlike some women in the village—because she loved all the men she entertained, and they loved her, every one of them. In a way, she was married to all the men in the village. Everybody knew it—the wives knew it; the itinerant Catholic priest knew it; the Presbyterian minister knew it—but nobody objected. Actually, I suspect the women (my mother included) did not mind their husband's visits to Im Kaleem. Oh, they wrung their hands and complained to one another about their men's unfaithfulness, but secretly they were relieved, because Im Kaleem took some of the pressure off them and kept the men out of their hair while they attended to their endless chores. Im Kaleem was also a kind of confessor and troubleshooter, talking sense to those men who were having family problems, especially the younger ones.

21   Before the telephone came to Magdaluna, Im Kaleem's house was bustling at just about any time of day, especially at night, when its windows were brightly lit with three large oil lamps, and the loud voices of the men talking, laughing, and arguing could be heard in the street below—a reassuring, homey sound. Her house was an island of comfort, an oasis for the weary village men, exhausted from having so little to do.

22   But it wasn't long before many of those men—the younger ones especially—started spending more of their days and evenings at Abu Raja's
dikkan. There, they would eat and drink and talk and play checkers and
backgammon, and then lean their chairs back against the wall—the
signal that they were ready to toss back and forth, like a ball, the latest
rumors going around the village. And they were always looking up from
their games and drinks and talk to glance at the phone in the corner, as
if expecting it to ring any minute and bring news that would change
their lives and deliver them from their aimless existence. In the mean-
time, they smoked cheap, hand-rolled cigarettes, dug dirt out from under
their fingernails with big pocketknives, and drank lukewarm sodas that
they called Kacula, Seffen-Ub, and Bebsi. Sometimes, especially when it
was hot, the days dragged on so slowly that the men turned on Abu
Saeed, a confirmed bachelor who practically lived in Abu Raja's *dikkan*,
and teased him for going around barefoot and unshaven since the Virgin
had appeared to him behind the olive press.

23   The telephone was also bad news for me personally. It took away my
lucrative business—a source of much-needed income. Before the telephone came to Magdaluna, I used to hang around Im Kaleem's courtyard
and play marbles with the other kids, waiting for some man to call down
from a window and ask me to run to the store for cigarettes or arrack, or
to deliver a message to his wife, such as what he wanted for supper. There
was always something in it for me: a ten- or even a twenty-five-piaster
piece. On a good day, I ran nine or ten of those errands, which assured a
steady supply of marbles that I usually lost to Sami or his cousin Hani,
the basket weaver's boy. But as the days went by, fewer and fewer men
came to Im Kaleem's, and more and more congregated at Abu Raja's to
wait by the telephone. In the evenings, no light fell from her window
onto the street below, and the laughter and noise of the men trailed off
and finally stopped. Only Shukri, the retired Turkish-army drill sergeant,
remained faithful to Im Kaleem after all the other men had deserted her;
he was still seen going into or leaving her house from time to time. Early
that winter, Im Kaleem's hair suddenly turned gray, and she got sick and
old. Her legs started giving her trouble, making it hard for her to walk. By
spring she hardly left her house anymore.

24   At Abu Raja's *dikkan*, the calls did eventually come, as expected, and
men and women started leaving the village the way a hailstorm begins:
first one, then two, then bunches. The army took them. Jobs in the cities
lured them. And ships and airplanes carried them to such faraway places
as Australia and Brazil and New Zealand. My friend Kameel, his cousin
Habeeb, and their cousins and my cousins all went away to become ditch
diggers and mechanics and butcher-shop boys and deli owners who wore
dirty aprons sixteen hours a day, all looking for a better life than the one

they had left behind. Within a year, only the sick, the old, and the maimed were left in the village. Magdaluna became a skeleton of its former self, desolate and forsaken, like the tombs, a place to get away from.

25   Finally, the telephone took my family away, too. My father got a call from an old army buddy who told him that an oil company in southern Lebanon was hiring interpreters and instructors. My father applied for a job and got it, and we moved to Sidon, where I went to a Presbyterian missionary school and graduated in 1962. Three years later, having won a scholarship, I left Lebanon for the United States. Like the others who left Magdaluna before me, I am still looking for that better life.

Questions for Discussion

1. Does this essay focus primarily on cause or on effect? Of what?
2. "The Telephone" is divided into two parts: paragraphs 1 to 10 and 11 to 25. Summarize the content of the two halves of the piece.
3. Explain the irony in paragraph 11, the turning point of the essay.
4. In addition to causal analysis, this essay contains strong elements of description and narration. Identify two paragraphs that you think are particularly effective examples of each.
5. The first effect of the telephone on the village community is told through the story of Im Kaleem, "the village *shlikki*" (paragraphs 20 to 22). What is this consequence, and why do you think the author chooses Im Kaleem's story to communicate it?
6. In paragraph 24, we are told that "the calls did eventually come." What happens then? Where do people go? What happens to Magdaluna itself? Do you think that these effects are all due to the arrival of the telephone in the village?
7. In your own words, describe how the author feels about the changes that swept through his world. Refer to specific details from paragraphs 24 and 25.

ARTS EDUCATION DOES PAY OFF

Livio Di Matteo

1   Canada's universities—particularly the humanities and social sciences—face a major challenge. The current approach to education emphasizes immediate tangible benefits. This has led to government funding initiatives in science and technology that fail to recognize the importance of a liberal arts education. Yet supporting a humanities and

social science education is justified on sound economic grounds, not just on the civic and academic grounds usually used.

2   The humanities and social sciences provide social benefits that private market mechanisms do not count. Just as a vaccination benefits people other than those inoculated by reducing disease transmission, the humanities and social sciences have spill-over benefits by transmitting wisdom to society. The inability to attach a market price to a literate and civil society of educated citizens does not make this type of education valueless.

3   The humanities and social sciences complement scientific and technical training, and provide innovative strategies for meeting future challenges. While science graduates can provide technical solutions to problems, only individuals trained in human science can deal with the economic, ethical, cultural and social implications of these solutions. For example, we are told that advances in genetics are making a vastly extended human lifespan possible in the not-so-distant future. How will this affect the distribution of income and employment, and the quality of life in our society? Is this type of analysis not of economic benefit to society?

4   Market benefits to humanities and social science graduates translate into jobs, as economist Robert Allen of the University of British Columbia recently demonstrated in a study. Prof. Allen found that unemployment rates for humanities and social science graduates did not substantially differ from those of graduates in other fields. Moreover, these graduates' age–income profiles can actually be steeper than those in the sciences or technical programs, where the latest technical knowledge depreciates quickly. Like fine wine, humanities and social science graduates appreciate with age as their skills deepen, generating a steeply rising income over their working life. Some universities, such as Dalhousie, are beginning to [issue transcripts that list] skills such as collaborative work, oral communication, and analytical work to their liberal arts graduates. This communicates what was once obvious, but now has to be marketed: Liberal arts graduates are prized because of their ability to think creatively and laterally, using skills acquired in analysis, synthesis, research and communication.

5   Having reduced their market intervention on the grounds that private forces work best, governments are now replicating that interventionist role in post-secondary education by targeting funding increases to programs in science and technology. These programs are worthy of funding, but for universities to function according to a private-sector model, governments should provide universities with block increases in funding and allow them to pursue those programs they are best at. Targeted

funding distorts resource allocation decisions by inducing universities to expand government-favoured programs. This leaves governments selecting educational winners and losers when the economy's future needs are uncertain.

6 Other issues present themselves, too. What about the long-run cost structure of universities, given that the per-student cost of producing science and engineering graduates is higher than in other fields? Who is responsible if such funding generates a graduate glut in any one discipline? Will government be accountable, or will the buck be passed to the universities for once again "failing" in their role to society?

7 Humanities and social science students make up approximately half of university enrolments. If you believe that "voting with your feet" is a test of market demand, this enrolment share should be sending a clear message to educational policy-makers as to how the public values these programs. Humanities and social science students should be entitled to adequate research and teaching facilities, and to professors who conduct leading-edge research. When it comes to resource allocation, why should half of university students be placed on a path to second-rate treatment when they are indeed "paying customers"?

8 It is time to restore some balance. The current targeted funding approach ignores the obvious demand for humanities and social science training. Governments can best serve the university system by ensuring adequate general funding and allowing universities, in consultation with government and the public, to make the resource allocation decisions. In neglecting the humanities and social sciences, governments have not fully consulted all constituencies, and their funding decisions implicitly attach a negative value to these disciplines. Canadian society will pay huge economic and cultural costs if such myopic policies are continued.

Questions for Discussion

1. Does the author approach his argument directly or indirectly? Where is the thesis statement? Identify the reasons the author cites to support his opinion.
2. Who is the target audience for this essay? How do you know?
3. What is the author's purpose: to win his readers' agreement, or to move them to action? What sort of action could they take to support the author on this issue?
4. Identify the kinds of evidence the author uses in this essay.

5. The author uses a number of rhetorical questions (questions to which no answer is expected). Are they effective in supporting his argument? Why?

6. In your own words, explain why the author thinks targeted funding is a poor idea. (See paragraphs 5 and 6.)

7. Do you agree with the author? Why or why not?

FLEEING *FACEBOOK*

Carmen Joy King

1 In March, at the peak of *Facebook* popularity, I quit. With four swift clicks of the mouse, I canceled my account. Gone was the entire online persona I had created for myself—profile pictures, interests and activities, work history, friends acquired—all carefully thought out to showcase to the world the very best version of me, all now deleted.

2 Ironically, the decision to destroy my carefully built-up virtual image came as a result of wanting to enhance my profile. All that particular week I'd been hungry for new quotes on my page, something to reflect the week I'd been having: something introspective. I perused a quotes website and found this one attributed to Aristotle: "We are what we repeatedly do."

3 I became despondent. What, then, was I? If my time was spent changing my profile picture on *Facebook*, thinking of a clever status update for *Facebook*, checking my profile again to see if anyone had commented on my page, Is this what I am? A person who re-visits her own thoughts and images for hours each day? And so what do I amount to? An egotist? A voyeur? Whatever the label, I was unhappy and feeling empty. The amount of time I spent on *Facebook* had pushed me into an existential crisis. It wasn't the time-wasting, per se, that bothered me. It was the nature of the obsession—namely self-obsession. Enough was enough. I left *Facebook*.

4 In the past, my feelings toward *Facebook* and similar social networking sites had swung between a genuine sense of connection and community [and] the uncomfortable awareness that what all of our blogs, online journals and personal profiles really amounted to was serious narcissism. As my feelings of overexposure continued to mount, the obvious solution would have been to set limits on my *Facebook* time, yet I still found myself sucked in for longer periods every time I visited. In part, it was the hundreds of little links to and hints about other people's lives that kept me coming back. But even more addictive were the never-ending possibilities to introduce, enhance and reveal more of myself.

5 The baby-boomers were at one time thought to be the most self-absorbed generation in American history and carried the label of the Me

Generation. In recent years this title has been appropriated, twisted and reassigned to the babies of those same boomers, born in the 80s and 90s, now called Generation Me or the Look-at-Me Generation. Author Jean Twenge, an associate professor of psychology at San Diego State University and herself a member of Generation Me, spent ten years doing research on this group's sense of entitlement and self-absorption. She attributed it to the radical individualism that was engendered by baby-boomer parents and educators focused on instilling self-esteem in children beginning in the 1970s. American and Canadian youth were raised on aphorisms such as "express yourself" and "just be yourself." To further illustrate her point, Twenge also found a large increase in self-reference words like "I," "me," "mine" and "myself" in news stories published in the 80s and 90s. These words replaced collective words such as "we," "us," "humanity," "country" or "crowd" found in the [news] stories of the 50s and 60s. This generation might be the least thoughtful, community-oriented and conscientious one in North American history.

6 In the end, what does all this online, arms-length self-promotion ultimately provide? Perhaps it's merely one component of the pursuit to alleviate some of the blackness encountered in the existential vacuum of modern life. As Schopenhauer once projected, modern humans may be doomed to eternally vacillate between distress and boredom. For the vast majority of people experiencing the fragmented, fast-paced modern world of 2008, a Sunday pause at the end of a hectic week may cause them to become all too aware of the lack of content in their lives. So we update our online profiles and tell ourselves that we are reaching out.

7 And yet, the time we waste on *Facebook* only makes our search for comfort and community more elusive. Online networking sites are marketed as facilitators of community-orientation but when I think about the millions of people—myself included—who spend large portions of their waking lives feeding off an exchange of thousands of computerized, fragmented images, it doesn't add up to community engagement. These images have no meaning beyond "I look pretty from this angle" or "I'm wasted" or "look who my new boyfriend is." And as we continue to chase even harder—accessing *Facebook* at work, uploading images from our cell phones—we spend our money on constantly upgraded electronic gadgets marketed to our tendency to self-obsess and present uninteresting and repetitive images of ourselves. There's got to be more than this.

8 And so I quit.

9 After I left *Facebook*, I wondered what all my friends, family and acquaintances were going to think when they noticed I'd disappeared off the *Facebook* earth. So some of my *Facebook* narcissism (am I being noticed, am I being missed) remains. But I'm also asking myself some new questions. How do I find balance between my online life and my

"real" life? How much exposure is healthy? How do I act responsibly for myself and engage with those I love? These are still "me" thoughts but they feel different than before. As I sit here, keyboard under palm, eyes on screen, I try to remind myself that my hands and eyes need to venture out into the community and look and touch the truly tangible that lies just beyond that other big screen: my window.

Questions for Discussion

1. Why do you think the author has framed this essay with a personal narrative (paragraphs 1–3 and paragraphs 8–9)?
2. In your own words, identify the reasons the author quit *Facebook*.
3. What purpose is served by citing the work of Jean Twenge (paragraph 5)? What other evidence could the author have introduced to support her argument?
4. How convincing is this essay? Did it make you re-examine your own use of *Facebook*?
5. Write an argument supporting or refuting the last sentence in paragraph 5.

THE COUNTRY THE WORLD FORGOT—AGAIN
Kevin Myers

1   Until the deaths last week of four Canadian soldiers accidentally killed by a US warplane in Afghanistan, probably almost no one outside their home country had been aware that Canadian troops were deployed in the region. And as always, Canada will now bury its dead, just as the rest of the world as always will forget its sacrifice, just as it always forgets nearly everything Canada ever does.

2   It seems that Canada's historic mission is to come to the selfless aid both of its friends and of complete strangers, and then, once the crisis is over, to be well and truly ignored. Canada is the perpetual wallflower that stands on the edge of the hall, waiting for someone to come and ask her for a dance. A fire breaks out, she risks life and limb to rescue her fellow dance-goers, and suffers serious injuries. But when the hall is repaired and the dancing resumes, there is Canada, the wallflower still, while those she once helped glamorously cavort across the floor, blithely neglecting her yet again.

3   That is the price which Canada pays for sharing the North American continent with the US, and for being a selfless friend of Britain in two global conflicts. For much of the 20th century, Canada was torn in two different directions: it seemed to be a part of the old world, yet had an

address in the new one, and that divided identity ensured that it never fully got the gratitude it deserved.

4   Yet [Canada's] purely voluntary contribution to the cause of freedom in two world wars was perhaps the greatest of any democracy. Almost 10 per cent of Canada's entire population of seven million people served in the armed forces during the First World War, and nearly 60,000 died. The great Allied victories of 1918 were spearheaded by Canadian troops, perhaps the most capable soldiers in the entire British order of battle.

5   Canada was repaid for its enormous sacrifice by downright neglect, its unique contribution to victory being absorbed into the popular memory as somehow or other the work of the "British." The Second World War provided a re-run. The Canadian navy began the war with a half-dozen vessels, and ended up policing nearly half of the Atlantic against U-boat attack. More than 120 Canadian warships participated in the Normandy landings, during which 15,000 Canadian soldiers went ashore on D-Day alone. Canada finished the war with the third-largest navy and the fourth-largest air force in the world.

6   The world thanked Canada with the same sublime indifference as it had the previous time. Canadian participation in the war was acknowledged in film only if it was necessary to give an American actor a part in a campaign which the US had clearly not participated—a touching scrupulousness which, of course, Hollywood has since abandoned, as it has any notion of a separate Canadian identity.

7   So it is a general rule that actors and filmmakers arriving in Hollywood keep their nationality—unless, that is, they are Canadian. Thus Mary Pickford, Walter Huston, Donald Sutherland, Michael J. Fox, William Shatner, Norman Jewison, David Cronenberg and Dan Aykroyd have in the popular perception become American, and Christopher Plummer British. It is as if in the very act of becoming famous, a Canadian ceases to be Canadian, unless she is Margaret Atwood, who is as unshakeably Canadian as a moose, or Celine Dion, for whom Canada has proved quite unable to find any takers.

8   Moreover, Canada is every bit as querulously alert to the achievements of its sons and daughters as the rest of the world is completely unaware of them. The Canadians proudly say of themselves—and are unheard by anyone else—that 1 per cent of the world's population has provided 10 per cent of the world's peace-keeping forces. Canadian soldiers in the past half-century have been the greatest peace-keepers on earth—in 39 missions on UN mandates, and six on non-UN peace-keeping duties, from Vietnam to East Timor, from Sinai to Bosnia.

9   Yet the only foreign engagement which has entered the popular non-Canadian imagination was the sorry affair in Somalia, in which out-of-control paratroopers murdered two Somali infiltrators. Their regiment

was then disbanded in disgrace—a uniquely Canadian act of self-abasement for which, naturally, the Canadians received no international credit.

10 So who today in the US knows about the stoic and selfless friendship its northern neighbour has given it in Afghanistan? Rather like Cyrano de Bergerac, Canada repeatedly does honourable things for honourable motives, but instead of being thanked for it, it remains something of a figure of fun. It is the Canadian way, for which Canadians should be proud, yet such honour comes at a high cost.

11 This weekend four shrouds, red with blood and maple leaf, head homeward, and four more grieving Canadian families know that cost all too tragically well.

Questions for Discussion

1. This essay was first published in *The Daily Telegraph*, a British newspaper, in 2002. What was your reaction to it? Would it have affected you differently if it had been written by a Canadian and published in a Canadian journal? Why?
2. Working with a partner, draft an outline for this argument. (*Hint*: The thesis statement is in two parts: the first sentence of paragraph 2 and the last sentence of paragraph 3.)
3. What are the main developmental strategies that the author has used to support his points? Identify three good examples of each.
4. What do you think of the dance hall analogy the writer develops in paragraph 2? Does it increase or decrease your sympathy for the role Canada has played in the world for almost a century? Why?
5. Consider the actors and filmmakers that the author lists in paragraph 7. Were you aware that these stars and directors were Canadian? Can you think of other examples of "closet Canadians"? Do you agree with the author's claim that "It is as if in the very act of becoming famous, a Canadian ceases to be a Canadian. . . ."? Why?

[*Note:* The following essay is a research paper documented in MLA style.]

NO SWEAT?

Rubi Garyfalakis

1 When I began investigating the use of sweatshops in the garment industry, I thought there would be a simple answer: sweatshops were morally wrong, and their products should be boycotted by conscientious North American consumers. As I looked more deeply into the issue, how-

ever, I found surprising and perplexing information that left me more aware and educated but less convinced than before. My research revealed that sweatshops are a complex issue, full of complications that make it a grey moral area. Through my journey, I ultimately found that there is no "right or wrong," "yes or no," "do or do not do" solution to this dilemma, and that our duty as moral, ethical consumers is difficult to determine. Although this realization can lead consumers to feel frustrated, helpless, and eventually indifferent, there are effective actions we can take.

2   I began my research believing that sweatshops were unethical. The definition of a sweatshop confirmed my conviction. According to ethics teachers and researchers Denis Arnold and Laura Hartman, a sweatshop is

> . . . any working environment in which the workers are subject to two or more of the following conditions: systematic health and safety risks caused by employer negligence; systematic forced overtime, coercion, or underpayment; or income for a 48-hour work week that is less than the amount needed to satisfy basic survival needs. (2)

Stories of such conditions are common in the media. For example, in Uzbekistan, thousands of children must pick 10 to 40 kg of cotton per day, earning a wage of 38 cents for their efforts. The children carry pesticides in plastic water bottles, a practice that results in skin burns as the pesticides splash onto the children's arms and hands.

3   Ethics professor C. D. Meyers claims that sweatshops contradict "the commonsense moral presumption against economic exploitation, which is supported by the dominant moral theories of today" (1). The exploitation of sweatshop workers is wrong because it is unfair: the exploiters gain at the expense of the exploited, who are not fairly compensated (Mayer 2–4). Sweatshop employers could afford to pay their workers more, but they do not because it benefits them to pay as little as possible. Essentially, sweatshops violate globally recognized basic labour rights, including the right to freedom from forced labour, the right to a limited number of hours in a workday, and the right to just and favourable working conditions (Arnold and Hartman 6). The evidence of blatant exploitation and violation of workers' human rights would probably lead any ethical consumer to conclude that sweatshops are morally wrong.

4   If only the problem were that simple. For those who like tidy problems with clear solutions, it is disturbing to find that there is another side to the sweatshop debate. To begin with, sweatshops are "the first rung on the ladder out of extreme poverty" (Sachs 11). They allow developing countries to expand their exports and consequently to improve their economies (Arnold and Hartman 2). Workers (usually women) choose to work in sweatshops because they are often the only means by which women can further their own ends. By working in sweatshops, women

make a small income, learn about business practices, and benefit from the improved social and economic conditions that come with economic growth. Arnold and Hartman explain that as the economy grows, more jobs are created; the labour market tightens, and companies are forced to improve their working conditions in order to attract employees (2-3). Theoretically, this analysis makes sense, but does it apply in practice? Do employees really benefit from working in sweatshops?

5   As I dug deeper into the research, I was surprised to learn that in some cases, sweatshops *can* have positive effects. A clear example is Bangladesh's garment industry. Thousands of women, mostly between the ages of eighteen and twenty-five, work in sweatshops to cut, stitch, and package clothing for common brands, such as GAP and Walmart, that are sold in Europe and North America (Sachs 11). Economic advisor Jeffrey Sachs reports that his interviews with Bangladeshi women working in sweatshops revealed an unexpected reality. Although all of the women admitted that they worked long hours, were subject to harassment, and were denied labour rights, they also affirmed that the job provided an opportunity greater than they could otherwise have hoped for, and that it had improved the quality of their lives (Sachs 12). With their small income, the women experienced some independence. Earning a salary gave them the opportunity to manage their own finances, have their own rooms, choose when and whom they wanted to marry, and choose when they wanted to have children. They could save to improve their living conditions or to return to school to improve their literacy or job-market skills.

6   Sweatshops provide work that is difficult and underpaid, but any job in an economically depressed region offers women an opportunity that had previously been unavailable, even unthinkable. Without the option of sweatshop work, women have no choice but to submit to arranged marriages in their early teens and to begin bearing children. The evidence suggests that in the highly patriarchal society of Bangladesh, sweatshops are helping to change attitudes toward women. Encouragingly, because of the garment industry, Bangladesh's economy has grown by 5% per year in the last decade (Sachs 13). If Arnold and Hartman's theory holds, improvements in working conditions will follow.

7   Well-meaning protestors in the first world have suggested that Bangladesh's sweatshops should pay higher wages or be shut down, but closing factories would take jobs away from women (Sachs 12). Thus the consumer faces a dilemma: the issue is not one of choosing between right and wrong, but of choosing the best possible (or least wrong) option.

8   What can concerned consumers do? Boycotting companies that contract their production to sweatshops may seem like a viable anti-sweatshop action; however, boycotts themselves raise complex issues.

First, they normally result in job losses for workers (*Labour Behind the Label*), thus only adding to the injustice because it is not the workers but the employers whom consumers want to punish. Second, most sweatshop workers choose the job because it is better than the available alternative; without their jobs, women have no choice but to settle for marriage—assuming they are still young enough to attract a husband. On the other hand, some studies show that boycotting can have an impact on companies because they become known as "ethical offenders" (Shaw et al. 5). Nike and GAP are two examples of companies that were forced by negative publicity to modify their labour practices to maintain their place in the competitive market. Unfortunately, most large companies that advertise their "positive action" on the labour front simply go through a public relations exercise: they develop and publicize new codes of conduct (5). Codes of conduct may look impressive on paper, but they do not guarantee action or change. Unless top-level management endorses and enforces a firm's code of conduct, little or nothing changes at the level of the sweatshops, which cling precariously to the bottom rung of the company hierarchy.

9   Nevertheless, a code of conduct is a start, and a start is better than nothing. But even the most determined consumers confront problems in deciding which companies or products to boycott. Identifying consumer goods produced wholly or in part by workers in sweatshops is nearly impossible. Over the last 30 years, North American and European multinational corporations have greatly increased the amount of production that they contract to the developing world (Arnold and Hartman 2). This massive relocation of work in the garment industry is part of an economic system called "triangular manufacturing": transnational companies based in Europe or North America receive orders for consumer goods, contract the production orders to lower-wage (usually third-world) economies, and ship the finished goods back to the buyers (Hale 3). As a result of triangular manufacturing, developing countries, where goods are produced and assembled, are forced to compete in a "race to the bottom." The winner is the country that can produce the most goods at the fastest pace and at the lowest cost. The race to the bottom requires suspending workplace and environmental regulations, resulting in below-par wages and dismal working conditions (*Labour Behind the Label*).

10   Another effect of triangular manufacturing is that it is virtually impossible to know where a product came from or where it was made. For example, a large amount of Uzbekistan's cotton, picked by child labourers, is sent to China, the world's largest exporter of garments and textiles (Belli 2). Uzbek cotton ends up in T-shirts that are made in China and sold in the USA. Because the label on the "made in China" T-shirt does not say

where the cotton is from, it is impossible to know whether children were exploited in the process of producing the garment (Belli 2). Similarly, a label claiming that a product is "organic" refers to how the cotton was produced. An "organic" product sounds good to the conscientious consumer, but the organically grown cotton may have been picked, packed, shipped, woven, cut, and sewn into completed garments by children in sweatshops (Belli 2). This confusion (and sometimes deception) is possible because there are no regulations for clothing labels. Unlike the fair trade food labels, there are no internationally recognized labels for clothing to ensure that fair trade standards were maintained throughout the chain of production (Shaw et al. 4). Consequently, consumers turn to clues such as the country of origin stated on the label, and try to avoid products made in countries notorious for exploitation, such as China. Stigmatizing certain countries is unfair, however, because it is based on prejudice, not proof, and it could potentially harm ethical companies in those countries who need to attract business in order to survive.

11   If boycotting has both pros and cons, "targeted" boycotting is virtually impossible, and product information is unreliable, how are consumers to shop ethically? One alternative is to shop from the limited niche market for ethical clothing. The options in Canada are basically limited to garments produced by two firms: American Apparel and No Sweat. American Apparel designs, knits, dyes, sews, markets, and distributes its products in Los Angeles (*American Apparel Investor Relations*), but it does not claim that the raw material it uses was grown in the United States. The cost of producing cotton in the United States forces this fair trade-conscious company to buy it from overseas (Belli 2). No Sweat is an online store that sells clothing and footwear produced by independent trade union members in Canada, the United States, and the developing world. Established in 2000, this company guarantees that its products are fairly traded and that all workers receive a living wage (*No Sweat*). While these two outlets sound good, they offer a limited selection at relatively high prices. As a student, I am tempted to resist the increased price level, but then I am reminded that, as Meyers points out, "whatever extra we have to pay for a new pair of sneakers is not comparable to the suffering that could be prevented by giving sweatshop workers a living wage" (2).

12   The lack of ethical alternatives and the confusion about product information in the garment industry make supporting sweatshops almost unavoidable for consumers. It would be easy to become discouraged and to conclude that there is nothing we can do about sweatshop injustices.

Such a conclusion would be a mistake, however, because each option has the potential to make a partial positive change. Boycotts help to raise awareness; they also send the message to large companies that labour policies matter. Buying from alternative stores shows support for companies who do uphold fair trade practices. Shopping at thrift stores may help to decrease the enormous demand for new clothing that fuels triangular manufacturing (Hale 2). Above all, each of these actions represents a rejection of complacency, sending the message that our current consumer culture is substantially flawed.

13 Sweatshops and the solution to the problem they represent are extremely complex. There is no clear moral answer to the issue, and there is no clear course of action for the ethical consumer in the developed world. It is our duty, however, to try our best to make moral choices when we shop for clothing. Although change must ultimately come from the top, our conscientious actions will help the change to begin from the bottom and to work its way up.

Works Cited

American Apparel Investor Relations. *American Apparel*. Web. 27 Nov. 2008.

Arnold, Denis G., and Laura P. Hartman. "Beyond Sweatshops: Positive Deviancy and Global Labour Practices." *Business Ethics: A European Review* 14.3 (July 2005): 206-22. Print.

Belli, Brita. "Fashion Victims." *E Magazine* 18.5 (Sept. 2007): 32-33. *Academic Search Premier*. Web. 28 Nov. 2008.

Hale, Angela. "What Hope for 'Ethical' Trade in the Globalised Garment Industry?" *Antipode* 32.4 (Oct. 2000): 349. *Academic Search Premier*. Web. 1 Dec. 2008.

Labour Behind the Label. UK Clean Clothes Campaign. Web. 1 Dec. 2008.

Mayer, Robert. "Sweatshops, Exploitation, and Moral Responsibility." *Journal of Social Philosophy* 38.4 (Winter 2007): 605-19. Print.

Meyers, C. D. "Moral Duty, Individual Responsibility, and Sweatshop Exploitation." *Journal of Social Philosophy* 38.4 (Winter 2007): 620-26. *Academic Search Premier*. Web. 28 Nov. 2008.

No Sweat. No Sweat Apparel. Web. 27 Nov. 2008.

Sachs, Jeffrey D. *The End of Poverty*. New York: Penguin Books, 2005. Print.

Shaw, Deirdre, Gillian Hogg, Elaine Wilson, Edward Shiu, and Louise Hassan. "Fashion Victim: The Impact of Fair Trade Concerns on Clothing Choice." *Journal of Strategic Marketing* 14.4 (Dec. 2006): 427-40. Print.

Questions for Discussion

1. Most research papers are written in the third person (*one*, *he*, *she*, *they*), and the author's voice is silent (no use of first person *I*). Yet this essay begins in the author's voice (paragraphs 1 and 2), then changes to third person, which is the dominant point of view of the rest of the essay (exceptions are paragraphs 5 and 13). Why do you think the author begins and ends the account of her research findings by inserting herself into the essay?

2. Identify the thesis statement of this essay and the topic sentences in paragraphs 2, 4, 8, and 11. Now identify the kind(s) of support the author has used to develop her topic in these paragraphs.

3. The author supports her argument that working in a sweatshop can be a positive experience for women in developing countries by focusing primarily on one country. What country does she choose to illustrate her point? How could she have strengthened her support for her argument?

GOOGLE NEVER FORGETS: A CAUTIONARY TALE

Max Fawcett

1   We all have one, be it a mother, a well-meaning grandparent or a particularly mischievous college buddy. They're the people who insist on sharing embarrassing stories—which are invariably supported either by a gallery of photographs or a library of shaky home videos—with those you had foolishly hoped would never see them. For example, my mother enjoys producing the front page of *The Vancouver Sun*, circa 1981, on which I am pictured stark naked and sucking on my bottle while sitting on the edge of a public swimming pool on a particularly hot summer day. The upside was the fact that, like my naked baby picture, these embarrassing moments could be managed, the mortifying game of show-and-tell limited to small audiences, and its effects mitigated with healthy doses of self-deprecating laughter.

2   The Internet, quite unintentionally, has changed that. Thanks to what amounts to a universally accessible photographic memory, the Internet essentially creates the digital equivalent of an unauthorized biography for everyone who leaves a digital footprint. This biography is full of things you might like to share and others you might not, from your comments in an online discussion group to your Grade 12 graduation pictures or some ill-conceived poetry you submitted to an online journal

a few years ago. Worse still is the fact that you have almost no control over the biography's content.

3   Douglas Coupland describes this as our digital "shadow," and he believes it has dangerous implications. As he told a *Time* reporter last spring:

> You've got this thing that follows you no matter where you go. It's going to survive your real shadow long after you're dead. It's composed of truth, half-truth, lies, vengeance, wishful thinking, accuracy, inaccuracy. It grows and grows and gets bigger. It's you but it's not you.

It is, in other words, like having the details of a particularly nasty high-school rumour tattooed on your forehead for the rest of your life. Worse still to Coupland is the fact that these shadows are no longer limited merely to the famous and assorted minor celebrities: "Mine's pretty large at the moment but I think in a few years, everyone's is going to be huge. It won't be just people in the public light any more," he said in the same interview.

4   The ghost writer behind these increasingly common unauthorized biographies is none other than Google, that most trusted and financially successful search engine. Google, you see, has betrayed your trust. While it was guiding you to a particularly good restaurant or helping you find a long-lost high-school friend, it was also collecting the dirt on you and sharing it with anyone who would listen.

5   The search engine business used to be a competitive one, with rival engines like Lycos, HotBot and AltaVista battling Google for market domination. But Google's code won out, in large part because it was so good at finding a good bed and breakfast in Napa Valley instead of napalm manufacturers or articles on the dangers of breakfast in bed when you punched "bed and breakfast + Napa" into the search field. But that superior code is also ruthlessly efficient at finding every reference, however obscure, tangential or dated it might be, when an individual's name is searched. As the *National Post*'s Samantha Grice wrote in March, "the Internet's helpful librarian can become an embarrassing mom who insists on hanging your dorkiest kid photos above the mantle and incessantly gushing about your less-than-stellar achievements."

6   I learned this lesson first hand, thanks to an Angelfire/Geocities website that I created in 1998. I was 18 years old, living in a student residence at UBC and, like many people at the time, relatively unfamiliar with the Internet. One of my floor-mates, a computer science student, appealed to my vanity (a winning strategy to this day, unfortunately) by suggesting that I create a webpage. After all, he argued, what was the harm? It was

free, and if I either got bored with it or didn't like what I had created I could just delete it and forget about the whole experience. He neglected to mention that I could also forget that it existed.

7   In 2004, I finally remembered. Vanity being one of my chief weaknesses, I was Googling myself (a process in which you enter your own name as a search term on Google and discover your digital reflection) and I discovered, with no small degree of horror, the webpage that I had forgotten. Appropriately titled—appropriate in that it exacted the greatest amount of embarrassment—"Max Fawcett, this is your life," the page was a quintessentially amateurish presentation of my interests at age 18. According to the site, "I'm an honors history student/freelance newspaper writer. On this page you will find my collection of wrestling, *South Park*, and other cool links." Surf through and you could—and according to the ticker positioned at the bottom of the page, 670 people did—find a "shrine" to "the greatest wrestler of all-time, Chris Jericho" as well as "an extensive collection of *South Park* links, images, and episodes." The cherry in this cocktail of shame is the email address provided, greekgod@angelfire.com, a reference both to the summer I had spent in Greece and the fact that, I assume, I was fairly high on myself at the time of the page's construction.

8   The cost of my "bad Google" has been limited to embarrassment, but for others the price of leaving a digital footprint can be much higher. Employers now routinely Google prospective hires, and one ill-considered comment on a weblog five years ago can mean the difference between making the final round of interviews and being passed over in favour of someone without an objectionable Google shadow. A recent Harris Interactive poll found that 23 percent of adult Internet users in the United States had searched online for information about their clients, customers, workers and potential employees.

9   Worse still is the fact that these Google-happy bosses often find what they're looking for. Nunavut Tourism employee Penny Cholmondeley—Polar Penny, to her online visitors—stumbled across this unfortunate reality on July 18, 2004, when she was terminated from her job for comments made on her weblog. Intended as a personal journal that would detail her summer in Canada's Arctic for her friends and family, the blog included the occasional unflattering picture of, or critical observation on Iqaluit. Without notice or an opportunity to defend herself, Cholmondeley was fired by Nunavut Tourism after it was tipped off about the existence of the blog by an anonymous source just before the

end of her six-month probation period. Polar Penny's experience isn't unique, either. Ironically enough, the next year, Google employee Mark Jen was fired after blogging about his first few days at work. Delta Air Lines employee Ellen Simonetti was fired because the airline discovered photos of her in her uniform that she had posted on a website.

10 Perhaps the most infamous Google shadow in history belongs to Mike Klander, once a powerful organizer for former prime minister Paul Martin and the author of an ill-considered blog posting in which he compared federal NDP candidate Olivia Chow to a certain breed of dog. The post and blog were quickly taken down, but not before Google's robots—the architects of everyone's Google shadow—captured and archived it. Klander resigned, but the blog became a major news story and gravely harmed Klander's boss, then Trinity-Spadina Liberal MP Tony Ianno, who was trying to defeat Chow for a third consecutive time to retain his seat. I'm not sure what Mr. Klander is like as a person, but this seems like an awfully high price to pay for what amounts to a bad joke.

11 The lesson here (ironically, one I'm not heeding, as the publication of this piece will breathe new life into that darkest corner of my Google shadow) is to be careful of what you put on display. The Internet, for all of its marvellous technological advances and still greater possibilities, is a more dangerous place than we'd like to admit, and that danger comes not from spam, viruses, worms or even those creepy old men who prowl chat rooms pretending to be 16-year-old girls, but instead from the fact that our every cyber-step, every cyber-thought and every search term is saved, sealed and put on display, without our consent and beyond our control. Consider yourself warned.

Questions for Discussion

1. Write a thesis statement that includes both the author's thesis (proposition) and his main points (reasons for believing his proposition).
2. What level of language does Fawcett use in this essay? Identify five or six examples to support your answer.
3. What is the author's main purpose: To amuse? Or to persuade?
4. The author discusses three consequences of reckless Google posts: personal, professional, and political. Identify one strong example that he uses to develop each point.
5. Did this essay persuade you to "be careful of what you put on display" on the Internet? Why?

STUPID JOBS ARE GOOD TO RELAX WITH
Hal Niedzviecki

1   Springsteen kicked off his world tour at Toronto's Massey Hall a while back. Along with record company execs and those who could afford the exorbitant prices scalpers wanted for tickets, I was in attendance. As Bruce rambled on about the plight of the itinerant Mexican workers, I lolled in the back, my job, as always, to make myself as unapproachable as possible—no easy feat, trapped as I was in paisley vest and bow-tie combo. Nonetheless, the concert was of such soporific proportions and the crowd so dulled into pseudo-reverence, I was able to achieve the ultimate in ushering—a drooping catatonia as close as you can get to being asleep while on your feet at a rock concert.

2   But this ushering nirvana wouldn't last long. For an usher, danger takes many forms, including vomiting teens and the usher's nemesis: the disruptive patron. And yes, to my semi-conscious horror, there she was: well-dressed, blond, drunk and doped up, swaying in her seat and . . . clapping. Clapping. In the middle of Springsteen's solo dirge about Pancho or Pedro or Luisa, she was clapping.

3   Sweat beaded on my forehead. The worst was happening. She was in my section. Her clapping echoed through the hall, renowned for its acoustics. The Boss glared from the stage, his finger-picking folksiness no match for the drunken rhythm of this fan. Then, miracle of miracles, the song ended. The woman slumped back into her seat. Bruce muttered something about how he didn't need a rhythm section. Placated by the adoring silence of the well-to-do, he launched into an even quieter song about an even more desperate migrant worker.

4   I lurked in the shadows, relaxed the grip I had on my flashlight (the usher's only weapon). Springsteen crooned. His guitar twanged. It was so quiet you could hear the rats squirrelling around the ushers' subterranean change rooms. The woman roused herself from her slumber. She leaned forward in her seat, as if suddenly appreciating the import of her hero's message. I wiped the sweat off my brow, relieved. But slowly, almost imperceptibly, she brought her arms up above her head. I stared, disbelieving. Her hands waved around in the air until . . . boom! Another song ruined, New York record execs and L.A. journalists distracted from their calculations of Bruce's net worth, the faint cry of someone calling, "Usher! Do something!"

5   For several years now, I have relied on stupid jobs to pay my way through the world. This isn't because I am a stupid person. On the contrary, stupid jobs are a way to avoid the brain-numbing idiocy of full-time

employment. They are the next best thing to having no job at all. They will keep you sane, and smart.

6   I'm lazy sometimes. I don't always feel like working. On the stupid job, you're allowed to be lazy. All you have to do is show up. Hey, that's as much of an imposition on my life as I'm ready to accept. Does The Boss go to work every day? I don't think so. He's The Boss.

7   Understanding the stupid job is the key to wading your way through the muck of the working week and dealing with such portentous concepts as The Youth Unemployment Crisis and The Transformation of the Workplace. So sit back and let me explain. Or, as I used to say behind the scowl of my shining grin: "Hi, how are you this evening? Please follow me and I will show you to your seat."

8   "Out of Work: Is There Hope for Canada's Youth?" blurted the October . . . issue of *Canadian Living*. My answer? There is more hope than ever. I'm not talking about ineffectual governments and their well-intentioned "partners," the beneficent corporations, all banding together to "create" jobs. After all, what kind of jobs do you think these corporations are going to create? Jobs that are interesting, challenging and resplendent with possibilities? Hardly. These are going to be stupid jobs. Bring me your college graduates, your aspiring business mavens, your literature lovers and we will find them rote employment where servility and docility are the best things they could have learned at university.

9   But hope, hope is something altogether different. Hope is the process whereby entire generations learn to undervalue their work, squirm out of the trap of meaningless employment, work less, consume less and actually figure out how to enjoy life.

10   I hope I'm right about this, because the reality of the underemployed, overeducated young people of Canada is that the stupid job is their future. As the middle-aged population continues to occupy all the "real" jobs, as the universities continue to hike tuition prices (forcing students to work and study part time), as the government continues to shore up employment numbers with make-work and "retraining," there will be more stupid jobs than ever. And these stupid jobs won't be reserved for the uneducated and poor. The fertile growth of the stupid job is already reaping a crop of middle-class youngsters whose education and upbringing have, somehow, given way to (supposedly) stalled prospects and uncertain incomes.

11   These are your grandchildren, your children, your sisters, your cousins, your neighbours. Hey, that might very well be a multicoloured bow-tie wrapped around your neck.

12   I took a few tenuous steps down the aisle. All around me, luxurious people hissed in annoyance and extended their claws. Clapping woman was bouncing in her seat. She was smiling. Her face was flushed and joyous. The sound of her hands coming together was deafening. I longed for the floor captain, the front-of-house manager, the head of security, somebody to come and take this problem away from me. I hit her with a burst of flashlight. Taking advantage of her momentary blindness, I leaned in: "Excuse me Miss," I said. "You can't do that." "What?" she said. "That clapping," I said. "Listen," she slurred. "I paid $300 to see this. I can do what I want."

13   My flashlight hand wavered. Correctly interpreting my silence for defeat, she resumed her clapping. Springsteen strummed louder, unsuccessful in his attempt to drown out the beat of luxury, the truth of indulgence. I faded away, the darkness swallowing me up. For a blissful moment, I was invisible.

14   A lot of young people think their stupid jobs are only temporary. Most of them are right, in a way. Many will move on from being, as I have been, an usher, a security guard, a delivery boy, a data co-ordinator, a publishing intern. They will get marginally better jobs, but what they have learned from their stupid jobs will stay with them forever. Hopefully.

15   If I'm right, they will learn that the stupid job—and by extension, all jobs—must be approached with willing stupidity. Set your mind free. It isn't necessary, and it can be an impediment. While your body runs the maze and finds the cheese, let your mind go where it will.

16   Look at it this way: you're trading material wealth and luxury for freedom and creativity. To simplify this is to say that while you may have less money to buy things, you will have a lot more time to think up ways to achieve your goals without buying things. It is remarkable how quickly one comes to value time to just sit and think. Oddly, many of us seem quite proud of having absolutely no time to think about anything. The words "I'm so busy" are chanted over and over again like a mantra, an incantation against some horrible moment when we realize we're not so busy. In the stupid job universe, time isn't quantifiable. You're making so many dollars an hour, but the on-job perks include daydreams, poems scribbled on napkins, novels read in utility closets and long conversations about the sexual stamina of Barney Rubble. How much is an idea worth? An image? A moment of tranquillity? A bad joke? The key here is to embrace the culture of anti-work.

17   Sometime after the Springsteen debacle, I was on a delivery job dropping off newspapers at various locales. I started arguing with my co-worker, the van driver, about work ethic. I suggested we skip a drop-off

or two, claiming that no one would notice and even if they did, we could deny it and no one would care. He responded by telling me that no matter what job he was doing, if he accepted the work, he was compelled to do it right. I disagreed. Cut corners, I argued. Do less for the same amount of pay. That's what they expect us to do, I said. Why else would they pay us so little? Not that day, but some weeks later, he came to see things my way.

18   What am I trying to tell you? To be lazy? To set fire to the corporation?

19   Maybe. Our options might be limited, but they are still options. Somewhere in the bowels of Massey Hall it has probably been noted in my permanent record that I have a bad attitude. That was a mistake. I wasn't trying to have a bad attitude. I was trying to have no attitude. . . .

20   What I should have told my friend in the delivery van was that when working the stupid job, passivity is the difference between near slavery and partial freedom. It's a mental distinction. Your body is still in the same place for the same amount of time (unless you're unsupervised), but your mind is figuring things out. Figuring out how many days you need to work to afford things like hard-to-get tickets to concerts by famous American icons. Or figuring out why it is that at the end of the week, most people are too busy or too tired to do anything other than spend their hard-earned dollars on fleeting moments of cotton candy ecstasy as ephemeral as lunch hour. Personally, I'd take low-level servitude over a promotion that means I'll be working late the rest of my life. You want me to work weekends? You better give me the rest of the week off. . . .

21   Montreal has one of the highest unemployment rates of any city in Canada. Young people in that city are as likely to have full-time jobs as they are to spend their nights arguing about Quebec separation. Not coincidentally, some of the best Canadian writers, comic artists and underground periodicals are from that city. We're talking about the spoken-word capital of North America here. Creativity plus unemployment equals art.

22   The burgeoning stupid job aesthetic is well documented in another youth culture phenomenon, the vaunted 'zine (photocopied periodicals published by individuals for fun, not money). Again, it doesn't take a genius to make the connection between the youth culture of stupid jobs and the urgency and creativity 'zine publishers display when writing about their lives. "So why was I dishonest and subversive?" asks Brendan Bartholomew in an article in the popular Wisconsin 'zine *Temp Slave*. "Well, I've been sabotaging employers for so long, it's become second nature. It's in my blood. I couldn't stop if I wanted to."

23   Slacking off, doing as little as possible, relishing my lack of responsibility, this is what the workplace has taught me to do. This is the stupid job mantra. It isn't about being poor. The stupid job aesthetic is not about going hungry. Canada is a country of excess. You cannot have a stupid job culture when people are genuinely, truly, worried that they are going to starve in the streets.

24   Nevertheless, the tenets of the stupid job revolution are universal: work is mainly pointless; if you can think of something better to do, you shouldn't have to work; it's better to have a low-paying job and freedom than a high-paying job and a 60-hour workweek. It was Bruce's drunken fan who highlighted the most important aspect of what will one day be known as the stupid job revolution: with money, you think you can do whatever you want, but you rarely can; without money, you can be like Bartholomew—a postmodern rat, a stowaway writing his diaries from the comfort of his berth at the bottom of the sinking ship.

25   My father's plight is a familiar one. He started his working life at 13 in Montreal. He's 55 now. His employer of 12 years forced him to take early retirement. The terms were great, and if he didn't own so much stuff (and want more stuff) he could live comfortably without ever working again. But he feels used, meaningless, rejected.

26   On his last day, I helped him clean out his office. The sight of him stealing staplers, blank disks and Post-it note pads was something I'll never forget. It was a memo he was writing to his own soul (note: they owe me).

27   But the acquisition of more stuff is not what he needs to put a life of hard work behind him. I wish that he could look back on his years of labour and think fondly of all the hours he decided not to work, those hours he spent reading a good book behind the closed door of his office, or skipping off early to take the piano lessons he never got around to. Instead of stealing office supplies, he should have given his boss the finger as he walked out the door. Ha ha. I don't care what you think of me. And by the way, I never did.

28   Despite his decades of labour and my years of being barely employed (and the five degrees we have between us), we have both ended up at the same place. He feels cheated. I don't.

Questions for Discussion

1. Which paragraph states the thesis of the essay?
2. What strategy does the author use in his conclusion? (See paragraphs 25 to 28.) Do you think it's effective? Why?

3. What were your expectations of the author when you read the title of the essay? Were you surprised to find words such as "exorbitant," "soporific," and "catatonia" in the first paragraph? What other elements of style and structure tell us that the author is far from "stupid"?
4. Is this essay primarily argument or persuasion? (See page 267.)
5. What is the basis of the author's disagreement with the van driver as they're dropping off newspapers? (See paragraphs 17 to 20.) Whom do you agree with? Who, in your opinion, has the better attitude toward the job? Why?
6. What proof does the author offer to support his point that art and creativity are likely to flourish among people who are unemployed or have "stupid jobs"?
7. What is the author's attitude toward consumerism? Does he think we buy too much or not enough? Where in the essay is his attitude most clearly revealed? Do you agree with him? Why?

FARMING IT OUT

Maria Amuchastegui

1   It was the Thursday before Easter that Henk Sikking Jr. got the doctor's call. The 28-year-old tulip farmer was getting ready to take his crew of Mexican migrant workers grocery shopping. The workers live on his property and get around with bicycles, but rely on their boss to take them on major shopping trips. He had arranged for a bus to take the workers into town.

2   Sikking's best worker, Hermelindo Gutiérrez, had gone to see the doctor earlier in the week, complaining of swollen feet and ankles. Sikking assumed that Gutiérrez had injured himself while driving one of the carts used to navigate the sprawling complex of greenhouses. The doctor was blunt. The bloodwork revealed that both of Gutiérrez's kidneys had failed. If Gutiérrez did not go to the hospital, he was going to die.

3   The family business, Pioneer Flower Farms, was started by Henk Sr., who immigrated to Canada from Holland in 1972. Henk Jr. is in charge of potted plants, his brother Peter runs the cut flowers division, while Henk Sr. oversees the entire operation. The farm is the main supplier of buds for Ottawa's annual tulip festival. Until he fell ill, the 32-year-old Mexican had been working at the St. Catharines, Ontario, greenhouse for six years, working his way up to become foreman. "He was my right-hand guy," said Sikking. "He pretty much ran the crew. He could speak English. He was really interested in the job."

4   Gutiérrez was diagnosed with kidney failure and admitted to the Hotel Dieu Hospital in St. Catharines. His co-workers suggested he call the Mexican consulate in Toronto to let them know he was sick. Before long, the consulate began to call Gutiérrez, demanding that he return to Mexico. Sikking knew that for Gutiérrez this was a death sentence. Unless he received a kidney transplant, he would require dialysis for the rest of his life. The rural village that he comes from does not have dialysis facilities. And Gutiérrez hadn't bothered to buy health insurance in Mexico because he spends most of the year working in Canada. Sikking said to Gutiérrez, "You're not going back. You got sick in Canada. It's Canada's responsibility to take care of you."

5   Gutiérrez came to Canada through the Seasonal Agricultural Workers Program (SAW), a federal guest-worker program that has been in existence since 1966. The original participants in the program were from Jamaica, Trinidad-Tobago and Barbados; Mexico followed suit in 1974; other Caribbean nations joined in 1976. According to statistics provided by Human Resources and Skills Development Canada (HRSDC), in 2004, 18,887 migrant workers came to Canada under the SAW program, 10,777 of whom were from Mexico.

6   Compared to the undocumented masses who make the dangerous trek to the US, migrant workers in Canada—theoretically at least—receive more social benefits and have more legal rights. According to Juan José Martínez de la Rosa, coordinator of the agricultural program at the Mexican consulate in Toronto, Mexico considers Canada's SAW program to be a "best practices" model for managed migration, especially compared to the US, where the vast majority of migrant workers are illegal immigrants. "It's a tangible, positive example of what can happen when two parties agree to administer migration, given the need of one party for labour, and the need of the other party to provide jobs. It's a way to manage the phenomenon of migration without the risk associated with border crossing by *indocumentados*."

7   For Mexico, and other countries that participate in the SAW program, the money sent home by migrant workers is an important source of hard currency. According to the World Bank, Mexico received $18.1 billion US in foreign remittances in 2004—about 2.5 percent of its GDP—making it the third-greatest recipient of remittances in absolute terms, after India and China. In 2003, remittances were Mexico's second-largest source of foreign exchange after oil, eclipsing foreign investment and tourism. The Canadian Department of Foreign Affairs estimated that in 2002, Mexico received about $80 million in remittances from participants in the SAW program. Mexican participation in the SAW program had more than doubled from 1994 to 2004.

8   Canada benefits, according to the HRSDC website, because the program provides farmers with a "reliable" source of labour. From the farmers' perspective, the chief attraction of guest workers is that they can't easily quit their jobs. "If you want 100 Canadians, you have to hire 300," said Sikking. The temporary work permits given to migrant workers are for specific farms; workers need the farmer's permission to transfer elsewhere. If workers complain about their work conditions, farmers have the power to have them repatriated to Mexico. If workers return to Mexico before completing half their work term, they have to reimburse the farmer for their airfare, a powerful disincentive to quit.

9   The farmers benefit, too, from securing workers who are comparatively cheap. The agreement between Canada and Mexico stipulates that migrants must be paid the "prevailing wage" that Canadians are paid for the same work. According to a United Food and Commercial Workers' (UFCW) draft 2005 report on the SAW program, the rate paid to migrant workers in 2006 will be $8.30 an hour. HRSDC's own stats, however, show the average for Canadian agricultural workers is closer to $10.50 an hour. Assuming a 40-hour work week, migrant workers gross about $332 per week before taxes. The actual hours worked are much longer: Gutiérrez initially assumed that his feet had swollen from working 16- and 17-hour days. Farmers don't always pay the required rate: In 2005, Mexican workers who were picking berries in Pitt Meadows, British Columbia, returned to Mexico of their own accord, complaining of being paid $24 for 10-hour days.

10   Still, $332 per week is a lot of money in Mexico. From the workers' perspective, the SAW program gives them a well-paying job and raises their family's standard of living. According to a report prepared for the North-South Institute by Mexican researchers Gustavo Verduzco and María Isabel Lozano, the same workers make an average of $55 US per week in Mexico. Verduzco and Lozano also found that the program may be helping to keep the workers' kids in school: the longer a worker participated in the SAW program, the higher the level of schooling reached by his children.

11   The Canadian government takes a big cut from the workers' paycheques. According to Verduzco and Lozano, about 20 percent of workers' paycheques is deducted in taxes, including EI, CPP and income tax; 77 percent of the workers have their income tax deductions refunded because they make less than $14,000 per year. The cost of housing and airfare to and from Canada is borne by the farmer.

12   In exchange, the workers receive some social benefits. Retired workers can collect CPP, even if they retire in Mexico. Health coverage varies by province, but in Ontario the workers get provincial health cards that are valid for the calendar year. In addition, the workers receive Worker's

Comp for work-related injuries, and are required to purchase private health insurance for expenses not covered by their provincial health cards. The Mexican workers have a group policy with RBC Insurance.

13   The workers' relative prosperity comes at a price. Although the workers are helping to subsidize Canadian social programs with their taxes, they don't receive all the benefits that Canadians receive. Many social benefits require Canadian residency. Because the workers have to leave Canada when their work permits expire, they are not eligible to receive those benefits. For example, migrant workers are not eligible for most EI benefits, despite paying EI premiums. In the case of medicare, workers who have returned to Mexico do not have coverage for conditions developed in Canada.

14   The exclusion of migrant workers from EI is currently the subject of a Supreme Court challenge. The federal government tried to have the case dismissed, arguing that the UFCW does not have standing in the case. The judge ruled in January [2006] that the UFCW does have the right to represent migrant workers, the first time a union has ever won the right to represent unorganized workers. It is illegal in Ontario for agricultural workers, both migrant and Canadian, to join trade unions and to strike. (They can join "associations," but the associations can't bargain on their behalf.) The rationale given by farmers and by the government is that crops are time-sensitive. If agricultural workers take collective action, farmers could lose their crops.

15   In the spring-bulb world, crops are planted in the fall and harvested in the spring. Sikking summons Mexican workers to his farm in two stages: in spring to coincide with the harvest, and again in fall to coincide with the planting. In the barn, workers are stationed along an assembly line, planting tulips. Some workers feed bulbs onto a conveyor belt. Others sort bulbs onto trays, 100 bulbs to a tray. The bulbs are watered, covered in dirt and sand, and placed in cold storage for four months, until they sprout roots. The bulbs are then are taken to the greenhouse for three weeks, where they will form buds. Tulips are classified as hardy bulbs because they can withstand low temperatures. They must be "forced" to bloom by being placed in cold storage.

16   Sikking is a tall man, with Elvis sideburns and a kindly face. He picks up a tulip bulb and holds it before him. "These are the best bulbs," he says proudly. Pioneer Flower Farms imports all its tulip bulbs from Holland. It is one of the largest flower-bulb forcing farms in North America, producing over 40 million blooms per year, 20 million tulips and 20 million other varieties. The farm includes 300,000 square feet of greenhouse and nearly two acres of cold storage. Eighty percent of the

farm's business is with the United States; its customers include [Metro], Costco and the National Capital Commission.

17 When Gutiérrez fell ill, he had just arrived at the farm for the spring harvest. He spent one week in the Hotel Dieu hospital. The consulate said they would send someone to see him, but no one ever came. Gutiérrez was discharged from the hospital and went back to the farm. He continued to receive dialysis treatment as an outpatient. During this time, the cost of his dialysis was covered by OHIP, Ontario's medicare.

18 One day, the phone rang at the farm, and it was the consulate. The consulate told Gutiérrez that he would have to go back to Mexico because he had a pre-existing condition that was not covered by his insurance, and because his treatment was too expensive. He offered Gutiérrez a payment of $3,500 from RBC Insurance on the condition that he return.

19 The Mexican Ministry of Labour is supposed to ensure that workers have received yearly medical checkups before sending them to Canada. When Gutiérrez was first admitted to the SAW program, he got a clean bill of health. When he was diagnosed with kidney failure, he had not had a medical checkup in several years.

20 "Do you have any idea what your treatment costs?" said the consulate.

21 Gutiérrez is modest and soft-spoken in the way of the Mexican campesino, but now he raised his voice. "I don't care what it costs," said Gutiérrez. "I've been working here seven years. I don't have health insurance in Mexico. I've brought everything to Canada, just like you. I want to be treated here."

22 "That doesn't matter," said the consulate. "You're going back to Mexico."

23 The consulate contacted Gutiérrez's wife in Mexico, and asked her to sign a power of attorney authorizing the consulate to forcibly return her husband to Mexico. She refused. When Gutiérrez found out about the conversation, he was furious. The consulate told Gutiérrez he was starting to become difficult, *sangrón*.

24 The consulate says it contacted Gutiérrez's family so that it could arrange for Gutiérrez to receive medical treatment in Mexico. Gutiérrez initially went along with the plan, and then backed out. According to Lourdes Borofsky, a Mexican community activist who does outreach with workers and advocated on Gutiérrez's behalf with the consulate, Gutiérrez didn't believe the consulate's promises. "He didn't believe it because he had heard of other cases in which workers are returned to Mexico and once they are there, the government totally forgets about them," said Borofsky. "They promise things and don't deliver. That's what he heard."

25   Gutiérrez did what migrant workers are supposed to do. Workers are told to contact their consulate if they have a health issue or a problem with their employer. But because the consulates have an interest in attracting farms and in ensuring the smooth functioning of the program, they often sacrifice individual workers.

26   In Gutiérrez's case, his work permit gave him the legal right to remain in Canada for eight months, until December 15, and his medicare was valid until December 31. According to Marina Wilson, a spokesperson for Citizenship and Immigration Canada, temporary workers aren't forced to leave Canada immediately if they become sick or injured. "They can stay for the duration of their permit. They still have status for as long as their work permit is valid. They are not deported if they break their leg on the job or if they develop a condition." Under Canadian law, migrant workers who fall ill in Canada can legally remain here until their work permits expire. Under the terms of their employment contract, farmers can send them back to Mexico for any "sufficient reason," including illness. According to a report prepared for the North-South Institute by human rights lawyer Veena Verma, "workers are not provided equal treatment with Canadian workers when the effect of the repatriation provisions make it difficult to enforce their rights." In theory, migrant workers are protected by the same laws that protect Canadians. In practice, because they can be repatriated at any time, they can't enforce their rights.

27   Jorge Aceytuno, a spokesperson for HRSDC, said that sick workers are generally returned to Mexico only if they have a long-term illness, and that Mexico makes arrangements for treatment to continue there. "If it's a short-term illness, it's in nobody's interest for the worker to go back," he said. He acknowledged that Mexico is not obligated by the Canada–Mexico agreement to provide health care for sick workers after they return. According to a report published in 2004 by the UFCW, the Canadian government washes its hands of its responsibility toward the workers. "The government believes its responsibility with regard to migrant workers begins and ends with the issuance of work visas," said the report. "The government has indicated that the consulates of the sending countries and their staffs are responsible for supporting and advocating on behalf of workers."

28   The small Mexican community in St. Catharines rallied around its beleaguered countryman. When Gutiérrez's co-workers realized he was having difficulty getting to his dialysis treatments (Sikking would sometimes lend Gutiérrez his van, but he couldn't always spare it), they chipped in $1,600 to buy him a used car.

29   The consulate then began to call Sikking, pressuring him to send his worker back to Mexico. RBC Insurance called Sikking too, offering

Gutiérrez a $3,000 payment. Sikking asked Gutiérrez if he had health insurance in Mexico; Gutiérrez said no. Sikking was afraid of what the government would think if it found out he helped his worker. "We depend on these guys for our livelihood," he said. Sikking's friends advised him to send Gutiérrez back. "People were saying, 'Don't take it personal, just send the guy back,'" said Sikking.

30   Gutiérrez recalled Sikking's reaction to the consulate's pressure. "When they insisted on removing me, my boss said, 'Hermelindo'—he always calls me Hermelindo—'You have worked for me. You have been a good worker. I am going to help you. I don't know how we're going to do it, but you're going to stay here.'" Someone at the office happened to know a human rights lawyer, Ryan Persad. Sikking paid the $2,000 retainer fee, and the lawyer filed a claim for refugee status. They are currently awaiting a court date.

31   Gutiérrez's case is not exceptional. Workers are routinely sent back to Mexico when they are gravely ill. There was a case in Hamilton of a worker who fractured his skull in a bicycle accident. The doctors had to remove a seven-centimetre piece of his skull to accommodate the swelling of his brain. "They took him out of the Hamilton hospital with his skull in a bag and a nurse to escort him back to Mexico," said Stan Raper, agricultural coordinator at the UFCW.

32   Workers can also be repatriated if they complain about their working or housing conditions. In 2003, a Caribbean worker was sent home after he complained that pesticides were seeping into his living quarters. In 2001, in an incident that caused the Canadian labour movement to take notice of migrant workers, Mexican workers at a greenhouse in Leamington, Ontario, organized a wildcat strike. The farmer had the ringleaders repatriated.

33   What makes Gutiérrez's case different is that his employer wants him to stay in Canada, against the wishes of the consulate. What is also different is the involvement of a private insurance company. RBC Insurance applied pressure to Sikking and to the consulate to persuade Gutiérrez to return to Mexico, offering him a financial incentive to go home. "They wanted him out of the country," said Sikking.

34   One day in September, Borofsky called Gutiérrez to see how he was doing. He had moved into a refugee settlement house in St. Catharines. "He didn't say he was depressed, but I could tell he was depressed," said Borofsky. "He was sad and afraid he wouldn't have anyone to talk to. And he said, 'I would like to spend Christmas with my family. I don't know if you could help me out.'"

35   Borofsky contacted Wayne Manne, a priest at Ste. Marguerite d'Youville parish in Brampton. He arranged for one of the members of

the congregation, who wishes to remain anonymous, to purchase plane tickets for Gutiérrez's wife, María del Rosario Romero, his 11-year-old daughter Sayuri and his eight-year-old son Sergio. The family arrived in Canada on a tourist visa, and planned to stay until April.

36   According to Kerry Preibisch, a sociology professor at the University of Guelph, the preference given by Mexico to hiring married men is one of the mechanisms used to ensure that workers go home. "This program works through cooperation between Canada and the labour-sending countries. They're not wanted as citizens by Canada, they're wanted as labourers. Allowing workers to stay in the country when they're not working jeopardizes the smooth functioning of the program," said Preibisch. "If you think about it, it's remarkable that every year, nearly 20,000 workers come up to Canada to fill labour shortages in agriculture, and then go back to their country."

37   Meanwhile, Gutiérrez continues to live at the settlement house and to receive dialysis, while awaiting a court date for his refugee hearing. The irony is that, although he has medicare and a willing organ donor, he can't afford a kidney transplant. Gutiérrez is not eligible to be on Canada's waiting list for donated organs since he is not a permanent resident, but he is sure that one of his brothers and sisters will be willing to donate a kidney. The cost of transplanting a kidney into Gutiérrez is covered by OHIP, but the cost of removing a kidney from his sibling is not.

38   Back on the farm, Mexican *cumbia* music pulsates from a boombox. Migrant workers carefully stack tulip buds into crates: red, pink and white. Using forklifts, the workers transport the crates from the assembly line area in the barn to the loading dock at the other end of the greenhouse complex. They load the crates into trucks and dispatch them to the National Capital Commission in Ottawa. At the tulip festival, the buds will bloom, a symbol of the safe refuge that the Dutch royal family found in Canada during the Second World War.

39   "What happened to Hermelindo happens to almost everyone," says Sikking. "If they're not getting medical treatment in Mexico, then I think they should get something here. Some of these guys have been working here 40 years."

Questions for Discussion

1. The author of this piece develops her argument indirectly, beginning with a narrative incident (paragraphs 1 through 4). Go through the essay and identify by number the paragraphs that continue the story.

2. The narrative that threads through this essay is not told in a straight line. Why did the author choose to develop her argument by alternating narrative incident with general/background information?

   Would it have been more effective to tell the story of Hermelindo Gutiérrez first, and then provide the background/context? Why?
3. Where in the essay does the author first clearly state her opinion that migrant workers are discriminated against in Canada?
4. In addition to narration, the author frequently uses direct quotations to develop her argument. Why?
5. The author acknowledges that both the workers (paragraphs 7, 10, and 12) and the employers—including the government—(paragraphs 8, 9, and 11) benefit from the Seasonal Agricultural Workers Program. She also acknowledges that there are risks on both sides. Nevertheless, one side benefits more than the other. Which one? Support your answer with specific reference to the essay.
6. Explain the irony in paragraph 38. Find at least one other example of irony in this piece.
7. The author quotes a University of Guelph sociology professor: "This program works through cooperation between Canada and the labour-sending countries. [The migrant workers] are not wanted as citizens by Canada, they're wanted as labourers. . . . If you think about it, it's remarkable that every year, nearly 20,000 workers come up to Canada to fill labour shortages in agriculture, and then go back to their country." Why do you think Canada does not want agricultural workers as citizens? Do you agree with the government's position?
8. The Gutiérrez story did not end where the author left it. While his wife and children were visiting Gutiérrez, the son was struck by a car. Use your research skills to find out what happened and update the story of the Gutiérrez family.
9. How did you react to this essay? Would your response have been the same if the author had stated her opinion up front and then listed and developed her reasons?

Workbook

He who would perfect his work must first sharpen his tools.
Confucius, 551–479 BCE

Someone who makes an error and does not correct it makes two errors.
Aristotle, 324–382 BCE

Look not where you fell, but where you slipped.
African proverb

Substitute "damn" every time you're inclined to write "very"; your editor will delete it, and the writing will be just as it should be.
Mark Twain, 1831–1910

A Review of the Basics

How to Use This Workbook

This part of *Essay Essentials* is a workbook designed to improve the correctness of your writing. In Sections 7.1 to 7.20, we look at the errors that give many writers trouble, whether they are writing student papers, professional reports, PowerPoint presentations, or office correspondence.

In each section, we do three things: explain a point, illustrate it with examples, and provide exercises in the text and on the website to help you master the point. The exercises are arranged in sets that become more difficult as you go along. By the end of the last set in each chapter, you should have a good grasp of the skill. You will lose that grasp, however, if you do not practise. To maintain and reinforce mastery of the skills you are learning, make a conscious effort to apply them every time you write.

You should work your way through this part of the book while you are working on Parts 1 through 6. If you have been out of school for some time or if your basic skills are not as strong as you'd like them to be, you may find it helpful to set up a schedule, matching a section of the workbook with a unit of the text. For example, while you are learning how to plan an essay in Part 1, you could set yourself the goal of working through Sections 7.1 through 7.6 on sentence structure; while learning how to write an essay in Part 2, you could work through Sections 7.7 through 7.9 on grammar. You would then cover Sections 7.10 through 7.15 on punctuation, along with Part 3, revising the essay. Finally, as you learn about the different kinds of essays in Part 5, you could cover Sections 7.16 through 7.20 on spelling.

Alternatively, you could go through this workbook section by section, addressing in order the errors your instructor identifies in your writing. Whichever approach you choose, we recommend that you complete every section of the workbook. If you do so conscientiously, we guarantee that as your papers improve in organization and effectiveness, your writing will also improve in correctness and clarity.

Here's how to proceed in each section.

1. Read the explanation. Do this even if you think you understand the point being discussed.
2. Study the highlighted rules and the examples that follow them.
3. Now turn to the exercises. Try at least one set even if you are confident that you understand the principle.
4. **Always check your answers to each set of exercises before going on to the next.** Only if you check your answers after every set can you avoid repeating your mistakes or—worse—reinforcing your errors. For those exercises marked with an asterisk (*), you will find the answers in the back of the book. For exercises on the website, the answers are marked automatically, so you will know instantly whether you have understood the material.
5. When you make a mistake, go back to the explanation and examples and study them again. Try making up some examples of your own to illustrate the rule. If you are truly stuck, check with your instructor. You can reinforce your understanding by doing the practice tests that you will find on the "More Practice" page of the *Essay Essentials* website.
6. At the end of each section, there is a mastery test marked with the icon shown in the left margin. Your instructor can provide you with the answers for these tests. Use these tests to help track your progress as you master basic writing skills.

On the inside front cover, you will find a "Quick Revision Guide." Use it to ensure that you have covered all the essentials before handing in your paper.

On the inside back cover, you will find a list of correction marks commonly used by instructors to draw your attention to specific errors. Use this list to be sure you've eliminated all errors your instructor has previously identified in your writing. (Teachers are paid, in part, to pay attention to student errors. So, even if you choose not to track your errors from one assignment to the next, you can be assured your teacher will.)

SECTION 7.1

Cracking the Sentence Code

There is nothing really mysterious or difficult about sentences; you've been speaking them since you were two. The difficulty arises when you try to write—not sentences, oddly enough, but paragraphs. Most college students, if asked to write 10 sentences on 10 different topics, could do so without error. However, when those same students write paragraphs, then fragments, run-ons, and other sentence faults appear.

The solution to sentence-structure problems has two parts.

Be sure every sentence you write
1. has both a subject and a verb
2. expresses a complete thought

If English is your first language, your ear may be the best instrument with which to test your sentences. If you read a sentence aloud, you may be able to tell by the sound whether it is complete and clear. Sometimes, however, your ear may mislead you, so this section will show you, step by step, how to decode your sentences to find their subjects and verbs. When you know how to decode sentences, you can make sure that every sentence you write is complete.

Read these sentences aloud.

Every skier should wear a protective helmet.
Although every skier should wear a protective helmet.

The second "sentence" doesn't sound right, does it? It does not make sense on its own and is in fact a sentence fragment.

Testing your sentences by reading them aloud won't work if you read your paragraphs straight through from beginning to end. The trick is to read from the end to the beginning. That is, read your last sentence aloud and *listen* to it. If it sounds all right, then read aloud the next-to-last sentence, and so on, until you have worked your way back to the first sentence you wrote.

Now, what do you do with the ones that don't sound correct? Before you can fix them, you need to decode each sentence to find out if it has both a subject and a verb. The subject and the verb are the bare essentials of a sentence. Every sentence you write must contain both. There is one exception:

In a **command**, the subject is suggested rather than stated.

Consider these examples.

Sign here. = [You] sign here. (The subject you is implied or understood.)
Charge it. = [You] charge it.
Play ball!   = [You] play ball!

Finding Subjects and Verbs[1]

A sentence is about *someone* or *something*. That someone or something is the **subject**. The word (or words) that tells what the subject *is* or *does* is the **verb**. In the following sentences, the subject is underlined once and the verb twice.

Snow falls.
Kim dislikes winter.
We love snowboarding.
Mt. Whistler offers excellent opportunities for winter sports.
In Canada, winter is six months long.
Some people feel the cold severely.

The subject of a sentence is always a **noun** (the name of a person, place, thing, or concept) or a **pronoun** (a word such as *I, you, he, she, it, we,* or *they* used in place of a noun). In the examples above, the subjects include persons (*Kim, we, people*); a place (*Mt. Whistler*); a thing (*snow*); and a concept (*winter*). In one sentence, a pronoun (*we*) is the subject.

Find the verb first.

---

[1]If you have forgotten (or have never learned) the parts of speech and the basic sentence patterns, you will find this information on the student page of the *Essay Essentials* website, http://www.essayessentials5e.nelson.com.

One way to find the **verb** in a sentence is to ask what the sentence says about the subject. There are two kinds of verbs.

- **Action verbs** tell you what the subject is doing. In the examples above, *falls*, *dislikes*, *love*, and *offers* are action verbs.
- **Linking verbs** link or connect a subject to a noun or adjective describing that subject. In the examples above, *is* and *feel* are linking verbs.

    Linking verbs tell you the subject's condition or state of being. (For example, "Tadpoles *become* frogs," "Frogs *feel* slimy.") The most common linking verbs are forms of *to be* (*am, is, are, was, were, have been*, etc.) and verbs such as *look, taste, feel, sound, appear, remain, seem*, and *become*.

Another way to find the verb in a sentence is to put a pronoun (*I, you, he, she, it*, or *they*) in front of the word you think is the verb. If the result makes sense, it is a verb. For example, you could put *it* in front of *falls* in the first sentence listed above: "it falls" makes sense, so you know *falls* is the verb in this sentence. Try this test with the other five example sentences.

Keep this guideline in mind as you work through the exercises below.

To find the subject, ask <u>who</u> or <u>what</u> the sentence is about.
To find the verb, ask what the subject <u>is</u> or <u>is doing</u>.

Exercise 7.1.1*

In each of the following sentences, underline the <u>subject</u> with one line and the <u>verb</u> with two. Answers for exercises in this section begin on page 546. If you make even one mistake, go to the website and do the exercise listed beside the Web icon that follows this exercise. Be sure you understand this material thoroughly before you go on.

1. I bought a used car.

2. The used car was cheap.

3. It needed some repairs.

4. Unfortunately, the repairs were expensive.

5. Insurance for the car was expensive, too.

6. Buying a car is costly.

7. According to the salesman, the car was a bargain.

8. Always get a second opinion.

9. After 10 years, cars sometimes develop serious problems.

10. Paying for repairs offsets the cheap price.

GO TO WEB

EXERCISE 7.1.1

Usually, but not always, the subject comes before the verb in a sentence.

Occasionally, we find the subject after the verb:

- In sentences beginning with *Here* + a form of *to be* or with *There* + a form of *to be*

Here and *there* are never the subject of a sentence.

Here <u>are</u> the test <u>results</u>. (Who or what <u>are</u>? <u>Results</u>.)
There <u>is</u> a <u>fly</u> in my soup. (Who or what <u>is</u>? A <u>fly</u>.)

- In sentences that are deliberately inverted for emphasis

Finally, at the end of the long, boring joke <u>came</u> the pathetic <u>punch line</u>.
Out of the stadium and into the pouring rain <u>marched</u> the <u>parade</u>.

- In questions

<u>Are</u> <u>we</u> there yet?
<u>Is</u> <u>she</u> the one?

But notice that in questions beginning with *who, whose, what, where,* or *which*, the subject and verb are in "normal" order: subject followed by verb.

<u>Who</u> <u>ate</u> my sandwich?   <u>Whose</u> <u>horse</u> <u>came</u> first?
<u>What</u> <u>caused</u> the accident?   <u>Which</u> <u>car</u> <u>runs</u> best?

Exercise 7.1.2*

Underline the subject with one line and the verb with two. Watch out for inverted sentences. If you make an error, do the Web exercises that follow.

1. Here is an idea to consider.

2. Who wants the last piece?

3. Eat slowly.

4. There, beyond the swimming pool, is the hot tub.

5. A moving chicken is poultry in motion.

6. Two days after the due date, Homer began his term paper.

7. Here are the results of your examination.

8. In 1834, William Lyon Mackenzie became mayor of York, a town in Upper Canada.

9. Later he led a rebellion against the government of Upper Canada.

10. Irish coffee contains ingredients from all four of the essential food groups: caffeine, fat, sugar, and alcohol.

GO TO WEB

EXERCISES 7.1.2, 7.1.3, 7.1.4

More about Verbs

The verb in a sentence may be a single word, as in the exercises you've just done, or it may be a group of words. When you are considering whether or not a word group is a verb, there are two points you should remember.

1. No verb preceded by *to* is ever the verb of a sentence.[2]
2. **Helping verbs**[3] are often added to main verbs.

---

[2] The form *to* + verb—e.g., *to speak*, *to write*, *to help*—is an infinitive. Infinitives can act as subjects or objects, but they are never verbs.

[3] If you are familiar with technical grammatical terms, you will know these verbs as **auxiliary verbs**.

The list below contains the most common helping verbs.

be (all forms of *to be* can act as helping verbs: e.g., *am, are, is, was, were, will be, have/had been*, etc.)	can could/could have do/did have/had may/may have might/might have	must/must have ought shall/shall have should/should have will/will have would/would have

The complete verb in a sentence consists of the main verb together with any helping verbs.

Here are a few of the forms of the verb *write*. Notice that in questions the subject may come between the helping verb and the main verb.

You <u>may write</u> now.
He certainly <u>can write</u>!
We <u>should write</u> home more often.
I <u>shall write</u> tomorrow.
He <u>could have written</u> yesterday.
She <u>is writing</u> her memoirs.
<u>Did</u> he <u>write</u> to you?

You <u>ought to write</u> to him.
We <u>will have written</u> by then.
He <u>had written</u> his apology.
I <u>will write</u> to the editor.
The proposal <u>has been written</u>.
Orders <u>should have been written</u>.
<u>Could</u> you <u>have written</u> it in French?

One verb form *always* takes a helping verb. Here is the rule.

A verb ending in *-ing* MUST have a helping verb (or verbs) before it.

Here are a few of the forms an *-ing* verb can take:

I <u>am writing</u> the report.
<u>Is</u> she <u>writing</u> the paper for him?
You <u>are writing</u> illegibly.
I <u>was writing</u> neatly.
You <u>will be writing</u> a report.
They <u>must have been writing</u> all night.
<u>Have</u> you <u>been writing</u> on the wall?

Beware of certain words that are often confused with helping verbs.

Words such as *not, only, always, often, sometimes, never, ever,* and *just* are NOT part of the verb.

These words sometimes appear in the middle of a complete verb, but they are modifiers, not verbs. Do not underline them.

I <u>have</u> just <u>won</u> a one-way ticket to Moose Factory.
She <u>is</u> always <u>chosen</u> first.
Most people <u>do</u> not <u>welcome</u> unasked-for advice.

Exercise 7.1.3*

Underline the subject once and the complete verb twice. Check your answers, and if you made even one mistake, try the Web exercises that follow.

1. He has talked nonstop for three hours.

2. I will be the first member of my family to graduate from college.

3. Could they return the loan tomorrow?

4. You cannot eat your dessert before dinner.

5. Carla should have been filing the letters and memos.

6. I will not be taking the car.

7. Paula's lawsuit should never have been allowed to proceed this far.

8. Have you ever been to Newfoundland?

9. There has never been a better time to travel.

10. How are the club members chosen?

GO TO WEB

EXERCISES   7.1.5, 7.1.6, 7.1.7, 7.1.8

More about Subjects

Often groups of words called **prepositional phrases** come before the subject in a sentence or between the subject and the verb. When you're looking for the subject in a sentence, prepositional phrases can trip you up unless you know the following rule.

The subject of a sentence is never in a prepositional phrase.

You must be able to identify prepositional phrases so that you will know where *not* to look for the subject.

A prepositional phrase is a group of words that begins with a preposition and ends with a noun or a pronoun that answers the question *what* or *when*.

The noun or pronoun is called the object of the preposition. It is this word that, if you're not careful, you might think is the subject of the sentence.

Below is a list of prepositional phrases. The words in blue print are prepositions; the words in black are objects of the prepositions.

about the book	*between* the desks	*near* the wall
above the desk	*by* the book	*of* the typist
according to the book	*concerning* the memo	*on* the desk
after the meeting	*despite* the policy	*onto* the floor
against the wall	*down* the hall	*over* a door
along the hall	*except* the staff	*to* the staff
among the books	*for* the manager	*through* the window
among them	*from* the office	*under* the book
around the office	*in* an hour	*until* the meeting
before lunch	*in* front *of* the desk	*up* the hall
behind the desk	*inside* the office	*with* a book
below the window	*into* the elevator	*without* the book
beside the book	*like* the book	*without* them

Before you look for the subject in a sentence, cross out all prepositional phrases.

The keyboard ~~of your computer~~ should be cleaned occasionally.

What <u>should be cleaned</u>? The <u>keyboard</u> (not the computer).

Regardless ~~of the expense~~, one ~~of us~~ should go ~~to the IT conference in Las Vegas~~.

Who <u>should go</u>? <u>One</u> (not the group).

Exercise 7.1.4*

In the following sentences, first cross out the prepositional phrase(s), then underline the subject once and the verb twice. Check your answers before going on to the Web exercises that follow.

1. Among English teachers, Santa's helpers are known as subordinate clauses.

2. After his death, Terry Fox became a national symbol of heroic courage.

3. In the state of Florida, it is illegal for single, divorced, or widowed women to parachute on Sunday afternoons.

4. In Kentucky, no woman may appear in a bathing suit on any highway in the state unless escorted by two officers or armed with a club.

5. In my wildest imaginings, I cannot understand the reason for these laws.

6. During a break in the conversation, Darryl's embarrassing comment could be heard in every corner of the room.

7. In my lawyer's dictionary, a will is defined as a dead giveaway.

8. To the staff and managers of the project, I extend my congratulations for an excellent job.

9. Against all odds, and despite their shortcomings, the St. John Miners made it into the playoffs of the Southern New Brunswick Little League.

10. Walk a mile in my shoes at high noon with your head held high in order to avoid clichés like the plague.

GO TO WEB

EXERCISES 7.1.9, 7.1.10

Multiple Subjects and Verbs

So far, you have been decoding sentences containing a single subject and a single verb, even though the verb may have consisted of more than one word. Sentences can, however, have more than one subject and one verb.

Multiple subjects are called **compound subjects**; multiple verbs are **compound verbs**.

Here is a sentence with a compound subject:

Esquimalt and Oak Bay border the city of Victoria.

This sentence has a compound verb:

She groped and stumbled her way down the aisle of the darkened movie theatre.

And this sentence has a compound subject and a compound verb:

The detective and the police sergeant leaped from their car and seized the suspect.

The parts of a compound subject or verb are usually joined by *and* (sometimes by *or*). Compound subjects and verbs may contain more than two elements, as in the following sentences:

Thoughtful planning, careful organization, and conscientious revision are the keys to good essay writing.

I finished my paper, put the cat outside, shut off my cellphone, and crawled into bed.

Exercise 7.1.5*

In the following sentences, cross out all prepositional phrases, then underline the subjects once and the verbs twice. Be sure to underline all the elements in a compound subject or verb. Check your answers before continuing.

1. Management and union met for a two-hour bargaining session.

2. They debated and drafted a tentative agreement for a new contract.

3. The anesthetist and the surgeon scrubbed for surgery and hurried to the operating room.

4. Frederick Banting and Norman Bethune are known around the world as medical heroes.

5. Kevin and Sandra hiked and cycled across most of Newfoundland.

6. My son or my daughter will meet me and drive me home.

7. Knock three times and ask for Stan.

8. In the 17th and 18th centuries, the French and the English fought for control of Canada.

9. Buy the base model and don't waste your money on luxury options.

10. Ragweed, goldenrod, and twitch grass formed the essential elements in the bouquet for his English teacher.

GO TO WEB

EXERCISES 7.1.11, 7.1.12, 7.1.13, 7.1.14

Here's a summary of what you've learned in this chapter. Keep it in front of you as you write the mastery test.

Summary

- The subject is *who* or *what* the sentence is about.
- The verb tells what the subject *is* or *does*.
- The subject normally comes before the verb (exceptions are questions and sentences beginning with *there* or *here*).
- The complete verb = a main verb + any helping verbs.
- By itself, a word ending in *-ing* is not a verb.
- An infinitive (a phrase consisting of *to* + a verb) is never the verb of a sentence.
- The subject of a sentence is never in a prepositional phrase.
- A sentence can have more than one subject and/or verb.

Exercise 7.1.6

This challenging exercise will test your ability to find the main subjects and verbs in sentences. In each sentence below, first cross out any prepositional phrases, and then underline each subject with one line and each verb with two lines. Be sure to underline all elements in a multiple subject or verb.

1. The politicians of all parties try in vain to change the world, but they seldom try to change themselves.

2. In the past, men and women had clearly defined roles and seldom broke away from them.

3. Police, firefighters, and paramedics comforted, rescued, and treated my aunt and uncle after their car accident.

4. Among the many kinds of cheese made in Canada are Camembert, Fontina, and Quark.

5. French fries, gravy, and cheese curds are the ingredients in traditional Quebec poutine.

6. Increasingly, in high-end restaurants, chefs are experimenting with Canadian foods like elk meat, fiddlehead greens, and Saskatoon berries.

7. On the Lovers' Tour of Lake Louise were two elderly women with walkers, a couple of elderly gentlemen with very young wives, half a dozen middle-aged divorcées, and me.

8. Negotiate in English, swear in German, argue in Spanish, and make love in French.

9. After the rain, the sun came out, the birds sang, and the tourists returned to their chairs by the pool.

10. According to its campaign literature, the incoming government will provide jobs for all Canadians, eliminate the national debt, find a cure for cancer, land a Canadian on Mars, and reduce income tax by 50 percent, all in its first year in office!

SECTION 7.2

Solving Sentence-Fragment Problems

Every complete sentence has two characteristics. It contains a subject and a verb, and it expresses a complete thought. Any group of words that is punctuated as a sentence but lacks one of these characteristics is a **sentence fragment**. Fragments are appropriate in conversation and in some kinds of writing, but normally they are unacceptable in school, technical, and business writing.

There are two kinds of fragments you should watch out for: the "missing piece" fragments and the dependent clause fragments.

"Missing Piece" Fragments

Sometimes a group of words is punctuated as a sentence but is missing one or more of the essential parts of a sentence: a subject and a verb. Consider these examples.

1. Found it under the pile of clothes on your floor.

   <u>Who</u> or <u>what</u> found it? The sentence doesn't tell you. The subject is missing.

2. Their arguments about housework.

   The sentence doesn't tell you what the arguments <u>were</u> or <u>did</u>. The verb is missing.

3. During my favourite TV show.

Who or what was or did something? Both subject and verb are missing.

4. The programmers working around the clock to trace the hacker.

Part of the verb is missing. Remember that a verb ending in *-ing* needs a helping verb to be complete.

Finding fragments like these in your work when you are revising is the hard part. Fixing them is easy. There are two ways to correct sentence fragments. Here's the first one.

To change a "missing piece" fragment into a complete sentence, add whatever is missing: a subject, a verb, or both.

1. You may need to add a subject:

Your <u>sister</u> found it under the pile of clothes on your floor.

2. You may need to add a verb:

Their arguments <u>were</u> about housework. (linking verb)
Their arguments about housework eventually <u>destroyed</u> their relationship. (action verb)

3. You may need to add both a subject and a verb:

My <u>mother</u> always <u>calls</u> during my favourite TV show.

4. Or you may need to add a helping verb:

The programmers <u>have been</u> working around the clock to trace the hacker.

Don't let the length of a fragment fool you. Students sometimes think that if a string of words is long, it must be a sentence. Not so. No matter how long the string of words, if it doesn't contain both a subject and a verb, it is not a sentence. For example, here's a description of a student overwhelmed by frustrating circumstances:

With his assignment overdue and penalty marks eating into the grade he had hoped to achieve, and his computer behaving erratically thanks to a virus that his roommate had downloaded while playing Texas Hold 'Em against a gamer somewhere in Arkansas, the same roommate who was now in the next room with four of his friends loudly cheering on their favourite team—the Calgary Flames—during the Western Conference semifinals against his own beloved Canucks.

At 75 words, this "sentence" is long—but it is a fragment. It lacks both a subject and a verb. If you add to the end of the fragment, "<u>Dennis broke down</u> and <u>sobbed</u>," you would have a complete sentence.

In the following exercises, decide whether each group of words is a complete sentence or a "missing piece" fragment. Put *S* before each complete sentence and *F* before each fragment. Make each fragment into a complete sentence by adding whatever is missing: the subject, the verb, or both. Then compare your answers with our suggestions. Answers for exercises in this chapter begin on page 547.

Exercise 7.2.1*

1. _____ About historical events.

2. _____ To decide on the basis of rumour, not facts.

3. _____ Trying to be helpful, I offered to check the files.

4. _____ To make my famous tuna casserole.

5. _____ The party members gathering in the campaign office.

6. _____ We won.

7. _____ Hands over your head.

8. _____ To go anywhere without my iPod.

9. _____ Having worked hard all her life.

10. _____ Wanting to please them, she had coffee ready on their arrival.

GO TO WEB

EXERCISES 7.2.1, 7.2.2, 7.2.3, 7.2.4

Exercise 7.2.2*

_____ Professional athletes making millions of dollars a year. _____ At the same time, owners of sports franchises growing fantastically rich from the efforts of their employees, the players. _____ The fans being the forgotten people in the struggle for control over major league sports. _____ The people who pay the money that makes both owners and players rich. _____ I have an idea that would protect everyone's interests. _____ Cap the owners' profits. _____ Cap the players' salaries. _____ And, most important, the ticket prices. _____ A fair deal for everyone. _____ Fans should be able to see their teams play for the price of a movie ticket, not the price of a television set.

Dependent Clause Fragments

Any group of words containing a subject and a verb is a **clause**. There are two kinds of clauses. An **independent clause** is one that makes complete sense on its own. It can stand alone, as a sentence. A **dependent clause**, as its name suggests, cannot stand alone as a sentence; it depends on another clause to make complete sense.

Dependent clauses (also known as **subordinate clauses**) begin with **dependent-clause cues** (subordinating conjunctions).

Dependent-Clause Cues

after	if	until
although	in order that	what, whatever
as, as if	provided that	when, whenever
as long as	since	where, wherever, whereas
as soon as	so that	whether
because	that	which, whichever
before	though	while
even if, even though	unless	who, whom, whose

Whenever a clause begins with one of these words or phrases, it is dependent.

A dependent clause must be attached to an independent clause. If it stands alone, it is a sentence fragment.

Here is an independent clause:

I am a terrible speller.

If we put one of the dependent-clause cues in front of it, it can no longer stand alone:

Because I am a terrible speller.

We can correct this kind of fragment by attaching it to an independent clause:

Because I am a terrible speller, I carry a smartphone with a dictionary.

Exercise 7.2.3*

Put an *S* before each item that contains an independent clause and is therefore a sentence. Put an *F* before each clause that is dependent and therefore a sentence fragment. Circle the dependent-clause cue in each sentence fragment.

1. _____ Although she practised it constantly.

2. _____ Since the horse stepped on her.

3. _____ As soon as the troops arrived, the fighting stopped.

4. _____ Whichever route the bikers choose.

5. _____ Before Biff bought his bike.

GO TO WEB

EXERCISES 7.2.5, 7.2.6, 7.2.7, 7.2.8

Exercise 7.2.4*

Identify the sentence fragments in the paragraph below by highlighting the dependent-clause cue in each fragment you find.

[1]Although many companies are now experiencing difficulty because of tough economic times. [2]Middle managers seldom breathe easily even during times of expansion and high profits. [3]In difficult times, middle managers are vulnerable to the cost-cutting axe. [4]As companies seek to reduce overhead. [5]In times of fast growth, the executive branch of many companies expands rapidly. [6]Which leads to a surplus of managerial talent, especially among junior executives. [7]And it is these younger, well-educated, ambitious young hires who can threaten middle managers. [8]Who have reached, or overreached, their potential. [9]Whether it is through termination, early retirement, or buyout. [10]Such mid-level executives are the first to feel the effects of a company's desire to streamline the hierarchy in good times or eliminate paycheques in bad times.

Most sentence fragments are dependent clauses punctuated as sentences. Fortunately, this is the easiest kind of fragment to recognize and fix. All you need to do is join the dependent clause either to the sentence that comes before it or to the one that comes after it—whichever linkage makes better sense.

Read the following example to yourself; then read it aloud (remember, last sentence first).

> Montreal is a sequence of ghettos. Although I was born and brought up there. My experience of French was a pathetically limited and distorted one.

The second "sentence" sounds incomplete, and the dependent-clause cue at the beginning of it is the clue you need to identify it as a sentence fragment. You could join the fragment to the sentence before it, but then you would get "Montreal is a sequence of ghettos, although I was born and brought up there," which doesn't make sense. The fragment should be linked to the sentence that follows it, like this:

> Montreal is a sequence of ghettos. Although I was born and brought up there, my experience of French was a pathetically limited and distorted one. (Mordecai Richler)

If, as in the example above, your revised sentence *begins* with the dependent clause, you need to put a comma after it. If, however, your revised sentence *ends* with the dependent clause, you don't need a comma between it and the independent clause that precedes it.

> My experience of French was limited although I was born and brought up in Montreal.

See Section 7.10, Rule 3 (page 455).

Exercise 7.2.5*

Turn back to Exercise 7.2.4 and revise it by joining each dependent clause fragment to an independent clause that precedes or follows it, whichever makes better sense.

GO TO WEB

EXERCISE 7.2.9

Exercise 7.2.6*

The following paragraph contains both independent and dependent clauses (fragments), all punctuated as if they were complete sentences. Letting meaning be your guide, join each dependent clause fragment to the independent clause that comes before or after it—whichever makes better sense. Be careful to punctuate correctly between clauses. (There are seven errors in this paragraph).

In spite of what everyone says about the weak economy and the scarcity of jobs, especially for young people. I have financed my college career with a variety of part-time and seasonal jobs. Right now, for instance, while completing my third year at college. I have not one, not two, but three part-time jobs. I am a short-order cook three nights a week for a local bar and diner. And a telemarketer for a cable company after school. Or whenever I have free time. I'm also a server at a specialty coffee store on weekends. Maintaining a social life. While juggling three jobs and the requirements of my third-year program is not easy, but I find it hard to turn down any opportunity for experience. Not to mention cash. I'm willing to put my social life on hold. For a while.

Exercise 7.2.7

As a final test of your skill in finding and correcting sentence fragments, try this exercise. Make each fragment into a complete sentence.

1. I had never eaten curry. But the first time I tasted it. I decided I liked it.
2. In France, they say that an explosion in the kitchen could have disastrous results. Such as linoleum blown apart.
3. Our family thinks my sister is too young to get married. Since she and her boyfriend want to be registered at Toys "R" Us.
4. It may surprise you to know that Canadians have made significant contributions to world cuisine. Two of the best known being baby pabulum and frozen peas.
5. Bathing the family cat. It's an activity that carries the same risks as tap dancing in a minefield. Or juggling with razor blades.
6. After working for three nights in a row trying to make my essay perfect so that I would get a high grade in my course. I lost my entire project when my brother crashed the computer while playing *Grand Theft Auto*.
7. I decided to take swimming lessons for two reasons. The first is fitness. Second, water safety.
8. There is good news. The man who was caught in an upholstery machine has fully recovered.
9. All of us are more aware of the effects of pollution now than we were 10 years ago. Because we are continually bombarded with information about the environment and our impact on it. In school, on television, and in newspapers.
10. My second favourite household chore is ironing. The first being hitting my head on the top bunk bed until I faint. (Erma Bombeck)

SECTION 7.3

Solving Run-On Problems

Some sentences lack certain elements and thus are fragments. Other sentences contain two or more independent clauses that are incorrectly linked together. A sentence with inadequate punctuation between clauses is a **run-on**. Run-ons tend to occur when you write in a hurry, without first organizing your thoughts. If you think about what you want to say and punctuate carefully, you shouldn't have any problems with them.

There are two kinds of run-on sentences to watch out for: comma splices and fused sentences.

Comma Splices and Fused Sentences

As its name suggests, the **comma splice** occurs when two complete sentences (independent clauses) are joined together with only a comma between them. Here's an example:

I am deeply in debt, I cut up my credit cards.

The tunes are good, the lyrics are not.

A **fused sentence** occurs when two complete sentences are joined together with no punctuation at all:

I am deeply in debt I cut up my credit cards.

The tunes are good the lyrics are not.

There are four ways to fix run-on sentences.

1. Make the independent clauses into separate sentences.

I am deeply in debt. I cut up my credit cards.
The tunes are good. The lyrics are not.

2. Separate the independent clauses with a comma followed by one of these words: *and, but, or, nor, for, so, or yet.*[1]

I am deeply in debt, so I cut up my credit cards.
The tunes are good, but the lyrics are not.

3. Make one clause dependent on the other by adding one of the dependent-clause cues listed on page 380.

Because I am deeply in debt, I cut up my credit cards.
I cut up my credit cards because I am deeply in debt.
Although the tunes are good, the lyrics are not.

Your turn:

The tunes are good _____.

4. Use a semicolon, either by itself or with a transitional word or phrase, to separate independent clauses. (See Section 7.11.)

I am deeply in debt; I cut up my credit cards.
The tunes are good; however, the lyrics are not.

Note: All four solutions to comma splices and fused sentences require you to use a word or punctuation mark strong enough to come between two independent clauses. A comma by itself is too weak, and so is a dash.

The sentences in the following exercises will give you practice in fixing comma splices and fused sentences. Correct the sentences where necessary and then check your answers, beginning on page 549. Since there are four ways to fix each sentence, your answers may differ from our suggestions. If you find that you're confused about when to use a semicolon and when to use a period, be sure to read pages 463–67 before going on.

---

[1]These words are called **coordinating conjunctions** because they are used to join equal (or coordinating) clauses. If you are not sure how to punctuate sentences with coordinating conjunctions, see Section 7.10, Rule 2 (page 454).

Exercise 7.3.1*

1. This is strong coffee, it has dissolved my spoon!
2. Just let me do the talking, we're sure to get a ticket if you open your mouth.
3. I keep buying lottery tickets, but all I ever win is free tickets.
4. If you have never tried it, hitting a golf ball may look easy, it's not.
5. As long as you smile when you speak, you can get away with saying almost anything.
6. Montreal used to be known as "Ville-Marie," before that it was known as "Hochelaga."
7. Students today really need summer jobs and part-time employment, their tuition and living costs are too high for most families to subsidize.
8. Because I'm not very good at calculating odds, I'm afraid to play poker with you.
9. It's very windy, a ball hit deep to centre field will likely go into the stands.
10. "I was married by a judge, I should have asked for a jury." (Groucho Marx)

GO TO WEB

EXERCISES 7.3.1, 7.3.2

Exercise 7.3.2*

1. For students in most technology programs, job prospects are good, however, a diploma does not guarantee job security.
2. Despite my parents' objections, I like having long hair, it makes me feel attractive.
3. Casual meetings are fine for small groups, more formal settings are appropriate for larger groups.
4. I'd be happy to help you, just call when you need me, I'll be here all day.
5. In Canada, winter is more than a season it's a bad joke.
6. Perfection is probably impossible to achieve, but that doesn't mean you should stop trying your best.
7. A Canadian who speaks three languages is called multilingual, one who speaks two languages is called bilingual, one who speaks only one language is called an English Canadian.
8. Skilled people are needed in specialized fields, currently, the top three are geriatrics, health care, and environmental technology.

9. I use a keyboard all the time my handwriting has become illegible.
10. I believe in a unified Canada, I believe that in 1867 the Fathers of Confederation were right, a federation of provinces can make a strong nation.

Exercise 7.3.3

As a final test of your ability to identify and correct run-on sentences, find and correct the 10 errors in the following paragraphs.

According to a news report, a private girls' school in Victoria was recently faced with an unusual problem, they solved it in a way that can only be described as creative, it is also a good example of effective teaching. Some of the grade 10 girls, forbidden by their parents to wear lipstick at home, began to apply it at school, in the second-floor washroom. That was the first problem, the second was that after applying the lipstick, they would press their lips to the mirror, leaving dozens of perfect lip prints. Every night, the maintenance crew would remove the prints, the next day the girls would reapply them and finally the principal decided that something had to be done.

She called the girls into the washroom, where she met them with one of the maintenance men and he stood by while the principal addressed the girls. She explained that the lip prints on the mirrors were causing a problem for the maintenance crew, they had to clean the mirrors every night instead of doing other work. To demonstrate how difficult the cleaning job was and how much time was wasted on this needless chore, the principal asked the maintenance man to clean one of the mirrors, the girls watched with interest he took out a long-handled squeegee and began scrubbing at the lipstick prints. When he had scrubbed for a while, he turned, dipped his squeegee into one of the toilets, and continued to work on the mirrors and since then, there has not been another set of lip prints on the washroom mirror.

SECTION 7.4

Solving Modifier Problems

Oscar was complimented on a great game and a fine job of goaltending *by his mother.*

Snarling furiously and baring his teeth, Maurice crawled through a basement window only to confront an angry watchdog.

When she was a first-year student, the English professor told Sophie she would *almost* write all her assignments in class.

These sentences show what can happen to your writing if you aren't sure how to use modifiers. A **modifier** is a word or phrase that adds information about another word in a sentence. In the examples above, the italicized words are modifiers. Used correctly, modifiers describe, explain, or limit another word, making its meaning more precise. Used carelessly, however, modifiers can cause confusion or, even worse, amusement.

You need to be able to recognize and solve two kinds of modifier problems: **misplaced modifiers** and **dangling modifiers**.

Misplaced Modifiers

Modifiers must be as close as possible to the words they apply to. Usually, readers will assume that a modifier modifies whatever it's next to. It's important to remember this, because, as the following examples show, changing the position of a modifier can change the meaning of your sentence.

Jason walked (only) as far as the corner store. (He didn't walk any farther.)

Jason (only) walked as far as the corner store. (He didn't jog or run.)

(Only) Jason walked as far as the corner store. (No one else went.)

Jason walked as far as the (only) corner store. (There were no other corner stores.)

To make sure a modifier is in the right place, ask yourself "What does it apply to?" and put it beside that word or word group.

When a modifier is not close enough to the word it refers to, it is said to be misplaced. A misplaced modifier can be a single word in the wrong place.

The supervisor told me they needed someone who could use both Word and Excel (badly.)

Is some company really hiring people to do poor work? Or does the company urgently need someone familiar with word and data-processing programs? Obviously, the modifier *badly* belongs next to *needed*.

The supervisor told me they (badly) needed someone who could use both Word and Excel.

Be especially careful with these words: *almost, nearly, just, only, even, hardly, merely, scarcely*. Put them right before the words they modify.

Misplaced: Caro (nearly) answered every question.

Correctly placed: Caro answered (nearly) every question.

Misplaced: After driving all night, we (almost) arrived at 7:00 a.m.

Correctly placed: After driving all night, we arrived at (almost) 7:00 a.m.

A misplaced modifier can also be a group of words in the wrong place.

She died in the home in which she had been born (at the age of 89.)

The modifier *at the age of 89* is too far away from the verb it is supposed to modify, *died*. In fact, it seems to modify *had been born*, making the sentence ridiculous. We need to rewrite the sentence:

She died (at the age of 89) in the home in which she had been born.

Look at this one:

I drove my mother to Saskatoon, where my aunt lives (in her old car.)

In her old car applies to *drove* and should be closer to it.

I drove my mother (in her old car) to Saskatoon, where my aunt lives.

Notice that a modifier does not always need to go right next to what it modifies; it should, however, be as close as possible to it.

Occasionally, as in the examples above, the modifier is obviously out of place. The writer's intention is clear, and the sentences are easy to correct. But sometimes modifiers are misplaced in such a way that the meaning is not clear, as in the following example:

David said (after the game) he wanted to talk to the press.

Did David *say* it after the game? Or does *he want to talk to the press* after the game? To avoid confusion, we must move the modifier and, depending on which meaning we want, write either

(After the game,) David said he wanted to talk to the press.

or

David said he wanted to talk to the press (after the game.)

In Exercises 7.4.1 and 7.4.2, rewrite the sentences that contain misplaced modifiers, positioning them as closely as possible to the words they modify. Check your answers to the first set before continuing. Answers for this section begin on page 550.

Exercise 7.4.1*

1. The telephone only rings when I am trying to work.

2. Geoff left on the counter the can of Pet Grrrmet for the dog that he had opened.

3. We almost enjoyed the whole movie; the ending was only disappointing.

4. Leo and Annie found an apartment in a high-rise within walking distance of the campus with two bedrooms and free Internet.

5. This is the computer best suited to the design team with a full-sized HD monitor and increased RAM.

6. To support our local school's fundraising, I gave a student $10.00 to wash my car in a team uniform.

7. A jury found the teenager guilty of killing her best friend for the second time.

8. Our instructor told us in September that he thought our class was a hopeless case.

9. A charming, youthful companion is sought by an aging but wealthy gentleman who likes to travel and looks good in designer gowns.

10. One of us could only go because there was enough money just to buy one ticket.

Exercise 7.4.2*

1. *Essay Essentials* is designed to help college and university students learn to write good prose with clear explanations and lots of exercises.

2. Each year, half a million Canadian men almost have a vasectomy.

3. James caught sight of a doe and her two fawns with his new binoculars.

4. Vancouver is a wonderful city for anyone who likes rain and fog to live in.

5. Some games are less demanding in terms of fitness and strength, such as Scrabble and checkers.

6. Thanks to my new camera, I can take professional-quality pictures with automatic functions.

7. We looked for a suitable retirement gift for our boss online.

8. The Canadian Human Rights Act prohibits discrimination against anyone who is applying for a job on the basis of race, religion, sex, or age.

9. One finds the best Chinese food in restaurants where the Chinese eat usually.

10. Tonight, Liam Neeson will talk about his wife, Natasha Richardson, who died after falling on a ski slope at Mont Tremblant with George Stroumboulopoulos.

Dangling Modifiers

A dangling modifier occurs when the sentence does not contain a specific word or idea to which the modifier could sensibly refer. With no appropriate word to modify, the modifier seems to apply to whatever it's next to, often with ridiculous results.

(After a good night's sleep,) my teachers were impressed with my unusual alertness.

This sentence seems to say that the teachers had a good night's sleep.

(Trying desperately to finish an essay,) my roommate's CD player made it impossible to concentrate.

The *CD player* was writing an essay?

Dangling modifiers are harder to correct than misplaced ones; you can't simply move danglers to another spot in the sentence. There are, however, two ways in which you can fix them. One way requires that you remember the following rule.

When a modifier comes at the beginning of a sentence, it almost always modifies the subject of the sentence.

This rule means that you can avoid dangling modifiers by choosing the subjects of your sentences carefully.

1. Ensure the subject is an appropriate one for the modifier to apply to.

Using this method, we can rewrite our two examples by changing the subjects.

(After a good night's sleep,) I impressed my teachers with my unusual alertness.

(Trying desperately to finish an essay,) I found it impossible to concentrate because of my roommate's CD player.

2. Another way to correct a dangling modifier is by changing it into a dependent clause (in blue print below):

After I had had a good night's sleep, my teachers were impressed with my unusual alertness.

When I was trying desperately to finish an essay, my roommate's CD player made it impossible to concentrate.

Sometimes a dangling modifier comes at the end of a sentence:

A Smart car is the one to buy when looking for efficiency and affordability.

Can you correct this sentence? Try it; then look at the suggestions at the foot of the page.

Here is a summary of the steps to follow in solving modifier problems.

Summary

1. Ask "What does the modifier apply to?"
2. Be sure there is a word or group of words *in the sentence* for the modifier to apply to.
3. Put the modifier as close as possible to the word or word group it applies to.

Here are two suggestions.
1. Add a subject: Looking for efficiency and affordability, I decided a Smart car was the one to buy.
2. Change the dangler to a dependent clause: A Smart car is the one to buy since I am looking for efficiency and affordability.

Exercise 7.4.3*

Most of the following sentences contain dangling modifiers. Correct each sentence by using whichever solution given on page 394 best suits your purpose. There is no one right way to correct these sentences; our answers are only suggestions.

1. Driving recklessly and without lights, the police stopped Gina at a roadblock.

2. My supervisor gave me a lecture about punctuality after being late twice in one week.

3. After criticizing both my work and my attitude, I was fired.

4. With enough memory to store her favourite movies and more than 10 000 songs, Hannah knew that the MacBook was the computer she needed.

5. After spending two weeks quarrelling over money, their relationship was over.

6. As a dedicated fan of Alice Munro, her last book is her best.

7. In less than a minute after applying the ointment, the pain began to ease.

8. Making her first formal presentation to her colleagues and her supervisor, Jake was probably more nervous than Allison was.

9. When handling hazardous waste, the safety manual clearly outlines the procedures to follow.

10. After spending the day in the kitchen preparing a gourmet meal, the guests drank too much wine to appreciate Kendra's efforts.

Exercise 7.4.4*

In the following sentences, correct the misplaced and dangling modifiers in any way you choose. Our answers on page 551 are only suggestions.

1. Only she was the baker's daughter, but she could loaf all day.

2. Being horribly hung over, the problem with a free bar is knowing when to quit.

3. Rearing and kicking, Sam finally got the terrified horse under control.

4. In a hurry to get to the interview on time, my résumé was left lying on my desk at home.

5. As a college student constantly faced with new assignments, the pressure is sometimes intolerable.

6. Listening to the rumours, the newlyweds are already on the road to separation.

7. As a nondrinker, the liquor in the duty-free outlet is of no interest.

8. The bride was given in marriage by her father, wearing a strapless gown with a short lace jacket.

9. Rolling on her back, eager to have her tummy scratched, Queen Elizabeth couldn't resist the little Corgi puppy.

10. Wearing a small Canadian flag on your backpack or lapel, people abroad will be less likely to assume you're American.

GO TO WEB

EXERCISES 7.4.1, 7.4.2, 7.4.3, 7.4.4

Exercise 7.4.5

As a final test of your ability to use modifiers, correct the misplaced and dangling modifiers in the sentences below, using any solution you choose.

1. Obviously having drunk too much, I drove poor Tanya to her apartment, made her a pot of coffee, and called her mother.

2. When trying for your Red Cross bronze medal, your examiner will evaluate your speed, endurance, and resuscitation techniques.

3. The Riel Rebellion this month will be featured in *Canadian History* magazine.

4. Sinking like a ball of fire below the horizon, our sailboat was the perfect vantage point from which to watch the setting sun.

5. Not being reliable about arriving on time, I can't hire her to supervise others who are expected to be punctual.

6. While they were in my pocket, my children managed to break my glasses by leaping on me from behind.

7. Combining comfortable accommodation and economical travel, my wife and I find a camper van ideal for travelling both here and abroad.

8. The only used motorcycles we could find had been ridden by bikers that were in pretty bad shape.

9. After submitting the lowest bid that met all the developer's criteria, not being awarded the contract was bitterly disappointing.

10. "This bus has a seating capacity of 56 passengers with a maximum height of four metres." (Sign on a double-decker bus in Charlottetown)

The Parallelism Principle

Brevity, clarity, and force: these are three characteristics of good style. **Parallelism** will reinforce these characteristics in everything you write.

When your sentence contains a series of two or more items, they must be grammatically parallel. That is, they must be written in the same grammatical form. Consider this example:

Sophie likes *swimming, surfing,* and *to sail.*

The three items in this series are not parallel. Two are nouns ending in *-ing*, but the third, *to sail,* is the infinitive form of the verb. To correct the sentence, you must put all the items in the same grammatical form. You have two choices. You can write

Sophie likes *swimming, surfing,* and *sailing.* (all nouns)

Or you can write

Sophie likes *to swim, to surf,* and *to sail.* (all infinitives)

Now look at this example with two nonparallel elements:

Most people seek happiness in *long-term relationships* and *work that provides them with satisfaction.*

Again, you could correct this sentence in two ways. You could write "Most people seek happiness *in relationships that are long-term* and *in work that provides them with satisfaction,*" but that solution produces a long and clumsy sentence. The shorter version works better: "Most people seek happiness in *long-term relationships* and *satisfying work.*" This version is concise, clear, and forceful.

> Correct faulty parallelism by writing all items in a series in the same grammatical form: all words, all phrases, or all clauses.

One way to tell whether the items in a series are parallel is to write them out in list form, one below the other. That way, you can see at a glance if all the elements are in the same grammatical form.

Not Parallel	Parallel
My brother is *messy,* *rude,* and *an obnoxious person.*	My brother is *messy,* *rude,* and *obnoxious.*
(This list has two adjectives and a noun phrase.)	(This list has three adjectives.)
I support myself by *delivering pizza,* *poker,* and *shooting pool.*	I support myself by *delivering pizza,* *playing poker,* and *shooting pool.*
(This list has two phrases and one single word as objects of the preposition *by*.)	(This list has three phrases as objects of the preposition *by*.)
Jules wants a job that *will interest him,* *will challenge him,* and *pays well.*	Jules wants a job that *will interest him,* *(will) challenge him,* and *(will) pay him well.*
(This series of clauses contains two future tense verbs and one present tense verb.)	(All three subordinate clauses contain future tense verbs.)

As you can see, achieving parallelism is partly a matter of developing an ear for the sound of a correct list. A parallel sentence has a smooth, unbroken rhythm. Practice and the exercises in this chapter will help. Once you have mastered parallelism in your sentences, you will be ready to develop ideas in parallel sequence—in thesis statements, for example—and thus to write clear, concise prose. Far from being a frill, parallelism is a fundamental characteristic of good writing.

Correct the sentences where necessary in the following exercises. As you work through these sentences, try to spot parallelism errors from the change in rhythm that the faulty element produces. Then revise the sentence to bring the faulty element into line with the other elements in the series. Check your answers to each set of 10 before going on. Answers for this chapter begin on page 551.

Exercise 7.5.1*

1. This program is easy to understand and using it is not difficult, either.

2. We were told to leave and that we should take everything with us.

3. We organized our findings, wrote the report, and finally our PowerPoint presentation was prepared.

4. Both applicants were unskilled, not prepared, and lacked motivation.

5. Elmer's doctor advised that he should be careful with his back and not to strain his mind.

6. The company is looking for an employee who has a car and knowledge of the city would be a help.

7. If consumers really cared, they could influence the fast-food industry to produce healthy, delicious food that didn't cost very much.

8. When I want to get away from it all, there are three solitary pleasures I enjoy: a walk in the country, reading a book, and music.

9. A recent survey of female executives claims that family responsibilities, being excluded from informal networks, and lacking management experience are the major factors keeping them from advancement.

10. If it is to be useful, your report must be organized clearly, written well, and your research should be thorough.

GO TO WEB

EXERCISES 7.5.1, 7.5.2

Exercise 7.5.2*

1. For my birthday, I requested either a Roots bag or a scarf from Dior.

2. In my community, two related crimes are rapidly increasing: drug abuse and stealing things.

3. Bodybuilding has made me what I am today: physically perfect, very prosperous financially, and practically friendless.

4. After reading all the explanations and all the exercises have been completed, you'll be a better writer.

5. Bruce claimed that, through repetition and giving rewards, he had trained his centipede to be loyal and demonstrate obedience.

6. During their vacation in New Brunswick, Trevor and Jane visited many beautiful locations and wonderful seafood.

7. I'm an average tennis player; I have a good forehand, my backhand is average, but a weak serve.

8. The problem with being immortalized as a statue is that you will be a target for pigeon droppings and artists who write graffiti.

9. Never disturb a sleeping dog, a baby that is happy, or a silent politician.

10. I'd like to help, but I'm too tired, and my time is already taken up with other things.

GO TO WEB

EXERCISES 7.5.3, 7.5.4, 7.5.5, 7.5.6

Exercise 7.5.3*

Make the following lists parallel. In each case, you can make your items parallel with any item in the list, so your answers may differ from ours.

Example:	**Incorrect:**	report writing	program a computer
	Correct:	report writing	computer programming
	Also correct:	write a report	program a computer

1. Incorrect: wine   women   singing
   Correct:

2. Incorrect: doing your best   don't give up
   Correct:

3. Incorrect: information   education   entertaining
   Correct:

4. Incorrect: individually   as a group
   Correct:

5. Incorrect: privately   in public
   Correct:

6. Incorrect: happiness   healthy   wisdom
   Correct:

7. Incorrect: employers   people working   workers on
                                full-time for an employer   contract
   Correct:

8. Incorrect: insufficient time   too little money   not enough
                                                        staff
   Correct:

9. Incorrect: French is the   English is used   philosophy is
                         language of love in business   often written
                                                             in German
   Correct:

10. Incorrect: lying about   to do whatever
                          all morning   I please
    Correct:

Exercise 7.5.4*

Correct the faulty parallelism in these sentences.

1. Not being able to speak the language causes confusion, is frustrating, and it's embarrassing.

2. Trying your best and success are not always the same thing.

3. The first candidate we interviewed seemed frightened and to be shy, but the second was a composed person and showed confidence.

4. To lick one's fingers and picking one's teeth in a restaurant are one way to get attention.

5. Our CEO claims his most valuable business assets are hitting a good backhand and membership at an exclusive golf club.

6. In order to succeed in this economy, small businesses must be creative and show innovation and flexibility.

7. Lowering our profit margin, raising prices, and two management lay-offs will enable us to meet our budget.

8. After an enjoyable dinner, I like to drink a cappuccino, a dark chocolate mint, and, occasionally, a good cigar.

9. Lying in the sun, consumption of high-fat foods, and cigarette smoking are three life-threatening activities that were once thought to be healthy.

10. Business travellers complain of long delays at airports, they are paying higher costs for services, and tighter restrictions on their freedom of movement.

Exercise 7.5.5

As a test of your mastery of parallel structure, correct the six errors in the following paragraph.

The dictionary can be both a useful resource and an educational entertainment. Everyone knows that its three chief functions are to check spelling, for finding out the meanings of words, and what the correct pronunciation is. Few people, however, use the dictionary for discovery as well as learning. There are several methods of using the dictionary as an aid to discovery. One is randomly looking at words, another is to read a page or two thoroughly, and still another is by skimming through words until you find an unfamiliar one. It is by this last method that I discovered the word *steatopygous*, a term I now try to use at least once a day. You can increase your vocabulary significantly by using the dictionary, and of course a large and varied vocabulary can be used to baffle your colleagues, employers will be impressed, and your English teacher will be surprised.

Refining by Combining

To reinforce what you've learned about sentence structure, try your hand at **sentence combining**, a technique that enables you to avoid a choppy, monotonous, or repetitious style while at the same time producing correct sentences. Sentence combining accomplishes three things: it reinforces your understanding of sentence structure; it helps you to refine and polish your writing; and it results in a style that will keep your reader alert and interested in what you have to say.

Let's look at two short, technically correct sentences that could be combined:

I prefer champagne.

My budget allows only beer.

There are several ways of combining these two statements into a single sentence.

1. You can connect them with an appropriate linking word, such as *for, and, nor, but, or, yet,* or *so* (the FANBOYS words).

I prefer champagne, *but* my budget allows only beer.

2. You can change one of the sentences into a subordinate clause.

Although I prefer champagne, my budget allows only beer.

My budget allows only beer *even though I prefer champagne.*

3. You can change one of the sentences into a modifying phrase.

(Living on a beer budget,) I still prefer champagne.

4. Sometimes it is possible to reduce your sentences to single-word modifiers.

I have (champagne) tastes and a (beer) budget.

In sentence combining, you are free to move parts of the sentence around, change words, add or delete words, or make whatever other changes you find necessary. Anything goes, as long as you don't drastically alter the meaning of the base sentences. Remember that your aim in combining sentences is to create effective sentences, not long ones. Clarity is essential, and brevity has force.

In the following exercises, try your solutions aloud before you write them. You may also want to refer to Sections 7.10 and 7.11 for advice on using the comma and the semicolon, respectively.

Exercise 7.6.1*

Combine each pair of sentences using a FANBOYS connecting word: *for, and, nor, but, or, yet,* or *so.* Suggested answers for the exercises in this chapter begin on page 553.

1. We cannot sell our cottage.
   We will live there instead.

2. There are three solutions given for this problem.
   All of them are correct.

3. The people in our firm work very hard.
   They wouldn't want it any other way.

4. We could spend our day off cleaning the house.
   We could spend the day fishing.

5. Great leaders do not bully their people.
   They do not deceive them.

6. I will not be able to finish my report by the deadline.
   There are only two hours before the deadline.

7. Jennifer knows that she will probably not get the vice-president's job.
   She wants the experience of applying for it.

8. Finish the estimate.
   Do not begin work until the estimate has been approved.

9. Today has been the worst day of my life.
   My horoscope was right today.

10. The department did not offer me a job.
    It did not even reply to my letter.

Exercise 7.6.2*

Using dependent-clause cues (see Section 7.2, page 380), combine the following sentences into longer, more interesting units.

Hint: Read each set of statements through to the end before you begin to combine them, and try out several variations aloud or in your head before writing down your preferred solution.

1. Leonardo da Vinci was a great artist and inventor.
   He invented scissors, among other things.

2. Cats can produce over 100 vocal sounds.
   Dogs can make only 10 vocal sounds.

3. It is said that men don't cry.
   They do cry while assembling furniture.

4. The name Wendy was made up for a book.
   The book was called *Peter Pan*.

5. Ten percent of Canadians are heavy drinkers.
   Thirty-five percent of Canadians abstain from alcohol.

6. Travel broadens the mind.
   Travel flattens the bank account.

7. We are seeking an experienced and innovative director.
   The candidate should be fluent in French.

8. One hundred thousand Vietnam veterans have taken their own lives.
   This is twice the number who were killed in action.

9. My cooking class went on a field trip to gather greens for a salad.
   We discovered that what we had thought was watercress was not watercress. It was poison ivy.

10. Ten of my classmates ate the salad.
    Eight were hospitalized.
    No one was critically ill.

Exercise 7.6.3

Combine the following sentences, using the connecting words listed in Exercise 7.6.1 and the dependent-clause cues listed on page 380.

1. Mario loses a girlfriend.
   He goes shopping for new clothes.

2. Failure breeds fatigue, according to Mortimer Adler.
   There is nothing more energizing than success.

3. We won't have enough stock to fill our orders.
   A shipment arrives today.

4. Friends may come, and friends may go.
   Enemies accumulate.

5. Marriage is for serious people.
   I have not considered it an option.

6. Divorce is an acknowledgement.
   There was not a true commitment in the first place.
   Some people still believe this.

7. In his essay "A Modest Proposal for a Divorce Ceremony," Pierre Berton proposed that Canada institute a formal divorce ceremony.
The divorce ceremony would be like a formal wedding ceremony.
All the symbolism would be reversed.

8. The bride, for example, would wear black.
Immediately after the ceremony, the newly divorced couple would go into the vestry.
They would scratch their names off the marriage register.

9. Twenty percent of adults in Canada are illiterate.
Fifty percent of the adults who can read say they never read books.
This is an astonishing fact.

10. Canada is a relatively rich country.
Most of us brush up against hunger and homelessness almost daily.
We encounter men, and less often, women begging.
They are on downtown street corners.

After you have combined a number of sentences, you can evaluate your work. Read your sentences out loud. How they *sound* is important. Test your work against the following six characteristics of successful sentences.

Summary

1. **Meaning:** Have you said what you mean?
2. **Clarity:** Is your sentence clear? Can it be understood on the first reading?
3. **Coherence:** Do the parts of your sentence fit together logically and smoothly?
4. **Emphasis:** Are the most important ideas either at the end or at the beginning of the sentence?
5. **Conciseness:** Is the sentence direct and to the point? Have you cut out all redundant or repetitious words?
6. **Rhythm:** Does the sentence flow smoothly? Are there any interruptions in the development of the key idea(s)? Do the interruptions help to emphasize important points, or do they distract the reader?

If your sentences pass all six tests of successful sentence style, you may be confident that they are both technically correct and pleasing to the ear. No reader could ask for more.

SECTION 7.7

Mastering Subject–Verb Agreement

Singular and Plural

One of the most common writing errors is lack of agreement between subject and verb. Both must be singular, or both must be plural. If one is singular and the other plural, you have an agreement problem. You have another kind of agreement problem if your subject and verb are not both in the same "person" (see Section 7.9, pages 433–451).

Let's clarify some terms. First, it's important to distinguish between **singular** and **plural**.

- "Singular" means one person or thing.
- "Plural" means two or more persons or things.

Second, it's important to know what we mean when we refer to the concept of **person**:

- "First person" is the person(s) speaking or writing: *I, me; we, us.*
- "Second person" is the person(s) being addressed: *you.*
- "Third person" is the person(s) being spoken or written about: *he, she, it; they, them.*

Here's an example of the singular and plural forms of a regular verb in the present tense.

	Singular	Plural
First person	I win	we win
Second person	you win	you win
Third person	she wins (*or* he, it, the horse wins)	they win (*or* the horses win)

The form that most often causes trouble is the third person because the verb endings do not match the subject endings. Third-person singular present tense verbs end in -*s*, but their singular subjects do not. Third-person plural verbs never end in -*s*, while their subjects normally do. Look at these examples.

A <u>fire</u> <u>burns</u>.
The <u>car</u> <u>skids</u>.
The <u>father</u> <u>cares</u> for the children.

The three singular verbs, all of which end in -*s* (*burns, skids, cares*), agree with their singular subjects (*fire, car, father*), none of which ends in -*s*. When the subjects become plural, the verbs change form, too.

Four <u>fires</u> <u>burn</u>.
The <u>cars</u> <u>skid</u>.
The <u>fathers</u> <u>care</u> for the children.

Now all of the subjects end in -*s*, and none of the verbs do.
To ensure **subject–verb agreement**, follow this basic rule:

Subjects and verbs must both be either singular or plural.

This rule causes difficulty only when the writer doesn't know which word in the sentence is the subject and so makes the verb agree with the wrong word. As long as you decode the sentence correctly (see Section 7.1), you'll have no problem making every subject agree with its verb.

If you have not already done so, now is the time to memorize this next rule:

The subject of a sentence is NEVER in a prepositional phrase.

Here's an example of how errors occur.

Only one of the 2000 ticket buyers are going to win.

What is the subject of this sentence? It's not *buyers*, but *one*. The verb must agree with *one*, which is clearly singular. The verb *are* does not agree with *one*, so the sentence is incorrect. It should read

Only <u>one</u> ~~of the 2000 ticket buyers~~ <u>is</u> going to win.

Pay special attention to words that end in *-one*, *-thing*, or *-body*. They cause problems for nearly every writer.

Words ending in *-one*, *-thing*, or *-body* are always singular.

When used as subjects, these pronouns require singular verbs.

anyone	anything	anybody
everyone	everything	everybody
no one	nothing	nobody
someone	something	somebody

The last part of the pronoun subject is the tip-off here: every*one*, any*thing*, no*body*. If you focus on this last part, you'll remember to use a singular verb with these subjects. Usually, these words cause trouble only when modifiers crop up between them and their verbs. For example, you would never write "Everyone are here." The trouble starts when you insert a group of words in between the subject and the verb. You might, if you weren't careful, write this: "Everyone involved in implementing the company's new policies and procedures are here." The meaning is plural: several people are present. But the subject (*everyone*) is singular, so the verb must be *is*.

More subject–verb agreement errors are caused by violations of this rule than any other. Be sure you understand it. Memorize it, and then test your understanding by doing the following exercise before you go any further.

Exercise 7.7.1*

Rewrite each of the following sentences, using the alternative beginning shown. Answers for this section begin on page 554.

Example: <u>She</u> <u>wants</u> to make a short documentary.
<u>They</u> <u>want</u> to make a short documentary.

1. He sells used books to other students.
   They

2. That new guideline affects all the office procedures.
   Those

3. Everyone who shops at Pimrock's receives a free can of tuna.
   All those

Grammar

4. The woman maintains that her boss has been harassing her.
The women

5. That girl's parents are looking for a suitable husband for her.
Those

So far, so good. You can match up singular subjects with singular verbs and plural subjects with plural verbs. Now let's take a look at a few of the complications that make subject–verb agreement such a disagreeable problem.

Five Special Cases

Some subjects are tricky. They look singular but are actually plural, or they look plural when they're really singular. There are six kinds of these slippery subjects, all of them common and all of them likely to trip up the unwary writer.

1. Compound subjects joined by *or*; *either . . . or*; *neither . . . nor*; or *not . . . but*

Most of the compound subjects we've dealt with so far have been joined by *and* and have required plural verbs, so agreement hasn't been a problem. But watch out when the two or more elements of a compound subject are joined by *or*; *either . . . or*; *neither . . . nor*; or *not . . . but*. In these cases, the verb agrees in number with the nearest subject. That is, if the subject closest to the verb is singular, the verb will be singular; if the subject closest to the verb is plural, the verb must be plural too.

Neither <u>the coach</u> nor <u>the players are</u> ready to give up.

Neither <u>the players</u> nor <u>the coach is</u> ready to give up.

Exercise 7.7.2*

Circle the correct verb in each of the following sentences.

1. Not your physical charms but your honesty (is are) what I find attractive.

2. Either your job performance or your school assignments (is are) going to suffer if you continue your frantic lifestyle.
3. The college has decided that neither final marks nor a diploma (is are) to be issued to students who owe library fines.
4. Not the rising costs of health care but unemployment (is are) Canadians' chief concern.
5. Neither the compensation nor the benefits you offer (tempt tempts) me to work for your firm.

2. Subjects that look like compound subjects but really aren't

Don't be fooled by phrases beginning with words such as *with*, *like*, *together with*, *in addition to*, or *including*. These prepositional phrases are NOT part of the subject of the sentence. Since they do not affect the verb, you can mentally cross them out.

Mario's <u>brother</u>, ~~together with three of his buddies~~, <u>is going</u> to the Yukon to look for work.

Obviously four people are looking for work. Nevertheless, the subject (<u>brother</u>) is singular, and so the verb must be singular (<u>is going</u>).

All my <u>courses</u>, ~~except economics~~, <u>are</u> easier this term.

If you mentally cross out the phrase *except economics*, you can easily see that the verb (<u>are</u>) must be plural to agree with the plural subject (<u>courses</u>).

Exercise 7.7.3*

Circle the correct verb in each of the following sentences.

1. Indian meals, like Chinese, (is are) best enjoyed by a group of six or more diners.
2. Our city, along with many other North American urban centres, (register registers) a dangerous level of carbon monoxide pollution in the summer months.
3. The Tour de France, like the Olympic Games, (is are) a world-class athletic competition.
4. Brad, in addition to Angelina's fans, often (wonder wonders) how many children are enough.
5. My English instructor, as well as my math, biology, and even my learning skills instructor, (put, puts) a lot of pressure on me.

Grammar

3. *Each (of), either (of), neither (of)*

Used as subjects, these words (or phrases) take singular verbs.

<u>Either</u> <u>is</u> acceptable to me.

<u>Each</u> <u>wants</u> desperately to win.

<u>Neither</u> of the stores <u>is</u> open after six o'clock. (Remember, the subject is never in a prepositional phrase.)

Exercise 7.7.4*

Circle the correct verb in each of the following sentences.

1. Unless we hear from the coach, neither of us (is are) playing tonight.
2. Each of these courses (involve involves) a field placement.
3. When my girlfriend asks if she looks fat in a dress she is trying on, I know that either of my answers (is are) bound to be wrong.
4. Each of the women (want wants) desperately to win the Ms. Comox Valley bodybuilding competition.
5. Strict discipline is what each of our teachers (believe believes) in.

4. Collective nouns

A **collective noun** is a word that names a group. Some examples are *company, class, committee, team, crowd, band, family, audience, public,* and *jury.* When you are referring to the group acting as a *unit,* use a *singular* verb. When you are referring to the *members* of the group acting *individually,* use a *plural* verb.

The <u>team</u> <u>is</u> sure to win tomorrow's game. (Here *team* refers to the group acting as a whole.)

The <u>team</u> <u>are</u> getting into their uniforms now. (The members of the team are acting individually.)

Exercise 7.7.5*

Circle the correct verb in each of the following sentences.

1. Our club (is are) planning to attend the bikers' rally.
2. The wolf pack (has have) been almost wiped out by local ranchers.

3. By noon on Friday, most of the dorm (has have) packed their laundry and headed for home.
4. After only two hours' discussion, the committee (was were) able to reach consensus.
5. The majority of Canadians, according to a recent survey, (is are) not so conservative about sex and morality as we had assumed.

5. Units of money, time, mass, length, and distance

When used as subjects, they all require singular verbs.

Four kilometres is too far to walk in this weather.

Remember that 2.2 pounds equals a kilogram.

Three weeks is a long time to wait to get your paper back.

Exercise 7.7.6*

Circle the correct verb in each of the following sentences.

1. No wonder you were annoyed if $70 (was were) what you paid for last night's pizza.
2. Tim told his girlfriend that nine years (seem seems) like a long time to wait.
3. Forty hours of classes (is are) too much in one week.
4. When you are anxiously looking for a gas station, 30 km (is are) a long distance.
5. Ninety cents (seems seem) very little to tip, even for poor service.

In Exercises 7.7.7 and 7.7.8, correct the errors in subject–verb agreement. (Some rephrasing may be required.) Check your answers to each exercise before going on.

Exercise 7.7.7*

1. Neither of the following sentences are correct.

2. The faculty, with the full support of the college administration, treats plagiarism as a serious offence.

3. Either good looks or intelligence run in our family, but never at the same time.

4. None of the computer experts have been able to untangle our billing problems.

5. The enjoyment of puns and jokes involving plays on words are the result of having too little else on your mind.

6. Anyone who jumps from one of Paris's many bridges are in Seine.

7. It is amazing how much better the orchestra play now that the conductor is sober.

8. The number of layoffs in the last quarter are truly alarming.

9. Her colleagues, along with her supervisor, agrees that Emily needs further training.

10. Canada's First Nations population are thought to have come to this continent from Asia thousands of years before the Europeans arrived in North America.

Exercise 7.7.8*

Quebec City, along with Montreal, Toronto, and Vancouver, are among Canada's great gourmet centres. Whereas Toronto and Vancouver are relative latecomers to this list, neither Quebec City nor Montreal are strangers to those who seeks fine dining. Indeed, travel and food magazines have long affirmed that including these two cities in a Quebec vacation are a "must." Montreal is perhaps more international in its offerings, but Quebec City provides exquisite proof that French Canadian cuisine and hospitality is second to none in the world. Amid the Old World charm of the lower city is to be found some of the quaintest and most enjoyable traditional restaurants, and the newer sections of town boasts equally fine dining in more contemporary surroundings. The combination of the wonderful food and the charm of the city are sure to entice any visitor to return. Either summer, when the city blooms and outdoor cafés abound, or winter, when Carnaval turns the streets into hundreds of connecting parties, are wonderful times to visit one of Canada's oldest and most interesting cities.

GO TO WEB

EXERCISES 7.7.1, 7.7.2, 7.7.3, 7.7.4

Summary

- Subjects and verbs must agree: both must be singular, or both must be plural.
- The subject of a sentence is never in a prepositional phrase.
- Pronouns ending in *-one*, *-thing*, or *-body* are singular and require singular verbs.
- Subjects joined by *and* are always plural.
- When subjects are joined by *or; either . . . or; neither . . . nor;* or *not . . . but*, the verb agrees with the subject that is closest to it.
- When looking for the subject in a sentence, ignore phrases beginning with *as well as, including, in addition to, like, together with*, etc. They are prepositional phrases.
- When *each, either,* and *neither* are used as subjects, they require singular verbs.
- Collective nouns are usually singular.
- Units of money, time, mass, length, and distance are always singular.

Grammar

Exercise 7.7.9

As a final check of your mastery of subject–verb agreement, correct the following sentences as necessary.

1. Each of the options you outlined in your concluding remarks are worth examining further.

2. My opinion of the college's accounting programs are that neither of them are what I need.

3. Every one of the dozen people we interviewed qualify for the position.

4. My whole family, with the exception of the cat, dislike anchovies on pizza.

5. The applause from a thousand enthusiastic fans were like music to the skaters' ears.

6. Neither of your decisions are likely to improve sales, let alone morale.

7. Three thousand dollars per term, the students agree, are too much to pay for their education.

8. Neither age nor illness prevents Uncle Alf from leering at the nurses.

9. The birth of triplets, after six other children in eight years, were too much for the parents to cope with.

10. Everything you have accomplished in the last three years are wasted if you fail this assignment.

Using Verbs Effectively

Good writers pay especially careful attention to verbs. A verb is to a sentence what an engine is to a car: it's the source of power—but it can also be a source of trouble. Now that you've conquered subject–verb agreement, it's time to turn to the three remaining essentials of correct verb use: **form**, **consistency**, and **voice**.

Choosing the Correct Verb Form

Every verb has four forms, called its **principal parts**:

1. The **infinitive** form: used with *to* and with *can, may, might, shall, will, could, should, would, must*
2. The **simple past** (also called the **past tense**)
3. The **present participle** (the **-ing**) form
4. The **past participle** form: used with *has* or *have*

Here are some examples:

Infinitive	Simple Past	Present Participle	Past Participle
dance	danced	dancing	danced
learn	learned	learning	learned
play	played	playing	played
seem	seemed	seeming	seemed

To use verbs correctly, you must be familiar with their principal parts. Knowing three facts will help you.

- The present participle, the -*ing* form, is always made up of the base form of the verb + *ing*.
- Your dictionary gives you the principal parts of all **irregular** verbs. Look up the base form, and you'll find the simple past and the present and past participles given beside it, usually in parentheses. For example, if you look up *sing* in your dictionary, you will find *sang* (simple past), *sung* (past participle), and *singing* (present participle) listed immediately after the verb itself. If the past tense and past participle are not given, the verb is **regular**.
- To form the simple past and the past participle of regular verbs: add -*ed* to the base form. The examples listed above—*dance, learn, play, seem*—are all regular verbs.

Unfortunately, many of the most common English verbs are irregular. Their past tenses and past participles are formed in unpredictable ways. The verbs in the list that follows are used so often that it is worth your time to memorize their principal parts. (We have not included the -*ing* form because, as we have noted above, it never causes any difficulty.)

The Principal Parts of Irregular Verbs

Infinitive	Simple Past	Past Participle
(Use with *to* and with helping/ auxiliary verbs)		(Use with *have, has, had*)
awake	awoke/awaked	awaked/awoken
be (am, is)	was/were	been
bear	bore	borne
beat	beat	beaten
become	became	become
begin	began	begun
bid (offer to pay)	bid	bid
bid (say, command)	bid/bade	bid/bidden
bite	bit	bitten
bleed	bled	bled
blow	blew	blown
break	broke	broken
bring	brought (*not* brang)	brought (*not* brung)

Infinitive	Simple Past	Past Participle
(Use with *to* and with helping/ auxiliary verbs)		(Use with *have, has, had*)
broadcast	broadcast	broadcast
build	built	built
burst	burst	burst
buy	bought	bought
catch	caught	caught
choose	chose	chosen
come	came	come
cost	cost	cost
cut	cut	cut
deal	dealt	dealt
dig	dug	dug
dive	dived/dove	dived
do	did (*not* done)	done
draw	drew	drawn
dream	dreamed/dreamt	dreamed/dreamt
drink	drank (*not* drunk)	drunk
drive	drove	driven
eat	ate	eaten
fall	fell	fallen
feed	fed	fed
feel	felt	felt
fight	fought	fought
find	found	found
fling	flung	flung
fly	flew	flown
forget	forgot	forgotten/forgot
forgive	forgave	forgiven
freeze	froze	frozen
get	got	got/gotten
give	gave	given
go	went	gone (*not* went)
grow	grew	grown
hang (suspend)	hung	hung
hang (put to death)	hanged	hanged
have	had	had
hear	heard	heard
hide	hid	hidden

Grammar

Infinitive	Simple Past	Past Participle
(Use with *to* and with helping/auxiliary verbs)		(Use with *have, has, had*)
hit	hit	hit
hold	held	held
hurt	hurt	hurt
keep	kept	kept
know	knew	known
lay (put or place)	laid	laid
lead	led	led
leave	left	left
lend	lent (*not* loaned)	lent (*not* loaned)
lie (recline)	lay	lain (*not* layed)
light	lit/lighted	lit/lighted
lose	lost	lost
mean	meant	meant
meet	met	met
pay	paid	paid
raise (lift up, increase, bring up)	raised	raised
ride	rode	ridden
ring	rang	rung
rise	rose	risen
run	ran	run
say	said	said
see	saw (*not* seen)	seen
sell	sold	sold
set (put or place)	set	set
shake	shook	shaken (*not* shook)
shine	shone	shone
sing	sang	sung
sink	sank	sunk
sit	sat	sat
sleep	slept	slept
slide	slid	slid
speak	spoke	spoken
speed	sped	sped
steal	stole	stolen
stick	stuck	stuck
strike (hit)	struck	struck

Infinitive	Simple Past	Past Participle
(Use with *to* and with helping/ auxiliary verbs)		(Use with *have, has, had*)
strike (affect)	struck	stricken
swear	swore	sworn
swim	swam	swum
swing	swung *(not* swang)	swung
take	took	taken
teach	taught	taught
tear	tore	torn
tell	told	told
think	thought	thought
throw	threw	thrown
wake	woke/waked	waked/woken
wear	wore	worn
weave	wove	woven
win	won	won
wind	wound	wound
wring	wrung	wrung
write	wrote	written

Grammar

Exercise 7.8.1*

Find and correct the incorrect verbs in the following sentences. When you have finished, check your answers on page 555.

1. Once I laid down, I found it very hard to get up again.

2. The staff have ate all the sandwiches that were ordered for the board's lunch.

3. Have you ever drove a Porsche?

4. Having finished his presentation, Greg set down to answer questions.

5. The contractor who was eventually chose was the one who submitted the lowest bid.

6. My computer has print the document in a font so small I can't read it.

7. After spending all day in class, I need to lay down for an hour or two.

8. When will I get back the money I loaned you last month?

9. After three years of constant use, our copier is practically wore out.

10. I should have knew that all generalizations are false.

GO TO WEB

EXERCISES   7.8.1, 7.8.2, 7.8.3, 7.8.4

Exercise 7.8.2

As a final test of your mastery of verb forms, correct the errors in the following sentences.

1. We swum in the pool until my toes were almost froze.

2. The stars shined like diamonds the night I told Emmy-Lou how I feeled about her and gave her the ring that costed me a week's pay.

3. Dan had drove very slowly on the gravel road, but once he reached the highway he speeded away into the night.

4. She had forgot how much I dislike the green dress and weared it at the wedding rehearsal.

5. If only we had knew then what we know now, we wouldn't have spoke so quickly.

6. We have never forgave her for the time when her cell rung during the scariest part of the movie.

7. It finally sunk in that he had stole my heart.

8. After the band had sang "The Lion Sleeps Tonight" seven times, we realized that they had been payed too much because they only knowed four tunes.

9. The priest has spoke with the condemned man who will be hung in the morning unless the governor gives him a stay of execution.

10. I played the guitar they loaned me and sung an old tune that I had wrote when I was much younger.

Keeping Your Tenses Consistent

Verbs are time markers. Changes in tense express changes in time: past, present, or future.

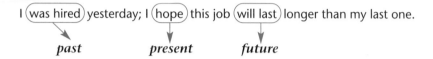

I (was hired) yesterday; I (hope) this job (will last) longer than my last one.

      past   *present*   *future*

Sometimes, as in the example above, it is necessary to use several different tenses in a single sentence to get the meaning across. But most of the time, whether you're writing a sentence or a paragraph, you use one tense throughout. Normally, you choose either the past or the present tense, depending on the nature of your topic. (Few paragraphs are written completely in the future tense.) Here is the rule to follow.

Don't change tense unless meaning requires it.

Readers like and expect consistency. If you begin a sentence with "I worried and fretted and delayed," your readers will tune in to the past-tense verbs and expect any other verbs in the sentence to be in the past tense, too. Therefore, if you finish the sentence with ". . . and then I decide to give it a try," your readers will be jolted abruptly out of one time frame and into another. This sort of jolting is uncomfortable, and readers don't like it.

Shifting tenses is like shifting gears: it should be done smoothly and only when necessary. Avoid causing verbal whiplash: keep your tenses consistent.

Wrong: Monika starts the car and revved the engine.
Right: Monika started the car and revved the engine.
Also right: Monika starts the car and revs the engine.

Wrong: Carrie flounces into the room and sat down. Everyone stares.
Right: Carrie flounced into the room and sat down. Everyone stared.
Also right: Carrie flounces into the room and sits down. Everyone stares.

Exercise 7.8.3*

In this exercise, most of the sentences contain unnecessary tense shifts. Use the first verb in each sentence as your time marker and change the tense(s) of the other verb(s) in the sentence to agree with it. Answers begin on page 555.

Grammar

1. After he accused me of cheating, I call him a liar.

2. My husband watches television until he went to sleep.

3. Hank Aaron broke Babe Ruth's record of 714 home runs in a lifetime when he hits number 715 in 1974.

4. Children are quite perceptive and will know when you are trying to hide something from them.

5. She went up to the counter and asks for a refund.

6. When George Clooney walked into the building, the women go crazy.

7. You should not go into that building until the police arrive.

8. Tim entered the room, took one look at Leroy, and smashes him right through the wall.

9. First you will greet the guests; then you show them to their rooms.

10. The largest cheese ever produced took 43 hours to make and weighs a whopping 15 723 kg.

Exercise 7.8.4*

Correct the 15 faulty tense shifts in this passage.

For some reason, when mistakes or accidents happen in radio or television, they were often hilariously funny. If, in the course of a conversation, someone said, "Here come the Duck and Doochess of Kent," listeners would probably be mildly amused. But many years ago, when an announcer makes that slip on a live radio broadcast, it becomes one of the most famous blunders in radio history. Tapes of the slip will be filed in "bloopers" libraries all over the world. This heightened sense of hilarity is the reason that so many people who work in radio dedicated their creativity to making the on-air announcer laugh while reading the news. To take one example, Lorne Greene's is the deeply serious voice that is heard on the CBC news during World War II. He is the victim of all kinds of pranks aimed at getting him to break up while reading the dark, often tragic, news of the combat overseas.

The pages of his news script are set on fire while he reads. He is even stripped naked as he reads, calmly, and apparently without strain. Lorne Greene will be a true professional. Many other newscasters, however, will have been highly susceptible to falling apart on air at the slightest provocation. And there were always people around a radio station who cannot resist giving them that little push.

GO TO WEB

EXERCISE 7.8.5

Exercise 7.8.5

To test and reinforce your mastery of correct verb forms and tense consistency, correct the 10 errors in the following paragraph. Use the italicized verb in the sentence as your time marker.

The art of writing *is* not dead. Thanks to the use of computers in homes and businesses, it will now be more important than ever to be able to write competently. Not everyone agrees with this statement. Many people will continue to think that electronic technology has eliminated the need to learn how to write, but it will be clear that reports of the death of the written word were premature. Computer networking, bulletin boards, e-mail, and electronic forums made it more important than ever to write well. In the past, when letters were written on paper, writers could have checked their messages over before mailing them to ensure that there were no errors or embarrassing miscommunications. Now, however, communication is instantaneous, and any writing faults will be immediately apparent.

The exposure of writing flaws, however, is not the only reason electronic communication links require the ability to write clear, unambiguous prose. Paper letters were normally mailed to a few people, at most. Electronic mail, on the other hand, will often be sent to dozens, even hundreds, of receivers; therefore, the message will need to be carefully composed if all recipients are to understand what the writer intended. In today's world of electronic communication, good writing skills will be more important than ever before.

Choosing between Active and Passive Verbs

Verbs have another quality besides tense (or time). Verbs also have what is called "voice," which means the quality of being either active or passive. In sentences with **active voice** verbs, the "doer" of the action is the grammatical subject of the sentence.

> **Active voice:** Good parents <u>support</u> their children.
> A car <u>hit</u> the raccoon.
> Someone <u>will show</u> a movie in class on Friday.

In sentences with **passive voice** verbs, the grammatical subject of the sentence is the "receiver" of the action (that is, the subject is passively acted upon), and the "doer" becomes an object of the preposition *by* or is absent from the sentence entirely, as in the third example below.

> **Passive voice:** Children <u>are supported</u> by good parents.
> The raccoon <u>was hit</u> by a car.
> A movie <u>will be shown</u> in class on Friday.

Always use an active verb unless you have a specific reason to choose a passive one.

You probably use the passive voice more often than you think you do. To be a better writer, you need to know the distinction between active and passive, to understand their different effects on the reader, and to use the passive voice only when it is appropriate to your meaning.

There are three good reasons for choosing a passive verb rather than an active one.

1. The person or agent that performed the action is unknown (or the writer does not wish to disclose the identity).

My books <u>were stolen</u> from my locker.

Giovanna's father <u>was killed</u> in Bosnia.

Unlike the streets of a typical prairie city, which <u>are laid out</u> on a grid, Vancouver's streets <u>are laid out</u> to follow the curves and bends of the harbour and the Fraser River.

2. You want to place the emphasis on the person, place, or object that was acted upon rather than on the subject that performed the action.

Early this morning, the Bank of Montreal at 16th and Granville <u>was robbed</u> by four men wearing balaclavas and carrying shotguns.

This sentence focuses the reader's attention on the bank rather than on the robbers. A quite different effect is produced when the sentence is reconstructed in the active voice:

Four men wearing balaclavas and carrying shotguns <u>robbed</u> the Bank of Montreal at 16th and Granville early this morning.

3. You are writing a technical or scientific report or a legal document.

Passive verbs are the appropriate choice when the focus is on the facts, methods, or procedures involved rather than on who discovered or performed them. Passive verbs also tend to establish an impersonal tone that is appropriate in these kinds of writing. Contrast the emphasis and tone of the following sentence pairs:

Grammar

Passive: The heat <u>was increased</u> to 200°C and <u>was maintained</u> at that temperature.

Active: My lab partners and I <u>increased</u> the heat to 200°C and <u>maintained</u> it at that temperature.

Passive: Having been found guilty, the accused <u>was sentenced</u> to two years.

Active: The jury <u>found</u> the accused guilty, and the judge <u>sentenced</u> him to two years.

In general, because active verbs are more concise and forceful than passive verbs, they add vigour and impact to your writing. The distinction between active and passive is not something you should worry about during the drafting stage, however. The time to focus on verbs and decide whether active or passive would best serve your purpose is during revision. When you find a passive verb in your draft, think about *who is doing what*. Ask yourself why the "who" is not the subject of the sentence. If there's a good reason, then use the passive verb. Otherwise, choose an active verb.

Exercise 7.8.6*

Rewrite the sentences below, changing their verbs from passive to active. Note that you may have to add a word or word group to identify the "doer" of the action of the verb.

Example: Matt's two front teeth <u>were knocked out</u> by Clark's shot.

Clark's shot <u>knocked out</u> Matt's two front teeth.

1. A meeting was called by the department head.

2. Your espresso will be made by the barista in a few minutes.

3. When it gets cold, the block heater is plugged in overnight.

4. For many years, steroids have been used by professional athletes to improve speed and endurance.

5. No photos may be taken during the performance.

6. These letters were written by my great-grandfather, who served in the army overseas.

7. This film was made for less than $100 000 by a crew of students.

8. While our neighbours were vacationing in Cuba, their house was broken into by thieves.

9. An error was made in the code you wrote for this program.

10. Teamwork is a valuable concept, especially when someone is needed to take the blame for the boss's mistakes.

Exercise 7.8.7*

Rewrite each of the sentences below, changing the verbs from active to passive or vice versa, and then decide which sentence is more effective.

1. Feist won another Juno.

2. Jian spiked the ball after scoring the go-ahead touchdown.

3. City Council passed a bylaw forbidding backyard bird feeders.

4. Later that night, a shadowy figure was seen entering the lab.

5. After standing in line all night, Courtenay managed to get four tickets to the Michael Bublé concert.

6. The 10 p.m. news revealed the truth behind the fake diploma scandal.

7. Passive voice is often used by people who want to shift responsibility from themselves to others.

8. After a long debate, the student council finally agreed to endorse Yasmin's idea of a class *Facebook* page.

9. A computer program that analyzes speech patterns has been developed by language psychologists.

10. After years of research among college students, it has been concluded by language psychologists that people who frequently use passive voice tend to be maladjusted.

Exercise 7.8.8

Rewrite the following paragraphs, changing the 15 misused passive verbs to active verbs. (Remember, passive voice verbs are sometimes appropriate.)

The last time Glenn had his hair cut by the barber at the local mall was the day of the big high-school graduation dance. One of the prettiest girls in the school had been invited to the prom by Glenn, and to make a good impression was what was wanted. The barber was thought to be talented, if a little unconventional: he had long hair and a vaguely dreamy smile. It was well known by everybody that he had been a hippie back in the 1970s; it was thought by some that his youthful excesses might be responsible for his soft voice and mumbling speech.

Glenn settled into the chair, and a few inaudible words were muttered by the barber. Glenn made a guess at what had been said and replied that the weather was fine. Another mumble from the barber. This time, Glenn thought he'd been asked which college he planned to attend in the fall, and he answered politely. At this point, the conversation was stopped, and the barber got on with his work.

Half an hour later, the sheet was swept away, and the chair was spun so that Glenn could see his image in the mirror. To his horror, it was discovered that he was practically bald, except for an 8-cm high strip of hair running from his forehead to the nape of his neck. Glenn's scream was heard through the entire mall. After the excitement died down, it was learned by the crowds of curious shoppers that when Glenn had been asked what kind of haircut he wanted, Glenn had replied, "Mohawk."

So the prom was attended by Glenn in a tux, a startling haircut, and with a very unsympathetic date. The following week, Glenn left for Hamilton and Mohawk College. His high-school sweetheart was never seen by him again.

SECTION 7.9

Solving
Pronoun Problems

Look at the following sentences. Can you tell what's wrong with them?

"Dev must choose between you and I," Miranda said.

When you are on a diet, it is a good idea for one to avoid Bagel World.

We had invited everybody to come with their partner, so we were a little surprised when Marcel showed up with his Doberman.

Everyone is expected to do their duty.

Gary's nose was badly sunburned, but it has now completely disappeared.

Most of the students that were protesting tuition increases were ones which had been elected to council.

These sentences all contain pronoun errors. After verbs, pronouns are the class of words most likely to cause problems for writers. In this chapter, we will look at the three aspects of pronoun usage that can trip you up if you're not careful: pronoun form, agreement, and consistency. We'll also look at the special problems of usage that can lead to sexist language.

Choosing the Correct Pronoun Form

First you need to be sure you are using the "right" pronouns—that is, the correct pronoun forms—in your sentences. Some examples of incorrect pronoun usage follow.

Her and me cannot agree on anything.

The reason for the quarrel is a personal matter between he and I.

How do you know which form of a pronoun to use? The answer depends on the pronoun's place and function in your sentence.

SUBJECT AND OBJECT PRONOUNS

There are two forms of personal pronouns: one is used for subjects, and the other is used for objects. Pronoun errors occur when you confuse the two. In Section 7.1, you learned to identify the subject of a sentence. Keep that information in mind as you learn the following basic rule.

When a subject or a complement is a pronoun, the pronoun must be in **subject form**. Otherwise, use the **object form**.

Subject Pronouns

Singular	Plural
I	we
you	you
he, she, it, one	they

She and *I* tied for first place. (The pronouns are the subject of the sentence.)

The lucky winners of the all-expenses-paid weekend in Paris are *they*. (The pronoun is the complement and refers to the subject of the sentence, *winners*.)

The student who regularly asks for extra help is *he*. (The pronoun is the complement and refers to the subject of the sentence, *student*.)

Object Pronouns

Singular	Plural
me	us
you	you
him, her, it, one	them

Between you and *me,* I think he's cute. (*Me* is not the subject of the sentence; it is one of the objects of the preposition *between.*)

Omar asked *him* and *me* for help. (*Him* and *me* are not the subject of the verb *asked*; *Omar* is, so the pronouns need to be in the object form.)

Be especially careful when using pronouns in compound subjects or after prepositions. If you can remember the following two rules, you'll be able to eliminate most potential errors.

1. A pronoun that is part of a compound subject is *always* in subject form.
2. A pronoun that follows a preposition is *always* in object form.

Grammar

Examples:

She and *I* had tickets to U2. (The pronouns are used as a compound subject.)

It is up to *you* and *her* to pay for the damage. (The pronouns follow the preposition *to.*)

When you're dealing with a pair of pronouns and can't decide which form to use, try this test.[1] Mentally cross out one pronoun at a time, then read aloud the sentence you've created. Applying this technique to the first example above, you get "*She* has tickets" and "*I* have tickets." Both sound right and are correct. In the second sentence, if you try the pronouns separately, you get "It is up to *you*" and "It is up to *her.*" Again, you know by the sound that these are the correct forms. (You would never say "*Her* had tickets," or "*Me* had tickets," or "It is up to *she.*") If you deal with paired pronouns one at a time, you are unlikely to choose the wrong form.

Note, too, that when a pair of pronouns includes "I" or "me," that pronoun comes last. For example, we write "between *you* and *me*" (not "between *me* and *you*"); we write "*she* and *I*" (not "*I* and *she*"). There is no grammatical reason for this rule. It's based on courtesy. Good manners require that you speak of others first and yourself last.

---

[1] This test is reliable only for those who are fluent in English. ESL students must rely on memorizing the rules.

Exercise 7.9.1*

Correct the pronouns in these sentences as necessary. Answers for the exercises in this section begin on page 557.

1. Murray and him fell asleep in class, as usual.

2. Would you like to work on the project with Emily and I?

3. Only two students failed to show up for the midterm exam: Nadia and me.

4. No one except her parents and I has any interest in following her tweets.

5. It's true that I got some ideas from she and Jacques, but I did not copy their essay.

6. When it comes to the argument over Mac vs. PC, her and me have agreed to disagree.

7. If him and I cannot solve this problem, you and her will have to do it.

8. Everyone agrees that Yoshi and her are the best players, but Leah and me have been practising.

9. Quentin and him agreed to split the price of a case with Mike and I.

10. Trina and me are planning a trip to Guatemala, where us and a dozen other Habitat for Humanity volunteers are going to build a school.

GO TO WEB

EXERCISES 7.9.1, 7.9.2

Using Pronouns in Contrast Constructions

Choosing the correct pronoun form is more than just a matter of not wanting to appear ignorant or careless. Sometimes the form you use determines the meaning of your sentence. Consider these two sentences:

Adam is more interested in his new car than *I*.

Adam is more interested in his new car than *me*.

There's a world of difference between the meaning of the subject form ("Adam is more interested in his new car than *I* [am]") and the object form ("Adam is more interested in his new car than [in] *me*").

> When using a pronoun after *than*, *as well as*, or *as*, decide whether you mean to contrast the pronoun with the subject of the sentence. If you do, use the subject form of the pronoun. If not, use the object form.

Jay would rather watch television than I. (*I* is contrasted with the subject, *Jay.*)

Jay would rather watch television than me. (*Me* is contrasted with the object, *television.*)

To test your sentence, try putting a verb after the pronoun. If the sentence makes sense, then the subject form is the form you want.

Jay would rather watch television than I [would].

Some writers prefer to leave the added verb in place, a practice that eliminates any possibility of confusion.

Exercise 7.9.2*

Correct the following sentences where necessary.

1. At 14, my younger brother is already taller than me.

2. No one likes partying more than him and Anne.

3. Would you like to join Daniel and I for dinner and a movie?

4. Only one person in this firm could manage the department as well as him.

5. At last I have met someone who enjoys grilled liver as much as me!

6. We can skate as well as them, but they are much better at shooting and defending than us.

7. More than me, Serge uses the computer to draft and revise his papers.

Exercise 7.9.3*

Revise the following paragraph to correct the errors in pronoun form.

(1) My boyfriend and me have different opinions when it comes to food. (2) I like fast food better than him. (3) He likes vegetables better than me. (4) In fact, between you and I, he is a vegetarian, though he would deny it. (5)

Grammar

When we go out with friends, it is difficult for they to know where to take him and I because our tastes are so different. (6) The only type of restaurant where us and them can all have what we like is Italian. (7) There, him and his friends can sample pasta primavera and eggplant parmigiana while my friends and I tuck into spaghetti and meatballs and pepperoni pizza. (8) We are probably not as healthy as they, but they don't seem to enjoy their food as much as us.

Now that you know how to choose the correct form of pronouns within a sentence, let's turn to the problems of using pronouns consistently throughout a sentence and a paragraph.

Pronoun–Antecedent Agreement

The name of this pronoun problem may sound difficult, but the idea is simple. Pronouns are words that substitute for or refer to the name of a person, place, or thing mentioned elsewhere in your sentence or your paragraph. The word(s) that a pronoun substitutes for or refers to is called the **antecedent**.

Dracula had his own way of wooing women. (The pronoun *his* refers to the antecedent *Dracula*.)

Soula respects her parents. (The pronoun *her* refers to the antecedent *Soula*.)

The computer is processing as fast as it can. (The pronoun *it* substitutes for the antecedent *computer*.)

Usually, as in these three examples, the antecedent comes before the pronoun that refers to it. Here is the rule to remember.

A pronoun must agree with its antecedent in
- number (singular or plural)
- person (first, second, or third)
- gender (masculine, feminine, or neuter)

Most of the time, you follow this rule without even realizing that you know it. For example, you would never write

Dracula had *your* own way of wooing women.

Soula respects *its* parents.

The computer is processing as fast as *she* can.

You know these sentences are incorrect even if you may not know precisely why they are wrong.

There are three kinds of pronoun–antecedent agreement that you do need to learn about. They lead to errors that, unlike the examples above, are not obvious, and you need to know them so you can watch out for them. The rules you need to learn involve **indefinite pronouns ending in -one, -body, or -thing; vague references; and relative pronouns.**

1. INDEFINITE PRONOUNS: PRONOUNS ENDING IN *-ONE*, *-BODY*, OR *-THING*

The most common pronoun–antecedent agreement problem involves **indefinite pronouns:**

anyone	anybody	anything
everyone	everybody	everything
no one	nobody	nothing
someone	somebody	something
each (one)		

In Section 7.7, you learned that when these words are used as subjects they are singular and take singular verbs. So it makes sense that the pronouns that stand for or refer to them must also be singular.

Antecedents ending in *-one, -body,* or *-thing* are singular and must be referred to by singular pronouns: *he, she, it; his, her, its.*

Please put everything back in *its* place.

Anybody can retire comfortably if *he* or *she* begins planning now.

Everyone is expected to do *his* share.

No one in *his* right mind would claim *he* enjoys living in this climate.

Now take another look at the last two sentences. Until about 30 years ago, the pronouns *he, him,* and *his* were used with singular antecedents to refer to both men and women. In order to appeal to the broadest possible audience, most writers today are careful to avoid this usage and other examples of what may be seen as sexist language.

In informal speech, it has become acceptable to use plural pronouns with -*one,* -*body,* or -*thing* antecedents. Although these antecedents are grammatically singular and take singular verbs, they are often plural in meaning, and in conversation we find ourselves saying

Everyone is expected to do *their* share.

No one has to stay if *they* don't want to.

This usage is acceptable in speech, but it is not acceptable in academic or professional writing.

Writers sometimes make errors in pronoun–antecedent agreement because they are trying to write without indicating whether the person referred to is male or female. A sentence such as "Everyone is required to do *their* oral presentation" is incorrect, as we have seen, but it does avoid making "everyone" male. It also avoids the awkwardness of "Everyone is required to do *his* or *her* oral presentation." There are two better ways to solve this problem.

1. Revise the sentence to leave the pronoun out.

Everyone is required to deliver an oral presentation in the last week of class.

or

An oral presentation is required of everyone in the last week of class.

Such creative avoidance of gender-specific or incorrect constructions can be an interesting challenge. The results often sound a little artificial, however. The second method is easier to accomplish.

2. Revise the sentence to make both the antecedent and the pronoun plural.

You are all required to deliver an oral presentation in the last week of class.

or

All students are required to deliver an oral presentation in the last week of class.

Here are two more examples for you to study.

Problem: Everybody has been given his or her assignment.
Revision 1: Everybody has been given an assignment.
Revision 2: All of the students have been given their assignments.

Problem: No one wants his copy edited.
Revision 1: No one wants copy editing.
Revision 2: Most writers object to having their copy edited.

Exercise 7.9.4*

In the following sentences, identify the most appropriate word(s) from the choices given in parentheses. (*Note:* The options may not be the best choices stylistically; just select the one that is grammatically correct in each case.) Check your answers on page 558 before continuing.

1. Everyone who enjoys a thrilling match will reserve (his their) seat for today's chess club meeting.
2. The elevator was broken, so everyone had to climb to the fourth floor to hand in (her their) course evaluation.
3. Each of her sons successfully completed (his their) diploma program.
4. Someone with a lot of cash left (her their) purse in the women's washroom.
5. Every reporter must decide for (himself themselves) how far (he they) will go in pursuit of a story.

Exercise 7.9.5*

Rewrite the sentences in Exercise 7.9.4 to eliminate sexist language.

Exercise 7.9.6*

Correct the following sentences where necessary, being careful to avoid awkward repetition and sexist language.

1. Virginia claims that every one of her male friends has a room of their own.

2. Almost everyone I know is concerned about finding a job that will be suitable for him or her.

3. Anybody who applies for a job with this institution can expect to spend a lot of their time in selection committee interviews.

4. Taking a picture of someone when they are not looking can produce interesting results.

5. Nearly every man who can cook will tell you that they enjoy preparing food.

---

2. VAGUE REFERENCE

Avoiding the second potential difficulty with pronoun–antecedent agreement requires common sense and the ability to think like your readers. If you look at your writing from your readers' point of view, it is unlikely that you will break the following rule.

Every pronoun must have a clearly identifiable antecedent.

The mistake that occurs when you fail to follow this rule is called **vague reference.**

Chris told his brother that he was losing his hair.

Who is going bald? Chris or his brother?
Here's another example:

The faculty are demanding higher salaries and fewer teaching hours, but the administration does not support them.

What does the administration not support: higher salaries, fewer classes, or the faculty themselves?
In sentences like these, you can only guess the meaning because you don't know who or what is being referred to by the pronouns. You can make such sentences less confusing by using either more names or other nouns and by using fewer pronouns. For example:

Chris told his brother Sam that Sam was losing his hair.

The faculty are demanding higher salaries and fewer teaching hours, but the administration does not support their demands.

Another type of vague reference occurs when there is no appropriate antecedent in the sentence for the pronoun to refer to.

I sold my skis last year and can't even remember how to do it anymore. (Do what?)

Reading is Sophia's passion, but she says she doesn't have a favourite. (A favourite what?)

My roommate smokes constantly, *which* I hate. (There is no noun or pronoun for *which* to refer to.)

I hate homework; this is my downfall. (*This* refers to homework, but homework is not my downfall. My hatred of doing it is.)

How would you revise these sentences? Try it, then see our suggestions in the footnote below.[2]

Be sure that every pronoun has a clear antecedent with which it agrees in number, person, and gender. Once you have mastered this principle, you'll have no further trouble with pronoun–antecedent agreement.

─────────────────────────────── **Exercise 7.9.7***

Correct the following sentences where necessary. There are several ways to fix these sentences. In some cases, the antecedent is missing, and you need to supply one. In other cases, the antecedent is so vague that the meaning of the sentence can be interpreted in more than one way. You need to rewrite these sentences to make the meaning clear.

1. I know that smoking is bad for me and everyone else, but I can't give them up.

2. If your pet rat won't eat its food, feed it to the kitty.

3. Our cat is a picky eater, which is inconvenient and expensive.

4. Whenever Stan and Matt played poker, he stacked the deck.

5. The gorilla was mean and hungry because he had finished it all in the morning.

─────────────────

[2]I sold my skis last year and can't even remember how to *slalom* anymore.

Reading is Sophie's passion, but she says she doesn't have a favourite *writer*.

My roommate is constantly smoking, *which* I hate.

I hate doing homework; *this* is my downfall.

6. Madonna has transformed herself at least five times in her career, which makes her unique.

7. Dani backed her car into a garbage truck and dented it.

8. Rocco was suspicious of handgun control because he thought everyone should have one for late-night subway rides.

9. Get your ears pierced during this week's special and take home an extra pair free.

10. Our car is in the shop, but this won't keep us from going to the party.

Exercise 7.9.8

To test your understanding of the pronoun problems we have covered so far, try this exercise, which contains all three kinds of pronoun–antecedent agreement errors. Correct the following sentences where necessary.

1. Each of her suitors had their faults, but Denise decided to overlook the shortcomings of the one that had the most money.

2. Embezzling is what he does best, but he hasn't been able to pull one off lately.

3. Everyone may pick up their exams in my office on Tuesday after 9:00 a.m.

4. None of the candidates came with their résumé, so we had to reject them all.

5. Every applicant must submit their portfolio of work, their essay on why they want to enter the program, and a neatly folded $50 bill.

6. When I go fishing, I expect to catch at least a few.

7. Every secretary knows that their boss is someone that could not survive for 15 minutes without competent secretarial assistance.

8. All the women in this beauty pageant are treated like a sister even though the competition is fierce.

9. Everybody that joins the tour will receive their own souvenir hat.

10. Before a Canadian votes, it is their responsibility to make themselves familiar with the candidates and the issues.

3. RELATIVE PRONOUNS

The third potential difficulty with pronoun–antecedent agreement is how to use relative pronouns—*who/whoever, whom/whomever, which*, and *that*—correctly. Relative pronouns refer to someone or something already mentioned in the sentence or paragraph. Here is the guideline to follow.

> Use *who/whom* and *whoever/whomever* refer to people.
> Use *that* and *which* to refer to everything else.

The student *who* won the Governor General's Academic Medal decided to go to Dalhousie.

For *whom* are you voting: the Liberals or the New Democrats?

The moose *that* I met looked hostile.

Her car, *which* is imported, is smaller than cars *that* are built here.

Tips:

1. Whether you need *who* or *whom, whoever* or *whomever*, depends on the pronoun's place and function in your sentence. Apply the basic rule of pronoun usage: if the pronoun is acting as, or refers to, the subject or the complement, use *who/whoever*. Otherwise, use *whom/whomever*.

   My husband was the idiot *who* entered a contest to win a trip to Moose Factory. (The pronoun refers to the subject of the sentence, *husband*.)

   The trip's promoters were willing to settle for *whomever* they could get. (The pronoun does not refer to the sentence's subject, *promoters*; it is the object of the preposition *for*.)

   An even simpler solution to this problem is to rewrite the sentence so you don't need either *who* or *whom*.

   My husband entered a contest to win a trip to Moose Factory.

   The trip's promoters were willing to settle for anyone they could get.

2. *That* is required more often than *which*. You should use *which* only in a clause that is separated from the rest of the sentence by commas. (See Comma Rule 4 on page 456.)

The moose *that* I met looked hostile.

The moose, *which* was standing right in front of my car, looked hostile.

Exercise 7.9.9*

Correct the following sentences where necessary.

1. The actress that saw her first grey hair thought she'd dye.

2. I am a long-time fan of David Cronenberg, a director that began his career in Canada.

3. I wonder why we are so often attracted to people which are opposite to us.

4. I'm one of those people that should stay out of the sun.

5. People that take afternoon naps often suffer from insomnia as a result.

6. The vacuum-cleaner salesperson which came to our door was the sort of person that won't take no for an answer.

7. Ms. Waldman is the teacher that helped me achieve the grades which I had thought were beyond me.

8. Marathon runners that wear cheap shoes often suffer the agony of defeat.

9. The math problems which we worked on last night would have baffled anyone that hadn't done all the problem sets.

10. We took the ancient Jeep, that we had bought from a friend that had lost his licence, to a scrapyard who paid us $200 for it.

GO TO WEB

EXERCISES 7.9.3, 7.9.4, 7.9.5, 7.9.6

Person Agreement

So far, we have focused on using pronouns correctly and clearly within a sentence. Now let's turn to the problem of **person agreement**, which means using pronouns consistently throughout a sentence or a paragraph. There are three categories of person that we use when we write or speak:

	Singular	**Plural**
First person	I; me	we; us
Second person	you	you
Third person	she, he, it, one; her, him *and all pronouns ending in* -one, -thing, -body	they; them

Here is the rule for person agreement.

Do not mix "persons" unless meaning requires it.

In other words, be consistent. If you begin a sentence using a second-person pronoun, you must use second person all the way through. Look at this sentence:

If *you* wish to succeed, *one* must work hard.

This is the most common error—mixing second-person *you* with third-person *one*.

Here's another example:

One can live happily in Vancouver if *you* have a sturdy umbrella.

1. We can correct this error by using the second person throughout:

You can live happily in Vancouver if *you* have a sturdy umbrella.

2. We can also correct it by using the third person throughout:

a. *One* can live happily in Vancouver if *one* has a sturdy umbrella.

or

b. *One* can live happily in Vancouver if *he* or *she* has a sturdy umbrella.

These examples raise two points of style that you should consider.

1. Don't overuse *one*.

All three revised sentences are grammatically correct, but they make different impressions on the reader, and impressions are an important part of communication.

- The first sentence, in the second person, sounds the most informal—like something you would say. It's a bit casual for general writing purposes.
- The second sentence, which uses *one* twice, sounds the most formal— even a little pretentious.
- Sentence 2(b) falls between the other two in formality. It is the one you'd be most likely to use in writing for school or business.

Although it is grammatically correct and nonsexist, sentence 2(b) raises another problem. Frequent use of *he or she* in a continuous prose passage, whether that passage is as short as a paragraph or as long as a paper, is guaranteed to irritate your reader.

2. Don't overuse *he or she*.

He or she is inclusive, but it is a wordy construction. If used too frequently, the reader cannot help shifting focus from what you're saying to how you're saying it. The best writing is transparent—that is, it doesn't call attention to itself. If your reader becomes distracted by your style, your meaning gets lost. Consider this sentence:

A student can easily pass this course if he or she applies himself or herself to his or her studies.

Readers deserve better. A paper—or even a single paragraph—filled with this clumsy construction will annoy even the most patient reader. There are two better solutions to the problem of sexist language, and they are already familiar to you because they are the same as those for making pronouns ending in *-one*, *-body*, or *-thing* agree with their antecedents.

- You can change the whole sentence to the plural.

  Students can easily pass this course if they apply themselves to their studies.

- You can rewrite the sentence without using pronouns.

  A student can easily pass this course by applying good study habits.

In each of the following sentences, select the correct word from the choices given in parentheses. Check your answers before continuing.

1. If you want to make good egg rolls, I advise (them her you) to buy the ready-made wrappings.
2. Every person working in this office should know that (they she) helped to finish an important project.
3. Anyone who wants to swim should bring (their your his her a) bathing suit and towel.
4. If you win tonight's lottery, will (one he you) tell (one's his your) friends?
5. When we toured the House of Commons, (you we he one) didn't see a single MP.

Correct the following sentences where necessary.

1. When a person lives in a glass house, they shouldn't throw stones.

2. Experience is something one acquires just after you need it.

3. Anyone who enjoys snowboarding can have your best holiday ever in western Alberta.

4. When she asked if Peter Tchaikovsky played for the Canucks, you knew she wasn't the woman for me.

5. From time to time, most of us think about the opportunities we've missed even if you are happy with what you have.

6. If you are afraid of vampires, one should wear garlic around one's neck and carry a silver bullet.

7. Any woman who wears a garlic necklace probably won't have to worry about men harassing them, either.

8. Can you really know another person if you have never been to their home?

9. Managers who are concerned about employee morale should think about ending your policy of threats and intimidation and consider other means to improve your efficiency.

10. A sure way to lose one's friends is to eat all the ice cream yourself.

Grammar

Exercise 7.9.12*

Revise the following passage to make the nouns and pronouns agree in person (first, second, or third) and number (singular or plural). Use the italicized word in the first sentence of each paragraph as your marker. There are 10 errors in this exercise.

When *people* see a dreadful occurrence on television, such as a bombing, an earthquake, or a mass slaughter, it does not always affect one. It is one thing for people to see the ravages of war oneself and another thing to see a three-minute newscast of the same battle, neatly edited by the CBC. Even the horrible effects of natural catastrophes that wipe out whole populations are somehow minimized or trivialized when I see them on TV. And although viewers may be horrified by the gaunt faces of starving children on the screen, you can easily escape into your familiar world of Egg McMuffins, Shake'n Bake, and Labatt Blue that is portrayed in commercial messages.

Thus, the impact of television on *us* is a mixed one. It is true that one is shown terrible, sometimes shocking, events that you could not possibly have seen before television. In this way, one's world is drawn together more closely. However, the risk in creating this immediacy is that one may become desensitized and cease to feel or care about other human beings.

GO TO WEB

EXERCISES 7.9.7, 7.9.8

Exercise 7.9.13

Revise the following paragraph, which contains 15 errors representing the three different kinds of pronoun–antecedent agreement errors. If you change a subject from singular to plural, don't forget to change the verb to agree. Some of your answers may differ from our suggestions and still be correct. Check with your instructor.

Everyone that has been to Newfoundland knows that an outport is a small fishing community along the coast of that vast island province. Ladle Cove, for example, is a tiny outport with fewer than 200 residents that live there all year. Despite its small population, Ladle Cove is a village which enjoyed a nation-wide moment of fame when a man that lives there met the Queen. Fred had left Ladle Cove, as just about every man does when they need to find work, and gone to St. John's. Fred wanted to work, but he had few marketable skills to help him get one. Fortunately, he had relatives in St. John's that helped him find a place to stay and eventually found him a job at Purity Foods, a company famous for their baked goods—and for Newfoundland's favourite treat, Jam Jam cookies.

During Queen Elizabeth's visit to St. John's, the officials that organized her tour decided it would be a good idea for her to visit a local industry which had a national reputation. Purity Foods was the logical choice. While touring the plant, the Queen stopped to talk to a few of the men and women that were on the production line. Near the end of the tour, that was being filmed by the national media, the Queen stopped by one of the workers that were making the famous Jam Jams: Fred. As the television lights glared and each reporter held their pencil poised over their notebook, the Queen leaned toward Fred and asked, "And what are we making here?" With a courteous bow in Her Majesty's direction, Fred replied, "Tenfifty an hour, Ma'am. Ten-fifty an hour."

The Comma

Many writers-in-training tend to sprinkle punctuation marks like pepper over their pages. Do not use punctuation to spice up your writing. Punctuation marks have a function: they indicate to the reader how the various parts of a sentence relate to one another. By changing the punctuation, you can change the meaning of a sentence. If you don't believe that, ask Rogers Communication about its recent two-million-dollar legal dispute with Aliant Inc. over the wording of a contract—the disagreement hinged on the placement of a comma!

Here are two examples that demonstrate how commas can influence meaning:

1. An instructor wrote the following sentence on the board and asked the class to punctuate it: "Woman without her man is nothing."

   The men wrote, "Woman, without her man, is nothing."
   The women wrote, "Woman! Without her, man is nothing."

2. Now it's your turn. Punctuate this sentence: "I think there is only one person to blame myself."

   If you wrote, "I think there is only one person to blame, myself," the reader will understand that you believe only one person—who may or may not be known to you—is to blame.

   If you wrote, "I think there is only one person to blame: myself," the reader will understand that you are personally accepting responsibility for the blame.

The comma is the most frequently used—and misused—punctuation mark in English. One sure sign of a competent writer is the correct use of commas, so it is important that you master them. This chapter presents five comma rules that cover most instances in which you need to use commas. If you apply these five rules faithfully, your reader will never be confused by missing or misplaced commas in your writing. And if, as occasionally happens, the sentence you are writing is not covered by one of our five rules, remember the default commandment of comma usage: when in doubt, leave it out.

Five Comma Rules

> 1. Use commas to separate three or more items in a series. The items may be expressed as words, phrases, or clauses.

Words   The required subjects in this program are *math*, *physics*, and *English*.

Phrases   Punctuation marks are the traffic signals of prose. They tell us *to slow down*, *notice this*, *take a detour*, and *stop*. (Lynne Truss)

Clauses   *Karin went to the movies*, *Jan and Danuta went to play pool*, and *I went to bed*.

The comma before the *and* at the end of the list is optional, but we advise you to use it. Misunderstandings can occur if it is left out.

Exercise 7.10.1*

Insert commas where necessary in the following sentences. Answers for exercises in this chapter begin on page 560.

1. A cup of coffee a croissant and a glass of juice are what I want for breakfast.

2. The food at the Thai Palace is colourful spicy delicious and inexpensive.

3. Life would be complete if I had a BlackBerry a Porsche a Sea-Doo and a job.

4. The gear list for the Winter Wilderness course includes woollen underwear snowshoes Arctic boots and a toque.

5. Holly held two aces a King a Queen and a Jack in her hand.

6. Please bring the videos maps and souvenirs of your trip to Australia.

Punctuation

7. In most of Canada, the four seasons are summer winter winter and winter.

8. My wife thinks that I should eat less exercise more and take a daily vitamin and mineral supplement.

9. Sleeping through my alarm dozing during English class napping in the library after lunch and snoozing in front of the TV after supper are the causes of my hyperactive nightlife.

10. Welcome home! Once you have finished your homework taken out the garbage and done the dishes, you can feed the cat clean your room and do your laundry.

---

2. Put a comma between independent clauses when they are joined by these connecting words:

for	but	so
and	or	
nor	yet	

(You can remember these words easily if you notice that their first letters spell FANBOYS.)

I hope I do well in the interview, for I really want this job.

I like Norah Jones, but I prefer Diana Krall.

We shape our tools, and our tools shape us. (Marshall McLuhan)

I knew I was going to be late, so I went back to sleep.

Be sure that the sentence you are punctuating contains two independent clauses rather than a single clause with one subject and a multiple verb. E.g.,

We loved the book but hated the movie.
(We is the subject, and there are two verbs, loved and hated. Do not put a comma between two or more verbs that share a single subject.)

We both loved the book, but Kim hated the movie.
(This sentence contains two independent clauses—We loved and Kim hated—joined by *but*. The comma is required here.)

Exercise 7.10.2

Insert commas where they are needed in the following sentences, then check your answers on page 560.

1. Either it is very foggy this morning or I am going blind.

2. We have an approved business plan and budget but we're still looking for qualified and experienced staff.

3. People on talk shows haven't said anything new in years nor have they solved a single one of the problems they endlessly discuss.

4. We discovered that we both had an interest in photography so we made a date to go to the Ansel Adams exhibition next week.

5. Canadians are proud of their country but they don't approve of too much flag-waving.

6. Take good notes for I'll need them in order to study for the exam.

7. I will rent a tux but I will not get a haircut or have my shoes shined.

8. I chose a quiet seat on the train and two women with bawling babies boarded at the next station.

9. I have travelled all over the world yet my luggage has visited at least twice the number of countries that I have.

10. Jet lag makes me look haggard and ill but at least I resemble my passport photo.

3. Put a comma after an introductory word, phrase, or dependent clause that comes before an independent clause.

Lucas, you aren't paying attention. (word)

After staying up all night, I staggered into class 15 minutes late. (phrase)

If that's their idea of a large pizza, we'd better order two. (clause)

Until she got her promotion, she was quite friendly. (clause)

Exercise 7.10.3

Insert commas where they are needed in the following sentences. Check your answers before you move on to Rule 4.

1. Remember a clear conscience is often just a sign of a poor memory.

2. If you think nobody cares try missing a few payments.

3. When the cannibals ate a missionary they got a taste of religion.

4. No matter how much I practise my singing never gets any better.

5. First cook the noodles in a large pot of boiling water.

6. If Barbie is so popular why do you have to buy friends for her?

7. Until I had my performance review I thought my manager had no appreciation of my efforts.

8. No matter how much you push the envelope it will still be stationery.

9. Ladies and gentlemen please put away all cellphones BlackBerrys and any other electronic devices you may have concealed on your person before entering the examination room.

10. In democracy it is your vote that counts; in feudalism it is your count that votes.

---

4. Use commas to set off any word, phrase, or dependent clause that is NOT ESSENTIAL to the main idea of the sentence.

Following this rule can make the difference between your reader's understanding and misunderstanding what you mean. For example, the following two sentences are identical, except for a pair of commas. But notice what a difference those two tiny marks make to meaning:

The children who were dressed in Halloween costumes got little bags of candy. (Only the children wearing Halloween costumes got candy.)

The children, who were dressed in Halloween costumes, got little bags of candy. (All the children wore costumes and were given candy.)

To test whether a word, phrase, or clause is essential to the meaning of your sentence, mentally put parentheses around it. If the sentence still makes complete sense (i.e., the main idea is unchanged; the sentence just delivers less information), the material in parentheses is *not essential* and should be set off from the rest of the sentence by a comma or commas.

Nonessential information can appear at the beginning of a sentence,[1] in the middle, or at the end of a sentence. Study the following examples.

> Alice Munro ⦃ one of Canada's best-known novelists ⦄ spends summers in Clinton and winters in Comox.

Many readers would be puzzled the first time they read this sentence. Because all the information is presented without punctuation, the reader assumes it is all equally important. In fact, the material in broken parentheses is extra information, a supplementary detail. It can be deleted without changing the sentence's meaning, and so it should be separated from the rest of the sentence by commas:

> Alice Munro, one of Canada's best-known novelists, spends summers in Clinton and winters in Comox.

Here's another example:

> The Queen ⦃ who has twice as many birthdays as anyone else ⦄ officially celebrates her birthday on May 24.

Again, the sentence is hard to read. You can't count on your readers to go back and reread every sentence they don't understand at first glance. As a writer, your responsibility is to give readers the clues they need as to what is crucial information and what isn't. In the example above, the information in broken parentheses is not essential to the meaning of the sentence, so it should be set off by commas:

> The Queen, who has twice as many birthdays as anyone else, officially celebrates her birthday on May 24.

In this next sentence, the nonessential information comes at the end.

> Writing a good letter of application isn't difficult ⦃ if you're careful ⦄.

The phrase "if you're careful" is not essential to the main idea, so it should be separated from the rest of the sentence by a comma:

> Writing a good letter of application isn't difficult, if you're careful.

And finally, consider this sentence:

> Writing a letter of application ⦃ that is clear, complete, and concise ⦄ is a challenge.

---

[1] Comma Rule 3 covers nonessential information at the beginning of a sentence.

If you take out "that is clear, complete, and concise," you change the meaning of the sentence. Not all letters of application are a challenge to write. Writing vague and wordy letters is easy. Anyone can do it. The words "that is clear, complete, and concise" are essential to the meaning of the sentence, and so they are not set off by commas.

> Writing a letter of application that is clear, complete, and concise is a challenge.

Exercise 7.10.4*

Insert commas where they are missing in the following sentences, then check your answers.

1. A good day in my opinion always starts with a few cuts of high-volume heavy metal.
2. This photograph which was taken when I was eight months old embarrasses me whenever my parents display it.
3. Mira's boyfriend who looks like an ape is living proof that love is blind.
4. Isn't it strange that the poor who are often bitterly critical of the rich buy lottery tickets?
5. A nagging headache the result of last night's party made me miserable all morning.
6. Our ancient car made it all the way to Saskatoon without breaking down a piece of good luck that astonished us all.
7. Professor Repke a popular mathematics teacher won the Distinguished Teaching Award this year.
8. We're going to spend the afternoon at the mall a weekly event that has become a ritual.
9. No one who watched Patrick Roy play could doubt that he was a superstar.
10. Classical music which I call Prozac for the ears can be very soothing in times of stress.

Exercise 7.10.5*

Insert commas where they are needed in the following sentences. Check your answers on pages 561–62 before continuing.

1. Unfortunately we'll have to begin all over again.
2. Lord Black your wife would like a word with you.
3. In college the quality of your work is more important than the effort you put into it.
4. Hopelessly lost my father refused to stop and ask for directions.
5. Finally understanding what she was trying to say I apologized for being so slow.

6. After an evening of watching television I have accomplished as much as if I had been unconscious.
7. Since the doctor ordered me to walk to work every morning I have seen three accidents involving people walking to work.
8. That same year Stephen Leacock bought his summer home in Orillia, Ontario.
9. When an optimist is pulled over by a police officer the optimist assumes it's to ask for directions.
10. Having munched our way through a large bag of peanuts while watching the game we weren't interested in supper.

---

5. Use commas between coordinate adjectives but not between cumulative adjectives.

Coordinate adjectives are adjectives that pass two tests: (1) they can be re-ordered without changing the meaning of the sentence, and (2) the word *and* can be inserted between them without changing the meaning of the sentence. For example,

Our company is looking for energetic, courteous salespeople.

The adjectives *energetic* and *courteous* could appear in reverse order, and you could put *and* between them: "Our company is looking for courteous and energetic salespeople."

In a series of **cumulative adjectives**, however, each adjective modifies the word that follows it. You cannot change their order, nor can you insert *and* between them.

The bride wore a pale pink silk dress, and the groom wore a dark blue wool suit.

You cannot say "The bride wore a silk pink pale dress" or "The groom wore a dark and blue and wool suit," so no commas are used with these adjectives.

One final note about commas before you try the review exercises: never place a SINGLE comma between a subject and its verb.

Wrong:	Those who intend to register for hockey, must be at the arena by 8:00 a.m.
Right:	Those who intend to register for hockey must be at the arena by 8:00 a.m.

Punctuation

Two commas, however, between a subject and its verb are correct if the commas set off nonessential material.

<u>Saied and Mohamed</u>, who intend to register for hockey, <u>have</u> never <u>played</u> before.

Exercise 7.10.6*

Insert commas where they are needed in the following sentences. Check your answers before continuing.

1. Dietitians recommend that we eat at least two servings daily of green leafy vegetables.
2. Do you want your portrait in a glossy finish or a matte finish?
3. Bright yellow fabric that repels stains is ideal for rain gear.
4. Toronto in the summer is hot smoggy and humid.
5. St. John's, on the other hand, is cool sunny and windy.
6. The dining room table was made of richly stained ornately carved walnut.
7. This ergonomic efficient full-function keyboard comes in a variety of pastel shades.
8. We ordered a large nutritious salad for lunch, then smothered it in calorie-laden creamy ranch dressing.
9. For my sister's birthday, her boyfriend gave her a cute cuddly seven-week-old puppy.
10. Today's paper has an article about a new car made of lightweight durable carbon fibre.

The rest of the exercises in this chapter require you to apply all five comma rules. Before you start, write out the five rules and keep them in front of you as you work through the exercises. At the end of each sentence, write the number(s) of the rule(s) you applied to correct it. After you've finished each exercise, check your answers and make sure you understand any mistakes you've made.

Exercise 7.10.7*

1. Your dogs Mr. Pavlov seem hungry for some reason.
2. I use SMS to communicate with my colleagues e-mail to keep in touch with clients and Canada Post to send greetings to my relatives.
3. There are I am told people who don't like garlic but you won't find any of them eating at Freddy's.

4. How you choose to phrase your resignation is up to you but I expect to have it on my desk by morning.
5. Pinot noir which is a type of grape grown in California Oregon British Columbia and Ontario produces a delicious red wine.
6. Looking for a competent computer technologist we interviewed tested investigated and rejected 30 applicants.
7. According to G. K. Chesterton "If a thing is worth doing it is worth doing badly."
8. Your superstitious fear of March 15 Julius is irrational and silly.
9. Canada a country known internationally for beautiful scenery peaceful intentions and violent hockey always places near the top of the United Nations' list of desirable places to live.
10. The lenses of my new sunglasses are high-functon impact-resistant UV-reflective optical plastic.

Exercise 7.10.8*

1. Whereas the Super Bowl tradition goes back about four decades the Grey Cup has a history that stretches back to the 19th century.
2. Otherwise Mrs. Lincoln said she very much enjoyed the play.
3. Our guard dog a Rottweiler caught an intruder and maimed him for life.
4. Unfortunately my Uncle Ladislaw was the intruder and he intends to sue us for every penny we have.
5. The year 1945 marked the end of World War II and the beginning of assistance to war-torn nations.
6. We bought a lovely old oak dining table at auction for $300.
7. If there were more people like Gladys global warming would be the least of our worries.
8. We are pleased with your résumé and are offering you an interview this week.
9. Deciding on the midnight blue velvet pants was easy but paying for them was not.
10. Igor asked "May I show you to your quarters or would you prefer to spend the night in the dungeon?"

Punctuation

GO TO WEB

EXERCISES 7.10.1, 7.10.2, 7.10.3

Exercise 7.10.9

To test your mastery of commas, provide the necessary punctuation for the following paragraph. There are 15 errors.

When my brother and I were growing up my mother used to summon us home from playing by ringing a solid brass bell that could be heard for miles. All of the other kids to our great embarrassment, knew when our mother was calling us and they would tease us by making ringing noises. We begged her to yell like all the other moms but she knew she had a foolproof system and wouldn't change. One day while we were playing with our friends in the fields behind our homes the bell rang in the middle of an important game. The other kids began their usual taunts that our mother was calling but this time we bravely ignored the bell. When it rang the second time we ignored it again. By the third ring, however we knew that we were in big trouble so we dashed for home. We agreed on the way that we would tell our mother that we just didn't hear the bell. We arrived hot sweaty and panting from our run. Before Mom could say a word my brother blurted out, "We didn't hear the bell until the third ring!" Fortunately for us our mother couldn't stop laughing and we escaped the punishment we deserved.

Summary

The Five Comma Rules

1. Use commas to separate items in a series of three or more. The items may be expressed as words, phrases, or clauses.
2. Put a comma between independent clauses when they are joined by *for, and, nor, but, or, yet,* or *so.*
3. Put a comma after an introductory word, phrase, or dependent clause that comes before an independent clause.
4. Use commas to set off a word, phrase, or dependent clause that is NOT ESSENTIAL to the main idea of the sentence.
5. Use commas between coordinate adjectives but not between cumulative adjectives.

The Semicolon

The semicolon and the colon are often confused and used as if they were interchangeable. They have distinct purposes, however, and their correct use can dramatically improve a reader's understanding of your writing. The semicolon has three functions.

1. A semicolon can replace a period; in other words, it can appear between two independent clauses.

You should use a semicolon when the two clauses (sentences) you are joining are closely connected in meaning, or when there is a cause-and-effect relationship between them.

I have used up all my sick days; now I call in dead.

Montreal is not the city's original name; it was once called Ville-Marie.

A period could have been used instead of a semicolon in either of these sentences, but the close connection between the clauses makes a semicolon more effective in communicating the writer's meaning.

2. Certain transitional words or phrases can be put between independent clauses to show a cause-and-effect relationship or the continuation of an idea.

Punctuation

Words or phrases used in this way are usually preceded by a semicolon and followed by a comma:

; also,	; furthermore,	; nevertheless,
; as a result,	; however,	; on the other hand,
; besides,	; in addition,	; otherwise,
; consequently,	; in fact,	; then,
; finally,	; instead,	; therefore,
; for example,	; moreover,	; thus,

The forecast called for sun; instead, we got snow.

My monitor went blank; nevertheless, I kept on typing.

"I'm not offended by dumb blonde jokes because I know I'm not dumb; besides, I also know I'm not blonde." (Dolly Parton)

In other words, *a semicolon + a transitional word/phrase + a comma* = a link strong enough to come between two related independent clauses.

Note, however, that, when these transitional words and phrases are used as nonessential expressions rather than as connecting words, they are separated from the rest of the sentence by commas (Section 7.10, Rule 4, page 456).

I just can't seem to master particle physics, however hard I try.

The emissions test, moreover, will ensure that your car is running well.

3. To make a COMPLEX LIST easier to read and understand, put semi-colons between the items instead of commas.

A complex list is one in which at least one component part already contains commas. Here are two examples:

I grew up in a series of small towns, including Cumberland, British Columbia; Red Deer, Alberta; and Timmins, Ontario.

When we opened the refrigerator, we found a limp, brown head of lettuce; two small containers of yogurt, whose "best before" dates had long since passed; and a hard, dried-up piece of something that might once have been cheddar cheese.

Exercise 7.11.1

Put a check mark next to the sentences that are correctly punctuated. Check your answers before continuing. Answers for this chapter begin on page 563.

1. _____ We've eaten all the food, it's time to go home.
2. _____ Many doctors claim weather affects our health; in fact, barometric pressure has a direct effect on arthritis.
3. _____ Your instructor would like to see you pass, however, there may be a small fee involved.
4. _____ Molly is going to Chicago, she is determined to meet Oprah.
5. _____ Many people dislike hockey; because some of the players act like goons rather than athletes.
6. _____ Lisa tried and tried; but she couldn't get Homer's attention.
7. _____ The new dean presented her report using PowerPoint slides interspersed with music; her presentation woke up the accountants.
8. _____ Tomorrow is another day, unfortunately it will probably be just like today.
9. _____ Rumours of a merger had begun to circulate by five o'clock; so it's no wonder many employees looked nervous on their way home.
10. _____ We knew the party had been a success when Uncle Irving, drunk as usual, tap-danced across the top of the piano, Aunt Liz, who must weigh at least 80 kg, did her Cirque du Soleil routine, and Marvin punched out two of his cousins.

Exercise 7.11.2

Correct the faulty punctuation in Exercise 7.11.1.

GO TO WEB

EXERCISES 7.11.1, 7.11.2

Punctuation

Exercise 7.11.3*

Insert semicolons where necessary in these sentences. Then check your answers.

1. A day without puns is like a day without sunshine, it leaves gloom for improvement.
2. The rain has to stop soon otherwise, we'll have to start building an ark.
3. Our finances are a mess the only way we can repay our debts would be to stop paying for rent and food.
4. We would like to meet on Tuesday, however, since you have another commitment, we will reschedule.
5. I work on an assembly line, we workers believe that if a job is worth doing; it's worth doing 11 000 times a day.
6. It is not impossible to become wealthy, if you're under 20, all you need to do is put the price of a pack of cigarettes into an RRSP every day, and you'll be a millionaire by the age of 50.
7. If, on the other hand, you continue to spend your money on smokes, the government will make the millions that could have been yours, you'll die early and broke.
8. As a dog lover and the owner of an Afghan, I suffer a great deal of abuse, for example, for my birthday, my wife gave me a book rating the intelligence of Afghans as 79th out of 79 breeds tested.
9. A plateau, according to the *Dictionary of Puns*, is a high form of flattery, this may be low humour, but it's a clever pun.
10. According to a *Bon Appetit* poll, four of the top ten restaurants in the world are in Paris, three—those ranking eighth, ninth, and tenth—are in the United States, two are in Tokyo and the other is in Thailand.

GO TO WEB

EXERCISE 7.11.3

Exercise 7.11.4

Test your mastery of semicolons and commas by correcting the punctuation in these sentences.

1. Growing old has never really bothered me in fact I consider aging a huge improvement over the alternative.
2. I visit a chiropractor twice a month, if I miss a treatment I have to crawl into work.

3. Our marketing campaign is based on sound principles, for example if we are sufficiently annoying people will buy our product just to make us go away.
4. The construction was so far behind schedule that we couldn't make up the time, consequently we lost our performance bonus our chance to bid on the next contract and an important client.
5. Among the many products being standardized by the European Community is the condom however a number of nations have officially complained that the standard size is too small.
6. Failing to stop at the light turned out to be the least of his offences the police were much more interested in his expired driving licence.
7. In her fridge we found a pound of butter dating from last August a mouldy piece of cake three containers of unidentifiable fur-bearing substances and an open can of beer.
8. A practice that works well in one country may not work in another for example every man in Switzerland is required to own a rifle. Such a policy might find acceptance in the United States however anyone who proposed it in Canada would be thought insane.
9. While some people find bird watching an exciting hobby and others are drawn to rock climbing or heli-skiing my own preference is for less strenuous pastimes such as those involving food.
10. To use or not to use the semicolon is sometimes a matter of the writer's choice, on the other hand, a few syntactical constructions require a semicolon, no other punctuation mark will do.

Punctuation

The Colon

The **colon** functions as an introducer. When a statement is followed by a list, one or more examples, or a quotation, the colon alerts the reader that some sort of explanatory detail is coming up.

When I travel, I am never without three things: sturdy shoes, a money belt, and my journal.

There is only one enemy we cannot defeat: time.

We have two choices: to study or to fail.

Early in his career, Robert Fulford did not think very highly of intellectual life in Canada: "My generation of Canadians grew up believing that, if we were very good or very smart, or both, we would someday *graduate* from Canada."

The statement that precedes the colon must be a complete sentence (independent clause).

A colon should never come immediately after *is* or *are*. Here's an example of what *not* to write.

The only things I am violently allergic to are: cats, ragweed, and country music.

This is incorrect because the statement before the colon is not a complete sentence.

1. Use a colon between an independent clause and a LIST or one or more EXAMPLES that define, explain, or illustrate the independent clause.

The information after the colon often answers the question "what?" or "who?"

I am violently allergic to three things: (what?) cats, ragweed, and country music.

Business and industry face a new challenge: (what?) rebuilding their pension funds.

The president has found the ideal candidate for the position: (who?) her brother.

2. Use a colon after a complete sentence introducing a quotation.

Lucille Ball observed that there were three secrets to staying young: "Live honestly, eat slowly, and lie about your age."

3. Finally, use a colon to separate the title of a book, film, or TV show from a subtitle.

Word Play: What Happens When People Talk

The Chronicles of Narnia: Prince Caspian

Trading Spouses: Meet Your New Mommy

If you remember the following summary, you'll have no more trouble with colons:

The colon follows an independent clause and introduces an example, a list, or a quotation that amplifies the meaning of that clause.

Punctuation

Exercise 7.12.1*

Put a check mark next to the sentences that are correctly punctuated. Check your answers before going on. Answers for this chapter begin on page 564.

1. _____ The most annoying sound in the world has to be that produced by: bagpipes.
2. _____ Three of Canada's highest awards in elite sports are the Stanley Cup, the Mann Cup, and the Grey Cup.
3. _____ Believe it or not, the country that produces the most films every year is: India.
4. _____ One topic has dominated the health concerns of the world since the late 1980s: AIDS.
5. _____ In the Okanagan Valley, the major fruit crops are: apples, peaches, and cherries.
6. _____ Sebastian wants to go home to be comforted by the only creature in the world who truly understands him: his beagle.
7. _____ Most students want their teachers to treat them with: courtesy, fairness, and respect.
8. _____ I have a real problem, my iPod is full.
9. _____ Our department's proposal is sure to receive funding, it has the CEO's approval.
10. _____ The company's bankruptcy resulted from a number of factors, including: the economic downturn, obsolete products, and excessively rich benefits for their unionized employees.

Exercise 7.12.2*

Insert colons in the following sentences where necessary and then check your answers. If you've made any mistakes, review the explanations on pages 468–69, study the examples, and be sure you understand why your answers were wrong before going on.

1. Right after we moved in, we discovered we had a problem termites.
2. I have set myself three goals this year to achieve an 80 percent average, to get a good summer job, and to buy a car.
3. After our bankruptcy, our credit card consultant asked us an interesting question "Why don't you cut up your credit cards?"
4. Many Canadian writers are better known abroad than they are at home Carol Shields, Neil Bissoondath, and Michael Ondaatje are three examples.
5. There are a number of inexpensive activities that will improve physical fitness; swimming, tennis, jogging, even brisk walking.

6. Jocelyn is trying to achieve two contradictory goals a significant weight loss and success as a restaurant critic.
7. Several of the animals on the international list of endangered species are native to Canada; the wood bison, the northern kit fox, and the whooping crane.
8. We'll finish the assignment by tomorrow only if we stay up all night and consume vast quantities of pizza and black coffee.
9. Canada's population is worn out and exhausted at the end of a long, hard winter, but most people are able to console themselves with one comforting thought, spring will arrive sometime in May or June.
10. There are several troublesome implications of biological engineering, but one in particular disturbs most people the cloning of human beings.

Exercise 7.12.3 *

Correct the incorrectly punctuated sentences in Exercise 7.12.1.

GO TO WEB

EXERCISES 7.12.1, 7.12.2, 7.12.3, 7.12.4

Exercise 7.12.4

The following paragraph contains 15 punctuation errors. Replace the incorrect punctuation marks—including the dashes—with colons and semicolons, as needed. (No other punctuation marks are required.)

Let's face facts, English is a crazy language. It lacks consistency! Students are often told to figure out the meaning of a word by considering its roots. How is this advice helpful when there is no egg in *eggplant*—no ham in *hamburger*—no dog in *hot dog*, no apple, let alone pine, in *pineapple*? English muffins were not invented in England, French fries did not originate in France.

And then there are plural noun forms, in English, these are wildly inconsistent. For example, the plural of *hoof* is *hooves*. The logical plural of *roof*

Punctuation

would be *rooves*, instead, it's *roofs*. Based on the analogy of *house* (singular) and *houses* (plural), the plural of *mouse* should be *mouses*, where did *mice* come from?

If you need further examples of the lunacy of our language, consider these, only in English do people recite at a play and play at a concert, ship by truck and send cargo by ship, and have noses that run and feet that smell. Only in English could the following paradoxes exist, a *slim chance* and a *fat chance* have the same meaning, a *wise man* and a *wise guy* are opposites. How can people be expected to figure out the meaning of sentences such as these—*They were too close to the door to close it, When I saw the tear in my silk shirt, I shed a tear*? It's a wonder anyone ever masters this loony language.

Adapted from Lederer, Richard. "English Is a Crazy Language." *Crazy English: The Ultimate Joy Ride through Our Language.* By Lederer. New York: Pocket Books, 1998. N. pag. Print.

Quotation Marks

Quotation marks are used to mark the beginning and end of direct speech (dialogue), quoted material, and some titles. For information on how to punctuate and insert quoted material into your papers, see pages 170–77. To review when to use quotation marks for titles, see page 183.

A **direct quotation** is someone's exact words, whether they are spoken or written. A quotation is usually introduced by a reporting expression such as *she said, he replied,* or *they commented.* Put quotation marks before and after the person's exact words.

Tim asked angrily, "Did you delete my address book?"

"No, a virus attacked the computer and ate your files," I replied.

Nearly 50 years ago, Marshall McLuhan observed, "The medium is the message."

Do not use quotation marks with **indirect quotations** (reported speech):

Tim asked angrily if I had deleted his address book. (These are not Tim's exact words, so no quotation marks are necessary.)

I replied that a virus had attacked his computer and destroyed his files. (Note that indirect quotations are often introduced by *that.*)

A half-century ago, Marshall McLuhan observed that the meaning of a message was determined by the medium through which it was delivered.

Use single quotation marks to enclose a quotation within a quotation:

"I don't understand what you mean by the term 'creative memory,'" said Lauren.

The final thing you need to know about direct quotations is how to punctuate them. Here are the rules to follow.

1. Use a comma to separate a reporting expression from a quotation.

Professor Lam announced, "You will write the midterm test on Tuesday."

"You will write the midterm test on Tuesday," announced Professor Lam.

2. If there is no reporting verb, use a colon after an independent clause to introduce a quotation.

Too late, I remembered Professor Lam's advice at the beginning of term: "Keep up with your work each week, and the tests will cause you no trouble."

3. Begin each quoted sentence with a capital letter. If a quoted sentence is divided into two parts, begin the second part with a small letter.

"Our national anthem," Justin informed us, "was written by Calixa Lavallée. First composed in French, it was later translated into English."

4. If the end punctuation is part of the direct quotation, put commas, periods, question marks, and exclamation marks *inside* the second quotation mark of a pair.

"Could you help me?" the woman asked. "I'm trying to find Melrose Avenue." Almost in tears, she went on, "I'm already late for my job interview!"

5. If the end punctuation is *not* part of the direct quotation, put it *outside* the second quotation mark. (It's part of your sentence, not the speaker's.)

Did you hear her say, "I'm late for my job interview"?

6. Put colons and semicolons *outside* the second quotation mark (unless they are part of the direct quotation).

Near tears, the woman begged, "Please help me"; we could hardly leave her standing there alone.

The woman cried, "Please help me"; she was near tears.

"Please help me; I'm late for my job interview," pleaded the woman.

Exercise 7.13.1*

Punctuate the following sentences correctly, using quotation marks and other punctuation marks where they are needed. Answers are provided on pages 565–66.

1. Did you see the look on her face asked Roderick.
2. Frank asked Jenna if she would like to play bridge.
3. I'd love to, she replied, if only I knew how.
4. Pardon me, boys, is this the Transylvania Station asked the man in the black cape.
5. When I pointed out to Wayne that he was wearing one green sock and one brown sock, he replied what's wrong with that? My brother has a pair just like it.
6. When I asked the guide if people jumped from the CN Tower very often, he replied no, just the once.
7. Pierre Trudeau once told Canadians that the state had no business in the nation's bedrooms.
8. Just as well, muttered Lola, because I wouldn't want the state to see what's growing on my bedroom windowsill.
9. I knew that Microsoft had lost its corporate mind when my computer flashed the following error message No keyboard detected. Press any key to continue.
10. The psychiatrist said to the woman whose husband thought he was a horse I can cure your husband, but it will take a long time and be very costly. Money is no object, replied the woman. He just won the Queen's Plate.

Punctuation

Question and Exclamation Marks

The Question Mark

Everyone knows that a question mark follows an interrogative (or asking) sentence, but everyone sometimes forgets to include it! Let this chapter serve as a reminder not to forget.

> The **question mark** is the end punctuation for all interrogative sentences.

The question mark gives your readers an important clue to the meaning of your sentence. "There's more?" is vastly different in meaning from "There's more!" and that difference is communicated to readers by punctuation.

The only time you don't end a question with a question mark is when the question is part of a statement.

Is anyone there? (question)

I asked if anyone was there. (statement)

Do you understand? (question)

I wonder whether you understand. (statement)

What costume have you decided on for the Halloween party? (question)

I'm curious to know what costume you've chosen for the Halloween party. (statement)

Supply the correct end punctuation for the following sentences. Then check your answers. Answers for this chapter are on page 566.

1. Do you ever wonder why we park in a driveway and drive on a parkway

2. I cannot understand how you can listen to that music

3. I find it hard to believe that you would question my integrity

4. I wonder if my apartment will ever be the same after their visit

5. What's another word for *thesaurus*

6. If we can't finish the project on time, will we lose the contract

7. I question the results you got on your survey

8. Did you know there are only 18 000 elephants in all of India

9. Human Resources wants to know why we hired an unqualified, inexperienced person for such a sensitive position

10. If corn oil comes from corn, where does baby oil come from

GO TO WEB

EXERCISES 7.14.1, 7.14.2

The Exclamation Mark

In informal or personal writings, the exclamation mark is a useful piece of punctuation for conveying **tone** to your readers. Consider the difference between these two sentences:

There's a man behind you.

There's a man behind you!

In the first sentence, information is being supplied, perhaps about the line-up at a grocery store checkout counter. The second sentence might be a shouted warning about a mugger.

> Use an **exclamation mark** as end punctuation in sentences requiring extreme emphasis or dramatic effect.

Exclamation marks have "punch" or dramatic effect only if you use them sparingly. If you use an exclamation mark after every third sentence, how will your readers know when you really mean to indicate excitement? Note also that exclamation marks are seldom used in academic or professional writing.

Practically any sentence could end with an exclamation mark, but remember that the punctuation changes the meaning of the sentence. Read each of the following sentences with and without an exclamation mark and picture the situation that would call for each reading.

He's gone   Don't touch that button

The room was empty   There she goes again

Exercise 7.14.2*

Supply the correct end punctuation for each of the following sentences. In many cases, the punctuation you use will depend on how you want the sentence to be read.

1. You must be kidding

2. Turn left Now

3. I can't believe I actually passed

4. Oh, great We're moving to Backwater, Alberta

5. Run It's right behind you

6. I'm freezing Turn up the heat

7. "Workers of the world, unite" (Karl Marx)

8. At last Someone is finally coming to take our order

9. For the last time, leave me alone

10. What a great game I've never seen a better one.

GO TO WEB

EXERCISES 7.14.3, 7.14.4, 7.14.5

Exercise 7.14.3

Supply appropriate end punctuation to the questions below. Note that some items include more than one sentence.

1. We asked whether there is intelligent life in Arkansas

2. Don't shoot I'm on your side

3. What in the world were you thinking when you had "file not found" tattooed on your arm

4. Whenever the power goes out, we wonder if the outage affects everyone or just us

5. Would you believe that the heaviest world-champion boxer, Primo Carnera, weighed 123 kg for a 1933 fight

6. That's one king-size heavyweight

7. Do you really believe that Al found a lamp that held a genie who gave him three wishes

8. That's outrageous

9. I often think about my future. Will I become an architect A fashion designer Or a movie director

10. Hooray This chapter is finished

Punctuation

Dashes and Parentheses

When you are talking with someone, you use your voice to punctuate: you pause for a short time (commas) or for a longer time (semicolons and periods), you shout (exclamation marks), or you query (question marks). In writing, punctuation substitutes for these vocal markers: it helps you ensure that your writing will make sense to your readers.

One way you can add variety and flexibility to your sentences is by inserting words or phrases that add to but are not essential to the sentence's meaning. That is, the word or words could be omitted and the sentence would still be complete and make sense. It might, however, lack grace or interest.

You can use three punctuation marks to add nonessential material to your sentences: commas, dashes, and parentheses. You are already familiar with the first one. Here is your opportunity to master the last two: the **dash**—which looks like this—and **parentheses** (round brackets). (If you are typing, the dash is two hyphens with no space between them or on either side.)

Dashes

Dashes are used to mark a break in thought or an abrupt shift in emphasis.

1. Use a dash or a pair of dashes to set off a series of items separated by commas.

I still love dried apricots, raisins, and pickled beets—foods my mother gave me as treats when I was a child.

Three qualities—perseverance, spirit, and skill—ensure a good game.

Atwood, Ondaatje, Laurence, Davies, Clarke, and Richler—for a country with a relatively small population, Canada has produced an extraordinary number of internationally acclaimed novelists.

2. Use a dash or a pair of dashes to set off from the rest of the sentence a climactic or emphatic moment.

Please welcome our new managers—Muhsin and Lisa.

Because they were afraid of the police, my so-called friends—Cory, Shane, and Mark—all betrayed me.

The apartment she showed me would have been fine, had it not been for the tenants—moths, cockroaches, and silverfish—already making it their home.

3. Use a dash to introduce a word, phrase, or clause that summarizes or restates what has just been said. (The dash in this context is interchangeable with a colon.)

I expect—and so does the college—that students at this level should be self-motivated.

Our neighbour—an animal-rights activist—keeps rabbits in his backyard.

If you really want to go—even though you haven't been invited—I'll take you.

Note that dashes set off material that is not grammatically part of the sentence. If you were to omit the words between the dashes, the sentence would still make sense.

Dashes can be misused if you use them too frequently. Unless you are writing informally—in a personal message, for instance—save dashes for the very occasional phrase to which you want to draw emphatic attention.

Punctuation

Exercise 7.15.1*

Add dashes where they are appropriate. Answers for this chapter begin on page 566.

1. One Aboriginal tribe in England painted themselves blue with dye made from a plant woad.
2. My purpose in moving from Vancouver to Hope like that of hundreds of people before me was to find affordable housing.
3. We will have to start without her again!
4. Skiing and skating if you like these sports, you'll love Quebec.
5. Tending to his garden, writing his memoirs, and dining with friends these were the pleasures Arnold looked forward to in retirement.
6. What is missing in his life is obvious rest and relaxation.
7. Zoe should do well in fact, I'm sure she will in the engineering program.
8. Alexei was amazed positively thunderstruck when he heard that Uncle Vladimir had won a million dollars.
9. Historians, diarists, and memoirists these are the recorders of our past.
10. Dashes a kind of silent shout allow you to insert an occasional exclamatory word or phrase into your sentences.

Parentheses

Like dashes, parentheses are used to enclose an interruption in a sentence. The difference between them is a matter of tone: dashes SHOUT—they serve to draw the reader's attention to the material they enclose—but parentheses (which should be used sparingly) "whisper." Parentheses are similar to theatrical asides; they are subordinate to the main action but are not to be missed.

1. Use parentheses around additional information that you wish to include but not emphasize.

Marita's teaching schedule (she is in class seven hours a day) gives her little time to meet with students individually.

They brought me to their village and presented me to their chief (a woman) and to the tribal councillors.

Note the difference in tone your choice of punctuation makes. Compare the examples above with the following versions.

Marita's teaching schedule—she is in class seven hours a day—gives her little time to meet with students individually.

They brought me to their village and presented me to their chief—a woman—and to the tribal councillors.

2. Use parentheses to enclose explanatory material that is not part of the main sentence.

"Looking Both Ways" (an essay in Part 5) was written by a student in her first year of college.

The Malagasy (people of Madagascar) like to eat a kapoaka of rice (enough to fill a condensed-milk can) three times a day.

3. Use parentheses to enclose reference data in a research paper. (See Chapter 13.)

Exercise 7.15.2*

Add parentheses where they are appropriate.

1. Five of the students I was asked not to name them have volunteered to be peer tutors.
2. The apostrophe is explained in Section 7.17 on pages 499–506.
3. Jason complained that being a manager he became one in March was like being a cop.
4. I have enclosed a cheque for one hundred and fifty dollars $150.
5. More members of the Canadian Forces died in World War I 1914–18 than in any war before or since.
6. Although Mozart lived a relatively short time he died when he was 36, he composed hundreds of musical masterpieces.
7. As news of her "miracle cures" spread patients began to come to her from all over the province, the doctor had to move her clinic to a more central location.
8. The new contract provided improved working conditions, a raise in salary 3 percent, and a new dental plan.

Punctuation

9. Ontario and British Columbia now produce award-winning, world-class wines from small estate wineries Inniskillin, Hillebrand, and Quails' Gate are three examples.

10. "One of the most important tools for making paper speak in your own voice is punctuation; it helps readers hear you the way you want to be heard" Baker 48–49.

GO TO WEB

EXERCISE 7.15.1

Exercise 7.15.3

Insert dashes and parentheses where appropriate in the following sentences.

1. The function of parentheses see the explanation on pages 482–83 is to mark off material that interrupts the main idea of the sentence and that the writer does not want to emphasize.

2. Dashes, on the other hand bold, dramatic dashes are used to set off an emphatic interjection.

3. We should we must find a way to cut expenses by at least 10 percent.

4. On their first and last date, Rupert took Freda bowling.

5. Proof of the need for investment in infrastructure see the appendix to the *Building Committee Report* is that the building has twice failed fire code inspections.

6. We wanted it to be warm for our week at the ocean, but it was so hot 40 degrees that we didn't even want to leave the hotel to go to the beach.

7. This comic book comics may not be great literature, but they are important cultural documents cost me 10 cents and is now worth more than $4000.

8. There are a few people obnoxious people like Dwight and Daisy who light up the room when they leave.

9. For my birthday, my sister gave me a pair of hand-knit socks I'm allergic to wool, a box of chocolates I'm on a diet, and a coffee mug with the Nortel logo on it.

10. Canadian sports broadcaster Foster Hewitt created a sports catch phrase "He shoots! He scores!" during an overtime game between the Rangers and the Leafs on April 4, 1933. The Rangers won.

Exercise 7.15.4

Correct the following paragraph, which contains 20 errors (each set of dashes and parentheses counts as two errors).

As a final review of punctuation here's a paragraph that should contain all the punctuation marks we have discussed in this section of the book however 20 pieces of punctuation are missing. Your job is to provide the missing punctuation. Let's quickly deal with punctuation marks one by one. The comma probably the hardest-working of them all is used to separate items in a series to set off nonessential material to join with a conjunction two separate independent clauses and to set off material that comes before a main clause. Whew. The semicolon can replace a period it often separates two independent clauses that are closely connected in meaning. The colon has a different function it follows an independent clause and introduces a list a clarification or a quotation. Did you remember that a colon should never follow "is" or "are". A question mark must be used at the end of all interrogative sentences. We all know this but sometimes we forget. Exclamation marks are used at the end of sentences for one purpose only to supply dramatic effect. But remember that they are seldom used in academic writing. Finally dashes and parentheses allow a writer to interrupt a train of thought and insert an "aside" into a sentence. That's it. If you have correctly inserted all the punctuation in this paragraph then you are ready to tackle hazardous homonyms.

Hazardous Homonyms

This chapter focuses on homonyms—words that sound alike or look alike and are easily confused: *accept* and *except*; *weather* and *whether*; *whose* and *who's*; *affect* and *effect*. A spell checker will not help you find spelling mistakes in these words because the "correct" spelling depends on the sentence in which you use the word. For example, if you write, "Meat me hear inn halve an our," no spell checker will find fault with your sentence—and no reader will understand what you're talking about.

Careful pronunciation can sometimes help you tell the difference between words that are often confused. For example, if you pronounce the words *accept* and *except* differently, you'll be less likely to use the wrong one when you write. You can also make up memory aids to help you remember the difference in meaning between words that sound or look alike.

Below is a list of the most common homonym hazards together with some word pairs that, while technically not homonyms, are often confused. Only some of the words on this list will cause you trouble. Make your own list of problem pairs and tape it on the inside cover of your dictionary or post it close to your computer. Get into the habit of checking your document against your list every time you write.

accept except	*Accept* means "take" or "receive." It is always a verb. *Except* means "excluding." I **accepted** the spelling award, and no one **except** my mother knew I cheated.
advice advise	The difference in pronunciation makes the difference in meaning clear. *Advise* (rhymes with *wise*) is a verb. *Advice* (rhymes with *nice*) is a noun. I *advise* you not to listen to free *advice.*

affect **effect**	*Affect* as a verb means "change." Try substituting *change* for the word you've chosen in your sentence. If it makes sense, then *afFECT* is the word you want. As a noun, *AFfect* means "a strong feeling." *Effect* is a noun meaning "result." If you can substitute *result,* then *effect* is the word you need. Occasionally, *effect* is used as a verb meaning "to bring about."

> Learning about the *effects* (results) of caffeine *affected* (changed) my coffee-drinking habits.
> Depressed people often display inappropriate *affect* (feelings).
> Antidepressant medications can *effect* (bring about) profound changes in mood.

a lot **allot**	*A lot* (often misspelled *alot*) should be avoided in formal writing. Use *many* or *much* instead. *Allot* means "distribute" or "assign."

>   *many*   *much*
> He still has a̶ ̶l̶o̶t̶ ̶o̶f̶ problems, but he is coping a̶ ̶l̶o̶t̶ better.
> The teacher will *allot* the marks according to the difficulty of the questions.

aloud **allowed**	*Aloud* means out loud, not a whisper. *Allowed* means permitted.

> We were not *allowed* to speak *aloud* during the performance.

amount **number**	*Amount* is used with uncountable things; *number* is used with countable things.

> You may have a large *number* of jelly beans in a jar but a small *amount* of candy.
> (Jelly beans are countable; candy is not.)

are **our**	*Are* is a verb. *Our* shows ownership.

> Marie-Claire Blais and Margaret Atwood *are* two of Canada's best-known writers.

> Canada is *our* home and native land.

assure **ensure** **insure**	*Assure* means "state with confidence; pledge or promise."

> She *assured* him she would keep his letters always.

> The prime minister *assured* the Inuit their concerns would be addressed in the next budget.

Spelling

Ensure means "make certain of something."

> The extra $20 will *ensure* that you get a good seat.

> No number of promises can *ensure* that love will last.

Insure means "guarantee against financial loss." We *insure* lives and property.

> Kevin *insured* the parcel before he sent it.

> We have *insured* both our home and our car against fire and theft.

choose
chose

Pronunciation is the clue here. *Choose* rhymes with *booze* and means "select." *Chose* rhymes with *rose* and means "selected." (Some people would *choose* booze before flowers.)

> Please *choose* a topic.

> I *chose* filmmaking.

cite
sight
site

To *cite* is to quote or mention. A lawyer *cites* precedents. Writers *cite* their sources in research papers. You might *cite* a comedian for her wit or a politician for his honesty. A *site* is a place (where something is *situated*).

> You have included only Internet sources in your Works *Cited* list.

> Tiananmen Square is the *site* of the massacre.

> Pape and Mortimer is the *site* of our new industrial design centre.

A *sight* is something you see.

> The view over the Plains of Abraham is an unforgettable *sight*.

> With his tattooed forehead and three nose rings, he was a *sight* to behold.

coarse
course

Coarse means "rough, unrefined." (Remember: The word *arse* is co*arse*.) For all other meanings, use *course*.

> That sandpaper is too *coarse*.
> You'll enjoy the photography *course*.
> Of *course* you'll do well.

complement compliment	A *complement* completes something. A *compliment* is a **gift** of praise.

> A glass of wine would be the perfect *complement* to the meal.
>
> Some people are embarrassed by *compliments*.

conscience conscious	Your *conscience* is your sense of right and wrong. *Conscious* means "aware" or "awake"—able to feel and think.

> After Katy cheated on the test, her *conscience* bothered her.
>
> Katy was *conscious* of having done wrong.
>
> The injured man was *unconscious* for an hour.

consul council counsel	A *consul* is a government official stationed in another country. A *council* is an assembly or official group. (Members of a council are *councillors*.) *Counsel* can be used to mean both "advice" and "to advise." (Those who give advice are *counsellors*.)

> The Canadian *consul* in Mexico was very helpful.
>
> The Women's Advisory *Council* meets next month.
>
> Maria gave me good *counsel*.
>
> She *counselled* me to hire a lawyer.

continual continuous	*Continual* refers to an action that goes on regularly but with interruptions. *Continuous* refers to an action that goes on without interruption.

> The student *continually* tried to interrupt the lecturer, who droned on *continuously*.
>
> There is a *continuous* flow of traffic during rush hour.

credible credulous creditable	*Credible* means "believable." A person who believes an incredible story is *credulous*.

> Nell was fortunate that the police officer found her story *credible*.
>
> My brother is so *credulous* that we call him Gullible Gus.

Creditable means "worthy of reward or praise."

> After two wasted semesters, Ellen is finally doing *creditable* work.

Spelling

desert dessert	A *DESert* is a dry, barren place. As a verb, *deSERT* means "leave behind." *DESSERT* is the part of the meal you'd probably like a double serving of, so give it a double *s*. The tundra is Canada's only *desert* region. While technically the night watchman did not *desert* his post, he did sleep on the job. *Dessert* is my favourite part of the meal.
dining dinning	You'll spell *dining* correctly if you remember the phrase "wining and dining." You'll probably never use *dinning*. It means "making a loud noise." The children are in the *dining* room. We are *dining* out tonight. The noise from the bar was *dinning* in our ears.
disburse disperse	*Disburse* means "to pay out money," which is what **bursars** do. *Disperse* means "to break up"; crowds are sometimes *dispersed* by the police. The college's financial-aid officer will *disburse* the students' loans at the end of this week. The protesters were *dispersed* by the police.
does dose	Pronunciation provides the clue. *Does* rhymes with *buzz* and is a verb. *Dose* rhymes with *gross* and refers to a quantity of medicine. John *does* drive quickly, doesn't he? My grandmother gave me a *dose* of cod liver oil.
farther further	You'll have no trouble distinguishing between these two if you associate *farther* with *distance* (think "far") and *further* with *time*. Ralph wanted me to walk a little *farther* so we could discuss our relationship *further*.
faze phase	*Fazed* usually has a *not* before it; to be *not fazed* means to be not disturbed, or concerned, or taken aback. *Phase* means "stage of development or process."

Unfortunately, Theo was not *fazed* by his disastrous grade report.

Since Mei Ling works full-time, she has decided to complete her degree in *phases*.

fewer
less

Fewer is used with countable things. *Less* is used with uncountable things.

In May, there are *fewer* students in the college, so there is *less* work for the faculty to do.

The *fewer* attempts you make, the *less* your chance of success.

With units of money or measurement, however, use *less*:

I have *less* than $20 in my wallet.

Our house is on a lot that is *less* than four metres wide.

forth
fourth

Forth means "for**ward**" or "onward." *Fourth* contains the number *four*, which gives it its meaning.

Please stop pacing back and *forth*.

The BC Lions lost their *fourth* game in a row.

hear
here

Hear is what you do with your **ear**s. *Here* is used for all other meanings.

Now *hear* this!

Ray isn't *here*.

Here is your assignment.

imply
infer

A speaker or writer *implies*; a listener or reader *infers*. To *imply* is to hint or say something indirectly. To *infer* is to draw a conclusion from what is stated or hinted at.

In her introduction of the speaker, Carol *implied* that she greatly admired the mayor.

I *inferred* from the mayor's remarks that he was very fond of Carol.

it's its	*It's* is a shortened form of *it is.* (The apostrophe takes the place of the *i* in *is.*) If you can substitute *it is,* then *it's* is the form you need. If you can't substitute *it is,* then *its* is the correct word.

> *It's* really not difficult. (*It is* really not difficult.)
>
> The book has lost *its* cover. ("The book has lost *it is* cover" makes no sense, so you need *its.*)

It's is also commonly used as the shortened form of *it has.* (In this case, the apostrophe replaces the *ha* in *has.*)

> *It's* been a good year. (It has been a good year.)

later latter	**Later** refers to time and has the word **late** in it. *Latter* means "the second of two" and has two *ts.* It is the opposite of *former.*

> It is *later* than you think.
>
> You take the former, and I'll take the *latter.*

loose lose	Pronunciation is the key to these words. *Loose* rhymes with *goose* and means "not tight." *Lose* rhymes with *booze* and means "misplace" or "be defeated."

> A *loose* electrical connection is dangerous.
>
> Some are born to win, some to *lose.*

martial marshal	*Martial* refers to warfare or military affairs. *Marshal* has two meanings. As a noun, it refers to a person of high office, either in the military or (especially in the United States) the police. As a verb, it means to arrange or assemble in order.

> She is a *martial* arts enthusiast.
>
> When the troops were *marshalled* on the parade grounds, they were reviewed by the army *marshal.*

miner minor	A **miner** works in a **mine.** *Minor* means "lesser" or "not important" or refers to a person of less than legal age.

> Liquor can be served to *miners,* but not if they are *minors.*
>
> For me, spelling is a *minor* problem.

moral morale	Again, pronunciation provides the clue you need. Moral refers to the understanding of what is right and wrong. Morale refers to the spirit or mental condition of a person or group.

People often have to make *moral* decisions.
The low *morale* of the workers prompted the strike.

peace piece	*Peace* is what we want on **Earth**. *Piece* means "a part or por-tion of something," as in "a **piece** of **pie**."

Everyone hopes for *peace* in the Middle East.
A *piece* of the puzzle is missing.

personal personnel	*Personal* means "private." *Personnel* refers to the group of people working for a particular employer or to the office responsible for maintaining employees' records.

The file was marked *"Personal* and Confidential."
We are fortunate in having qualified *personnel.*
Fatima works in the *Personnel* Office.

principal principle	*Principal* means "main." A *principle* is a ru**le**.

A *principal* is the main administrator of a school.
Oil is Alberta's *principal* industry.
I make it a *principle* to submit my essays on time.

quiet quite	If you pronounce these words carefully, you won't confuse them. *Quiet* has two syllables; *quite* has only one.

The librarian asked us to be *quiet*.
We had not *quite* finished our homework.

roll role	Turning over and over like a wheel is to *roll*; a bun is also a *roll*. An actor in a play has a *role*.

His *role* called for him to fall to the ground and *roll* into
a ditch, all the while munching on a bread *roll.*

Spelling

simple simplistic	*Simple* means uncomplicated, easily understood. Something described as *simplistic* is too simple to be acceptable: essential details or complexities have been overlooked.

> This problem is far from *simple.* Your solution to it is *simplistic.*

stationary stationery	*Stationary* means "fixed in place." *Stationery* is writing paper.

> Sarah Ferguson works out on a *stationary* bicycle.
> No matter how far you push the envelope, it is still *stationery.*

than then	*Than* is used in comparisons. Pronounce it to rhyme with *can. Then* refers to time and rhymes with *when.*

> Rudi is a better speller *than* I.
> He made his decision *then.*
> Eva withdrew from the competition; *then* she realized the consequences.

their there they're	*Their* indicates ownership. *There* points out something or indicates place. It includes the word *here,* which also indicates place. *They're* is a shortened form of *they are.* (The apostrophe replaces the *a* in *are.*)

> It was *their* fault.
> *There* are two weeks left in the term.
> You should look over *there.*
> *They're* late, as usual.

too two to	The *too* with an extra *o* in it means "more than enough" or "also." *Two* is the number after one. For all other meanings, use *to.*

> He thinks he's been working *too* hard. She thinks so, *too.*
> There are *two* sides *to* every argument.
> The *two* women knew *too* much about each other ever *to* be friends.

weather whether wether	*Whether* means "which of the two" and is used in all cases when you aren't referring to climatic conditions (*weather*). A *wether* is a castrated ram, so that word's uses are limited.

Whether you're ready or not, it's time to go.

No one immigrates to Canada for its *weather.*

were
where
we're

If you pronounce these three carefully, you won't confuse them. *Were* rhymes with *purr* and is a verb. *Where* is pronounced "hwear," includes the word **here**, and indicates place. *We're* is a shortened form of *we are* and is pronounced "weer."

You *were* joking, *weren't* you?

Where did you want to meet?

We're on our way.

who's
whose

Who's is a shortened form of *who is* or *who has*. If you can substitute *who is* or *who has* for the *who's* in your sentence, then you are using the right spelling. Otherwise, use *whose*.

Who's coming to dinner? (*Who is* coming to dinner?)

Who's been sleeping in my bed? (*Who has* been sleeping in my bed?)

Whose calculator is this? ("*Who is* calculator" makes no sense, so you need *whose*.)

woman
women

Confusing these two is guaranteed to irritate your female readers. *Wo**man*** is the singular form; compare **man**. *Wo**men*** is the plural form; compare **men**.

A *woman's* place is wherever she chooses to be.

The *women's* movement promotes equality between *women* and men.

you're
your

You're is a shortened form of *you are*. If you can substitute *you are* for the *you're* in your sentence, then you're using the correct form. If you can't substitute *you are*, use *your*.

You're welcome. (*You are* welcome.)

Unfortunately, *your* hamburger got burned. ("*You are* hamburger" makes no sense, so *your* is the word you want.)

Spelling

In Exercises 17.16.1 and 17.16.2, choose the correct word from those in parentheses. If you don't know an answer, go back and reread the explanation. Check your answers after each set. Answers for this chapter begin on page 567.

Exercise 7.16.1*

1. The limited (coarse course) selection will (affect effect) our academic development and subsequent job opportunities.
2. (Are Our) you going to (accept except) the offer?
3. Eat your vegetables; (than then) you can have your (desert dessert).
4. If (your you're) overweight by 20 kg, (loosing losing) the excess will be a long-term proposition.
5. It's (quiet quite) true that they did not get (hear here) until the party was over.
6. It is usually the saint, not the sinner, (who's whose) (conscience conscious) is troubled.
7. He (assured ensured insured) me he would keep the (amount number) of changes to a minimum.
8. (Its It's) hard to tell the dog from (its it's) owner.
9. To (choose chose) a (coarse course) of action against your lawyer's (advice advise) would be foolish.
10. (Continual Continuous) (dining dinning) out becomes boring after a while.

Exercise 7.16.2*

1. By reading between the lines, we can (infer imply) (wether weather whether) the author intends his (forth fourth) chapter to be taken seriously.
2. (Who's Whose) (principals principles) are so firm that they wouldn't pay (fewer less) tax if they could get away with it?
3. The (affect effect) of trying to (disperse disburse) a mob of (less fewer) than 20 people was to cause a riot involving hundreds.
4. The chief librarian did not mean to (imply infer) that (farther further) cuts to services are being considered by the board, which, in the circumstances, has done a very (credible credulous creditable) job.
5. After the accident, the (moral morale) of the (miners minors) did not recover for many months, but the owners appeared not to be (fazed phased) by the disaster.
6. It is (simple simplistic) to claim that our society's (morals morales) have declined over the last 20 years; to do so (infers implies) that morality is an absolute value.

7. It's (your you're) fault that we are (continually continuously) harassed by salespeople because your welcoming smile (assures insures ensures) that they will return again and again.

8. Are you (conscious conscience) of the fact that (choosing chosing) this (site cite sight) for your business will take you (farther further) away from your client base?

9. Gloria could not (accept except) the fact that the (councillors counsellors) rejected her plan to (phase faze) out parking in the downtown core.

10. The (amount number) of people (aloud allowed) to participate depends on (fewer less) (then than) a dozen (woman women) who are entrusted with making the decision.

Exercise 7.16.3*

Each of the items below is followed by two statements. Identify the one that makes sense as a follow-up to the introductory sentence.

1. All former students will be welcomed back to class.
   a. We will except all former students.
   b. We will accept all former students.
2. The lawn mower next door has been running nonstop for over an hour.
   a. The continual noise is driving me crazy.
   b. The continuous noise is driving me crazy.
3. This author only hints at how the story ends.
   a. She implies that they live happily ever after.
   b. She infers that they live happily ever after.
4. Your proposal is not worth our consideration
   a. It's simple.
   b. It's simplistic.
5. We're looking for a female role model.
   a. The women must lead by example.
   b. The woman must lead by example.
6. How many assistants will be required?
   a. The amount of helpers we will need is hard to estimate.
   b. The number of helpers we will need is hard to estimate.
7. While their skill sets are very different, together, the two make a good team.
   a. She compliments his weaknesses.
   b. She complements his weaknesses.
8. Are you permitted to talk during the lectures?
   a. It is not allowed.
   b. It is not aloud.

Spelling

9. Where did she wake up?
   a. She regained her conscience in the hospital.
   b. She regained her consciousness in the hospital.
10. How close are we to the cottage?
   a. We have only a little farther to go.
   b. We have only a little further to go.

GO TO WEB

EXERCISES   7.16.1, 7.16.2, 7.16.3, 7.16.4

Exercise 7.16.4

Now test your mastery of homonyms by correcting the 10 errors in the following paragraph.

I would advice anyone who's schedule seems to be full to try the solution I came up with less then three months ago. I pulled the plug on my TV. Overwhelmed with assignments and unable to chose among priorities, I realized I was making the problem worse by sitting for three or four hours a night in front of the tube. I decided I should spend more time on my coarses and less on watching television. To avoid temptation, I put the TV set in the closet. The results have been more dramatic then I thought possible. My apartment is now a haven of piece and quiet, and some of my assignments are actually handed in before their due. Occasionally there is a twinge of regret that I no longer know whose doing what to whom in the latest reality contest, but overall, I'm much happier for choosing to loose the tube.

The Apostrophe

Most punctuation marks indicate the relationship among parts of a sentence. Apostrophes and hyphens, on the other hand, indicate the relationship between the elements of a word. That's why we've chosen to discuss them in this section, along with other spelling issues.

Misused apostrophes display a writer's ignorance or carelessness. They can also confuse, amuse, and sometimes annoy readers.

- Sometimes you need an apostrophe so that your reader can understand what you mean. For example, there's a world of difference between these two sentences:

  The instructor began class by calling the students' names.

  The instructor began class by calling the students names.

- In most cases, however, misused apostrophes just amuse or irritate an alert reader:

  The movie had it's moments.

  He does a days work for every weeks salary.

  The Lion's thank you for your contribution.

It isn't difficult to avoid such mistakes. Correctly used, the apostrophe indicates either **contraction** or **possession**. It never makes a singular word plural. Learn the simple rules that govern these uses and you'll have no further trouble with apostrophes.

Contraction

Contraction is the combining of two words into one, as in *they're* or *can't*. Contractions are common in conversation and in informal written English. Unless you are quoting someone else's words, however, you should avoid them in the writing you do for school or work.

The rule about where to put an apostrophe in a contraction is one of those rare rules that has no exception. It *always* holds.

> When two words are combined into one, and one or more letters are left out, the apostrophe goes in the place of the missing letter(s).

Here are some examples.

I am	→ I'm	they are	→ they're
we will	→ we'll	it is	→ it's
she is	→ she's	it has	→ it's
do not	→ don't	who is	→ who's

Exercise 7.17.1*

Correct these sentences by placing apostrophes where needed. Answers for this section begin on page 568.

1. Who knows whats wrong with this sentence?
2. Shes only a whiskey maker, but he loves her still.
3. Its a long way from Halifax to Vancouver, but we think were ready: weve been in training since August.
4. No matter how much well push the envelope, itll always be stationery.
5. Wasnt it Mark Twain who said, "Its easy to stop smoking; Ive done it dozens of times"?

GO TO WEB

EXERCISES 7.17.1, 7.17.2

Exercise 7.17.2*

In some formal kinds of writing—academic, legal, and technical, for example—contractions are not acceptable. A good writer is able not only to contract two words into one, but also to expand contractions into their original forms. In the following paragraph, find and expand the contractions into two-word phrases (e.g., he'll = he will).

I'm writing to apply for the position of webmaster for BrilloVision.com that you've advertised in the *Daily News*. I've got the talent and background you're looking for. Currently, I work as a Web designer for an online publication, Vexed.com, where they're very pleased with my work. If you click on their website, I think you'll like what you see. There's little in the way of Web design and application that I haven't been involved in during the past two years. But it's time for me to move on to a new challenge, and BrilloVision.com promises the kind of opportunity I'm looking for. I guarantee you won't be disappointed if I join your team!

Possession

The apostrophe is also used to show ownership or possession. Here is the rule that applies in most cases.

Add *'s* to the word that indicates the *owner*.
If the resulting word ends in a double or triple *s*, delete the last *s*, leaving the apostrophe in place.[1]

---

[1]Many writers today prefer to keep the final *s* when it represents a sound that is pronounced, as it is in one-syllable words such as *boss* and *class*, and in some names such as *Harris* and *Marcus*.

Spelling

Here are some examples that illustrate the rule.

woman + 's = woman's voice   women + 's = women's voices
student + 's = student's transcript   students + 's = students' ş transcripts
player + 's = player's uniform   players + 's = players' ş uniforms

To form a possessive correctly, you must first identify the word in the sentence that indicates possession and determine whether it is singular or plural. For example, "the managers duties" can have two meanings, depending on where you put the apostrophe:

the manager's duties (the duties belong to one *manager*)
the managers' duties (the duties belong to two or more *managers*)

To solve an apostrophe problem, follow this two-step process:
1. Find the owner word.
2. Apply the possession rule.

Problem: Carmens hair is a mess.
Solution: 1. The word that indicates possession is *Carmen* (singular).
2. Add *'s* to *Carmen*.

Carmen's hair is a mess.

Problem: The technicians strike halted the production.
Solution: 1. The word that indicates possession is *technicians* (plural).
2. Add *'s* to *technicians*, then delete the second *s*, leaving the apostrophe.

The *technicians'* strike halted the production.

Sometimes the meaning of your sentence is determined by where you put the apostrophe.

Problem: I was delighted by the critics response to my book.

Now you have two possibilities to choose from, depending on your meaning.

Solution A: 1. The owner word is *critic* (singular).
2. Add *'s* to *critic*.

I was delighted by the *critic's* response to my book.

Solution B: 1. The owner word is *critics* (plural).

2. Add *'s* to *critics*, then drop the second *s*, leaving the apostrophe.

I was delighted by the *critics'* response to my book.

Both solutions are correct, depending on whether the book was reviewed by one critic (A) or by more than one critic (B).

Possession does not have to be literal. It can be used to express the notion of "belonging to" or "associated with." That is, the owner word need not refer to a person or group of people. Ideas or concepts (abstract nouns) can be "owners" too.

a month's vacation = a vacation of one month
a year's salary = the salary of one year
"A Hard Day's Night" = the night that follows a hard day

Note that a few words, called **possessive pronouns**, are already possessive in form, so they don't have apostrophes.[2]

yours	ours	whose
hers, his, its	theirs	

His music is not like *yours.*

Whose lyrics do you prefer, *theirs* or *ours?*

The dog lost *its* bone.

Four of these possessive pronouns are often confused with the contractions that sound like them. It's worth taking a moment to learn how to avoid this confusion. When you are trying to decide which spelling to use,

1. Expand the contraction into its original two words.
2. Then substitute those words for the contraction in your sentence.
3. If the sentence still makes sense, use the contraction. If it doesn't, use the possessive spelling.

---

[2]If you add an apostrophe to any of these words, you create an error. There are no such words as *your's, her's, their's,* or *our's.*

Spelling

Possessive		Contraction	
its	= *It* owns something	it's	= it is/it has
their	= *They* own something	they're	= they are
whose	= *Who* owns something	who's	= who is
your	= *You* own something	you're	= you are

Error: They're (they are) going to sing they're (~~they are~~) latest song.
Revision: They're going to sing *their* latest song.

Error: You're (~~you are~~) parents were thrilled by you're (~~you are~~) achievement.
Revision: *Your* parents were thrilled by *your* achievement.

Exercises 7.17.3 and 17.17.4 will test and reinforce your understanding of both contraction and possession.

Exercise 7.17.3*

Correct the following sentences by adding apostrophes where necessary.

1. The cars brakes are worn and its tires are nearly bald.
2. Diplomatic ambassadors wives or husbands are often as important to a missions success as the ambassadors themselves.
3. Near Chicoutimi is one of the countrys most beautiful parks, where the skills of canoeists, fishermen, and wildlife photographers can be put to the test on a summers day.
4. Janes career got its start when she sang seafarers songs in the yacht clubs dining lounge.
5. A countrys history is the main determinant of its national character.

Exercise 7.17.4*

In each of the sentences below, choose the correct word from those in parentheses. Check your answers before going on.

1. Where (your you're) going, (your you're) biggest problem will be maintaining (your you're) tan.
2. (Someones Someone's) got to take responsibility for the cats and dogs (whose who's) owners have abandoned them.
3. The (ships ship's ships') captain agreed to donate a (weeks week's weeks') salary to the Scott Mission.
4. Contrary to some (people's peoples) opinions, postal (workers worker's workers') contracts are most often settled by both (sides side's sides') willingness to bend long before a strike is necessary.
5. My (turtles turtle's) legs are shorter than your (turtles turtle's), but I bet (its it's) going to run (its it's) laps faster than (yours your's).

EXERCISES 7.17.3, 7.17.4

Plurals

The third apostrophe rule is very simple. Memorize it, apply it, and you will instantly correct many of your apostrophe errors.

Never use an apostrophe to make a word plural.

The plural of most English words is formed by adding *s* to the root word (not *'s*). The *s* alone tells the reader that the word is plural: e.g., *memos, letters, files, broadcasts, newspapers, journalists*. If you add an apostrophe + *s*, you are telling your reader that the word is either a contraction or a possessive.

Incorrect: Never use apostrophe's to make word's plural.
Correct: Never use apostrophes to make words plural.

Exercise 7.17.5*

Correct the misused and missing apostrophes in the following sentences. There are 10 errors in this exercise.

1. Two silkworm's had a race; they ended up in a tie.

2. When you feel like a snack, you can choose between apples and Timbit's.

3. Teds career took off when he discovered how easy it was to sell childrens toy's to grandparents.

4. A beginning golfer needs three different kinds of clubs: wood's for long shots, iron's for short ones, and a putter for the last four or five shots.

5. Good writing skill's wont guarantee success in you're career, but poor writing skill's are guaranteed to hold you back.

Exercise 7.17.6

Before you try the final exercise in this chapter, carefully review the information in the Summary box below. Then test your mastery of apostrophes by correcting the 15 errors in the passage below.

The following advisory for American's heading to Canada was compiled from information provided by the U.S. State Department and the CIA. It is intended as a guide for American traveller's:

Canada is a large foreign country, even bigger than Texas. It has 10 states (called provinces) and it's only neighbour is America. Canadas contributions to Western civilization include back bacon, hockey players, geese, doughnut's, and the Mountie's red uniform's.

Canadians stand in line without complaining, seldom raise they're voices, and cheer politely when the home or visiting teams players do something worthwhile. Canada has two language's: French and American. Some linguistic oddities include "eh," which can turn any statement into a question, and the pronunciation of *ou* as *uoo*, as in *huoose* or *abuoot*.

The bright colour's and funny picture's of Canadian currency may make the unwary tourist think of it as play money, but each blue Canadian five-dollar bill is worth about four real dollars. The one- and two-dollar coins, called loonies and toonies, make good souvenir's.

The Canadian government is somewhat left-leaning, providing health care for all and refusing to execute criminal's. Tourists are advised to avoid political discussions and to remember that politician's in Canada are like politician's anywhere: popular with some people, unpopular with others.

Summary

- When contracting two words into one, put an apostrophe in the place of the missing letter(s).
- Watch for owner words: they need apostrophes.
- To indicate possession, add *'s* to the owner word. (If the owner word already ends in *s*, just add the apostrophe.)
- Possessive pronouns (e.g., *yours, its, ours*) do not take apostrophes.
- Never use an apostrophe to form the plural of a word.

The Hyphen

The **hyphen** (-) has three different functions:

- as part of the correct spelling of a word (e.g., mother-in-law, self-esteem)
- to divide a word at the end of a line
- to separate or join two or more words or parts of words. There are five rules to follow.

1. Use a hyphen to divide a word at the end of a written or typed line.

Your dictionary tells you where words can be divided. Most dictionaries mark the syllables of a word with a dot: syl·lables = syl-lables.

Never divide a word of only one or two syllables. Use a hyphen at the end of a line for words of three or more syllables (e.g., commu-nity). If the word is already hyphenated (e.g., self-reliance, ex-president), break it after the hyphen.

2. Use a hyphen to separate a prefix from the main word when two of the same vowels occur together.

Examples: re-elected, co-operate, anti-imperalism

When the two vowels are different, however, no hyphen is required:

semiautomatic, realign, preamble

3. Use a hyphen with compound numbers from twenty-one to ninety-nine, with fractions, and with dimensions.

Examples: forty-six, one-eighth, ninety-eight, six- by eight-metre room

Spelling

4. Use a hyphen to join two or more words that serve as an adjective *before* a noun.

Examples: The (first-born) child is often the best loved.

The (best-loved) child is often the first born.

(Word-of-mouth) advertising is very effective.

A good writer has a (well-thumbed, up-to-date) dictionary.

5. Use a hyphen to avoid ambiguity.

Consider the differences in meaning between the following pairs of statements:

Examples: I resent everything you asked for. (I'm angry.)

I re-sent everything you asked for. (I sent it all again.)

The contractor re-covered the roof with asphalt shingles. (He repaired the roof.)

The contractor recovered his money. (He got his money back.)

The government's plan provided for nursing-home care. (care in a nursing home)

The government's plan provided for nursing home-care. (care at home by nurses)

The prime minister will address small business owners. (Do you really want to say he will talk only to short people?)

The prime minister will address small-business owners. (These people are owners of small businesses.)

Exercise 7.18.1*

Most of the following sentences require one or more hyphens. Review the rules in the boxes above, then try your hand at correcting these sentences. Answers for this chapter are on page 569.

1. Joy wants to sublet her fifth floor apartment.
2. In 1950, at the age of forty seven, George Orwell died of tuberculosis.
3. Just before the critical play, the hard fought game was preempted by the prime minister's address.
4. Hand knit sweaters are usually more expensive than factory produced ones.
5. Alan claims he is addicted to hip hop but allergic to classical music.

GO TO WEB

EXERCISE 7.18.1

Exercise 7.18.2*

In the following sentences, some hyphens are missing, and some are included where they don't belong. Correct the errors in these sentences.

1. A rubber band pistol was confiscated during algebra-class because it was considered a weapon of math disruption.

2. Would you re-lay this message to Mr. Chan: the masons want to relay the bricks tomorrow.

3. Our next door neighbour teaches high-school, but she doesn't like being introduced as a high school teacher.

4. We had a presentation by Atheists-Anonymous, a non prophet organization.

5. Because Angela was an attorney at law and had once been an all Canadian athlete, no one was surprised when she became Minister-of-Recreation.

Spelling

Exercise 7.18.3

This last exercise is a mastery test. Insert hyphens where they are needed and delete them where they are not.

1. At 20 years-of-age, Trudy began to reorganize her life.
2. Because she is the instructor who is the most up to date with trends in the industry, Alysha is the coordinator of our program.
3. Only one third of the team seemed to be reenergized by the 20 minute break.
4. Vernon wore his hand tailored three piece suit to his former-girlfriend's wedding.
5. In spite of its country garden atmosphere, the hotel's up to the minute décor and facilities could not be faulted.
6. The space shuttle will reenter the atmosphere in exactly eighty five seconds.
7. Tim began to recover from his career threatening injury after taking an antiinflammatory.
8. Some very successful businesses are coowned by the employees; these cooperative ventures ensure that workers' hard earned dollars are put to work on their-own behalf.
9. Computer generated graphics are ninety nine percent of our over the counter business.
10. Trevor was treated for post traumatic stress after his no hope, last minute attempt to pass chemistry.

Capital Letters

Capital letters belong in a few specific places and nowhere else. Some writers suffer from "capitalitis." They put capital letters on words without thinking about their position or function in a sentence.

Capitalize the first letter of a word that fits into one of the six categories listed below:

1. The first word of a sentence, a direct quotation, or a sentence from a quoted source.

Are you illiterate? Write to us today for free help.
The supermodel cooed, "I just love the confidence makeup gives me."
Lister Sinclair claims that the only thing Canadians have in common is that "We all hate Toronto."

Exercise 7.19.1*

Correct the seven missing or misused capital letters in the following sentences. Answers for exercises in this chapter begin on page 569.

1. Nancy whispered, "there's a light in the Frankenstein house."

2. time is nature's way of keeping everything from happening at once.

3. Learning to speak and write Standard english is, for many people, like learning another Language.

4. Richard Harkness, writing in *The New York Times*, said, "a committee is a group of the unwilling, picked from the unfit, to do the unnecessary."

Spelling

5. in conclusion, I want you to consider the words of Wendell Johnson: "*always* and *never* are two words you should always remember never to use."

---

2. The names of specific people, places, and things.

Names of people (and their titles):

Shania Twain, Governor General Michaëlle Jean, the Rev. Jeremiah Wright, the Hon. Eugene Forsey, Senator Mike Duffy

Names of places, regions, and astronomical bodies (but not general geographic directions):

Stanley Park, Lake Superior, Cape Breton Island; Nunavut, the Prairie Provinces, the Badlands; Saturn, Earth, the Moon, the Asteroid Belt; south, north

Names of buildings, institutions, organizations, companies, departments, products, etc.:

the Empress Hotel; McGill University, Red Deer College; the Liberal Party, the Kiwanis Club; Petro-Canada, Future Shop; the Department of English, the Human Resources Department; Kleenex, Nissan, Labatt's

Exercise 7.19.2*

Add capital letters where necessary in the following sentences. There are 30 errors in this exercise.

1. Do you find that visa is more popular than American express when you travel to faraway places such as mexico, france, or jupiter?

2. Our stay at the seaview hotel, overlooking the pacific ocean, certainly beat our last vacation at the bates motel, where we faced west, overlooking the city dump.

3. As the fundraiser for our alumni association, I am targeting companies like disney, canadian tire, the bank of montreal, and the cbc, all of which employ our graduates.

4. The broadcast department of niagara college has ordered six sony cameras for their studios in welland, ontario.

5. After a brief stay in the maritimes, captain tallman and his crew sailed west up the st. lawrence river.

---

3. Names of major historical events, historical periods, religions, religious texts, and religious holidays.

World War II, the Depression; the Renaissance; Islam, Judaism, Christianity, Buddhism, Hinduism; the Torah, the Koran, the Bible, the Upanishads; Ramadan, Yom Kippur, Easter

Exercise 7.19.3*

Add the 20 capital letters that are missing from the following sentences.

1. The crusades, which were religious wars between muslims and christians, raged through the middle ages.

2. The hindu religion recognizes and honours many gods; islam recognizes one god, allah; buddhism recognizes none.

3. The koran, the bible, and the torah agree on many principles.

4. The jewish festival of hanukkah often occurs near the same time that christians are celebrating christmas.

5. After world war I, many jews began to immigrate to Palestine, where they and the muslim population soon came into conflict.

Spelling

GO TO WEB

EXERCISE 7.19.1

4. The days of the week, months of the year, and specific holidays, but not the seasons.

Wednesday; January; Remembrance Day, Canada Day; spring, autumn

Exercise 7.19.4*

The following sentences contain both missing and unnecessary capitals. Find and correct the 15 errors.

1. Next monday is valentine's day, when messages of love are exchanged.

2. By thursday, I'll have finished my st. patrick's day costume.

3. My favourite months are january and february because I love all Winter sports.

4. In the summer, big meals seem to be too much trouble; however, after thanksgiving, we need lots of food to survive the winter cold.

5. A National Holiday named flag day was once proposed, but it was never officially approved.

5. The main words in titles of published works (books, magazines, websites, films; essays, poems, songs; works of art; etc.). Do not capitalize minor words (articles, prepositions, conjunctions) in titles unless the word is the first word in the title.

The Colony of Unrequited Dreams
Of Mice and Men
Maclean's
Facebook

The Thinker
"An Immigrant's Split Personality"
"In Flanders Fields"
"O Canada"

Exercise 7.19.5

Add the 30 capital letters that are missing from the following sentences.

1. The review of my book, *the life and times of a hog rider*, published in *the globe and mail*, was not favourable.

2. Clint eastwood fans will be delighted that the two early movies that made him internationally famous, *a fistful of dollars* and *for a few dollars more,* are now available on DVD.

3. Joseph Conrad's short novel *heart of darkness* became the blockbuster movie *Apocalypse now*.

4. My essay, "a bright and silent place," was published in the april issue of *landscapes* magazine.

5. Botticelli's famous painting, "birth of venus," inspired my poem "woman on the half shell."

Pay special attention to this next category. It is one that often causes trouble.

6. The names of specific school courses.

Marketing 101, Psychology 100, Mathematics 220, English 110,

but

a) not the names of general school subjects

   e.g., marketing, sociology, mathematics

b) *unless* the subjects are languages or pertain to specific geographical areas whose names are capitalized

   e.g., English, Greek, the study of Chinese history, modern Caribbean literature, Latin American poetry

(Names of languages, countries, and geographical regions are ALWAYS capitalized.)

Spelling

Exercise 7.19.6*

Add capital letters where necessary in the following sentences. There are 10 errors in this exercise.

1. We began our study of sociology with the concept of relationships.

2. After passing Professor Bacchus's course, introduction to wine, I registered for oenology 200.

3. After studying geography for two years, I began taking courses in ancient greek and modern history.

4. While math is her strong subject, Louisa has trouble with accounting, english, and conversational french.

5. The prerequisite for theology 210 is introduction to world religions, taught by Professor O'Connor.

GO TO WEB

EXERCISE 7.19.2

Exercise 7.19.7

The following exercise is the mastery test and contains 30 errors. Before you begin, it would be a good idea to review the six capitalization rules presented in this chapter.

1. On the first official friday of Spring, we always celebrate by going fishing on lake winnipeg.

2. Failing Sociology is like eating soup with a fork: it's difficult, but you can do it if you really try.

3. July First is Canada day, when we celebrate the anniversary of confederation, which occurred in 1867.

4. Although Ms. Lau is a member of the new democratic party, she is quite Conservative in her thinking on Economic and social issues.

5. She may look like a sheep, but I'll have you know she's a purebred afghan hound.

6. Trying to learn english as quickly as possible, Wong Bao Lin took two Night School classes a week and listened to audiotapes several hours every day.

7. When travelling abroad, canadians can readily identify each other by their mountain equipment co-op backpacks, tilley hats, and roots clothing.

8. If I drop Math and Accounting, I will be able to concentrate on english and Marketing, but it will mean adding a semester to my program.

9. Citroen, Renault, and Peugeot are french cars that sell well in Europe, but have never caught on in north America.

10. Sally and Kendra are packing away the essentials like cigarettes, doritos, and Beer in preparation for the end of the World, which, they are convinced, will occur on December 31, 2015.

Spelling

SECTION 7.20

Numbers

Numbers may be expressed as words (*one, four, nine*) or as figures (*1, 4, 9*), depending on the kind of document you are writing and what the numbers refer to. In a few circumstances, a combination of words and figures is required. In scientific and technical papers, numbers are normally given in figures; in humanities papers, numbers that can be expressed in one or two words are spelled out. For your assignments, ask your instructor which style he or she prefers. For general purposes, including most business writing, follow the guidelines given below.

When to Use Words

1. Use words to express whole numbers *one* through *nine* and simple fractions. Use figures for numbers *10* and above.

The novel's three parts chronicle the nine-week journey of the five Acadian teenagers.

China and India together account for more than one-third of the Earth's population.

Approximately 35 years ago, Paul Henderson scored the most famous goal in the history of Canadian hockey.

There are two exceptions to this general rule.

A. Spell out any number that begins a sentence, or rewrite the sentence so that the number does not come first.

Incorrect: 157 students submitted essays to the awards committee.

Correct: One hundred and fifty-seven students submitted essays to the awards committee.

Also correct: The awards committee received essays from 157 students.

B. Use *either* figures *or* words to express numbers that modify the same or similar items in one sentence. (That is, be consistent within a sentence.)

We are looking for three accountants, fifteen salespeople, and two customer service representatives. (*not* "three, 15, and two")

Only 9 of the 55 applicants had both the qualifications and the experience we required. (*not* "nine of the 55 applicants")

2. Treat ordinal numbers (*first, second*, etc.) as you would cardinal numbers (*one, two*, etc.).

Up to its sixth or seventh month, an infant can breathe and swallow at the same time.

In a 1904 speech, Sir Wilfrid Laurier predicted that the 20th century would belong to Canada. Maybe our luck will improve in the 21st century.

Exercise 7.20.1*

Applying the first two highlighted rules in this chapter, correct any errors in the following sentences. Answers begin on page 571.

1. This applicant claims to speak more than 7 languages, but from her résumé, I'd say that English is not 1 of them.

2. This is the 3rd time the Accounting Department has filed its report more than 2 days late.

Spelling

3. 54 eager people have signed up for the 2nd annual office pool.

4. Of the twelve cuts on her new DVD release, the 1st is my favourite.

5. Gavin, who works for the garage where I take my car, was unable to answer ten of the twenty-three questions on the Mechanic Certification Exam.

6. In the Great Fire of 1666, 1/2 of London burned down, but only 6 people lost their lives.

7. If the diesel mixture contains 3/4 of a litre of regular gasoline, it will make your truck easier to start in those 4 or 5 really cold weeks of winter.

8. When I was twenty-seven and had been unemployed for nearly 3 years, I decided to return to college for 2 years of practical training.

9. In the United States, 1 of the reasons that hemp is illegal is that about eighty years ago, cotton growers lobbied against its cultivation because they saw it as competition.

10. Only eight out of forty-seven trivia players were able to name Jay Silverheels of Brantford, Ontario, as the original Tonto in *The Lone Ranger.*

GO TO WEB

EXERCISE 7.20.1

When to Use Figures

As a general rule, you should use figures when you are presenting precise or technical numerical information or when your sentence or paragraph contains several numbers.

> 3. Use figures to express dates, specific times, addresses, and percentages; with abbreviations or symbols; and with units of currency.

Dates	April 1, 2010, *or* 1 April 2010
Times	8:45 a.m. *or* 08:45, 7:10 p.m. *or* 19:10 (Use words with *o'clock*: e.g., *nine o'clock, four o'clock* sharp)
Addresses	24 Sussex Drive, 2175 West 8th Street
Percentages	19 percent, a 6.5 percent interest rate (Use the % sign only with figures in tables or illustrations.)
With abbreviations or symbols	7 mm, 293 km, 60 km/h, 40 g, 54 kg, 18°C, 0.005 cm, 1.5 L, 8½", p. 3
Amounts of money	79 cents *or* $0.79, $2, $100, $30 000, $20 million, $65 billion (Use words if the unit of currency follows whole numbers one through nine: e.g., *two dollars, seven euros*, unless the number includes a decimal: e.g., *1.5 trillion pesos*.)

Exercise 7.20.2 *

With Rule 3 in mind, correct the errors in the following sentences.

1. Researchers at Cornell University conducted a study that showed that sixty-six percent of all businessmen wear their ties too tight.

2. More than ten percent of those studied wore their ties so tight that blood flow to the brain was diminished.

3. 99 percent of the people who read the report wondered why Cornell had conducted such a study.

4. 1 plan is to retire on December seventeenth, 2055, when I will be 80.

5. At precisely eight-ten p.m. on June third, your flight will leave for Whitehorse.

6. You will arrive at approximately 10 o'clock on June fourth if you make all your connections.

7. I won 5 dollars from Ted by proving that February Eighteen Sixty-five was the only month in recorded history not to have a full moon.

Spelling

8. You must be present at one thirty-three West Eighteenth Street by exactly 7:00 o'clock to claim your prize.

9. So far this year, I have spent thirty-eight thousand dollars—twenty percent more than my anticipated income for the entire year—and it's only May fifteenth!

10. At the Indianapolis Speedway, the race cars burn approximately four L of fuel for each lap, while the ship *Queen Mary 2* moves just fifteen cm for every 4 L of fuel it burns.

GO TO WEB

EXERCISE 7.20.2

When to Use Both Words and Figures

4. When one number immediately follows another, spell out the one that makes the shorter word.
5. For numbers over a million, express introductory whole numbers 10 and above in figures, and the quantity in words (*million, billion, trillion,* etc.). (If the numbers involve decimals, use figures.)

The Grey Cup is contested by *two 12-man* teams of heavily padded and helmeted warriors.

Our local car dealers sold more than *200 four-wheel*-drive vehicles the day after our first big storm.

The human stomach contains more than *35 million* digestive glands.

The Earth's population was estimated to be *6.79 billion* as of July 1, 2009.

The following exercises will test your ability to apply all of the rules and exceptions presented in this chapter.

Exercise 7.20.3[*]

Correct any errors in the expression of numbers in the following sentences.

1. The speedboat is powered by 2 80-horsepower outboard motors.

2. 1 8-cylinder SUV emits more pollution than two four-cylinder Volkswagens or 3 Toyota gas–electric hybrids.

3. Because she sold seven $2 000 000 homes last year, she topped the agency's earnings list.

4. Eighty-two percent of people whose net worth is over three million dollars say they got rich by hard work.

5. 200 people were invited to celebrate my parents' twenty-fifth wedding anniversary on August Thirty-first, 2009.

6. A total of 10 fifteen-year-old girls and 4 fifteen-year-old boys applied for the commercial acting position we advertised.

7. Our lawyer told us that thirty-eight % of people who die between the ages of 45 and 54 have not prepared a will.

8. Canada's population of about 33 000 000 puts us in thirty-sixth place on the list of most populous countries.

9. 10 years ago, the average speed on urban freeways was fifty kph, but it has been steadily declining and is expected to be thirty kph within the next 5 years.

10. 7 000 ecstatic fans celebrated their team's unexpected two–one win in the Memorial Cup final, partying in the streets until four-thirty a.m.

GO TO WEB

EXERCISE 7.20.3

Exercise 7.20.4

Before you tackle this final exercise, review the five highlighted rules given in this chapter. It's a good idea to copy them onto a single sheet of paper and keep them handy. There are 15 errors in this paragraph.

Roughly ninety-nine % of a human's body mass is composed of just 6 elements: oxygen (sixty-five %), carbon (eighteen percent), hydrogen (10 percent), nitrogen (three percent), calcium (1-1/2 percent), and phosphorous (one percent). The remaining one percent of the recipe consists of tiny amounts of potassium, sulphur, sodium, chlorine, and magnesium, plus even smaller traces of iron, copper, molybdenum, zinc, and iodine. According to science reporter Scott LaFee of *The San Diego Tribune*, "The average human body contains enough sulphur to kill all the fleas on an average-sized dog, enough carbon to make nine hundred pencils, enough potassium to fire a toy cannon . . . enough phosphorous to make two thousand, two hundred match heads, enough water to fill a ten-gallon [thirty-eight L] container, and enough iron to make a three inch [eight cm] nail."

List of Terms:
A Vocabulary of Writing

The following list contains definitions of some common terms referring to syntax and style. For some of the terms, you will find further information in the book or on the *Essay Essentials* website (www.essayessentials5e .nelson.com). If a term you are looking for is not listed, check the index or consult your dictionary. For punctuation marks, see Sections 7.10 through 7.15 and Sections 7.17 and 7.18.

abstract, concrete   See **noun**.

active voice   See **voice**.

adjective   A word that modifies (describes) a noun or a pronoun. Adjectives usually answer the questions What kind? How many? Which? For example, The *best* exercise; *three* strikes; *my morning* class. Nouns, phrases, and clauses can also function as adjectives: *ground* control; *up-to-the-minute* news. See also "Parts of Speech" on the *Essay Essentials* website.

adverb   A word that modifies a verb, adjective, or another adverb. Adverbs usually answer the questions When? How? Where? Why? How much? For example, Nino talks loudly (*loudly* modifies the verb *talks*); he is a very loud talker (*very* modifies the adjective *loud*); he talks really loudly (*really* modifies the adverb *loudly*). Adverbs often—but not always—end in *-ly*. A phrase or a clause can also function as an adverb. See also "Parts of Speech" on the *Essay Essentials* website.

agreement   Grammatical correspondence in person and number between a verb and its subject, or in person, number, and gender between a pronoun and its antecedent. See Sections 7.7 and 7.9.

analogy   A comparison between two dissimilar things that share at least one element or characteristic in common; e.g., Time is like a river. Just as the river flows from higher to lower ground, so time flows from the past into the future. Analogies are often used for stylistic or dramatic effect as well as to explain or illustrate a point.

anecdote A short account of an event or incident, used to illustrate a point and sometimes intended to entertain. See paragraphs 1–4 of Hal Niedzviecki's "Stupid Jobs Are Good to Relax With."

antecedent From Latin for "coming before; preceding." An antecedent is the word or words that a pronoun refers (usually back) to or stands for: My sister thinks she is always right (*sister* is the antecedent of the pronoun *she*).

article Often classed as adjectives, the definite article *the* and the indefinite articles *a* and *an* are "determiners" that precede nouns: *the* umpire; *a* baseball bat; *an* orange.

auxiliary A "helping" verb used with a main verb to form different tenses. The auxiliary verbs are *be, have, do, may, can, ought, must, shall, will* and their various forms.

clause A group of words containing a subject and a verb. If the group of words can stand by itself as a simple sentence, it is an **independent** (or **main**) **clause**: Great minds think alike. A **dependent** (or **subordinate**) **clause** cannot stand alone as a sentence; it must be linked to a main clause: *Because great minds think alike,* I am sure you will agree with me. See Section 7.2.

cliché A phrase that has become meaningless through overuse. See Chapter 9.

coherence The logical consistency and stylistic connections between ideas, sentences, and paragraphs in a piece of writing. See Chapter 8.

collective noun A noun that names a group; for example, class, faculty, jury, choir. Collective nouns are singular when the group is considered as a unit, plural when the focus is on individual members: The <u>class</u> <u>wants</u> a midterm break. The <u>class</u> <u>have</u> not yet <u>handed</u> in *their* papers. See **agreement**.

colloquialism A word or group of words that is appropriate in casual conversation and informal—but not formal—writing. Some common examples are guy, kid, flunk.

comma splice Two independent clauses joined with a comma: The comma splice is a type of run-on sentence, it is a serious error. See Section 7.3.

complement A word or phrase that completes the meaning of a verb. Also called a **subjective completion**, a complement is a noun, pronoun, or adjective that follows a linking verb: Jamie is the *manager* (noun complement); The winner was *she* (pronoun complement); Her paper will be *excellent* (adjective complement).

complex sentence A sentence consisting of one independent clause and one or more subordinate clauses. See also "Sentences: Kinds and Parts" on the *Essay Essentials* website.

compound	Two or more grammatical elements (words, phrases, clauses) joined so that they function as a unit: *Hans, Peter, and Walter* are brothers (compound subject); Hans *works and studies* (compound verb); Peter expects an *A or a B+* (compound object). Also called **multiple** subjects, verbs, objects, or complements.
compound sentence	A sentence consisting of two or more independent clauses. See also "Sentences: Kinds and Parts" on the *Essay Essentials* website.
compound-complex sentence	A sentence consisting of two or more independent clauses and one or more subordinate clauses. See also "Sentences: Kinds and Parts" on the *Essay Essentials* website.
concrete, abstract	See **noun**.
conjunction	A part of speech. **Coordinating** conjunctions (*for, and, nor, but, or, yet, so*) join equal grammatical elements such as nouns, verbs, phrases, or clauses. **Subordinating** conjunctions are words or phrases that join dependent clauses to main clauses. Some examples are *although, because, after, in order that, as soon as*. See **dependent clause cues** in Section 7.2. For **correlative** conjunctions, see "Parts of Speech" on the *Essay Essentials* website.
conjunctive adverb	An adverb such as *however, therefore, thus,* and *nevertheless* used to indicate a logical relationship between two independent clauses. Conjunctive adverbs are preceded by a semicolon and followed by a comma: Jordan hates math; *therefore,* he is not going to be an engineer.
connotation	The positive or negative meaning associated with a word; for example, *slender* and *skinny* both mean *thin*, but to describe someone as *slender* is a compliment, while to describe someone as *skinny* suggests disapproval.
contraction	The combining of two words into one, spelled with an apostrophe to mark the missing letter or letters: *isn't* (is not), *here's* (here is), *should've* (should have). Contractions are not appropriate in formal writing unless they are part of quoted speech.
dangling modifier	See **modifier**.
declarative sentence	See "Sentences: Kinds and Parts" on the *Essay Essentials* website.
demonstrative	See **pronoun**.
denotation	The specific meaning of a word; the dictionary definition. Compare **connotation**.
dependent clause	See **clause**.
dependent-clause cue	A word or phrase that introduces a dependent clause. See Section 7.2.

diction A writer's choice and use of words. Diction is a feature of style and can be colloquial, informal, or formal. Within the context of a sentence, paragraph, or paper, diction can be appropriate (consistent and suitable to the target audience) or inappropriate (inconsistent and unsuited to the target audience).

direct object See **object**.

ellipses The three spaced periods (. . .) used to indicate that a word or words have been omitted from a quoted passage. See Chapter 12.

exclamatory sentence See "Sentences: Kinds and Parts" on the *Essay Essentials* website.

fragment A group of words, punctuated as a sentence, that cannot stand alone as a sentence. The word group may be missing a subject, verb, or both subject and verb, or it may be a dependent clause. See Section 7.2.

fused sentence Two independent clauses with no punctuation between them: The fused sentence is a type of run-on it is a serious error. See Section 7.3.

gender Nouns and pronouns may be masculine (father, boy, stallion; he, his, him), feminine (mother, girl, mare; she, hers, her); or neuter (laughter, book; it).

gender-biased language See **sexist language**.

grammar The description and study of how the elements of language function, by themselves and in relation to one another. See also "Grammar Basics" on the *Essay Essentials* website.

helping verb See **auxiliary**.

homonyms Two or more words that are identical in sound (e.g., meet, meat, mete) or spelling (e.g., bank—a place to deposit money; bank—a slope) but different in meaning. See Section 7.16.

imperative sentence Also called a **command**. See "Sentences: Kinds and Parts" on the *Essay Essentials* website.

indefinite pronoun See **pronoun**.

independent clause See **clause**.

indirect object See **object**.

infinitive A verb form usually consisting of *to* + the base form of the verb: to be, to walk, to read, to procrastinate. An infinitive or infinitive phrase can function as a noun, adjective, or adverb, but never as the main verb in a clause; e.g., I offered to help (*to help* functions as a noun, direct object of the verb *offered*).

interrogative sentence   See "Sentences: Kinds and Parts" on the *Essay Essentials* website.

irony   A way of saying one thing while implying something else, often the opposite of what the words themselves signify. For an extended example of irony, see "The Country the World Forgot—Again" (pages 334–36). Situations can also be ironic: in "Toothpaste" (pages 308–10), for example, we learn that a hygiene product is made from disgusting materials; in "The Telephone" (pages 323–29), the instrument that was supposed to enhance the life of a village in fact destroys it.

irregular verb   A verb that does not form its past tense and past participle by adding -*ed* or -*d*; for example, write, wrote, written; sing, sang, sung. See Section 7.8.

jargon   Strictly, the specialized technical vocabulary of a particular profession. More broadly, **pretentious language**: wordy, confusing language that is intended to impress the reader. See Chapter 9.

linking verb   See **verb**.

misplaced modifier   See **modifier**.

modifier   A word or group of words that describes, qualifies, or restricts another word, phrase, or clause in a sentence. A modifier can act as an adjective or as an adverb. If there is no word in the sentence to which the modifier can logically refer, or if the modifier refers grammatically to a word it doesn't actually modify, it is a **dangling modifier**: Standing on the dock, many fish could be seen. A **misplaced modifier** is not placed close enough to the word it is intended to modify: Our team has *nearly* lost half its regular players. See Section 7.4.

noun   A word that names a person, place, thing, idea, quality, action, or event, and that can be made possessive. **Concrete** nouns name things we know through our five senses and can be **proper** (naming a particular person, place, thing, etc.: John, Alberta, July, the *Bluenose*, World War II), or **common** [naming one or more members of a class of things or qualities: boy(s), province(s), month(s), ship(s), war(s)]. **Abstract** nouns name ideas or qualities that we know with our minds: truth, excellence, anger. See also "Parts of Speech" on the *Essay Essentials* website.

number   The form of a verb, a noun, or a pronoun may be singular or plural.

object   A noun or noun substitute (pronoun, phrase, or clause) that receives the action expressed by a transitive verb, or that completes a prepositional phrase. Objects of transitive verbs can be **direct** (David wanted a *raise*; Mira promised *to give David a raise*) or **indirect** (Mira gave *David* a raise). The object of a preposition usually follows the preposition (in the *book*, before the *class*), except in direct questions (*What* are you writing *about*?) and indirect questions (I'm not sure *what* to write *about*).

parallelism   Use of the same form for words, phrases, or clauses that have equal grammatical value and similar function in a sentence or paragraph. Parallel elements match each other in structure as well as meaning: Hot weather makes people *tired*, *cranky*, and *quarrelsome*; *What I said* and *what I meant* are two different things. See Section 7.5.

paraphrase   To paraphrase is to rephrase another writer's idea in your own words. A good paraphrase reflects both the meaning and the tone of the original passage. It is usually approximately the same length or shorter than the original. Be sure to acknowledge the source of any material you paraphrase.

participle   A verb form regularly ending in *-ing* or *-ed* that can be used as an adjective (the *weeping* willows, a *completed* work) or with an auxiliary as part of a verb phrase (am *succeeding*, have been *rented*). For past participles of irregular verbs, see Section 7.8 or a dictionary.

parts of speech   The nine categories into which traditional grammar classifies words according to their function in a sentence: noun, pronoun, verb, adjective, adverb, conjunction, preposition, article, expletive. See also "Parts of Speech" on the *Essay Essentials* website.

passive voice   See **voice.**

person   A quality of pronouns and verbs that shows whether they refer to someone speaking (**first person:** I, we), to someone being spoken to (**second person:** you), or to someone or something being spoken about (**third person:** he, she, it, they, everyone).

personal pronoun   See **pronoun.**

phrase   A group of meaning-related words lacking a subject and/or a verb; compare **clause.** The different kinds of phrases function as grammatical units (parts of speech) and syntactical elements (subject, verb, object, etc.). For example,

Please order more *legal-size file folders*. (noun phrase acting as object of verb *order*)

I *must have been sleeping* when you called. (verb phrase acting as main verb in independent clause)

prefix   One or more letters that can be added to the beginning of a word (1) to make a new word or (2) to change its part of speech.

1. a + sexual = asexual
   contra + diction = contradiction
   mis + spell = misspell
   un + thinkable = unthinkable

2. de + nude (noun) = denude (verb)
   in + put (verb) = input (noun)
   con + temporary (adjective) = contemporary (noun, adjective)

Some prefixes require a hyphen: e.g., *anti*-reform, *all*-Canadian, *mid*-season, *self*-control. See Section 7.18.

preposition	A word that links a noun, pronoun, or phrase (object of the preposition) to some other word(s) in the sentence. Prepositions may be a single word (from, upon, within, to, for) or a phrase (apart from, on account of, in spite of).
prepositional phrase	A group of words consisting of a preposition and its object(s), along with any modifiers. Prepositional phrases usually function as adjectives or adverbs:

Mine is the second office *on the right*. (adjective modifying noun *office*)

Please go *into my office*. (adverb modifying verb *go*)
See the list of prepositional phrases on page 372.

pretentious language	Wordy, roundabout, or unintelligible language. Also called *gobbledygook*. Pretentious writing is a kind of jargon characterized by wordiness, long words, vague abstract nouns, and frequent use of the passive voice. See Chapter 9.
principal parts	The forms of a verb from which all its tenses are derived: the **infinitive** (or **base**) **form** (walk, write, drink), the **present participle** (walking, writing, drinking), the **past tense** (walked, wrote, drank), and the **past participle** (walked, written, drunk). The principal parts of irregular verbs are listed in the dictionary. See Section 7.8.
pronoun	A word that stands for or refers to a noun or another pronoun (its antecedent). There are several kinds of pronouns:

personal:	I, we, you, he, she, it, they (subject forms) me, us, him, her, it, them (object forms)
possessive:	my, our, your, his, her, its, their
demonstrative:	this, these, that, those
relative:	who, which, that, whom, whose
interrogative:	who, whose, whom, which, what
indefinite:	any, some, all, one, everybody, anything, each, either, few, none, several, etc.

See **antecedent**, **number**, **person**, and Section 7.9.

run-on	Two or more independent clauses lacking appropriate punctuation between them. See Section 7.3.
sentence	The basic unit of connected speech and writing. A sentence can assert, question, request, command, or exclaim. See "Sentences: Kinds and Parts" on the *Essay Essentials* website.

sexist language	Writing that calls attention unnecessarily to the sex of the person being written about: actress, waitress, female author. Also, the use of masculine nouns and pronouns to refer to persons of both sexes: A good *salesman* listens to *his* customers. See Chapter 9.
slang	A highly colloquial word or phrase, used by speakers belonging to a particular group; e.g., high-school students, music lovers, or sports fans. Slang is not appropriate in academic or professional writing. See Chapter 9.
style	A characteristic of written language; good style, whether formal or informal, is concise, clear, and pleasing.
subject	In a sentence, the person, place, thing, or concept that the sentence is about (see Section 7.1). In a paper, what the essay is about—the topic (see Chapter 2).
subordinate clause	See **clause**.

suffix	One or more letters added to the end of a word (1) to change its meaning, (2) to change its grammatical function, or (3) to change its part of speech.
	
	1. king + dom = kingdom
	  tooth + less = toothless
	  few + er = fewer
	
	2. love (base form) + s = loves (3rd-person singular, present tense)
	  student (singular) + s = students (plural)
	  eat (base form) + en = eaten (past participle)
	
	3. happy (adjective) + ness = happiness (noun)
	  happy (adjective) + ily = happily (adverb)
	  hope (noun) + ful = hopeful (adjective)

tense	The quality of a verb that indicates time: past, present, or future. The tense of a verb is indicated by its ending (play*s*, play*ing*, play*ed*) and by any auxiliary verbs associated with it (*will* play, *has* played, *must have* played).

Simple tenses

present: ask, asks
past: asked
future: will ask

Perfect tenses

has (have) asked
has (have) asked
will have asked

The simple and perfect tenses can also be **progressive**: am asking, have been asking, will be asking.

thesis	The idea or point about a subject that an essay sets out to prove or explain. See Chapter 4.
tone	A writer's attitude toward his or her subject and intended audience, conveyed through style and ideas. Tone is an emotional quality, and there are as many different kinds of tone as there are emotions: objective, angry, sarcastic, humorous, solemn, anxious, concerned, etc. See Chapter 8.

LIST OF TERMS: A VOCABULARY OF WRITING · 533

transition	Any device used to connect ideas within a sentence, a paragraph, or a paper. See Chapter 8.
unity	The quality of oneness in a sentence, paragraph, or essay. A piece of writing should focus on a single topic or thesis; everything in the piece should relate directly to the topic or thesis; there should be no unrelated ideas or digressions.
usage	The customary or conventional way of using words and combinations of words in a language. The incorrect use of words and expressions (called "abusages" in this book) is a sign of non-standard English. See Chapter 9.
verb	A part of speech that indicates one of three states:

action: Ravi stopped the ball. (physical action)
          Nina believed the team would win. (mental action)

occurrence: Father's Day falls on the third Sunday in June.

condition: Minnie felt ill.

Transitive verbs require a direct object: I *hate* chemistry; Minnie *lifts* weights.

Intransitive verbs do not require an object: Please *listen* and *learn*.

Linking verbs require a noun or adjective as their complement: Phil is the *manager* of our department (noun); Phil is *ambitious* (adjective).

The most common linking verb is *be* (*am, is, are, was, were,* etc.) Other linking verbs are *appear, become, feel, grow, look, taste, remain, seem, smell,* and *sound.*

See also **auxiliary** verb and "Parts of Speech" on the *Essay Essentials* website.

voice	A quality of verbs, which may be either **active** or **passive**. With an active voice verb, the subject of the verb is performing the action (I *read* your essay); with a verb in the passive voice, the subject of the sentence is being acted upon (Your essay *was read* by me). See Section 7.8.

NEL

APPENDIX B

Answers for Selected Exercises

Answers for Chapter 1: Your Audience and You (pages 9–24)

Exercise 1.1

1. Audience: Literate readers who are interested in exploring a serious analysis of what is often treated as a trivial topic.

    Writer's role: To provide information.

    Language: Formal. Sentences vary in length; one is quite long and complex. While there are no technical terms, the writer assumes the reader has a broad general vocabulary and good reading ability. Use of third-person point of view contributes to the impersonal tone.

2. Audience: Experts in woodworking.

    Writer's role: To provide information in an accessible way. The writer is not instructing the reader, but outlining the function of the tool and some of its possible applications.

    Language: General level, combining technical vocabulary with an informal tone. Sentences vary in length. Writer addresses reader as "you."

3. Audience: Educated business owners or high-level managers who are interested in doing business in China.

    Writer's role: To inform Canadian entrepreneurs who have little experience with Chinese business culture that it is very different from the Canadian culture, and that considerable preparation is needed if one is to be successful in that market.

    Language: Formal. Sentences are long and complex; vocabulary is highly sophisticated and includes a few examples of business jargon: e.g., "principals," "power brokers." Tone is serious.

4. Audience: General readers. (The author wrote a popular newspaper column for many years.)

    Writer's role: Primarily to entertain. Readers who have been to Paris will smile with recognition; those who haven't, will smile at Nicol's imagery and will learn something about Parisian traffic.

Language: Mostly general level, with some informal constructions (e.g., contractions, sentence fragment). Writer addresses readers as "you," as if speaking directly to them.

5. Audience: English professor

Writer's role: To demonstrate that she can write a good research paper. The paragraph supports its topic with a quotation, two paraphrases, and the student's own observations and questions.

Language: Formal. No contractions or colloquialisms. Writer uses the third-person approach, which contributes to the impersonal, objective tone. Sentences vary in length. Note the parallel constructions in sentences 6 and 7: these reinforce the formality of the paragraph.

Answers for Chapter 2: Selecting a Subject (pages 25–29)

Exercise 2.1

1. significant
2. significant
3. significant
4. significant
5. revise
6. significant
7. revise

Exercise 2.2

1. revise
2. revise
3. revise
4. single (the subject is the *importance of accuracy*, not the two media)
5. single
6. revise
7. revise

Exercise 2.3

1. specific
2. revise
3. specific
4. revise
5. revise
6. revise
7. revise

Exercise 2.4

1. supportable
2. supportable
3. supportable
4. revise
5. revise
6. revise
7. supportable

Exercise 2.5
1. not specific
2. not single
3. not supportable
4. satisfactory
5. not specific

Answers for Chapter 3: Managing the Main Points (pages 30–47)

Exercise 3.6
1. cellphone (not distinct, overlaps with *telephone*)
2. distance from suppliers and markets (not related)
3. repetitive (not related: repetition is a programming problem, not a characteristic of commercials)
4. procrastination (not distinct, overlaps with *poor study habits*)
5. *find a reliable real estate agent* overlaps with *seek expert advice*; also not necessarily relevant—not all people need an agent
6. *competitors offer better pay* overlaps with *salary lower than industry standard*

Exercise 3.7
1. chronological (5, 1, 4, 3, 2)
2. climactic (2, 1, 3, 4)
3. random
4. climactic (3, 1, 2. This order reflects the amount of time it takes for a smoker to quit using each method and also the amount of agony the smoker will suffer in the process.)
5. random

Answers for Chapter 4: Writing the Thesis Statement (pages 48–58)

Exercise 4.1
1. Students who try to combine a full-time job with a full-time program face problems at school, at work, and at home.
2. To be successful in a broadcasting career, you must be talented, motivated, and hard-working.
3. Establishing a local area network would promote teamwork and increase efficiency in the office.
4. The business traveller can learn much from the turtle. Carry everything you need with you. Move slowly but with purpose and consistency. Keep your head down until you are sure you know exactly what is going on.
5. Cellphones must be turned off during class because they disrupt everyone's concentration, they prevent the user from learning, and they distract and annoy the teacher, to the detriment of all.

6. Although easily dismissed as merely animated entertainment, <u>*The Simpsons* is</u> <u>effective social commentary, tackling with humour and gusto</u> such issues as <u>the</u> <u>environment</u>, <u>social justice</u>, and <u>race relations</u>.

7. Large energy producers and some provincial governments say we cannot afford to live up to the terms of the Kyoto Accord, which seeks to reduce the production of greenhouse gases. <u>But can we afford not to comply with this international agreement</u>? <u>Can we afford to compromise the health of Canadians by continuing to pollute</u>? <u>Can we afford to risk the effects of global warming on our environment</u>? <u>Can we afford to fall behind the rest of the world in research and development leading to a solution to the problem of greenhouse gases</u>?

Exercise 4.7 (suggested answers)

1. When choosing between two fast-food restaurants, consider food, atmosphere, service, and price.

2. Urban overcrowding results in traffic jams, air pollution, homelessness, and both street and domestic violence.

3. Successful small businesses are usually those with adequate capital, a marketable product, dedicated personnel, and a workable business plan.

Answers for Chapter 6: Understanding Paragraph Form and Function (pages 67–84)

Exercise 6.3

1. Canada makes no economic sense.

2. All sports can be made ridiculous because the essence of sport is rules.

3. In reality, taste buds are exceedingly small.

4. Scholarly explanations of humor fall into three major categories.

5. With the huge variety of computers now on the market, the determining factor in a purchase should be the job the machine will be expected to do.

Answers for Chapter 8: Keeping Your Readers with You (pages 97–110)

Exercise 8.1

1. sentence 6
2. sentence 4
3. sentence 5
4. sentence 5
5. sentence 6

Exercise 8.2

1. Therefore, ...
2. Finally, . . . but . . . .

3. Unfortunately, however, ...
4. On the other hand, ...
5. Still . . .

Exercise 8.4
The transitions in this exercise are identified by category. See the numbered list of coherence strategies on pages 102–3.

1. Finally (5), developing the proper attitude is the key to winning tennis. I define *winning tennis* (1) as playing the game to the best of your ability, hitting the ball as well as you can, and enjoying the feeling of practised expertise (4). Winning tennis (1) has little to do with defeating an opponent. Naturally (5), if you learn the basics, practise sufficiently, and concentrate (4), you will win many matches, but that is the reward of playing well, not the reason for playing well (4). People who swear and throw their racquets when they lose are very useful: they (3) are the most satisfying players to trounce. But I do not understand why they (3) play a game (2) that causes them such pain. Tennis players who enjoy the feel of a well-hit ball and the satisfaction of a long, skilfully played rally are winners, regardless of the score.

2. Travel abroad offers you the best education you can get. For one thing (5), travel (1) is a course in communication skills. In order to function in a foreign language, you must practise every aspect of the communication process (1, 2), from body language to pronunciation. In fact (5), just making yourself understood is a lesson in creativity, a seminar in sign language, and a lab in communication theory (2, 4). Another educational aspect of travel (5) is the history, geography, and culture (4) that you learn about almost unconsciously. Everywhere you go, you encounter memorable evidence of historic events (2) you may dimly recall from school, and you are continually confronted by the practical realities of geography (1) as you try to find your way around. As for culture (1, 5), no book or course of study could provide you with the understanding and appreciation of another society that living in it (3) can. A third way (5) in which travel (1) educates is through teaching you about yourself. Your ability— or inability—to cope with unfamiliar customs, with language difficulties, and with the inevitable problems of finding transportation and accommodation (4) will tell you more than you might want to know about yourself (2). Without the safety net of family and friends, perhaps without even the security of knowing where you'll spend the night, you develop self-reliance or you go home. Either way (5), you learn valuable lessons. While you may not get a diploma from Travel U., you'll learn more about the world, about people, and about yourself (1, 4) than you will in any classroom.

Exercise 8.6 (suggested revision)
Those who support fighting in hockey argue that "It's part of the game" or that "It's what fans want" or "It prevents dangerous, dirty play," but even a quick look at the facts shows that such arguments are baseless. Like hockey, sports such as football, soccer, and basketball are fast, aggressive, and violent, but fighting is banned in all of them. If fighting was what fans demanded, then there would be few viewers for the Olympics or for World Championship tournaments. The fact that these events draw

unequalled ratings demonstrates that hockey fans do not need fights to draw them to the game. Meanwhile, NHL ratings are in decline in Canada, and the rest of the world views hockey as a third-rate sport. Hockey can be beautiful, fast, skilful, and creative, but when players whose only skill is fighting are sent into the game, it becomes nothing more than a brutal street brawl.

Answers for Chapter 9: Choosing the Right Words (pages 111–28)

Exercise 9.1 (suggested answers)

1. I wondered why the baseball kept getting bigger. Then it hit me.
2. Would you repeat the instructions about wordiness? I didn't hear them because I was texting while you were speaking.
3. Our competitor's products, although inferior to ours, are now selling better than ours.
4. My writing is as good as Ashley's and deserves an equivalent (*or:* as good a) mark, especially since I use more words to say the same thing.
5. I prefer *Facebook* to *MySpace* because *MySpace* is owned by Fox, whose politics are far to the right of mine.
6. I doubt that this innovation will succeed.
7. A firm understanding of English fundamentals is a prerequisite to success in college or university, business, and the community.
8. "As a new teacher," we told our English instructor, "you need to understand that grammar, spelling, and punctuation rules stifle our creativity."
9. I think that the [many] social media we use today will soon converge, and the electronic world will resemble the "real" world so closely that the boundaries between the two will blur.
10. We have eliminated any unlawful descriptors, such as race, age, gender, religion, and marital status, from our personnel documents. Now they are all practically identical.

Exercise 9.4 (suggested answers)

1. When the rain began, we turned on the windshield wipers.
2. Young people often have difficulty communicating with parents and others in authority.
3. The witness lied when she claimed that the accused had confessed in a meeting with her.
4. The results of our study demonstrate that our survey instrument is as valid as any other.
5. Cancelling IMF loans to Pacific Rim countries could affect the relationship between developed and developing nations.

Exercise 9.6 (suggested answers)

1. The well-known writer and director Nora Ephron often regrets that she cannot go out in public without attracting the attention of fans and photographers.
2. Amy King first joined the company as a salesperson; only 10 years later, she was promoted to president.
3. An executive sitting in the first-class cabin rang for the flight attendant, a friendly woman who quickly arrived to assist him.

4. The list of ingredients on food packages contains information that may be important to consumers, especially if they are the parents of young children.
5. The typical family is often hard-pressed to find time for family recreation.

Exercise 9.7 (suggested answers)
1. **Regardless** of what you think, the problem between her and **me** has nothing to do with you.
2. If you want to be in the office pool, I need $5.00 **from** you today because there will be no spots left by tomorrow.
3. If I **hadn't texted** you this morning to remind you that you were **supposed** to write your chemistry exam, you would **have** missed it.
4. I didn't feel like seeing **anybody**, so I went home, turned on the TV, and **did nothing** for the rest of the night.
5. This **used** to be a good place to work, but now we're **supposed** to work a full shift every day, or a penalty is deducted **from** our pay.
6. When Barack Obama was elected president, **most** U.S. liberals hoped that **much** of the prejudice in that country had finally been put to rest.
7. **Regardless** of media hype, Barack Obama is not the first person of African descent to head a G8 country; that distinction had **already** been won by Canada's Michaëlle Jean.
8. It's **irresponsible** of us to blame television or any other **medium** for causing violence.
9. Television is partly responsible, however, for the fact that **many** ungrammatical expressions sound **all right** to us.
10. Between you and **me**, the reason I didn't speak to **anyone** about Elmo's cheating on the test is **that** he would **have broken** my arm.

Answers for Chapter 10: Rewriting, Editing, and Proofreading (pages 131–42)

Exercise 10.1 (suggested answer)
In this suggested answer, we have reorganized the main points to conform to the usual way of presenting them (reduce, reuse, recycle); added supporting evidence and transitions (in colour); deleted repetitious, irrelevant, or insignificant material (by drawing a line through it); and revised inappropriate words and tone (**changes appear in bold**). We've also added some explanatory comments in the margin. The first-stage revision below still contains errors, but we will address them when we come to the editing and proofreading phases.

Since our rewrite will not match yours (rewording, transitions, and supporting details can be supplied only by an individual writer), how can you tell if your revision makes the changes that need to be made at this stage? If you have rearranged the main points, added transitions and supporting details, and reworded at least some of the inappropriate passages, you're on the right track.

1   ~~We are having a garbage crisis.~~ Canadians are experiencing a huge cultural shift,   — *Weak opening*

one that has been caused not by politics, or films, or music, but by garbage. We are

drowning in garbage. ~~There is~~ So much waste ~~being~~ **is produced** in North America   — *Lapse in tone*

that we no longer ~~have any idea of~~ **know** were to put it. Take Toronto, for instance.

~~Toronto's garbage problem is so great that they are trucking~~ The city produces so   — *Redundant*

much garbage that **it trucks** thousands of tonnes ~~of it~~ to Michigan every year. A

short-term solution ~~that is~~ **unsustainable**. ~~just plain stupid, and how long can it~~

~~last? We must act now, and we must act as individuals.~~ We cannot wait for the   — *Lapse in tone*

Government to save us from this crisis. ~~We produce~~ the garbage; we must solve the   — *Wordy*

problem. ~~that much is perfectly obvious to anyone. In very practical, down to earth,~~

~~concrete terms, here are some things we can do to~~ We cannot afford to delay: we   — *Reorder points*

must act now to reduce, reuse, and recycle. Yes, the "3 Rs" of environmental respon-

sibility, the same rules we've paid so little attention to for years.   — *Transition added*

2   First**, we** must reduce the amount of garbage we produce. We can do this be

refusing to buy products that are ~~over packaged~~ **overpackaged**, like fast food ~~that~~

~~comes~~ in styrafoam containers tucked into plastic bags for carrying, **and foil-**

wrapped chocolates ~~that have a paper wrapping, a box, lining paper,~~ **in** a plastic

tray ~~for the candies, and foil wrap around each chocolate~~ **inside a fancy, paper-**   — *Wordy*

lined, nonreclyclable cardboard box. By not purchasing such wasteful items, we

say to the manufacturer, either reduce the packaging of your product or lose busi-   — *Wordy*

ness to your competition. We can also ~~be less wastful in our own habits~~ **reduce**

waste by car-pooling, for example, and by turning up the temperature in our homes

a few degrees in summer and down a few degrees in winter. David Suzuki gives

sound advice in his TV commercials: switch to low-energy light bulbs, wear a   *The point is not*
adequately
sweater indoors when it's cold, and supplement fossil fuel heating systems with a   *supported in this*
paragraph. We've
wood-burning stove or fireplace. How could anyone sitting in front of a warm, cozy   *added some detail*
and new
wood fire complain about "having to cut back"?   *examples.*

[The paragraph that follows was originally the fourth paragraph in our first

draft, but most of the information in it more logically belongs in the discussion of

reducing waste.]

Transition added

3   ~~We can reuse most things.~~ Another way to reduce the amount of garbage we produce is to reuse goods whenever possible. ~~Composting vegetable garbage is a good way to put waste to valuable use. Or~~ We can carry our groceries home in washable cloth or reusable plastic containers rather than disposable plastic bags. Instead of paper towels, we can use frayed towels and tattered cotton T-shirts as cleaning rags around the house. We can build and renovate with reclaimed lumber instead of new wood. **Items** we no longer need or want can be offered to others through lawn sales and flea markets. We can even advertise lawn sale leftovers on Craigslist or Kijiji. You'll be surprised how many people are interested in free "stuff"!

The first draft provided little support for this point. We've added details and examples to develop the paragraph adequately.

Composting is a recycling activity. See paragraph 4.

4   Once we have reduced our consumption and trained ourselves to reuse rather than replace, the last step is to ~~We must~~ recycle everything we can ~~instead of sending it to the dump. Old cloths can be sent to the Salvation Army.~~ Composting vegetable garbage is a good way to put waste to valuable use. **Unwanted or outgrown items of clothing** can be **donated** to the Salvation Army, Goodwill, or other charitable organizations that support everyone from refugees to radical environmentalists. As can furniture, appliances, books, and most other household items. There are dozens of ways to make useful items from things that would otherwise ~~be thrown away~~ **become landfill**, such as quilts from old clothes; bird feeders from plastic jugs; and fire logs from newspapers. ~~We don't need to consume as much as we do, and it won't hurt us to use things longer instead of buying new items before the old ones are completely worn out.~~ Many companies now manufacture products from recycled ~~goods~~, some of which are quite surprising, would you believe high-fashion, waterproof jackets made from recycled plastic bottles? We should ~~be on the lookout for their~~ **learn about these** products, ~~to support these~~ **companies'** efforts, and ~~to~~ **thus further** ~~reduce the~~ waste that is dumped into landfills. ~~And whatever we can't use ourselves can be sent to organizations that help others where they will have a life away from a landfill.~~

Transition sentence added

The examples in this paragraph have been rearranged to reflect our production of recyclable waste, from daily to infrequently to rarely.

Redundant— point has already been made

Too colloquial

Redundant

5   ~~This is an absolute necessity.~~ This cultural shift is one that all of us who care about our families, our country, and our planet should whole-heartedly support. If we do not stop producing so much waste, we will inevitibly destroy our own enviornment. Unlike most efforts to improve ~~things~~ **our lives**, the move to

Poor sentence: What does "This" refer to?

Vague

reduce, reuse, and recycle ~~has one other advantage, it doesn't cost any money~~ **costs us nothing**. ~~In fact, it can~~ **save** ~~every~~ households~~**s**~~ ~~that practises it~~ hundreds of dollars a year. Everyone wins when we commit to the "3 Rs."

Wordy

Reordered

Memorable statement added

Exercise 10.2 (suggested answers)
1. I **expect** a salary **commensurate** with my qualifications *** and experience.
2. I have **learned** Microsoft Word and **Excel spreadsheet programs**.
3. In 2007, I **received** a **plaque** for being salesperson of the year.
4. Reason for leaving last job: **maternity** leave.
5. You will want me to be a **manager** in no time.
6. I am a perfectionist and rarely**, if ever,** forget details.
7. Marital status: single. ***
8. In my previous job I**, I learned to trust no one**. (Not an admission you should make in a job application.)
9. As **indicated**, I have over five **years' experience in** analyzing investments.
10. I was responsible for **running** *** a Western chain store. (*Better:* I was responsible for managing a Western chain store.)

Exercise 10.3 (suggested answer)
[We developed this suggested answer by checking each sentence and paragraph of the answer to Exercise 10.1 against the "Editing Checklist" on pages 139–40. Changes we have made to sentence structure, grammar, spelling, and punctuation appear in **bold type**.]

1   Canadians are experiencing a huge cultural shift, one that has been caused not by politics, or films, or music, but by garbage. We are drowning in garbage. So much waste is produced in North America that we no longer know **where** to put it. Take Toronto, for instance. The city produces so much garbage that it trucks thousands of tonnes of it to Michigan every year**, a** short-term solution that is unsustainable. We cannot wait for the **government** to save us from this crisis. We produce the garbage; we must solve the problem. We cannot afford to delay: we must act now to reduce, reuse, and recycle. Yes, **we're talking about** the "3 Rs" of environmental responsibility, the same rules we've paid so little attention to for years.

2   First we must reduce the amount of garbage we produce. We can do this **by** refusing to buy products that are overpackaged, like fast food in **Styrofoam** containers tucked into plastic bags for carrying, and foil-wrapped chocolates in a plastic tray inside a fancy, paper-lined, nonrecyclable cardboard box. By not purchasing such wasteful items, we say to the manufacturer, "Either reduce the packaging of your product or lose business to your competition." We can also reduce waste by carpooling, for example, and by turning up the temperature in our homes a few degrees

in summer and down a few degrees in winter. David Suzuki gives sound advice in his TV commercials: switch to low-energy light bulbs, wear a sweater indoors when it's cold, and supplement fossil fuel heating systems with a wood-burning stove or fireplace. How could anyone sitting in front of a warm, cozy wood fire complain about "having to cut back"?

3 [Paragraph 3 contains no editing errors.]

4   Once we have reduced our consumption and trained ourselves to reuse rather than replace, the last step is to recycle everything we can. Composting vegetable garbage is a good way to put waste to valuable use. Unwanted or outgrown items of clothing can be donated to the Salvation Army, Goodwill, or other charitable organizations that support everyone from refugees to radical environmentalists**, as** can furniture, appliances, books, and most other household items. There are dozens of ways to make useful items from things that would otherwise become landfill, such as quilts from old clothes**,** bird feeders from plastic jugs**,** and fire logs from newspapers. Many companies now manufacture products from recycled goods, some of which are quite surprising**: W**ould you believe high-fashion, waterproof jackets made from recycled plastic bottles? We should learn about these products, support these companies' efforts, and thus further reduce the waste that is dumped into landfills.

5   This cultural shift is one that all of us who care about our families, our country, and our planet should whole-heartedly support. If we do not stop producing so much waste, we will **inevitably** destroy our **environment**. Unlike most efforts to improve our lives, the move to reduce, reuse, and recycle costs us nothing. In fact, it can save households hundreds of dollars a year. Everyone wins when we commit to the "3 Rs."

Exercise 10.4

According to a recent survey in ***Maclean's*** magazine, only 43 percent of Canadians are satisfied with their jobs. What can you do to ensure that you will not be one of the 57 percent who are unhappy with the work they do? There are three questions to consider when seeking employment that will provide satisfaction as well as a paycheque.

First**,** are you suited to the kind of work you are applying for**?** If you enjoy the outdoors, for example, and like to be active, **you are** not going to be happy with a nine-to-five office job, no matter how much it pays.

Second**,** is the job based in a location compatible with your **preferred** lifestyle**?** No matter how much you like your work, if you go home every night to an **environment** you are miserable in, it will not be long before you start **transferring** your **dissatisfaction** to your job. If you like the amenities and **conveniences** of the city, you probably will not enjoy working in a small town. If, on the other hand, you prefer the quiet and security of small-town life, you may find the city a stressful place in which to live.

Finally, is **the company you are applying to** one that you want to work for**?** Do you need the security of generous **benefits**, a good pension plan, and incentives to stay and grow with one company? Or are you an **ambitious** person who is looking for variety, quick advancement, and a high salary**?** If so, you may have to forgo security in favour of commissions or cash incentives and be willing to move as quickly and as often as opportunities occur. Some **careful** self-analysis now, before you start out on your career path, will help you **choose** a direction that will put you in the 43 percent minority of satisfied Canadian workers.

Answers for Chapter 13: Documenting Your Sources (pages 180–217)

Exercise 13.2 (Answers in MLA style)

Works Cited

Cleeland, Nancy. "As Jobs Heat Up, Workers' Hearts Take a Beating." *Vancouver Sun* 30 Mar. 2005: A2. *eLibrary Canada*. Web. 26 Apr. 2009.

Dubrin, Andrew J. *Getting It Done: The Transforming Power of Self-Discipline.* Princeton: Pacesetter, 1995. Print.

Ford, Janet. Message to the author. 5 June 2009. E-mail.

Mercer, Rick. "Everything You Wanted to Know about Canada but Were Afraid to Ask." *Rick Mercer Report.* CBC Television. 3 Feb. 2009. *YouTube*. Web. 6 Feb. 2009.

"Stress, Definition of Stress, Stressor, What Is Stress? Eustress?" *American Institute of Stress.* n.d. Web. 2 May 2009.

White, Linda A. "Child Care, Women's Labour Market Participation and Labour Market Policy Effectiveness in Canada." *Canadian Public Policy* 27.4 (2001): 385-405. Print.

Exercise 13.4 (Answers in APA style)

References

American Institute of Stress. (n.d). *Stress, definition of stress, stressor, what is stress? eustress?* Retrieved from http://www.stress.org/topic-definition-stress.htm

Cleeland, N. (2005, March 30). As jobs heat up, workers' hearts take a beating. *The Vancouver Sun*, p. A2. Retrieved from eLibrary Canada database.

Dubrin, A. J. (1995). *Getting it done: The transforming power of self-discipline.* Princeton, NJ: Pacesetter.

Mercer, R. (2009, February 3). Everything you wanted to know about Canada but were afraid to ask. [Video file]. *The Rick Mercer report.* CBC Television. Retrieved from http://www.youtube.com/watch?v=yi1yhp-_x7A

White, L. A. (2001). Child care, women's labour market participation, and labour market policy effectiveness in Canada. *Canadian Public Policy, 27*(4), 385–405.

Note: The APA does not include e-mail messages in the References list. The e-mail from Janet Ford would appear as a parenthetical citation in the paper itself: (J. Ford, personal communication, June 5, 2009).

Answers for Section 7.1: Cracking the Sentence Code (pages 365–76)

Exercise 7.1.1
1. I bought a used car.
2. The used car was cheap.
3. It needed some repairs.
4. Unfortunately, the repairs were expensive.
5. Insurance for the car was expensive, too.
6. Buying a car is costly.
7. According to the salesman, the car was a bargain.
8. [You] Always get a second opinion.
9. After 10 years, cars sometimes develop serious problems.
10. Paying for repairs offsets the cheap price.

Exercise 7.1.2
1. Here is an idea to consider.
2. Who wants the last piece?
3. [You] Eat slowly.
4. There, beyond the swimming pool, is the hot tub.
5. A moving chicken is poultry in motion.
6. Two days after the due date, Homer began his term paper.
7. Here are the results of your examination.
8. In 1834, William Lyon Mackenzie became mayor of York, a town in Upper Canada.
9. Later he led a rebellion against the government of Upper Canada.
10. Irish coffee contains ingredients from all four of the essential food groups: caffeine, fat, sugar, and alcohol.

Exercise 7.1.3
1. He has talked nonstop for three hours.
2. I will be the first member of my family to graduate from college.
3. Could they return the loan tomorrow?
4. You cannot eat dessert before dinner.
5. Carla should have been filing the letters and memos.
6. I will not be taking the car.
7. Paula's lawsuit should never have been allowed to proceed this far.
8. Have you ever been to Newfoundland?
9. There has never been a better time to travel.
10. How are the club members chosen?

Exercise 7.1.4

1. ~~Among English teachers,~~ Santa's helpers are known as subordinate clauses.
2. ~~After his death,~~ Terry Fox became a national symbol ~~of heroic courage.~~
3. ~~In the state of Florida,~~ it is illegal ~~for single, divorced, or widowed women~~ to parachute ~~on Sunday afternoons.~~
4. ~~In Kentucky,~~ no woman may appear ~~in a bathing suit on any highway in the state~~ unless escorted ~~by two officers~~ or armed ~~with a club.~~
5. ~~In my wildest imaginings,~~ I cannot understand the reason ~~for these laws.~~
6. ~~During a break in the conversation,~~ Darryl's embarrassing comment could be heard ~~in every corner of the room.~~
7. ~~In my lawyer's dictionary,~~ a will is defined as a dead giveaway.
8. ~~To the staff and managers of the project,~~ I extend my congratulations ~~for an excellent job.~~
9. ~~Against all odds,~~ and ~~despite their shortcomings,~~ the St. John Miners made it ~~into the playoffs of the Southern New Brunswick Little League.~~
10. [You] Walk a mile ~~in my shoes at high noon with your head held high in order to avoid clichés like the plague.~~

Exercise 7.1.5

1. Management and union met ~~for a two-hour bargaining session.~~
2. They debated and drafted a tentative agreement ~~for a new contract.~~
3. The anesthetist and the surgeon scrubbed ~~for surgery~~ and hurried ~~to the operating room.~~
4. Frederick Banting and Norman Bethune are known ~~around the world~~ as medical heroes.
5. Kevin and Sandra hiked and cycled ~~across most of Newfoundland.~~
6. My son or my daughter will meet me and drive me home.
7. [You] Knock three times and ask ~~for Stan.~~
8. ~~In the 17th and 18th centuries,~~ the French and the English fought ~~for control of Canada.~~
9. [You] Buy the base model and don't waste your money ~~on luxury options.~~
10. Ragweed, goldenrod, and twitch grass formed the essential elements ~~in the bouquet for his English teacher.~~

Answers for Section 7.2: Solving Sentence-Fragment Problems (pages 377–84)

Exercise 7.2.1 (suggested answers)
We have made the sentence fragments into complete sentences to give you an idea of how the sentences might be formed. Different sentences can be made out of the fragments in this exercise; just be sure each sentence has a subject and a verb.

1. F   My favourite movies are about historical events.
2. F   It is silly to decide on the basis of rumour, not facts.
3. S

4. F   <u>It takes</u> only 20 minutes to make my famous tuna casserole.
5. F   The party <u>members</u> gathering in the campaign office <u>called</u> for a recount.
6. S
7. F   [<u>You</u>] <u>Put</u> your hands over your head.
8. F   <u>I</u> don't <u>want</u> to go anywhere without my iPod.
9. F   Having worked hard all her life, <u>she was</u> happy to retire.
10. S

Exercise 7.2.2 (suggested answers)

__F__ Professional <u>athletes</u> <u>make</u> millions of dollars a year. __F__ At the same time, <u>owners</u> of sports franchises <u>grow</u> fantastically rich from the efforts of their employees, the players. __F__ The <u>fans</u> <u>are</u> the forgotten people in the struggle for control over major league sports. __F__ <u>They</u> <u>are</u> the people who pay the money that makes both owners and players rich. __S__ I have an idea that would protect everyone's interests. __S__ Cap the owners' profits. __S__ Cap the players' salaries. __F__ And, most important, [<u>you</u>] <u>cap</u> the ticket prices. __F__ This <u>plan</u> <u>would ensure</u> a fair deal for everyone. __S__ Fans should be able to see their teams play for the price of a movie ticket, not the price of a television set.

Exercise 7.2.3

1. F   Although
2. F   Since
3. S
4. F   Whichever
5. F   Before

Exercise 7.2.4

1. Although many companies. . . .
4. As companies seek. . . .
6. Which leads to a surplus. . . .
8. Who have reached. . . .
9. Whether it is through termination. . . .

Exercise 7.2.5

Although many companies are now experiencing difficulty because of tough economic times, **m**iddle managers seldom breathe easily even during times of expansion and high profits. In difficult times, middle managers are vulnerable to the cost-cutting axe **as** companies seek to reduce overhead. In times of fast growth, the executive branch of many companies expands rapidly, **w**hich leads to a surplus of managerial talent, especially among junior executives. And it is these younger, well-educated, ambitious young hires who can threaten middle managers **w**ho have reached, or overreached, their potential. Whether it is through termination, early retirement, or buyout, **s**uch mid-level executives are the first to feel the effects of a company's desire to streamline the hierarchy in good times or eliminate paycheques in bad times.

Exercise 7.2.6

    In spite of what everyone says about the weak economy and the scarcity of jobs, especially for young people**,** I have financed my college career with a variety of part-time and seasonal jobs. Right now, for instance, while completing my third year at college**,** I have not one, not two, but three part-time jobs. I am a short-order cook three nights a week for a local bar and diner**, a**nd a telemarketer for a cable company after school **o**r whenever I have free time. I'm also a server at a specialty coffee store on weekends. Maintaining a social life **w**hile juggling three jobs and the requirements of my third-year program is not easy, but I find it hard to turn down any opportunity for experience**, n**ot to mention cash. I'm willing to put my social life on hold **f**or a while.

Answers for Section 7.3: Solving Run-On Problems (pages 385–88)

Exercise 7.3.1

1. This is strong coffee**. I**t has dissolved my spoon!
2. Just let me do the talking**. W**e're sure to get a ticket if you open your mouth.
3. Correct
4. If you have never tried it, hitting a golf ball may look easy, **but** it's not.
5. Correct
6. Montreal used to be known as "Ville-Marie." **B**efore that it was known as "Hochelaga."
7. Students today need summer jobs and part-time employment **because** their tuition and living costs are too high for most families to subsidize.
8. Correct
9. It's very windy, **so** a ball hit deep to centre field will likely go into the stands.
10. "I was married by a judge**;** I should have asked for a jury." (Groucho Marx)

Exercise 7.3.2

1. For students in most technology programs, job prospects are good**;** however, a diploma does not guarantee job security.
2. Despite my parents' objections, I enjoy having long hair **because** it makes me feel attractive.
3. Casual meetings are fine for small groups, **but** more formal settings are appropriate for larger groups.
4. I'd be happy to help you**. J**ust call when you need me**;** I'll be here all day.
5. In Canada, winter is more than a season**. I**t's a bad joke.
6. Correct
7. A Canadian who speaks three languages is called multilingual**;** one who speaks two languages is called bilingual**; and** one who speaks only one language is called an English Canadian.
8. Skilled people are needed in specialized fields**;** currently, the top three are geriatrics, health care, and environmental technology.

9. **Because** I use a keyboard all the time, my handwriting has become illegible. (*Or:* I use a keyboard all the time**, so** my handwriting has become illegible.)
10. I believe in a unified Canada**. I** believe that in 1867 the Fathers of Confederation were right**:** a federation of provinces can make a strong nation.

Answers for Section 7.4: Solving Modifier Problems (pages 389–97)

Exercise 7.4.1
1. The telephone rings only when I am trying to work.
2. Geoff left on the counter the can of Pet Grrrmet that he had opened for the dog.
3. We enjoyed almost the whole movie; only the ending was disappointing.
4. Leo and Annie found an apartment with two bedrooms and free Internet in a high-rise within walking distance of the campus.
5. With a full-sized HD monitor and increased RAM, this is the computer best suited to the design team.
6. To support our local school's fundraising, I gave a student in a team uniform $10.00 to wash my car.
7. For the second time, a jury found the teenager guilty of killing her best friend.
8. In September, our instructor told us that he thought our class was a hopeless case. (*Or*: Our instructor told us that he thought our class was a hopeless case in September.)
9. A charming, youthful companion who likes to travel and looks good in designer gowns is sought by an aging but wealthy gentleman. (*Better:* An aging but wealthy gentleman seeks a charming, youthful companion who likes to travel and looks good in designer gowns. See "Choosing between Active and Passive Verbs" within Section 7.8.)
10. Only one of us could go because there was enough money to buy just one ticket.

Exercise 7.4.2
1. With clear explanations and lots of exercises, *Essay Essentials* is designed to help college and university students learn to write good prose.
2. Each year, almost half a million Canadian men have a vasectomy.
3. With his new binoculars, James caught sight of a doe and her two fawns.
4. Vancouver is a wonderful city to live in for anyone who likes rain and fog.
5. Some games, such as Scrabble and checkers, are less demanding in terms of fitness and strength.
6. Thanks to my new camera with automatic functions, I can take professional-quality pictures.
7. We looked online for a suitable retirement gift for our boss.
8. The Canadian Human Rights Act prohibits discrimination on the basis of race, religion, sex, or age against anyone who is applying for a job.
9. One usually finds the best Chinese food in restaurants where the Chinese eat.
10. Tonight, Liam Neeson will talk with George Stroumboulopoulos about his wife, Natasha Richardson, who died after falling on a ski slope at Mont Tremblant.

Exercise 7.4.3

1. Because she was driving recklessly and without lights, the police stopped Gina at a roadblock.
2. After I had been late twice in one week, my supervisor gave me a lecture about punctuality.
3. After criticizing both my work and my attitude, she fired me.
4. With enough memory to store her favourite movies and more than 10 000 songs, the MacBook was the computer Hannah knew she needed.
5. After they spent two weeks quarrelling over money, their relationship was over.
6. As a dedicated fan of Alice Munro, I believe her last book was her best.
7. In less than a minute after applying the ointment, I felt the pain begin to ease.
8. Jake was probably more nervous than Allison, who was making her first formal presentation to her colleagues and her supervisor.
9. When handling hazardous waste, [you] follow the procedures in the safety manual.
10. After spending the day in the kitchen preparing a gourmet meal, Kendra felt her efforts weren't appreciated because the guests drank too much wine.

Exercise 7.4.4

1. She was the baker's only daughter, but she could loaf all day. (*Or:* She was only the baker's daughter, but she could loaf all day.)
2. Being horribly hung over, I realized that the problem with a free bar is knowing when to quit.
3. Sam finally got the terrified horse, which was rearing and kicking, under control.
4. In a hurry to get to the interview on time, I left my résumé lying on my desk at home.
5. As a college student constantly faced with new assignments, I find the pressure is sometimes intolerable.
6. Listening to the rumours, I'll bet the newlyweds are already on the road to separation.
7. The liquor in the duty-free outlet is of no interest to me because I do not drink.
8. The bride, who was wearing a strapless gown with a short lace jacket, was given in marriage by her father.
9. Queen Elizabeth couldn't resist the little Corgi puppy, which was rolling on her back, eager to have her tummy scratched.
10. If you wear a small Canadian flag on your backpack or lapel, people abroad will be less likely to assume you're American.

Answers for Section 7.5: The Parallelism Principle (pages 398–403)

Exercise 7.5.1

1. This program is easy to understand and to use.
2. We were told to leave and take everything with us.
3. We organized our findings, wrote the report, and finally prepared our PowerPoint presentation.
4. Both applicants were unskilled, unprepared, and unmotivated.

5. Elmer's doctor advised him not to strain his back or his mind.
6. The company is looking for an employee who has a car and who knows the city.
7. If consumers really cared, they could influence the fast-food industry to produce healthy, delicious, inexpensive food.
8. When I want to get away from it all, there are three solitary pleasures that I enjoy: walking in the country, reading a book, and listening to music.
9. A recent survey of female executives claims that family responsibilities, exclusion from informal networks, and lack of management experience are the major factors keeping them from advancement.
10. If it is to be useful, your report must be clearly organized, well written, and thoroughly researched.

Exercise 7.5.2
1. For my birthday, I requested either a Roots bag or a Dior scarf.
2. In my community, two related crimes are rapidly increasing: drug abuse and theft.
3. Bodybuilding has made me what I am today: physically perfect, financially prosperous, and practically friendless.
4. After reading all the explanations and completing all the exercises, you'll be a better writer.
5. Bruce claimed that, through repetition and reward, he had trained his centipede to be loyal and obedient.
6. During their vacation in New Brunswick, Trevor and Jane visited many beautiful locations and ate wonderful seafood.
7. I'm an average tennis player; I have a good forehand, an average backhand, but a weak serve.
8. The problem with being immortalized as a statue is that you will be a target for pigeon droppings and graffiti.
9. Never disturb a sleeping dog, a happy baby, or a silent politician.
10. I'd like to help, but I'm too tired and too busy.

Exercise 7.5.3

1. wine	women	song
2. do your best	don't give up	
3. information	education	entertainment
4. as individuals	as a group	
5. privately	publicly	
6. happy	healthy	wise
7. employers	full-time employees	contract workers
8. lack of time	[lack of] money	[lack of] staff
9. French is the language of love	English is the language of business	German is the language of philosophy
10. lying about all morning	doing whatever I please	

Exercise 7.5.4
1. Not being able to speak the language is confusing, frustrating, and embarrassing.
2. Trying your best and succeeding are not always the same thing.
3. The first candidate we interviewed seemed frightened and shy, but the second was composed and confident.

4. Licking one's fingers and picking one's teeth in a restaurant are one way to get attention.
5. Our CEO claims his most valuable business assets are a good backhand and membership at an exclusive golf club.
6. In order to succeed in this economy, small businesses must be creative, innovative, and flexible.
7. Lowering our profit margin, raising our prices, and laying off two managers will enable us to meet our budget.
8. After an enjoyable dinner, I like to drink a cappuccino, eat a dark chocolate mint, and, occasionally, smoke a good cigar.
9. Lying in the sun, consuming high-fat foods, and smoking cigarettes are three life-threatening activities that were once thought to be healthy.
10. Business travellers complain of long delays at airports, higher costs for services, and tighter restrictions on their freedom of movement.

Answers for Section 7.6: Refining by Combining (pages 404–8)

Exercise 7.6.1

1. We cannot sell our cottage, **so** we will live there instead.
2. There are three solutions given for this problem, **and** all of them are correct.
3. The people in our firm work very hard, **yet** they wouldn't want it any other way.
4. We could spend our day off cleaning the house, **or** we could spend the day fishing.
5. Great leaders do not bully their people, **nor** do they deceive them.
6. I will not be able to finish my report, **for** there are only two hours before the deadline.
7. Jennifer knows that she will probably not get the vice-president's job, **but** she wants the experience of applying for it.
8. Finish the estimate, **and** do not begin work until it has been approved.
9. Today has been the worst day of my life, **so** my horoscope was right.
10. The department did not offer me a job, **nor** did it even reply to my letter.

Exercise 7.6.2 (suggested answers)

1. Leonardo da Vinci was a great artist and inventor **who** invented scissors, among other things.
2. Cats can produce over 100 vocal sounds, **whereas** dogs can make only 10.
3. **Although** it is said that men don't cry, they do while assembling furniture.
4. The name Wendy was made up for a book **that** was called *Peter Pan*.
5. **Although** 10 percent of Canadians are heavy drinkers, 35 percent abstain from alcohol.
6. Travel broadens the mind **even though** it flattens the bank account.
7. We are seeking an experienced and innovative director **who** is fluent in French.
8. One hundred thousand Vietnam veterans have taken their own lives, **which** is twice the number who were killed in action.
9. **After** my cooking class went on a field trip to gather greens for a salad, we discovered that what we had thought was watercress was poison ivy.
10. Eight of my ten classmates **who** ate the salad were hospitalized, **although** no one was critically ill.

Answers for Section 7.7: Mastering Subject–Verb Agreement (pages 409–18)

Exercise 7.7.1

1. They sell used books to other students.
2. Those new guidelines affect all the office procedures.
3. All those who shop at Pimrock's receive free cans of tuna.
4. The women maintain that their boss has been harassing them.
5. Those girls' parents are looking for suitable husbands for them.

Exercise 7.7.2

1. is
2. are
3. is
4. is
5. tempt

Exercise 7.7.3

1. are
2. registers
3. is
4. wonders
5. puts

Exercise 7.7.4

1. is
2. involves
3. is
4. wants
5. believes

Exercise 7.7.5

1. is
2. has
3. have
4. was
5. are

Exercise 7.7.6

1. was
2. seems
3. is
4. is
5. seems

Exercise 7.7.7

1. Neither of the following sentences **is** correct.
2. The faculty, with the full support of the college administration, **treat** plagiarism as a serious offence.
3. Either good looks or intelligence **runs** in our family, but never at the same time.

4. None of the computer experts **has** been able to untangle our billing problems.
5. The enjoyment of puns and jokes involving plays on words **is** the result of having too little else on your mind.
6. Anyone who jumps from one of Paris's many bridges **is** in Seine.
7. It is amazing how much better the orchestra **plays** now that the conductor is sober.
8. The number of layoffs in the last quarter **is** truly alarming.
9. Her colleagues, along with her supervisor, **agree** that Emily needs further training.
10. Canada's First Nations population **is** thought to have come to this continent from Asia thousands of years before the Europeans arrived in North America.

Exercise 7.7.8

Quebec City, along with Montreal, Toronto, and Vancouver, **is** among Canada's great gourmet centres. Whereas Toronto and Vancouver are relative latecomers to this list, neither Quebec City nor Montreal **is a stranger** to those who **seek** fine dining. Indeed, travel and food magazines have long affirmed that including these two cities in a Quebec vacation **is** a "must." Montreal is perhaps more international in its offerings, but Quebec City provides exquisite proof that French Canadian cuisine and hospitality **are** second to none in the world. Amid the Old World charm of the lower city **are** to be found some of the quaintest and most enjoyable traditional restaurants, and the newer sections of town **boast** equally fine dining in more contemporary surroundings. The combination of the wonderful food and the charm of the city **is** sure to entice any visitor to return. Either summer, when the city blooms and outdoor cafés abound, or winter, when Carnaval turns the streets into hundreds of connecting parties, **is a** wonderful **time** to visit one of Canada's oldest and most interesting cities.

Answers for Section 7.8: Using Verbs Effectively (pages 419–32)

Exercise 7.8.1

1. lay
2. eaten
3. driven
4. sat
5. chosen
6. printed
7. lie
8. lent
9. worn
10. known

Exercise 7.8.3

1. After he accused me of cheating, I **called** him a liar.
2. My husband watches television until he **goes** to sleep.
3. Hank Aaron broke Babe Ruth's record of 714 home runs in a lifetime when he **hit** number 715 in 1974.
4. Children are quite perceptive and **know** when you are trying to hide something from them.
5. She went up to the counter and **asked** for a refund.
6. When George Clooney walked into the building, the women **went** crazy.
7. Correct
8. Tim entered the room, took one look at Leroy, and **smashed** him right through the wall.

9. First you will greet the guests; then you **will show** them to their rooms.
10. The largest cheese ever produced took 43 hours to make and **weighed** a whopping 15 723 kg.

Exercise 7.8.4

For some reason, when mistakes or accidents happen in radio or television, they **are** often hilariously funny. If, in the course of a conversation, someone said, "Here come the Duck and Doochess of Kent," listeners would probably be mildly amused. But many years ago, when an announcer **made** that slip on a live radio broadcast, it **became** one of the most famous blunders in radio history. Tapes of the slip **were** filed in "bloopers" libraries all over the world. This heightened sense of hilarity is the reason that so many people who work in radio **dedicate** their creativity to making the on-air announcer laugh while reading the news. To take one example, Lorne Greene's **was** the deeply serious voice that **was** heard on the CBC news during World War II. He **was** the victim of all kinds of pranks aimed at getting him to break up while reading the dark, often tragic, news of the combat overseas. The pages of his news script **were** set on fire while he **read**. He **was** even stripped naked as he **read**, calmly, and apparently without strain. Lorne Greene **was** a true professional. Many other newscasters, however, **have been** highly susceptible to falling apart on air at the slightest provocation. And there **are** always people around a radio station who cannot resist giving them that little push.

Exercise 7.8.6

1. The department head called a meeting.
2. The barista will make your espresso in a few minutes.
3. When it gets cold, we plug in the block heater overnight.
4. For many years, professional athletes have used steroids to improve speed and endurance.
5. You may not take photos during the performance.
6. My great-grandfather, who served in the army overseas, wrote these letters.
7. A crew of students made this film for less than $100 000.
8. Thieves broke into our neighbours' house while they were vacationing in Cuba.
9. You made an error in the code you wrote for this program.
10. Teamwork is a valuable concept, especially when we need someone to take the blame for the boss's mistakes.

Exercise 7.8.7

1. Another Juno was won by Feist. (Active voice is more effective.)
2. The ball was spiked by Jian, after scoring the go-ahead touchdown. (Active voice is more effective.)
3. A bylaw forbidding backyard bird feeders was passed by City Council. (Passive voice is more effective because it focuses on the law rather than on who passed it.)
4. Later that night, the security guard saw a shadowy figure entering the lab. (Passive voice is more effective because it focuses on the intruder rather than on who saw him or her.)
5. Four tickets to the Michael Bublé concert were bought by Courtenay after standing in line all night. (Active voice is more effective.)

6. The truth behind the fake diploma scandal was revealed on the 10 p.m. news. (Passive voice is more effective because it focuses on the scandal rather than on when it was revealed.)

7. People who want to shift responsibility from themselves to others often use passive voice. (Passive is more effective.)

8. After a long debate, Yasmin's idea of a class *Facebook* page was endorsed by the student council. (Passive voice is more effective because it focuses on the idea rather than who supported it.)

9. Language psychologists have developed a computer program that analyzes speech patterns. (Passive voice is more effective because it focuses on the specific program rather than on the anonymous group who developed it.)

10. After years of research among class students, language psychologists have determined that people who frequently use passive voice tend to be maladjusted. (Active voice is more effective.)

Answers for Section 7.9: Solving Pronoun Problems (pages 433–51)

Exercise 7.9.1

1. Murray and **he** fell asleep. . . .
2. Would you like to work on the project with Emily and **me**?
3. Only two students failed to show up for the midterm exam: Nadia and **I**.
4. No one except her parents and **me** has any interest. . . .
5. It's true that I got some ideas from **her** and Jacques. . . .
6. When it comes to the argument over Apple vs. PC, **she** and **I** have agreed to disagree.
7. If **he** and I cannot solve this problem, you and **she** will have to do it.
8. Everyone agrees that Yoshi and **she** are the best players, but Leah and **I** have been practising.
9. Quentin and **he** agreed to split the price of a case with Mike and **me**.
10. Trina and **I** are planning a trip to Guatemala, where **we**. . . .

Exercise 7.9.2

1. At 14, my younger brother is already taller than **I** [am].
2. No one likes partying more than **he** and Anne.
3. Would you like to join Daniel and **me** . . . ?
4. Only one person in this firm could manage the department as well as **he** [could].
5. At last I have met someone who enjoys grilled liver as much as **I** [do]!
6. We can skate as well as **they**, but they are much better at shooting and defending than **we** [are].
7. More than **I** [do], Serge uses the computer. . . .

Exercise 7.9.3

1. My boyfriend and **I**. . . .
2. I like fast food better than **he** [does].
3. He likes vegetables better than **I** [do].
4. In fact, between you and **me**. . . .
5. . . . it is difficult for **them** to know where to take him and **me**. . . .

6. The only type of restaurant where **we** [and **they**] can all have what we like is Italian.
7. There, **he** and his friends. . . .
8. We are probably not as healthy as they, but they don't seem to enjoy their food as much as **we** [do].

Exercise 7.9.4
1. his
2. her
3. his
4. her
5. himself, he

Exercise 7.9.5
1. Everyone who enjoys a thrilling match will reserve a seat. . . .
2. . . . everyone had to climb to the fourth floor to hand in the course evaluation.
3. Correct
4. Someone with lots of money left a purse in the women's washroom.
5. Reporters must decide for themselves how far they will go. . . .

Exercise 7.9.6
1. Virginia claims that every one of her male friends has a room of his own.
2. Almost everyone I know is concerned about finding a suitable job.
3. Anybody who applies for a job with this institution can expect to spend a lot of time in selection committee interviews.
4. Taking pictures of people when they are not looking can produce interesting results.
5. Nearly every man who can cook will tell you that he enjoys preparing food.

Exercise 7.9.7
1. I know that smoking is bad for me and everyone else, but I can't give up cigarettes.
2. If your pet rat won't eat its food, feed the pellets to the kitty.
3. Our cat is a picky eater; her food preferences are inconvenient and expensive.
4. Whenever Stan and Matt played poker, Stan stacked the deck.
5. The gorilla was mean and hungry because he had finished all his food in the morning.
6. Madonna has transformed herself at least five times in her career, an accomplishment that makes her unique.
7. Dani backed her car into a garbage truck and dented her fender.
8. Rocco was suspicious of handgun control because he thought everyone should have a gun for late-night subway rides.
9. Get your ears pierced during this week's special and take home an extra pair of earrings free.
10. Our car is in the shop, but we're still going to the party.

Exercise 7.9.9
1. The actress **who** saw her first grey hair thought she'd dye.
2. I am a long-time fan of David Cronenberg, a director **who** began his career in Canada.

3. I wonder why we are so often attracted to people **who** are opposite to us.
4. I'm one of those people **who** should stay out of the sun.
5. People **who** take afternoon naps often suffer from insomnia as a result.
6. The vacuum-cleaner salesperson **who** came to our door was the sort of person **who** won't take no for an answer.
7. Ms. Waldman is the brilliant teacher **who** helped me achieve the grades **that** I had thought were beyond me.
8. Marathon runners **who** wear cheap shoes often suffer the agony of defeat.
9. The math problems **that** we worked on last night would have baffled anyone **who** hadn't done all the problem sets.
10. We took the ancient Jeep, **which** we had bought from a friend **who** had lost his licence, to a scrapyard **that** paid us $200 for it.

Exercise 7.9.10
1. you
2. she
3. a
4. you, your
5. we

Exercise 7.9.11
1. People who live in glass houses shouldn't throw stones.
2. Experience is something **you acquire** just after you need it.
3. Anyone who enjoys snowboarding can have **the** best holiday ever in western Alberta.
4. When she asked if Peter Tchaikovsky played for the Canucks, **I** knew she wasn't the woman for me.
5. From time to time, most of us think about the opportunities we've missed even if **we are** happy with what **we** have.
6. If you are afraid of vampires, **you** should wear garlic around **your** neck and carry a silver bullet.
7. Any woman who wears a garlic necklace probably won't have to worry about men harassing **her**, either.
8. Can you really know another person if you have never been to **his or her** home?
9. Managers who are concerned about employee morale should think about ending **their** policy of threats and intimidation and consider other means to improve ***efficiency.
10. A sure way to lose **your** friends is to eat all the ice cream yourself.

Exercise 7.9.12
When people see a dreadful occurrence on television, such as a bombing, an earthquake, or a mass slaughter, it does not always affect **them.** It is one thing for people to see the ravages of war **themselves** and another thing to see a three-minute newscast of the same battle, neatly edited by the CBC. Even the horrible effects of natural catastrophes that wipe out whole populations are somehow minimized or trivialized when **people** see them on TV. And although viewers may be horrified by the gaunt faces of starving children on the screen, **they** can easily escape into **their**

familiar world of Egg McMuffins, Shake'n Bake, and Labatt Blue that is portrayed in commercial messages.

Thus, the impact of television on us is a mixed one. It is true that **we are** shown terrible, sometimes shocking events that **we** could not possibly have seen before television. In this way, **our** world is drawn together more closely. However, the risk in creating this immediacy is that **we** may become desensitized and cease to feel or care about other human beings.

Answers for Section 7.10: The Comma (pages 452–62)

Exercise 7.10.1

1. A cup of coffee, a croissant, and a glass of juice are what I want for breakfast.
2. The food at the Thai Palace is colourful, spicy, delicious, and inexpensive.
3. Life would be complete if I had a BlackBerry, a Porsche, a Sea-Doo, and a job.
4. The gear list for the Winter Wilderness course includes woollen underwear, snowshoes, Arctic boots, and a toque.
5. Holly held two aces, a King, a Queen, and a Jack in her hand.
6. Please bring the videos, maps, and souvenirs of your trip to Australia.
7. In most of Canada, the four seasons are summer, winter, winter, and winter.
8. My wife thinks that I should eat less, exercise more, and take a daily vitamin and mineral supplement.
9. Sleeping through my alarm, dozing during English class, napping in the library after lunch, and snoozing in front of the TV after supper are the causes of my hyperactive nightlife.
10. Welcome home! Once you have finished your homework, taken out the garbage, and done the dishes, you can feed the cat, clean your room, and do your laundry.

Exercise 7.10.2

1. Either it is very foggy this morning, or I am going blind.
2. We have an approved business plan and budget, but we're still looking for qualified and experienced staff.
3. People on talk shows haven't said anything new in years, nor have they solved a single one of the problems they endlessly discuss.
4. We discovered that we both had an interest in photography, so we made a date to go to the Ansel Adams exhibition next week.
5. Canadians are proud of their country, but they don't approve of too much flag-waving.
6. Take good notes, for I'll need them in order to study for the exam.
7. I will rent a tux, but I will not get a haircut or have my shoes shined.
8. I chose a quiet seat on the train, and two women with bawling babies boarded at the next station.
9. I have travelled all over the world, yet my luggage has visited at least twice the number of countries that I have.
10. Jet lag makes me look haggard and ill, but at least I resemble my passport photo.

Exercise 7.10.3

1. Remember, a clear conscience is often just a sign of a poor memory.
2. If you think nobody cares, try missing a few payments.
3. When the cannibals ate a missionary, they got a taste of religion.
4. No matter how much I practise, my singing never gets any better.
5. First, cook the noodles in a large pot of boiling water.
6. If Barbie is so popular, why do you have to buy friends for her?
7. Until I had my performance review, I thought my manager had no appreciation of my efforts.
8. No matter how much you push the envelope, it will still be stationery.
9. Ladies and gentlemen, please put away all cellphones, BlackBerrys, and any other electronic devices you may have concealed on your person before entering the examination room.
10. In democracy, it is your vote that counts; in feudalism, it is your count that votes.

Exercise 7.10.4

1. A good day, in my opinion, always starts with a few cuts of high-volume heavy metal.
2. This photograph, which was taken when I was eight months old, embarrasses me whenever my parents display it.
3. Mira's boyfriend, who looks like an ape, is living proof that love is blind.
4. Isn't it strange that the poor, who are often bitterly critical of the rich, buy lottery tickets?
5. A nagging headache, the result of last night's party, made me miserable all morning.
6. Our ancient car made it all the way to Saskatoon without breaking down, a piece of good luck that astonished us all.
7. Professor Repke, a popular mathematics teacher, won the Distinguished Teaching Award this year.
8. We're going to spend the afternoon at the mall, a weekly event that has become a ritual.
9. Correct
10. Classical music, which I call Prozac for the ears, can be very soothing in times of stress.

Exercise 7.10.5

1. Unfortunately, we'll have to begin all over again.
2. Lord Black, your wife would like a word with you.
3. In college, the quality of your work is more important than the effort you put into it.
4. Hopelessly lost, my father refused to stop and ask for directions.
5. Finally understanding what she was trying to say, I apologized for being so slow.
6. After an evening of watching television, I have accomplished as much as if I had been unconscious.

7. Since the doctor ordered me to walk to work every morning, I have seen three accidents involving people walking to work.
8. That same year, Stephen Leacock bought his summer home in Orillia, Ontario.
9. When an optimist is pulled over by a police officer, the optimist assumes it's to ask for directions.
10. Having munched our way through a large bag of peanuts while watching the game, we weren't interested in supper.

Exercise 7.10.6
1. Dietitians recommend that we eat at least two servings daily of green, leafy vegetables.
2. Correct
3. Correct
4. Toronto in the summer is hot, smoggy, and humid.
5. St. John's, on the other hand, is cool, sunny, and windy.
6. The dining room table was made of richly stained, ornately carved walnut.
7. This ergonomic, efficient, full-function keyboard comes in a variety of pastel shades.
8. We ordered a large, nutritious salad for lunch, then smothered it in calorie-laden, creamy ranch dressing.
9. For my sister's birthday, her boyfriend gave her a cute, cuddly, seven-week-old puppy.
10. Today's paper has an article about a new car made of lightweight, durable carbon fibre.

Exercise 7.10.7
1. Your dogs, Mr. Pavlov, seem hungry for some reason. (Rule 4)
2. I use SMS to communicate with my colleagues, e-mail to keep in touch with clients(,) and Canada Post to send greetings to my relatives. (Rule 1)
3. There are, I am told, people who don't like garlic, but you won't find any of them eating at Freddy's. (Rule 4, Rule 2)
4. How you choose to phrase your resignation is up to you, but I expect to have it on my desk by morning. (Rule 2)
5. Pinot noir, which is a type of grape grown in California, Oregon, British Columbia(,) and Ontario, produces a delicious red wine. (Rule 4, Rule 1)
6. Looking for a competent computer technologist, we interviewed, tested, investigated(,) and rejected 30 applicants. (Rule 3, Rule 1)
7. According to G. K. Chesterton, "If a thing is worth doing, it is worth doing badly." (Rule 3, Rule 3)
8. Your superstitious fear of March 15, Julius, is irrational and silly. (Rule 4)
9. Canada, a country known internationally for beautiful scenery, peaceful intentions(,) and violent hockey, always places near the top of the United Nations' list of desirable places to live. (Rule 4, Rule 1)
10. The lenses of my new sunglasses are high-function, impact-resistant, UV-reflective optical plastic. (Rule 5)

Exercise 7.10.8

1. Whereas the Super Bowl tradition goes back about four decades, the Grey Cup has a history that stretches back to the 19th century. (Rule 3)
2. Otherwise, Mrs. Lincoln said, she very much enjoyed the play. (Rule 4)
3. Our guard dog, a Rottweiler, caught an intruder and maimed him for life. (Rule 4)
4. Unfortunately, my Uncle Ladislaw was the intruder, and he intends to sue us for every penny we have. (Rule 3, Rule 2)
5. Correct
6. We bought a lovely, old, oak dining table at auction for $300. (Rule 5)
7. If there were more people like Gladys, global warming would be the least of our worries. (Rule 3)
8. Correct
9. Deciding on the midnight blue velvet pants was easy, but paying for them was not. (Rule 2)
10. Igor asked, "May I show you to your quarters, or would you prefer to spend the night in the dungeon?" (Rule 4, Rule 2)

Answers for Section 7.11: The Semicolon (pages 463–67)

Exercise 7.11.1

1. incorrect	6. incorrect
2. correct	7. correct
3. incorrect	8. incorrect
4. incorrect	9. incorrect
5. incorrect	10. incorrect

Exercise 7.11.2

1. We've eaten all the food; it's time to go home.
2. Correct
3. Your instructor would like to see you pass; however, there may be a small fee involved.
4. Molly is going to Chicago; she is determined to meet Oprah.
5. Many people dislike hockey because some of the players act like goons rather than athletes.
6. Lisa tried and tried, but she couldn't get Homer's attention.
7. Correct
8. Tomorrow is another day; unfortunately, it will probably be just like today.
9. Rumours of a merger had begun to circulate by five o'clock, so it's no wonder many employees looked nervous on their way home.
10. We knew the party had been a success when Uncle Irving, drunk as usual, tap-danced across the top of the piano; Aunt Liz, who must weigh at least 80 kg, did her Cirque du Soleil routine; and Marvin punched out two of his cousins.

Exercise 7.11.3

1. A day without puns is like a day without sunshine; it leaves gloom for improvement.
2. The rain has to stop soon; otherwise, we'll have to start building an ark.
3. Our finances are a mess; the only way we can repay our debts would be to stop paying for rent and food.
4. We would like to meet on Tuesday; however, since you have another commitment, we will reschedule.
5. I work on an assembly line; we workers believe that if a job is worth doing, it's worth doing 11 000 times a day.
6. It is not impossible to become wealthy; if you're under 20, all you need to do is put the price of a pack of cigarettes into an RRSP every day, and you'll be a millionaire by the age of 50.
7. If, on the other hand, you continue to spend your money on smokes, the government will make the millions that could have been yours; you'll die early and broke.
8. As a dog lover and the owner of an Afghan, I suffer a great deal of abuse; for example, for my birthday, my wife gave me a book rating the intelligence of Afghans as 79th out of 79 breeds tested.
9. A plateau, according to the *Dictionary of Puns*, is a high form of flattery; this may be low humour, but it's a clever pun.
10. According to a *Bon Appetit* poll, four of the top ten restaurants in the world are in Paris; three—those ranking eighth, ninth, and tenth—are in the United States; two are in Tokyo; and the other is in Thailand.

Answers for Section 7.12: The Colon (pages 468–72)

Exercise 7.12.1

1. incorrect	6. correct
2. correct	7. incorrect
3. incorrect	8. incorrect
4. correct	9. incorrect
5. incorrect	10. incorrect

Exercise 7.12.2

1. Right after we moved in, we discovered we had a problem: termites.
2. I have set myself three goals this year: to achieve an 80 percent average, to get a good summer job, and to buy a car.
3. After our bankruptcy, our credit card consultant asked us an interesting question: "Why don't you cut up your credit cards?"
4. Many Canadian writers are better known abroad than they are at home: Carol Shields, Neil Bissoondath, and Michael Ondaatje are three examples.
5. There are a number of inexpensive activities that will improve physical fitness: swimming, tennis, jogging, even brisk walking.
6. Jocelyn is trying to achieve two contradictory goals: significant weight loss and success as a restaurant critic.
7. Several of the animals on the international list of endangered species are native to Canada: the wood bison, the northern kit fox, and the whooping crane.

8. Correct
9. Canada's population is worn out and exhausted at the end of a long, hard winter, but most people are able to console themselves with one comforting thought**:** spring will arrive sometime in May or June.
10. There are several troublesome implications of biological engineering, but one in particular disturbs most people**:** the cloning of human beings.

Exercise 7.12.3

1. The most annoying sound in the world has to be that produced by bagpipes.
2. Correct
3. Believe it or not, the country that produces the most films every year is India.
4. Correct
5. In the Okanagan Valley, the major fruit crops are apples, peaches, and cherries.
6. Correct
7. Most students want their teachers to treat them with courtesy, fairness, and respect.
8. I have a real problem: my iPod is full.
9. Our department's proposal is sure to receive funding: it has the CEO's approval.
10. The company's bankruptcy resulted from a number of factors, including the economic downturn, obsolete products, and excessively rich benefits for their unionized employees. (*Or:* The company's bankruptcy resulted from a number of factors: the economic downturn, obsolete products, and excessively rich benefits for their unionized employees.)

Answers for Section 7.13: Quotation Marks (pages 473–75)

Exercise 7.13.1

1. "Did you see the look on her face**?**" asked Roderick.
2. Correct
3. "I'd love to," she replied**,** "if only I knew how."
4. "Pardon me, boys, is this the Transylvania Station**?**" asked the man in the black cape.
5. When I pointed out to Wayne that he was wearing one green sock and one brown sock, he replied**,** "What's wrong with that? My brother has a pair just like it."
6. When I asked the guide if people jumped from the CN Tower very often, he replied**,** "No, just the once."
7. Correct
8. "Just as well," muttered Lola, "because I wouldn't want the state to see what's growing on my bedroom windowsill."
9. I knew that Microsoft had lost its corporate mind when my computer flashed the following error message**:** "No keyboard detected. Press any key to continue."
10. The psychiatrist said to the woman whose husband thought he was a horse**,** "I can cure your husband, but it will take a long time and be very costly." "Money is no object," replied the woman. "He just won the Queen's Plate."

*Answers for Section 7.14: Question and Exclamation Marks
(pages 476–79)*

Exercise 7.14.1

1. question mark
2. period
3. period
4. period
5. question mark

6. question mark
7. period
8. question mark
9. period
10. question mark

Exercise 17.14.2

1. You must be kidding!
2. Turn left! Now!
3. I can't believe I actually passed!
4. Oh, great! We're moving to Backwater, Alberta! (*Or:* We're moving to Backwater, Alberta.)
5. Run! It's right behind you!
6. I'm freezing! Turn up the heat!
7. "Workers of the world, unite!"
8. At last! Someone is finally coming to take our order.
9. For the last time, leave me alone!
10. What a great game! I've never seen a better one. (*Or:* I've never seen a better one!)

Answers for Section 7.15: Dashes and Parentheses (pages 480–85)

Exercise 7.15.1

1. One Aboriginal tribe in England painted themselves blue with dye from a plant—woad. (*Or:* . . . dye from a plant: woad.)
2. My purpose in moving from Vancouver to Hope—like that of hundreds of people before me—was to find affordable housing.
3. We will have to start without her—again!
4. Skiing and skating—if you like these sports, you'll love Quebec.
5. Tending to his garden, writing his memoirs, and dining with friends—these were the pleasures Arnold looked forward to in retirement. (*Or:* . . . friends: these were the pleasures. . . .)
6. What is missing in his life is obvious—rest and relaxation! (*Or:* . . . is obvious: rest and relaxation.)
7. Zoe should do well—in fact, I'm sure she will—in the engineering program.
8. Alexei was amazed—positively thunderstruck—when he heard that Uncle Vladimir had won a million dollars.
9. Historians, diarists, and memoirists—these are the recorders of our past. (*Or:* . . . and memoirists: these are the recorders.)
10. Dashes—a kind of silent shout—allow you to insert an occasional exclamatory word or phrase into your sentences.

Exercise 7.15.2

1. Five of the students (I was asked not to name them) have volunteered to be peer tutors.
2. The apostrophe is explained in Section 7.17 (pages 499–506).
3. Jason complained that being a manager (he became one in March) was like being a cop.
4. I have enclosed a cheque for one hundred and fifty dollars ($150).
5. More members of the Canadian Forces died in World War I (1914–18) than in any war before or since.
6. Although Mozart lived a relatively short time (he died when he was 36), he composed hundreds of musical masterpieces.
7. As news of her "miracle cures" spread (patients began to come to her from all over the province), the doctor had to move her clinic to a more central location.
8. The new contract provided improved working conditions, a raise in salary (3 percent), and a new dental plan.
9. Ontario and British Columbia now produce award-winning, world-class wines from small estate wineries (Inniskillin, Hillebrand, and Quail's Gate are three examples).
10. "One of the most important tools for making paper speak in your own voice is punctuation; it helps readers hear you the way you want to be heard" (Baker 48-49).

Answers for Section 7.16: Hazardous Homonyms (pages 486–98)

Exercise 7.16.1

1. course, affect
2. Are, accept
3. then, dessert
4. you're, losing
5. quite, here
6. whose, conscience
7. assured, number
8. It's, its
9. choose, course, advice
10. Continual, dining

Exercise 7.16.2

1. infer, whether, fourth
2. Whose, principles, less
3. effect, disperse, fewer
4. imply, further, creditable
5. morale, miners, fazed
6. simplistic, morals, implies
7. your, continually, ensures
8. conscious, choosing, site, farther
9. accept, councillors, phase
10. number, allowed, fewer, than, women

Exercise 7.16.3

1. b
2. b
3. a
4. b
5. b
6. b
7. b
8. a
9. b
10. a

Answers for Section 7.17: The Apostrophe (pages 499–506)

Exercise 7.17.1

1. Who knows **what's** wrong with this sentence?
2. **She's** only a whiskey maker, but he loves her still.
3. **It's** a long way from Halifax to Vancouver, but we think **we're** ready: **we've** been in training since August.
4. No matter how much **we'll** push the envelope, **it'll** always be stationery.
5. **Wasn't** it Mark Twain who said, "**It's** easy to stop smoking; I've done it dozens of times"?

Exercise 7.17.2

I am writing to apply for the position of webmaster for BrilloVision.com that **you have** advertised in the *Daily News*. **I have** the talent and background **you are** looking for. Currently, I work as a Web designer for an online publication, Vexed.com, where **they are** very pleased with my work. If you click on their website, I think **you will** like what you see. **There is** little in the way of Web design and application that I **have not** been involved in during the past two years. But **it is** time for me to move on to a new challenge, and BrilloVision.com promises the kind of opportunity **I am** looking for. I guarantee you **will not** be disappointed if I join your team!

Exercise 17.7.3

1. The **car's** brakes are worn and its tires are nearly bald.
2. Diplomatic **ambassadors'** wives or husbands are often as important to a **mission's** success as the ambassadors themselves.
3. Near Chicoutimi is one of the **country's** most beautiful parks, where the skills of canoeists, fishermen, and wildlife photographers can be put to the test on a **summer's** day.
4. **Jane's** career got its start when she sang **seafarers'** songs in the yacht **club's** dining lounge.
5. A **country's** history is the main determinant of its national character.

Exercise 17.7.4

1. you're, your, your
2. Someone's, whose
3. ship's, week's
4. people's, workers', sides'
5. turtle's, turtle's, it's, its, yours

Exercise 17.7.5

1. Two **silkworms** had a race; they ended up in a tie.
2. When you feel like a snack, you can choose between apples and **Timbits**.
3. **Ted's** career took off when he discovered how easy it was to sell **children's toys** to grandparents.
4. A beginning golfer needs three different kinds of clubs: **woods** for long shots, **irons** for short ones, and a putter for the last four or five shots.
5. Good writing skills **won't** guarantee success in **your** career, but poor writing **skills** are guaranteed to hold you back.

Answers for Section 7.18: The Hyphen (pages 507–10)

Exercise 7.18.1

1. Joy wants to sublet her **fifth-floor** apartment.
2. In 1950, at the age of **forty-seven**, George Orwell died of tuberculosis.
3. Just before the critical play, the **hard-fought** game was **pre-empted** by the prime minister's address.
4. **Hand-knit** sweaters are usually more expensive than **factory-produced** ones.
5. Alan claims he is addicted to **hip-hop** but allergic to classical music.

Exercise 7.18.2

1. A **rubber-band** pistol was confiscated during **algebra class** because it was considered a weapon of math disruption.
2. Please **relay** this message to Mr. Chan: the masons want to **re-lay** the bricks tomorrow.
3. Our **next-door** neighbour teaches **high school**, but she doesn't like being introduced as a **high-school** teacher.
4. We had a presentation by **Atheists Anonymous**, a **non-prophet** organization.
5. Because Angela was an **attorney-at-law** and had once been an **all-Canadian** athlete, no one was surprised when she became **Minister of Recreation**.

Answers for Section 7.19: Capital Letters (pages 511–17)

Exercise 7.19.1

1. Nancy whispered, "**T**here's a light in the Frankenstein house."
2. **T**ime is nature's way of keeping everything from happening at once.
3. Learning to speak and write **s**tandard **E**nglish is, for many people, like learning another **l**anguage.

4. Richard Harkness, writing in *The New York Times*, said, "**A** committee is a group of the unwilling, picked from the unfit, to do the unnecessary."

5. **I**n conclusion, I want you to consider the words of Wendell Johnson: "*Always* and *never* are two words you should always remember never to use."

Exercise 7.19.2

1. Do you find that **V**isa is more popular than American **E**xpress when you travel to faraway places such as **M**exico, **F**rance, or **J**upiter?

2. Our stay at the **S**eaview **H**otel overlooking the **P**acific **O**cean certainly beat our last vacation at the **B**ates **M**otel, where we faced west, overlooking the city dump.

3. As the fundraiser for our alumni association, I am targeting companies like **D**isney, **C**anadian **T**ire, the **B**ank of **M**ontreal, and the **CBC**, all of which employ our graduates.

4. The **B**roadcast **D**epartment of **N**iagara **C**ollege has ordered six **S**ony cameras for their studios in **W**elland, **O**ntario.

5. After a brief stay in the **M**aritimes, **C**aptain **T**allman and his crew sailed west up the **S**t. **L**awrence **R**iver.

Exercise 7.19.3

1. The **C**rusades, which were religious wars between **M**uslims and **C**hristians, raged through the **M**iddle **A**ges.

2. The **H**indu religion recognizes and honours many gods; **I**slam recognizes one god, **A**llah; **B**uddhism recognizes none.

3. The **K**oran, the **B**ible, and the **T**orah agree on many principles.

4. The **J**ewish festival of **H**anukkah often occurs near the same time that **C**hristians are celebrating **C**hristmas.

5. After **W**orld **W**ar I, many **J**ews began to immigrate to Palestine, where they and the **M**uslim population soon came into conflict.

Exercise 7.19.4

1. Next **M**onday is **V**alentine's **D**ay, when messages of love are exchanged.

2. By **T**hursday, I'll have finished my **S**t. **P**atrick's **D**ay costume.

3. My favourite months are **J**anuary and **F**ebruary because I love all **w**inter sports.

4. In the summer, big meals seem too much trouble; however, after **T**hanksgiving, we need lots of food to survive the winter cold.

5. A **n**ational **h**oliday named **F**lag **D**ay was once proposed, but it was never officially approved.

Exercise 7.19.5

1. The review of my book, ***The Life and Times of a Hog Rider***, published in ***The Globe and Mail***, was not favourable.

2. Clint **E**astwood fans will be delighted that the two early movies that made him internationally famous, ***A Fistful of Dollars*** and ***For a Few Dollars More***, are now available on DVD.

3. Joseph Conrad's short novel ***Heart of Darkness*** became the blockbuster movie *Apocalypse Now*.

4. My essay, "**A B**right and **S**ilent **P**lace," was published in the **A**pril issue of *Landscapes* magazine.

5. Botticelli's famous painting, ***Birth of Venus***, inspired my poem "**W**oman on the **H**alf **S**hell."

Exercise 7.19.6

1. Correct
2. After passing Professor Bacchus's course, **I**ntroduction to **W**ine, I registered for **O**enology 200.
3. After studying geography for two years, I began taking courses in ancient **G**reek and modern history.
4. While math is her strong subject, Louisa has trouble with accounting, **E**nglish, and conversational **F**rench.
5. The prerequisite for **T**heology 210 is **I**ntroduction to **W**orld **R**eligions, taught by Professor O'Connor.

Answers for Section 7.20: Numbers (pages 518–24)

Exercise 7.20.1

1. This applicant claims to speak more than **seven** languages, but from her résumé, I'd say that English is not **one** of them.
2. This is the **third** time the Accounting Department has filed its report more than **two** days late.
3. **Fifty-four** eager people have signed up for the **second** annual office pool.
4. Of the **12** cuts on her new DVD release, the **first** is my favourite.
5. Gavin, who works for the garage where I take my car, was unable to answer **10** of the **23** questions on the Mechanic Certification Exam.
6. In the Great Fire of 1666, **one-half** of London burned down, but only **six** people lost their lives.
7. If the diesel mixture contains **three-quarters** of a litre of regular gasoline, it will make your truck easier to start in those **four** or **five** really cold weeks of winter.
8. When I was **27** and had been unemployed for nearly **three** years, I decided to return to college for **two** years of practical training.
9. In the United States, **one** of the reasons that hemp is illegal is that about **80** years ago, cotton growers lobbied against its cultivation because they saw it as competition.
10. Only **8** out of **47** trivia players were able to name Jay Silverheels of Brantford, Ontario, as the original Tonto in *The Lone Ranger*.

Exercise 7.20.2

1. Researchers at Cornell University conducted a study that showed that **66** percent of all businessmen wear their ties too tight.
2. More than **10** percent of those studied wore their ties so tight that blood flow to the brain was diminished.
3. **Ninety-nine** percent of the people who read the report wondered why Cornell had conducted such a study.
4. **One** plan is to retire on **December 17**, 2055, when I will be 80.
5. At precisely **8:10 p.m.** on **June 3**, your flight will leave for Whitehorse.

6. You will arrive at approximately **ten o'clock** on **June 4** if you make all your connections.
7. I won **five dollars** from Ted by proving that February **1865** was the only month in recorded history not to have a full moon.
8. You must be present at **133 West 18th** Street by exactly **seven o'clock** to claim your prize.
9. So far this year, I have spent **$38 000**, or **20** percent more than my anticipated income for the entire year, and it's only **May 15**!
10. At the Indianapolis Speedway, the race cars burn approximately **4 L** of fuel for each lap, while the ship *Queen Mary 2* moves just **15** cm for every **4** L of fuel it burns.

Exercise 7.20.3

1. The speedboat is powered by **two** 80-horsepower outboard motors.
2. **One** 8-cylinder SUV emits more pollution than two 4-cylinder diesel Volkswagens or **three** Toyota gas–electric hybrids.
3. Because she sold seven **$2-million** homes last year, she topped the agency's earnings list.
4. Correct
5. **Two hundred** people were invited to celebrate my parents' **25th** wedding anniversary on **August 31**, 2009.
6. A total of **ten 15-year-old** girls and **four 15-year-old** boys applied for the commercial acting position we advertised.
7. Our lawyer told us that **38 percent** of people who die between the ages of 45 and 54 have not prepared a will.
8. Canada's population of about **33 million** puts us in **36th** place on the list of most populous countries.
9. **Ten** years ago, the average speed on urban freeways was **50 kph**, but it has been steadily declining and is expected to be **30 kph** within the next **five** years.
10. **Seven thousand** ecstatic fans celebrated their team's unexpected **2–1** win in the Memorial Cup final, partying in the streets until **4:30 a.m.**

Index

Credits

This page constitutes an extension of the copyright page. We have made every effort to trace the ownership of all copyrighted material and to secure permission from copyright holders. In the event of any question arising as to the use of any material, we will be pleased to make the necessary correction in future printing. Thanks are due to the following authors, publishers, and agents for permission to use the material indicated.

Page 6: "What I Have Lived For." Bertrand Russell. *The Autobiography of Bertrand Russell.* (Prologue). Boston: Little, Brown, 1967. 3–4.

Pages 23–24: "The Needle and the Damage Done." Matthew McKinnon. Originally published in *up! magazine* 20 December 2008. © Matthew McKinnon. Reprinted by permission of the author.

Pages 126–28: "Little Red Riding Hood Revisited." Russell Baker. Originally published in *New York Times Magazine* 13 January 1980. © 1980 The New York Times.

Pages 231–32: "Looking Both Ways." Amanda van der Heiden. Reprinted by permission of ProWord Communications, Inc.

Pages 236–38: "How to Play Winning Tennis." Brian Green. Reprinted by permission of the author.

Pages 238–39: "Forging: The Black Art." Paul Allen. Reprinted by permission of the author.

Pages 243–44: "On-the-Job Training." Alice Tam. Reprinted by permission of the author.

Pages 245–46: "Methods of Conflict Resolution." Eva Tihanyi. Reprinted by permission of the author.

Pages 252–53: "The Canadian Climate." D'Arcy McHayle. Reprinted by permission of the author.

Pages 253–54: "Shopping Around." Aniko Hencz. Reprinted by permission of the author.

Pages 259–60: "The Enemy in the Mirror." Brian Green. Reprinted by permission of the author.

Pages 261–63: "The Slender Trap." Trina Piscatelli. Reprinted by permission of the author.

Pages 272–73: "A City for Students." Aliki Tryphonopoulos. Reprinted by permission of the author.

Pages 274–75: Walter Isaacs, "Of Pain, Predators, and Pleasure." Reprinted by permission of the author.

Page 281: "Thinking Unbound." Joseph Scheppach. *Lufthansa Magazine* June 2002: 56.

Pages 282–84: Excerpted from *Beauty Tips from Moose Jaw* by Will Ferguson. Copyright © 2004 Will Ferguson. Reprinted by permission of Knopf Canada. First published in Great Britain by Canongate Books Ltd., 14 High Street, Edinburgh, EH1 1TE. Used by permission of Grove/Atlantic, Inc. Reproduced by permission of The Text Publishing Co. Pty. Ltd. Australia.

Pages 285–87: "How I Write." Richard Lederer. Reprinted by permission of the author.

Pages 288–93: From *Outliers* by Malcolm Gladwell. Copyright © 2008. By permission of Little, Brown & Company.

Pages 293–95: "Getting Pancake Sauce from Trees." Geoffrey Rowan. Originally published in the *Globe and Mail* as "They Get Pancake Sauce from Trees." March 15, 1994: A11. Reprinted by permission of *The Globe and Mail*.

Pages 295–98: "The Magic of Moviegoing." Rick Groen. Originally published in the *Globe and Mail* 4 January 2002. Reprinted by permission of *The Globe and Mail*.

Pages 298–300: "Get Radical. Get Some Rest." Matt Carmichael. Excerpted from *Resurgence* May–June 2008. © Matt Carmichael / Resurgence / Planet Syndication.